D1452082

POLEMICS
in Marxist
Philosophy

POLEMICS
in Marxist
Philosophy

George
Novack

Monad Press · New York

This volume is dedicated to
JOSEPH HANSEN
for his valued partnership in philosophy and politics
through more than four decades.

George Novack's other books include *Democracy and Revolution* (1971), *Empiricism and Its Evolution* (1968), *Humanism and Socialism* (1973), *An Introduction to the Logic of Marxism* (1969), *Pragmatism versus Marxism* (1975), *Origins of Materialism* (1965), and *Understanding History* (1972). He has also edited *America's Revolutionary Heritage* (1976) and *Existentialism versus Marxism: Two Conflicting Views on Humanism* (1965). In addition, he has authored or coauthored numerous pamphlets and articles on philosophy, political theory, and history. His literary collaborators have included Isaac Deutscher, C. Wright Mills, and Ernest Mandel.

He has been involved in civil liberties cases since the 1930s, including the defense of the Scottsboro Boys and the International Commission of Inquiry into the Moscow Trials (the Dewey Commission).

Frontispiece photograph by Brian Shannon

Published by Monad Press for the Anchor Foundation
Distributed by Pathfinder Press
                410 West Street
                New York, NY 10014

First printing 1978

Contents

Acknowledgments

All of the essays in this book have appeared in print previously:
"My Philosophical Itinerary: An Autobiographical Foreword"
was published in the June 28 and July 5, 1976, issues of
Intercontinental Press, © 1976 by Intercontinental Press; reprinted by permission.

"Freedom for Philosophy" was published in the March 29, 1976,
issue of *Intercontinental Press*, © 1976 by Intercontinental Press;
reprinted by permission.

"Marxism and Existentialism" originally appeared as "Marxism
and Existentialism: Are the Two Compatible?" in the Spring 1965
International Socialist Review. It forms part of a longer introduction to *Existentialism versus Marxism: Conflicting Views on
Humanism* (New York: Dell, 1965).

"In Defense of Engels" is based on a talk given at the 1975
Socialist Workers Party convention. It was published in the
February 23, 1976, issue of *Intercontinental Press*, © 1976 by
Intercontinental Press; reprinted by permission.

"Georg Lukács as a Marxist Philosopher" originally appeared in
the January and July-August 1972 *International Socialist Review*, © 1972 by International Socialist Review; reprinted by
permission.

"The Jesting Philosopher: The Case of Leszek Kolakowski"
originally appeared in the January 1975 *International Socialist
Review*, © 1975 by International Socialist Review; reprinted by
permission.

"Sebastiano Timpanaro's Defense of Materialism" was first published in the March 21, 1977, issue of *Intercontinental Press*,
© 1977 by Intercontinental Press; reprinted by permission.

"Back to Kant? The Retreat of Lucio Colletti" was first published in the November 14 and November 21, 1977, issues of *Intercontinental Press*, © 1977 by Intercontinental Press; reprinted by permission.

"Is Nature Dialectical?" originally appeared in the Summer 1964 and Winter 1965 issues of the *International Socialist Review*.

"American Philosophy and the Labor Movement" first appeared in the Spring 1962 issue of the *International Socialist Review*.

"Leon Trotsky on Dialectical Materialism" was first published in the Fall 1960 issue of the *International Socialist Review*.

(The last three articles listed here were first published under the pseudonym William F. Warde.)

Footnotes indicating specific locations of cited quotations are included at the back of the book, so as not to interfere with the text. Where no annotation is provided, the source has generally been given in the text.

The glossary was compiled by Leslie Evans, who also assisted the author in compiling the bibliography.

⌂

My Philosophical Itinerary:
An Autobiographical Foreword

The essays in this book differ from the usual run of philosophical writings in the United States in two salient respects. They have been written by a convinced dialectical materialist. And they were prompted not by topics discussed in professional philosophical journals and conferences, but by theoretical and methodological questions that have aroused controversy within and around the international socialist movement over the past two decades.

The diffusion of Marxist ideas has varied greatly from one country to another since their emergence in the mid-nineteenth century. The United States was the second country in the world (after Germany) to constitute a national party based on the principles elucidated by Marx and Engels: the Workingmen's Party of 1876, later known as the Socialist Labor Party. Yet a century later their ideas have exercised only a marginal influence on America's intellectual and political life. For weighty historical reasons, the United States has up to now been the most resistant among the major countries to the consideration and acceptance of scientific socialism.

Thanks to the War of Independence, the United States acquired the most advanced political regime in the world for that time. When the bicentennial anniversary came around, it had the most highly developed industry. And yet it was the most retarded in matters of social theory.

Marxist philosophers have been a rare breed in this country, whose political and ideological level is far lower than its capacity to build computers and nuclear missiles. Whereas in postwar

11

France political commitment has consorted with philosophical conviction, these areas are kept wide apart on this side of the Atlantic.

The separation of theorizing from practical affairs is carried to an extreme in the philosophical departments of the universities, where, as a rule, the specialists of various persuasions pursue their vocation in complacent detachment from social and political problems. They tend to disparage Marxism because, among other reasons, its ideas are inseparable from the stakes in the class struggle; they usually refuse to accord dialectical materialism the same full citizenship rights in the domain of contemporary thought as the varieties of positivism or existentialism.

Most faculties have not allowed the doctrines of Marxism to be presented by qualified adherents. Under such circumstances a revolutionary socialist thinker who was also a political activist would have been wise to emulate the unorthodox Benedict Spinoza, who, to maintain his independence, chose to grind lenses for a living rather than take a chair at Heidelberg.

Mindful of these realities, although I have been preoccupied with philosophical questions for half a century, I have not dropped anchor in any university harbor. The choppy waters of radical politics have been the milieu of my activities. For more than forty years I have dedicated my energies to promoting the cause of socialism as a member of the Socialist Workers Party and have taken a leading part in its work as a journalist and editor, a campaigner for civil liberties and labor rights, and a shaper of its policies on national and international issues. This has necessitated applying the Marxist method to the urgent problems of the class struggle, where competing theories are put to the test by their consequences in practical operation.

Not until the ferment among the youth opened up American campuses to socialist views in the late 1960s was I asked to speak at numerous colleges around the country. Professor Walter Kaufmann of Princeton testifies to the explosion of interest in Marx at that time. "When Jacques Maritain joined the department of philosophy at Princeton University in 1948, one professor was apprehensive that the great neo-Thomist might try to convert his students to Roman Catholicism, and he considered it reassuring that Maritain would not teach undergraduates. Yet the only suggestion Maritain ever made about the undergraduate curriculum was that Marx should be taught, as he was in Paris. In the late 1960s students almost everywhere wanted to have courses on Marx; and many were persuaded by Marx's early writings or by Engels or some passages in Lenin, or by Kojève or Lukács, that one cannot fully understand Marx without knowing something about Hegel." (*Times Literary Supplement,* London, January 2, 1976.)

Thus the "dangerous thoughts" of Marxism, barred from entering by the front door, came in through windows opened up by the students.

I was sometimes asked before and after my talks: Where do you teach?—as though it was unthinkable for anyone to philosophize without Ph.D. credentials and some sort of academic affiliations. Here is an extended version of my answer to such queries about my background and qualifications.

*   *   *

As the only son of immigrant Jews from Eastern Europe, I escaped the lot of a rabbinical student thanks to the voyages of my father and mother to the New World late in the nineteenth century. This fortuitous circumstance has buttressed my belief in the determinative effect of their social situation on people's destinies. Growing up in the suburbs of Boston, I was directed in high school toward Harvard, where an older cousin living in the same house had enrolled before me. To my family this upward step on the educational ladder was to provide a passport to success and wealth in one of the professions or as a business executive. Alas for the dreams of parents for their children! My university training was to be put to quite different uses.

I was an omnivorous reader of anything in print, from recipes on cereal boxes and adventure stories to novels and poetry; the free public library did almost as much to educate me as the schoolrooms. I had a passion for creative literature, but that yielded to other interests at Harvard, where I shifted my field of concentration from the English department to philosophy. Just as certain youths with a scientific bent aspire to learn radio technology or the properties of the chemical elements, I wanted to know where the ideas in people's minds came from and how they developed.

This concern with the nature of ideas was a strong incentive for studying philosophy and later becoming a Marxist. The adversaries of Marxism often allege that we Marxists are interested only in the pursuit of power, not in ideas. The productions of its leading exponents are the best refutation of this libel. Ideas have their own power, and the way to power is guided by ideas. But they are products and parts of the total process of social development. Dialectical materialists consider them to be conceptual reflections—and projections—of the conditions of the natural and social environment in which people act. The proponents of Marxism could hardly underplay the creative role of ideas when their own system has been the most far-reaching and fruitful ideology ever let loose on this planet.

Another deepgoing motive for my embrace of philosophy came from a yearning to find out "the secret of life." What, I wondered from adolescence on, gave meaning to the endeavors of human beings and how could I, as an individual in my own time and place, relate to this scheme of things and contribute to its realization? This spiritual, intellectual, and scientific problem, which has sustained the fictions and fantasies of religion, is in some form posed to every thinking person.

The conclusions of science had rendered belief in divine ghosts a ridiculous anachronism. I shed faith in God and immortality early and easily, despite the perfunctory ceremonials of a fast-fading Judaism in my home, and sought enlightenment from some secular source. After discarding the virtues of philanthropic good works as a satisfactory replacement, I was momentarily excited by the excessive individualism and poetic exaltation of Friedrich Wilhelm Nietzsche's *Thus Spake Zarathustra* and captivated by Havelock Ellis's unrestrictive attitude toward sex and his prescription for making an art out of the good life.

This self-centered estheticism was one ingredient of a restless and diffuse discontent with the prevailing conditions of American life as well as with the kind of teaching I encountered at Harvard, where I spent five years but quit three times, without getting a degree. My quest for a philosophy of life was from the first coupled with a critical attitude toward the domination of the dollar. This was honed by Upton Sinclair's exposures of the grip of big business upon the educational system and the press in *The Goose-Step, The Goslings,* and *The Brass Check.*

My fervor for social justice and cultural renovation boiled over when I read *The Golden Day,* Lewis Mumford's criticism of the shortcomings and commercialism of nineteenth-century American culture. At the end of the book Mumford invoked Walt Whitman's invitation to remold America along plebeian-democratic lines: "Allons! The road is before us." As naively idealistic youth will do, I took this injunction more literally than the author intended, and wanted to send him word that I was all set to join the glorious crusade "to conceive a new world" he projected. When I later migrated to New York and became acquainted with Mumford, I soon saw the unrealism of his utopian plans for remaking this country into "a complete and harmonious society" without a political confrontation with the power of the ruling plutocracy.

I participated in the Third World Congress of Philosophy held at Harvard in the summer of 1926 in a most humble role. At the request of my tutor, Raphael Demos, I took care of the laundry of visiting celebrities. In addition to this glimpse of the underside of the philosophic community, I listened to, among other contributions, the talk given by John Dewey on "Philosophy and Civilization," later published in the collection of his articles under that title.

My main occupation that summer was racing through the shelves of the philosophical section in the stacks at Widener Library, indiscriminately gobbling up such publications as the proceedings of the Aristotelian Society, ransacking their pages for light on the riddle of existence. (According to these British scholars, the answers seemed to be located in problems arising from the theory of knowledge rather than the nature of reality.)

My development thereafter followed a standard pattern for Marxists—from youthful idealism through pragmatism to a matured materialism. When I was inducted into philosophy at Harvard in the mid-1920s, its faculty offered a bewildering bill of fare for the neophyte to digest. They expounded religious idealism (William Hocking), pragmatic realism (Ralph Perry), Thomism (Maurice de Wulf), and differing approaches to logic (Henry M. Sheffer, Ralph M. Eaton, C. S. Lewis).

Echoes from the halcyon days of William James, Josiah Royce, and George Santayana still reverberated through Emerson Hall, the seat of the philosophy department; and the last survivor of that galaxy, the venerable George Herbert Palmer, could be seen shuffling through Harvard Yard. The disconnected writings of C. S. Peirce were then being collected and edited by one of my teachers, Charles Hartshorne.

However, the attention of the more serious students was drawn toward Bertrand Russell's collaborator, A. N. Whitehead, the erudite modernizer of Platonism with scientific-mathematical trimmings. He read several chapters of his major treatise *Process and Reality* to our class. Obscure and enigmatic as much of its metaphysics was, it appealed to my need for a comprehensive, rational interpretation of the universe. For a while I became an entranced disciple of Whitehead, although as an atheist I was disconcerted to hear that my guru occasionally sermonized at King's Chapel in Boston. This immersion in Whitehead's system, with its fusion of scientific, mathematical, and philosophical concepts, immensely widened my intellectual horizon. I also learned from his *Science in the Modern World* that the clash of doctrines speeds progress.

At the foremost institution of higher learning in the United States, I was taught nothing about Marxism or socialism in the midst of that conservatized decade which was promised endless prosperity. I learned about Plato's theory of forms, Aristotle's doctrine of the Golden Mean, David Hume's skepticism, and the wager on God's existence laid down by William James. But not a whisper about modern materialism either in my philosophy or history courses.

After leaving the academic cocoon of Harvard for New York, where I had to work for a living in the publishing business, I passed over for a time to pragmatism. Dewey's instrumentalism was not only popular among friends who had studied under him at Columbia, but suited my political and social orientation. This was of the *Nation-New Republic* type, spiced with a dash of Menckenian cynicism and elitism about the crass bourgeoisie and its dupes among the "booboisie." (As a left liberal, I voted for Democrat Al Smith in the 1928 presidential election, the first and last time I supported a capitalist candidate.) Most probably, if I had not gone to Manhattan and become integrated into its literary milieu, my career would have been very different. The transit was indeed fortunate for me, even though I did not foresee its consequences.

The social catastrophe and economic paralysis that climaxed the twenties upset my whole outlook and permanently estranged me from loyalty to capitalism or hopes for its reformation. Along with a legion of leftward-moving intellectuals, I became persuaded of the necessity for socialism and undertook sustained study of the theoretical bases of Marxism in philosophy, sociology, history, and economics.

I had the greatest difficulty in overcoming resistance to the labor theory of value in the political economy elaborated by Marx and Engels and to the dialectical logic that guided their investigations. Notions of this kind were foreign to my previous training. I could not wholeheartedly embrace Marxism until the correctness of these key ideas became clear to me.

Under the impact of the Great Depression, it proved easier for most new-hatched radicals to switch political positions from liberalism to socialism than to change the philosophical foundations underneath the two outlooks. That required a thorough transmutation in one's habits of thinking; the novel ideas had to be absorbed into the very marrow of one's being. Thus the process of learning the dialectical materialist method effected as much of a revolution in my mode of thought as in my politics.

There is a world of difference between teaching philosophy for a living, which can be done without the force of personal conviction, and adopting a satisfactory philosophy to live by. The two need have no affinity. That was not the case with me. I earnestly sought a set of beliefs that could provide a compass to steer by in daily affairs as well as in scientific matters. Marxist philosophy alone filled these requirements.

On the way to Marxism I paused to consider other options. During the summer of 1931 I assiduously annotated the just-published *Reason and Nature*, the major work of Morris Cohen. The College of the City of New York professor was admired by acquaintances of mine, such as his former pupil Sidney Hook, for his wit, learning, and logical acumen. His method of logical rationalism was regarded as the most eligible alternative to Dewey's instrumentalism.

Cohen's approach to reality and thought was predicated on his "principle of polarity," which stated that opposites involved each other and therefore both sides had to be carefully weighed in all situations and all problems. This prudential maxim was a devitalized version of the unity of opposites at the core of Hegel's dialectics; it cut out the impetus of conflict that eventually results in resolving real contradictions. The process of negation as the motive force of progressive development was missing from his scheme of things.

Cohen's primary principle, with its arguments for rational order in all realms, was out of kilter with the turmoil of the times. It was a formula for the liberal consensus—there were always two sides to every question and they had to be mutually accommodated in the end. This was the very essence of the liberal reformism I was rejecting. From different premises Cohen's rationalism arrived at the same conclusion as Dewey's instrumentalism—that conflicting claims and interests in morals, politics, and sociology had to be reconciled rather than thought through and fought out until the more correct idea or progressive agency prevailed.

*   *   *

Through the 1930s most radicals followed the Communist Party. My path diverged from theirs. I was part of the first group of leftist intellectuals in New York, where national trends in politics were set, who became disillusioned with both Stalinism and Social Democratic reformism. Experience had demonstrated that their policies could not effectively combat fascism and lead the working class to power. Late in 1933, following the shock of Hitler's victory in Germany, I joined the American Trotskyist movement. Through sharp confrontations with larger rivals, its members were constantly embroiled in ideological controversy, and as a writer for its publications I had to improve my grasp of socialist theory in a hurry.

It may be of interest to note the impediments we novices had to overcome to break loose from prevailing currents of thought and assimilate the teachings of Marxism. The main block on the road was the deep-rooted and pervasive empiricism that has saturated American life and thought for so many generations and has affected the socialist movement as well.

Earlier American socialists took little interest in dialectical materialism and made no significant efforts to disseminate its method of thought. We had no such reliable and talented teachers as the Russian Marxists had in George Plekhanov, the Germans in Franz Mehring, and the Italians in Antonio Labriola. Lacking either native traditions or homegrown literature, we had to rely upon imports from abroad, as our prerevolutionary colonial predecessors did.

Even so, the available writings on the subject had big gaps. There was no complete edition of Karl Marx and Frederick Engels in English. The main items in the inventory at hand were such classics as *Anti-Dühring, Ludwig Feuerbach and the Outcome of Classical German Philosophy*, and part of *The German Ideology*. These were flanked by some of Plekhanov's essays and Labriola's excellent *Socialism and Philosophy*. Neither Marx's early writings, such as the *Economic and Philosophic Manuscripts of 1844*, nor Lukács's *History and Class Consciousness* were yet accessible in English. To be sure, we had Marx's *Capital* as the consummate example of his dialectical and historical method to learn from, though its fourth part, *Theories of Surplus Value,* had still to be translated. The very existence of the *Grundrisse* was unsuspected. Not until 1940 did we have access to Engels's *Dialectics of Nature,* which enabled us to see how the dialectical approach could be applied to the theoretical problems posed by the developments of natural science.

In view of the prominence the theme of alienation has since acquired, it is surprising in retrospect that Marxists then paid hardly any attention to it. I cannot recall a single discussion of the topic during the 1930s, although Sidney Hook's *From Hegel to Marx* had some references to this idea. It came forward only after the Second World War.

It took almost fifteen years for the regeneration of dialectical materialism by the leaders of the Russian revolution to begin reaching American shores. A translation of V. I. Lenin's *Materialism and Empirio-Criticism* appeared in 1926, but his important *Philosophical Notebooks* were unknown. Nikolai Bukharin was represented by his somewhat mechanical treatise *Historical Materialism* and by his articles in the compilations *Science at the Crossroads* (1931) and *Marxism and Modern Thought* (1935). Leon Trotsky's views on philosophy were only slightly known through his *Literature and Revolution.*

Somewhat later in the decade several popularizations of uneven merit appeared, such as August Thalheimer's *Introduction to Dialectical Materialism,* T. H. Jackson's *Dialectics,* and Edward Conze's misleading and superficial *An Introduction to Dialectical Materialism.* I mention these to indicate the kind of handbooks students like me might turn to for guidance.

Since the Social Democrats were largely indifferent to theory in general, and Marxist philosophy in particular, we were dependent upon whatever Moscow saw fit to issue in English. The classics were a boon. But beyond these the Soviet apparatus, bound by the edicts of the cultural commissars and Stalin's canonical scripture *Dialectical and Historical Materialism,* offered only debased and dogmatic versions of Marxist philosophy.

The liveliest discussions on philosophic questions took place outside the precincts policed by the official Communist ideologues. These revolved around the debates between Sidney Hook and Max Eastman that continued through the decade. As an avowed adversary, Eastman waged an untiring battle against dialectical materialism in a series of books and articles in left-wing periodicals. At the end of the thirties, disheartened by the crimes of Stalinism, he abjured socialism altogether.

Hook defended Marxism against Eastman's arguments in a special manner. He adapted his own theory of knowledge to Dewey's instrumentalism and borrowed deviant ideas from the works of Georg Lukács and Karl Korsch, whose lectures he had attended. I had personal relations with both Hook and Eastman, and Hook had played a part in winning me to Marxism, but I did not share either one's positions. While I thoroughly disagreed with Eastman's hostility to the philosophic foundations of scientific socialism, I was disquieted by Hook's abandonment of the dialectics of nature and the labor theory of value, two cornerstones of Marxist theory.

When Hook published *Towards the Understanding of Karl Marx* in 1933, I could see the discrepancies between his interpretations on a number of questions and the positions actually held by Marx, Lenin, and Rosa Luxemburg. I drafted an open letter addressed to Hook (which, however, remained unfinished and unsent), calling attention to these differences and asking him to comment on them.

Around that time, from his exile in Turkey, Leon Trotsky wrote a letter to the *Nation* taking Hook to task for casting doubt on the scientific character of the Marxist method. So did writers for the *New International*, the theoretical monthly of revolutionary Marxism, to which Hook and I contributed. However, until 1939-40 most of us in the American Trotskyist movement who were concerned with matters of theory did not fully appreciate the importance of a correct philosophical method or the grave political consequences implicit in departures from it.

This relationship was made crystal clear when a tense struggle erupted within the Socialist Workers Party following the Soviet-Nazi pact and the onset of the Second World War. At issue was the nature of the Soviet Union and the necessity to defend it against imperialist attack—without making any concessions to its Stalinist misleadership. James Burnham and Max Shachtman headed the minority that sought to change the traditional Trotskyist position on these questions; Leon Trotsky and James P. Cannon led the majority.

At the outset of the conflict I was somewhat disoriented and uncertain about which side had the correct political line. As the debate expanded, the underlying philosophical issues in dispute with Burnham, the ideological inspirer of the opposition, were brought to the fore by Trotsky's polemical initiatives. Once the issues were posed on that theoretical level, I could see that Burnham was upholding non-Marxist views in both his politics and his philosophy.

My comprehension was facilitated by the fact that I had previously had disagreements with Burnham, who was a professor of philosophy at New York University, a colleague of Hook's, and the coauthor with Philip Wheelwright of a textbook on logic based on positivist rather than materialist premises. In October 1936 Burnham, Shachtman, and I had gone to Philadelphia, where the National Committee of the Socialist Party was meeting, in order to solicit support for the American Committee for the Defense of Leon Trotsky, of which I was national secretary. Its purposes were to obtain asylum for the exile, then interned in Norway, and to promote the formation of a commission of inquiry into the monstrous charges against him in the Moscow trials. (This was later headed by John Dewey.)

While waiting hours in an anteroom for a hearing, the three of us discussed some matters pertaining to philosophy and logic. Burnham opposed the historical necessity of socialism on the general ground that no categorical determinism existed either in nature or in society; any and every proposition about reality was no more than probable. In arguing against this positivist attitude, I asked: "Don't you think you will die some day, as all other human beings have done up to now, and isn't this an absolutely necessary statement—or do you believe you might be immortal?" With logical consistency, Burnham replied: "My death is not absolutely necessary and certain; it is only extremely probable." This rejection of materialist determinism and lawfulness convinced me that we stood far apart on fundamental questions of science and logic. So I was already forewarned that despite our then political agreement, Burnham held non-Marxist views in philosophy.

At Trotsky's suggestion I took up the cudgels in defense of dialectical materialism against Burnham's offensive, and in the party discussion in New York City that wound up the furious faction fight I debated him on the philosophical issues involved. My first work on Marxist philosophy, *An Introduction to the Logic of Marxism*, came out of this experience. It was based on talks originally given to SWP members in 1942 as part of a program under the tutelage of the learned John G. Wright to enhance their understanding of the essentials of the Marxist mode of thought.

This exposition of the elements of dialectical logic, which has since gone through six printings and also proved popular in its Spanish translation, contravened an almost unanimous campaign against the philosophic basis of Marxism. Three books published in 1940-41 repudiated the dialectic on various grounds as a worthless hangover from Hegelian idealism in the Marxist outlook. These were *Marxism: Is It Science?* by Max Eastman, *Reason, Social Myth and Democracy* by Sidney Hook, and *To the Finland Station* by the literary critic Edmund Wilson, who was indoctrinated on this point by them.

The trio's negative verdict settled the matter for most American intellectuals. The materialist dialectic was virtually banished from the scene for the next three decades. It found few defenders outside the Trotskyist ranks. From then on I held an isolated outpost on the philosophical front.

The eclipse of Marxism's fundamental philosophical tenets was one aspect of the stampede away from socialism that set in during 1939 and culminated in the conformism and anticommunism of the postwar period. Though the opponents of dialectics balked at recognizing the objective reality of contradiction, they themselves passed through a highly contradictory course of development after 1929. They forsook reformism for the socialist program of revolution, and then, as they slid back, reverted to a toothless liberalism or even served as armor-bearers in the camp of imperialist reaction.

I observed the gyrations of this mercurial layer of intellectuals at first hand; many of my former associates were prominently involved. The sharp swings in their standpoints proved in practice how, under the impact of changing circumstances, groupings and individuals can turn into their opposites.

Georg Lukács observed in *The Young Hegel*: "The political and social fate of Germany led him to place the phenomenon of contradictoriness in the forefront of his thought; we see how he comes to *experience* contradiction as the foundation and the driving force of life."[1]

The young people of my generation first experienced the full force of the contradictions inherent in capitalism after the crash of 1929. Then the presence of poverty and misery amidst plenty, and the spectacle of millions of unemployed beside the most productive apparatus in the world, made contradiction a visible reality.

I could also see my own political evolution from a liberal do-gooder to a revolutionary socialist, and the changes in my systematic thought—my early idealism partially negated by pragmatism and then fully transcended by dialectical material-ism. This too exemplified dialectical development.

The radicalization and deradicalization of this segment of my contemporaries was not to be explained on ideological grounds alone. This double turnabout was at bottom provoked by the vicissitudes of U.S. capitalism and the alignments of class forces on a national and world scale. This correlation between changing views and material circumstances bore witness to the operation of that historical determinism which was so abhorrent to the liberal mentality.

*   *   *

I was initially attracted to Marxism not by its theory of being or knowledge, but by the materialist conception of history. The liberal outlook that envisaged the gradual growth of American capitalism toward greater equality and abundance for all had lost its credibility under the blows of the Great Depression. Its exponents had not foreseen the crisis of capitalism and could not explain its occurrence or tell how to cope with its devastating consequences.

Marxist theory, on the other hand, did account for the break-down of capitalism and the causes of its evils, and showed the way to replacing its exploitation with a society freed of class distinctions. Furthermore, the method of historical materialism cast a scientific searchlight upon the entire course of human development that led up to the debacle of the bourgeois system in its strongest sector.

·Its prediction that capitalist relations could be overthrown by the mass action of the workers and peasants under proper leadership, and that a social order could be constructed on new principles, was being empirically verified by the achievements of the planned economy ushered in by the October 1917 revolution in Russia.

I had been curious about the mainsprings of history from an early age. I recall a discussion with a college chum in one of the Harvard dormitories about the historical conceptions of Henry and Brooks Adams that were current at the time. I remarked, "If only we could know what the laws of history were, we would be able to predict what was ahead of us." I pored over Oswald Spengler's *Decline of the West* when it came out in English translation in 1926, although it was not difficult to detect its reactionary bias and methodological weaknesses.

If the phenomena of nature were subject to laws, why, I asked, should history be exempt from them? A character in Evelyn Waugh's satirical novel *Decline and Fall* complained: "I couldn't understand why God had made the world at all." In a similar vein skeptical scholars admitted that they could not figure out how history had been made, even though it had been made by human beings. Surely the totality of their strivings and accomplishments was not thoroughly inscrutable. Marxism not only affirmed its lawfulness but disclosed the essence of its laws, such as those imposed by commodity production and exchange.

The consistent historical-mindedness of Marxism, which was so repugnant to critics such as Karl Popper, impressed me as a logical extension on a higher level of the universal concept of evolution, the bedrock of modern science. The blind evolution of inorganic and organic nature was the precondition for the emergence of humankind from a branch of the primates. Through its development of the labor process, our species had acquired its distinctive capacities and characteristics and made its way up from an apelike condition to civilization.

This view of humanity's past provided a solid foundation for the belief in social progress. Like most Americans, I had spontaneously breathed in this notion from the surrounding atmosphere. That had been one of the attractive features of Dewey's meliorism. Such an outlook was being placed in doubt by pessimists who identified the collapse of capitalism with the end of civilization. Through Marxism my belief in progress acquired a more rational grounding.

If progress was illusory, how was humanity's ascent from the animal kingdom to be scientifically explained? Moreover, denial of the reality or worth of social progress logically signified that our remote ancestors might just as well have continued to go on all fours or been content gathering roots and fruits and hunting wild game instead of engaging in the agriculture and stock raising that paved the way for civilization.

Such a conclusion ran counter to the actual upward climb of humanity in the past; in my eyes it was even less justified for the future. The advances of science, technology, and industry and the social revolutions of our century were accelerating the pace of change at an unprecedented rate, opening up endless vistas of exploration and achievement. It was shortsighted and defeatist to sell human creativity—and working class combativity—short.

Marxism singled out the growth of the productive forces as the prime motive power that propelled humanity forward and saved it from stagnation. The qualitative leaps to more efficient modes of production provided an objective criterion for placing one social formation on a higher rung than another, despite the objections of relativists and primitivists. More urgently, it validated the transition from capitalism to socialism on a world scale as the next necessary stage in human advancement and explained why the working class was the agency whose functions enabled it to bring this about.

Also, as a sociology of knowledge, historical materialism clarified the origins and spread of the idea of progress itself—which had become a mass sentiment and a mighty force for the improvement of human conditions from the eighteenth century on. This was more than a theoretical point. It dovetailed with the needs of reconstructing the social order. The findings of historical science harmonized with the aims of revolutionary activity, and the study of history was thereby linked with the practice of politics. The purpose of learning as much as possible about the past was to make contemporary history more consciously and effectively.

The conceptions held by historians of what constitutes history permeate their writing of it. My own approach coincided with the definition given by E. H. Carr in his excellent exposition *What Is History?* "Historiography is a progressive science in the sense that it seeks to provide constantly expanding and deepening insights into a course of events which is itself progressive."[2]

Through Marx I came to Georg Wilhelm Friedrich Hegel, his idealist predecessor in the study of dialectics. Hegel had been the first to correlate the history of philosophy with what was then called the philosophy of history—investigation into the laws governing the movement of humanity. Despite its idealist armature, Hegel's attempt to uncover a logical consistency in universal history through his system of dialectical development was a highly suggestive landmark in human thought. His view of the historical process portrayed the interplay of its objective and subjective sides; the human participants were both purposive agents and passive sufferers. The ultimate outcome of their collective efforts often exceeded or diverged widely from their intentions or expectations. The ironic and antagonistic character of progress in societies with exploiting classes was still more profoundly illuminated, along materialist lines, in the writings of Marx and Engels.

*   *   *

It may be asked: Why should people engrossed in working class politics make a fuss about dialectical versus nondialectical thinking? Because in complicated cases the one method yields far better results than the other. That was shown by two unexpected developments that have baffled and tripped up most of the ex-radicals over the past few decades. One involved the first workers' state; the other the American labor movement.

The rulership of the Soviet Union was drastically changed from the workers' democracy of its first years, under Lenin and Trotsky, to Stalin's tyranny. Soviet society thereupon acquired an extremely contradictory makeup; a totalitarian regime was saddled upon the nationalized and planned economy made possible by the October revolution.

Purely empirical thinking could not fathom this novel and enigmatic phenomenon. The fugitives from socialism regarded Stalinism as the continuator, not the antithesis, of Leninism, and refused to distinguish between the reactionary political superstructure of the USSR and the progressive nature of its underlying mode of production. This was the theoretical bridge over which they crossed to a bitter anticommunism.

They responded in an equally obtuse manner to the reversal in the combativity of the workers at home. The energetic drive that unionized the major industries against the resistance of the corporations had filled them with confidence in the capacities of the proletariat.

Then, as the mass of workers quieted down and the unions became conservatized and bureaucratized during the postwar period, their hopes in the potential of the workers went sour. Just as they could perceive nothing worth salvaging in the Stalinized Soviet Union, which was transformed from an inspiration into a menace, so they disqualified the working class as the main force for social change and began looking for substitutes in other quarters.

Thanks to an understanding that the class struggle was bound to pass through abrupt twists and adverse turns, we American Trotskyists were able to avoid these grave errors of judgment that helped to detach so many disappointed individuals from the cause of socialism.

*   *   *

Over the years I gave many lectures and wrote a number of works on historical topics. These ranged from consideration of the entire span of social evolution to the place occupied in it by our own country. Unlike the cultures of the Old World, North American civilization was a specific outgrowth of the global expansion of the capitalist system. This fundamental fact has shaped its course and endowed it with very distinctive characteristics. The main line of our national history has essentially consisted in the formation and transformation of bourgeois forms of social relations as their elements were perfected from the European conquest to the domination of the monopolists.

The Frenchman Alexis de Tocqueville observed: "America is a land of wonders in which everything is in constant motion." The incessant and rapid changes generated by the dynamics of capitalist development gave rise to acute clashes of its inner forces that erupted in the War of Independence at the end of the eighteenth century and the Civil War in the mid-nineteenth. These tremendous upheavals were successive stages in the triumphant advance of the bourgeois democratic movement on American soil.

The progress of the United States in the hundred years from the close of Reconstruction to the celebration of the bicentennial has posed a question few contemporary historians are prepared to tackle. Did the revolutionary experiences of the American people definitively end after the settlement of accounts with the slavocracy? The ordinary citizen believes that they are safely stowed in the past, while the plutocrats whose precursors were the greatest beneficiaries of the earlier revolutions arrogantly assume that their supremacy will be everlasting.

Ruling classes are notoriously shortsighted. And, however strenuously they resisted its consequences, America's rulers underestimated the significance of the fact that the ascendant trend of twentieth century development on the world arena was not the consolidation of capitalism but the growth of its socialist antagonist. Since 1917, capitalist power and property have been abolished in fourteen countries, and the anticapitalist tide has swept as close as Cuba to our shores.

The United States had risen to the summit of world power during this weakening of international capitalism, and it could not be immunized from the accumulated effects of its decline, as the defeat in Southeast Asia indicated. This country would not remain the one inviolable sanctuary protected from the intrusion of revolutionary ideas and forces. Just as American capitalism had been lifted to the top on the basis of two immense popular uprisings, so its descent would sooner or later usher in an even more momentous and convulsive series of crises and class conflicts.

This broad conception of the march of American civilization and its perspectives has animated all my writings on American history.

What, then, are the prospects for democracy? We socialists have had to contend with two widespread misconceptions on this subject. One is the notion taught to every schoolchild: that bourgeois democracy provides the unsurpassable model of government, that the republic founded in 1789 is the freest and most representative on earth. While this article of faith has been jolted from time to time by exposures of the control wielded by agents of big business in Washington, it retains its hold on the majority of the population.

I was imbued from an early age with respect for democracy, and never relinquished the ideal of equality, liberty, and justice for all. Once I became aware that the democracy accorded under capitalist rule was a counterfeit and that its inequalities were structurally irremediable, I looked to the struggle for workers' power and socialism as the road to the realization of true democracy.

I held fast to this conviction despite the degeneration of the Soviet state after Lenin's death. But the evils of Stalinist bureaucratism were a heavy liability in the effort to win new forces to socialism. We Trotskyists relentlessly exposed and combatted this suppression of the most elementary civil rights as part of Stalin's betrayal of socialism. The liberals joined with right-wing propagandists to brandish the indefensible practices of Stalinism under our noses as irrefutable proof that socialist revolution inevitably resulted in totalitarianism.

My book *Democracy and Revolution* addressed itself to these burning problems. Since the record of the struggles for popular sovereignty and greater human rights in the Western world over the past 2,500 years was hardly known even to the educated public, I reviewed the vicissitudes of the democratic movements through their three main stages: the precapitalist forms of political democracy, the bourgeois democratic era, and the post-capitalist societies of our own day. The narrative demonstrated how central the revolutionary action of the masses had been in originating, extending, and safeguarding the liberties of the people against repressive and reactionary types of rule. After a description of the six decisive steps in the bourgeois democratic revolution from the establishment of the Dutch republic to the American Civil War, it was made clear why that epoch came to an end in the last part of the nineteenth century: World capitalism entered its imperialist phase, and the bourgeoisie was everywhere ineluctably converted into a conservative, antidemocratic, and counterrevolutionary force.

The prospects for the survival, preservation, and expansion of the democratic rights of the people, I explained, are totally bound up with the anticapitalist movement of the working class, which aims to win decisive economic and political power and construct a deeper, *socialist* democracy.

The concluding chapters explained the reasons why the existing postcapitalist regimes, located in backward countries hemmed in by imperialism, have fallen short of this goal. On the other hand, the very different circumstances that would attend a victorious socialist revolution in so developed a country as the United States could avert the curses of bureaucratic deformation and bring forth "a new birth of freedom" for the American people, far exceeding the achievements of our past revolutions. However late Americans might be in coming to socialism, they will amaze themselves and others by what they make of its discovery.

*   *   *

The disproportions of development from which backward countries suffer are painfully evident to informed observers. It is not so clear that on a higher plane the United States is also incapacitated in important respects by the lopsidedness of its own development. Here the fundamental material prerequisites for socialism are at hand, but very few of the subjective factors have ripened. Unlike their counterparts in other industrialized lands, the American workers have yet to establish a political organization of their own, independent of the two capitalist parties. The powerful unions they have organized exist alongside a low degree of political class consciousness and ideology. The anomalies of this situation have compelled American Marxists to take heed of the irregularities as well as the regularities of the historical process.

In the opening chapter of his masterwork, *The History of the Russian Revolution,* Leon Trotsky first formulated the law of uneven and combined development as a key to analyzing a comparable tangle of contradictions in tsarist Russia. This struck me as one of the most precious additions to Marxist teachings in our time. In *Understanding History* I gave an extended exposition of this law and illustrated its usefulness for clarifying complex historical phenomena and unusual social formations. It held out the possibility that the peculiar combination of advanced and backward features that characterized contemporary American society could at a critical juncture generate sudden leaps forward in class consciousness and organization that would alter America's destiny.

This law had philosophical implications as well as historical and political applications. It stated that the extreme unevennesses in social life could lead to the merging of elements on different levels of development and result in surprising deviations from the norm. This was a particular expression of the interpenetration of opposites that characterized the dialectical nature of development. The essential lawfulness that has operated throughout history concretely manifests itself in a highly irregular manner. Typical or "pure" forms are normative abstractions that are indispensable for analytical purposes but are only imperfectly embodied in reality. This discrepancy between the ideal model and the actual facts runs through the whole course of human thought and has to be kept in mind in dealing with a multiplicity of scientific and social problems.

My interests in philosophy and history came together in the second book I published. Curiously enough, its seed was planted back in the freshman course in philosophy I took at Harvard. The assigned textbook, *A Student's History of Philosophy* by A. K.

Rogers, informed us that the Greeks were the first philosophers. However, the author offered a shallow psychological explanation of why this people rather than others pioneered this branch of knowledge. He attributed the feat to the distinctive qualities of the Greek mind, its creative spirit and feeling for the finite. But where did that exceptional mentality come from?

The puzzle of "the Greek miracle" nagged at me as I delved into the background of philosophy. Taking to heart Aristotle's dictum that one who sees things from their beginnings has the best view of them, I decided to investigate the configuration of causes that impelled the Milesians to displace religion and mythology with systematic rational theorizing from naturalistic premises. *The Origins of Materialism* is one of the few accounts in English that dig down to the roots of that line of thought in Greco-Roman civilization.

My approach to the birth process of the materialist outlook can be gauged by the following passage from the chapter "The Revolution in Aegean Society":

The supreme outcome of all these revolutionary changes was the production of new forms of general consciousness. Magic was the characteristic world view of tribalism; religion of the earliest kingdoms and city-states. Now something genuinely new emerged in the practice and minds of men: the first shoots of philosophy and science.

These could not have appeared until the historical soil for their growth and cultivation had been prepared and enriched by the elements we have described: the introduction of iron, metallic money, alphabetic writing, weights and measures; a new type of slave production; the shattering of the remaining institutions of tribal society and the breakup of agriculturally based theocratic despotisms; the ascent of trade, manufacturing and colonizing to new levels; the birth of powerful new progressive social forces in the maritime city-states of Greece which carried class antagonisms to a new pitch of intensity and created new types of legal, political and cultural institutions. Such were the indispensable historical preconditions for the formation of philosophy.[3]

These general causal factors bore their first methodological fruit in the materialist thinkers of Miletus.

*　　　　*　　　　*

On visits to college campuses early in the 1960s I ran into the prevalence of existential attitudes and ideas arising from discontent with the status quo and stimulated by the literary productions of Jean-Paul Sartre, Albert Camus, and Simone de Beauvoir. The single philosophical issue that could arouse discussion among critical-minded students revolved around the relation between these left existentialists and Marxism. There was considerable confusion regarding their compatibility.

Such was the motivation for the anthology *Existentialism versus Marxism.* My contributions argued that the two philosophies were not complementary but conflicting; the attempt by Sartre and his disciples to mate a creed of ultra-individualism and subjectivism with the materialist and collectivist postulates of scientific socialism was a hopeless, retrograde, and sterile enterprise.

This was the first of several books that critically examined such leading tendencies of contemporary philosophy as empiricism and positivism, liberalistic humanism, and Dewey's instrumentalism. My aim was to counterpose the answers to the principal problems of philosophy given by these schools of thought to the views of dialectical materialism.

The culminating work in this series was *Pragmatism versus Marxism*, which distilled all that I had learned about the achievements of generalized thought in this country from Jonathan Edwards to John Dewey. It presented a distinctive interpretation of the main course of philosophical development from the eighteenth century to the twentieth as it was molded by the special features of American capitalist civilization and culture.

Here is how the central thesis on the essential continuity in the progress of American thought is described in the introduction:

> The mainstream of our national thought since the eighteenth century has flowed through the channel of bourgeois democracy. This set of ideas has passed through three principal stages. The democratic creed first blossomed on American soil during the Age of the Enlightenment in the form of the rationalism, empiricism, and anti-Calvinist Deism, shading off into materialism, which attended the first American revolution. In its second phase it became revitalized in the fountain of Transcendentalism fed by the social conflicts which were to erupt in the Civil War. The pragmatic school—culminating in Dewey's instrumentalism, which arose as the philosophical rationale for middle class liberalism at the turn of the century—was its third incarnation.[4]

My appraisal of Dewey's philosophy set forth its strong and weak points and then explained why its basic ideas and procedures fell short of the latest developments in science and society and could not satisfy the requirements of further progress in American thought. It concluded that, just as socialism must replace capitalism in the strivings of the American people for a better way of life, so deficient petty-bourgeois modes of thought such as pragmatism have to be superseded by the teachings of Marxism as the guide to working class activity.

In between these larger works I wrote articles and pamphlets on a variety of current political issues extending from the Afro-American liberation struggle to the Sino-Soviet split. There was no separation between these theoretical and scholarly pursuits and my organizational duties. I followed Marx's injunction that it is not enough for thinkers to interpret the world in one way or another; they must work collectively to change it along socialist lines.

Philosophical theory is not to be elaborated for its own sake or for academic preferment but as a tool for casting light on the urgent problems brought forward by modern knowledge and experience, especially as they pertain to the movement for liberation from capitalist oppression. Theorists are not privileged to abstain from all the chores of party building and shuffle them off onto the lowly activists. They are called upon to participate directly in the everyday struggles of the people, taking due account of the value of their specialized capacities in the overall allocation of functions.

This was the model set by those personalities who most admirably exemplified the aims and ideals of scientific socialism, and I tried to emulate them to the measure of my abilities. I was fortunate enough to collaborate with two of them during their lifetimes: Leon Trotsky and James P. Cannon, founder of the American Trotskyist movement. I first met the Soviet exile when he landed in Mexico in January 1937, between the first and second Moscow frame-up trials. The conduct of his life and the content of his ideas have been the foremost influence upon my own.

*　　　　*　　　　*

Though it is not for me to assess the worth of my philosophical activities, I can at least point to the service they performed during a period marked by wholesale apostasy and abandonment of Marxist positions.

Professor John Lachs of Vanderbilt University, author of *Marxist Philosophy: A Bibliographical Guide,* wrote in 1967:

There has, of late, been a revival of interest in Marxist philosophy in the United States. The Society for the Philosophical Study of Dialectical Materialism has organized symposia on Marxist thought in connection with meetings of the American Philosophical Association since 1962. The recently founded American Institute for Marxist Studies sponsors discussions and publishes pamphlets. A number of new magazines devoted, at least in part, to the examination of Marxist principles have commenced publication in the last few years. In spite of these facts, there is no major Marxist theoretician in the United States today, and no American has ever made a lasting contribution to the development or defense of dialectical and historical materialism.[5]

This severe judgment disregards the fact that since the deaths of its creators very few individuals anywhere have had the distinction of extending the theoretical acquisitions of Marxism. These innovators can be counted on the fingers of one hand. Nonetheless, numerous qualified adherents have popularized the doctrines of philosophic materialism and justified the validity of its dialectics against stiff opposition. I can claim to belong to this company, having consistently upheld the principles of dialectical materialism over the past four decades against its adversaries, detractors, and misinterpreters in this country.

Under the circumstances, that was no sinecure. The blaze of interest in Marxism kindled among intellectuals and workers during the Great Depression had died down by the end of the 1930s; it was virtually extinguished in the reaction brought on by the Second World War and its witch-hunting cold war aftermath. Socialism came to be regarded as a dream that had turned into a Stalinist nightmare; the sociologist Daniel Bell proclaimed "the end of ideology"; and Marxism was dismissed as an obsolescent nineteenth-century set of ideas unsuited to American conditions. Its philosophic aspects could receive scant attention in such a climate.

Dialectical materialism was treated with disdain by the recreant intellectuals who, under the banner of an anemic liberalism, had transformed themselves from an avant-garde of socialism into anticommunist crusaders on the cultural front. At the same time, all shades of academic opinion looked upon Marxism as exclusively a theory of society, whose philosophic pretensions were of little account.

This appraisal went uncontested by the New Lefts, who came forward in the late 1960s without any coherent theory; most of them scorned dialectics as a crotchet of the Old Left. In the five years of its existence the Socialist Scholars Conference did not devote a single one of its programs to consideration of those philosophic problems that fellow radicals were debating in other countries of the West and East. This depreciation of philosophic materialism was helped along by those praxis interpreters of Marxism who rejected the universal scope of Marxist thought, the scientific character of its philosophy, and the dialectics of nature.

The arguments in these essays are directed not only against the positions of non-Marxists but also against mistaken ideas held by certain avowed socialists. It may seem to some readers that their polemical zeal detracts from the judicious objectivity that is mandatory in philosophizing. The Greek thinkers who discovered dialectics and sought for the truth through the clash of opposing views would have ridiculed this sort of objection.

Since philosophy is by its very nature an enterprise of criticism, it tends to acquire a polemical edge. A polemic is a militant reply, in the form of reasoned arguments, to attacks upon a position or proposition worthy of defense. This can be mild in manner or muted in tone, as academic etiquette requires, or harsh and vigorous, as necessity may dictate. What is decisive is not the manner but the gist of the matter. Have the pros and cons of the question been trenchantly set forth so that the issues at stake become clarified by the confrontation of opposing views?

Many works in philosophy have had a polemical aim. The innovative thinkers of the bourgeois era vigorously attacked the incorrect and obsolete ideas of their opponents. The contentious Bruno assailed the Oxford pedants who took offense at his propagation of a new cosmology of infinite worlds based on the Copernican revolution. The versatile Francis Bacon no less relentlessly attacked the "barren virgins" of medieval metaphysics in the name of the inductive and experimental method of his natural philosophy.

John Locke was a more even-tempered reasoner. Yet the second chapter of *An Essay on Human Understanding* aims a barrage at the advocacy of any innate principles in the mind as the source of human ideas, in order to clear the site for the foundation of his empirical theory of knowledge. Hegel's *Phenomenology of Mind* is a sustained polemic against the positions of Immanuel Kant, Johann Gottlieb Fichte, Friedrich Wilhelm Joseph von Schelling, and Friedrich Heinrich Jacobi, his predecessors and contemporaries in classical German philosophy.

Now, as then, the sparks of controversy can light the way to truth. In reality, the critics are less offended by the polemical fire than by the kind of partisanship it betokens. Marxism candidly avows that in philosophy it aligns itself with materialism, in logic with dialectics, in politics with revolutionary change, and in sociology and economics with the standpoint of the working class in its anticapitalist struggles. Nor does this taking of definite positions detract from its scientific character.

So unambiguous an attitude is uncongenial to thinkers who thrive on confused and half-formed ideas, though some readily cast off their cloak of neutrality when they happen to be arguing against Marxism or communism. (See the polemics of Karl Popper.) They categorically deny that their own philosophic ideas are disposed to favor the aims, aspirations, or outlook of any particular social grouping. This posture is not only a delusion but is as impossible to adhere to in philosophy as in politics.

Such a disclaimer cannot withstand criticism on another count. The function of philosophers is to introduce the maximum of consciousness into their reflections on social as well as scientific problems. To disregard—or even worse to deny—the presence of social influences, class loyalties, and political implications in one's positions is to exhibit an inferior degree of understanding of the nature of philosophic ideas and a lack of awareness about their actual connections with other manifestations of cultural life.

For a thinker in our time it is not possible to remain aloof from the battle of social forces. Philosophy does not attain its goal or justify itself solely through exchanges among scholars or lectures in classrooms. True ideas in this field, as in others, are valued by the influence they can exert upon the conscious activity of people living in a society torn by conflicting interests and intense passions. The supreme merit of Marxism as a living philosophy and a philosophy of life consists in the conscious fusion of its theory with practical affairs that involve and affect broad masses in action.

After 1940, living in the stronghold of imperialism, it was

difficult to keep faith in the prospects of socialism and hold fast to its principles without a long view of history and a worldwide outlook. I had to watch most of my generation fall by the wayside and conclude a separate peace with the ruling powers in the universities, the publishing field, the professional and business worlds. Today, at the age of seventy, I am one of a very few: a radical intellectual of 1930s vintage who remains active as an unrepentant Marxist and full-time professional in the revolutionary movement.

How is it, I am sometimes asked, that you managed to survive when so many others succumbed to disillusionment and discouragement and withdrew from the arena? A main reason for this staying power is the firm grounding I acquired in Marxist theory.

Trotsky taught his followers by precept and example how necessary it was to preserve the heritage of world revolutionary thought and pass it on to others, especially in reactionary periods when the working class is dormant and its vanguard pushed into a corner. Revolutionists had to retain and fight for the ideological conquests of the past, maintaining the continuity of Marxist thought in order to prepare the way for the next surge forward when the tide turned in a more favorable direction. That has been the principal objective of my work.

The growing discontent with the quality of life under capitalism, the discreditment of liberal reformism, and the manifest helplessness of New Left eclecticism have recently replenished the forces of revolutionary socialism and created an ampler audience for authentic Marxist ideas in the United States. The long darkness is beginning to pass.

This collection will, I hope, benefit those inquiring minds who want to learn what Marxist philosophy really stands for. Dialectical materialism is not an irrelevant and exotic doctrine but the only method that can measure up to the theoretical and political requirements of this tempestuous age of transition from capitalist decay to socialist progress.

March 1, 1976

ଶ

Freedom for Philosophy

[This essay is preceded by an introductory note written by the author for a Gujarati translation published in India before the ousting of Indira Gandhi's repressive regime.]

In the first year of the nineteenth century G. W. F. Hegel wrote: "The lawgivers of Athens prescribed the death-sentence for political abstention at times of political unrest. Philosophical abstention, the decision not to defend one's own position but to resolve in advance to submit to whomever fate crowns with victory and general acclaim, is the decision to condemn oneself to the death of one's speculative reason."[1]

The eminent German thinker was here concerned with asserting not only the right but, even more, the duty of individual judgment and uninhibited expression of belief. This issue, which had been fought out in the sphere of religion during the Protestant Reformation under the watchword "freedom of conscience," was extended into the political and juridical realms through the plebeian-democratic movements of the bourgeois era.

Subsequently guarantees of freedom of thought and expression have been incorporated in the constitutions of most governments, East and West, whether these rest on a capitalist or a socialist economic basis. They are registered in articles 18 and 19 of the Universal Declaration of Human Rights.

However, these liberties remain fragile and are often honored more in the breach than in the observance. They are continually in danger of restriction and, in extreme cases, of destruction altogether by dictatorial or totalitarian regimes, as Augusto Pinochet's Chile freshly demonstrates.

This essay was originally written to make clear the position of Marxism in regard to freedom of thought and expression. This question has come to the fore because of the stringent regimentation of intellectual and cultural, as well as political, life in countries such as the Soviet Union and China, which have passed beyond capitalism but remain very far from the establishment of a socialist democracy of producers and consumers and lack even the most elementary civil liberties required for its preparation.

The status of philosophy can serve as a touchstone for the actual condition of civil rights in those countries. For, if the professional thinkers and qualified teachers of the younger generation in the universities are unable to speak their minds and publish their views without fear of censorship or reprisal, then the vast majority of citizens are certainly no better off.

It is significant that many of the philosophical faculties in the leading universities of Eastern Europe have become centers of dissent and their members subjected to crackdowns and expulsions by party and government authorities. Their criticisms of the status quo articulate the grievances of other layers of society, which are not so well placed to make their voices heard.

Recently I asked one of those philosophers, who had himself been penalized by the officialdom in his country, why the philosophical departments harbored more dissidence than others. He explained that the professors and students in faculties such as engineering, law, medicine, and even economics, could pursue their studies, gain their diplomas, and engage in professional careers without giving too much consideration to fundamental theoretical, political, and cultural questions. Such indifference to burning issues was more difficult in the field of philosophy, which attracted individuals who were less career-oriented, more interested in ideas, and more concerned with seeking satisfactory answers to the problem of life.

They therefore tended to react more quickly and vigorously against the discrepancies between official doctrine and the realities they observed around them, and were less disposed to overlook the gap between the ideals and promises of socialism and the performance of the party in power. Sooner or later these contradictions brought about friction and conflict between the authorities and the students and professors who reciprocally influenced one another.

Experience has shown that any abridgment of democratic rights by a bourgeois regime comes to be directed against the toiling masses and also that the suppression of freedom of speech and opinion in the bureaucratized workers' states is designed to shield the governing caste from criticism from below. That is why Marxists are duty-bound to oppose any restrictive measures or practices that prevent the people at any level from expressing themselves in public or in private.

The utmost latitude for democracy is the most favorable condition for the development of the workers' movement and the cause of socialism not only in the period of preparing for the conquest of power but also after they have succeeded in doing so. Any exceptions to this rule under conditions of full-scale civil war must be regarded as a temporary evil to be eliminated as soon as possible.

When I wrote this essay, I certainly did not expect it would be translated into Gujarati. However, the curtailing of civil liberties, persecutions for opinion, and imprisonments under Prime Minister Indira Gandhi's "emergency" renders its message immediately relevant to the peoples of India. These actions have been defended in the United States with the arguments that poor people don't need democracy and that the withdrawal of civil liberties affects only a small group. "What is the value of freedom of dissent or of a free press to an illiterate farmer or a grossly underpaid teacher in an Indian village?" one apologist wrote.

He forgets that human rights are indivisible. The exercise of civil liberties—the rights of thought, expression, movement—are no less important than social and economic rights—the right to a job, to medical treatment, to education, to social security. When the poorest or their spokesmen and real representatives are deprived of their freedoms, the powers that be, safe from criticism or opposition, can continue to neglect or give low priority to the demands of those most in need of assistance. Thus the restoration and extension of basic freedoms is the precondition for progress.

I hope that the ideas set forth in this essay can help guide those who aspire to remain true to the traditions and teachings of genuine Marxism unadulterated by Stalinism or its Maoist variant.

February 14, 1977

Recent developments in Yugoslavia, Czechoslovakia, Hungary, Poland, and China have called attention to the status of philosophy in the postcapitalist countries and sharply posed the question of the relations between the Marxist world outlook and the unhampered exercise of philosophic inquiry.

Collisions between state and clerical authorities and philosophers long antedate the advent of the Communist regimes of the twentieth century. They are almost as old as philosophizing itself, which is inclined to be critical of established ideas and institutions. Anaxagoras was banished from Athens for impiously declaring that the moon was not divine but made of stone. Socrates had to drink the hemlock after being accused of corrupting the youth with his teachings.

The Inquisition condemned Bruno as a heretic, imprisoned him for eight years, and burned him alive. In the seventeenth century René Descartes and Benedict Spinoza were persecuted for their unorthodox views, while the English government imprisoned the free-thinking deists Peter Anset and Thomas Woolston on the charge of blasphemy for questioning the credibility of miracles and other biblical doctrines.

With the separation of church and state, ecclesiastical controls over free thought were loosened in most Western countries. For instance, the clerical grip upon the teaching of philosophy in the denominational colleges dating from colonial times began to break up in the United States. After the Civil War the flourishing of competitive capitalism and the elevation of philosophy into a professional academic discipline were conducive to a comparable competitiveness in the ideological marketplace. In the last quarter of the nineteenth century Harvard under President Charles Eliot set the pattern for this diversity. According to George Santayana, who benefited from this liberalism, the administrators would have invited a Buddhist, a Muslim, and a Catholic scholastic to the philosophic faculty if they had found suitable candidates.

However, this permissiveness had its limits. C. S. Peirce was not allowed to lecture to the Harvard students because of his irregular marital relations; political radicalism was unwelcome. As Professor Barrows Dunham—who was himself victimized by the Haverford College administration during the reign of McCarthyism—observed in *Thinkers and Treasurers*, the boundaries of free enterprise in ideas "are medieval philosophy on the one hand and Marxist philosophy on the other. The life of

Western philosophy and the lives of its philosophers are spent in trying not to go back to the thirteenth century and not to go forward to the twenty-first."[2]

American universities nowadays pride themselves upon upholding unrestricted freedom of thought, including its philosophic expression. Yet few university philosophy departments treat dialectical materialism seriously, even though this world view has the broadest international influence and has been espoused by some of the keenest minds of this century. They usually have an opponent, rather than a qualified and convinced advocate, present its ideas to students.

Like other democratic rights under capitalist rule, freedom of philosophic inquiry is accorded in the abstract and abridged in reality. While the discrimination against adherents of Marxism is normally more tacit than explicit, it now and then becomes exposed to view. Witness, in recent years, the exclusion of the Stalinist Angela Davis from the University of California at Los Angeles and of the Trotskyist Morris Starsky from Arizona State and Cal State–Dominguez Hills. These cases demonstrate that theoretical agreement with certain Marxist doctrines may be tolerated, but political activism can bring about victimization by witch-hunting administrators.

In the ideological atmosphere of Western Europe and Britain the situation is somewhat less restrictive. There, avowed Communists, and even Maoists and Trotskyists, are to be found on university faculties and are less penalized for their theoretical views and political affiliations. However, in West Germany, where professors are state employees, revolutionists are by law liable to ouster for their ideas. This is an old tradition; after getting his diploma as a Doctor of Philosophy at Jena in 1842, Marx was prevented by the stiflingly reactionary atmosphere from obtaining an academic post.

Thus it is apparent, in the capitalist democracies as elsewhere, that politics does affect the functioning of philosophy, whether or not its professional practitioners care to recognize the fact. Indeed, the prevailing view among most academic philosophers in the United States is that their specialty has little or nothing to do with politics and that the mutual estrangement of the two is normal and desirable.

They are content to leave the practice, if not the theory, of politics to representatives of the men of property and power. Such tendencies as the linguistic analysts, the existentialists, and the idealists maintain that while individual thinkers may in their private capacity as citizens be occupied with political issues and activities, their philosophic work as such has no intrinsic connection or concern with politics. Since the politicos reciprocate this indifference, philosophy nowadays has no perceptible effect on the course of practical politics and does not even influence political discussions.

Such a disjunction between philosophy and politics is anathema to Marxism, which bases itself upon the unity of theory and practice in all spheres. Its founder proclaimed that for a thinker to explain the world is not enough—the point is to change it along revolutionary lines.

Moreover, such indifferentism to political action even runs counter to the recommendations of John Dewey's instrumentalism, which provided a rationale for the mass reform movement of Progressivism before and after the First World War. After Dewey's death in 1952, his pupil Sidney Hook sought to step into his shoes. As a right-wing Social Democrat, Hook became an apologist for the U.S. State Department's policies. In a collection issued by his fellow scholars in honor of his sixty-fifth birthday, Hook was acclaimed as "without peer, the leading philosopher deeply involved in social affairs." This happens to be the case so far as the holders of academic chairs in this country are concerned.

This fact tells a great deal about the state of American philosophy in this generation. France has Jean-Paul Sartre as its premier philosopher, Poland has Leszek Kolakowski, England had its Bertrand Russell—and we, alas, have Sidney Hook! The three Europeans stand out as fierce critics of their societies, defenders of rebel youth, and partisans of the oppressed. Hook has been the favorite philosopher of the *New York Times* and of that corrupt witch-hunter, the late Senator Thomas Dodd of Connecticut. One of the most energetic cold warriors in intellectual circles, Hook argued in 1949 that Communists were conspirators and should be barred from teaching in the schools and universities. This ex-revolutionist voted for Richard Nixon in 1972.

*   *   *

The widespread belief that philosophy and politics are alien pursuits is not the only misconception about their proper relationship. No less erroneous is the antithetical notion, commonly maintained under tyrannical, clerical, and totalitarian regimes, that philosophy must serve as a counselor for the policies of the class or caste that rules the state.

Such a view was predominant in feudal Europe, where philosophy was the handmaiden of theology. More recently, the servile role assigned to philosophy was crassly exhibited in fascist Italy. Benito Mussolini and his blackshirt gangs seized power in 1922 without benefit of any ideology beyond chauvinism and anticommunism. After consolidating his hold, he felt the need for some more elaborate creed as a figleaf for his naked personal dictatorship on behalf of the Italian capitalists.

In 1929 Il Duce decided that his party must "provide itself with a body of doctrine." He accordingly ordered his official philosopher, the former minister of public instruction, Giovanni Gentile, to have it ready in two months—"between now and the National Congress."

Hitlerism had greater power but fewer philosophical pretensions than its Italian precursor. The Nazis made do in the domain of ideology with ultranationalism and racial mysticism combined with the suppression of all independent philosophic thought. The Hitlerite treatment of philosophy was dramatically symbolized by two acts in 1933: the capitulation of Martin Heidegger, the principal theoretician of existentialism in the German university system, to the Nazi government and party, and the bonfires that burned the heretical literatures of Marxism and liberalism.

It is understandable that fascism, the mortal foe of liberal democracy as well as of proletarian socialism, could not allow philosophy to function freely in a critical atmosphere. If such freedom were permitted in that one area, it could not easily be prevented from spilling over into others. The fascists know by instinct that every philosophy has political implications. Muzzling mouths and manacling minds are as indispensable as armed gangs to ensuring the maximum of totalitarian "coordination."

But it had been quite unexpected that regimes ruling in the name of socialism and professing to adhere to Marxism would also totally subordinate philosophy to the dictates of the state power. This first happened in the Soviet Union after Lenin's death, as a bureaucratic caste usurped power from the workers.

Under Stalin, teachers and historians of philosophy could not deviate an iota from the officially sanctioned interpretations of

Marxist doctrine. They had to parrot the prescribed formulas in dealing with problems of theory if they wanted to hold their posts, publish their writings, or even stay out of jail.

Held in a bureaucratic vise, Marxist philosophy had all life-giving juices squeezed out of it and became converted into its opposite. Instead of being a flexible instrument of critical analysis to deal with the development of the contradictory elements in all things, this brand of "dialectical materialism" hardened into a set of dogmatic formulas that disregarded the complexities of the historical process. It was merely a device to justify each shift in the increasingly counterrevolutionary policies of the all-powerful bureaucracy.

This resulted in the ossification and distortion of Marxist thought in and around Communist circles. It set up the opinions of one individual, Joseph Stalin, as the irrefutable standard of truth. Anyone who refused to acknowledge the infallibility of the words uttered by the oracle in the Kremlin was subject to correction, not by superior argument, but by the intervention of the secret police.

This vassalization of philosophic thought to the arbitrary requirements of bureaucratic despotism seriously handicapped the development of the natural and social sciences. The dismissal of the verified results of genetics; the misjudgment of Einstein's theory of relativity and its philosophical implications; the initial disparagement of cybernetics and information theory; the denial of the validity of formal logic within its limits; and the derogation of Sigmund Freud's contributions—whatever his misconceptions on other matters—to depth psychology and psychopathology testify to the harm inflicted by Stalinist dogmatism and intellectual terrorism upon Soviet science and philosophy.

In the past fifteen years, some of this burden has been lightened, though it is still far from being lifted. Natural scientists can proceed within the bounds of their specialties with little fear of punishment for "dangerous thoughts" frowned upon by the authorities. The situation has also somewhat eased in philosophy, though Soviet philosophers are far from enjoying freedom of expression even within the framework of the Marxist world outlook.

Unfortunately, the cult of the individual in philosophy did not die with Stalin. After being buried in Moscow, it was resurrected in Peking. Maoism prescribes that politics—and bureaucratic politics at that!—takes command of philosophy as totally as it does everything else, including the arts and sciences.

"The great red banner of Mao's thought" covers the entire field of philosophy and is virtually a substitute for it in the People's Republic. Mao is awarded the same monopoly in philosophy as Stalin once held—and with as little justification. It was reported in 1971 that Professor Feng Yu-lan of Peking University, who was then seventy-six years old and considered to be the most eminent Chinese philosopher, was rewriting Chinese philosophy from the standpoint of Mao Tse-tung Thought. The journal *Philosophical Research,* published by the Institute of Philosophy in Peking, the highest faculty in China, was discontinued in 1966, at the beginning of the Great Proletarian Cultural Revolution, on the ground that only 5.1 percent of the institute's time was spent on the study of Mao's writings.

Neither Stalin nor his most prominent imitator deserves such eminence on the basis of their contributions to philosophy in general or to Marxist theory in particular. Stalin's writings on philosophical questions were a watered-down, often vulgarized, version of some of the elementary ideas of dialectical and historical materialism he had garnered from Marx, Engels, Plekhanov, and Lenin. In opposition to them, Stalin expunged the negation of the negation from his exposition of the laws of dialectical development. This surgical operation was especially reprehensible because it omitted any logical explanation for the progressive nature of evolution at that climactic revolutionary point where the new replaces the old and lifts things to a higher stage.

Mao learned his philosophy as a pupil of the Stalinist school. His two essays on the subject—*On Practice* and *On Contradiction*—are in large measure paraphrases of what he derived from the standard Stalinized texts, with some sprinkling of illustrative examples drawn from Chinese life and literature.

The method of dialectical materialism should expose fetishes wherever they are to be found—from political economy to the state and religion. Yet many naive radicals have fallen victim to fetishism through the mistaken notion that command of the state apparatus invests those who exercise it with exceptional capacities of theoretical insight. They have had an almost hypnotic adoration for the philosophic prowess of a Stalin or Mao. This illusion serves as a supplementary prop of bureaucratic rule and induces the devotees to acquiesce in the subjection of philosophy to the needs of the state—which violates the critical essence of the dialectical method.

*   *   *

The friction between heterodox philosophers and the Stalinized regimes has flared up most openly in Eastern Europe, where the philosophical faculties of universities from East Berlin to Budapest have been centers of ideological opposition to bureaucratic rule and censorship. The late Georg Lukács made speeches against the harm done by the dogmatism of the Stalin era during debates organized by the Petöfi Circle in June 1956. This was part of the ferment that exploded in the Hungarian revolt that October. Lukács became minister of culture in the ill-fated Nagy government; he was deported to Romania after its overthrow, and only permitted to return the following spring. Yet today under the Janos Kadar administration his followers, such as Agnes Heller, cannot get their works published.

In Czechoslovakia, on April 28, 1975, police raided the home of the philosopher Karel Kosík and confiscated a thousand pages of an unpublished manuscript. They accused him of concealing writings that would show he was criminally engaged in "subversion against the Republic," a charge that carries a one- to five-year sentence. They did the same to his friend, the noted writer Ludvig Vaculik. Kosík, a longtime member of the Communist Party, was expelled in 1969 after Moscow's occupation of his homeland; he was removed the next year from the faculty of philosophy at Prague's Charles University. In a letter to Jean-Paul Sartre, Kosík said he felt as though he were "buried alive." His publications are banned from bookshops and public libraries. He is unable to attend scholarly meetings and cannot accept invitations to lecture at European universities. He is one of thousands of oppositional intellectuals under attack by the Gustav Husak government.

The tribulations of Poland's two best-known Marxist philosophers, Leszek Kolakowski and Adam Schaff, exemplify the situation in that country. The young Kolakowski, the rising star of Polish philosophy, became the most popular voice among the dissenting intellectuals in the antibureaucratic resistance leading up to the "little October" of 1956. In a satirical poem entitled

"What Is Socialism?" he defined the Stalinized state as a place "where philosophers and writers always say the same thing as the generals and ministers, but always after them."[3] When he persisted in criticizing the lack of political and cultural liberties under Wladyslaw Gomulka as under his predecessor, Kolakowski was deprived of his chair in the philosophy faculty of Warsaw University in 1968, blacklisted by the authorities, and forced into exile. He now teaches at Oxford.

A no less telling illustration of how little leeway is allowed for the expression of theoretical differences was the punishment meted out to Adam Schaff, the foremost Polish Communist philosopher and a member of the party's Central Committee since 1959. As a guardian of party orthodoxy, Schaff had scored Kolakowski for his heresies and in 1959 had been instrumental in having him removed as editor in chief of *Philosophical Studies*.

Six years later Schaff published a book, *Marxism and the Human Individual*, that expressed some of the same sentiments and made certain concessions to the trend of thought initiated by his former pupil. He propounded the thesis that the abolition of private property does not signify the end of all forms of alienation in postcapitalist societies but only some of them. Socialism, he wrote, has not completely overcome any one of the known forms of alienation—not even the economic one. He went on to castigate the chauvinism, anti-Semitism, bureaucratism, privileges, and limitations upon freedom of science and critical thought in Poland. He even argued that a full-fledged socialist society will retain certain kinds of alienation stemming from the complex tasks, extensive administrative apparatus, and specialization of labor bound up with modern industrialization.[4]

Gomulka's henchmen condemned Schaff for these views. They were especially alarmed by his recommendations for liberalizing intellectual life. He was expelled from the Central Committee in 1968 and now divides his teaching year between Warsaw and Vienna.

The most stubborn and protracted struggle has taken place in Yugoslavia. For several years the government of Marshal Josip Broz Tito sought to dismiss from Belgrade University's philosophy department six professors and two graduate students who were founders and contributors to the Marxist philosophical journal *Praxis*. This review, internationally celebrated as the foremost medium for the exchange of philosophic views in the entire Soviet bloc, was adamantly opposed to the ideological regimentation of Stalinism and stood for the elaboration of a socialist humanism. It organized yearly seminars at Korcula, where noted left thinkers of such diverse persuasions as Lucien Goldmann, Georg Lukács, Ernst Bloch, Herbert Marcuse, Erich Fromm, and Ernest Mandel participated. Since February 1975 the magazine has been unable to appear because of the government's interference.

The measures taken against the critical-minded professors spring from an ongoing struggle between the state officials, who want to maintain and reinforce their monopoly of control over intellectual and political life, and the democratizing forces among the youth, the intellectuals, and the workers, striving for policies of a more socialist character. All the professors have been known as dissidents since 1968, when they supported the students who occupied the University of Belgrade and set forth a list of economic and political demands that included the establishment of genuine workers' self-management in state enterprises and an end to social inequalities.

Tito himself accused the professors of being "anarcho-liberal" defiers of party discipline and doctrine. In April 1973 a member of the CP's Presidium, Peter Stambolic, said that the view they upheld "tends to undermine confidence among young people in the organizational and leadership qualities of the Communist Party."

For a time the professors successfully resisted the regime, thanks to the support of students, fellow faculty members in various Yugoslav cities, and colleagues abroad. However, legislation on the political and ideological "fitness" of teaching personnel, adopted in early 1974 by the government, stated that professors must agree with the program of the ruling party. Following its adoption, the eight instructors at Belgrade were accused of engaging in "anti–self-management" and "antisocialist" activities and threatened with removal from their posts.[5] On January 28, 1975, the dissidents were dismissed by the Serbian legislature. According to Vladimir Stankovitch, minister of education, they had "abused their function as educators by preparing and orienting youth toward political confrontation and revolt."

In an open letter the professors described their dismissal as an arbitrary action contrary "to all the principles of self-management." They detailed the long campaign against them, including the withdrawal of passports, attempts to compromise their intellectual and moral integrity, and even "the sentencing to forced labor of students who dared to defend us."

The group had earlier been accused by the central party organ, *Kommunist*, of establishing links with West European "Trotsky-ists." Their open letter acknowledged that they do have "relations abroad"—not "with financial magnates, businessmen, generals, intelligence services, kings, or emperors, but with philosophers, thinkers, well-known intellectuals, that is, with men who are not, as the official propaganda claims, enemies of socialism and our country, but quite the contrary, their tested friends."

The charge of unpatriotic activities, the professors noted, has always been invoked by "police with a Stalinist mentality" as a cover for stifling opinions they do not agree with.[6]

They also pointed out that the accusation of corrupting the youth is almost as old as philosophy itself. And so, the persecu-tion of philosophical heretics has come full circle from ancient Athens to Yugoslavia today.

*   *   *

After these horrible examples of the subjection of philosophiz-ing to reactionary politics from the history of both East and West over the past fifty years, it is necessary to ask what the relations of philosophy to the state and society should be according to genuine Marxist standards. The adversaries of Marxism contend that freedom of thought and expression cannot be expected of any regime professing revolutionary socialism since it must be totalitarian by nature.

These preachers of original sin fail to distinguish between a monolithic bureaucratized workers' state that fears dissent like a plague and an authentically Marxist regime, which would not simply tolerate but encourage free inquiry and the confrontation of differing views in all spheres.

Trotsky once remarked that politics is the culture of the proletariat on the road to power. Philosophical outlook and logical method are crucial in guiding this political thought. However, that does not give the proletarian party or state the right to dictate to philosophy—any more than any other party or state. Considerations of political expediency should not be al-lowed to write or rewrite the history of philosophy, dominate its life, or prescribe its course of development.

It is perfectly in order for a Marxist party, or a government guided by such a party, to propagate the doctrines and method of dialectical materialism openly and consistently along with its program. Indeed, Marxists are obligated to do so in order to give the rising generation a correct lead in the field of generalized thought and to oppose whatever is reactionary, obsolescent, and wrong among the ideas implanted in the minds of the people by the old system.

But that is entirely different from adopting a state philosophy and then compelling everyone, from university scholars to schoolchildren, to pay obeisance to that viewpoint. That is as bad as enforcing a state religion. In fact the two are not very far apart. A philosophic standpoint or system that is imposed by official compulsion takes on the traits of a religion: blind faith, hypocrisy, discrepancy between theory and practice, dogmatism, and the withering of critical thought.

It can also lead to censoring and prohibiting alternative trends of thought. These restraints upon the clash of opinions react back upon the orthodox philosophy and further enfeeble it. When it encounters no serious, open challenges to its positions and formulas, official thought grows dull, slothful, and unsure of itself. It inclines to evade the most burning, sensitive, and complicated questions of everyday life that trouble the thought and conscience of the people. It begins to lose the allegiance of the best minds among the mature and alienates the flower of the youth. It ceases to progress.

This process of degradation afflicted philosophy in the Soviet bloc under Stalin. It is the source of the grave, still unresolved crisis in the realm of philosophy felt throughout the Communist world. More and more of the keenest thinkers in the Soviet bloc are dissatisfied with the post-Stalin dogmatism and keep hacking away at it, though in most cases with dull weapons and inconclusive results. The situation in China is, if anything, worse. Mao-style ideas, turned into a catechism to be repeated by rote, have made a travesty of dialectical materialism.

Even if such a philosophy were authentically Marxist in spirit, its enforced prescription by the state would have harmful effects; it is even worse when a falsified version is imposed. A living and effective philosophy must earn and win conviction by the force of its arguments rather than by arguments of force. It must gain assent by its concordance with the facts of experience, the insight of its analyses, and the truth of its conclusions. It must evolve, change, and advance in the light of practice.

Genuine Marxism is such a philosophy. It has no fear of opposing or divergent views. Why should it shrink from any competition of ideas? Despite innumerable attempts to repress them, the ideas of scientific socialism have gained a worldwide hearing and adherence over the past hundred years. No one can claim to be politically literate today without some acquaintance with them.

Dialectical materialism wants free competition in philosophy as well as in the arts and sciences, just as Marxist politics favors a plurality of parties in a socialist democracy. This would foster the most propitious atmosphere for the advancement of creative thought and endeavor in all fields.

Having made this clear, it is necessary to note that there is no shade of philosophy without class bias and political implications. A philosophy may sincerely proclaim that it has nothing to do with public affairs or political questions, that its ideas have no necessary applications to practical life. But this does not preclude politics from having something to do with it, as the German professors in their academic hideouts discovered when Hitlerism took over, or as American thinkers became aware of when McCarthyism was rampant.

Philosophy is not a purely intellectual exercise dealing exclusively with some esoteric regions inaccessible to ordinary mortals or with subjects locked up in the minds of Ph.D.s. Its ideas are shaped not only by the existing state of social development and inventory of culture and science, but by the world outlook, material needs, vital aims, and aspirations of diverse sectors of society. Philosophy has social functions, and its use and influence extend beyond college courses and professional journals. Its methods of thought serve as tools of social forces, as weapons in the struggles of contending classes. John Dewey's instrumentalism was the expression and instrument of the liberal reformers of the Progressive movement, just as Marxism is the theory and method of revolutionary socialism.

*   *   *

Marxists will draw different conclusions from the *via dolorosa* of philosophy under the postcapitalist regimes than the anti-Marxists. The latter take these repeated instances of repression as proof positive of the inherent incompatibility of free, critical thought with any postcapitalist regime. The Marxist approach looks forward to the norms of a socialist democracy rather than turning back toward the outlook of a decaying bourgeois liberalism.

For Marxists it is first of all imperative to defend all those scholars who have been penalized by Stalinist regimes for their oppositional ideas whether or not one agrees with their views. This is an indispensable act of solidarity with the increasing demand of the workers and students for observance of the elementary human rights explicitly incorporated in the constitutions of their countries and often in their government's international agreements. When I presented this point of view at an Australian university, a Maoist philosophy professor scornfully remarked that I sounded more like the John Stuart Mill of *On Liberty* than a Marxist. (He should more accurately have said a Stalinist.) His point had more pertinence than he realized.

The citizens living under malignant bureaucratic dictatorships do not enjoy even those democratic rights that the revolutionary forces fought for and to some degree won during the rise of bourgeois society. It is an irony of history—and an illustration of the contradictory course of social progress—that advocates of "socialism with a human face" have to demand freedom of opinion and the right of expression against official inquisition and censorship, just as bourgeois democrats previously fought for the separation of church from state and freedom of religious belief, along with other liberties.

Their cause is just and fully worthy of support, for the sake of both democracy and socialism. Marxism agrees with liberalism that freedom of thought and expression are goods to be cherished and a right of the people to be safeguarded against restriction by reactionary forces.

The two schools of thought clash over the struggle for power between classes—at the point of confrontation between revolution and counterrevolution. Classical liberalism elevates bourgeois democratic rights above the concrete conditions and necessities of the class struggle and regards them as supreme commandments—like Immanuel Kant's categorical imperative, they are never under any circumstances to be curtailed or violated. (To be sure, the adherents of liberalism abrogated these rights in practice whenever it suited their interests or convenience.)

Historical materialists take a more realistic, relativistic, and forthright approach to this question, as to others. They deny that there are any sacrosanct principles of social organization and conduct that are binding upon everyone at all times and in all cases, that must be strictly adhered to, come what may. There can be exceptions to all rules. In determining what position to adopt on any particular issue and in any specific situation, the Marxist takes into account not only the relevant general principles, but more decisively, what class interests are at stake. Behind every abstraction put forward by the forces involved in a conflicting situation, it is necessary to discern the material interests each side is protecting and promoting.

In the academic field, for example, departmental autonomy is considered essential for maintaining high standards of scholarship and shielding the faculty from adverse outside interference. Is this rule never to be breached? In Yugoslavia, where the state authorities have grossly trampled upon the autonomy of the philosophy faculty, this principle has to be upheld and defended.

It is otherwise when the same principle is invoked in the United States to protect the privileged positions of an elite of white male professors. Thus, Sidney Hook was outraged when repeated documented complaints forced the Office of Civil Rights of the Department of Health, Education and Welfare to file suits against the pattern of racial and sexual discrimination in numbers, salaries, and positions in colleges receiving federal funds. The professor complained that "the effect of ultimata to the universities to hire blacks and women under threat of losing crucial financial support is to compel them to hire unqualified Negroes and women and to discriminate against qualified non-blacks and men."[7] His arguments, under cover of "faculty freedom," against affirmative action to eliminate the effects of long-standing discrimination, bear the same reactionary stamp as the efforts of union bureaucrats in the building trades to maintain a white job monopoly against the demands of the oppressed minorities.

Similar considerations apply in cases of civil war and other life-and-death situations for the revolutionary cause. Under such exceptional circumstances it may be warranted and sometimes imperative for a workers' regime to restrict ordinary civil rights for a time. Proletarian revolutions are not unique in this respect. Curbs on legal and civil rights were instituted during all the major revolutions of the bourgeois era, including our own War of

Independence and the Civil War. The worker-peasant revolutions of the twentieth century have been compelled to do the same in the conquest and consolidation of their power.

Notwithstanding this necessity, the leadership of the revolution is duty-bound to recognize that these are temporary wartime expedients and should not be perpetuated once the new regime is stabilized and civil peace restored. Such restraints are not the norm for a workers' state, as the Stalinists hold; they are abnormal and episodic measures that should be lifted as soon as feasible. What was done along this line by the bourgeoisie's liberal parliamentary regimes in the nineteenth century is all the more incumbent upon the workers' states in the twentieth. They should not only promise but actually achieve expanded freedoms in all areas for their citizens, without the restrictions imposed by the private ownership of social wealth that abridges and corrupts so many guaranteed rights.

The Marxist approach to this touchy question has been well stated by Roy Medvedev, the noted Soviet historian and dissident, whose own family has been the target of repression by high government officials. "The right of dissent should not be thought peculiar to bourgeois democracy. It is a most important feature of any democracy. There are exceptional situations in which certain important democratic freedoms, including freedom of speech and opposition, can be temporarily restricted. Such a situation really did exist in our country during the first years of Soviet rule, but there was no reason for the state of emergency to apply during the building of socialism and communism. In today's world, fifty-three years after the October Revolution, it is certainly both absurd and extremely harmful to be intolerant toward dissent and opposition, political or otherwise."[8]

In an article written in 1938 Leon Trotsky agreed that the proletariat in power might, for a certain time during a civil war, have to take special measures against the actively counterrevolutionary bourgeoisie, such as curtailing freedom of the press.

Naturally, if you are forced to use artillery and planes against the enemy, you cannot permit this same enemy to maintain his own centers of news and propaganda within the armed camp of the proletariat. Nonetheless, in this instance, too, if the special measures are extended until they become an enduring pattern, they in themselves carry the danger of getting out of hand and of the workers' bureaucracy gaining a political monopoly that would be one of the sources of its degeneration. . . .

The real tasks of the workers' state lie not in clamping a police gag on public opinion but rather in freeing it from the yoke of capital. This can be done only by placing the means of production, including the production of public information, in the hands of society as a whole. Once this fundamental socialist step has been taken, all currents of public opinion that have not taken up arms against the dictatorship of the proletariat must be given the opportunity to express themselves freely. It is the duty of the workers' state to make available to them, in proportion to their numbers, all the technical means they may require, such as presses, paper, and transport. One of the main causes of the degeneration of the state apparatus is the Stalinist bureaucracy's monopolization of the press, which threatens to reduce all the gains of the October Revolution to utter ruin.[9]

It will be retorted that the necessity to ward off the counterrevolutionary forces of capitalist restoration and imperialism is the same justification used today by the Soviet government and its emulators for maintaining censorship and suppressing civil rights. There is not a single element of Marxism that the bureaucrats do not pervert, including this one.

But the Soviet Union has already existed for over half a century and is not threatened by civil war or the near prospect of military invasion. Its progress is actually threatened by the stifling of domestic freedoms. Its peoples are entitled to the rights guaranteed by their constitution. It is one thing for the police power to be used against counterrevolutionaries engaged in activities directly aimed at overthrowing the socioeconomic gains made since 1917; it is an entirely different matter to wield them against artists, writers, philosophers, or plain workers and peasants who think differently than the powers that be.

Just as healthy lungs need fresh air to breathe, so the free exchange of ideas and circulation of information is indispensable to the citizens of any country if their political and cultural life is to flourish.

A strong and healthy workers' state cannot be undermined by open criticism frankly expressed; it can only be morally and intellectually benefited by such ventilation. In fact, the restrictions are imposed by the bureaucrats not to defend the institutions of the revolution, but to shield their material privileges and autocratic power from public scrutiny and accountability. They are the greatest menace today to the gains made through the October revolution.

Some members of the Frankfurt school maintain that philos-

ophers must by the very nature of their activity be hostile to
society and the state, regardless of its content and direction,
because their reason for existence is to be critical of what exists.
They view the philosopher as an eternal and unchangeable
adversary of all institutions. This smacks more of anarchism
than of Marxism.

Yet the observation does contain a grain of truth. Discontent
with things as they are has been the psychic motive force of all
human progress—philosophy included. Philosophy as a rational,
scientific approach to the world emerged out of the criticism of
religion and mythology. To philosophize is to criticize—and the
dialectical method is vigorously critical. It is predicated upon the
contradictory nature of changing reality and takes no state of
affairs or stage of knowledge as fixed or final.

All the same, the Frankfurt conception of the functioning of
philosophy erects into an absolute an office that is relative to the
surrounding historical conditions. There need not be unbridgeable antagonism between intellectuals and the state, however
uncomfortable their cohabitation. Philosophers holding the most
varied views can uninhibitedly proceed with their inquiries if the
social and political order is basically progressive and more
responsive to human welfare than its predecessor, if the regime
permits the free exercise of thought and expression, and if its
policies promote social and scientific advancement.

For its own material and moral advantage a healthy workers'
state would take pains to ensure that no impediments whatsoever
are placed upon intellectual expression and scientific research
and that their fruits are made accessible to all. The socialist
movement aims to provide more democratic rights for the collectivity and the individual than have ever been extended under the
most liberal capitalism. So long as this obligation is unfulfilled, it
will have fallen short of its historical mission and failed to realize
the potential of its revolutionary humanism.

Marxism and Existentialism

Existentialism and Marxism are the most widely discussed and widely held philosophies of our time. The first is dominant in Western Europe and gaining increasing popularity in the United States. The second is not only the official doctrine of all Communist countries but, in one form or another, is accepted as a guide by many movements and parties throughout the world.

Over the past twenty years the proponents of these two schools of thought have engaged in continual debate with one another. The center of this controversy has been France. There existentialism has found its most talented spokesmen in Nobel Prize winner Jean-Paul Sartre and his associates, who have developed their positions in direct contact and contest with Marxism. They live on a continent where, unlike the United States, socialism has influenced public life for almost a century, and in a country where the Communist Party gets a quarter of the vote, is followed by most of the working class, and exerts heavy pressure upon radical intellectuals. These circumstances have compelled the so-called Mandarins of the Left to make clear their attitude toward Marxism at every stage in the evolution of their views.

The development of Sartre has been especially paradoxical. He worked out his original existentialist ideas under the sway of nonmaterialist thinkers such as Edmund Husserl and Martin Heidegger as a deliberate challenge to Marxism. In *Being and Nothingness* (1943) and *Materialism and Revolution* (1947) Sartre

presented his philosophy as an alternative to dialectical materialism. Then in the late 1950s he made a turnabout and embraced
Marxism, at least in words—which for him, as he explains in the
first volume of his recent autobiography, have had a reality
greater than the objective world.

In his latest philosophical treatise, *The Critique of Dialectical
Reason* (1960), the first section of which has been published in
English as *Search for a Method,* he declares that existentialism
has become a subordinate branch of Marxism which aspires to
renew and enrich it. Thus the phenomenologist of existence who
condemned dialectical materialism as false and a foe to human
freedom in the 1940s now proposes to marry Marxism and
existentialism.

To what extent, if any, can these philosophies be conjoined?
Can a synthesis of the two be viable? This article intends to show
that the contending world outlooks cannot be harmonized or
integrated into one containing "the best features" of both. A
legendary alchemist thought that by putting together fire and
water he would concoct that most desirable of delights, "fire-
water." Actually, the one nullifies or extinguishes the other when
they come into contact. It is the same with Marxism and
existentialism. Their fundamental positions over a broad spectrum of problems extending from philosophy and sociology to
morality and politics are so divergent that they cannot really be
reconciled.

This piece can do no more than indicate the main lines of their
disagreement on the most important issues. Let us first consider
their opposing conceptions on the nature of reality and then on
science, which is the highest expression of our endeavors to
investigate and know the world.

1. Science and the Absurdity of Reality

For existentialism the universe is irrational; for Marxism it is
lawful. The propositions of existentialist metaphysics are set in a
context of cataclysmic personal experience. They all flow from
the agonizing discovery that the world into which we are thrown
has no sufficient or necessary reason for existence, no rational
order. It is simply there and must be taken as we find it. Being is
utterly contingent, totally without meaning, and superfluous.

Human existence as such is equally meaningless. "It is absurd
that we were born, it is absurd that we die," writes Sartre in

Being and Nothingness. We do not know where we came from, why we are here, what we must do, or where we are going. "Every existing thing is born without reason, prolongs itself out of the weakness of inertia and dies by chance," says one of Sartre's characters in *Nausea.*

If the world is devoid of meaning and impervious to rational inquiry, a philosophy of existence would seem a contradiction in terms. In contrast to religious mysticism, philosophy aims to illuminate reality by means of concepts, the tools of reasoning. How is it possible to explain an unconditionally absurd universe or even find a foothold for theory in it?

Soren Kierkegaard did contend that it was neither possible nor desirable to think systematically about the reality of life, which eluded the grasp of the abstracting intellect. Albert Camus rejected existentialist theorizing on similar grounds. It is hopeless, he asserted, to try to give rational form to the irrational. The absurdity of existence must be lived through, suffered, defied; it cannot be satisfactorily explained.

However, the professional thinkers of this school do not choose to commit philosophical suicide. They have proceeded, each in their own way, to elaborate a philosophy of "being in an absurd world." There is logic to their illogicality. If everything is hopelessly contradictory, why should the enterprise of philosophy be an exception? The human mission, they say, is to find out the meaning of meaninglessness—or at least give some meaning through our words and deeds to an otherwise inscrutable universe.

For dialectical materialism, reality has developed in a lawful manner and is rationally explicable. The rationality of nature and human history is bound up with matter in motion. The concatenation of cosmic events gives rise to cause-and-effect relations that determine the qualities and evolution of things. The physical preceded and produced the biological, the biological the social, and the social the psychological in a historical series of mutually conditioned stages. The aim of science is to disclose their essential linkages and formulate these into laws that can help pilot human activity.

The rationality, determinism, and causality of the universal process of material development do not exclude but embrace the objective existence and significance of absurdity, indeterminism, and accident.

However, these random features of reality are no more fundamental than regularity. They are not immutable and irremovable aspects of nature and history but relative phenomena which in the course of development can change to the extent of becoming their own opposites. Chance, for example, is the antithesis of necessity. Yet chance has its own laws, which are lodged in the occurrence of statistical regularities. Quantum mechanics and the life insurance business exemplify how individual accidents are convertible into aggregate necessities.

Exceptions are nothing but the least frequent alternatives, and when enough exceptions pile up they give rise to a new rule of operation which supersedes the formerly dominant one. The interplay of chance and necessity through the conversion of the exception into the rule can be seen in the economic development of society. Under tribal life, production for immediate personal consumption is the norm whereas production for exchange is a rare and casual event. Under capitalism, production for sale is the general law; production for one's own use is uncommon. What was categorically necessary in the first economic system is fortuitous in the second. Moreover, in the transition from one economy to the other the bearers of chance and necessity have changed places, have become transformed into each other.

Social structures that are rational and necessary under certain historical circumstances become absurd and untenable at a further stage of economic development and are scrapped. Thus feudal relations, which corresponded to a given level of the powers of social production, became as anachronistic as Don Quixote and had to give way before the more dynamic forces and more rational forms of bourgeois society.

The existentialists go wrong, say the Marxists, in making an eternal absolute out of the occurrence of chance events and unruly phenomena. These are not unconditioned and unchangeable but relative and variable aspects of being.

As a result of their conflicting conceptions of reality, the two philosophies have entirely different attitudes toward science. If the universe is irrational through and through, then science, which is the most sustained and comprehensive effort to render the relations and operations of reality intelligible and manageable, must be nonsensical and futile. The existentialists mistrust and downgrade the activities and results of science. They accuse the scientists of substituting conceptual and mathematical abstractions for the whole living person, proffering the hollow shell of rationality for its substance, neglecting what is most important in existence, and breeding an unbridled technology which, like Frankenstein's monster, threatens to crush its creator.

Marxism, which holds fast to the rationality of the real, esteems scientific knowledge and inquiry as the fullest and finest expression of the exercise of reason. It believes that the discovery of physical and social laws can serve to explain both the regularities and irregularities of development, so that even the most extreme anomalies of nature, society, and the individual can be understood.

2. The Predominance of Ambiguity

In the eyes of the existentialists, ambiguity presides over existence. It is easy to see why. Ambiguity is a state between chaos and order, darkness and light, ignorance and knowledge. If the universe is ruled by chance, everything is inevitably and ineradicably indeterminate. The absence of cause-and-effect relations endows reality with a duplicity and disorder which renders it hopelessly obscure.

This uncertainty is exceedingly acute in the individual. We are torn by warring elements within ourselves. This predicament is all the more difficult because we are trapped in a maze of conflicting possibilities. We must act in a fog where indistinct shapes move in no definite direction and toward no ascertainable destination. Since the given situation has no intrinsic structure, trends, or signs which make one alternative superior to another, the existentialist is entitled to pick whatever solution seems most appealing. What comes out is then a matter of chance or caprice.

"The essential form of spiritual life is marked by ambiguity," observes Heidegger in *An Introduction to Metaphysics*. Simone de Beauvoir tells us that "from the very beginning, existentialism defined itself as a philosophy of ambiguity." She has attempted to found an ethics on the tragic ambivalence of the human being, who is tossed like a shuttlecock between pure externality and pure consciousness without ever being able to bring them into accord.

Maurice Merleau-Ponty likewise made ambiguity the leading principle of his social and political outlook. Human beings, he maintained, are thrust willy-nilly into situations where many conflicting forces are at work. These do not have any central line of development or indicate any particular outcome. We must arbitrarily select one of the multifarious possibilities and act upon it amidst uncertainty and confusion. Our option makes and throws light on our character but cannot remove either the inherent ambiguity of the situation or the risk of the undertaking. Everything in life is a gamble.

Merleau-Ponty objected to historical materialism because it did not give accident primacy over necessity in history. He applied his sweeping indeterminism to the outcome of the struggle for socialism: "The possibility remains of an immense compromise, of a decaying of history where the class struggle, powerful enough to destroy, would not be powerful enough to build and where the master-lines of History charted in *The Communist Manifesto* would be effaced." This was the theoretical source of the skepticism which lay behind his reluctance to join the Communist Party, and which later led to his rejection of the Stalinized Soviet Union as in any respect socialist.

The personages in the works of existentialist writers exemplify the enigmatic duplicity of the human being. They do not have stable characters or predictable courses of conduct. They plunge into unexpected and uncalled-for actions which contravene their previous commitments. Their lives and motives are susceptible to multiple meanings and inconclusive interpretations—which the authors are not concerned to clarify, since misunderstanding must accompany the ambiguity of existence. The latest example of this is Edward Albee's play *Tiny Alice,* whose symbolism and significances have puzzled not only the drama critics but the author and director as well.

The problem of ambiguity is very real; it arises from the contradictory content of things. While the universe has a determinate structure and a discernible order of evolution, its elements are so complex and changing that the forms of their development can assume highly equivocal and puzzling appearances. The question is whether these paradoxical manifestations must remain forever indecipherable and unsettled or whether the diverse and misleading forms can be correlated by scientific means into some lawful pattern which gets at the essence of things.

The existentialists refuse to concede that the outcome of a situation depends upon the relative weight of all the factors at work within it; they want to make the settlement depend entirely upon the will of the individual. This runs into conflict with their observation that the results of our activities are often at odds with our intentions, desires, and expectations. If this is so, what

other underlying forces determine the outcome? The existentialists have no answer but accident. For them, arbitrariness remains the arbiter of all events.

The materialist dialectician takes up where the baffled existentialist leaves off, proceeding from the premise that what can
become definite in reality can find clear-cut formulation in
thought. No matter how hidden, complicated, and devious the
contradictions encountered in reality may be, they can with time
and effort be unravelled. The dialectical essence of all processes
consists precisely in the unfolding of their internal oppositions,
the gradual exposure and greater determination of their polar
aspects, until they arrive at their breaking point and ultimate
resolution. As the contending forces and tendencies within things
are pushed to the extreme, they become more and more sharply
outlined and less and less ambiguous. The struggle of opposites is
brought to a conclusion and maximum clarification through the
victory of one irreconcilable alternative over the other. This is the
logical course and final outcome of all evolutionary processes.

Marxists do not regard ambiguity as an impenetrable and
unalterable property of things or thoughts but as a provisional
state which further development will overcome. Any unsettled
situation can give way to greater determination. Reality and our
understanding of it need not be forever ambiguous, any more
than water must remain fluid under all circumstances.

Order and disorder are relative features of things. The greatest
chaos has sources of order within it, behind it, and ahead of it.
The most crystallized form of order contains elementary traces of
irregularity which can in time spread out, upsetting and overturn-
ing its symmetry and stability. Moreover, ambiguity can be as
much of a challenge and an opportunity as an obstacle. It prods
knowledge and practice forward. Science advances and action
becomes more effective as humanity succeeds in displacing what
is indeterminate and problematic with definite ideas about
objectively determined things.

The existentialists make much of the ineradicable ambiguity of
history. They emphasize that history does not move in a straight
line or a uniform manner from one point to another; indeed some
among them question whether humankind has progressed at all.
Marxism does not deny that history is full of irregularities,
relapses, stagnation, and oddities. Despite its zigzags, however,
history has moved onward and upward from one stage to the
next, from savagery to civilization, for ascertainable reasons. It

exhibits necessities as well as ironic contingencies, final settle-
ments as well as unresolved issues. The French feudalists, the
colonial Loyalists, the Southern slaveholders, the German Nazis,
and the Russian capitalists can attest to that.

3. Individuals and Their Environment

For purposes of analysis, reality can be divided into two
sectors: one public, the other private. There is the objective
material world that exists around us, regardless of what anyone
feels, thinks, or knows about it. Against this is the inner domain
of personal experience, the world as it appears to each one of us,
as we perceive, conceive, and react to it. Although these two
dimensions of human existence are never actually disjoined, and
although they roughly correspond with each other, they do not
coincide in certain essential respects. They can therefore be
considered separately and studied on their own account.

Existentialism and Marxism take irreconcilable views on the
nature of the relationship between the objective and subjective
sides of human life, on the status, the interconnection, and the
relative importance of the public and private worlds.

Marxism says that nature is prior to and independent of
humanity. Human existence, as a product and part of nature, is
necessarily dependent upon it. Existentialism holds that the
objective and subjective components of being do not exist apart
from each other, and that in fact the subject makes the world
what it is.

The contrast between the idealistic subjectivity of the existentialist thinkers and the materialist objectivity of Marxism can be
seen in the following assertion of Heidegger in *An Introduction to
Metaphysics:* "It is in words and language that things first come
into being and are." In accord with the conception that other
aspects of reality acquire existence only to the extent that they
enter human experience, Heidegger makes not simply the meaning but the very existence of things emanate from our verbal
expression of them. To a materialist such human functions as
speech and thought reflect the traits of things but do not create
them. The external world exists regardless of our relations with it
and apart from the uses we make of its elements.

The whole of existentialism revolves around the absolute
primacy of the conscious subject over everything objective,
whether it be physical or social. The truth and values of existence

are to be sought exclusively within the experiences of the individual, in our self-discovery and self-creation of what we authentically are.

Marxism takes the reverse position. It gives existential priority, as any consistent materialism must, to nature over society and to society over any single person within it. Nature, society, and the individual coexist in the closest reciprocal relationship, which is characterized by the action of human beings in changing the world. In the process of subduing objective reality for their own ends they change themselves. The subjective comes out of the objective, is in constant interaction and unbreakable communion with it, and is ultimately controlled by it.

These opposing conceptions of the object-subject relationship are reflected in the conflict between the two philosophies on the nature of the individual and the individual's connections with the surrounding world. The category of the isolated individual is central in existentialism. The true existence of a person, it asserts, is thwarted by things and other people. These external forces crush the personality and drag it down to their own impersonal and commonplace level.

The individual can attain genuine value only in contest with these external relationships. We must turn inward and explore the recesses of our being in order to arrive at our real selves and real freedom. Only at the bottom of the abyss where the naked spirit grapples with the fearful foreknowledge of death are both the senselessness and the significance of existence revealed to us.

Thus existentialism pictures the individual as essentially divorced from other humans, at loggerheads with an inert and hostile environment, and pitted against a coercive society. This desolation of the individual is the wellspring of inconsolable tragedy. Having cut off the individual from organic unity with the rest of reality, from the regular operation of natural processes and the play of historical forces, existentialism is thereafter unable to fit the subjective reactions and reflections of the personality to the environing conditions of life. Indeed, says Sartre, our attempts to make consciousness coincide with "facticity," the world of things, are a futile business.

By a grim paradox, the solitary human mind is completely sovereign in shaping its real existence. With nothing but its own forces to lean on and its own judgment as a guide, it must confront and solve all the problems of life.

Existentialism is the most thoroughgoing philosophy of individualism in our time. "Be yourself at all costs!" is its first commandment. It champions the spontaneity of the individual menaced by the mass, the class, the state. It seeks to safeguard the dignity, rights, initiatives, even the vagaries of the autonomous personality against any oppressive authority, organized movement, or established institution.

With individual liberty as its watchword and supreme good, existentialism is a creed of nonconformism. "I came to regard it as my task to create difficulties everywhere," wrote Kierkegaard in describing how he turned to an existentialist view of life. The existentialists are averse to routine, externally imposed ideas, or disciplined modes of behavior, and whatever is uncongenial to the desires of the ego. All submission to projects not freely chosen is evidence of bad faith, says Sartre.

The targets of existentialism's protest are as diversified as the interests and inclinations of its exponents. These have ranged from religious orthodoxies to philosophical systematizing, from capitalist exploitation to Stalinist regimentation, from bourgeois morality to workers' bureaucratism. Kierkegaard set about to disturb the peace of mind of the hypocritical Danish middle class. Nietzsche heralded the superman who was to rise above the herdlike crowd and transcend good and evil. The favored heroes of Camus and Sartre are rebels and outsiders. Simone de Beauvoir and Sartre analyze writers such as the Marquis de Sade and Jean Genet, whose ideas and lives have outrageously flouted the ordinary canons of moral conduct.

It must be said that the heresies of the existentialists do not always succeed in shedding completely the values of the society they rebel against. Kierkegaard assailed the sluggishness and self-deception of the smug citizens around him only to embrace the Christian God with more passionate intensity. And Sartre, who attacks stuffed shirts and stinkers for their egotism, clings to the concept of the totally free person beholden solely to himself as the pivot of his philosophy and moral theory.

Existentialism proclaims the urge of the individual to develop without hindrance. But its constitutional aversion to the organized action of mass movements determined by historically given circumstances renders it incapable of finding an effective solution of this problem for the bulk of humanity. That is why it is nonconformist rather than revolutionary.

Historical materialism takes an entirely different approach to the relationship between individual and environment. We are essentially social beings; we develop into individuals only in and through society. For Marxists, the isolated individual is an abstraction. All distinctive things about humans, from tool-making, speech, and thought to the latest triumphs of art and technology, are products of our collective activity over the past million years or so.

Take away from the person all the socially conditioned and historically acquired attributes derived from the culture of the collectivity and little would be left but the biological animal. The specific nature of the individual is determined by the social content of the surrounding world. This shapes not only our relations with other people but our innermost emotions, imagination, and ideas.

Even the special kind of solitude felt by people today is an outgrowth of the social system. One of the major contradictions of capitalism is that it has brought humans into the closest "togetherness" while accentuating conditions that pull them apart. Capitalism socializes the labor process and knits the whole world into a unit while separating people from one another through the divisive interests of private property and competition. Frederick Engels noted this when he described the crowds in the London streets in his first work, *The Condition of the Working Class in England in 1844*: "This isolation of the individual, this narrow self-seeking, is the fundamental principle of our society everywhere. . . . The dissolution of mankind into monads, of which each has a separate *principle*, the world of atoms, is here carried out to its utmost extreme." The "barbarous indifference, hard egotism and nameless misery" which he observed over a century ago still strongly permeate our acquisitive society.

Like the existentialists, the socialist movement has made one of its chief aims and persistent concerns the defense and expansion of individuality—however much this has been violated in practice by bureaucratic powers speaking in the name of socialism. But Marxism differs from existentialism by denying that individualism as a philosophy can provide an adequate method of social change and political action. Since the social structure shapes and dominates the lives of individuals, it has to be transformed by the collective struggle of the working people in order to eliminate the conditions that repress individuality and create an environment suited to the unhampered cultivation of the capacities of each living human being.

4. Freedom, Necessity, and Morality

According to its supporters, the supreme merit of existentialism is its capacity to explain and safeguard human freedom. It is superior to Marxism, they claim, because it does not subjugate human life to determinism, which robs us of free choice and moral responsibility for our deeds.

The problem of freedom and necessity arises from two apparently contradictory facts of life. Science teaches, and practice confirms, that nature and society have regularities which are expressed in laws. At the same time, people deliberately select between different lines of action. How can universal determinism coexist with freedom of choice?

The existentialists cut this Gordian knot by depriving determinism of any sway over human beings. What is nonhuman may be subject to objective causation but a person cannot be reduced to the status of a thing. To be human is to be totally free, that is to say, completely self-determined by successive acts of will. When external circumstances compel us to be or do anything against our will, we are not behaving like human beings but like automatons. It is only by detaching ourselves from the given situation that we can freely decide the character and course of our lives.

Marxism resolves the antithesis between scientific determinism and human choice in an altogether different manner. Humanity really becomes free by uncovering and understanding the laws of nature, society, and thought. Our aims become effective to the extent that verified scientific knowledge enables us to control and change the world around us. The existentialist demand for absolute personal freedom does not correspond to anything real or realizable. People must act under the constraint of their conditions of life and cannot cast off their causal weight.

Human activity is an unequal synthesis of extrinsic determination and self-determination. People react consciously and vigorously to their environment and take initiatives to alter certain aspects of it. The measure of control exercised by the objective and subjective components of the causal process changes and develops in the course of time according to the growth of our mastery over nature and society. History has proceeded, by and large, toward greater freedom, toward a growth in our ability to decide and direct an increasing number of activities.

The existentialists regard determinism as an inveterate foe of human aims and aspirations. In reality, determinism can display either a hostile or friendly face to us, depending upon the given circumstances. Humans became free in this century to travel through the atmosphere for the first time and even to leave this planet. This was achieved by finding out the principles of aerodynamics and propulsion and then utilizing them to construct the instruments to realize the aim of flight. In making aircraft we have succeeded in putting the determinism of the material world to work for us, rather than against us.

The same is true of social determinism. People have been enabled to enlarge their freedom not by ignoring and rejecting the determinants of history but by recognizing them and acting in accord with their requirements. The American people acquired and extended their liberties by seeing the need for abolishing British domination and Southern slaveholding when national progress demanded such revolutionary deeds.

Far from being incompatible with freedom, as the existentialist thinks, natural and social necessities are the indispensable foundation of all the freedoms we have.

The existentialists, however, are more concerned about the narrower dilemmas of personal responsibility than with the broader problem of the interaction of freedom and necessity in social and historical evolution. Both existentialism and Marxism agree that our conduct has to be regulated and judged by relative human standards. We are accountable only to ourselves and for ourselves, and have no right to sanctify or justify our decisions by reference to any supernatural source.

What, then, is the basis of morality? Where do our standards of right and wrong come from? The ethics of existentialism is uncompromisingly libertarian. We create both ourselves and our morality through our utterly uncurbed choices. Authentic freedom manifests itself in the causeless selection among alternative possibilities and fulfills itself in the deliberate adoption of one's own set of values.

The Marxist theory of morality does not rest upon an inborn capacity of the individual to make unconditioned and unmotivated choices but upon historical and social considerations. Its position can be summarized as follows: (1) Morality has an objective basis in the conditions, relations, needs, and development of society. Its rational character is derived from a correspondence with given historical realities and an understanding of specific social necessities. (2) Morality has a variable content and a relative character, depending upon changes in social circumstances. (3) Under civilization to date, morality inescapably takes on a class character. (4) There are no absolute standards of moral behavior and judgment. Human acts are not good or bad, praiseworthy or iniquitous, in themselves. All moral codes and conduct must be evaluated by reference to the prevailing conditions and the concrete social needs, class interests, and historical aims they serve.

The rival theories of morality are put to a test in cases which pose conflicting lines of action. The philosophical and literary works of the existentialists concentrate upon such "either-or" situations. To accept God or reject Him. To join one side rather than the other. To turn traitor or remain loyal to one's comrades. To live or die.

Existentialism insists that there cannot be any sufficient and compelling grounds within the situation itself, the individual's connections with it, or the person's own character to warrant choosing one rather than the other of mutually exclusive alternatives. Humans, says Sartre, are the beings through whom nothingness enters the world. This power of negation is most forcefully expressed in our perfect liberty to do what we please in defiance of all external circumstances. The exercise of fully conscious, uninhibited preference distinguishes people from animals and one person from another. "By their choices shall ye know them."

The historical materialists reply that, while we can make choices in situations permitting real alternatives—that is the crux of personal morality—these decisions are not made in a void. Making up one's mind about the possibilities of a confusing or conflicting situation is only a part of the total process of moral action.

Voluntary acts are links in a chain of events beginning with objective circumstances and ending with objective consequences. The given situation, personal character, motivation, decision, action, and results form a continuity of phases which are lawfully connected and feed back upon one another. The uniqueness of individual choice does not consist in its self-sufficiency or release from essential relations with other facts, but in contributing its special quality of approval or dissent, collaboration or resistance, to them.

The existentialists deny any causal ties between the psychological act of choice and the circumstances in which it takes place. They sheer away the moment of personal decision from all that precedes and follows it, from the environing conditions, motivations, and consequences of human action. However, there is no empirical evidence that choice occurs apart from and unaffected by the totality of concurrent conditions; this is a purely metaphysical assumption.

In fact, the power of choice is far from unlimited. A multitude of social, historical, and biographical factors enter into the process of moral determination. The real opportunities open to the individual are restricted by natural and social history, by the forces operating in a particular situation and the trends of their development. These provide objective criteria which make it possible to ascertain beforehand whether one alternative is preferable to another, or, after the fact, whether one was better than another. Moreover, the individual is predisposed, though not predestined, by previous experiences and existing connections to take one path rather than another. Otherwise human behavior would be completely unpredictable.

The highest good in the existentialist scale of values is personal sincerity, which is certified by devotion to a freely chosen object of faith. This psychological quality, which is considered the most powerful manifestation of freedom, is the sole principle of moral worth. The feelings of the autonomous individual determine what is right or wrong in any given case.

Marxists judge actions to be good or bad not according to the intentions or emotions of the agents, but by their correspondence with social and class needs and their service to historical aims. They are considered justified or unjustified to the extent that they help or hinder progress toward the goals of socialism. Good deeds must be judged by their consequences. They must actually lead to increasing our command over nature and to diminishing social evils.

5. The Destiny of Humanity

The ambivalence of existentialism is most conspicuous in its view of human destiny. It is at the same time a philosophy of the utmost despair and of breathless effort to go beyond it. Existentialism swings back and forth between these extremes. At one end stand the principal characters in *Waiting for Godot,* a classic of the existentialist theater. They wait and wait but nothing important happens, nothing changes, no one comes. Their expectations continuously disappointed, they are sunk in the futility of an empty existence which must go on without hope or help.

But most writers and thinkers of this school cannot remain in the unrelieved apathy and inertia dramatized by Samuel Beckett. His ending is their point of departure. After looking the worst in the face, they challenge the tragic absurdity of existence. Merleau-Ponty distinguishes between "bad" existentialism, which wallows in pure negativism, and "good" existentialism, which strives to project itself beyond despair. Camus regards the revolt against nihilism as the basis of everything worthwhile.

The mark of freedom, says Sartre, is conscious refusal to submit to any externally imposed condition of life. The authentic person will pass from total negation to self-affirmation in action, from nay-saying to yea-saying. Individuals forge genuine selves by bucking against the "practico-inert" around them and surpassing their given situation through involvement in a characteristic venture, a cause, a future.

The existentialists take many divergent paths out of the original abysmal human condition. The religious, such as Kierkegaard, Gabriel Marcel, Martin Buber, Paul Tillich, try to find a way to God. The unbelievers seek a solution, a transcendence, in this world. This quest has led the most radically inclined among them toward the revolutionary struggle of the working masses. As Julian Symons wittily put it, they would rather be "waiting for Lefty" than "waiting for Godot."

Yet they cannot completely merge themselves with the aims of any movement because of their stand on the insurmountable ambiguity of everything. Existentialism remains fundamentally a creed of frustration in the midst of fulfillment. The most brilliant success turns into failure as coal into ashes. The hazardous leap from what is to what should be inevitably falls short of realization. For Camus every act of rebellion against oppression is justified in itself but installs a new form of servitude. For Sartre the act of transcendence negates itself and in the very process of materialization, trickles out, and dies. It must be followed by a fresh exertion of creative revolt—which in turn will not reach its goal.

Thus we hunger but are never fully fed. We ask for nourishing bread and receive a stone. The most promising road forward winds up in a blind alley. Life is not only a gamble; it is in the end a cheat. We are swindled by the limitations of time, history, and death, which nullify our fondest hopes. "The sorrows of our proud and angry dust are from eternity and will not fail." But human beings always will.

Sartre has epitomized this pessimism coiled in the heart of existentialism in the famous aphorism from *Being and Nothingness:* "Man is a useless passion." So grim a humanism, in which every venture must turn out to be a lost cause, can stimulate spasmodic expenditures of energy in social struggle. But the expectation that defeat lurks in ambush spreads skepticism and cripples the steadfastness of the inwardly divided individual at every step.

The pessimistic irrationalism of the existentialists clashes head-on with the militant temper of Marxism, which feels sure of the victory of humanity over all obstacles. For the historical materialist, humanity is above all the creative producer that has succeeded through its own titanic efforts in elevating itself from animality to the atomic age—and is just on the threshold of its authentically human career.

This belief in the rationality of social evolution and in the necessity of the socialist revolution to usher in the next stage of human progress is the theoretical source of the optimism which suffuses scientific socialism. Marxism points to the historical achievements recorded in humanity's rise over the past million years and incorporated in the accumulated knowledge, skills, and acquisitions of world culture as tangible proofs of the worth of human work and as a pledge of the future.

The indomitable struggles for a better life among the downtrodden, the "wretched of the earth," the key role of the industrial workers in modern economy, the successes of the first experiments in nationalized property and planned economy even under extremely adverse conditions, give confidence to Marxists that the most difficult problems of our age are susceptible of solution through the methods of proletarian-peasant revolution and socialist reconstruction.

As in the past, many surprises, setbacks, disappointments, and detours will be encountered enroute. These are part of the price exacted by the fact that we have to climb and sometimes crawl upward unaided by anything but our own collective efforts. Yet every great social and political revolution has added new stature and power to humankind despite the pains and even disenchantments attending it. The offspring of history have been worth the agonies of birth and the difficulties of their upbringing.

6. Alienation in Modern Society

Why do so many people nowadays feel that the major forces governing their lives are inimical and inscrutable and beyond their capacity to control or change? Where does this state of helplessness come from and what can be done to remove it? Their disagreements on the causes and cure of alienation in modern society constitute an impassable dividing line between the two philosophies.

Both existentialism and Marxism recognize that people have become dehumanized by the alienations they suffer in contemporary life. Alienation expresses the fact that the creations of the human mind and hand dominate their creators. The victims of this servitude become stripped of the qualities of self-determination and self-direction which raise them above the animal level.

For existentialism, human alienation has neither beginning nor end. It is not a historical phenomenon but a metaphysical fate. It is a primordial, indestructible feature of human existence, the quintessence of "human nature." The free and conscious human being is irreconcilably estranged from the world into which we have been hurled. Although we can interject meaning, value, usefulness into it, this does not efface its alien and absurd nature.

Hostility is likewise built into the structure of interpersonal relations. The world whose meaning I create differs from that of others. This produces incessant friction between me and other people, who strive to impose their views on me, nullify my authentic existence, and divert me from my own needs and aims to serve their alien needs.

Finally, individuals are ill at ease with themselves. Our inner being is rendered unhappy by the perpetual tension of conflicting impulses and claims. The goals we set are unrealized or result in something other than we expected or desired.

Since all these sources of alienation are ineradicable, we can do no more than clear-sightedly confront and stoically bear up under this somber state, trying to cope with it as best we can. All the diverse ways in which the existentialists seek to transcend their fate—religion, artistic creation, good works, liberalism, social revolution—are by their own admission only palliative and superficial. They make life tolerable and meaningful but do not and can not end alienation. Free people are obliged to try to overcome their alienation in ways most suitable to themselves— that is their glory. But their efforts prove unavailing—that is their melancholy destiny.

Alienation plays the same part in the existentialist metaphysics as Adam's fall from grace in Christian theology. It is the equivalent of original sin. Just as Jehovah expelled the erring pair from Paradise and condemned their descendants to sin and suffering on earth forever after, so through the fatality of our existence as humans we are eternally and ineluctably withdrawn from others and enclosed within ourselves. There is no release or redemption from such estrangement.

Instead of indicating any exit from the state of alienation, existentialism makes it the permanent foundation of human life, reproducing and justifying it in metaphysical terms.

Marxism gives a materialist and historical analysis of alienation. It is the product of our impotence before the forces of nature and society and our ignorance of the laws of their operation. It diminishes to the extent that our powers over nature and our own social relations, and our scientific knowledge of their processes of development, are amplified.

The idolatries of magic and religion by which people prostrate themselves before supernatural beings of their own imaginative manufacture are the most primitive forms of alienation. But the alienations peculiar to civilization are based not upon subjection to nature, but upon subjection to others through the exploitation of labor.

This type of alienation originates in a highly developed division of labor and the cleavage of society into antagonistic classes. Bereft of the conditions of production, the masses of direct producers lose control over their lives, their liberties, and their means of development, which are at the mercy of hostile social forces. This is obvious under slavery, which was the first organized system of alienated labor. The alienation of labor is far more complex and refined under capitalism, where it attains ultimate expression.

The wage workers are subjected to uncontrollable external forces at every step of capitalist economy. Having none of the material prerequisites of production, they must go to work for their owners. Even before physically participating in production, they surrender their labor power to the entrepreneur in return for the payment of the prevailing wage. While at work, the conditions and duration of the job are determined by the capitalist and his foremen. As men and women on the assembly line can testify, workers become degraded into mere physical accessory factors of production. Instead of intelligently exercising their capacities, they are constrained to perform monotonous, repetitious tasks which strain their endurance. The plan, process, and aim of production all confront them as hostile and hurtful powers.

At the end of the industrial process the product does not belong to the workers who made it but to the capitalist who bought their labor power. It goes into the market to be sold. There the masses of commodities and money function like an untameable force which even the biggest groups of capitalists cannot control, as the fluctuations of the business cycle and periodic crises demonstrate.

On top of this, the competitiveness of capitalism pits the members of all classes against one another and generates unbridled egotism and self-seeking. The members of bourgeois society, whatever their status, are immersed in an atmosphere of rivalry rather than communal solidarity.

Thus the alienations within capitalism come from the contradictory relations of its mode of production and the class antagonisms and competive conditions engendered by them. The divisions rooted in the economic foundations of capitalism branch out into all aspects of social life. They appear in the collisions of class interests and outlooks on a national and international scale, in the opposition of monopolist-dominated governments to the mass of the people, in the struggle of the creative artist against commercialism, in the contrast between metropolitan slums and ghettos and luxury apartments and hotels, in the subordination of science to militarism, and in myriad other ways. Its cruelest and sharpest large-scale expression today in the United States is the deep-going estrangement between the Black people and the whites.

These stigmata mangle human personalities, injure health, stamp out the chance of happiness. They produce many of the mental and emotional disturbances which make up the psychopathology of everyday life in the acquisitive society.

Can the alienations of modern humankind be overcome? The

existentialists contend that they cannot. Marxism replies that these characteristics of a barbarous past and exploitative present can be removed by revolutionizing outworn social structures. Now that we have achieved superiority over nature through science and technology, the next great step is to gain supremacy over the blind and anarchic forces in our lives. The sole agency that is strong enough and strategically placed to carry through this task of instituting conscious collective control over economic and political life is the alienated labor embodied in the industrial working class.

The material means for liberating humanity from the causes and consequences of alienation can be brought into existence only through the socialist revolution, which will concentrate economic, political, and cultural power in the hands of the toiling majority. Planned economy along socialist lines on an international scale can lead to such plenty that the circumstances permitting and even necessitating rule over the many by the few will be wiped out forever.

When all the compulsory inequalities in the conditions of life and in access to the means of self-development are done away with, then the manifestations of these material disparities in the estrangements of one section of society from another will die away. The equal and fraternal relations at the base of the future socialist culture will facilitate the formation of integrated personalities no longer at odds with each other or with themselves.

7. The Meaning of Life and Death

The cleavage between the two outlooks comes to a sharp focus over the meaning of life and death. Humanism has traditionally upheld the supreme value of life on earth against the religious emphasis on death, resurrection, and immortality. For humanists, death was to be countered by making the sole span of existence allotted to mortal creatures as productive and joyous as possible.

Despite their disbelief in divinity, even the secular existentialists invert these values and reinstate the fact of death to the centrality it has had in Christian theology and church practice. Like a medieval meditation upon mortality, Karl Jaspers opines: "Philosophizing means learning to die." Camus insists in *The Myth of Sisyphus* that suicide—that is, what answer to give to the question: Is life worth living?—is the only philosophical issue.

Heidegger defines life as a being-for-death. "When you stand by the cradle of a new-born child, there is only one statement you can make of him with entire certainty," he says. He must die.

According to existentialism, life acquires its deepest meaning not from its own aims and activities, but only when one awakens to the full implications of one's doom. Most people try to shut out this awful awareness by cowardly evasion. The ordinary citizen becomes immersed in everyday activities and distracting pleasures, the artist in creative work, the philosopher in spinning cobwebs of thought. These are nothing but diversions and illusions so long as the individual refuses to confront the realization of eventual annihilation with unflinching and complete consciousness.

Death is the foundation of morality and liberation because it compels each of us to decide whether life is worthwhile and what to do with it. Every act of moral choice is literally a life-and-death matter. All the freely created values of life are stacked up against the overwhelming prospect of death.

Heidegger declares that death is the only thing nobody else can do for me. If we embrace our finitude, our being-for-death, we internalize it and integrate it into the totality of our existence and thus give it meaning. To Sartre, on the other hand, death is a meaningless external fact, a limit that cannot be interiorized in the sum total of our lives. The consciousness of death does not make us human. It merely heightens our individuality by prodding us to decide in defiance of conventional values. "The choice that each of us has made of his life was an authentic choice because it was made face to face with death," he says.

For Heidegger death gives life all meaning; for Sartre it removes all meaning from life. These opposing evaluations show how difficult it is to extract a common position from the existentialists. But, despite the extreme variations in their answers to this problem, the terrifying shock of the recognition of death overshadows their reflections on the meaning and worth of life.

The Marxist approach is more in accord with the humanist mainstream. It is the first law of nature—as well as dialectical materialism—that everything has its day and then must perish. Nothing and no one is immune from this law. The processes of life and death emerged on this planet as the result of new biochemical reactions several billion years ago. Humankind is the highest product of this development.

Is life worth living? And if so, how should the inevitable

approach and advent of death be met? Marxism replies to the first question with a ringing affirmative. No matter what the toil, turmoil, and pain of personal and social experience, life is the supreme value for humankind. Not life as it is but life as liberated humanity will make and remake it. The paramount practical-moral aim of socialism is to improve the quality of life without limit. By increasing humanity's power over nature and decreasing the power of one person over another, a boundless potential of happiness and creative achievement can be released from generation to generation.

The prospect of our own death and the death of others we love and admire often causes anguish and sorrow. Such grief is a normal sentiment among civilized people and is morbid only when it becomes obsessive. The dread of death is not the primal and central fact of human existence, an eternal attendant of the human condition, as the existential metaphysicians contend. It is a historically conditioned psychological reaction. Many primitive peoples do not experience it.

Excessive preoccupation with death belongs to the psychopathology of civilization. The malfunctioning and disproportionate wearing out of our bodies, the multiple insecurities, disorders, stresses, sufferings, and alienations of a crisis-ridden, class-divided society make life difficult and burdensome. Paradoxically, for all their hysterical fear of death many people desperately welcome and even hasten the ending of a too hard life.

The socialist movement aspires to transform and eventually eradicate such attitudes and feelings by changing the conditions of life and labor for all. The remodeling of humanity must begin with the transformation of social relations from antagonism into cooperation, with its ever-enlarging possibilities of satisfying human desires. But it will not stop there. The scientists of the future, in teamwork with highly conscious individuals, will plan to reshape the physiological side of life and subordinate that to the control of reason and will. Biology and medicine will ease the processes of birth and postpone the incidence of death. The coming biological-social type of human will manifest a new psychology in which, among other things, people will no longer have reason to dread death. So long as it cannot be indefinitely put off or averted, the end of living will be greeted not as a frightful calamity, but as the ransom of time.

The existentialist displacement of the seat of value from life to death reflects both the ordeals of our age and a loss of vitality

among sensitive souls who despair of triumphing over the dark
and destructive forces of a sick social order. On the other hand, a
lust for life, conscious participation in the collective struggle for a
better world, and an indestructible confidence in the real possibilities of unbounded progress characterize the working class
humanism projected by Marxism. It is intent on making life what
it could and should be—a serene and splendid adventure for all
members of the human family.

8. Can Existentialism and Marxism Be Reconciled?

Are existentialism and Marxism compatible? Are they opposites or affinities? Can they be synthesized into a coherent unit?

Most interpreters and adherents of existentialism, especially
the theists among them, do not think the two are reconcilable.
They reject Marxism totally because it fails to recognize what to
them is the most meaningful aspect of being: the sovereign
subjectivity and dignity of the individual. They maintain that
materialist theory debases people to mere objects while socialist
practice stamps out personal freedom.

Orthodox Marxists no less firmly insist that the contending
philosophies have far too many principled differences to be
welded into one.

In between stand a variegated group who agree with Sartre
that the two can be fused into a single alloy that will reinforce
both. In the United States the noted psychoanalytical sociologist
Erich Fromm is the most ardent champion of the thesis that
existentialism and Marxism are substantially identical. In
Marx's Concept of Man (1961), which presents Fromm's concept
of Marx, he asserts that Marx's thinking is humanist existentialism. The doctrines appear alike to him since both protest against
the alienation in modern society and seek ways to overcome it.
"Marx's philosophy," he writes, "constitutes a spiritual existentialism in secular language and because of this spiritual quality
is opposed to the materialistic practice and thinly disguised
materialistic philosophy of our age. Marx's aim, socialism, based
on his theory of man, is essentially prophetic Messianism in the
language of the nineteenth century."

This transmutation of the materialist Marx into a precursor
and preacher of existentialism is typical of radical humanists of
very different backgrounds and beliefs; Fromm is their chief
American representative. They locate the "true" Marx in the

early *Economic and Philosophic Manuscripts of 1844,* which mark transitional stages of his development, instead of in the ripe conclusions of his mature thoughts. They contend that Marx has been misrepresented as a crude dialectical materialist by his orthodox disciples from Engels to Lenin—until the radical humanists revealed that he really was an ethical existentialist.

Fromm's equation of dialectical materialism with existentialism is as ill-founded as his astonishing statement that "Marx's atheism is the most advanced form of rational mysticism." The atheistic Marx is no more a mystic than the Marx of scientific socialism is an existentialist.

Ever since socialism became a powerful movement and Marxism its dominant ideology, attempts have been made to disqualify the dialectical and materialist principles of its method in favor of a different theoretical basis. At various times and places Kantianism, ethical idealism, positivism, pragmatism, and even Thomism have been nominated as replacements. None of these proposed supplements and substitutes (or their eclectic combinations) have proved convincing or viable. The Marxist system has such an integrated structure, from its philosophical and logical premises to its political economy and historical outlook, that it cannot easily be chopped up and recombined with other theories.

Sartrean existentialism is the latest and most popular candidate for the office of eking out the real or alleged deficiencies of Marxist thought. It is unlikely to be more successful than its predecessors.

The existentialists aver that the individual's sincerest act and tragic responsibility is the necessity to choose between anguishing alternatives and take the consequences. Sartre shrinks from doing this in philosophy. The confrontation of existentialism with dialectical materialism is a genuine case of "either-or." But Sartre wants to embrace *both* Kierkegaard *and* Marx without choosing between them.

"To the marriage of true minds, let us admit no impediment," Shakespeare said. The trouble is that dialectical materialism and existentialism are contrary-minded and oriented along diametrically different lines. They clash at almost every point on the major issues of philosophy, sociology, morality, and politics. It is a bootless task to try to mate these opposites.

This has not—and will not—deter either radical-minded existentialists or socialist eclectics from trying to coalesce the one with the other. The controversy between the philosophers of existence and the dialectical materialists, as well as those who mix the two, has steadily expanded its area over the last two decades. It is still in full swing and far from concluded.

The first commandment of existentialism is, as has been said, "Be yourself!" This is not a bad maxim, and it ought to be applied as strictly to philosophies as to personalities. Let existentialism be what it really is—the ideological endproduct of liberalism and individualism—and not pretend to be something else. Let Marxism likewise be what it should be: that dialectical materialism which is the scientific expression and practical guide of the world socialist revolution of the working masses.

But let not the two be intermixed and confused. Their mismating can produce only stillborn offspring, whether in philosophy or in politics.

ด

In Defense of Engels

Our discussions this week [at the Socialist Workers Party's 1975 convention] have revolved around the new turn in the world situation brought on by the end of the postwar boom and what this portends for the prospects of the class struggle and our work in the United States. The dialectics of capitalism's development, arising from its incurable contradictions, is becoming asserted with ever greater force. After thirty years of prosperity come stagflation and large-scale unemployment. After the explosive and unchecked expansion of Washington's military might on the world arena comes the defeat in Southeast Asia.

The socialist movement is now looking ahead and tooling up for corresponding shifts in the attitudes of the American workers. They can be expected to change from raw material for capitalist exploitation into a more self-conscious and independently acting force for political and social change.

These reversals at hand and in the making present a philosophical as well as a political challenge to us. The revolutionary vanguard requires a world outlook and a logical method capable of analyzing these unfolding processes and foreseeing their underlying trends. Fortunately, we have at our disposal the ideas of Marxism, the theoretical foundation of scientific socialism.

However, Marxism itself is in a state of crisis nowadays in the international socialist movement. Several generations have been miseducated by the Stalinist degradation and distortion of Marxist theory that has been coupled with the political degeneration of the Soviet Union. The thoughts on philosophy of Mao Tsetung have further addled the minds of many militants.

Finally, just as the long detour of the world revolution through the colonial countries has induced rebels in the advanced to embrace and extend this peculiar pattern and adapt to Castroism or Maoism, so in philosophy many left intellectuals have been beguiled by the ideas held by the young Lukács; Karl Korsch; the Frankfurt school, including Herbert Marcuse, Max Horkheimer, and Theodor Adorno; Erich Fromm; Jean-Paul Sartre; and similar nonmaterialist interpreters of Marxism.

These considerations make it advisable to assure that the philosophic orientation of our cadres is clear and correct as we contemplate the advent of more favorable conditions for anticapitalist action on a mass scale in this country.

*   *   *

I will focus upon Frederick Engels and his contributions to the elaboration of dialectical materialism, for the following reason. The cocreator of scientific socialism has come under heavy fire in recent years on the ground that he switched Karl Marx's thought onto the wrong track and distorted his teachings on philosophy. Just as Leon Trotsky is portrayed by the Stalinists as the antagonist of Vladimir Ilyich Lenin after 1917, so Engels is separated by his detractors from Marx and depreciated in a like manner on the philosophic front. He is accused of deforming Marx's method in a mechanistic way, thereby being the progenitor of Social Democratic deviations and Stalinist dogmatism. This fabrication has been broadly accepted and embroidered by New Left ideologists in both East and West because it undermines those elements of dialectical materialism the critics want to discredit and discard.

This variegated grouping applies "salami tactics" to the body of Marxist thought, although they do not all slice it up the same way. The most unrestrained slicers cut Marx himself in half by discovering a contradiction between the young Marx and the mature Marx. He is supposed to have shifted his views in the wrong direction between his early humanistic writings and the publication of *Capital.* They unjustifiably introduce a sharp break in the normal process of growth through which Marx deepened his understanding of many things from one decade to the next.

However, most of the revisionists find Marx guiltless of misinterpreting himself, or let him off lightly as ambiguous. The other half of the team is singled out as the main culprit and bears the brunt of the attack as the prime falsifier of Marx's real beliefs. The core of the indictment against Engels is that his version of dialectical materialism is essentially different from Marx's historical materialism. The true, innovative, humanistic Marx is to be found in such writings of the 1840s as the *Economic and Philosophic Manuscripts of 1844* and the "Theses on Feuerbach" (which, incidentally, Engels recovered and published after Marx's death). This humanity-centered philosophy of praxis, according to the allegation, was disfigured and displaced by the deterministic, mechanistic, positivistic, and scientistic rendering of dialectical materialism Engels presented in his writings. (Praxis is a Greek word for human activity, popularized by contemporary philosophers.)

The false antithesis between Marx and Engels contradicts the basic facts about their relationship. It is, bluntly speaking, a hoax; and serious socialists should beware of being taken in by it. When Engels first visited Marx in Paris in the summer of 1844, he later wrote: "We found that we were in complete accord in all theoretical domains; this was when our joint work began." It continued without letup until Marx died in 1883.

History has rarely witnessed so close, harmonious, and unabated an intellectual and political partnership. Their correspondence testifies to the communion of thought and lively interchange of ideas on a multitude of subjects that found expression in their writings. Although Engels modestly assigned himself the role of "second fiddle" to Marx, the development of the dialectical method and historical materialism was a collective creation. Engels and George Plekhanov later named the synthesis dialectical materialism. Marx and Engels elaborated its fundamental principles together in the 1840s. Most of what they wrote thereafter, whether in the form of newspaper articles, manifestos, pamphlets, or books, was either discussed beforehand or submitted to each other's searching critical scrutiny.

Whatever differences of opinion they had on this or that minor matter, there is no record of disagreement on any important theoretical or political question during their forty-year collaboration. Engels was so familiar with Marx's criticism of political economy that he alone could be entrusted with piecing together and putting into publishable shape the second and third volumes of *Capital*.

Anti-Dühring, by Engels, was the fullest exposition of Marxist philosophy issued while Marx was alive. It was a preliminary sketch for *Dialectics of Nature* and shares the same theoretical viewpoint. *Anti-Dühring* was undertaken on Marx's insistence. He endorsed every word in the book, which Engels read to him before sending it to the printers. Chapter 10 of part II was written by Marx. Therefore any dissent from the ideas presented in its pages is ipso facto a disagreement with Marx as much as Engels. The latter made this clear when he wrote in the preface to its second edition: "I must note in passing that inasmuch as the mode of outlook expounded in this book was founded and developed in far greater measure by Marx, and only in an insignificant degree by myself, it was self-understood between us that this exposition of mine should not be issued without his knowledge."[1] Engels likewise noted in the preface to the first edition of *The Origin of the Family, Private Property, and the State* that he had drawn extensively upon Marx's prolific observations and conclusions in writing that book.

Long after their deaths, the mythmakers are attempting to do what was impossible during their lifetimes—pit the one revolutionist against the other. This gambit is not new. In a letter to Eduard Bernstein, written April 23, 1883, shortly after Marx's death, Engels said: "The fable about the nasty Engels who had led the benign Marx astray has been repeated many times since 1844."

Indeed, it has been considerably magnified from that time to this. George Plekhanov and Karl Kautsky are said to have extended the derelictions of Engels in the next generation. To spice the dish, it is implied, if not always stated, that Plekhanov's bad conduct in 1905, 1914, and 1917, and Kautsky's betrayals from 1914 on, are traceable at least in part to the philosophic deviations derived from their mentor. To top off this indictment, just as Georg Wilhelm Friedrich Hegel has been held responsible to some extent for the Kaiser's Prussianism and Hitler's totalitarianism, so Engels is alleged to have fed the version of "diamat" (dialectical materialism) disseminated by the Stalinist school because his dialectical materialism subordinated the human individual to the laws of nature and history. To round out the rogues' gallery, Lenin is charged with carrying forward this vulgar materialistic mode of thought in *Materialism and Empirio-Criticism*, although he began coming to his senses in the *Philosophical Notebooks*.

If we are to credit this caricature of the development of Marxist philosophy, all the leading exponents of European socialist thought from Engels to Lenin, Rosa Luxemburg, and Trotsky misunderstood Marx's ideas and went astray—until the contemporary critics arrived to set matters straight.

This melange of misrepresentations has been taken up by academic Marxologists, who willingly retail such misinformation to untutored pupils and unwary readers. Here is how the British philosopher Anthony Quinton formulates the tale in a review of recent books on Hegel in the May 29, 1975, *New York Review of Books*: "The official Marx of the interwar years, discredited by the theological ornamentation of Stalin's slave state, was the late scientistic Marx of *Das Kapital*, as interpreted by the naively positivist Engels, whose task it was to generalize Marx's theory of history and society into the comprehensive philosophy of dialectical materialism."

Quinton naturally prefers the libertarian image of Marx dreamed up by the petty-bourgeois humanists who, he says, emphasize "man as the creator of himself and the world." Unlike this newfangled Marx, the original Marx knew that while humanity did create itself, it did not have the godlike capacity of creating the world—only of changing it. The power of humanity is limited to adapting the materials of nature to serve its needs and purposes.

This Oxford scholar is forthright enough to place the mature Marx alongside Engels as the fountainhead of the original sin of scientism, which is a highfalutin euphemism for materialism. Many of the semi-Marxists are not so candid or consistent. These timid iconoclasts hesitate to wield the hammer against the granite figure of Marx himself. They fear to question his authority, and hold him blameless for the transgressions of his partner.

A comical specimen of their tortured reasoning is offered by the reformist socialist George Lichtheim in his last book, entitled *From Marx to Hegel*. He opposes what he calls "the peculiar ontological system of metaphysical materialism invented by Engels and termed 'dialectical materialism' by Plekhanov and Lenin."[2] Lichtheim writes, "The 'dialectical' materialism, or monism, put forward in the *Anti-Dühring*, and in the essays on natural philosophy eventually published in 1925 under the title *Dialectics of Nature*, has only the remotest connection with Marx's own viewpoint, though it is a biographical fact of some importance that Marx raised no objection to Engels' exposition of the theme in the *Anti-Dühring*."[3]

This offhand remark not only blatantly sweeps aside the nature of the working relations between the pair but disregards Marx's whole character. That militant materialist would not have remained indifferent to misrepresentations of his philosophical method by so close a colleague, any more than Plekhanov, Lenin, or Trotsky would have. He would not have allowed such an offense to pass without making his own counterviews known to the socialist public.

*   *   *

After settling their basic philosophical principles in their own minds, Marx and Engels divided the tasks at hand in the exposition of their common ideas. While Marx immersed himself in the prodigious labor of investigating the problems of political economy, Engels undertook to popularize their philosophic positions. The most important of these works were *Anti-Dühring*, from which *Socialism: Utopian and Scientific* was extracted, and later *Ludwig Feuerbach and the Outcome of Classical German Philosophy*. These were to be crowned by *Dialectics of Nature*, which remained unfinished at his death. In addition to *Capital*, which stands as the supreme example of the application of their method, these classical writings are the prime sources for our knowledge about Marxist philosophy.

From the inventory of previous philosophizing, Marx and Engels retained the materialist conception of the world and dialectical logic, making these acquisitions the cornerstones of their systematic thought. The distinctive character of the revolution they effected in philosophy was to fuse these two disconnected elements into a synthetic world outlook that posed the necessity for the working class to transform society and offered a theoretical guide for this emancipation struggle. Materialism was extended from natural to social phenomena and to the development of the thought process; the idealist dialectic of Hegel was turned upside down and given a solid scientific basis in the realities of the universal evolution of matter in motion.

Marxism redefined and revitalized philosophy by linking it with the class struggle and political activity, by converting it into an instrument to be added to the arsenal of the revolutionary proletariat in its struggle to change the world through class action, and by absorbing the results of the growing scientific knowledge about nature, history, and the mind into its principles.

The unfounded allegation that Marx and Engels held divergent philosophical views sets up Engels as a whipping boy for Marx himself. The objections raised against his positions are actually aimed against the tenets of the dialectical materialism they held in common. The detractors ought to come out from ambush and challenge Marx fairly and squarely.

If all the criticisms they make of Engels were accepted as valid, few parts of Marxist theory would be left intact. They begin with nothing less than an abandonment of its materialist foundation.

From its origins in antiquity, the materialist philosophy has been based on a specific interpretation of the nature of reality; its highest expression in dialectical materialism is no exception. Materialism maintains that nature alone, based on matter in motion, has a self-sufficient existence; everything in human life is derived from and dependent upon the objective world. Idealism, on the contrary, denies that nature is primary, making it subordinate to mind or spirit. In Hegel's system, for example, nature is the alienated reflection of the logical process—or, as Marx said, the son begets the mother.

These are the two fundamental opposing camps in the history of philosophy. However, their contraposed positions do not exhaust the possibilities in this field. A heterogeneous array of thinkers and tendencies have, on one ground or another, refused to align themselves in a clear-cut manner with one side or the other. They try to combine elements from both the materialist and idealist viewpoints and they oscillate unsteadily between these two poles.

These eclectics commonly skate around the crucial question of whether nature or social and intellectual phenomena come first. The humanist exponents of praxis stand on the left flank of this category. They affirm that neither nature nor thinking but human activity is the essence of reality, and therefore praxis is the fulcrum of Marxist theory.

They consider this intermediate variant superior to vulgar materialism, as they call it, or out-and-out idealism. Yet their standpoint fails to face up to the need to define the fundamental relation of practice to the external world. When hard pressed, most of the praxologists dispose of the problem by arguing that this question really has no meaning and needs no definite answer because nature and thought are inseparably united in and through practice. While this happens to be true as far as it goes, it leaves undecided whether matter or mind, the objective or the subjective, takes priority in existence. Their ambiguity and evasiveness on this issue is actually a half-concession to idealism, which holds that there is no object without a subject and that the object is solely a shadow or "reflective moment" cast by the subject—variously called in the history of philosophy, God, spirit, mind, *nous,* the Word, etc.

The "critical theorists" of the Frankfurt school, as they are known, believe that the objective world cannot be severed from the subject because it is itself a product of human activity. In viewing the object only through the mediation of the human subject and rejecting determinism as a metaphysical aberration, they revert to the standpoint of the left Hegelians, which Marx and Engels, using Ludwig Feuerbach's materialism as a bridge, threw off early in their intellectual evolution.

Materialism teaches that nature has objective reality before and apart from the human subject. This paramount premise has been confirmed by the discoveries of the natural sciences, from astrophysics to biochemistry, showing the evolution of the cosmos over billions of years. The earth and its lower organisms had a prolonged history before humanity came on the scene with its distinctive productive activities.

Practice, to be sure, thereupon became the motive force in *social* history. But it cannot be considered the basis of material being. The praxis school tends to make social life eclipse the natural matrix of which it is an outgrowth. The value we rightly attach to the activities, achievements, and further progress of our species, which is the focus of our attention, should not contract our vision of reality as a whole. Anthropocentrism is as outdated as the view that the earth is the center of the universe. It is extremely parochial at a time when rockets are invading outer space, researchers are looking for signs of life on remote planets, and scientists are exploring ever deeper into the atom.

Thus George Lichtheim, whom Quinton describes as "one of the most active and enthusiastic exponents of this current of thought," writes: "The external world, as it exists in and for itself, is irrelevant to a materialism which approaches history with a view to establishing what men have made of themselves."[4] This is in the same vein as the statements by Georg Lukács in *History and Class Consciousness* that "Existence is the product of human activity" and "nature is a societal category."[5] The discovery of nature is a social enterprise and the *concept* of nature is a social-historical category, but not nature itself. Leszek

Kolakowski, too, tells us in *Marxism and Beyond*: "The world is a human product."[6]

Finally, Alfred Schmidt, a younger member of the Frankfurt school who has devoted an entire book to *The Concept of Nature in Marx,* says: "Nature exists for man only as it is mediated by history."[7] He contrasts Engels with his "naturalized Hegelianism" to Marx, who subordinated nature to its "appropriation through social labor." "Nature," he writes, "only appears on the horizon of history, for history can emphatically only refer to men. History is first, and immediately, practice."[8]

This is a half-truth: it applies to human but not to natural history. As Marx and Engels stated in *The German Ideology,* "We know only a single science, the science of history. History can be contemplated from two sides, it can be divided into the history of nature and the history of mankind. However the two sides are not to be divided off; as long as men exist, the history of nature and the history of men are mutually conditioned."[9] Schmidt disregards the decisive qualification in the quotation: "as long as men exist." Several million years ago humanity did not yet exist, although nature did. That fact is what the philosophic materialism of Marx and Engels is predicated on. It embraces but goes beyond the horizon of human history as such.

We can agree with other socialist humanists that the problems of human life—and the revolutionary theory and practice of coping with them—are central to the teachings of Marxism. But the point at issue is not the center but the circumference of materialist philosophy, that which identifies the total field of its concerns. Does dialectical materialism deal only with what is specifically human or with all of reality? Most critics of Engels contend that the broader concern with ontology, the theory of being, is an outworn metaphysical relic of Hegelianism; Marxism limits itself to social experience.

Their narrow conception of Marxism as historical materialism alone is an unwarranted abridgment of the dialectical materialism Marx and Engels developed. This issue has far-reaching implications. The world outlook and procedure of science itself was made possible only when its first practitioners cast aside animism, religion, teleology, and other anthropocentric notions. They learned to separate themselves from nature, and nature from themselves, and approach the world objectively, as it really was in its own right, having an independent existence and operating in accord with its own laws.

According to Karl Klare, editor of a collection of articles on the leading figures of so-called Western Marxism from Lukács to Marcuse, their signal achievement has been "to restore human consciousness, human subjectivity to the heart of Marxism."[10] Genuine Marxism does not need any injection of subjectivity. But these critical theorists, who find the determinism and lawfulness upheld by dialectical materialism to be the source of Social Democratic fatalism and Stalinist totalitarianism, felt that the socialist movement could not be reoriented without it. The trouble is that they gave Marxism such an overdose of subjectivity as to throw it off balance both in theory and in practice.

Marxism was the first system of thought to give a correctly balanced account of the objective and subjective aspects of human activity. It views the object-subject relation as a unity of opposites in which one can be transformed under certain conditions into the other. In the same process whereby the flint was chipped into a hand ax, thus mingling the physical raw material with the subjective (human) factor of labor, the concept of the tool and its purpose were objectivized by the maker in the artifact itself. The idea became materialized as the natural thing was humanized.

The primary basis of the object-subject relation is to be found in the interaction between humankind and nature that is incorporated in productive activity. Here nature is objective to the human subject; this object-subject relationship develops as the forces of nature are converted to social use by labor. The essence of history consists in the progressive modification of nature by the productive activity of humankind, and in the correlative transformation of humankind itself as the powers of production grow.

The early Lukács and the Frankfurt school term the artificial environment in which we live, work, and think "second nature." They focus exclusively upon the phenomena in this domain and try to shove the original and underlying nature into the shade. In doing so they give greater weight to the subjective factors in human history and social life than to the objective conditions of development.

Historical materialism teaches that what is subjective (human) is governed by objective realities, laws, and necessities. This is summarized in the statement that social being determines social consciousness. This does not mean, as some critics contend, that the subjective element is negligible or powerless. Quite the contrary, it is omnipresent in human affairs and can play a more or less influential part, depending upon the material circumstances of the case. At climactic junctures in the process of historical determination the subjective factor can even be decisive, as I have discussed in the article "The Role of the Individual in History Making."[11] Recognition of this fact necessitates the building of the revolutionary party, a conclusion that most New Left apostles of praxis refuse to draw. Their subjectivity shrinks from accepting this objective necessity.

The Marxist conception of the reciprocal interplay of the two factors affords ample room for effective action by the subject. The subjective, like the objective, is a relative category that shifts its field of reference. It can refer to the human collective in respect to the natural environment, or to a class within the given social formation, a party of the class, an ideological grouping, or a single person and his or her consciousness. As a physical organism the individual is an object to himself or herself and others, while as a social being she or he is a subject with a spiritual, that is, a private psychological and intellectual, inner life.

As a doctrine of class struggle and a guide to revolutionary action, Marxism least of all plays down the part that can be exercised by the will and initiative of human beings in all departments of endeavor, from altering their habitat to forming and transforming social relationships and redirecting the course of events through their deliberate intervention. But we humans have been able to do all this only under the historically created conditions that have lawfully determined the nature, direction, and scope of our transformative powers. These conditions have not yet come under our collective control as they will under socialism.

The crux of the argument with the praxis theorists, its practical political point, is that they tend to exaggerate the subjective element and underestimate the predominance of the real objective conditions. This one-sidedness is conducive to voluntarism, ultraleftism, and adventurism in politics. Lukács's essays collected in *History and Class Consciousness,* for instance, reflect the ultraleft course against which Lenin, Trotsky, and other leaders of the Third International fought in 1921. This did not prevent Lukács from swinging around, withdrawing from political activism in the Hungarian Communist Party, and accommodating himself for two decades, albeit with teeth clenched, to the Stalinist regime.

Extreme subjectivism in theory and politics can readily turn into its opposite. Often it ends up in capitulation to the existing alignment of forces, as demonstrated by so many of the ultraleft stars of the 1960s in this country, from Rennie Davis and Tom Hayden to Bobby Seale and Eldridge Cleaver.

The philosophical problem of the object-subject relation goes back to the Greeks. The first materialists, from Thales to the Atomists, concentrated their attention upon the nature of physical being. The Sophists and Socrates turned aside from these cosmological considerations to focus upon social, moral, and logical problems. They taught that humanity first had to know itself.

However one-sided this shift was, it was then a necessary step in the development of philosophic thought. This alternation of attention between the objective and subjective sides of reality has recurred on higher levels at subsequent stages of philosophy's progress. In the concrete course of its elaboration, Marxism itself first examined the most urgent economic, social, and political questions and only later, as we shall see, took up the theoretical problems posed by the development of natural science.

However much this overemphasis was justified and even inescapable in preceding phases of philosophizing, such one-sidedness becomes retrogressive when it is reproduced by the praxologists at this late date. The Polish Communist thinker Adam Schaff rightly distinguishes between the Milesian and Socratic lines in philosophic tradition and then wrongly urges Marxists to abandon the Milesians for the humanistic starting point and outlook of Socrates. But Socrates was the inspirer of idealism, the one who diverted Greek thought from materialism. Schaff's injunction to follow his lead would impel socialists in the same direction. If examples from antiquity are in order, we, like Lenin, recommend the path of the pioneer materialists, Democritus and Lucretius, instead.

Let us go from the history of philosophy to contemporary politics. The divergent consequences of adhering to the objective method of Marxism or slipping into some subjective approach are exemplified in the debate over one of the most crucial issues of world politics: What is the nature of the Soviet Union? According to historical materialism, the fundamental character of a social system is determined by the prevailing relations of production as expressed in the property form its state defends. In the light of these objective criteria the Soviet Union, the product of the

October revolution, must be defined as a workers' state, a progressive formation qualitatively different from and superior to a capitalist economy. This sociological characterization is made more precise by the political qualification that the Soviet Union today is not a healthy but a diseased workers' state because of the suppression of proletarian democracy.

Many of the praxis-oriented thinkers reject both this method and its conclusion and resort to more superficial criteria in ·assessing the nature of the USSR. Some, noting the persistence of commodity relations, classify it as a regime of "state capitalism." Others designate it as a bureaucratic-collectivist state, a completely new kind of society. Still others throw up their hands and confess their incapacity to fit this historical anomaly into any sociological categories. All of them hold that unless the workers have democratic control over the economy and state, it cannot have any progressive social substance. They give political relations precedence over socioeconomic realities.

Their failure to understand what the Soviet Union really is can lead to incorrect and even reactionary positions. This kind of subjective sociology is carried to an extreme by the Maoists, followed in their manner by the left economists Charles Bettelheim, Paul M. Sweezy, and Martin Nicolaus. Because of the sharp differences between Moscow and Peking on the state level, the Maoists call the Soviet Union a capitalist, imperialist, even fascist power, just as Moscow plastered similar labels on Yugoslavia after Josip Broz Tito resisted Joseph Stalin. Such lines of thought, which originated in Stalin's misbegotten theory of "social fascism," are a travesty of Marxism.

*   *   *

The independent existence of material reality, the primacy of objective conditions, and the objectivity of knowledge all fit together in the structure of Marxist philosophy. The Marxist theory of knowledge is predicated on the capacity of the human mind to reflect the surrounding world more or less correctly. It is inseparable from the Marxist conception of material being. The properties and relations of things that we sense, perceive, and handle are conceptualized through the abstractive and generalizing powers of logical thought. The content of our true ideas corresponds with, that is, more and more approximates, what objectively exists.

The praxologists undercut the premises of this materialist conception of knowledge by severing the intrinsic connection between the ontology (the theory of existence) and the epistomology (the theory of knowledge) of dialectical materialism. Lichtheim argues that Marx's historical materialism, which he distinguished from the philosophic materialism of Engels and Plekhanov, had "no connection whatever" with their "indefensible theory of cognitive perception."[12]

A major stumbling block in the way of this attempt to demonstrate a divergence between Marx and Engels and stealthily dispose of their materialist theory of knowledge is Marx's clear and categorical statement in the afterword to the second edition of *Capital* in 1873: "With me . . . the ideal is nothing but the material world reflected in the mind of man, and translated into forms of thought."[13] Schmidt characterizes this assertion as "unfortunate"—as indeed it is for the thesis that Marx did not hold the same reflective theory of knowledge as Engels.

The critics often mix up the Marxist view with the position that people passively receive sensations and perceptions that are reproduced in the mind as direct replicas or mirror images of objects. Such a simplified and mechanical explanation of knowledge was held by the empiricists, sensationalists, and pre-Marxian materialists. The eighteenth-century materialist Denis Diderot likened the brain to wax on which things left their imprint.

Dialectical materialism goes far beyond this crude conception. It views human beings not as mere spectators of their environment or reactors to its stimuli, but as doers, inquirers, and strugglers who engage in labor and other practical activities directed by their ideas, and who have developed their conceptual equipment in accord with changing historical circumstances and social relations. In the process of knowledge the active, productive subject works out generalizations, ideal models, and categories which when tested in social practice disclose their correspondence with or variance from the essential features of things. The whole development of knowledge from primitive ignorance to present-day science bears witness to the creative capacities and social character of the human reason.

As a faculty and product of developing human beings, knowledge has its subjective sides. But if our sensations, perceptions, and ideas did not truly reflect events occurring outside us and give reliable information about the phenomena, conditions, and laws of reality, the process of cognition would be worse than useless; it would have no practical value in orienting us to what is happening or in dealing with difficult situations and changing them.

Subatomic physics is in the forefront of scientific research today. It has taken science and society 2,500 years to work out the theory of the atomic constitution of matter; and an immense amount is still to be learned about this aspect of the universe. But we undeniably know that atoms actually exist. We know many of their properties through the verification of hypotheses concerning their content.

* * *

A favorite charge is that Engels was a one-sided "economic determinist" who slighted the relative autonomy of political and other forces. This is particularly untenable in light of the series of letters he wrote to Konrad Schmidt, Franz Mehring, and other correspondents in the early 1890s. He derided the narrow-minded individuals who attributed all social phenomena to economic causes alone and disregarded the many-sided interaction of all factors from the material substructure to the intellectual heights in the process of social determination.

However, Engels never forgot to add what the praxologists usually overlook: that economic conditions are ultimately decisive in historical developments. As he wrote to J. Bloch, "There is an interaction of all these elements [political, legal, philosophical, religious, and so on] in which, amid all the endless *host* of accidents . . . the economic movement finally asserts itself as necessary."[14] His observation that "what these gentlemen lack is dialectics" applies not only to those mechanical minds who see nothing but economic causes and ignore the influence of super-structural factors, but also to those fugitives from materialism who refuse to acknowledge the determinative role of economics in the formation of social-cultural features.

Engels can easily be absolved of having a mechanical approach to social causation because he did not even have a mechanistic conception of natural processes. He adopted a consistently dialectical method in respect to both sectors of reality. The objections of the critics are directed not at his alleged mechanical-mindedness, but at his insistence that human affairs as well as physical phenomena are governed by lawfulness, a conception that is fundamental to scientific method but anathema to nonmaterialist humanists.

Marx and Engels contended that through dialectical and historical materialism socialism had matured from its infantile utopianism into a thoroughly scientific approach to the world. This claim is discounted or disqualified by the adversaries of Engels. They deny that Marxism is a scientific theory based upon a correct knowledge of objective reality in the same sense as the natural sciences.

The more sweeping critics say that scientific socialism is a gross misnomer. In their opinion, as an ideology designed to further the aims and interests of a particular class, it possesses no objectively demonstrable validity.

This line of thought is shared by Leszek Kolakowski, Ernst Fischer, and members of the Frankfurt school, who regard Marxism not as a fully scientific mode of thought but as a system of values and norms along humanistic lines—which Engels, followed by Plekhanov, Kautsky, and Lenin, converted into a misleading positivistic and scientistic ideology later exploited by Stalinism.

In his book *Art and Coexistence,* published in 1966, Fischer holds that Marxism is not a pure ideology (that is, a mystified consciousness of the world) but a mixture of science and utopianism. Ernst Bloch's philosophy of hope makes utopian idealism the pivot of Marxism.

Decades ago Sidney Hook argued that Marxism could not be an objective science because, unlike the socially neutral natural sciences, it incorporates the narrow and subjective class interests of the proletariat. He regarded Marxism as simply a pragmatically useful set of directives to assist the activity of the working class in its struggles.

Marxism admits no opposition between the objective truths of science and the interests of the working class; the two are inseparable. Marxism is *both* the outlook of its revolutionary-socialist contingent *and* a scientific mode of thought that gives the most correct and correctible interpretation of reality. This invests it with the exceptional quality of being revolutionary. The credentials for its scientific character come not only from theoretical considerations but from practical proofs provided by actual developments of world society, such as the current economic crisis.

In contrast to guesswork and intuition, scientific forecasting is founded on the study of law-governed causal connections as they really exist and operate. Marxism passes this practical test. Its value as a reliable and effective guide to proletarian activity and its usefulness in predicting the main trends of social and political development have been confirmed by both the positive and negative experiences of the class struggle.

Such currents of thought as positivism, pragmatism, and existentialism deny that philosophy must have a foundation in science. They restrict that characteristic to the natural sciences or at most to some branches of social science. Unlike the physical sciences, philosophy, they say, is not concerned with the nature and laws of the world at large but only with human activities, aspirations, and values. If philosophy as such has no intrinsic relation with the whole of reality, then dialectical materialism is in the same boat and is bereft of scientific validity.

Praxis-oriented thinkers agree that Marxist philosophy does not have the same status as the special branches of science. That is the meaning of the contrast they draw between the "scientistic" Engels and the humanistic early Marx. Figures such as Adorno want to keep philosophy apart from science in order to safeguard subjectivity.

To support this contention they sometimes point to the fact that, whereas philosophy originally contained within itself many of the branches of science from astronomy to psychology, these have since set up in business for themselves. This process of divestiture has left philosophy with no content of its own save the realm of human values. Philosophy is in the miserable condition of King Lear, who handed over all his possessions to his daughters and was left destitute and helpless with no domain of his own.

This picture of the interrelations between philosophy and the sciences presents only one side of their progress. While one science after another has split off from philosophy, the sciences as a whole have come closer together at many points, as biophysics and biochemistry testify. These growing interconnections and their results have provided a more comprehensive and solid basis for the categories of scientifically guided philosophic thought. The laws discovered in their specific fields of operation have yielded the groundwork for elaborating and verifying the most general laws of motion in the universe.

This brings us to the most controversial issue in the anti-Engels campaign and to its main target: *Dialectics of Nature*.

This book is held up as the prize exhibit of the unscientific character of dialectical materialism and dismissed as a fantastic metaphysical hangover from Marxism's Hegelian heritage.

This makes it all the more essential to explain what Engels was aiming to accomplish in this fragmentary and unfinished work. *Dialectics of Nature* is not a marginal addition or an excrescence in Marxist literature, as the anti-Engels forces contend. It is an integral part of the whole world outlook of modern materialism.

Let us see what place this undertaking occupies in the development of the thought of its creators. In common with the titans of philosophy from Democritus and Aristotle through Thomas Aquinas to René Descartes and Hegel, Marx and Engels responded to the necessity of elaborating a unitary and systematic interpretation of reality, encompassing the physical world, society, and the cognition of both of them.

Unlike the metaphysicians, they did not present a closed, fixed, final structure of philosophic generalizations. What they did aspire to work out was as coherent and consistent an understanding of matter in motion as the scientific knowledge and theoretical insight of their time allowed. This synthesis could then serve as a powerful instrument of further analysis.

In *Capital* Marx formulated the laws governing the development of capitalism; and in other writings on historical materialism, notably in the introduction to *The Critique of Political Economy,* he indicated the general laws that determined the nature and regulated the march of humanity in precapitalist times as well. Under the spur of the most pressing requirements of the working class movement, Marx and Engels had to start with an analysis of the driving forces of social activity. They went on, as soon as they could, to examine the vast realm of nature and the findings of the natural sciences as a further test of their outlook. This next step was a logical extension of their theorizing.

That gigantic task involved assessing the results of the advances in the natural sciences from the standpoint of the materialist dialectic, just as they were doing in the social sciences, beginning with political economy. By mutual agreement, as their correspondence amply shows, Engels set about to study the conclusions of the natural sciences to see whether and in what ways they demonstrated the presence of the dialectical laws and categories in the world. He did not seek to impose these logical laws upon the phenomena of nature but rather to find out what laws of motion were actually exhibited within the facts that scientific research had extracted in one field after another—but had insufficiently generalized. He first explored the inorganic and then the organic sciences.

The notations assembled in *Dialectics of Nature* were organized around the following key concept. The physical world harbors a hierarchy of diverse forms of motion, each of which has a distinctive and irreducible quality of its own. These modes of motion are not uniformly and exclusively mechanical as the Newtonian determinists believed, although the laws of mechanics are widely operative in the macrocosmos. There are many other, different types of motion—chemical, electronic, physiological, and so on—determined by the structure and properties of the field under observation. All these forms of motion are materially interconnected, and under the appropriate conditions are convertible one into the other. In the process of transformation, the energy is conserved although the form is changed.

The individual sciences deal with the laws specific to their domains. But running through these particular kinds of movement are more general laws, which constitute the dialectics of nature. One such law, for example, is the transformation of quantity into quality. Another is the conversion of possibility through probability into categorical necessity.

The dialectical method dictated that the essential features of each of the diverse forms of motion are to be concretely investigated not only in and for themselves, as the specialists of the separate sciences do, but also in their generality, in their mutual determinations and transitions from one into the other. The most important points in this study are the borderlines conjoining one form of motion with another, through which they undergo a qualitative transformation—mechanical motion generating heat, electricity converting into mechanical movement. Over time the dialectical development of nature has given rise to more highly organized types of matter.

Marx and Engels gave special attention to those critical turning points in the development of things where they pass over into their opposites. The two most momentous transitions in universal evolution were the leaps taken from the inorganic to the organic—from physicochemical processes to living beings—and, billions of years later, from animal to human. In human history the two most important are the passage from precivilized to civilized institutions, described in *The Origin of the Family,*

Private Property, and the State, and from class formations to the socialist future, envisaged in the *Communist Manifesto, Capital,* and other writings.

The *Dialectics of Nature* does not confine itself to a study of the evolutionary processes in the physical world, but as a materialist humanism should, heads toward its culmination in the creation of our species. Since the myth of divine creation was junked, the riddle of anthropogenesis, which asks how and by what means human beings originated, had baffled investigators. In the article "The Part Played by Labour in the Transition From Ape to Man," included in *Dialectics of Nature,* Engels outlined a materialist and dialectical solution to this problem. The labor theory of social origins showed how the process of cosmic development led by its own laws several million years ago to the emergence from nature of its own opposite, the human species, which had its own special kinds of activity and laws of development as a social being. This triumphant achievement of the Marxist method has been substantiated by many scientific discoveries since its first formulation.

The labor theory of humanization rounds out the dialectics of nature. Engels wrote that "the key to the understanding of the whole history of society lies in the historical development of labour."[15] The ending of *Dialectics of Nature* is linked with the beginning of *Capital* through this evolutionary approach to the labor process. The former shows how laboring created humankind, while the first chapter of *Capital* analyzes the nature of the commodity as a compound of the two forms of labor, concrete and abstract labor. Later in his exposition Marx traces labor activity back to the beginning of humanity's struggle with nature for survival.

In addition to mapping out the objective dialectics of nature, Engels had much to say about the dialectical, i.e., contradictory, ways in which scientific knowledge itself has developed. He pioneered in the new field of the history of science that has so energetically been pursued by scholars in recent years.

What conclusions can be drawn from these observations that are pertinent to our theme? First, the dialectics of natural evolution itself passed over into the dialectics of social evolution, a qualitative jump of the utmost importance. The first process was the material root, the precondition, the necessary basis, for the second. Contrary to the praxis theorists, who deny its existence or belittle its importance, the dialectics of nature existentially precedes the dialectics of the subject-object relation that they take as the be-all and end-all of Marxist method. Although these two modes of dialectical development operate in tandem within human history, the secondary process is dependent on the primary one. This is a cardinal principle of materialism.

Second, the dialectics of nature is not an invention of Engels that he smuggled into dialectical materialism behind Marx's back or after his death. It is a conception they worked out together. In *Capital*, Marx appealed to the law of the transformation of quantity into quality as having shown its worth in natural science as elsewhere.[16]

Third, the dialectics of nature is an essential part of Marxist philosophy, which would otherwise be incomplete, remaining a structure of sociology or anthropology without a firm and harmonious foundation in the acquisitions of the natural sciences that form the basis of all knowledge. In ruling out the operation of the laws of dialectics in natural processes and confining them to social phenomena, the myopic praxologists disrupt the unitary character and universal scope of Marxist theory, which reflects the material unity amidst qualitative diversity of the external world. They divide reality into two contraposed compartments— the physical, from which the laws of dialectics are absent, and the social, where they prevail because humans are actively involved.

Thus the existentialist Maurice Merleau-Ponty, along with Sartre, insists that matter has no principle of productivity or novelty. He writes: "If nature is dialectical, it is because it is that nature is perceived by man and inseparable from human action, as Marx made clear in the *Theses on Feuerbach* and in *The German Ideology*."[17] To the contrary, what Marx made clear was that the dialectics of nature proceeds on its own, long precedes human existence, perception, and action, and in fact gave birth to them. Alfred Schmidt asserts: "It is only the process of knowing nature which can be dialectical, not nature itself."[18] Both of these commentators offer a subjectivist version of the dialectical process, which is basically objective in character.

The revolution in the natural sciences over the past hundred and fifty years has transformed the world through the impact of industrial technology. Revolutionary developments of such magnitude have to be incorporated into the philosophy of the most revolutionary class in this age of permanent revolution. This fact obliges socialist thought to encompass the achievements of the sciences in all areas, as Marx, Engels, Lenin, Luxemburg, and Trotsky recognized.

It may be asked: What use have natural scientists made of the dialectical approach to the understanding of nature? There is a pronounced disparity in this respect between Soviet and Anglo-American scientists. Except for the eminent geneticist H. J. Muller in the 1930s, American scientists have regarded it as unserviceable, just as the academic economists have found the teachings of Marx unserviceable in political economy. Their empirical training and positivist outlook lead them to believe that nature exhibits no general laws apart from the specific laws of physics, chemistry, biology, etc., and that the search for such laws has no value.

The study of the dialectics of nature aims to answer two related questions. Are there more general laws of motion intermingled with and arising from the specific laws to be found in limited domains such as astronomy, genetics, electronics? The ordinary scientists, along with the positivist-minded philosophers, do not even raise this question, let alone provide an answer. Marxism does. It maintains that the relation of the specific laws of motion to the dialectical ones is comparable to the relation between arithmetic and algebra. The one exists on a higher level of generality and abstraction than the other.

Are there laws of motion operative in and universally applicable to all three divisions of being—nature, society, and the thought process? Marxism answers affirmatively and seeks to find out and describe what these are. Most other philosophies give a negative answer and accuse the dialectical materialists of going on a wild goose chase. Most praxis theorists agree with them.

One considerable handicap to serious consideration of the dialectical characteristics of nature has been the appalling spectacle of the obscurantism imposed upon the sciences under Stalin. The advances made in relativity physics, genetics, the resonance theory in chemistry, and cybernetics were rejected on the false ground that they failed to conform to the arbitrary specifications of all-powerful arbiters of Soviet thought such as Andrei Zhdanov. In the name of defense of materialist dialectics these discoveries were castigated and banned as idealistic aberrations. In this way Stalinism has cast the same discredit on dialectics in nature as on the name of socialism.

Since the dictator's death the situation has eased so far as most Soviet natural scientists are concerned. The best of them are no longer burdened by these taboos, and the convinced dialectical materialists among them can employ that method more flexibly and creatively. One of the most perceptive is B. M. Kedrov, who under Stalin was removed in 1948 as editor of the chief Soviet philosophical journal, *Problems of Philosophy*. He is now director of the Institute of the History of Science and Technology of the USSR Academy of Sciences. His writings on the development of scientific thought are superior in insight to most productions of the Western scholars on this subject. I am indebted to him for some of the ideas about Engels's work presented here.

One of the fullest accounts of the interaction between Marxist philosophy and the natural sciences among the leading Soviet scientists today has been given by the Columbia University scholar Loren Graham. Here is his concluding opinion:

> Contemporary Soviet dialectical materialism is an impressive intellectual achievement. The elaboration and refinement of the early suggestions of Engels, Plekhanov, and Lenin into a systematic interpretation of nature is the most original creation of Soviet Marxism. In the hands of its most able advocates, there is no question but that dialectical materialism is a sincere and legitimate attempt to understand and explain nature. In terms of universality and degree of development, the dialectical materialist explanation of nature has no competitors among modern systems of thought. Indeed, one would have to jump centuries, to the Aristotelian scheme of a natural order or to Cartesian mechanical philosophy, to find a system based on nature that could rival dialectical materialism in the refinement of its development and the wholeness of its fabric.[19]

This well-informed judgment is far better founded than the cursory dismissal of the worth of natural dialectics by the critics of Engels, who have little understanding of the broad theoretical problems posed by the advances of contemporary natural science.

*   *   *

The main source of inspiration for the nonmaterialist reinterpretations of Marxism that have become so popular is the collection of essays by Georg Lukács, *History and Class Con-*

sciousness. There he claimed that Marxism does not concern itself with any theory of nature but is exclusively a class explanation of human history and an exposition of society. Lukács accused Engels of being an exponent of an empiricism, scientism, and crass materialism that amounted to a bourgeois philosophy. Karl Korsch, an ultraleft leader of the German Communist Party who was expelled in 1926, likewise Hegelianized Marxism, although he did not agree on all points with Lukács, with whom he has been coupled.

Toward the end of his long career Lukács reconsidered and repudiated the views expressed in his early essays, saying they were predicated on false assumptions. He further recommended a return to the theoretical traditions of Engels, Plekhanov, and Lenin, whom he no longer dissociated from Marx. But the errors that men commit live after them, and despite the self-criticism of the older and wiser Lukács, these misconceptions have acquired a life of their own.

They were eagerly snapped up by left existentialists such as Sartre and Merleau-Ponty, who found the expunging of materialist objectivity and opposition to determinism consonant with their voluntaristic conception of individuals freely deciding their destiny. In his polemic against "the myth of objectivity" in "Materialism and Revolution," Sartre mistakenly claimed that Marx had held that subjectivity could not be dissociated from objectivity—until his "destructive encounter with Engels."[20] He repeats this theme in his more recent work, *The Critique of Dialectical Reason.*

The reaction against the materialist foundations of Marxism has been further promoted by such luminaries of the Frankfurt school as Adorno, Horkheimer, Marcuse, and their disciples. The line of thought fathered by Lukács has also been fostered by a broad spectrum of philosophers and sociologists in revolt against Stalinist orthodoxy from Yugoslavia to Hungary to Poland. These ideas have percolated from Europe to New Left intellectuals in the English-speaking countries. The quarterly publication *Telos* is at present the most assiduous propagandist for the Hegelianizing of Marxism in the United States.

While the views they have espoused may come as a fresh revelation to these radicals, they are a warmed-over dish to revolutionists of my vintage. This train of ideas was inaugurated as long ago as 1933 by Sidney Hook with his book *Towards the Understanding of Karl Marx.*

In the preface he gives credit to Lukács's *History and Class Consciousness* and Korsch's *Marxism and Philosophy* for confirming his "own hypothesis of the practical-historical axis of Marx's thought." Hook reproduced many of the major Lukácsian theses. Marxism is not based on a scientific explanation of objective reality, he held. The materialist dialectic does not apply to natural phenomena but solely to human history; it is a dialectic of social change. Marxism is not a body of doctrines derived from a scientific analysis of nature, society, and human thought; it is simply a method without any essential, determinate content and would be valid without its specific conclusions. Like the early Lukács and Horkheimer, Hook contested the inevitability of socialism as the progressive outcome of the class struggle under imperialism; it would come about from a voluntary choosing among options by a conscious proletariat.

Hook denied that there had been a complete identity in the doctrines and standpoint of Marx and Engels from the beginning of their friendship. On the contrary, he said Engels gave a wrong twist to his partner's positions in both economics and philosophy, transforming Marx's economic propositions into a closed deductive system and shifting his naturalistic activism to a simplified materialism that he called dialectical but was really mechanical. Engels also misconstrued Marx's theory of knowledge by insufficiently stressing the importance of the active practical element and retaining a crude theory of ideas as passive reflections of the material world. These innovations became hardened into dogma by the Social Democratic theoreticians before the First World War, he said.

During the 1930s Hook paraded as a free-thinking philosopher of the extreme Left intent on combatting the twin perversions of Marxism by the reformist Social Democrats and the Stalinists. Despite his pretensions, he was actually engaged in trimming dialectical materialism to a pragmatic pattern that fitted the political opportunism that carried him away from the revolutionary struggle.

At the time of their appearance, Hook's deviations were severely criticized by Trotsky. Hook had sketched them in an article in the *Nation* entitled "Marxism: Dogma or Method?" In his reply, "Marxism as a Science," Trotsky pointed out that the very posing of the question in that way was wrong. The materialist dialectic is not only a method but one whose applications to capitalist economy and the historical process have produced the positive results contained in the Marxist doctrines of political economy and historical materialism.

To Hook's contention that Marxism is not a science but merely a realistic method of class action, Trotsky rejoined that it could not be realistic unless it was based upon true knowledge of objective reality. To Hook's argument that Marxism was a matter of practical needs and class aims, and not of scientific objectivity, Trotsky answered that a doctor must have *both* the wish to cure the patient *and* accurate knowledge of anatomy, physiology, pathology, and other sciences. The same held true for revolutionists confronted with a sick society.[21]

It was around this time that newly hatched Trotskyist intellectuals like me became inoculated against the views of Lukács, Korsch, and their American followers. Unfortunately, other leading comrades such as Felix Morrow, Albert Goldman, and James Burnham were not.

The continuity in the assimilation of Marxist philosophy was so sharply broken between the 1930s and the 1970s that this earlier dispute between the pro-Lukácsians and their opponents is virtually unknown. The New Left intellectuals who are refurbishing the ideas of the early Lukács may be disconcerted to learn that Hook was their precursor in pitting Engels against Marx, tossing out the dialectics of nature, and interpreting Marxism as a sociology of revolutionary praxis. This theoretical weakness had its effect upon his regressive political course from 1940 on.

Marxism is, to be sure, the theory of revolutionary action par excellence. But it could not serve this purpose unless it was a scientific doctrine based upon true knowledge of the material conditions of development—because these determine the nature, scope, and effectiveness of social change and political activity. By cutting away or sliding over the totality of objective factors, the revisionists invite the intrusion of pragmatism, voluntarism, and subjectivism in place of an authentic materialist method.

*   *   *

What relevance do these apparently abstruse theoretical disputes, past and present, have to our current work and historical tasks? The members of our movement were first impressed with the practical importance and political relevance of a correct philosophical method in the 1939-40 struggle that split the Socialist Workers Party (recorded in Trotsky's *In Defense of Marxism* and Cannon's *The Struggle for a Proletarian Party*). The polemics of that time over the relation between dialectical materialism and revolutionary politics were necessary to clarify the fundamental nature of the Soviet Union as a degenerated workers' state and reaffirm the proletarian duty of defending it against imperialism.

At present there are no such tense differences over philosophy or politics in our party. However, a variance of views on some questions of method does exist within the world Trotskyist movement. These can be calmly and objectively discussed. Unlike the Healyite sectarians, we do not believe that philosophic ideas are the most important and determining element at all times in class politics. The notion that philosophy takes command is not a materialist and dialectical but a mechanistic and idealist approach to the place philosophy occupies in the total activity and development of the revolutionary movement of the working class.

Nonetheless, experience has demonstrated that a light-minded attitude toward one's theoretical outlook, or even worse a stubborn defense of nonmaterialist premises, can have serious consequences for practical activity. Underlying philosophical differences can come to the surface in the form of opposing political conclusions. What these might be can be ascertained only by analysis of the concrete circumstances of the case.

Individuals can stray from the right road in various directions. Despite their affinities in misinterpreting certain principles of Marxist thought, Lukács, Korsch, and Hook, for example, subsequently traveled along divergent paths and ended up at different destinations, as determined by their personal situations and the environing pressures on them. Lukács was trapped in the Stalinist apparatus; Korsch quit politics and even repudiated Marxism in the 1950s; and Hook, who endorsed the Communist ticket in 1932, supported the Republican presidential candidate forty years later. The unstable eclecticism of their positions can hold out equally divergent futures for present adherents of the praxis school.

The doctrines upon which our movement is based are not named scientific socialism without good and sufficient reason. Our party endeavors to educate its members in all aspects of

Marxism from the most general problems of theory to everyday tactics. We want to create well-equipped revolutionists who know enough not to be captivated by passing fads. We have to polish the tools of thought given by Marxism and keep them sharp by continuous application.

•   *   *   *

The philosophical situation within the international socialist movement nowadays is very complex. Three main tendencies are contending with one another. There are those who propagate the deformations of Marxist thought that emanate from Moscow or Peking. In opposition to them are genuine exponents of the dialectical materialist method as derived from the unalloyed teachings of its founders. In between is a variety of tendencies in flux, which overlap materialism at one end and border on subjectivism at the other.

The wide differences of opinion among the dissidents in the Soviet bloc require us to distinguish between them. We support the democratic rights of all of them without qualification; we do not support those theoretical positions and political perspectives that deviate from revolutionary Marxism. On the philosophical level many of them are resisting the stultifying effects of Stalinism and questing for the truth along previously forbidden lines. Here too we solidarize with their fight against thought control and official dogmas, without sharing their errors.

The Stalinist debasement of Marxist teachings constitutes an ideology in the worst sense; it is a rationale for the special interests of a privileged caste. Moscow's "red professors" blunted the critical edge of the dialectical method and turned its laws and categories into a set of rigid formulas applied in a stereotyped manner dictated by state prescription. The logic of Marxism was not only schematized but eviscerated.

Stalin, for instance, in his obligatory catechism *Dialectical and Historical Materialism*, omitted mention of the law of the negation of the negation, which sets forth the pattern of progressive development in which the new replaces the old on a higher level as the outcome of the conflict of opposing forces. This omission in theory, it was hoped, would shield the bureaucracy from negation in practice. Marxism, instead of being a school of unfettered thought, became a school of scholastic mumbo jumbo.

In the course of challenging this ideology, numerous oppositionists have questioned some of the postulates of Marxist philosophy. Since the Stalinists, in the name of dialectical materialism, so grossly falsify the real state of affairs, many no longer consider dialectical materialism to be a scientific doctrine. They have likewise turned against historical determinism in indignation against the inquisitors who justify their abuses on the pretext that, as executors of the laws of history, they are entitled to pursue the class struggle more harshly after the conquest of power than before. Some counterpose to this the fervent moral idealism of the individual defying arbitrary rule. They seek an ethical instead of a class basis for their shaken faith in the prospects of socialism.

Those humanist dissidents who disavow the governance of lawfulness and necessity in social life, and stress the autonomous freedom of the nonconformist personality, are themselves driven by the imperious necessity of throwing off bureaucratic oppression and unmanacling their own minds. Their insistence on the unhampered exercise of critical thought and the right of uncensored expression reflects a powerful progressive ferment at work within the Soviet bloc.

However, too often they still accept the say-so of the Stalinists that they are faithful disciples of Engels and Lenin, and that to break away from Stalinism is equivalent to repudiating scientific socialism. In unthinking reflex many have placed a minus sign wherever Stalinism affixed a plus. Such critics make the same methodological mistake in philosophy as in party organization, where they lump together the autocratic centralization of the monolithic Communist parties with the Leninist conception of democratic centralism, and reject both.

The ideological havoc wrought by Stalinism is evidenced in the paradoxical fact that many of the most courageous champions of democratization have been caught up in the anti-Engels current. Some among them, such as certain members of the *Praxis* group in Yugoslavia, Kolakowski in Poland, and Karel Kosík in Czechoslavakia, have been penalized for their justified criticisms of the regime. In response to the indiscriminate accusations flung at them by the watchdogs of the status quo, they have clung all the more firmly to their heretical views.

The evolution of the two most prominent Polish Communist philosophers, Leszek Kolakowski and Adam Schaff, typifies this swing away from classical Marxism toward eclecticism. From their common starting points in Stalinist orthodoxy before 1956, both master and pupil have at different paces and in differing degrees discarded key elements of dialectical materialism en route to their present beliefs. Schaff spurns the dialectics of nature and doubts the possibility of eradicating alienation in the future socialist society, as though it were a built-in human trait, not a historically conditioned phenomenon. Kolakowski has almost entirely lost his Marxist bearings. The root of the trouble is their failure to overcome the insidious effects of Stalinist misdeeds and miseducation, even in resisting them, and their failure to use their newfound freedom of thought to advance to consistent Marxist positions.

So the worth of Engels and the tradition stemming from his work has become an unmerited casualty of the conflict between the repressive rulers and dissident thinkers in Eastern Europe, who have permitted the falsifications of Stalinism to blur some of the truths of Marxism.

It should be recognized that these heterodox theorists are grappling as best they can with the novel issues and unprecedented problems posed by the anomalous development of the postcapitalist regimes in their countries. And they have to undertake their inquiries in ceaseless conflict with the authorities bearing down upon them.

To explain the reasons for the direction their thought has taken is not to justify any of their incorrect views. In philosophy as in politics those who disengage from Stalinism can move along opposite lines. They can either find their way to the viable traditions of dialectical materialism that Stalinism smothers and obscures—or else adopt nonmaterialist, nonproletarian positions.

Up to now only a few have managed to embark on the first course in their search for a new orientation. Just as certain Social Democrats before the First World War attempted to amalgamate Marxism with borrowings from Immanuel Kant, the empiriocritics, and others, so New Left thinkers East and West are prone to cook up a stew that mixes Marxist conceptions with ingredients from nonmaterialist sources ranging from existentialism, structuralism, and pragmatism to neo-Hegelianism, phenomenology, and linguistic analysis. It is the season for raising hybrids rather than developing purebred Marxism.

Where, amidst this swirling confusion, do we as Trotskyists stand? We adhere to the principles originating with Marx and Engels and to the course marked out by their ablest followers in philosophy. Plekhanov, Lenin, Luxemburg, and Trotsky are our teachers, and we regard the heritage received from them as among our most precious possessions. We are resolved to carry forward and develop their ideas as the only scientific basis for revolutionary working class politics.

Georg Lukács
as a Marxist Philosopher

[The following three articles consist of an assessment by George Novack; a criticism by the French Marxist Etienne Abrahamovici; and Novack's reply.]

I

An Assessment by George Novack

For the past fifty years Georg Lukács stood in the front rank of European Marxist philosophy, literary criticism, and esthetics. The most controversial and influential of his voluminous works, *History and Class Consciousness,* finally appeared in an English translation in June 1971, around the same time that the renowned Hungarian thinker died in Budapest at the age of 86.

This book has had a curious history. Lukács passed through three phases as a Marxist theoretician. *History and Class Consciousness* belongs to the earliest, which extended from the defeated Hungarian revolution of 1918-19 to his withdrawal from active participation in Communist Party politics after 1929. The next period of his intellectual production was dominated and disfigured by Stalin's totalitarian tyranny. Lukács had greater latitude to express his real views in print during the final years from 1956 to his death, although he had to remain mindful of the party authorities.

After *History and Class Consciousness* was published in Vienna in 1923, it was condemned for distorting Marxist doctrines by Gregory Zinoviev and Nikolai Bukharin at the Fifth

Congress of the Third International in June-July 1924. The Soviet philosopher Abram Deborin, among others, pointed out that Lukács's attempt to counterpose Engels to Marx led him to philosophical idealism; that he wrongly rejected the applicability of the dialectical method to nature as well as the objective reality of nature independent of human cognition; and that he did not take a materialist approach to history and society.

Lukács himself disavowed the work after fresh attacks in 1933, not solely out of submission to the Stalinist thought police but because further reflection, stimulated by reading Lenin, had changed his mind and brought his views on certain key questions more into harmony with the positions of the founders of Marxism.

Meantime his semicontraband work enjoyed a subterranean reputation among left intellectuals of Eastern and Western Europe repelled by the sterile scholasticism and conformism of the Stalinist school. They picked up its quasi-Hegelian mode of interpretation, its severance of Engels from Marx, its rejection of numerous principles of dialectical and historical materialism, and utilized its heresies not only as weapons against Stalinist dogmatism but as a warrant for disqualifying authentic Marxist views.

Left existentialists such as Jean-Paul Sartre and Maurice Merleau-Ponty were especially assiduous in this endeavor. As the de-Stalinization of intellectual life has quickened in Eastern Europe, many heterodox socialist humanists there have followed suit. They are finding echoers in England and the United States—where, after some delay, the latest ideological fads from the Continent are usually snapped up with relish by academically trained radicals.

Lukács complained about this abuse of his early, outgrown, and erroneous version of Marxist theory, but his protestations have gone largely unheeded. His book is too useful for those who want to "trim Marx's beard" to suit their own theoretical purposes. *History and Class Consciousness* continues to be a favored fount of inspiration for assorted philosophers and sociologists who have ransacked its pages for arguments against the materialist foundations of the Marxist method.

The early Lukács has been popularized by the critics of Marxism for the same reasons that many of these people declare themselves so fond of the young Trotsky. Just as opponents of democratic centralism in party organization have resurrected

Trotsky's pre-1905 criticisms of Lenin's principles of organization—which Trotsky himself explicitly disavowed as incorrect, from 1917 on—many of the deviations Lukács cast off through deeper understanding have been flaunted as the true interpretation of Marxist method.

In justice it must be said that the virtues as well as the faults of *History and Class Consciousness* have been responsible for its attraction and influence. Lukács was, in Stephen Spender's phrase, "a millionaire of learning." He moved with consummate ease through the corridors of Western philosophy and dealt with contemporary problems of thought in a powerfully analytic manner. Ordinary professors of philosophy appeared like petty provincials beside him.

History and Class Consciousness is the product of what he rightly called his apprenticeship in Marxism. In addition to its place in his personal development, it has value as a historical document. For all its flaws, it represented an original and independent effort by a gifted intellectual, saturated in the advanced bourgeois culture of his day in Middle Europe, to transcend its limitations and come to terms with the Marxist outlook.

He was far from successful in this apprentice venture, as he himself acknowledged, and he did not fully attain that goal even at the last, as we shall see. However, in *History and Class Consciousness* Lukács, thanks to his grounding in German classical philosophy, highlighted the dialectical element of the Marxist method, which had been thrust into the background while Karl Kautsky held sway over the international Social Democracy. Lukács was the first since Marx to dwell upon the importance of the concepts of alienation and reification in the revolutionary criticism of the capitalist system. And, unlike the mechanical determinists, he saw that active, working, thinking, struggling human beings were not only the products but the producers of the historical process of social development.

Toward the end of his long and sinuous "road to Marx," Lukács wrote a candid appraisal of the book he had published a half century before. This reassessment, which can be taken as his final judgment on its merits and demerits, is reprinted as an introduction to the English edition. In any definitive summary of the worth of the work it is therefore necessary to bracket the original text with the self-criticism made from the vantage point of his ripened reflection in 1967.

The commentary in the preface presents his real views, since the most terrible constraints of the bureaucratic inquisitors who had previously forced recantations from him had been relaxed by that time. However much devotees of the younger Lukács may disagree, these afterthoughts have no less interest to students of his intellectual trajectory than his more widely known earlier views. Together they encompass the budding and the final fruit of his philosophical evolution along Marxist lines.

*   *   *

What did Lukács come to regard as incorrect in *History and Class Consciousness?* He first places the book in its specific historical setting. The essays were written and revised from 1919 to 1922. During that time he was afflicted, he says, with "messianic sectarianism." He means two different things by this. On one hand, he then awaited an imminent European proletarian revolution. At the same time he was a spokesman for the ultraleft currents that were rampant in the earliest years of the Communist International.

Lukács had come to Communism with a prior anarcho-syndicalist training that affected his political orientation until the mid-1920s. Lenin and Trotsky took the lead in combatting these adventurist tendencies at the Third World Congress of the Comintern; the former wrote his famous polemic *Left-Wing Communism: An Infantile Disorder* as part of that campaign. He singled out Lukács for special mention in 1920, criticizing his voluntarism and purely verbal Marxism which failed to take into account the precise historical circumstances at that point in the revolutionary struggle.

Thus the idealistic deviations of Lukács in the most general field of Marxist theory went hand in hand with the unrealistic strategy he then advocated for the proletarian vanguard. This partially accounts for the vehemence of the criticisms directed against *History and Class Consciousness* at the Fifth World Congress. Practical questions of strategy and tactics as well as issues of Marxist theory were involved in the controversy. Furthermore, Zinoviev, the patron of the Hungarian Communist leader Béla Kun, had an ax to grind with Lukács in connection with different proposals for reorganizing and redirecting the underground Hungarian CP.

From this accounting of the genesis of *History and Class*

Consciousness Lukács proceeds to pass judgment on its main positions. He is most severe on its fundamental methodological standpoint, which, he says, "strike[s] at the very roots of Marxian ontology."[1] *History and Class Consciousness* sets forth the premise that Marxism is exclusively a theory of society, a philosophy of human history. This misconstruction ignores and repudiates its intrinsic connection with the external world.

The book goes so far as to convert nature into a social category, implying that it is the work of humankind and even of its consciousness. Lukács wrote without qualification that "existence is the product of human activity," a statement valid only for *social* existence. For dialectical or any other materialism, nature has an independent objective existence prior to and apart from its relations with humankind, which is a product and a part of material reality. *History and Class Consciousness* inverts this real relationship between nature and humanity in the manner of idealism.

The repudiation of materialism in this work is unsparing. Lukács characterized the materialism of the Enlightenment, which Lenin urged Marxists to study, as merely "the ideological form of the bourgeois revolution."[2] Lukács approvingly cited his old teacher, the neo-Kantian Heinrich Rickert, who said that materialism was "inverted Platonism."[3] Whereas for him the dialectic was proletarian, he considered the materialist position to be essentially metaphysical and bourgeois.

The later Lukács, by affirming the universal scope of Marxist theory and the independent objectivity of nature, explicitly dissociated himself from those left existentialists such as Sartre, who tear Marxism from its anchorage in the material world as a whole and try to restrict its province, content, and concern to the strictly human realm. By cutting off social from natural evolution, they reduce Marxism to a pure "anthropology" disjoined from ontology.

In order to slice up dialectical materialism in this fashion, the revisionists are obliged to disrupt the historical continuity of the transmission of classical Marxist theory best expressed in the writings of Karl Marx, Frederick Engels, George Plekhanov, Vladimir Ilyich Lenin, Rosa Luxemburg, and Leon Trotsky. The gambit of this tendency is to divorce Engels, as an alleged exponent of empiricism, scientism, and vulgar, or metaphysical, materialism, from Marx as they refashion him. Though it was impossible to pit the one against the other during their lifetimes, these falsifiers have contrived to separate and oppose them after their deaths. They depict Engels not as the intimate collaborator of Marx and the most trustworthy interpreter of the dialectical materialism they created together, but as the original adulterator and distorter of Marx's thought. They accuse the guiltless Engels of doing what they themselves actually carry out.

Lukács's attack upon Engels along these lines has done much to popularize and sanction this distortion of the relations between the two founders of scientific socialism. When he concedes that Marxism incorporates a general theory of being going beyond society, he makes partial amends for his unfounded attempt to wedge apart the collaborators and their philosophical synthesis.

In accord with his restoration of materialism to its proper place, Lukács says in the preface to the new edition that the version of Marxism in *History and Class Consciousness* suffers from an overriding subjectivism. It presents an abstract and idealistic conception of praxis because it omits or disregards the central role of labor—productive activity—as the mediator of the metabolic interaction between society and nature.

History and Class Consciousness took its point of departure not from labor, the cardinal characteristic in the formation and development of humankind, but from a far more advanced stage in history when commodity relations were in full effect. The book does in fact narrow the scope of historical materialism to bourgeois society and the proletarian struggle against it. "Historical materialism in its classical form . . . means the *self-knowledge of capitalist society*," it says.[4] Actually the Marxist method covers all the successive stages of social organization at different levels of economic development, from the most primitive to capitalism and beyond.

*   *   *

The work is especially celebrated for the pioneering prominence it gave to the problem of alienation, which has since become a preoccupation of diverse currents of modern philosophy from existentialism to Marxism. Lukács observes that "*History and Class Consciousness* had a profound impact in youthful intellectual circles; I know of a whole host of good Communists who were won over to the movement by this very fact. Without a doubt the fact that this Marxist and Hegelian question was taken up by a

Communist was one reason why the impact of the book went far beyond the limits of the party."[5] In the same breath the later Lukács points out that he treated the problem "in purely Hegelian terms." He criticizes the original text on two points: the nature of object-subject relations and the confusion of objectification with alienation.

The handling of the object-subject relation has always drawn a principled dividing line between the materialist and idealist standpoints. Materialism maintains that the objective (in nature or in society) has an existence prior to and independent of the subject, whether this refers to humanity vis-à-vis nature, the inner lives of people, or the individual. The object and the subject are united but not identical.

Idealism, on the contrary, claims that there is no object without a subject; these two aspects of reality are inseparable and identical in the last analysis. Georg Wilhelm Friedrich Hegel, for example, pictured the dialectical process of universal history as the originally unified Spirit, or Absolute Idea, fissioning into external nature, bursting into consciousness, and passing through one grade of incompletely subjective existence to another, until at the highest stage of Absolute Spirit all alienation was abolished by the return of self-consciousness to itself. There at last the pristine identity of the subject and object was fully realized.

In *History and Class Consciousness* Lukács substituted the proletariat for the logical Idea of Hegel. Humanity is alienated from its true existence, object is opposed to subject, until the proletariat arrives at the class consciousness provided by Marxism. By this act of cognition the proletariat overcomes the disjunction between the knowing subject and the object of knowledge and frees itself along with the rest of humanity from its alienated state. This identical subject-object, incarnated in the class-conscious proletariat and created by its self-knowledge, rather than by its revolutionary struggle and reconstruction of society, is, as Lukács says, "a purely metaphysical construct" that out-Hegels Hegel.[6]

Hegel's idealistic conception of alienation depended upon his equation of objectification with alienation. According to his lights, every externalization of an object and its representation was an alienated form of its true existence. In order to overcome alienation it was necessary to throw off objectivity and totally absorb this false form of existence into the identical subject-object that the Absolute Spirit was destined to realize at the end of its travail.

History and Class Consciousness transposed this idealist scheme into social-historical terms. It converted all the achievements of humanity objectified in society up to the advent of the class-conscious proletariat into so many expressions of alienated activity enveloped with illusory reifications. It did not distinguish between those results of social practice that sustained humanity and elevated it and those that degraded and deformed people. Objectification, Lukács came to recognize, was a "natural phenomenon" that produced alienated relationships only under certain historical conditions and in specific ways. Forced labor has an alienated quality, free labor has not, though in both cases the laboring activity assumes an objective existence in its product.

Those humanistic socialists nowadays who see the subject-object relation manifested in social-historical praxis as the be-all and end-all of Marxist philosophy, rather than as a component of it, fall into the same subjective trap from which the later Lukács extricated himself. The objective, that is, the environmental determining conditions of life, both physical and social, cannot be swallowed up by the subjective elements without breaking with materialism and sliding over to some sort of anthropocentric or idealistic misconception of reality.

*   *   *

History and Class Consciousness has other weaknesses than those discussed by Lukács. His reasoning there is conducted on a level of rarefied abstraction that rarely makes contact with the relevant facts of historical actuality. This flight into "pure thought" is more proper to rationalism than to the Marxist method, which seeks to fuse the broadest generalizations with the empirical data connected with the problems under consideration. This procedure is all the more inadmissible in view of Lukács's subsequent insistence on the indispensability of "the specific" in genuinely dialectical thinking.

His contention that "scientific experiment is contemplation at its purest" is an invalid paradox, stemming from his aversion to the materialist basis of science and Marxist philosophy.[7] A natural and social science that aims to change the world and not simply contemplate it is the supreme form of social practice, as the later Lukács acknowledged.

History and Class Consciousness says that "immediacy," that is, the dwelling upon external appearances, is the chief characteristic and insurmountable limitation of the bourgeois mode of thought. This is too sweeping and absolute an assertion; it nullifies the tremendous advances and achievements in scientific knowledge during the bourgeois era that spurred its economic development. Galileo's and Isaac Newton's laws of motion revolutionized physics by going behind the appearances of phenomena to grasp and formulate their concealed essence. The classical economists arrived at the labor theory of value by penetrating through the market and monetary relations manifested as semblances in the circulation of commodities and bringing to light some of the basic determinants in the production process under capitalism. On this point Lukács undialectically failed to distinguish between the progressive and reactionary stages and aspects of a social formation.

Lukács was more of a Hegelian than a Marxist when he asserted that "the structure and hierarchy of the categories . . . are the central theme of history."[8] This inverts the relation between the ideas and the practical activities of humanity. The main line of history is traced through the successive levels of social productive power embodied in the modes of production extending from tribal collectivism to the transition from capitalism to socialism. "The structure and hierarchy of the categories"—whether these are economic, political, or philosophical—are conceptual reflections of this historical process.

The dialectical method of Marxism is not presented in *History and Class Consciousness* as a logical instrument for analyzing matter in motion in the physical, social, and intellectual realms. It is rather a selection or system of abstract categories (totality, reification) on which Lukács erects his theoretical constructions. The particular categories he favors are far more in evidence in his book than such dialectical laws of being and becoming as the unity and struggle of opposites, the change of quantity into quality, the interplay of form and content, etc.

Lukács treats the proletariat and its consciousness as a fixed entity, an absolute with permanent characteristics, rather than as an evolving social force undergoing extremely contradictory and uneven development, which, on the basis of its determinate role in the structure and operations of capitalism, is capable of acquiring opposing characteristics. As circumstances change, this class can pass over from an atomized to a highly organized

economic and political state and from a passively nonrevolution-
ary to an energetically revolutionary disposition. Under objectively imposed conditions of political defeat and industrial
setbacks this process can also temporarily move in the opposite
direction.

He suggests that the proletariat need only become aware of its
social nature and historical mission for reification to be overcome, although the eradication of this phenomenon arising from
commodity relations involves more than a change of consciousness; it requires nothing less than the socialist transformation of
society.

He pictures the proletariat coming to class consciousness as a
free agent ready for revolutionary action—without giving proper
weight to the determining objective conditions necessary for a
decisive drive to the conquest of power. This one-sidedness
reflects the rhetorical ultraradicalism Lenin criticized.

Finally, his rationalistic approach appears in the statement
that *"the strength of every society is in the last resort a spiritual
strength. And from this we can only be liberated by knowledge."*[9]
This is at best a misleading half-truth. Whenever the spiritual
and ideological resources of ruling classes that keep the oppressed in tow become expended, their agents resort to more
material means of repression, as colonial and civil wars demonstrate. This is the ultimate strength—as well as the Achilles'
heel—of capitalist domination which the organized counterpower
of the revolutionary masses has to confront and overcome.

*   *   *

While Lukács corrected serious theoretical errors in his original
exposition, his enterprise of self-criticism remained incomplete
and fell short in certain essential respects. He reinstituted the
ontological objectivity that is the cornerstone of any materialist
philosophy, but he evaded saying whether or not the processes of
nature have a dialectical character. This default is all the more
glaring since in *History and Class Consciousness* he was among
the first to upbraid Engels for extending dialectics to natural
phenomena on the ground that "the dialectical process . . . is
enacted essentially *between the subject and the object*."[10] It does
not, according to this thesis, take place within natural events.
Because dialectics presumably emerged only with humanity, the

physico-chemical transmutation of nonliving into living matter several billion years ago on earth could not be classified as a major manifestation of the law of qualitative jumps produced by preceding quantitive changes.

The limitation of dialectical processes and their laws to human history and thought violates the monism of the Marxist world view, which is based on the material unity of the cosmos in all its qualitative diversity. This partitioning of reality is not simply contrary to the position held by Marx, Engels, and Lenin. It fails to face up to the question: What do the results of the natural sciences, as well as the history of science itself, disclose about the most general character of the laws of motion and change in the physical world? According to Marxist philosophy, the most recent as well as the previous discoveries of the natural sciences—from the theory of inorganic and organic evolution to the incompleted findings about elementary-particle physics—confirm the validity of the dialectical conception of the processes of nature. It is plain that Lukács, unlike Engels and Lenin, did not feel at ease in coping with the philosophical problems posed by the latest developments in natural science.

For Hegel the laws of dialectics were mere laws of thought; for Marxism they are the most comprehensive laws of all the divisions of being: nature, society, and thought. For the revisionists, however, they are exclusively laws of human history. By evading the issue of the logical character of the changes in prehuman and extrahuman phenomena Lukács lends aid and comfort to the truncators of Marxist philosophy, from the French existentialists to the neohumanists, who deny the dialectics of nature and try to reduce Marxism to a theory of social development and the metabolism between nature and society, as he himself thought in *History and Class Consciousness.*

Second, Lukács did not abandon the one-sided explanation of the ideological genesis of dialectical materialism whereby he established too direct and exclusive a derivation of Marx's philosophy from Hegel. On this point he disregards the care for mediation that he rightly sees as essential to the use of the dialectical method.

Though he no longer believed that materialism was a bourgeois fetish, he maintained in his preface that "Marx followed directly from Hegel" and that "Plekhanov and others [others would include Engels and Lenin] . . . vastly overestimated Feuerbach's role" in the formation of dialectical materialism.[11] This opinion clearly controverts not only the evidence of Marx's early writings from 1843 to 1845 but the considered testimony of Engels, who wrote *Ludwig Feuerbach and the Outcome of Classical German Philosophy* to demonstrate their indebtedness to the eminent German materialist.

The unwarranted depreciation of Feuerbach's contribution to the development of modern materialism comes from Lukács's inveterate habit of minimizing the materialist elements in both the background and structure of Marxism. All of his thought bore the impress of the Hegelian prejudices he absorbed from the Central European academic milieu of his pre-Marxist years, even though it was somewhat less pronounced in his most mature works. As Ernst Bloch wittily remarked in his original review of *History and Class Consciousness*: ". . . Marx has not placed Hegel on his feet so that Lukács can put Marx back on his head."

This bias was obvious in his continued belief that, as he wrote in *History and Class Consciousness,* "concrete totality is . . . the category that governs reality."[12] He derived this conception from Hegel's proposition that "the truth is in the whole." The injunction to see all things and events in their interconnections and integrations and to recognize that the whole takes precedence over any one of its parts is an essential feature of the dialectical method. It is especially useful in counteracting the piecemeal and pluralistic approach to phenomena held up as a model by the empiricists, pragmatists, and positivists.

Nonetheless, it cannot be exalted into the central and supreme concept of Marxist thought as Lukács made out in *History and Class Consciousness,* where he wrote: "The category of totality, the all-pervasive supremacy of the whole over the parts, is the essence of the method which Marx took over from Hegel and brilliantly transformed into the foundations of a wholly new science."[13] This one-sided view of the concept of totality as preeminent above the rest, to which Lukács has given currency, has been seized upon as the magic talisman of dialectical thought by many other Marxist and quasi-Marxist theorists, such as Henri Lefèbvre, and Sartre in *The Critique of Dialectical Reason,* all of whom subordinate or suppress the materialist aspects of Marxism and Hegelianize it as they please.

Parenthetically, Lukács ignores his own prescription for a totality in Marxist philosophy when he refuses to accept the unbreakable connections between the dialectics of nature and the dialectics of the changing relations between nature and humanity in the historical development of social organization. This is an unresolved dualism in his ultimate position.

Finally, Lukács holds to the view that Marxism is not a body of doctrines and principles or a set of empirically tested and testable conclusions derived from their applications. It is simply and solely a method of reasoning, of critical analysis. This is a view shared with the Frankfurt school of Theodor Adorno, Max Horkheimer, and Herbert Marcuse—and even with Sidney Hook. He endorses the definition of orthodoxy contained in the following passage from the first essay in *History and Class Consciousness*: "Let us assume for the sake of argument that recent research had disproved once and for all every one of Marx's individual theses. Even if this were to be proved, every serious 'orthodox' Marxist would still be able to accept all such modern findings without reservation and hence dismiss all of Marx's theses *in toto*—without having to renounce his orthodoxy for a single moment."[14]

What an astounding opinion to be enunciated by a materialist who believes that social practice is the test of truth, or a dialectician who understands the unity of form and content! If every one of the Marxist theses on the course of history, such as the class struggle as the prime motive force in civilized societies, and all the conclusions in *Capital* from the labor theory of value, the twofold nature of labor, the source of surplus value, the increasing concentration and centralization of capital, up to the expropriation of the expropriators can be proven false, what good are they? A method in philosophy, history, or political economy that arrived at no true, dependable, or enduring conclusions and led only to errors would be theoretically insupportable and worthless in practice. It could solve no problems.

The notion that Marxism can be boiled down to a residue of method is a purely idealistic conception taken straight from Hegel—or rather, a one-sided extraction from his thought. Method by itself, without specific content, has no more reality, efficacy, or value than a disembodied spirit. It is a hollow shell. The propositions that make up the actual substance of Marxism as they have been amplified and verified over the past hundred years cannot be so cavalierly discounted. They constitute the essential and irreplaceable content of its system of thought and provide the guidelines of its procedures.

Any one of the particular propositions of Marxism in any area is open to question, critical examination, modification, and even discard if the facts require. Dogmatism is alien to dialectical materialism. But by hypothesizing the possibility of expunging the entire concrete content of Marxism from its definition, Lukács opens the door to philosophical skepticism and to the repudiation of the fundamental principles and distinctive positions that demarcate Marxism from all other schools of thought and give it the power of truth that can be fruitful in practice.

*   *   *

This review focuses upon Lukács's most controversial work and does not deal with the entire shelf of studies in the history and problems of philosophy, literature, and esthetic theory in which his talents were displayed. As a thinker and scholar in diverse fields of culture from philosophy to the arts Lukács was outstanding among his contemporaries. If he did not provide the right answers in all cases, his discussions illuminated most of the important questions in dispute among Marxist philosophers today.

How ignominious his political career was in contrast! As late as November 1918 he was against the October revolution. In 1919, after joining the Hungarian CP, he served as minister of education in the floundering revolutionary regime of Béla Kun, which collapsed in less than six months.

As has been noted, he belonged to the ultraleft camp in the Comintern in the days of Lenin and Trotsky. He took no definite position in the factional struggles that convulsed the international Communist movement during the 1920s and decided its direction thereafter. He so thoroughly cured himself of ultraleftism by the mid-1920s that he swung over to the right wing and hardly swerved from that course for the rest of his life.

Lukács retired from the arena of practical party politics in 1929 when he discovered that Béla Kun was planning to expel him from the Hungarian CP as a "liquidator." He renounced the struggle for his ideas presented in the "Blum Theses" (his party pseudonym) and published a recantation in order to avoid the fate of his fellow philosopher Karl Korsch, who was expelled from the German Communist Party in 1926.

He did the same on several subsequent occasions, disclaiming or suppressing his real views in order to stay in the Stalinist ranks and escape reprisals. The self-justification he offered fifty

years later was that his compliance enabled him to participate
actively in the struggle against fascism, although he admittedly
disagreed with Stalin's theory of "social fascism," which helped
Hitler come to power. The only effective way to have waged the
antifascist struggle was against the disastrous policies of Stalinism, as the Trotskyists did.

But from first to last Lukács was consciously and adamantly
opposed to Trotskyism. He lauded "socialism in one country" as
one of Stalin's greatest contributions and unreservedly accepted
peaceful coexistence, popular frontism, and their consequences.
He adapted himself to the cultural policies of the Kremlin and
echoed the slanders against the German people in its wartime
propaganda.

Returning to Hungary after 1945, he continued to devote
himself to literary pursuits and did not engage in public political
life until after the Soviet CP's Twentieth Congress in 1956.
During the memorable debates at the Budapest Petöfi Circle in
June of that year he came forth as a slashing critic of the
Stalinist cultural policy from which he had suffered. Swept along
by the momentum of the mass upsurge in 1956 as he had been in
1918, Lukács associated himself with the dissenting Communists
around Imre Nagy, was named to the Central Committee when
Nagy took over the premiership, and temporarily assumed the
portfolio of People's Culture in the new government.

At the height of the revolt, on October 31, he stated in an
interview with a Polish journalist that Communism in Hungary
had been totally disgraced. Following the brutal suppression of
the popular uprising he was interned in Romania, but he was
allowed to return to Budapest as early as April 1957. He refused
to renounce the revolt and was again denounced as an unregener-
ate revisionist. However, he and Janos Kadar, the present
Hungarian premier, were the only survivors among the founding
leaders of the new Communist Party organized by Nagy. Later
reconciled with the Kadar regime, he returned to the CP as one of
its honored ornaments.

Lukács customarily followed the line of least resistance. Although he recoiled from the worst abominations of Stalinism and
strongly condemned them so far as de-Stalinization allowed, he
loyally adhered to the Kremlin's political line. In the Sino-Soviet
dispute he sided with Moscow despite the cogent criticisms the
Maoists directed against Khrushchev's opportunism. Though he
admitted that alienation was intense in the bureaucratized

workers' states, except for the brief interlude of 1956 he was averse to any direct mass struggle for socialist democracy.

He espoused the thesis of the convergence of the postcapitalist and the industrialized capitalist countries and even—believe it or not—praised the Kennedy-type "brain trust" as an organizational form more valid than "the specific position of Marx and Lenin in socialist countries." At the end of his life he made no public declaration on the invasion of Czechoslovkia. He was privately distressed and opposed the intervention but did not speak out against it for fear, he said, of "being associated with antisocialist hysteria." Nor did he protest the exclusion of Aleksandr Solzhenitsyn, whose novels he deemed praiseworthy, from the Union of Soviet Writers.

His career followed much the same pattern as that of Ilya Ehrenburg, who likewise by dint of maneuvering and luck managed to elude the firing squads, welcome de-Stalinization, and come to a natural death in old age. It bears witness to the damage the Stalinist epoch inflicted upon many of the ablest minds drawn to the liberating cause of socialism.

The terrible mental, moral, and physical pressures the Stalinist system could bring to bear, which broke so many people, do not in themselves suffice to account for the capitulatory course pursued by Lukács. There is a consistency between certain characteristics of his theorizing and his line of action.

In consonance with his extremely abstract approach to the nature of the proletariat in *History and Class Consciousness,* Lukács outlined a conception of the role of the vanguard party that was further elaborated in his brochure *Lenin,* published early in 1924. He viewed the party as the tangible embodiment of proletarian class consciousness, which had the task of actively preparing and organizing the revolution instead of passively awaiting its advent. This model of the Leninist form of organization represented a considerable advance over the Social Democracy and even the shortcomings of Rosa Luxemburg's ideas.

However, from then on Lukács uncritically projected this version of the ideal party as the tangible embodiment of proletarian class consciousness upon the Russian Communist Party, heedless of circumstances. The real situation in the Soviet Union and the Communist International after Lenin's death did not correspond to its specifications.

This opponent of fetishism as a bourgeois vice succumbed to a malignant form of fetishism. Despite all the crimes committed by the Stalinist apparatus, he held fast to the illusion that the heads of the Soviet Union and the leaders of the Russian CP remained faithful to the program of Lenin and the cause of international socialism. Fixing his attention on the formal continuity between the party of Lenin and that of Stalin, he, like millions of others, failed to recognize that the Bolshevik organization had changed into its opposite, like the Social Democracy before it. From a party that served the working class and promoted its socialist aims, it had become perverted under Stalin into an agency dominated by a privileged bureaucracy that betrayed the workers' interests.

By making a fetish of Stalin's CP, Lukács surrendered the critical essence of the dialectical method. By refusing to see the gross disparity between its pretensions and its conduct and to draw all the necessary conclusions from this contradiction, as Trotsky did, he ignored the priority that Marxist materialism gives to the facts of experience in the class struggle. The lapses of this dialectician into formalism and fetishism are connecting links between his habits of thought and his political practice through the three phases of his development.

*　　　*　　　*

History and Class Consciousness, said Lukács fifty years afterwards, was a highly contradictory amalgam of ideas arising from conflicting trends within himself as he changed over from one class standpoint to another in the middle of a world crisis. This is a sound estimate of that celebrated work.

Half a century later many other young intellectuals are in a similar situation. They are breaking away from the views and values of the bourgeois world and its "pernicious academia" and entering the anticapitalist ranks. This obliges them to reconstruct their previous theoretical outlook in accord with the authentic doctrines of Marxism.

Many who have adopted more or less revolutionary positions in politics, economics, and sociology stop halfway and persist in clinging to non-Marxist ideas in philosophy and logic. They have yet to carry through the arduous task of replacing their former petty-bourgeois ideology with a scientific proletarian one all along the line.

Some appeal to *History and Class Consciousness* as an authority for their erroneous conceptions of the Marxist method of thought. Lukács's self-criticism should put them on notice that the essays are replete with misleading interpretations. He lamented that "it is precisely those parts of the book that I regard as theoretically false that have been most influential."[15]

The work is also a warning that it is often easier to dilute and distort the teachings of Marxism than to assimilate them fully and apply them to fertilize further thought. Lukács shed many of his earlier mistakes in philosophy with the help of Lenin's writings. Then he became a disciple of Stalin, spurning the continuation of Leninism in the movement of Trotskyism. If the new generation of revolutionary intellectuals can avoid the errors for which Lukács and the world working class paid so heavily, both Marxist philosophy and politics will be the beneficiaries.

II

Etienne Abrahamovici's Criticism of Novack's Assessment

It is entirely natural that the death of Lukács should provoke a critical evaluation of his works and outlook. It is still more natural that this evaluation, on the part of revolutionary Marxists, should be extremely critical, since Lukács's political career was particularly disgraceful. But the evaluation of his principal work, *History and Class Consciousness,* made by George Novack is itself questionable. If, as Lukács said, "It is precisely those parts of the book that I regard as theoretically false that have been most influential," this fact must be explained more precisely than George Novack has done.

The renown of *History and Class Consciousness* extended far beyond the circles of the Communist movement of the time for a simple reason—because the work came within the Marxist tradition, not insofar as it was Marxist, but insofar as it aptly renewed the connection with dialectics. Certainly Lukács's work is strongly imbued with idealism, owing as Novack observes, to the "Hegelian prejudices he absorbed from the Central European academic milieu." But it has in common with the works of Marx something which the industrious epigones of Marxist philosophy from George Plekhanov to Louis Althusser do not—it is in dialectical continuity with Western philosophical thought. He places Marxism where it belongs—as the philosophy of praxis in the strict sense of the term, the philosophy that can think praxis and that is an element of this praxis.

One of Lukács's essential contributions is to put Marxism back in its place as transcending traditional philosophy and particularly its finest ornament—Hegel. Lukács continues with what Marx and Engels had several times sketched out—to situate Marxist theory both as a continuation of and as a break with the field of culture, to show its necessity and validity. Lukács handles in peerless fashion the Marxist analysis of Marxist theory and its relationship to the problems that Western philosophy put to itself. There, it involves Marxist analysis in the field of ideology; understanding, of course, that the material prerequisites for that ideology and the possibility of analyzing it were established by Marx himself.

All this is to say that George Novack's article is unjust to Lukács's fundamental work. This injustice arises out of the fact that *History and Class Consciousness* is in reality used as a reference by anti-Marxist and idealist tendencies, as well as from the fact that Lukács changed into a henchman of Stalinism. These are not sufficient arguments—any Marxist, anti-Stalinist work can be used as support for anti-Marxist ideas, given that even today Stalinism and Marxism are difficult to distinguish from one another. As for Lukács's own political itinerary, it is completely reprehensible. From the Marxist point of view it is entirely correct to link the theoretical and the political positions of a member of the international communist movement. But erroneous political stands do not ipso facto incriminate theoretical positions—otherwise, we would backslide into philosophical Stalinism. Fortunately this is not the case. Elsewhere, Novack, contradicting himself, included Plekhanov in the historical continuity of orthodox Marxism, even though the positions of the latter proved to be increasingly doubtful, to the point of being counterrevolutionary. Why this (undeserved) indulgence toward Plekhanov and this sternness with Lukács?

What is still more peculiar and contradictory is that Novack seems to rehabilitate the mature Lukács. He does not mention the role of literary lackey of Stalinism that Lukács played for a time. In short, Novack presents the de-Stalinized Lukács as an almost irreproachable Marxist, even if elsewhere he mentions Lukács's political positions, which are at least doubtful. In fact, Novack takes as good coin Lukács's preface, of which one might ask whether it is not just a way of acquitting himself in the eyes of the post-Stalinist inquisition. For, after all, when one asserts, as Novack does, that Lukács disavowed his work not only because he submitted to Stalinism, but because he changed his opinion and returned to the positions of the founders of Marxism, one might wonder whether Stalinism is not ultimately the guardian of Marxist orthodoxy.

To say that by rejecting *History and Class Consciousness* under pressure from the bureaucracy he returned to the well-spring, is to say that Stalinist philosophy is orthodox, and a paragon of antirevisionism, which would be peculiar on the part of a Marxist such as Novack. In fact, Lukács was hardly de-Stalinized, and the evolution he underwent tended not toward revolutionary Marxism, but toward certain forms of bourgeois thought, elsewhere transcended, like most philosophers who emerge from the stifling confines of Stalinism.

At bottom, Novack asserts several questionable views. As far as materialism is concerned, he reproaches Lukács for presenting French materialism as the "ideological form of the bourgeois revolution," which is an entirely Marxist evaluation (cf. the "Theses on Feuerbach," particularly Theses I, IX, and X). That Lenin recommends studying French materialism, as he recommends studying Hegel, only points up the understanding that Lenin had of Marxism as a theory that emerged historically from bourgeois society, and not as a dogma issued from worlds unknown. It seems, moreover, that Novack does not make an adequate distinction between mechanical materialism and dialectical materialism, since several times he mentions materialism in general, without one's knowing too much of the content of that materialism. One of the great achievements of Marxism was precisely to differentiate itself from static materialism, in order to show the interaction between the subjective and the objective, the dialectic of praxis: "The materialist doctrine that men are products of circumstances and upbringing, and that, therefore, changed men are products of other circumstances and changed upbringing, forgets that circumstances are changed precisely by men and that the educator himself must be educated."[16]

It is entirely conceivable that in the struggle he is waging against idealism, Novack emphasizes the crude materialist aspect of Marxism, and underestimates the dialectical content, which is moreover in conformity with the conception that is currently most widespread, due to the Stalinist and Social

Democratic distortions. But therein may lie a danger, notably, when Novack states that "Materialism maintains that the objective (in nature or in society) has an existence prior to and independent of the subject." This would be Marxist if he added that this independence and priority is itself modified by the subject and that, moreover, the distinction between the subject and the object is itself a product of the dialectical evolution of nature and society. If one rejects this dialectical concept of the subject and the object, one makes the subject an alien in the material world, a negligible epiphenomenon. That concept is too often attributed to Marxism, whereas Marx emphasized the creative aspect of the subject as well as the circumstances under which it appeared.

Here we return to the whole problem of the dialectic of nature: the charges of idealism directed at Lukács can be understood only if one draws an absolute distinction between humanity and nature. Now, humanity and nature are two aspects of the same dialectic totality. From the point of view of the totality, humanity is natural and nature is humanized. "History itself is a *real* part of *natural history*—of nature's coming to be man."[17]

One cannot present a dialectic of nature which is distinct from the dialectic of human history. Today, for example, the transformation of quantity into quality, the interpenetration and struggle of opposites, are natural phenomena of social origin. As J. N. Brohm demonstrates in his preface to Jakubovsky's book *Les Superstructures idéologiques dans la conception matérialiste de l'histoire* [Ideological Superstructures in the Materialist Conception of History], isolating nature from social practice leads to metaphysical statements, and to speak of a dialectic of nature is meaningless, since the term of this dialectic is human society. Now, a dialectic that stops halfway is no longer a dialectic.

To state that the dialectic of nature is inseparable from Marxist theory is to side with the Stalinists, to encourage all the tendencies that turn Marxism into a simple mechanistic determinism. In this sense Lukács, leaving aside his formulations, was correct in posing the problem. Let us not forget that the condemnation of *History and Class Consciousness* dates from the Fifth Congress of the Communist International, the one where Zinoviev attempted to impose, in the name of Leninism, an inner-party regime foreshadowing that of Stalinism. Let us not forget that "Histmat" and "Diamat" are inventions of the Stalinists, who codified, congealed, and distorted the theoretical gains of Marxism. In fact, Marxist orthodoxy was definitively constituted as such the moment Stalinism rose on the horizon.

To condemn Lukács in the name of an orthodoxy that is itself problematical is, in the end, to petrify Marxist theory. After the night of Stalinism, revolutionary Marxism must reconstitute itself by taking up again whatever there is in the past that might enrich us today, even if the works themselves are debatable. Novack boosts Plekhanov—why not Lukács?

III

George Novack's Response to Abrahamovici

Comrade Abrahamovici raises five important issues in regard to my observations on the changes in Lukács's philosophical views. These are: Plekhanov's place in the tradition of Marxism; the appraisal of eighteenth-century French materialism; the relation of the objective to the subjective factors in history; the status of the dialectic of nature; and the role of practice in Marxist theory. Here are my comments on these topics.

The main line of Marxist philosophical thought for three successive generations is to be traced from Marx and Engels (without separating one from the other, as Lukács originally did) through Plekhanov and Antonio Labriola to Rosa Luxemburg, Lenin, and Trotsky. Lukács and his followers counterpose to this tradition an Engels-Kautsky-Plekhanov version of Marxism, which is allegedly mechanistic and positivist.

Plekhanov educated the entire school of Marxists who led the Russian revolution in the ideas of dialectical and historical materialism. He was a persuasive exponent and forceful defender of the philosophical principles of scientific socialism against the idealists, subjectivists, positivists, and eclectics of his day. He brought forward the importance of Hegel's logic in the formation of Marxism over a third of a century before Lukács, and far more correctly integrated it into the materialist outlook.

Lenin described his philosophical works as the best in international Marxist literature and insisted that they be included in "the series of compulsory manuals of communism." Trotsky wrote: "Plekhanov did not create the materialist dialectic but he was its convinced, passionate, and brilliant crusader in Russia from the beginning of the eighties. And this required the greatest penetration, a broad historical outlook, and a noble courage of thought."[18]

To those who sought to discredit Plekhanov's theoretical achievements on account of his notorious political lapses in 1905, 1914, and 1917, Trotsky replied: "The great Plekhanov, the true one, belongs entirely and wholly to us. It is our duty to restore to the young generation his spiritual figure in all its stature."[19]

These are sounder judgments than Abrahamovici's derogation of Plekhanov as one of the epigones, i.e., feeble dogmatic disciples, of Marx. Plekhanov was a more reliable guide in the interpretation of dialectical materialism than the early Lukács, and even the mature Lukács.

What, then, prompts Abrahamovici to rate Lukács above Plekhanov as a teacher of Marxist theory? This mistaken evaluation flows from the fact that his conception of the scope and content of Marxist philosophy is narrower and more subjectivistic than Plekhanov's consistent materialism. It approaches that of those exponents of the praxis school and Marxizing existentialists who, like the early Lukács, want to restrict the domain of dialectical materialism to social-historical phenomena and wave aside its more fundamental relation to natural phenomena.

Plekhanov's great strength was his steadfast adherence to a comprehensive materialist outlook that ranged from the evolution of the cosmos to the history of the most important tendencies in philosophy. He had a profound knowledge of the eighteenth-century French materialists. He explained how Marxist philosophy, as the consummation of 2,500 years of materialist inquiry, stood in dialectical continuity with the Enlightenment thinkers who fought against the ideology of the old regime and heralded the bourgeois democratic revolution. He took care to distinguish their fundamentally correct and progressive materialist positions from the limitations and errors that marked this stage of development (the nonevolutionary and mechanistic view of nature and society, the contemplative theory of knowledge, the idealistic misinterpretation of history.) In *History and Class Consciousness* Lukács did not accept this dialectical criticism of the French materialists (and Feuerbach) but swept aside the materialist premises these precursors of the bourgeois era had in common with Marxism.

To note that Lukács later shifted to positions on several key questions that more closely accorded with the materialism of Marx, Engels, and Lenin is not to make Stalinism into the custodian and model of orthodox Marxism, as Abrahamovici suggests. That was to Lukács's credit. The trouble with Lukács is that he did not fully settle accounts with his philosophical past and dispose of all the misunderstandings about the Marxist method spread by *History and Class Consciousness*.

It is just as necessary to have a correct materialist view of the relations between subject and object as it is to have a dialectical conception of the two categories. This begins with the connection between humanity and nature. The external world existed billions of years before humanity and is independent of it. On the other hand humanity (the subject) cannot and does not exist apart from nature (the object) but is a product and part of its evolution on earth. This scientific and philosophical objectivity distinguishes the materialist standpoint from all types of subjectivism and idealism.

Diverse truncators of Marxism seek to blur this all-important distinction by centering upon the interactions between the subject and object in the historical process. While nature and labor constitute two sides of a single dialectical totality in social evolution, all the modifications introduced by human beings in nature throughout history cannot conceal or cancel out the evolutionary precedence and existential priority of the external world.

The materialist conception of history extends the same principle of the primacy of the objective over the subjective to social phenomena. Social being (that is, the material conditions of life and labor) is primary; social consciousness is secondary. Such objective factors as the level of the productive forces, the technology, and the organization of labor expressed in the economic system, are far more decisive in shaping the course and character of historical events than morality, art, religion, philosophy, and other spiritual and subjective elements.

The predominance of the objective over the subjective factors has immense political as well as theoretical and methodological importance, since the activities, achievements, and consciousness of peoples, classes, parties, and individuals are governed by the objective conditions of their development. Recognition and application of this truth is indispensable for correct orientation in the class struggle.

Comrade Abrahamovici is apprehensive lest an affirmation of the independent and antecedent character of objective causes reduce humanity to a "negligible epiphenomenon" and nullify its creative role. This criticism has been made of Marxist materialism countless times.

The dialectical determinism of Marxism avoids the one-sidedness of the mechanists. It is based upon the reciprocity of cause and effect in the universal interconnection and interaction of events. In the course of development what was originally a consequence can turn into a more and more efficacious cause that influences the phenomena that produced it. Humankind, the offspring of nature, proceeds to change its environment to suit its purposes; ideas and programs generated by material circumstances can become a powerful force for change when acted upon by large numbers of people. Indeed, the proletariat, produced by capital, can destroy its procreator.

Nonetheless, in every process it is necessary to ascertain which element and set of elements plays the decisive determining part, since, save in exceptional and episodic cases, cause and effect do not affect each other to an equal extent.

The voluntarists who ascribe the decisive role in social development to the human will do not give sufficient weight to objective conditions and historical necessities. Moreover, they maintain that the materialist insistence on the primacy of objective causes is mechanistic and leads to passivity and fatalism. The true revolutionary, they believe, always makes the energy, consciousness, and will of the subjective side paramount in theory and in practice.

Dialectical materialists proceed from the objective to the subjective both in the investigation of history and in the struggle for the proletarian revolution. They are likewise aware that once the objective prerequisites have matured, the consciousness, initiative, and intervention of classes, parties, leaders, and individuals can become decisive—and they act accordingly.

Just as scientific knowledge of nature in its technological applications can transform the economy, so scientific knowledge of the laws of social development acted upon by the revolutionary forces can change society and redirect history. Doesn't this accord ample room to the creativity of humanity vis-à-vis nature and to the creative role of the subject in history and politics?

Abrahamovici apparently denies that there is or was a dialectic of nature distinct from the dialectic of human history. Such a position disregards the significance of the fact that our species is itself a product of the dialectical development of inorganic and organic matter. The dialectical development of human history grew out of this dialectic of nature; the primate was converted into the hominid and subsequently grew beyond it as laboring humanity more and more created the further conditions of its development.

It is true that the two are thoroughly integrated in the system of Marxism, which considers the dialectical movement of history as a prolongation on a qualitatively higher level of the dialectics of matter (but a break or leap in that continuity, because it operates according to different laws).

However, the crux of the controversy does not lie in the ontological and evolutionary links between natural and social processes but rather within the domain of nature itself. Nature went through a prolonged evolution before humanity emerged, and most events in the universe today occur without the presence and intervention of human beings. What was and is the logical pattern of these processes? That is the question. Marxism teaches that they conform to such dialectical laws as the interpenetration and struggle of opposites, the transformation of quantity into quality and vice versa, the disruption of continuity in the production of novelty, etc.

The major leaps from one qualitative state to another take place on the borderlands of evolution where one state of matter passes over into a higher one. At a certain point chemical processes gave rise to biochemical and later physiological ones; fish developed into amphibians which led on to land-living creatures. The transmutations of inorganic into organic matter and of living beings into humans have been the momentous examples of dialectical change in nature.

Comrade Abrahamovici brings two arguments against the independent existence of the dialectics of nature. In defense of Lukács he says that there can be no absolute distinction between humanity and nature. That depends upon which side of their relations is considered. It is true only where human history and society are concerned; it does not hold true for nature before the advent of humanity.

He then seeks to fortify his anthropocentric approach by

asserting that cases of the transformation of quantity into quality are "natural phenomena of social origin." The essence of his error is bared in this ambiguous phrase. The founders of Marxism held that the dialectical law of the transformation of quantity into quality characterized all forms of motion. It is, wrote Engels, a "general law of development of nature, society, and thought."

This mode of change is not primarily or exclusively a phenomenon of social origin, though it applies to society and was discovered and formulated as a universal law of development by certain logicians under special historical and intellectual circumstances. But these considerations do not negate its autonomous operation within nature before social existence and apart from it.

Contrary to Abrahamovici's contention, the dialectics of nature as the precondition and framework of the dialectic of history is not metaphysics, as the positivists claim, nor a deformation of Marxist thought derived from Stalinist "Diamat." It is the conception shared by Marx, Engels, Plekhanov, Lenin, and Trotsky.

The early Lukács and Karl Korsch rejected this view. In recent years they have been joined by a growing procession of "anthropological" and "humanistic" Marxists including Herbert Marcuse, Henri Lefèbvre, Kostas Axelos, Erich Fromm, and numerous Yugoslav, Czechoslovak, and Polish Communist philosophers. While most of them adhere to the dialectical conception of society, they concur with the existentialists (Martin Heidegger, Jean-Paul Sartre, Maurice Merleau-Ponty, Jean Hyppolite), with American pragmatists such as Sidney Hook, and with almost every representative of academic philosophy in the West, that the dialectic of nature is a Hegelian excrescence that has no place in a scientific explanation of the world and ought to be excised from a true philosophy.

In contrast, despite their revulsion against bureaucratic dogmatism and intellectual terrorism, some of the foremost Soviet scientists and philosophers, such as Fock, Blokhintsev, Omel'ianovskii, and Aleksandrov in physics, Schmidt and Ambartsumian in cosmogony and cosmology, Oparin in biochemistry, and B. Kedrov in the history of science, have willingly adopted the dialectical materialist interpretation of nature and are using its method and ideas in dealing with difficult and complex theoretical problems of contemporary science. More can be learned from their positions and procedures than from the echoers of the early Lukács.*

Abrahamovici defines Marxism as "the philosophy of praxis in the strict sense of the term." Marxism, to be sure, accords an exceptional and distinctive place to social practice in its conception of history and in its theory of knowledge. Practice, the activities of people in changing nature and their own interrelations, is the starting point, basis, and aim of knowledge. Productive activities form and transform human relations and generate the whole of culture. Practice and experiment in everyday life, as in science and industry, provide the supreme criterion of the truth or falsity of all ideas and judgments.

At the same time, human practice does not encompass all of reality, and the objective basis of dialectics goes beyond it. Social productive activities are limited to the reciprocal relationship whereby humanity utilizes, modifies, and masters the environment and changes itself. They came into existence only with the laboring process that elevated us above the ape. The independence of nature and the inescapable dependence of humankind upon it, the prime postulate of all forms of materialist philosophy from the Greeks to Marx, are what the disciples of the praxis school seek to occlude or repudiate.

For us the development of humanity through its creative and perfectible social practice and its attendant scientific theory and validated scientific knowledge is the crowning chapter in the evolution of the material world. As Trotsky wrote in his 1910 article on Tolstoy's death: "As the basis of the universe and of life we know and acknowledge only primeval matter, obedient to its own internal laws; in human society, as well as in the individual human being, we see only a particle of the universe, subject to general laws."[20]

Obviously, Comrade Abrahamovici and I do not see eye to eye on the current philosophical situation in socialist circles and its tasks. In philosophy, as in politics, I observe three main tendencies contending against one another amidst the considerable confusion provoked by the disintegration of Stalinist monolithism. These are the still-powerful leftovers of the Stalinist distortions of Marxist ideas; sundry varieties of revisionism, eclecticism, and subjectivism; and genuine exponents of the dialectical materialist method.

---

*For an extensive account of their work, see *Science and Philosophy in the Soviet Union* by Loren R. Graham (New York: Alfred A. Knopf, 1972).

The confusionists who belong to the second grouping assiduously try to tar the last with the Stalinist brush in order to bar the road to Marxist clarity and sanction their own misconceptions. For this reason Comrade Abrahamovici's warning against becoming aligned with the Stalinist deformations of Marxist thought by defending the materialist dialectic in all its dimensions is misdirected. Much greater is the danger of making concessions to the trend of thought fed by *History and Class Consciousness,* which ignores the anchorage of Marxist philosophy in the objective world, denies the dialectic of nature, and seeks to substitute some sort of nonmaterialist premises for authentic Marxist positions.

The Jesting Philosopher:
The Case of Leszek Kolakowski

Certain contemporary thinkers stand out as exemplars apart
from the merits of their positions and the validity of their ideas.
They facilitate our understanding of the influential tendency they
represent through a felicitous or forceful expression of its salient
traits. Both in the events of his career and in the evolution of his
views, the iconoclastic Polish philosopher-in-exile Leszek Kolakowski belongs in that category.

Born in 1927, he displayed as a very young scholar the gifts
that thrust him to the head of his intellectual generation. After
graduating from the philosophical faculty of Lódz University in
1950, he became assistant to Professor Tadeusz Kotarbinski and
then to Professor Adam Schaff, two of the foremost Polish
philosophers. He taught in the department of philosophy at the
University of Warsaw and was a member of the editorial board of
the principal philosophical journal, *Philosophical Thought*, until
he was removed in 1959.

This versatile man of letters has produced four kinds of
writings: works in the history of philosophy, essays, plays, and
folktales that are political parables. As a historian of philosophy
he has taken a special interest in religious thought, ranging from
Thomism and Thomas More to mysticism and the Protestant
heretics. This preoccupation would be unusual for a West European or Anglo-American Marxist, though it is less eccentric in the
cultural atmosphere of Poland, which is weighted down with the
traditions and presence of the Catholic church. Himself at odds

with an established creed and vengeful authority, he has been drawn to the study of earlier unorthodoxies and the fate of their upholders.

Kolakowski joined the Communist Party in 1945 at the age of eighteen, was hatched as a philosopher in the school of Stalinism, and until the mid-1950s was a zealous partisan of its doctrines. The political and ideological upheaval culminating in the Polish October of 1956 was the watershed in his development. It aroused his critical capacities, caused him to doubt his previous certitudes, and made him come to grips with the major problems confronting the Polish people at that crossroads in their postwar history. Almost overnight Kolakowski came to embody the moral conscience of the Communist reformation that yearned to liberate Poland from vassalage to the Kremlin and its native adjutants.

In 1956 two pieces of his aimed at the injustices of Stalinism were censored by the authorities. "What Is Socialism?" satirized the prevailing state of affairs. The Stalinized state was ironically defined as a place in which there are "more spies than nurses and more people in prisons than in hospitals. . . . in which the philosophers and writers always say the same thing as the generals and ministers, but always after them."[1]

The essay "The End of the Age of Myths" adumbrated two themes that he later expounded at length: a growing suspicion that the promises and program of Communism were illusory, and an affirmation of the power of critical reason above all else.

The period from 1955 to 1968 comprised his most glorious years. He was not only highly popular among the Communist youth in the universities but an inspiration to dissenters throughout Eastern Europe. He was deservedly admired by the anti-Stalinist Left in the West because of his resistance to bureaucratic persecution and insistence on freedom of thought.

In 1956 he pinned *Forty-eight Theses* to the bulletin board of Warsaw University. One of them declared that the task of intellectuals in the Communist movement was "not merely to express enthusiasm for the wise decisions of the Communist Party, but also to make sure that these decisions were really wise. Communism needs intellectuals for their ability to think and not for their opportunism."[2] A regime unable to gain the freely given cooperation of the intelligentsia, Kolakowski warned, must rely "exclusively on the force of the police and the army."

His words were prophetic. In May 1957 he was singled out as a dangerous revisionist by party leader Wladyslaw Gomulka in a plenary session of the Central Committee. The following October the party newspaper denounced him as an adversary of the party who wanted "to substitute pious dreams for activity and moral principles for revolutionary strategy."[3]

In his recoil against Stalinist practices and precepts Kolakowski veered away from Marxist materialism as well and became more and more eclectic in his philosophizing. Nonetheless, the party leaders put up with his deviations for a decade because of his world reputation. Then, in a speech at Warsaw University on the tenth anniversary of the "little revolution" of October 1956—which the government itself failed to observe out of deference to the Kremlin—Kolakowski told the assembled students and faculty members that little progress had been made in political and cultural freedom. This truth caused his expulsion from the party. The resentment in intellectual circles against his censure culminated in a letter of protest to the Central Committee signed by twenty-two prominent writers, all party members.

Following the student demonstrations of March 1968, Kolakowski was deprived of his chair at the university and blacklisted by the authorities. Like Ernst Bloch in East Germany, he was forced into exile; he has since taught philosophy at McGill University in Montreal, at the University of California at Berkeley, and at Oxford University. (Bruno, the sixteenth-century heretic, also sought refuge in Oxford.)

Although the regimes of Gomulka and Edward Gierek have pleasantly coexisted with the Catholic hierarchy, they have found it impossible to live at ease with an outspoken heterodox thinker who had the ear of the Communist students in their country and would not remain silent about their bureaucratic trampling upon elementary democratic rights. As Kolakowski said, the ideal state for the neo-Stalinists is one that "wants all its citizens to have the same opinions in philosophy, foreign policy, economics, literature, and morality."[4]

Kolakowski showed great courage in sticking to his opinions and voicing them against intense pressures to conform and recant. He publicly defended Jacek Kuron and Karol Modzelewski, young revolutionists who were imprisoned for their antibureaucratic writings. Many people, East and West, looked hopefully to him to point the way in regenerating Marxist philosophy and politics.

Almost twenty years have elapsed since Kolakowski cast off the manacles of Stalinist ideology and set out to rescue Marxism from its falsifiers. What is the balance sheet of his "free thinking"? It is an ironic one. Instead of promoting Marxism, he has bit by bit jettisoned its principles and abandoned its viewpoint. He has moved from early adherence to Stalinist schematism through abstract rationalism and moralism to eclecticism and skepticism. This has led to a benevolence toward religion and a conciliation with bourgeois liberalism. Let us trace the steps in the liquidation of his Marxist positions.

*   *   *

Once Stalinist ideology was exposed as counterfeit, the question was posed: What, then, is Marxism? Kolakowski's initial response was to draw a distinction between Marxism as institutional and Marxism as intellectual. The doctrines of institutionally approved Marxism, i.e., Stalinism, were false and dead; the original content of Marxism, i.e., what Marx himself taught, retained its validity, precision, and usefulness.

Although this was a salutary lever to pry himself loose from Stalinism, it was only a way station along his new road. It was coupled with two ominous negations that entailed a departure from dialectical materialism. He disqualified the scientific character of Marxism and extolled it instead as a progressive myth, an interpretation reminiscent of Georges Sorel's reasoning and close to Ernst Bloch's philosophy of hope.

The Marxist ideal, he said, contained the dynamic of utopianism, which could inspire the masses to struggle for a better world. "There are myths which played a great and creative role in human history and contributed more to man's progress than the conviction that it is necessary to live always on the barren land, where man was born."[5] Marxism was a creed that the masses believed in and acted upon; its principles and conclusions were not anchored in a true understanding of natural and social development.

Consequently Marxism could no longer be prized as the philosophy with the most correct method of thought, based upon a verified body of knowledge about the world. It was demoted to no more than one among other valuable contributions to the sum of human knowledge developed in the nineteenth century, like Darwinism and electromagnetic theory. Although it was useful to clarify theoretical problems in economics, sociology, and history, it could no longer claim to be, as Jean-Paul Sartre hailed it, "the philosophy of the age."

Moreover, there are numerous varieties of Marxism, and who except a dogmatist can say which one is truer or more faithful to its leading principles? This attitude toward Marxism was similar to that of enlightened bourgeois scholars. They will concede that, though outdated in many respects, the ideas of historical materialism form part of the heritage of modern culture and can be useful within strict limitations. However, its method is considered fundamentally unsound and its main conclusions unfounded. This is especially the case when it comes to practical politics in effecting social change. Kolakowski himself began to doubt that Marxism was the best guide to action or even that revolutionary activity by the working class was necessary and desirable.

These opinions eased the way for him to question the rest of his Marxist ideas; he shredded them piece by piece until very little of his original beliefs was left. His corrosive criticism steadily dematerialized the doctrines of Marxism, starting with the relationship between nature and society.

The basis of any philosophy is its theory of being. Dialectical materialism maintains that nature exists before humanity and independently of it. The keystone of the materialist view of reality is the understanding that we are a product and part of the universe beyond ourselves.

Kolakowski not only departs from this materialist position; he reverses it. "The world," he writes, "is a human product."[6] He argues that even the arrangement of the species into classes does not express objectively existing facts of animate nature but is the result of subjective classification.

In place of the independent existence of nature as the basis and source of everything, including humanity, Kolakowski makes the world emanate from human nature. He claims that we cannot conceive of nature apart from our contacts with it, although astrophysicists and paleontologists do so without difficulty. He calls this attitude a "philosophical anthropology." It is rather an extreme anthropocentrism.

Marx did hold that *society* and *human history* have been made and remade by humanity through its collective practice based on the labor process. But the external world is prior to the social life that arose out of it and remains in symbiosis with it.

In the course of history, nature as objective reality "in itself" becomes more and more transformed by social activity and the growth of knowledge into a reality "for us." But this humanization of the earthly environment and mastery of its processes does not wipe out the autonomous existence of the cosmos apart from humankind. In the interplay between humanity and nature Kolakowski has "the reality for us" swallow up the "reality in itself" by making the features of nature wholly dependent upon the creativity of man.

This subjectivist approach is a long distance from materialism. It lands him in the vicinity of the Kantian position that the nature of experience is constituted by the forms of sensibility and the categories of reason. Thus Kolakowski asserts that "the reality which our language divides into species is born at the same time as language itself," as though the classifying and naming of things somehow brought them into being.[7] When he says that Marx held the notion that ". . . the object cannot be conceived without the subject that constructs it," he falsely converts Marx into a disciple of Kant, who thought that way.[8]

In line with his inversion of the real relations between nature and humanity, Kolakowski propounds a theory of knowledge that is equally nonmaterialist and nonobjective. In an article "Karl Marx and the Classical Definition of Truth," written in 1958 and reprinted with modifications in 1971, he rejects the Marxist conception that cognitive activity discloses ("reflects") the properties and relations of objectively existing things and that the mind is able to acquire true knowledge because the content of consciousness corresponds to the realities of the material world.

In its stead he concocts a theory of knowledge extracted from misinterpretations of the *Economic and Philosophic Manuscripts of 1844*. He foists on the young Marx the notion that knowledge does not have representative content but only a functionally useful character. Since every act of cognition incorporates a value judgment arising out of practical considerations, he reasons that its satisfaction of some human need or interest prevents knowledge from reflecting reality as it is. He thus presents an instrumentalist version of the truth of ideas. They do not divulge the content of objective reality but simply serve as an efficient means of orientation in the world.

Indeed, he says that "things are reified consciousness" created by language, and that Marx—the materialist who knew that things precede ideas—thought so too.[9] In knowing, he argues, we do not arrive at conceptual reflections of an independent reality but at value-laden images belonging exclusively to ourselves. Our minds do not mirror, with rough accuracy, the properties of the external world. On the contrary, nature as "reified consciousness" produced by human nature gives back to us what we created in the first place. "In this sense," Kolakowski narcissistically concludes, "we can say that in all the universe man cannot find a well so deep that, leaning over it, he does not discover at the bottom his own face."[10]

He magnifies the subjective aspects of thought and knowledge to the point where their fundamental objective content is eclipsed. However, the whole trend of scientific progress is toward the exposure and eradication of extraneous subjective elements from our picture of the world and their replacement with more impersonal knowledge of objective reality and its laws. The heliocentrism of Nicholas Copernicus displaced and explained the subjective appearance of the movement of the heavens around the earth. Johannes Kepler deprived circular motion of the preferred position it had held in planetary astronomy since the Greeks. Galileo stripped physics of secondary qualities (color, odor, taste, texture) which in his day could be discussed only in subjective terms. Charles Darwin's theory of natural selection expelled teleology, the purposeful creativity humans possess, from living nature. And Albert Einstein's relativity established that there is no privileged frame of reference in universal motion.

For eons humans have spun more fantasies about the moon than any other celestial object. These false notions may be metaphorically said to have reflected humanity's own face, i.e., its imagination. However, the latest explorations have obtained more precise and correct scientific data about the earth's satellite. The more scientists and astronauts have learned about the features of its surface and the properties of its interior, the less subjective and the more objective our picture has become. Instead of seeing reflections of our own face in the water, these truths tell us not only what the moon really is today but what it was before we arrived and even before humanity emerged on earth.

Kolakowski's statement that wherever we go in the universe we will discover nothing but projections of our own selves is an unwarranted concession to idealism, whose paramount principle is that the world depends upon the cognitive consciousness (there is no object without a subject). Materialism holds, to the contrary, that the deeper we probe into the microcosmos and macrocosmos, the more we find things that are not our own subjective projections, such as X-rays, elementary particles, and quasars, and the more we find out about them.

*   *   *

Having broken with the materialist theory of being and its epistemology, Kolakowski could not retain the monistic view of Marxism as an integrated philosophic outlook with a systematic scientific structure encompassing nature, society, and thought in the fullness of their interrelated development. "Marxism as an all-embracing system is dead," he declared in the introduction to *Marxism and Beyond.* He denied that dialectical materialism is the necessary basis of Marxism, that the dialectic of nature precedes the dialectic of human evolution, and that society is an outgrowth of nature that has gone beyond it as its supreme expression.

Historical materialism is the most imperative part of the total theory of dialectical materialism. Its general principles apply to a particular phenomenon, the history of the human species over the past two million years. Like many socialist humanists of the praxis school, Kolakowski truncates universal evolution by divorcing the development of society from the dialectic of nature in which it is rooted. He contracts the scope and content of Marxism to historical materialism alone, and accords an autonomy to social practice that downplays its inseparable unity with the nature to which it simultaneously stands in opposition. This amputation cuts away the material platform upon which the Marxist world outlook rests.

According to Marxism, society—the result of human productive activity—has a relative autonomy in respect to its environing reality, as the solar system, which is not the product of human activity, is relatively independent of the other planetary systems in our galaxy. Since the hominids came out of the primate state, society has evolved in accord with new and additional laws arising out of the peculiar features belonging to human activity and achievements. These constitute the content of historical materialism.

Kolakowski denies that the totality of human activities expressed in the progress of society has been governed by ascertainable laws available to scientific inquiry and valid understanding. At one point he remarked: "I do not intend either to defend or to question any form whatsoever of a deterministic view of the world."[11] Despite this agnostic disclaimer, he now disavows that the principles of causality at the base of historical materialism have been operative in the rise of humanity to its present estate. Here is his latest pronouncement on this matter: "Determinism is a condition of scientific thinking, but it is so as a rule of thought—not as metaphysical knowledge of the nature of things—a knowledge that contains certain values pertaining to philosophy and a view of the world, but which is scientifically sterile and, of course unprovable in a rigorous and literal sense."[12]

In contrast to such a superficial, positivist definition of determinism, Marxism explains that determinism, dialectically interpreted and applied, can be a rule of thought and a condition of scientific thinking precisely because it has been ascertained to be operative in all areas of reality. It is not "metaphysically" but actually an essential aspect of the nature of things and our knowledge of them.

If Marxism adheres to the causal determination of phenomena in general, it more particularly teaches that the mode of production of material wealth is the principal determinant in social development. This determinism runs through the whole course of history as the processes of production have unfolded in a lawful manner. The productive relations of people are determined by the level of their productive forces; the productive relations in turn determine the nature of the given social formation; the social formation determines the character and characteristics of the higher functions and institutions, ranging from politics and morality to science, art, and philosophy. For example, it is the social structure that makes the state, not the other way around.

By 1966 Kolakowski had decided that the historical process had no such materialistic, deterministic, scientific foundation. The actions of an individual, he wrote, are explicable because they are purposive, but the same is not true of historical events, considered singly or all together. In "Historical Understanding and the Intelligibility of History" he stated flatly: "History is unintelligible and incomprehensible."[13]

Every general interpretation of history, he says, is either theological or teleological. Since no causal order can be perceived in its development, no scientific insight into history has been achieved or is possible. With one sweep he renders null and void all the knowledge about historical causation and the links in the chain of social evolution accumulated since Herodotus and Thucydides. Even liberal historians would not be so skeptical of the validity and worth of the overall findings in their field.

Although history for him is thoroughly opaque and contains no lawfulness that can invest it with objective significance, he contends that history can be given meaning "by an act of faith." Thus faith supersedes science. This denial of lawfulness in history and of the reality of social progress has the political implication that while the goal of socialism—a classless and free society—may be worth striving for, it has no solid ground in the movement of history or its scientific comprehension. It is, in fact, unattainable, since alienation is ineradicable, he contends.

The law-governed activities of the mass of humanity under the given conditions of life and labor have not shaped history. It has been endowed with meaning and direction by the ideal, the intention, the aim of the individual—retrospectively and, presumably, prospectively. "History becomes significant by virtue of the imposed intelligibility of which we are the authors."[14] This indeterministic misconception of the nature of history signalizes Kolakowski's passage from Marxism to existentionalist subjectivism in regard to historical, social, and political development. The absurd universe makes sense only through the projected aim of the individual.

At the beginning of his hegira, Kolakowski wrote that his criticism was "not the expression of intent to see history as a projection of the present into the past."[15] What he disclaimed in 1957 he espoused by 1970. The propulsion of his rupture with materialism proved stronger than his will.

*   *   *

Kolakowski is tormented not only by the contradictions of the present but by those of the past too. He complains that history has shown no consideration for its individual participants and has ridden roughshod over them—an observation as old as the Bible and the ancient Greeks. Once the theological argument—that such was God's will—was exploded, how was this cruel anomaly to be explained? Immanuel Kant and Georg Wilhelm Friedrich Hegel, among others, grappled with the problem in their philosophies of history. Marxism sought the answer through the theory of evolution.

Humankind has made its way upward from animality in a thoroughly empirical manner, without the benefit of forethought, foresight, or plan. This fumbling trial-and-error development has nevertheless been governed by laws that operated behind the backs of people in what Marx called a "natural-historical" fashion. The fact that history has unfolded not in a reasonable and conscious manner but along terrible, tortuous pathways, unjust not simply to individuals but to whole peoples and generations, is not surprising to a scientific mind. How could it have been otherwise? No social agency was on hand with the power and means to supervise the process and steer it according to our current understanding and morality.

Kolakowski contends that no human values have been realized through all this travail. This erases the tremendous progressive achievements through the ages. Whatever material and spiritual values we now enjoy have been acquired as a result. Of still greater import is the fact that this precious inventory bequeathed from the past has created the possibility for a decisive and radical alteration in the ways of historical progress.

The program of scientific socialism holds out the prospect that, once the anarchy of capitalist production is eliminated on a global scale and human relations are reorganized along collectivist lines, deliberate direction of further evolution by associated humanity can become determinative for the first time in history.

But how will that optimistic outlook, even if realized, make amends to the victims of the juggernaut of history? Kolakowski plaintively asks. Since we cannot repeal or make over what has happened before us, the only way we can fulfill our obligations to our predecessors and do justice to the dead is by making the world a better place to live for ourselves and especially for posterity.

The practical question is: How is this to be done? Here history merges with living politics. Kolakowski wants to know how the individual can reconcile the demands of the immediate present with the claims of the future. Every new generation faces this dilemma. The solution for the individual is to find out where the main line of progress is located and then come to terms with it in his or her daily doings and lifelong aims.

According to Marxism, the revolutionary struggle of the oppressed for liberation from capitalism and colonialism is that

central factor, supplemented by the struggle against bureaucratism. Kolakowski once believed that; he no longer does so. In his
view there is no historical necessity for the proletarian revolution.
The present is so ambiguous and uncertain and the future so
shrouded in mist, he can no longer discern any clear way forward
for humanity. That accounts for his floundering in unresolvable
contradictions in reference to history and contemporary politics.

*   *   *

Kolakowski's principal theme is the relation of determinism to
morality, a question that has troubled honest persons in the
Soviet bloc from the time of Nikita Khrushchev's disclosures of
Stalin's bestialities to Aleksandr Solzhenitsyn's recent report in
The Gulag Archipelago. The "intellectual thugs of the official
line," as C. Wright Mills characterized them, perverted the
concept of determinism, as they do so many other elements of
Marxism, by claiming that Stalinist terrorism was necessitated
by defense of the interests of the working class, the revolution,
and socialism. Kolakowski challenged this fraud. In reality the
methods and measures of the "police statesmen" were dictated by
the need to protect the privileges of the uncontrolled bureaucracy
against the people.

However, their abuse of a correct philosophical principle does
not warrant its abandonment; causality is a cardinal presupposi-
tion of scientific research and knowledge in all fields. Kolakowski
kept asking: How can historical determinism be reconciled with
one's individual moral responsibility for one's actions? This
dilemma, which springs from one of the vexing contradictions of
social life, has taxed the ingenuity of moralists, theologians, and
philosophers for thousands of years.

It must first be ascertained what objective basis there is, if any,
for ethical evaluations and obligations, for distinguishing right
from wrong, good from evil. The secular moralities that have
done away with clerical sanctions and that recognize the historically conditioned and relative character of moral codes and
conduct find their grounding in two sources.

Liberal morality derives its substance and standards from
those rules of behavior that have proved necessary for the
perpetuation of society and the welfare of humanity as a whole.
The same binding principles of morality apply equally, universally, and categorically to all members of the human race: rich

and poor, rulers and ruled, oppressors and oppressed. Morality is therefore assigned a superclass, or classless, character.

The view of morality upheld by historical materialism does not deny that certain indispensable elementary moral precepts have emerged in the progress of humanity. Some interests are so fundamental and common that they must be acknowledged and have been by and large observed in most communities. To speak the truth, to refrain from killing, not to harm little children, are some of these cautionary rules. The enterprise of science, for example, could not be pursued without obeying the ethical precept of truthfully reporting observed facts.

However, such obligatory norms are extremely abstract; when it comes to concrete cases, they have a limited and variable application. The general injunctions are often crossed up by deviations, exceptions, transgressions. Kolakowski takes note of the relativity, changeability, and contradictoriness of moral values when he writes: "Human life is an absolute value, but . . . we are permitted and sometimes obliged to kill."[16] The ultimate determinant of whether or not it is just to take another's life is not the categorical imperative "Thou shalt not kill," but the concrete circumstances of the case. Despite this commandment, it is right to shoot down a murderer who is running amok with a machine gun, or to resist to the death a fascist or militarist assault upon democracy. The given circumstances are decisive.

If moral situations and values are so conditional, unstable, and antithetical, on what grounds can moral preferences be justified? Why act in one way rather than another? Marxism and liberalism give different answers to this crucial question.

Historical materialism teaches that morality is a product of social development; that in civilized society it serves not all persons equally, but class interests; that these interests are contradictory, since what benefits one class injures another. The worth of conflicting moral values and judgments has to be objectively evaluated according to the roles the contending class forces play in blocking or promoting social progress and the relations of the individual to them. Clearly the moral views and values of the slave will clash with those of the master. Although the class relations are more complex under capitalism, the moral situation is not essentially different.

Thus the choice of one line of conduct over another concretely flows not so much from the common concerns of all members of the human family, but from the divergent and conflicting interests of the component classes to which people belong. The monumental hypocrisy of the morality of bourgeois democracy has been freshly demonstrated by the disclosures that the top officials in Washington systematically lied about Vietnam, Cambodia, and various domestic affairs. Although this flouts the moral code they preach, it is necessary for their rulership. It is equally necessary for their supporters among the clergy and liberal reformers to insist that the masses live up to moral norms that the master class violates at will. This duplicity is essential to the mechanics of continued capitalist domination.

Kolakowski has repudiated the Marxist teaching on the class content and criteria of moral values for the ethical stand of liberalism. "Moral convictions are part of the self-defensive behavior of the human race," he tells us.[17] This is only partially—and not impartially—true. At bottom the clashes of moral codes and convictions are even more part of "the defensive behavior" of the contending classes. But he no longer attaches importance to this predominant ingredient of flesh-and-blood ethics in contemporary society.

Since he has found it impossible to cleave to invariant moral norms, he has swung all the way over to an unrestricted relativism that sets aside objective criteria for moral behavior. There are no rules of morality to be guided by. What the individual decides according to his or her conscience is the ultimate warrant for moral conduct. From a denial of the *absolute* character of morality, he proceeds to a negation of its *objective* and *class* character.

Kolakowski has buttressed the independence of the moral sphere from class considerations with a chaotic ontology. The world is so "full of holes," so disorderly and incoherent, that individuals can find no basis in reality and no established values to guide or guarantee their course of conduct. Every moral decision has to be taken in total freedom regardless of circumstance, amidst all the uncertainty, ambiguity, and anguish depicted by the existentialists.

Freedom of choice, the capacity to select one alternative over another, exists in a relative way, being determined and restricted by material conditions, including the class struggle. Physical, social-historical, and personal factors all enter as determinants into the decision-making that goes on in the human brain, though not in equal measure.

Moral choice is not detached from or elevated above society and its class relations but is inextricably bound up with their processes. The decision of the individual to do this rather than that is the pivotal link in a concatenation of causation that is rooted in surrounding circumstances and bears its fruit in practical consequences. The decisions of classes, parties, and groups that shape the course of history and politics are likewise motivated by the objective circumstances pressing upon them.

The role of objective circumstances is especially pertinent in assessing the degree of moral responsibility of individuals or organizations. As a frank opponent of absolutes in morality, Marxism adheres to the doctrine of limited liability in matters of ethics. The responsibility of individuals extends only so far as the situation they are in can be controlled or modified by their decisions and deeds. Otherwise they are exempt from blame.

Kolakowski, on the other hand, adopts the existentialist view that individuals are completely responsible for all their actions. He defends "the belief in the total responsibility of each human being for the part he plays in all the determinants at work in the humanized world, i.e., quite simply, the world."[18] This is a logical corollary of the proposition that we are free agents creating our own destiny.

Such absolutism flies in the face of the facts of life. David Hume pointed out that it was not causation but coercion that exempted one from responsibility for one's acts. Neither the force of circumstances nor the circumstances of force can be disregarded in making moral judgments.

We can apply this realistic criterion to his own case. Kolakowski cannot be blamed if for some years in the early 1960s he was compelled by repression to withdraw temporarily from open political controversy with Gomulka's regime and immerse himself in other forms of literary and intellectual expression. The responsibility lies with the government that objectively determined his output.

Kolakowski is justly outraged by the violence of the architects and administrators of the Gulag Archipelago. The ethics of Marxist humanism is likewise opposed to violence against people. Revolutionary socialism aims to extirpate the root causes of violence in society.

But this moral position does not mean that all manifestations of violence can be placed on a par. Otherwise we would have to condemn every progressive civil and national war in history, every rising of slaves against their owners. The defensive

violence of the Vietnamese against the military aggressions of
the imperialist interventionists, the defensive violence of the
Blacks against the cops and of strikers against strikebreakers is
fully justified and has progressive moral value, whereas the
actions of the opposing side in these struggles are morally evil as
well as politically and socially reactionary. Since Kolakowski is
no pacifist, he might well agree with this.

However, he would not agree that, while correct moral evaluations play an important role in political and social affairs, they
are subordinate to the class interests at stake. The criteria of
morality reside not primarily within ourselves but in the connections we have outside ourselves—and these are with class
relations and forces. The liberals who inveigh against the
amorality of Marxism are actually concealing the fact that they
too are defending specific class interests, albeit in a two-faced
manner.

Kolakowski now offers us liberal moralizing as an antidote to
Stalinist criminality. The one is as unacceptable to a Marxist as
the other; both are injurious to the working masses. The
Kennedys, Johnsons, Nixons, and Humphreys who pose as moral
leaders of the nation, and the liberal ideologues such as Professor
Arthur M. Schlesinger, Jr., who draft their state papers, are more
sanctimonious in mouthing moral sentiments but no less criminal than the Kremlin rulers. They are ready to trample on the
most elementary decencies. Their record of villainies extends
from corrupting governments to slaughtering hundreds of thousands of innocent people in Southeast Asia to promote their
imperialist designs.

Millions of youth in the West have been appalled by their lies
and injustices. Many of these young people have advanced from
the moral indignation and ideological confusion that marked the
first flush of New Left radicalism to the Marxists' scientific
explanations of what imperialism is and how to fight against it.

Unfortunately, Kolakowski has no sympathy with or understanding of the impulses of these rebels, who have aligned
themselves with the Cubans, Vietnamese, and African liberation
fighters, as well as with the Black masses in the U.S. ghettos. He
haughtily stigmatizes them as anarchistic cultural "barbarians,"
symptomatic of "a genuine sickness of civilization," for siding
with "masses of illiterate peasants from the most backward parts
of the world":

The contemporary enthusiasm of intellectuals for peasant and *lumpen-proletarian* movements or for movements inspired by the ideology of national minorities is an enthusiasm for that which in these movements is reactionary and hostile to culture—for their contempt of knowledge, for the cult of violence, for the spirit of vengeance, for racism. Racism is still racism even when it is the racism of a discriminated minority, as in the case of certain forms of the American black movement.[19]

He does not see the essential difference between the progressive defensive nationalism of the oppressed and the reactionary racism of the oppressor. And he neglects to note that the same elements of the Left he attacks also demonstrated solidarity with their fellow students and intellectuals in Warsaw, Budapest, and Prague. How would he have felt if they had failed to do so—if they had listened to Moscow's toadies, who condemned the rebellious university students and Communist oppositionists like himself as counterrevolutionaries?

Kolakowski falls into the same kind of error in assessing the problem of culture as he does in the domain of morals. He rightly argues against the sectarian nonsense that bourgeois culture contains nothing of value that the revolutionary socialist movement has to preserve and build upon. The contempt displayed during the onset of the Great Proletarian Cultural Revolution for the works of Shakespeare, Beethoven, and Pushkin is a Maoist obscurantism foreign to genuine Marxism. No less erroneous and pernicious has been the concomitant idea of a specifically proletarian culture and the sterile cult of socialist realism in the arts. Lenin and Trotsky, as he notes, were opposed to this bureaucratic conception imposed by Stalinism.

However, Kolakowski affixes a universal, classless seal upon culture as such, and even inclines to identify its content with the universal spiritual values cultivated by the rising bourgeoisie. In this respect, too, he slides over from Marxism to liberalism.

*   *   *

Kolakowski stands out as a distinctive personality among contemporary European thinkers. His wit, irony, juggling of paradoxes, and acumen make his writings easier and pleasanter to read than the ponderous treatises of the equally learned Martin Heidegger and Theodor Adorno or the abstract argumentations of Georg Lukács. Yet however welcome the savor of his style,

however interesting the mannerisms of his thought, these qualities are less instructive than the features of his career and the
trend of his reflections.

He mirrors the misfortunes, confusions, and aberrations of a
significant section of the Communist or ex-Communist theoreticians of the post-Stalin era. The crumbling of the official ideology
ushered in an anguishing crisis of belief and perspective among
the most sensitive intellects, young and old, in the Soviet bloc,
psychologically akin to the loss of faith in a religion. The most
cherished ideas were placed in doubt and all first principles had
to be examined afresh. The acuteness of that convulsion, which is
far from ended, vibrates through Kolakowski's writings.

Once the fetishism of Moscow's word as revealed truth was
overturned, those Communist dissidents who wanted to remain
revolutionists had to find out what authentic Marxism was and
whether it was still viable as a replacement for their lost
confidence in its Stalinist perversion.

Kolakowski embarked on this quest, sincerely intending to
rescue Marxism from its debasers. Regrettably, his break from
Stalinist ideology was followed not by the reconstruction of
Marxist theory, but by the piecemeal dismantling of its tenets.

Like other thinkers in the West who, from different starting
points, have professed the desire to progress beyond Marxism
and overcome its deficiencies (such as Mills, George Lichtheim,
and Sartre, to name only the best known), Kolakowski actually
recycled views that Marxism had contended with and transcended during its formation. Thus he went back to the rationalism of the Enlightenment by making individual abstract reason
the paramount force in directing history and determining morality. He reverted to the standpoint of the utopians in assigning an
ethical basis to social change. Ludwig Feuerbach, the materialist
who helped Marx throw off Hegelian idealism, unambiguously
affirmed that nature was primordial and human nature or
consciousness secondary in existence. Kolakowski turned their
relationship around by making human nature the originator of
reality.

Similar relapses can be observed among other proponents of
"open-ended" Marxism in Eastern Europe. After forsaking Stalinism, they could either go forward to discover and develop the
authentic Marxist ideas and traditions Stalinism had suppressed
and distorted, or else fall back into outworn and incorrect modes
of thought prevalent in the West. Since the limited de-

Stalinization afforded them a certain leeway for independent thought, some Soviet natural scientists and philosophers have been trying, amidst official obstacles, to make their way out of the Stalinist morass toward the critical dialectics of classical Marxism and to elaborate its ideas without abandoning its materialist premises. They are additionally handicapped because they do not have access to the treasury of Trotskyism, which maintained and promoted living Marxism in the post-Lenin decades.

Kolakowski is more fortunate in this respect. He does know what Trotskyism stands for. However, he considers its ideas no less dogmatic and indefensible than those of Stalinism. Reviewing *Trotsky: The Great Debate Renewed,* a book which raises all the issues of the role of Trotskyism in the Marxist movement in the form of a debate between Trotskyists and non-Trotskyists, Kolakowski wrote in the Fall 1972 *Partisan Review* that he found the discussion "sectarian" and "boring."

Yet this scholar earnestly discusses the controversies introduced by the sects of the Great Reformation in 1517-23. He apparently considers the issues and ideas brought forward by the most advanced Marxist theoreticians after Lenin to be less important and relevant than those connected with the Reformation and Counter-Reformation in the transition from the feudal to the bourgeois world outlook. How can anyone concerned with political life today downgrade the problem of the nature and destiny of the first and most powerful workers' state, the prerequisites for socialism, the tasks of the world revolution, and the fate of humankind itself?

His frivolous attitude toward the discussion of such deadly serious questions shows how corrosive Kolakowski's skepticism has become. It has eaten away his attachments to Marxism.

Although he has been influenced by Sartre, Kolakowski has moved in an opposite direction. While Sartre was edging toward Marxism without surrendering his existentialist method, Kolakowski kept moving away from Marxist positions. The moralistic stance he arrived at brought him into closer affinity with Albert Camus, who from the heights of an abstract humanism failed to take sides with the Algerians in their independence struggle against French domination.

As with other persecuted dissidents in the Soviet bloc, two distinct issues are intermingled in Kolakowski's case. One relates to his right to pursue the search for the truth and publish his findings, even to fall into error along the way, without interference from the authorities. We revolutionary Marxists have vigorously upheld this democratic right to freedom of thought and expression against bureaucratic restriction.

But a further obligation is involved in regard to the defense of the heritage of Marxist thought. Its authentic content is not only hounded and misrepresented under the neo-Stalinist regimes from Warsaw to Peking. It is being nibbled at by many of those who have suffered at their hands and are seeking a new political and philosophical orientation.

It is imperative, but insufficient, to break with Stalinism in all its variants. That much has been done by a multitude of nonconformists and disillusioned dissidents since the 1930s. The decisive question is: Where do they go from there?

The thirst for truth and justice that impelled Kolakowski to expose Stalinism should have led to some positive replacement for what he found wanting. The burning problems that have shaken up the Stalinist world call out for theoretical and practical solutions in Marxist terms. Kolakowski has proved unequal to this formidable task.

He prefers to maintain the posture of a jester who mocks everything, sacred or profane. He told an interviewer, "I have never been a political leader and I have no wish to be one."[20] This disavowal is what the young American radicals he disparages would call a cop-out, an evasion of responsibility. While he had to don the cap and bells to get around Gomulka's censors, this costume is unsuitable for permanent wear now that he can speak more freely.

He is not the kind of academic specialist whose views interest only professional colleagues. Although he is primarily a man of ideas, not of action, he willy-nilly became a public figure, an intellectual beacon to whom many on the Left looked for enlightenment and guidance. He cannot so lightly shrug off the civic obligations he courageously fulfilled in the past.

To get himself off that hook, he invokes inconsistency as a supreme merit. Inconsistency is unavoidable, he assures us, because of the contradictory nature of all things and above all "the eternal and incurable antinomy in the world of values," which cannot be reconciled in any synthesis.

Though this posture may do for an artist, it is a poor recommendation for a serious philosopher who was once a Marxist. Kant wrote in the *Critique of Practical Reason* that the highest obligation of the philosopher is to be consistent. There is a qualitative difference between those inconsistencies imposed, often unconsciously, upon thinkers by the operation of uncontrollable contradictions in their historical situation and place in the evolution of human thought (as happened with Michel Eyquen Montaigne, David Hume, and Kant himself) and those that simply exhibit an incapacity or unwillingness to arrive at a principled method and stabilized positions. Benedict Spinoza, whom Kolakowski takes as a model, was one of the most rigorous of systematizers.

Hegel, Johann Wolfgang von Goethe, Marx, and other judges of world literature have regarded *Rameau's Nephew* by Denis Diderot as an incomparable portrayal of a personality riddled with inconsistencies. However, Diderot is esteemed as a philosopher not so much for the dialectical artistry depicting that paradoxical figure of his times as for his resolute efforts to work out a consistent materialist outlook. But Kolakowski would rather range himself alongside the fictional character of *Rameau's Nephew* than emulate its creator.

Kolakowski's inconsistencies testify to the discordances of a thought that has been drifting from one point to another ever since he cut loose from his original moorings, without arriving at any settled convictions. He is baffled by the complex social realities of our transitional time and cannot satisfactorily analyze them for lack of a correct scientific method.

Admittedly, specific contradictions are vexing to sort out in theory and often require prodigious and prolonged exertions to resolve in practice. But a philosophic approach that simply throws up its hands and asserts that they are fundamentally unmanageable and insoluble falsifies the development of both society and thought, as well as paralyzing and crippling action. Moreover, it discounts the achievements philosophy and logic have actually made, from the Greeks to dialectical materialism, in comprehending the nature and evolution of contradictions in reality.

His procedure in coping with the antinomies of existence and morality falls behind those followed by the German classical philosophers, not to speak of Marx, who went far beyond them. Kant did not rest after exposing the antinomies of theoretical reason but went on to seek a solution for them in practical reason. Hegel proceeded from the recognition of contradictions as the essence and motive force of reality to set forth the dialectical laws through which they necessarily develop and are transcended. Kolakowski erects as an absolutely insurmountable obstacle what Hegel grasped as a great breakthrough to understanding.

The dialectical logic of Marxism took advantage of these and other advances of thought to explain how the conflicting forces in natural, historical, and intellectual evolution work themselves out through the struggle of opposites and in accord with the law of the negation of the negation, among others.

Having cast aside such conquests of modern philosophy, Kolakowski confesses that he cannot find a rational way out of the maze of contradictions in which he is entangled, and indeed there is no need to do so. He recognizes no final judgments, no definitive solutions to problems. The theoretical formlessness of his "radical rationalism" and his instrumentalist conception of truth are little different from the "radical empiricism" of the pragmatic William James, who wrote in his last essay: "What is concluded, that we might conclude in regard to it?"

". . . The situation of incompleteness is the organic and constitutive situation of human life, and aside from death all endings are sham endings," Kolakowski recently wrote in "Culture and Fetishes."[21] This is an oddly one-sided observation for so acute a dialectician, who should know that endings belong to the process of reality as much as beginnings and that every ending is a new beginning on a different level. Doesn't this apply to the stages of his own evolution—and hasn't he definitively finished with Stalinism?

This accent on incompleteness has a practical purpose. It justifies avoiding commitment to any class, cause, position, or principle, on the ground that there are no "closed structures" or determinate situations to base oneself on.

His formal tolerance is hospitable to some very backward views. In *The Presence of Myth*, Kolakowski maintains that myth cannot be eradicated from human activities and ideas. Thus in a world of relative values where everything is permitted, "one can bed down just as comfortably on the idea of tragedy [the existential meaninglessness of life] as on the [Christian] idea of eternal salvation, or the [Marxist] idea that consciousness is determined by being."[22] Instead of rationality, arbitrariness rules the world of this ex-Marxist celebrator of "radical rationalism."

Why take exception to Kolakowski's skepticism? one of his admirers may ask. Didn't Marx once say that his favorite motto was "doubt everything" and hasn't Kolakowksi done exactly that?

The essential difference is that, as the result of the critiques of his predecessors, the founder of dialectical materialism placed philosophy and the social sciences on truer, stronger, more durable theoretical foundations. Kolakowski, on the contrary, has assembled out of his questioning a pastiche of ill-assorted views that "show the influence, in about equal measure, of the philosophical ideas of Spinoza, Kant, Hegel, Marx, Dilthey, Mannheim, Husserl, Sartre, Heidegger, and Camus."[23] To this menu should be added a portion of fashionable structuralism.

Nowadays Kolakowski envisages a theory of convergence in philosophy parallel to that of the Soviet scientist Andrei Sakharov in politics and economics. Since "the purity of Marxism as a global system" is untenable, whatever remains valid and valuable in its contributions will become assimilated into some prospective amalgam of ideas prevalent in the West. "Marxist traditions are being mingled with ideas coming from a variety of non-Marxist sources—phenomenology and existential philosophy, neo-Hegelian historicism, the analytical school."[24] He shares this syncretism, the fusion or confusion of incompatible beliefs, with heterodox colleagues among the philosophical faculties of East Europe.

Kolakowski can give a coherent presentation of a specific school of thought such as positivism. Yet he cannot do as much for his own. He says it is impossible to understand the whole or make the world "clear and coherent." His vision of reality has been so fractured that he cannot put the pieces together again in any orderly pattern. Like the protagonist of T. S. Eliot's *Waste Land*, he stands amidst the debris of his former beliefs in a desolate landscape without any coherence to his thought. A subjectivist world, an unintelligible history, a capricious morality—"these fragments I have shored against my ruins."

*   *   *

All this appears to be but a prelude to a further act in the drama. From the negation of dialectical materialism that marked his interim development he has shifted to tentative affirmations of a patently retrogressive character in both philosophy and political outlook. His eclecticism has served as a pontoon bridge by which he has crossed over from Marxism to liberalism—and perhaps "beyond."

Kolakowski's manipulation of inconsistency is most conspicuous in his new attitude toward religion. He who was once an outspoken atheist and foe of the Catholic church now calls himself "an inconsistent atheist." While he does not believe in God, he holds religion in the highest esteem. "I would say that men have no fuller means of self-identification than through religious symbolism, and that the need for this realization cannot be dismissed or set aside." Religion is "an irreplaceable part of human culture, man's only attempt to see himself as a whole, that is to say, as both object and subject."[25] What Marxist materialism regards as the epitome of self-alienation and abasement has become for him the means of human fulfillment.

The hand he extends to religion is accompanied by accommodation to upholders of the capitalist establishment. He initiated a conference in May 1973 at the University of Reading on a theme first announced as: "What is wrong with the socialist idea?" and later modified to: "Is there anything wrong with the socialist idea?" This symposium was patronized by well-known cold warriors.

He now scorns the project of a world socialist revolution and views "the failure of socialism" in the East against the brighter backdrop of democratic liberalism in the Western world.

E. P. Thompson, himself an ex-Stalinist ideologue of the British New Left and a founder of *New Left Review*, felt "a sense of injury and betrayal" at Kolakowski's apostasy. In *The Socialist Register 1973* he addressed an open letter, a hundred pages long, pleading with the Polish exile to reconsider and reverse his course. "I ask you if you can show the same tenacity and resistance to assimilation within capitalist ideology that you have shown with the Stalinist," he wrote.[26]

Has Kolakowski gone too far from his starting point to heed this appeal, turn back, and retrace his steps? Almost a quarter of a century ago, in 1950, Isaac Deutscher, another Polish exile living in England—who, however, remained faithful to Marxism his whole life long—sketched the orbit of his counterparts of the preceding generation.

Nearly every ex-Communist broke with his party in the name of communism. Nearly every one set out to defend the ideal of socialism from the abuses of a bureaucracy subservient to Moscow. Nearly every one began by throwing out the dirty water of the Russian revolution to protect the baby bathing in it.

Sooner or later these intentions are forgotten or abandoned. Having broken with a party bureaucracy in the name of communism, the heretic goes on to break with communism itself. He claims to have made the discovery that the root of the evil goes far deeper than he at first imagined, even though his digging for that "root" may have been very lazy and shallow. He no longer defends socialism from unscrupulous abuse; he now defends mankind from the fallacy of socialism. He no longer throws out the dirty water of the Russian revolution to protect the baby; he discovers that the baby is a monster which must be strangled. The heretic becomes a renegade.[27]

Kolakowski is treading perilously close to this borderline, although he still claims to be a sort of socialist and looks to a union of the workers and intellectuals as "the most important factor in future Polish developments."

Thompson was disquieted by the desertion of a fellow fighter for an honest socialism. And it is a disappointing loss to the cause of the working class that so gifted a person could not make the transit from Stalinism to revolutionary Marxism but has apparently succumbed to the blandishments of bourgeois liberalism after valiantly resisting the bureaucratic gangsters in his homeland.

*   *   *

His personal evolution has a broader political and ideological significance. Kolakowski's demoralization is indicative of the collapse of the exhilarating expectations of liberation aroused among the Polish intellectuals, youth, and working masses in the last months of 1956. Their bitter disenchantment at what ensued has induced many there and throughout Eastern Europe to renounce their former hopes in official Communism or its reformation.

Kolakowski has been trebly victimized by Stalinism. In his formation as a philosopher it deformed and deterred his understanding of Marxism. Then its agents tried to gag and crush him. In the present stage it has driven him into a skepticism verging on cynicism. Both then and now he failed to comprehend the real nature of the reactionary incubus that has fastened itself upon the bureaucratized workers' states. First in a positive then in a negative way, he has taken Stalinism to be not the antithesis but the representative of Marxism. He thereby became, in spite of himself, a prisoner of its ideology.

He was called upon to explain why the October revolution degenerated and how Stalinism and the Soviet Union under its heel were to be scientifically defined. These questions could not be clarified without a method of thought capable of analyzing the contradictory nature and development of concrete social and historical processes. That could be done only through dialectical materialism.

Kolakowski has deprived himself of the instrument of Marxism for deciphering the enigmatic character of the degenerated and deformed workers' states. His subjectivist interpretation of history prevents him from correctly appraising the objective significance of October 1917 as the event that inaugurated a new era of world history, the first gateway to the socialist future. Consequently he is all at sea when he confronts these anomalous societies.

He observes that they are "a new phenomenon not to be assimilated with any past form."[28] This is not very edifying. He then dismisses the notion that they have anything socialist about them or are transitory formations on the way to socialism.

How, then, are the postcapitalist states and what he calls their "ruling class" to be classified? He can not tell us what they are, wherein they resemble or differ from capitalist ones, or where they are going. All he knows is that Marxism and Leninism invariably lead to bureaucratic totalitarianism. Here's one point where determinism prevails!

This much any anticommunist professor in an English or American university can tell his students. They have a right to expect deeper sociological insight from a philosopher with his background and knowledge.

*　　　*　　　*

What is the way forward for contemporary Marxists out of the mystification of all variants of the official Communist ideology, from Brezhnev to Mao? This requires a dual rejection—of the Stalinist deformations and debasement of scientific socialism on the one hand, and of the obfuscations of the revisionist tendencies on the other. We must build on the solid foundations and enduring achievements of Marxist thought from its origins.

Kolakowski belongs to the growing array of ex-Communist and semi-Marxist thinkers who put forward their aberrant views through the technique of "divide and rule." They do so along two lines. They break up the comprehensive structure of Marxist theory and its body of knowledge by disjoining its philosophic foundations from its sociological and political applications. And they oppose historical to "philosophical" materialism. They dismember the development of dialectical materialism by ranging the young Marx against the mature Marx; Marx against Engels and Plekhanov; Marx against Lenin; the Lenin who wrote *Materialism and Empirio-Criticism* against the wiser Lenin who jotted down his marginal reflections in *Philosophical Notebooks*. One or all of these are also played off against Luxemburg and Trotsky.

Such counterpositions are unwarranted in regard to the philosophical and logical method these eminent revolutionists used. Whatever their disagreements on other matters, they all cultivated the same dialectical and materialist procedures. Through these mentors and their followers, Marxist theorizing has had a discernible line of progressive development, an enrichment of content, and a continuity of growth over the past hundred years.

Marxism rests upon two irreplaceable pillars. One is a consistent materialism; the other is a dialectic that encompasses the three qualitatively different divisions of phenomena—nature, society, and thought—in a single unified world outlook.

In repudiating both of these fundamental principles the jesting philosopher played a cruel joke on himself. He who aspired to overcome the defects and defaults of institutionalized Marxism has discarded its doctrines and says that even the name is indifferent to him, not worth arguing about. He who hoped to reform Stalinism from within now contrasts the virtues of bourgeois democracy to its villainies from without. The logic of his revisionist course had landed him by 1974 where he least expected to be in 1956.

Like many others in the East and West who have proclaimed that they were proceeding "beyond Marxism" to some less doctrinaire philosophy or more up-to-date method, Kolakowski has succeeded only in taking steps backward from Marxism's achievements. The "open-ended" Marxism that plunges ahead without a compass of principled class positions has led its proponents into dead ends that have done more to muddle than to clarify the theoretical and practical problems confronting the revolutionary movement.

Kolakowski in philosophy and Solzhenitsyn in literature are twin examples of those ex-Stalinist dissenters in the Soviet bloc who, in justifiably abhorrence of the monstrous crimes of Stalinism, unjustifiably rejected Bolshevism on the ground that it is responsible for totalitarian tyranny, and who charge Marxism with being the ideological source of the evil. The fact that it has transformed some of the finest minds under its sway into adversaries of socialism and Marxism and pushes them toward reaction is one more crime to be chalked up against Stalinism.

Those who have exchanged their delusions about Stalinism for illusions about democratic imperialism do a disservice to the cause of the oppressed. Not all of the current oppositionists have moved in this direction. The more progressive among them, like Pyotr Grigorenko, want to rehabilitate Leninism and cleanse Marxism of the Stalinist filth. That is the right road to follow in both philosophy and politics. Over the past half century, ever since the Communist Left Opposition challenged the initial manifestations of Soviet bureaucratism, the world Trotskyist movement has blazed the trail in this endeavor.

Sebastiano Timpanaro's
Defense of Materialism

After an earthquake shakes a building to its foundations, much time and effort are required to put everything back in its proper place. So those Communist thinkers who were jolted loose from Stalinist orthodoxy by the political upheavals of the past two decades have, after casting off their former beliefs, found it difficult to reorient their ideas in accord with authentic Marxist criteria.

Two contemporary Italian Marxist philosophers, Sebastiano Timpanaro and Lucio Colletti, have intervened in this painful process of readjustment in Western Europe. Their contributions have been translated into English by the London bimonthly *New Left Review* and its publishing firm, which have taken the lead in publicizing the views of Western Marxism.

This category comprises an extremely heterogeneous band of ideologues, who are linked together not so much by common positions as by their opposition to the official doctrines emanating from Moscow and by their abandonment of essential elements of dialectical materialism. According to Timpanaro, "the common denominator of all these philosophical pastiches is anti-materialism."[1]

Timpanaro is a classical philologist of international repute and a student of eighteenth- and nineteenth-century European culture. He has also written a critique of Freud's *Psychopathology of Everyday Life*. From 1945 to the present he has belonged to a series of left socialist organizations, evidently escaping the ill effects of Stalinism that have mangled the minds of so many of his contemporaries. The emancipated mentality that irradiates his writings enables him to cope more effectively with the complex theoretical problems posed to Marxists since the Second World War.

He is, above all, a stalwart materialist. As such, he stands in refreshing contrast to the horde of fugitives from philosophical materialism among the Western reinterpreters of Marxism and their East European counterparts. His fidelity to the foundations of scientific socialism is rare enough to merit special commendation.

The essays in his book are a sustained polemic against the more prominent antimaterialists who profess allegiance to Marxism but sacrifice some of its principles in their writings. These include such figures as Louis Althusser; the early Georg Lukács; Karl Korsch; Herbert Marcuse, Alfred Schmidt, and other luminaries of the Frankfurt school; and Jean-Paul Sartre. In connection with them he takes up the positions of Claude Lévi-Strauss and Noam Chomsky.

He states his own intellectual affinities in this way: "Hence the author's unconcealed sympathy for Engels, Lenin and Trotsky, who do not receive a very good press these days from the revolutionary left in the West, which prefers to go back to the early Lukács, Korsch 'or Rosa Luxemburg (interpreted in a voluntarist sense which does not correspond to her real thought)."[2]

Timpanaro sets his criticism of the current adulterators of Marxist theory in the broad historical context of intellectual development over the past century. Marxism, as the scientific outlook of the revolutionary working class, has had to make its way through a cultural and political terrain occupied by bourgeois and petty-bourgeois forces and ideas that have exerted unremitting pressures upon its adherents. Consequently, from one generation to the next, the propagators and defenders of dialectical materialism have been obliged to counter attempts to introduce incongruous ideas, derived from alien class sources, into its structure.

The deviators have been most strongly influenced by two opposing trends of bourgeois thought. One has been neoidealism; the other neopositivism. Despite their very different standpoints and methods, they have in common a hostility to modern materialism as elucidated by the creators of Marxism and their most qualified disciples. Most of the Western Marxists have gone astray by succumbing to certain attractive tenets of one or the other of these types of thought.

Just as Lenin took up the cudgels against empiriocriticism in 1908, so his true followers must nowadays ward off the encroachments of a comparable eclecticism. They have to conduct a two-front campaign: against a relapse into semi-Hegelianism by exponents of the praxis school on one side, and against the formalistic structuralists on the other. Timpanaro subjects both of these fashionable currents of thought to searching examination.

Their three-sided controversy revolves around the question: How is the relation between objective reality and social life to be conceived? The mechanical materialists who espouse behaviorism or biologism try to slur over or obliterate the qualitative distinction between animal and human behavior. The praxologists, on the other hand, assert or imply that the "second nature," the artificial environment created by humanity in the historical development of social life, has entirely absorbed primordial nature into itself. They thereby head toward some form of a voluntaristic spiritualism.

Timpanaro steers clear of both errors. He writes, ". . . to reduce man to what is specific about him with respect to other animals is just as one-sided as to reduce him (as vulgar materialists do) to what he has in common with them."[3] This is his definition of a genuine materialism:

By materialism we understand above all acknowledgement of the priority of nature over "mind," or if you like, of the physical level over the biological level, and of the biological level over the socio-economic and cultural level; both in the sense of chronological priority (the very long time which supervened before life appeared on earth, and between the origin of life and the origin of man), and in the sense of the conditioning which nature *still* exercises on man and will continue to exercise at least for the foreseeable future. Cognitively, therefore, the materialist maintains that experience cannot be reduced either to a production of reality by a subject (however such production is conceived) or to a reciprocal implication of subject and object. We cannot, in other words, deny or evade the element of passivity in experience: the external situation which we do not create but which imposes itself on us. Nor can we in any way reabsorb this external datum by making it a mere negative moment in the activity of the subject, or by making both the subject and the object mere moments, distinguishable only in abstraction, of a single effective reality constituted by experience.[4] [Objectivity would be a better term than passivity for designating the active role of the external world in human experience.]

The praxis theoreticians, from the Lukács of *History and Class Consciousness* to Antonio Gramsci and Sartre, commit the unpardonable transgression of shuffling away the existence of nature independent of humanity by insisting that the object is inseparable from the subject. However, humanity's action and effect upon nature does not eliminate the priority of nature's action and effect upon humanity. For all materialists, pre-Marxist and Marxist alike, the objective world antedates humanity and underlies its history. Any indecisiveness on this cardinal proposition inexorably pulls the wobblers toward antimaterialist conclusions of one sort or another.

Such a breakaway from the first premise of materialism is the impetus behind the attacks upon the philosophical traditions upheld by Frederick Engels, George Plekhanov, and Vladimir Ilyich Lenin. The negative evaluations made of Engels by various thinkers from Lukács to Colletti have a logical outcome. It is no matter of chance, Timpanaro says, that "those who have embarked on a 'Marxism without Engels' have arrived, coherently enough, at a 'Marxism without Marx.'"[5] The theoretical views of the cocreators of dialectical materialism are so firmly welded together that the positions of the one cannot be disavowed without discarding those of the other.

One line of argument invoked by the praxis and pragmatic indicters of Engels is that Marxism is purely and simply a method of inquiry that would retain its value and validity regardless of the sum and substance of its specific doctrines. It is, so to speak, a kind of intellectual activity, a technique of criticism, detachable from the body of its principles and conclusions. This approach fails to distinguish between what is absolutely essential to a particular philosophy and what is dispensable and episodic in its expressions. To reject the primacy of nature in particular, and objective conditions in general, is to cut the heart out of Marxist philosophy. Timpanaro protests against reducing Marxism to a revolutionary sociology by purging it of all aspects of a general conception of reality.

Such an abridgment enables its practitioners to discard whatever elements of dialetical materialism are uncongenial to them or unsuited to their purposes. Timpanaro emphasizes that scientific socialism can no more be reduced to its methodology alone than can science in general. The adherents of Marxism must attend to the results of its researches, which reflect objective realities, since its verified conclusions about the nature of things exist in organic unity with its postulates and procedures.

As a rule the antimaterialists are repelled by science, which some even regard as a form of "bourgeois false objectivity," just as existentialists dismiss it as an unauthentic perversion of real being. Timpanaro scorns such irrationalism as obscurantist. He asserts the need for a philosophy that is a vision of the world based on the results of the sciences. He is keenly aware that Marxism must keep in step with all advances of the natural and social sciences and integrate their acquisitions of knowledge into its system—without, however, forsaking its own dialectical and materialist standpoint.

While nature, and humanity as a biological being, can be treated as constants in respect to the more rapid transformations of society, this does not negate humankind's dependence on nature and its ever-present activity. To deny this is to give a finger to the idealists and subjectivists. "To maintain that, since the 'biological' is always presented to us as mediated by the 'social,' the 'biological' is nothing and the 'social' is everything, would once again be idealist sophistry," Timpanaro points out. "If we make it ours, how are we to defend ourselves from those who will in turn maintain that, since all reality (including economic and social reality) is knowable only through language (or through the thinking mind), language (or the thinking mind) is the sole reality, and all the rest is abstraction?"[6]

*   *   *

Timpanaro evaluates the impact of structuralism, with its blending of linguistics, psychoanalysis, and metaphysical idealism, upon Marxism as perspicaciously as he refutes attempts to sever historical materialism from its roots in physical and biological phenomena. His extensive discussion article "Structuralism and its Successors" is the most concise and cogent treatment of this antimaterialist and unhistorical methodology by a Marxist scholar.

As a philologist by profession, Timpanaro is especially qualified to discuss the achievements and shortcomings of the divers tendencies in the development of linguistics as an autonomous historical science during the nineteenth and twentieth centuries. He pays tribute to the merits while recognizing the ambiguities of the celebrated Swiss linguist Ferdinand de Saussure, who introduced the sharp distinctions between speech and language and between synchrony and diachrony that form the theoretical pillars of the structural method. However, he absolves Ferdinand de Saussure himself from the rigid mathematical-Platonist idealism of his disciples in this field, who have subordinated the changing empirical data of language to the system of abstract concepts derived from or imposed upon it. What were flexible dichotomies in de Saussure's thought have hardened into a one-sided system of timeless polarities in the more formalist currents of structural linguistics. Timpanaro insists that while language functions synchronically it evolves diachronically. These two interactive aspects cannot be separated from or counterposed to each other in the study of language. He holds that there is "a great ideological distance between Marxism and structural linguistics."[7]

Timpanaro praises the noted linguist Noam Chomsky for his courageous anti-imperialist stands and crusades for civil liberties at home and abroad. And he acknowledges the worth of his researches in transformational grammar. At the same time he censures the MIT professor for reverting to the device of "innate ideas" (inherent structures of the mind) as the source of language. This kind of explanation was long ago discredited by empiricism and is by now too antiquated even for bourgeois thought, he says. Its Cartesian philosophy is antiempirical, antimaterialistic, and nonevolutionary. Its dualism introduces a hiatus between the human and other animals that no intermediate steps can bridge. Chomsky's effort to overcome this gap by turning innate ideas into hereditary predispositions "wavers between an antediluvian spiritualism and a genuinely 'vulgar' materialism."[8]

In any case, Chomsky does not claim to be a Marxist; he is a libertarian. Timpanaro draws a clear line between the scientific gains made by the leading structural linguists in their specialty, from de Saussure to Chomsky, and their French extralinguistic imitators, who have extrapolated their conceptions in an illegitimate manner. He reserves the most scathing criticism for "that mélange of linguistics, ethnology and psychoanalysis which began to take shape in French culture during the nineteen fifties and sixties, and which has increasingly shown, in the works of

Lévi-Strauss, Foucault and Lacan, an ambition to elevate itself to the status of philosophy, of a 'science of man in general.' "[9] He charges them with charlatanry.

Though Claude Lévi-Strauss rules like an emperor over Western anthropology today, Timpanaro reveals the shoddiness of the theoretical garments he sports. While Lévi-Strauss tips his hat in the direction of Marxism, his method of investigation and exposition turns historical materialism on its head. It is a primary postulate of Marxism that social being determines social consciousness; Lévi-Strauss makes out social life to be a product of the collective consciousness, albeit a special sort of hidden, unconscious, and invariant universal mind.

His major work, apart from his later analysis of myths, is *The Elementary Structures of Kinship*. This is built around the thesis that the most primitive and fundamental form of kinship grouping comes from the reciprocal exchange of women by men to cement social solidarity. This explanation takes for granted the predominant role of the male sex in primitive society.

Lévi-Strauss's male bias is woven into a highly idealistic method of procedure. It is of course necessary to search for the elementary forms of things—as physicists have looked for atoms and nuclear particles, and biologists for genes. Similarly, Marx singled out the commodity form as the nuclear unit of capitalist relations. However, complex and multifarious phenomena can be reduced to the essential structural elements that underlie and cause them, along two different paths that give very different results.

One relates surface appearances to real though unevident components and forces, as chemists reduce molecular compounds to combinations of elements. The other way is to construe the outward show of events as the incarnation of universals that are in principle unverifiable by empirical means. The first is a genuinely scientific and materialistic practice; the second method gravitates toward Platonic idealism.

Thus Lévi-Strauss attributes the basic unit of kinship he claims to have discovered to invariant structures ingrained in the human mind, which has a propensity to construct logical categories by means of binary contrasts. These polarities are responsible for the forms of reciprocity found in primitive society. His structures emanate not from the material conditions of savage life but from mental predispositions and universal logical categories. Like Chomsky, Lévi-Strauss ultimately relies upon the untenable doctrine of innate ideas for the explanation of language and other social phenomena.

The notions of the linguistic structuralists and Lévi-Strauss have heavily influenced the French Communist philosopher Althusser, of whom Timpanaro has a low opinion. " . . . his terminological acquisitions were far more numerous than his actual conceptual advances," he says.[10] And his structuralism "emerges most prominently in his concept of science (anti-empiricist . . .), in his low estimation of diachrony, and in his expulsion of man from the human sciences."[11]

Althusser's antipathy to dialectics strikes at the historical-mindedness that is essential to scientific socialism. The distortion of Marxism resides in his structuralist procedure of analyzing capitalism, which is a transitory and contradictory socioeconomic formation undergoing continual change, in a purely synchronic and static manner, whereas Marx sought to explain its laws of motion and the dynamics of its development from birth to death.

Timpanaro does not touch upon Althusser's peculiar conception of dialectical materialism as the theory of successive stages in the production of scientific thought. While Marxist philosophy aims to base itself upon a strictly scientific explanation of the changing world, it has its own specific content and orientation that transcends the limits of the specialized sciences and answers questions about the nature of reality and its knowability beyond their terms of reference. Marxism propounds not only a theory of knowledge but a theory of being. The substance of its philosophy comprises the most general laws of the development of nature, society, and thought, and its method of inquiry is guided by them. Althusser's definition severs the science of thinking and the thinking of science from the study of the nature of reality.

The Western Marxists can be classified into two camps: the champions of "humanism" and the advocates of "scientism." In France today Sartre exemplifies the first and Althusser the second. However much they contend with one another, they represent equally one-sided deformations of socialist theory. Marxism is both humanistic and scientific; it does not recognize any insurmountable opposition between human activities and aspirations and the researches into reality that are indispensable to their realization.

Timpanaro judges the flawed ideas of many reigning idols among the left intellectuals by strict Marxist standards. Any one of his essays is worth dozens of the exegetical treatises rolling from the academic presses on Sartre, Theodor Adorno, and the like. Nonetheless several of the ideas he advances seem open to question.

While staunchly upholding one of the two main pillars of the Marxist world view, its materialist foundation, he displays a more ambiguous attitude toward its dialectical conception of reality. In defending Engels against Colletti's unfounded criticism, for example, he states: "The intrinsically idealistic character of the dialectic was not clearly recognized by either of them [Marx and Engels]."[12] More specifically, he recommends that "the Hegelian residues in *Dialectics of Nature*" be screened out, although he acknowledges the importance of the attempt to unite the natural with the social.[13] He proposes that the heritage of Marxism be updated and reformulated in more precise scientific concepts.

Marxists have to tread a narrow line between assimilating the valid achievements of modern science and becoming swamped by some unassimilable ideology that exploits them. It is unclear from Timpanaro's remarks whether he is simply urging that Marxist thought keep abreast of all major advances in science and knowledge, to which no exception can be taken, or whether he seeks to narrow the scope of dialectics and deny that its laws apply to natural phenomena. His assertion that the dialectic is essentially idealistic conflicts with the oft-stated opinion of Marx and Engels that the dialectical conception of reality has historically taken two very different philosophical forms and that its materialist version is not only compatible with but necessary to a fully scientific interpretation of the universal laws of development.

The rigid antithesis between nature and a changing human history, which even Hegel shared, was transcended when Charles Lyell, Charles Darwin, and others historicized the understanding of nature in the nineteenth century. Thereupon the question was posed: What laws and categories are operative in the incessant movement and transformations of the universe that are reflected in the mind and can be formulated in logical terms? Marx and Engels alike agreed that only the laws of dialectical development, materialistically understood, can satisfy this demand of modern scientific thought. Otherwise it is not possible to arrive at a unified and integrated world outlook with its proper logic. When

Timpanaro says that "attempts to salvage a materialist dialectic are of rather doubtful utility in relation to the tasks facing Marxists today," he is making unwarranted concessions to the standpoints of Althusser and Colletti on this crucial controversy.[14]

Further, in the area of historical materialism, Timpanaro retreats too much before the attacks of the Gramscians in the dispute over the relationship between the material basis of society and its superstructure. This "is still largely an open question within Marxism," he says.[15] Again it is uncertain what this remark is intended to imply. When the antideterminists refer to the unsettled relation between the base and superstructure, they mean that there are no coercive laws of socioeconomic development and that the generalization that the mode of production of the means of life fundamentally shapes and limits all other social-cultural phenomena and processes has no categorical character. Since Timpanaro obviously would not go along with this, it is difficult to tell what to his mind is in principle left indeterminate in regard to this question.

Apart from considerations of abstract analysis, one concrete way of refuting unjustifiable complaints about the allegedly doctrinaire, one-sided, and mechanical character of the method expounded by Engels is to refer to the best productions of the most qualified practitioners of historical materialism extending from Karl Marx's *Eighteenth Brumaire of Louis Bonaparte* to Leon Trotsky's *History of the Russian Revolution.* "By their fruits shall ye know" what the method really is and can accomplish in skillful hands.

In regard to Trotsky's masterwork of historiography we should challenge the critics: What essential aspects of that world-transforming event were ignored or slighted? What mainsprings of its development, from the international framework to its national background, were left unexplained? Was the role of ideas or the influence of the individual omitted? What other work is superior to its insights into the operations of twentieth-century history?

Trotsky has something else to his credit. In his *History of the Russian Revolution,* he employed the same Marxist method in analyzing the actual course of events after the fact as he did in predicting the main line of their development beforehand through his theory of permanent revolution. What historian of our time has harmonized theory and practice in so decisive a fashion?

Agnosticism about the correctness of historical materialism can be dispelled and its scientific adequacy weighed in the light of such literary works and political deeds.

*   *   *

Timpanaro is suspicious of any embrace of humanism, which he attributes to an aversion to the theories of technological conformity. He opposes the humanists in too sweeping a manner by identifying all expressions of the humanistic outlook with its nonscientific and petty-bourgeois versions. He thus falls in behind the sectarian attitudes of the Maoists and Althusser toward the humanistic element in Marxism.

It is as wrong to condemn humanism *en bloc* and surrender its designation and valid content to the adversaries of Marxism as it is to hand over democracy per se to these forces because of their deceitful abuse of the term. The revolutionary materialism of scientific socialism has to realize the fullest and finest promises of a genuine humanism. This viewpoint has been formulated as follows in my book *Humanism and Socialism*:

> Scientific socialism is *retrospectively* humanistic because it views humanity as the author and re-creator of itself without assistance from any supernatural being. It is *presently* humanistic because the movement for a better world it speaks for is the only one capable of lifting humanity out of poverty and inequality and safeguarding its further existence. It is *prospectively* humanistic in the highest sense because it aims to eradicate all the oppressive institutions and alienating relations bound up with class society, which have prevented the bulk of humankind from fulfilling its potential for creative practice.[16]

Timpanaro has nothing to do with the ultraleft stupidities of Maoist-influenced theorists such as Charles Bettelheim, Paul Sweezy, and Martin Nicolaus, who regard the Soviet Union as a capitalist economy and an imperialist state. He explicitly condemns the "typically Stalinist" techniques of Maoist domestic policy (the cult of the individual, the suppression of dissident views, and the accusations of being "capitalist-roaders" hurled at Mao's former associates in the leadership).

At the same time he appears overindulgent toward the Peking regime. He says that because of its reactionary immobility, Moscow no longer constitutes a point of reference for the revolutionary forces of the world. While this is correct, he claims that in a certain measure the People's Republic does constitute such a point of reference, because "China is a reality still in movement" and, despite the authoritarianism at the top, Mao's regime desired "to create a communist democracy at the base."[17] Possibly Peking's recent alignment with the most bellicose imperialist forces in the West would lead him to revise this judgment.

Timpanaro believes that Marxism remains underdeveloped in certain areas, and he discusses three of its supposed deficiencies. One concerns the materialist theory of the role of the individual in history, a subject that has been thrust to the fore by the combined impact of technological conformism under capitalism and the totalitarian steamroller of Stalinism. This problem has been treated by the French writer Lucien Sève in *Marxism and the Theory of Personality* and by the Polish philosopher Adam Schaff in *Marxism and the Human Individual*. Timpanaro decries the tendency to subordinate the ever-present biological constitution of humankind to the social aspects of the human condition in such a way as to compromise materialism.

He suggests two further improvements in Marxism with pleas for a larger place for hedonism and pessimism. Both proposals seem of dubious value.

He maintains that the pleasure-giving experiences and enjoyment of life that should accompany a materialist outlook have been scanted, not only by the distorters of Marxism, but by its founders. It is indubitable that, because of their backwardness and bureaucratic rulership, all the postcapitalist regimes to date have frowned upon hedonism in principle and in practice (except for the top bureaucratic circles). They are repressive on many levels. What needless suffering is caused by the restrictive sexual code imposed upon the Chinese youth today, and how little it accords with "communist democracy at the base"!

The teachings of Marx and Engels can scarcely be held liable for that. They early learned from direct experience and from Jean-Jacques Rousseau, Denis Diderot, Charles Fourier, and others the malign consequences of religious morality and the positive good in satisfying the natural needs of human beings— their instinctual drives, emotional urges, and need of love. Marxism is opposed to asceticism as a pattern of moral life. It envisages the cultured fulfillment of the needs of every individual, whether these be sexual, gustatory, or sportive. It aims to abolish class relations because, among other evils, their repressive domination inhibits or prevents the satisfaction of the imperious desires and demands of normal human beings. The conditions of life under socialism will foster the rounded development of each person's potential, from biological impulses to intellectual, artistic, and inventive capacities.

Despite this historical perspective, Timpanaro urges contemporary Marxists to "reconsider an entire tradition of hedonist-materialist thought which culminates in Leopardi."[18]

Giacomo Leopardi (1798-1837), the tormented Italian philosophical poet, himself bemoaned "the inevitable unhappiness of all mortals" and complained that "I am nothing in this globe, which is nothing in the world." He wanted to liberate humanity by demolishing its illusions.

Marxism, in contrast to Christianity or existentialism, is an optimistic credo based upon the vista of a qualitatively accelerated and illimitable progress once the impediments of class society and the inadequate powers of production are removed. Is it really necessary to inject a dose of pessimism into its outlook as an inoculation against a too facile optimism or a superficial conception of progress?

Apparently Timpanaro's brief for the importation of pessimism does not have a social-political motivation. He is not defeatist in respect to the proletariat's capacity to triumph over capitalism and go forward to create egalitarian social relations. His pessimism has not a short-term but a long-range basis. He doubts the possibility of overcoming the ills that people are naturally heir to, such as sickness, death, disappointment in love, frustrated ambitions.

Futurology is a nascent offshoot of social science, and the problem Timpanaro poses comes under its jurisdiction. To what extent can the limitations nature imposes on us be overcome in the far future? Thomas Huxley asked this same question in the last century: What are the limits of the powers of man over nature and nature over man?

Presuming the survival of our species and the establishment of a planned world economy, it would indeed be foolhardy at the present state of our knowledge and powers to say what will be insurmountable for posterity. The soaring of our imaginations is as historically restricted as more physical flights. Aristotle, the greatest mind of antiquity, believed that civilized peoples could not get along without social servitude. Most Americans today consider the coming of socialism to their country, which we envisage as a realistic prospect, to be an absurd eventuality.

The fantasies of one generation, like landing on the moon, may become the realities of the next. Most of the inventions that have revolutionized technology in the twentieth century were not only unattainable but unimaginable a hundred years ago. The search for the presence of life on distant planets, which was formerly the province of science fiction, is now pursued by sober government agencies. The gene, the building unit of the cell, which was not thought of until this century, has just been completely synthesized—a triumphant vindication of the materialist conception of living organisms that Timpanaro espouses.

This indicates that the biological characteristics and capacities of human beings are no more fixed and finalized than their social behavior and cultural traits. Genetics can become as potent an instrumentality of change as nuclear physics, holding out the same tremendous promise—and perils. Scientific medicine and knowledge of psychic disorders are still in their infancy.

Of course, a realistic revolutionist must face the facts as they are and not indulge in cheap optimism about a smooth, uninterrupted pathway of progress without setbacks, detours, and disasters. However, this is scarcely a temptation for generations that have gone through two world wars, fascism, the terrible retrogression of Stalinism, the counterrevolutionary resistance of monopoly capitalism, and the defaults of the leaderships of the major working class parties. The evolution of the Soviet Union shows what difficult and unexpected pitfalls can beset the world socialist movement.

Marx and Engels stressed the contradictory nature of all progress and the price that must be paid for every historical advance. Certainly twentieth-century experience has confirmed that truth to the hilt. The course of development is bound to be contradictory all along the way.

Current conditions provide more than enough reasons for pessimism and defeatism. The progressive outlook of the revolutionary proletariat bends the stick in the opposite direction. Marxists are the partisans of the victory not only of the working masses over all exploiters and bureaucrats, but of associated humanity over further obstacles, near and far.

The existentialists, infected with the sense of fatalism pervading bourgeois circles, allege that the human situation on earth is inherently senseless and that all collective and individual projects end in failure and disappointment. Marxists take exception to any such philosophy of gloom and doom. The present state of affairs as well as our previous history can be rationally explained and a way out of our agonizing predicaments shown. What humanity unconsciously created can be consciously reconstructed to come closer to satisfying our needs and aspirations.

Our forerunners refused to submit to nature's tyranny, and we have far less reason to do so. Having overcome the sources of social oppression, our socialist successors will tackle with renewed vigor and success such causes of nature's oppression as sickness and premature death.

Timpanaro is skeptical about the long-run possibilities of alleviating and eradicating the pains of these biological afflictions. His pessimism flows from a tacit assumption that the biological makeup and destiny of our species will forever remain the same and nothing can be done about it.

Since humans are not immortal, nature wins out over all individuals in the end. As Leopardi wrote in his *Dialogue Between Nature and an Icelander:* "The life of the universe is a perpetual circle of production and destruction, each of which is linked to the other in such a way that each constantly serves the other." But humans do not passively submit to this circular process; they seek to gain more and more control over it for their own purposes.

We could append the following argument to the Leopardian dialogue between the two antagonists.

Nature: "Vain creature! You can command me only by obeying me."

Humanity: "To be sure, but we have the better part of the bargain. We shall continue to trick you and turn you into an obedient servant through science and technology. We'll see whether blind nature or conscious collective humanity gets the upper hand. Up to now, despite everything, we've come a long way from the primate condition. That's not vainglorious boasting but the plain truth. And our journey into the future has barely begun!"

Natural selection favors successful reproduction of the plant or animal population and not necessarily of any or all particular individuals within it. Until now social selection has largely operated in a similar natural-historical manner. It has favored the most productive and thereby the most amply reproductive groupings. Individuals have been cruelly treated and sacrificed as history has proceeded at their expense. With the raising up and leveling out of the powers of production of the entire global population made possible by socialism, this animal-like mode of development can be reduced and eliminated so that every person will have an equal chance and the least favored will be given the utmost aid to overcome their handicaps.

Timpanaro's proposed philosophical pessimism is closer in spirit to existentialism than to the perspectives of modern materialism. It is out of phase with the psychology and outlook of an ascending class which has the mission of remaking the world and changing the course of human development.

*　　　*　　　*

I have taken up these more debatable themes in Timpanaro's book at some length because in the main its positions are so convincing and correct. This collection of essays admirably fulfills the goal Timpanaro set himself of being a stimulus to rethinking Marxism in the light of everything new that has occurred since World War II in the capitalist world, in China, and elsewhere. Every page of his book testifies that the critical spirit of genuine Marxism is very much alive in the Italian Left.

Back to Kant?
The Retreat of Lucio Colletti

Lucio Colletti presents a complex case for three reasons. The course of his philosophizing has been erratic; his views are still in flux; and they are becoming more distant from the basic principles of dialectical materialism. Criticism of his positions must be aimed at a moving target.

Since 1970, Colletti has held the chair in the philosophy of history at the University of Salerno. He sketched his ideological and political evolution in an interview with Perry Anderson, the editor of *New Left Review,* which appeared in the July-August 1974 issue of that magazine. Like many Italian left intellectuals, Colletti progressed from the Crocean school of historical idealism to Marxism, somewhat as certain American radicals earlier abandoned John Dewey's instrumentalism for Marxism. In 1950, at the age of twenty-five or twenty-six, he joined the Italian Communist Party during the Korean War, under much the same anti-imperialist impulses as moved Jean-Paul Sartre to align himself with the French Stalinists.

Colletti was one of the editors of the CP's cultural journal, *Società,* from 1958 to 1962. On *Società* he followed the views of Galvano Della Volpe, who stressed the study of the general laws of capitalist development rather than the peculiarities of the backwardness of Russia or Italy. Emphasis on the latter, Colletti says, served as a springboard for the rightist and revisionist line of the CP leadership, justifying its strategy of sticking to limited "democratic" objectives. These differing theoretical orientations "led to divergent political conclusions" and the party authorities closed down the journal in 1962.

Colletti quit the CP in 1964, after Nikita Khrushchev was deposed, recognizing that neither the leadership of the Soviet Union nor its Italian followers would return to the revolutionary program of Karl Marx and V. I. Lenin. From 1966 to 1967 he was editor of the independent Marxist monthly *La Sinistra*. Although he esteems Leon Trotsky and his work, and has been harangued by Maoists and others as a Trotskyist, he has never been a Fourth Internationalist.

His antipathy to dialectical logic induced Colletti to enlist in the anti-Engels brigade. He is resolved to rescue Marx from Frederick Engels's insidious embraces, though he is no more successful in this operation than previous distorters of their relationship.

The first section of Colletti's introduction to the anthology *Karl Marx: Early Writings*, which attributes not only the designation but the general philosophical theory of dialectical materialism to Engels alone, typifies his efforts to counterpose the intellectual development and world views of the two men. He regards "Marxism's most specific terrain of development" to be "the socio-economic one," not the philosophical.[1]

Zigzagging under fire of criticism, he has been obliged to concede that Marx shared some of Engels's "errors." Yet he continues to insist that in the main the "founding fathers" held different philosophical positions.

All Marx's work is essentially an analysis of modern capitalist society. His basic writings are the *Theories of Surplus-Value*, the *Grundrisse* and *Capital*: all the rest is secondary.[2]

Engels strayed much further afield:

While in the case of Engels, one of his major writings is indubitably the *Dialectics of Nature*—a work 90 per cent of which is hopelessly compromised by an ingenuous and romantic *Naturphilosophie*, contaminated by crudely positivist and evolutionist themes.[3]

This declaration not only cavalierly dismisses *The German Ideology*, *The Communist Manifesto*, and other joint productions of the two men, but misrepresents their later work. It disregards the facts. Engels many times discussed the themes in the

Dialectics of Nature with Marx. (In a letter to Marx dated May 30, 1873, Engels formulated the principal conceptions set forth in that unfinished writing.) He treated most of the same topics along the same lines in *Anti-Dühring*, which Marx read through and approved before publication, contributing a chapter to it. Marx had much to say about precapitalist formations in the *Grundrisse*; and was accumulating material on the institutions of precivilized societies (recently published as *Ethnological Notebooks*) that Engels worked up after his death in *Origin of the Family, Private Property, and the State.* Marx is as ideologically "compromised" and "contaminated" as his collaborator.

Marx is counterposed to Engels in order to scuttle the materialist dialectic they developed and used in all the political and literary activities of their maturity. (Colletti makes this purpose clear in his article "Marxism and the Dialectic," published in the September-October 1975 *New Left Review*.)

Colletti tries to shore up the myth of an antidialectical Marx betrayed by the dialectical Engels by arguing that Kant's epistemological positions provide better guidance for the revolutionary movement than Hegel's. In his 1974 interview he claims:

But from a strictly epistemological point of view, there is only one great modern thinker who can be of assistance to us in constructing a materialist theory of knowledge—Immanuel Kant.[4]

This recommendation flows from his drastic "reexamination" of Marxist theory. The following assertions indicate how far he has already gone in this direction. (1) Dialectical materialism is "a scholastic metaphysic."[5] (2) Marxism has no epistemological theory. (3) "The social sciences have not yet found a true foundation of their own."[6] (4) "Marxism lacks a true political theory."[7] (5) "So far as 'political' theory in the strict sense is concerned, Marx and Lenin have added nothing to Rousseau, except for the analysis (which is of course rather important) of the 'economic bases' for the withering away of the State."[8]

In common with most of the praxis school, Colletti deprives Marxism of any universal ontological character. He categorically states in *From Rousseau to Lenin*: "Marxism is a theory of the *laws* of development of human society"—and nothing more.[9] Such a stripped-down version of Marxism disregards its organic connection with antecedent materialist philosophy, which presented a distinctive theory of universal being. Marx and Engels did not throw out this basic position but amplified and enriched its view of the world by extending it to cover the origin, works, and ideas of productive and active human beings. While Colletti retains some rooms they added to the structure of materialist thought, he proposes to remove its foundation.

Not much of the content of Marxism is left intact after such ruthless iconoclasm in philosophy, logic, sociology, and politics. Indeed, Colletti acknowledges that in his eyes "the entire framework of traditional philosophical Marxism has been shattered."[10]

He wants to recement the pieces by substituting Kant's theory of knowledge for the materialistic dialectics embedded in Marxist thought. This project to disown Hegel's contribution to Marxism and substitute Kant's should set alarm bells ringing in the minds of anyone familiar with the philosophical controversies within and around the socialist movement over the past century. First, it controverts the account given by the cocreators of Marxism about the preconditions of their philosophical development. They characterized Kant as the initiator and G. W. F. Hegel as the consummator of classical German idealism. Hegel worked out certain answers to problems propounded by Kant on the nature of reality and knowledge that the latter was unable to solve in the idealist terms of his era. German philosophy advanced from the dualism, subjectivism, and agnosticism of Kant's idealism to the monism, objectivity, and rationality of Hegel's. These gigantic accomplishments were an irreplaceable element in the formation of dialectical materialism. This view of Marx and Engels on the genealogy of their ideas must be accorded considerable authority. For example, in the well-known "Afterword to the Second German Edition" of *Capital*, written in 1873, Marx said:

I criticized the mystificatory side of the Hegelian dialectic nearly thirty years ago, at a time when it was still the fashion. But just when I was working at the first volume of *Capital*, the ill-humored, arrogant and mediocre epigones who now talk large in educated German circles began to take pleasure in treating Hegel in the same way as the good Moses Mendelssohn treated Spinoza in Lessing's time, namely as a "dead dog." I therefore openly avowed myself the pupil of that mighty thinker, and even, here and there in the chapter on the theory of value, coquetted with the modes of expression peculiar to him. The mystification which the dialectic suffers in Hegel's hands, by no means prevents him from being the first to present its general forms of motion in a comprehensive and conscious manner.[11]

Engels, writing some years later, had this to say on the relation between Kant and Hegel:

> In addition there is yet a set of different philosophers—those who question the possibility of any cognition (or at least of an exhaustive cognition) of the world. To them, among the moderns, belong Hume and Kant, and they have played a very important role in philosophical development. What is decisive in the refutation of this view has already been said by Hegel, in so far as this was possible from an idealist standpoint.[12]

When European thinkers after Marx and Engels have turned in a reactionary direction, they have sought to break up this sequence of progress in philosophy by casting Hegel aside and reverting to Kant's starting point, especially in epistemology. The first to do so from a bourgeois viewpoint was Arthur Schopenhauer, who proposed, following the defeat of the 1848 revolutions, that the advances made after Kant, through Johann Gottlieb Fichte, Friedrich Wilhelm Joseph von Schelling, and Hegel, be set aside as aberrations and Kant's metaphysics be restored to supremacy. (It is instructive that the "critical philosopher" Max Horkheimer in his last phase embraced Schopenhauer.)

A similar path has been traversed since then by a varied procession of critics and revisers of Marxism in liberal and Social Democratic circles. The roster begins with Tomas Masaryk, the professor who became the first president of Czechoslovakia, Eduard Bernstein, Konrad Schmidt, Ludwig Woltman, and Charles Rappoport around the turn of the century, and later Max Adler and his Viennese school and Hendrik de Man, the Belgian socialist-turned-reactionary. All of them scorned materialist dialectics and rallied around the banner of a return to Kant.

So Colletti is not blazing any new trail in proposing to depose the materialist dialectic in favor of Kant's approach to knowledge. He is rather setting foot on a path that has taken others away from the philosophical foundation of Marxism and obscured a correct insight into the process of its formation.

The question he poses of Kant and Hegel's connection with the prehistory of dialectical materialism is not insignificant. It involves a dialectical progression of philosophical positions in which the central ideas expressed by each personality had a determinate character. Hegel's dialectics transcended Kant's more limited insights, within the idealist framework; Ludwig

Feuerbach's materialism shattered that framework without doing justice to the laws of dialectical logic or to historical development. Then Marx and Engels fused the materialist outlook with dialectical logic in an original synthesis that revolutionized philosophy. It would be as wrong to scramble the results of this order of philosophical development as to exalt Adam Smith above David Ricardo in the elaboration of political economy in Great Britain.

What did Kant set out to do and how does Hegel fit into the picture? Before Kant, the epistemology of the early bourgeois era had swung back and forth between antithetical poles. The materialists, empiricists, and sensationalists taught that experience was the sole source of all ideas in the mind, whereas the rationalists, idealists, and spiritualists held that certain universal and necessary ideas came from the mind alone. Experience only provided the occasion for the operation of the innate and eternal principles supporting God, immortality, logic, and morality.

Kant's "critical theory" was designed to overcome the inconclusive strife of the rival schools and reconcile the contradiction in their respective positions by salvaging what he considered to be the truths in both. He agreed with the empiricists that our knowledge of all phenomena is derived from experience. But experience itself, he added, consists of two different kinds of elements. One is the raw data of sensation and perception; the other is the forms of sensibility (space and time) and the categories of the understanding, such as causality, which gave order and significance to them. This metaphysics of experience satisfied the requirements of a rationalist idealism based on innate principles.

However, Kant's compromise solution to the problem of knowledge exacted a very heavy toll in fundamental respects. He divided reality into two opposing realms: the thing-in-itself, the "noumenal" realm, of which we have no direct evidence and can never know, although it exists; and the thing-for-us of the "phenomenal" realm, which is all that theoretical reason can know. Thus the nature of things is inaccessible to theoretical reason, which is confined to cognition of phenomenal appearances.

Kant did not stop at this point, which headed directly toward phenomenalism and skepticism. The thing-in-itself that is beyond the range of the understanding can be reached in another way, through what Kant called practical reason. This does possess universality and necessity because it is based on the imperative of moral law as the compulsory norm of human behavior. Thereby the convictions about God, immortality, and freedom of the will that are not validated by scientific knowledge could nonetheless be reasonably held as a matter of pure faith. As Kant stated in the preface to the second edition of the *Critique of Pure Reason*, "I must . . . abolish *knowledge*, to make room for *belief*."[13]

Heinrich Heine pertinently observed that after ruthlessly decapitating God as an object of scientific knowledge, Kant took pity and restored the divinity to preeminence for the solace of his manservant.

Every thinker thereafter had to come to grips with the problems Kant raised and his conclusions. Hegel was the most successful within idealist limits.

He contested Kant's absolute disjunction between the thing-in-itself and the thing-for-us. Reality is a unified whole in which the objective and subjective sides are not simply disjoined from each other but also form a unity. The objective world of things can be truly known. We learn what the nature of anything is from the properties, qualities, and relations presented to us. Every manifestation of an object contains and expresses a bit of its character, and the nature of any thing actually exists in the totality of its appearances. The thing-in-itself is simply a name for the state of our ignorance, an empty shell.

Hegel also refused to acknowledge any irremovable opposition between reason and reality or prescribe any limits to the power or province of reason (the logical idea). He summarized his view in the aphorism that "the real is rational and the rational is real."

Whereas Kant held that the raw material of experience was unformed, while perfectly pure forms existed in the sensibility and the mind, Hegel maintained that there was no content without its appropriate form and no form without some specific content. "The truth is concrete."

For Kant, contradiction existed only between propositions; it was a purely mental or linguistic phenomenon. Hegel insisted on the universality and objectivity of contradiction as an expression of the being of all things, the source of their change and development even into their opposites through the process of negation.

Hegel's objective idealism had the merit of overcoming the subjectivism, dualism, formalism, and agnosticism that marked Kant's system and theory of knowledge. He set forth an integrated conception of reality in which all its sectors were of one piece and there were no impassable boundaries between them. This one world was completely accessible to scientific understanding through dialectical reasoning.

Hegel therewith resolved the contradiction between the objective and subjective elements of experience that Kant was unable to overcome. Marxism did and can derive far more from his logic and epistemology than from those of his predecessor. Kant had tackled the vexing problem of contradiction very vigorously with all the strength of his powerful intellect and did much to clarify some of its puzzles. Indeed, he was the first to employ the term dialectical logic.

Hegel went forward from the point where Kant had to halt and broke through the stalemate of his metaphysics. He recognized the valid insights of Kant's reasoning. There is a unity of opposites in the thought processes. But that is only the beginning of wisdom, not its end. These antithetical aspects express the reality, the truth, of all things in their becoming. These have a dual nature, are in constant flux, and can in time be transformed into their opposites.

Whereas Kant could conceive of contradiction only in a subjective, static, and formalistic manner, Hegel brought out its historical, dialectical, and objective character. He explained that any given contradiction undergoes change through time and develops. In the *Logic* he made clear in abstract concepts how the difference implicit in a contradiction originates out of an identity, how its terms first come forth in the form of indifferent difference, and then become more and more sharply differentiated and counterposed until at the climactic point in their interrelation and interaction the constituent sides of the phenomenon become arrayed in polar opposition to each other. Carried to the extreme of its unfolding, every contradictory relation breaks up and its components pass over into a new form and a different grade of contradiction.

Marxism incorporated into its own structure of thought all that was viable and valid in Hegel's dialectical logic, which had itself developed by way of antithesis to the largely formalistic logic of Kant. However, it did not take over that logic in its original idealist form, which was unsuitable to its purposes and contrary to its materialist principles. Marxism carefully winnowed the wheat from the chaff and situated the dialectical laws and categories in their proper context, placing them on a solid materialist basis by viewing them as the most general laws of the development of nature and society, which are reflected in the mind in the form of historically conditioned categories.

Thus the idealist and materialist interpretations of dialectical logic are mutually exclusive, although Colletti construes them as identical. Insofar as both methods of thought have a dialectical content, they belong to the same species of logic and form a unity. But the actual mode of their existence is fundamentally different.

Eighteenth-century materialism had been nonevolutionary and paid insufficient attention to the distinctive features of the thought process. Classical German idealism from Kant to Hegel bequeathed two indispensable achievements to Marxism that enabled it to correct these deficiencies. One was the dialectical method, which studied phenomena in their contradictory development, interconnections, and transmutations, and set forth the patterns of their logic. The dialectic was the revolutionary element capable of further fruitful development (just as the labor theory of value was the revolutionary element in classical bourgeois political economy); its idealist matrix was the reactionary side of Hegel's doctrine that Marx and Engels discarded.

The other achievement was the emphasis placed by dialectical materialism upon the constructive activity of cognition, which had played a passive role in the pre-Marxian materialist outlook. Marxism took over the insights into the creativity of thought coming from the idealists, integrating them into the materialist premise that the objects of thought existed prior to any human subject and were perceived and cognized by them in the course of social-historical development. The mind worked upon the raw materials given by sensation and perception.

Then Marxism added the new discovery that this unity of the objectively real content of things and their thought forms, which was emphasized by the idealists, arose out of and was verified by social-historical practice. Human thought about nature, society, and itself was primordially engendered by its productive activities; the creation of ideas goes hand in hand with the development of social labor.

This exposition of the course of thought from Kant and Hegel through Feuerbach to Marx points up both the elements of continuity and the basic difference between the idealist and materialist conceptions of dialectical logic. It is a requisite in explaining why Kant's epistemology is unsuited for assimilation by a revolutionary materialism.

*   *   *

Before demonstrating how Colletti's project is a hopeless attempt to yoke incompatible theories together, one of his preliminary arguments has to be disposed of: his unfounded assertion that "Marxism is not an epistemology, at least in any fundamental sense."[14]

The problem of knowledge occupies a central place in Marxism. Marxist literature is replete with discussions that start and end with clear and definite conclusions about the nature of knowledge. These treat of the primacy of being over thought; the origins of human reasoning, language, and generalized concepts through social labor; the role of the process of material production in the generation and elaboration of ideas; the class content of ideas in civilized societies; the function of hypotheses and their conversion into laws as science grows; the causes and characteristics of class consciousness, etc. What is the motivation for the ceaseless debates around the theory of reflection and correspondence, i.e., the conformity or nonconformity of ideas with facts, if Marxist philosophy lacks its own specific theory of cognition?

Colletti, for his part, takes up the Kantian conception of epistemology, which he defines as "the search for the *limiting conditions* placed on thought."[15] This is a negative, and thus one-sided, formulations of its content. Epistemology is concerned with the conditions of our ability to know reality and to know it truly and effectively; it also deals with the sources, forms, and methods of cognition in their historical development.

Colletti's own conception of knowledge smacks more of positivism and pragmatism than Marxism. He argues against Timpanaro, for example, that "ideas are only hypotheses."[16] This discounts the existence of those theories that have been so conclusively and convincingly verified by experience, experiment, and reason that they present truthful knowledge and disclose the laws governing the development of things. While the hypothetical element may not be totally and forever eliminated from such acquisitions of scientific knowledge, it has been reduced to the point where it is negligible. If all ideas without exception are essentially hypothetical, there can be no certainty that the external world exists or assurance that the proposition "all humans are mortal" is true. Such an epistemology would corrode the foundation of the materialist outlook.

Colletti's arbitrary and sweeping erasure of the Marxist theory of knowledge (materialist dialectics) serves the purpose of appointing Kant's epistemology, tailored to Colletti's specifications, to make good the alleged deficiency. However, the Kantian approach to knowledge differs from Marx's as night from day. The one cannot be grafted upon the other with fruitful results.

Engels dealt with this question as long ago as 1888 in his work on Ludwig Feuerbach, where he wrote:

If . . . the Neo-Kantians are attempting to resurrect the Kantian conception in Germany and the agnostics that of Hume in England . . . this is, in view of their theoretical and practical refutation accomplished long ago, scientifically a regression and practically merely a shamefaced way of surreptitiously accepting materialism, while denying it before the world.[17]

First of all, Kant has a dualistic theory of being. He divides reality into two disconnected realms, the noumenal (the thing-in-itself) and the phenomenal (the thing-for-us), the latter alone being amenable to scientific inspection. Marxism has a unitary conception of being. In this respect it is linked with the tradition of Benedict Spinoza and Hegel and differs from that of René Descartes, David Hume, and Kant.

On the relation of thought to being, Kant held an agnostic position, divorcing what we sense and know from the reality of things. As he wrote in *Prolegomena to Every Future Metaphysics That May Be Presented as a Science* (1783):

Indeed when we rightly regard the objects of sense as mere phenomena we thereby admit that each such object is based upon a thing-in-itself of which we are not aware as it is constituted in itself, but only as known through its appearances, that is, by the manner in which our senses are affected by this unknown something.[18]

Marxism teaches, to the contrary, that knowledge of the objective world is not only possible but actually possessed in ever-increasing measure as our ideas are tested in production, social practice, and the advance of science.

Marxism approaches the problem and content of knowledge in a materialist and evolutionary way; Kant views the conditions of knowledge in a metaphysical manner, resting on those a priori ideas of pure reason that make knowledge possible. Marxism denies that there are any notions in the mind before and apart from the powers of sensation, perception, and abstraction, although we can interrogate objective reality with preconceptions, hypotheses, and theories that have previously been derived from experience, and we can extend the area of knowledge as extrapolations from it. However, experience has both the first and the last word on the validity, necessity, and universality of all our ideas.

For Kant, space and time are simply subjective forms of sensibility; they are not objectively rooted. For Marxism, space and time are both attributes of reality and categories of experience. In fact, they can be experienced and thought about precisely because of their objective existence.

The relation of the fact of space and time to their subjective expressions is one instance of the inseparable unity of form and content. The correlation of these two categories is entirely different for Kant and for Marx. In the former's system, the one can be absolutely independent of the other. For dialectical materialism the content of every object has some kind of concrete form and that form is a necessary part of the content at that point in its becoming. The form is not inserted into the content from without but expresses the ensemble of its elements in their interconnection and unfolding.

Kant's doctrine of the nature of the categories is thoroughly idealist. They are a priori, purely subjective, and nonhistorical forms of contemplation and reason. The category of causality, for example, does not reflect a general and essential property of the relations of phenomena in the external world that operates regardless of human experience. It is an ideal form, a regulative principle through which our minds introduce order into the items of experience.

For Marxism, all categories have an empirical content and a historical evolution. They are not timeless but derived from practical historical experience, proceeding from the data of sensation and perception to the fashioning, by the mental processes, of abstraction and generalization. They are conceptual reflections of real features produced by the objective conditions and needs of practical life.

In the preface to the second edition of *Critique of Pure Reason*, Kant announced that his revolutionary reversal in epistemology was this: hitherto cognition had to conform to the object; henceforth the object must conform to our cognition. Objects conform to the mind through the application of the a priori ideas. The materialist theory of knowledge holds that ideas must conform to the object if they are to arrive at the truth about them and be practically effective. These contrary positions cannot be reconciled or amalgamated.

Colletti says he does not wish to import everything from Kant's teachings into socialist theory, but only the usable parts of his epistemology. Unlike Bernstein and Schmidt, he disavows Kant's ethics. He sees that Kant's classless and axiomatic interpretation of morality has nothing in common with the standpoint of the revolutionary working class, which looks at morality as a mutable phenomenon whose evaluations are historically conditioned and, in civilized societies, acquire a class character.

He further claims that Kant's ethics has no affinity with his epistemology, a statement that would have shocked Kant and roused Marx and Engels to laughter. Kant's conception of morality is firmly predicated on his a priorism and noumenalism and cannot be severed from them. They are at the heart of the "limiting conditions" Kant placed on thought. The categorical imperative that should dictate conduct and determine the worth of human actions is the supreme specimen of the universality, necessity, and absolute character of an a priori idea. All individuals, floating in the unknowable "noumenal" realm, belong to the same moral community without distinction, have the same obligations, and their actions are to be judged by the same inflexible and invariable standard.

Nonetheless, Colletti contends that "in Kant there is a radical distinction between the domain of knowledge and the domain of morality, which Kant himself emphasised."[19]

While it is true that Kant separated the two, he applied the same a priorism to both. Just as the pure forms of sensibility and categories of the understanding are outside experience and are the necessary conditions for having any knowledge, so the categorical imperative, a universal and timeless law of moral conduct, originates outside human history and is absolutely independent of the specific circumstances and context of the human agents involved. Kant's ethical theory, which supposedly stands above the classes, is metaphysical, not dialectical; abstract, not concrete; bourgeois and not proletarian. It constitutes a consistent extension, a symmetrical complement, of his epistemology.

As idealists, both Kant and Hegel subordinated the real to the logical, whereas dialectical materialism subordinates the logical to the material reality, the power and findings of reason to factual existence. Kant set out to ascertain the limits of pure reason and found them to be inherent and eternally insurmountable. Marxism acknowledges that human reason has its limits. But these are historically conditioned and provisional. There are no a priori impassable barriers to the extension of the powers of reason and the growth of knowledge about the universe or of the mind itself. The accelerated growth of science demonstrates both the power and potential of reason and indicates that this capacity is only in its infancy.

Indeed, the rapid advances of philosophic thought after Kant's efforts to impose inherent limits upon the operation of human reason soon showed the fallaciousness of his project. To be sure, the exposure of its failure was one of the stimuli of further progress. Kant performed a signal service to philosophy by focusing his systematic criticism upon the defects of metaphysical thinking, thereby emphasizing the need for a superior mode of reasoning to succeed it. Hegel's dialectics were a step toward filling that need.

The two modes of thought clash most directly in their contrary conceptions of the nature and status of contradiction, as Colletti recognizes. For Kant, contradictions exist only in the mind, in logically contradictory propositions, in the denial of what is affirmed, and vice versa. Reality does not contain any contradictions but only "real oppositions," conflicts between forces.

For Hegel, contradiction, the unity of opposites, the merging of identity and difference, is the very essence of reality, the root of all being. Only insofar as anything contains a contradiction does it display motion and development.

Colletti accepts Kant's definition of contradiction and defends it against Hegel's with all the arguments he can muster. He justifies his choice on the ground that the principle of noncontradiction is at the basis of science itself, whereas dialectical contradiction befits a scarcely disguised religion: "It is a waste of time (indeed it is positively damaging) to speak of a *dialectic of things*."[20]

Colletti admits in nature only the existence of fixed *oppositions* between things of definite and determinate properties. It is certainly true that real oppositions abound in nature, and dialectics does not do away with them. The question is: Are these oppositions absolute and unchangeable? Fish live in water, reptiles on land. These are opposing modes of existence. Yet we know that through a series of intermediate forms fish that left their former habitat evolved into reptiles. The animal mode of existence is opposed to that of the human. Yet humanity grew out of primate stock and its conditions, negating the previous way of life. Such transformations demonstrate that real oppositions are not immutable and can be broken in the evolution of forms of life. A living creature is qualitatively different from a dead one, but sooner or later necessarily becomes converted into that state. That law of nature confirms not the notion of fixed opposites, but the dialectical conception of the unity of opposites that become exhibited in the qualitative change of a thing into its other.

The strongest point in Colletti's plea for Kant is that, contrary to Hegel, he affirmed "the principle of real existence," and thereby supplied the essential component of a materialist theory of knowledge. (Colletti even says that Marx took over this principle from Kant! Marx actually derived it from the 2,500-year treasury of materialist thought.)

Colletti's argument seems plausible until it is scrutinized more closely. Mere recognition of an objective reality external to the subject does not suffice to make a philosophy materialist. For that, the preexistence and independence of nature, matter in motion, is required. The theistic realism of the Thomist school, for example, teaches that the mind must conform to something independent of it. But it then adds that this world is God-created; an immaterial being accounts for its existence. Kant's "noumenal" realm of things-in-themselves plays the same role for him.

From Hegel's standpoint, which regarded the whole of reality as an objectification of the Absolute Idea, Kant's admission of the thing-in-itself appeared as a concession to the materialists. But from the standpoint of dialectical materialism, his epistemological notions that the noumenal realm is unknowable and the mind prescribes its laws to nature places Kant squarely among the idealists.

Colletti elects Kant over Hegel on the ground that his epistemology provides a better basis for historical materialism. However, on the level of epistemology, Hegel's dialectics as the logic of evolution and revolution has far more to offer a rounded materialist method than Kant's formalism and dualism. Moreover, Hegel's insight that labor was the self-creating process of the human species contributed to the formation of historical materialism.

Although Colletti seeks to extract from Kant a surety for materialism, Kant's system was an eclectic combination of idealist and empirical elements, in which the idealism was uppermost and defined its essential nature. Materialism affirms the objective existence of the external world, its unified materiality, and the knowability of the nature of reality. His internally contradictory system was alien both to a consistent materialism and to an absolute idealism.

Kant, who explicitly rejected materialism, has ever since been put up as a patron of nonmaterialist tendencies in modern thought. On the other hand, Hegel's monism, his dialectics, and the inner consistency of his systematic thought, the concordance of his conclusions with his cardinal premises, have assisted in the making of Marxism, despite the unalloyed idealism of his philosophy.

Colletti argues on his behalf that Kant takes science to be the only true form of knowledge, and not simply finite pseudoknowledge, as Hegel does. However, Hegel insisted that the nature of things was open to reason, whereas Kant restricted the knowledge of things available to science to appearance and not to their reality or totality.

The thing-in-itself has an equivocal character. It takes on a materialist sense since it has an independent status apart from the forms of sensibility and thought. Yet because of its knowability, the notion is an epistemological variant, couched in the terms of the mechanical world outlook, of the Platonic, and of the Christian conception of the world—the real one, as opposed to the phenomenal world of everyday experience.

For dialectical materialism, there is only one world, in which the appearance and essence of things are intermingled and mutually interpenetrative, not estranged from each other.

Colletti motivates his reversion to Kant and repudiation of dialectics on the ground that Marxism has to be brought into line with modern science. He is here coping with a pressing problem. The harm wrought by the deformations of dialectical materialism and bureaucratic interference in the sciences under the domination of Stalin and his heirs and the continued indifference of

Western scientists to the materialist dialectic have thrown the theoretical method of Marxism into doubt and disrepute.

Colletti seeks to get over this crisis in the vicissitudes of Marxism by jettisoning many of its cardinal principles and going back to the positivist tradition stemming from Hume and Kant, claiming that the latter's epistemology is indispensable to science and for constructing a correct materialist theory of knowledge.

The philosophical problems he brings forward have a long lineage. They can be traced back to the antithetical positions on the nature of change upheld by Heraclitus, who first discerned the copresence and mutual interpenetration of nonbeing and being as an explanation for the changes in reality, in contrast to Parmenides, who denied the reality of nonbeing and therewith the mobility and mutability of things. The conflicting tendencies in Western philosophy descended from Heraclitus and Aristotle were reproduced on a far higher level of scientific knowledge and theoretical development in the positions on the problem of knowledge put forward by Spinoza and Hegel on the one hand and Hume and Kant on the other.

Colletti explicitly aligns himself with the alternative school of Aristotle and Kant. The latter believed in the unquestionable solidity and infallibility of the laws of formal logic elaborated by the former, just as he believed that Euclid's theorems represented the sole possible system of geometry, that Isaac Newton's mechanics were the last word in physical theory, and that the human species had not and could not have evolved from lower animals.

The development of logic, mathematics, physics, and biology since his day has demonstrated that these conceptions have a restricted validity and sphere of application. Non-Euclidean geometries were not only theoretically formulable but were later shown to be applicable to cosmic spatial relations; the Newtonian laws of motion were seen to be a special case of the broader relativity laws of motion; the principles and method of non-Aristotelian logic were more powerful and percipient that the limited rules of his formal logic; Darwin's breakthrough destroyed the myth of special creation by demonstrating the descent of all living things from a common primordial origin.

Colletti fails to grasp the full significance of these epoch-making advances and settles back into the well-worn grooves of predialectical thought, which he wrongly identifies with the proper method and summary results of contemporary science.

However, the type of thought he clings to was predominant and appropriate only to that earlier stage of science when Newton reigned supreme and mechanics was the foremost branch of natural science.

Hegel defined "reflective thought" in contrast to dialectical thinking as the activity that consists in determining oppositions and passing from one to the other without demonstrating their unity, interconnection, and mutual transformability. In recurring to Kant, Colletti wants to hold logic down to this lower grade of thought, which has been surpassed by logic and science alike.

In the late nineteenth and twentieth centuries, science itself passed beyond the points reached by Aristotle, Newton, Hume, and Kant. In discussing the current relation of science to Marxism, Colletti disregards the logical implications of the most outstanding achievement of the scientific mind: the verification of the universality of evolution in nature, society, and the thought process. The universe in which we live is itself evolving and expanding, and all heavenly bodies undergo evolution. There is now no known exception to the rule first enunciated by Heraclitus, that everything is in flux. This scientific truth, which lies at the basis of dialectical logic, limits the validity of the premises of formal thinking.

Let us select several examples from the sciences. The property of mass is one thing; the property of energy is another. The two are in fact different and even opposite states of matter. And so they were regarded in physics up to the time of Albert Einstein. Einstein demonstrated first in theory that mass and energy did not invariably exist in and of themselves; they were convertible one into the other under the appropriate material conditions; and he worked out a precise mathematical formula for this conversion. The conceptual and mathematical unification of these opposites was a dialectical discovery of the first order that inaugurated a new era for physics. The practical verification of the conversion of one of these "real opposites" into the other was dramatically demonstrated by atomic fission.

The opposed states of matter lost none of their concrete individual reality. What they did forfeit was the absolute separateness previously attributed to them in physical reality and their conceptual autonomy in physical theory.

Relativity theory performed a similar metamorphosis in regard to space and time. These were treated as independent, self-subsistent principles in Newton's and Kant's scheme of things.

Einstein fused the two aspects of material reality into the synthetic concept of space-time. From the logical and epistemological standpoint, Hegel's dialectics triumphed over Kant's formalism.

Recently, Soviet scientists produced element 107 by bombarding a bismuth target having 83 protons in its nucleus with chromium nuclei, which have 24 each (83 plus 24 equals 107 protons). The discreteness of things is relative and transitory; it can be broken down when an entity is transmuted into something quite different from what it was.

Going from physics to chemistry, in the latter half of the nineteenth century, the elements were arranged into the periodic table and aggregated into groups according to their atomic weights. At this juncture they were still treated as separate and immutable entities. Since the turn of the century, the elements have been discovered to be subject to change. The sun has been converting hydrogen into helium for almost five billion years. Practically all of the chemical elements in the periodic table have been artificially transmuted into neighboring elements under experimental conditions.

Colletti's supposition that contradiction has no place in nature directly contravenes the view of Marx, who held that contradictions are to be found in all sectors of reality—the physical world, society and its history, and our thinking about them. Thus in the section "The Metamorphosis of Commodities" in chapter 3 of volume I of *Capital* Marx writes:

> We saw in a former chapter that the exchange of commodities implies contradictory and mutually exclusive conditions. The further development of the commodity does not abolish these contradictions, but rather provides the form within which they have room to move. This is, in general, the way in which real contradictions are resolved. For instance, it is a contradiction to depict one body as constantly falling towards another and at the same time constantly flying away from it. The ellipse is a form of motion within which this contradiction is both realized and resolved.[21]

This paragraph from *Capital* refutes Colletti all along the line. First of all, in regard to the presence of contradiction in nature. Centripetal motion is one thing; centrifugal motion quite another. So far the Kantian logic of real opposites applies; these are diametrically different forms of motion.

Yet there are bodies that can be placed in both categories, that simultaneously partake of centrifugal and centripetal motion. They traverse elliptical orbits. Our own earth is one of them. Thus Colletti cannot logically account for the annual procession of the planet we live on by sticking exclusively to Kant's logic and ignoring Hegel's dialectics.

It is evident that each thing exists as a distinct entity in its singularity and that as such it stands counterposed to everything else and most fully to its own contrary. These features of reality became codified in the laws of formal logic. Then keener minds noticed that each distinctive thing or distinct state of being not only stands alone, by itself and in itself, but is also internally connected with another side of itself which forms an essential constituent of its own nature. This state of affairs is confirmed by their transformation into their own opposites in the course of further development.

This deeper insight into the nature of things and their change-ability became the basis of dialectical logic, which is the logic of motion, not of rest; of change, not invariability; of the overcoming of hard-and-fast distinctions and divisions in all domains. Thus centripetal and centrifugal motions surrender their separate identities in the case of elliptical motion, which is both one and the other, just as light has been shown to possess both particulate and wavelike properties.

The worth of Colletti's recommendations can be judged by how they are used to interpret *Capital*. Do they illuminate Marx's method of thought—or do they distort it? Engels wrote:

It is the merit of Marx that . . . he was the first to have brought to the fore again the forgotten dialectical method, its connection with Hegelian dialectics and its distinction from the latter, and at the same time to have applied this method in *Capital* to the facts of an empirical science, political economy.[22]

In the afterword to the second German edition of *Capital* Marx stated: "That the method employed in *Capital* has been little understood is shown by the various mutually contradictory conceptions that have been formed of it." He plainly says: "My dialectical method is, in its foundations, not only different from the Hegelian, but exactly opposite to it," because it views the ideal as "nothing but the material world reflected in the mind of man, and translated into forms of thought."[23]

Although he cites the above passage in his chapter on "Kant, Hegel, and Marx" in *Marxism and Hegel,* Colletti refuses to take Marx and Engels at their word. He argues that Marx was guided not by the dialectical method, but by "the logico-deductive method" à la Kant. To be sure, Marx employed deduction in his inquiries and even in his presentation, going from the general to the particular and the individual, as well as induction that proceeds in the opposite way. But these two types of inference used in ordinary reasoning are not the axis of his procedure. That is located in the dialectical developments dealt with at every step of the exposition. The Hegelophobic Colletti skirts these. His presentation sounds like a report on a modern factory that emphasizes the hand tools occasionally used by the workers and that slights the machine tools used in most of the operations.

On the level of logic, Colletti disqualifies the unity of opposites, which is the nucleus of the dialectical method. It is, he says, an "old metaphysical commonplace."[24] He defines this law of development in a one-sided way as solely an expression of mutual negatives. On the concept of dialectical opposition, he writes:

This is traditionally expressed by the formula "A not-A." It is the instance in which one opposite cannot stand without the other and vice-versa (mutual attraction of opposites). Not-A is the negation of A. In itself and for itself it is nothing; it is the negation of the other *and nothing else.*[25]

A for its part is simply the negation of not-A. This leaves out the affirmative side of a two-sided relation. Each term or pole in a unity of opposites, which is the essence of contradictoriness, has both a positive and negative aspect; one or the other may be uppermost in any given context.

This can readily be verified by turning to the first two sections of chapter 1 of *Capital,* where Marx discusses the two factors of commodities and the dual character of the labor embodied in them. Use-value is the negation of exchange-value, and vice versa. The one exists as a physical property that satisfies some human want; the other is a purely social attribute made manifest in the exchange of labor products. Nonetheless, these mutually exclusive characteristics coexist as inseparable aspects of the commodity. Its existence is unthinkable without both these qualities. Their interdependence is disclosed from the beginning in the elementary form, in which the exchange-value of one commodity is reflected in the use-value of another.

The contrast between concrete and abstract labor is not only mutually exclusive but reciprocally interactive. Each of these two forms of labor has its own characteristics. The specific activity of labor such as tailoring, carpentering, etc., forms the utility of objects; the undifferentiated expenditure of labor-power creates value in exchange. The labor represented by use and the labor represented by value are antithetical; the one is qualitative, the other quantitative. Abstract labor does not possess the characteristics that belong to labor as a creator of use-values, while concrete labor has no part in the formation of exchange-value. Yet both are structural aspects of the commodity, each contributing its own necessary element to the unity of opposites that constitutes it. Logically speaking, that material entity, the commodity, is a synthesis of the double antitheses of use-value and exchange-value, concrete and abstract labor. The capitalist labor process creates at one and the same time both use-value and exchange-value, the latter being the sole source of surplus-value.

Colletti reminds us that Kant himself refers to the example of debt. The debtor-creditor relationship is a highly contradictory economic reality in which the positive and negative aspects cannot be dissociated. A liability to the debtor is an asset to the creditor.

Colletti tries to make fun of dialectics by asking whether a car crash, "a typical instance of a 'real opposition', i.e. of two opposed forces, constitutes a daily verification of dialectical materialism."[26] This feeble jest exhibits a poor understanding of the ABCs of dialectics. A car crash is not a genuinely dialectical opposition because the relation between the two objects is only external and accidental, not internal and necessary, as the connections between use-value and exchange-value, and between concrete and abstract labor, are in the commodity.

Colletti has to get around the predominant role of the materialist dialectic in the method of *Capital* because of his belief that contradictions are purely subjective. The mind, he thinks, can create and consider contradictory statements, but material formations beyond the mind cannot contain contradictory features or forces. This at once places him at odds with Marx, who is concerned from first to last with analyzing the contradictory relations of capitalist society that supply its dynamics and that will, as they come to a head, lead to its undoing.

In his 1975 essay "Marxism and the Dialectic," Colletti makes a revision of his own previous interpretation of Marx's method in

Capital. This emendation is worth examining at some length for what it shows about the distance between Colletti and Marx.

There are two major camps among modern revisers of Marxism: the Hegelianizing thinkers who, like the young Georg Lukács and the Frankfurt school, retain dialectics while scanting its material content; and those such as Louis Althusser, Della Volpe, and Colletti, who uphold materialism while rejecting the dialectical method by seeking to hitch Marxism to the cart of the positivist ideology commonly associated with the natural sciences in the West.

The members of both schools (except Althusser) reject the idea of a dialectics of nature—and as a consequence seek to separate Marx from Engels—though for very different reasons. The Hegelianizing Marxists accept the view that society, *because* it is a human product, involves genuine contradiction, indeterminate states, and evolutionary change through the clash of opposites. Their rejection of Engels is founded on the fear of diminishing the role of human will and reason by granting an analogy between the forms of change in society and those in nature. Their outlook is essentially anthropocentric. If material determinism is granted in society as well as nature, human beings will never escape from blind necessity and achieve freedom.

The goal of Colletti and Althusser—despite Colletti's many trenchant criticisms of the latter—is to efface the existence of evolutionary states and revolutionary transcendence, that is, of genuine contradiction. Whereas the aim of the Hegelianizers is largely accomplished when they have severed Marx from Engels, the disjunction of the founding fathers of scientific socialism is only the beginning for the antidialectical materialists. They then have to cope with the problem that Marx is absolutely unequivocal on the operation of dialectical contradiction within society.

Colletti writes in his 1975 essay:

> If we leave to one side the few and isolated statements where Marx appears to ratify the "dialectic of matter", we must on the other hand take into account the impressive and incontrovertible fact that he left behind him *Capital,* the *Grundrisse,* the *Theories of Surplus Value*—in other words, not a cosmogony but an analysis of modern capitalism.[27]

Unfortunately for Colletti, Marx's entire analysis of modern capitalism is based on a methodology that Colletti considers a "scarcely disguised religion."[28] For many years Colletti, following his mentor Della Volpe, sought to meet this dilemma head-on by arguing that Marx was methodologically mistaken and that he confused simple oppositions of definite forces with contradictions in the full sense. Now he writes in hindsight, summarizing the opinion he formerly shared with Della Volpe:

What the *Diamatiker* [practitioners of dialectical materialism] described and describe as *contradictions* in the real world were in effect contrarieties, i.e. real oppositions and hence *non-contradictions*. Consequently Marxism, while continuing to speak of conflicts and of *objective oppositions* in reality, no longer had to claim for itself (and worse, seek to impose on science) a special logic of its own—the dialectic—that was at variance with and opposed to the logic followed by the existing sciences. Further: Marxism could henceforth continue to speak of struggles and of objective conflicts in nature and in society, making use of the non-contradictory logic of science; and better yet, it would henceforth be a science and practise science itself.[29]

Colletti's distinction here, taken from Kant (who owed it to Aristotle), between oppositions ("contrarieties") and contradictions, is a useful one. He scores some points by showing that some Marxists have occasionally cited as examples of contradictions phenomena that do not involve internal differentiation or the unity of opposites. But that hardly exhausts the matter. There are above all the processes of reciprocal action in the course of evolutionary development with their qualitative transmutations that involve other forms of change, evolution, and opposition that cannot be disposed of so easily.

This leaves him the choice of following Althusser, who has characterized the entire corpus of Marx's work, with the exception of the late *Notes on Wagner*, as tainted with Hegelian *Naturphilosophie*, or else to seek some common ground with the thinking of Marx for the analysis of, at least, modern capitalist society. Colletti set himself on the latter course in his 1975 essay, where he grants that his own previous views were insufficient and that in capitalist society, if in no other place, genuine contradiction can be found.

This admission might be regarded as a positive development on Colletti's part, a partial reconciliation with the views of Marx. As we shall see, however, Colletti's grounds for his new position are quite different from Marx's and constitute a move away from Marx toward the nonmaterialist outlook of the Hegelian school.

For Marx, all of class society and each of its distinctive stages is characterized by an organic unity of opposites represented by the ruling class and the exploited producers, whether the latter are slaves, serfs, or wage-laborers. The dialectical process that Marx saw at work in social evolution, whose motor is the class struggle, was summarized by him in his famous "Preface to the Critique of Political Economy" (1859). There he wrote:

In the social production of their existence, men inevitably enter into definite relations, which are independent of their will, namely relations of production appropriate to a given stage in the development of their material forces of production. The totality of these relations of production constitutes the economic structure of society, the real foundation, on which arises a legal and political superstructure and to which correspond definite forms of social consciousness. The mode of production of material life conditions the general process of social, political and intellectual life. It is not the consciousness of men that determines their existence, but their social existence that determines their consciousness. At a certain stage of development, the material productive forces of society come into conflict with the existing relations of production or—this merely expresses the same thing in legal terms—with the property relations within the framework of which they have operated hitherto. From forms of development of the productive forces these relations turn into their fetters. Then begins an era of social revolution. The changes in the economic foundation lead sooner or later to the transformation of the whole immense superstructure.[30]

Here it is plain that the central dialectical contradiction in class society rests in its very bedrock in the evolution of the forces of production within the framework of a definite set of productive relations. The forces of production are not a fixed magnitude. The concept of contrariety is inadequate to explain the accumulation of quantitative changes in the forces of production that reach at a certain point a qualitative sundering of the old relations of production. The specific unity of opposites explodes in the destruction of the old society and the transformation of the superstructure to the mold of a new socioeconomic formation.

This is not an analysis restricted to capitalist society. Moreover, the two poles of the social contradictions Marx discusses are both genuine material realities, albeit ones that are bound together in a single totality. This is quite different from the Kantian concept of contradiction defended by Colletti. Colletti maintains with Kant that contradiction exists solely in the mind, not in the perceived external reality. He seeks to prove that Hegel in effect shares this view by arguing that contradiction for Hegel involved two poles, the pole of material phenomena and the pole of organizing reason, the Absolute Idea. Either one taken alone was for Hegel unreal. Colletti concludes triumphantly that because the poles of social contradiction, in particular the counterposed antagonistic social classes, have obvious materiality, they do not meet Hegel's definition of "contradiction."

But it is precisely here that he ignores Marx's placing of the Hegelian dialectic on material foundations. Naturally, for Marx, both poles of social contradiction, the classes in struggle with each other over the material resources and administration of society, are "real." Nevertheless, they are specific classes *only* in relation to each other. There can be no class of slave owners without the existence of slaves, and no slaves without masters.

*   *   *

Colletti's new epistemological position does not depart from his former view that dialectical opposition can exist only in the mind and not in reality. How, then, can dialectics be characteristic of a whole society and not just the mental processes of its individual members? That is the dilemma he has to resolve.

His answer is to seek unique features of capitalist society that reproduce on a social scale what he sees as the illusions of individual thought. He finds these in alienation and the fetishism of commodities. Thus for Colletti, what is most fundamentally contradictory about capitalist society is not, as Marx would have it, the opposition of labor and capital, or the opposition between the expanding forces of production and the fetters of private property. It lies instead in the false way in which capitalism induces people under its spell to *perceive* their social relations. Colletti does not acknowledge first and foremost the contradictory character of the production and reproduction of social life, but rather the contradictions manifested in the circulation of commodities and in the ideological reflection of this process.

To make clear what this issue is about, let us restate Marx's view on the fetishism of commodities, which he presents in the first chapter of volume I of *Capital*. In precapitalist society, Marx writes, "relations of personal dependence form the given social foundation." As a result, labor and the products of labor "take the shape, in the transactions of society, of services in kind and payment in kind."[31] In such a society the relations of lordship and bondage are obvious and transparent for all to see.

It is otherwise under capitalism, where distribution is mediated by the market and the exchange of commodities. Exchange seems to take place not between people but between money and commodities, that is, between things. Value appears to be a quality inherent in material objects, not a *social* relationship founded on a society-wide division of labor based on private property in the means of production. Labor appears as a private, individual occupation, not as a component of social labor.

To the producers, therefore, the social relations between their private labors appear as what they are, i.e. they do not appear as direct social relations between persons in their work, but rather as material [*dinglich*] relations between persons and social relations between things.[32]

For example, gold is in nature only a metal with special properties; that is its substantial reality. The Incas, who did not use gold as money but for ornament, personified this thing as "the tears of the sun."

Peoples who have progressed beyond such anthropomorphic metaphors may nonetheless believe that gold is "naturally" money. When they say that gold is per se more valuable than iron, this judgment mistakes the physical properties that make this metal suitable to serve as money for the essential social relationships that endow gold with its value. Value and its money form are exclusively *social* attributes. Gold becomes money only by functioning as the universal equivalent of the value of commodities, the outcome of a prolonged socioeconomic development.

The fetishism of commodities is an inseparable feature of the capitalist mode of production. It flows from the anarchic, decentralized, unplanned character of capitalist economy. It underlies the generation of false consciousness among the mass of the producers, by giving rise to the illusion of equal exchange between capital and labor. Money (wages) is exchanged for a commodity (labor power), an exchange that hides the relation of exploitation between the employer and the worker. (More on this later.)

For Marx, the fetishism of commodities is an expression not of the most profound and determinant contradictions of capitalism, which lie in the realm of production, but a necessary form of appearance of these contradictions on the level of mass psychology. Colletti seeks to found a general theory of capitalist contradiction on the opposition between the forces of production organized by capitalist society, which he takes as a noncontradictory given, and the superstructural reflection of the relations of production summed up in the concepts of alienation and fetishism. While the latter gives him the mental, "unreal" side of the contradiction he seeks, it is a move away from the material basis of the dialectical conflict presented in Marx's analysis.

The fetishism of commodities is not, as Colletti implies, the central feature of capitalism or the source and seat of its principal contradictions. The fundamental contradictions of capitalism flow from the conflict between the developing forces of production and the relations of production, the conflict between the socialized character of the production and circulation process and the private appropriation of their results, and the growing antagonism between the proletariat and the bourgeoisie.

Fetishism is one of the manifestations of the exchange relations of capitalist economy. That is its objective basis. It is a false form of consciousness, a distorted impression imposed on people's minds because of the indirect ties of production. A close analogy is the deceptive perception we have that the sun moves around the earth every twenty-four hours, whereas in reality the earth is spinning on its own axis.

The fetishism of commodities itself exemplifies the dialectical interdependence of appearance and reality. Thus a certain commodity such as cattle or gold turns into money because all other commodities express their value in it. That is the reality of the metamorphosis. However, they seem to express their value in it because it is money. Such a notion conceals and reverses the actual state of affairs and its evolution.

In contrast to commodity fetishism, the process of alienation is deeply embedded in the underlying productive relations of capitalism. Although economic, political, cultural, and psychological manifestations of alienation are more widespread and acute in contemporary bourgeois society, alienation preceded capitalism and will persist in the period of transition to socialism. Under capitalism the dominant element is the alienation of wage-labor, which has been effected by the prerequisites of the capitalist mode of production. These are the dispossession of the laborers from all the material means of production and their concentration in the hands of capitalist owners who are thereby entitled to appropriate surplus labor. Having previously been deprived of any control over the conditions of production, the workers' own labor is alienated from them by the sale of their labor-power to the boss. All the alienated relations that run through the fabric of capitalist society are derived from or reinforced by its economic forms of production and property.

Colletti contends that Marx's political economy is above all a theory of alienation.[33] He also writes that "the theory of value was entirely at one with the theory of alienation and fetishism."[34] This identification of the law of value with two outgrowths of its operation misrepresents the prime purpose of *Capital*, which is to present a scientific explanation of the laws of development of the capitalist mode of production. As part of his work, Marx does deal with the processes of alienation and fetishism among his other contributions to economic and social science. He integrates his studies on these subjects into a comprehensive exposition of the movement of the capitalist system from its origins to its replacement by a higher form of economic life.

Ironically, by pivoting his interpretation of *Capital* around alienation and fetishism rather than the dialectical development of its productive forces and relations as Marx, the historical materialist, does, Colletti takes a step toward Hegel's manner of thought and is partially Hegelianizing Marx's political economy, a transformation he considers the worst of abominations. It was not Marx but Hegel who identified the theory of alienation with the working of contradiction in society. Hegel construed labor as alienating by its very nature: by externalizing this human capacity it deprived humans of something that previously belonged to them; and because needs always exceed production, they can never be satisfied. Marx thought that labor undergoes alienation only under certain historical conditions which can be overcome at a higher level of socioeconomic development.

Colletti knows this full well. But by converting alienation and fetishism into the focal points of *Capital* and its contradictions, he retranslates Marx's economic categories into philosophical terms. This reverses the course of Marx's own thought, which began in its earliest stage with the abstract notions of speculative philosophy and moved forward to the specific concepts expressing the relations of production proper to political economy.

When Colletti writes that money is "a product of alienation," he reminds us of the German literati who, as the *Communist Manifesto* pointed out, "wrote their philosophical nonsense beneath the French original. For instance, beneath the French criticism of the economic functions of money, they wrote 'Alienation of Humanity'."[35] While money does give rise to many kinds of alienated relations and is based upon the alienation of a value of no use to its owner in exchange for something useful, in economic history and in the terms of political economy, money is the product of the differentiation of a particular use-value out of the multitude of others to serve as a general and universal equivalent of value. This is its prosaic historical origin.

This makes the money-commodity into the antithesis of all other commodities. Here again we meet with the operation of the unity of opposites that Colletti scorns. This invaluable instrument of theoretical analysis not only enabled Marx to decipher the twofold character of commodities and of labor that baffled his predecessors. It also made it possible to trace the metamorphosis of property rights in their evolution from elementary and marginal commodity production to the capitalist mode with its intensive exploitation of wage labor and its form of wealth as "an immense collection of commodities."

Marx explained how the law of private property based on commodity production and circulation was transformed into its direct opposite in line with its internal dialectic. The laws of commodity production originally justified a property right in individual labor, as with such small producers as peasants and artisans who face each other on the market as commodity owners with equal rights. The means to obtain the other commodity, or the commodity of others, is through the sale of the commodity previously produced by one's own labor.

However, under capitalist relations, private property functions in the opposite manner—on the side of the capitalist as the right to appropriate the unpaid labor or produce of others, on the side of the worker or small independent commodity producer, as the impossibility of appropriating one's own product. This reversal of property rights, which is a boon to the capitalist and a curse to the worker, small peasant, and artisan, is logically inexplicable without invoking the unity and struggle of opposites ruled out by Colletti.

As capitalism develops, the alienation of labor and the fetishism of commodities exert their most powerful and pernicious effect in connection with the exchange relations between the capitalist and the worker. The legally validated claim that equal values are represented on each side of the bargain in the labor market conceals the mechanism of exploitation whereby labor is alienated from the worker. It appears as though the workers are paid for the full value of their work. Yet they receive only enough of it to survive and reproduce their kind while the capitalist pockets the unpaid surplus labor.

The objective basis of their irrepressible struggle is the conflict over the division of the value the laborers produce; the more the workers manage to get, the less goes to the capitalist and vice versa. Surplus labor time exists only in antithesis to necessary labor time (again, unity of opposites!).

However, the reality of these productive relations is masked by the illusion arising from the fact that, in accord with the rules of the market, equal values are being exchanged in the sale and purchase of labor-power, the only commodity the worker possesses. Marx's conclusions on labor value and surplus-value exposed the fallacy behind this illusion by showing how the laws of commodity circulation became transformed into their opposite in the productive relations between the capitalist possessors and the disinherited workers. What appears as equal exchange on the surface is exploitation in reality.

It is not alienation and commodity fetishism by themselves but the specific exploitative relations between capital and labor that distinguish the capitalist mode of production, its socioeconomic formation, historical period, and stage of economic evolution from all others. To be sure, alienation and commodity fetishism play their parts in producing and maintaining this oppressive relationship by enveloping its manifestations in mystification so that things are not what they seem to be at first glance but are in fact their exact opposite. The capitalists do not support the workers by giving them jobs; the workers support the monied parasites by yielding up their surplus labor. The critical analyses of Marxist political economy demystify and explain these phenomena by distinguishing the real movement of the class relationships from their outward semblances.

Consider interest-bearing capital, which is the perfected and most mystified form of the fetishism of capital. Here it seems as though "money breeds money" autonomously, without any connection with the process of production where the real action of exploitation takes place. On the surface the loan and its repayment appear simply as a transaction between one capitalist and another. All the determining factors of capital are obliterated and its real elements invisible, though interest is actually in origin and substance a part of the unpaid labor appropriated by the operating capitalist from the worker in the shape of surplus-value. While the inner nature of capitalist production is objectively manifested in the interest accruing from the mere ownership of capital, it does so in a completely inverted and deranged guise.[36]

When a savings bank advertises: "Let your money work for you," it is appealing to a fetishistic notion. Under capitalism the social relationships refracted through money enable its owner to receive interest on loans. Despite the appearance, the thing itself, money, does no work. Only people engage in labor—and the interest is in reality a fraction of the abstract labor expended by the working class and made manifest as value.

Both commodity fetishism and alienation are themselves contradictory phenomena. It is a contradiction that the product of the workers' labor belongs not to them but to the boss, who buys their labor-power, and that the total product in the form of value becomes an alien and uncontrollable power dominating the working class and society as a whole. These contradictions do not exist simply in the minds of people, who may not give them the slightest thought, or in the pages of *Capital*. They are materialized in the antagonistic interests between the exploiters and exploited. If his conclusions were consistent with his logical premises, Colletti's conception of contradiction would convert these objective relations of production into mere relations between contrary propositions.

Is it not a contradiction that the laboring majority has no control over the material conditions of production required for their livelihood, whereas the capitalist minority has a monopoly of them, by which it seizes the surplus-value of the work force? Under capitalism, "the relationship of labour to the conditions of labour is turned upside-down, so that it is not the worker who makes use of the conditions of labour, but the conditions of labour which make use of the worker."[37]

This coercive relation, which places the workers at the mercy of the capitalist slave drivers, is an objective fact. Although Colletti runs into contradictions like these at every turn, he refuses to acknowledge their objective character simply because his shallow and subjective view of contradiction precludes him from doing so.

To back up his misreading of *Capital*, Colletti asserts that Marx shares his view that contradiction is a feature peculiar to capitalism because of its inverted relations.

From Marx's perspective, contradition is the *specific* feature of capitalism, the characteristic or quality which singles it out not only with respect to all other forms of society, but with respect to all other cosmic phenomena.[38]

This arbitrary limitation has no foundation either in cosmic reality, human history, or Marx's thought. The exploitative relations between slaveholder and slave, feudal lord and serf, were no less contradictory and antagonistic, even though the modes of extracting surplus labor by the owners and controllers of the means of production were different. The contradictions within the commodity between use-value and exchange-value, between concrete private labor and abstract social labor, and between the world of commodities and money are all to be found in the elementary commodity production and circulation of precapitalist times, though in an immature and restricted state. They come to full bloom in the contradiction between capital and wage-labor under generalized commodity production, in which the use-value of labor-power is the source of the surplus-value indispensable for capital accumulation. And surely there are plenty of contradictions in the postcapitalist formations of our century, even though they are not the same as those that characterize capitalist relations.

Colletti indulges in a rather tortuous argument to demonstrate that the false mental perceptions induced by commodity fetishism and alienation are the only source of capitalist contradiction. Since for him, one side of his newly conceded "dialectical opposition" in capitalist society must remain "unreal," he is unable to share with Marx the concept of an actual unity of opposites in struggle. Instead he conceives of two separate poles whose relation to each other is unclear. On the one side is the actual capitalist economy, where the laws of political economy have as much objective validity and determinate reality as the laws of nature. But:

From the other point of view these laws, which appear to have a material or objective character, are nothing other than the *fetishistic objectification* of human social relations which are beyond the control of men themselves. They do not represent natural objectivities, but alienation.[39]

Colletti in fact disjoins what he calls contradiction in capitalist society into two mutually exclusive parts, whose interaction he admits he cannot describe. On the "real" side of the equation are the productive forces and the relations of production; on the other, the unreal realm of reified consciousness. This is reflected in his misconception of the "two Marxes."

*   *   *

Many Western sociologists are troubled by the problem of whether Marxism can be both scientific and revolutionary. Colletti is among them. He tries to solve this false dilemma by splitting Marx into two parts, concerned alternately with these two irreconcilable "opposites." On the one side there is Marx the scientific political economist, who delineates the laws of economic motion of capitalism, and on the other there is Marx the moral philosopher, who demands the overthrow of capitalism's fetishistic objectification of human social relations.

This antithesis between scientific work and revolutionary activity is as false as Colletti's postulation of the "two Marxes." Through the scientific method of historical materialism, Marx arrived at the revolutionary conclusions in theory which he put into practice throughout his adult life. Depressed and disoriented by the evils of Stalinism and the delay in the advent of proletarian victories in the West, Colletti, like others, cannot envisage the harmonious unity between science and revolution that characterizes genuine Marxism.

If we look closely at his construct, a striking fact emerges. In the summarizing conclusion to his 1975 essay, Colletti writes:

For Marx, capitalism is contradictory not because it is a *reality* and all realities are contradictory, but because it is an *upside-down*, inverted reality (alienation, fetishism).[40]

If these words mean what they seem to mean, then Colletti has not really budged from his infatuation with Kant and his rejection of materialist dialectics. What he recognizes as "real" in capitalist society is only its economic substructure, in which he denies any intrinsic dialectical contradiction, in accord with Kant's epistemology. He takes the mystified ideological superstructure of capitalist society and denies it any status as "reality."

The only contradiction he really admits is the unresolvable one Kant himself granted, that between the thing-for-ourselves of "phenomenal" reality—the province of science—and, across an unbridgeable gulf, the "noumenal" mental world of moral practice—the province of morality, will, and faith. Starting from Kant's epistemology and logic, there is no interaction between the two poles. The "two Marxes" of Lucio Colletti have become "real opposites," and "never the twain shall meet" within his framework of thought.

The real Marx had a unitary view of the contradictions of capitalist society. The negating pole of the main contradiction for him was not the generation of false consciousness through commodity circulation but the growth of the productive forces and with them the development of the proletariat, its organization and class consciousness. The actual Marx saw the progressive resolution of capitalist contradictions in the revolutionary reconstruction of society. The Kantianized Marx of Lucio Colletti suffers from the same inability to unite theory and practice that characterized Kant as a philosopher. Colletti admits as much in his final pessimistic conclusion:

The social sciences have not yet found a true foundation of their own. Hence I do not know whether the existence of these two aspects [of Marx] is fatal or advantageous. What is not at issue is the fact that our task now is to find out whether and how they can be reconciled.[41]

Colletti alleges that there is no reference to revolution in *Capital.* So gross an oversight comes from his disregard for the dialectical denouement of its evolution. While Marx's work is centered on setting forth the laws of motion of the capitalist system, it unmistakably points to the outcome of the whole historical tendency of capitalist accumulation. In chapter 32 of volume I of *Capital,* Marx explains the consequences of the expropriation of the smaller and weaker individual private producers by the big capitalists, which makes them in turn ripe for collective expropriation by the revolutionary workers. The process of alienation wherein the capitalists and workers occupy opposite poles is at bottom a process of exploitation and enslavement which the workers resist and, under extremely explosive circumstances, revolt against:

Along with the constant decrease in the number of capitalist magnates, who usurp and monopolize all the advantages of this process of transformation, the mass of misery, oppression, slavery, degradation and exploitation grows; but with this there also grows the revolt of the working

class. . . . The centralization of the means of production and the socialization of labour reach a point at which they become incompatible with
their capitalist integument. This integument is burst asunder. The knell
of capitalist private property sounds. The expropriators are expropriated.[42]

This lawful process is dialectical. Capitalist monopoly is the
negation of individual private property in the means of production:

But capitalist production begets, with the inexorablility of a natural
process, its own negation. This is the negation of the negation.[43]

At the time the first volume of *Capital* was published this
might have seemed like an unjustifiable extrapolation prompted
by Hegelian metaphysics or "subjective utopianism." There are
many who still think so. Since then, the expropriators have been
expropriated one way or another in fourteen countries. Although
the dispossession of capitalist power and property may proceed
too slowly and haltingly for our desires, and while the course
taken by the socialist revolution on the world arena has been
highly contradictory to date, it has gone forward in our century
in accord with the laws discovered by Marx.

The still partial resolution of the irreconcilable historical
conflict between capital and labor brings us back to the respective logics of Kant and Hegel as construed by Colletti. He
approves the following statement by Kant:

In a real opposition one of the opposed determinations can never be the
contradictory contrary of the other [note this well (Colletti's interjection—
G.N.)], since in such a case the contrast would be of a logical character. . . .[44]

Kant thereby categorically counterposes real forces to contradictory relations, although the one is not at all incompatible with
the other. This distinction, which Colletti regards as all-
important, comes to grief when it is applied to capital-labor
relations.

The class struggle between the capitalists and the workers
involves a clash of real social forces—and these stand in dialectical contradiction to one another. Each has antithetical material
interests to defend that pull them in divergent directions. Yet at

the same time, on the plane of social relations, they are organically interconnected within the capitalist framework, the existence of one being dependent upon the existence of the other.

According to Hegel's conception of the movement of contradiction, the negative pole in the relation of opposites has the potential of annulling the positive pole, and, when the state of equilibrium, of dominance and subordination, is broken, proceeds to do so. Thus, in the course of development, the antagonistic interests of the contending classes lead to the disruption of the social and political equilibrium and ultimately to the downfall of the previously superior power.

It is the sharpening of the main inner contradictions, as capitalism develops, between the capitalists and the workers, between the outmoded national boundaries and the international operation of the capitalist economy, and between socialized production and private appropriation that generate the crisis-ridden condition of the system today. Such is the logic of the basic structural features of its development. That is not how Colletti conceives of the matter. He concludes: "Capitalist oppositions are, for Marx, dialectical contradictions and not real oppositions."[45]

What else can this mean but that there is no *necessary* antagonism in the relations between capital and labor, no definite connection between the laws of motion of the capitalist economy and the preparation of proletarian revolution? Such a theoretical position draws him closer to the outlook of an ethical socialism than to scientific socialism. Revolutionary action is reduced to a moral imperative.

In a broadcast given over BBC to mark the centennial of the publication of the first volume of *Capital*, Isaac Deutscher had this to say about the role of dialectics in that work:

Dialectics is indeed the grammar of Marxist thinking. But just as one shows one's mastery of grammar not in reciting its rules, but in living speech, so one shows one's grasp of dialectics not in mulling over its formulas, but in coming to grips with specific, large and vital issues in history and contemporary affairs. No doubt, the rules of dialectics have to be learned; a good manual, like a good grammatical textbook, has its uses. But a one-sided preoccupation with abstract methodology is often a form of ideological escapism, even if those who indulge in it love to dwell on "Praxis" and spell "Praxis" with a capital "P". *Das Kapital* is the supreme example of the dialectical mind in action, of the dialectical mind using all its power of abstraction to plow up layer after layer of empirical social experience. Marx was, of course, greatly concerned with the problems of his philosophical workshop as well, and with the nature of his intellectual tools, those he had inherited from others and those he himself invented. But the workshop and the tools were not ends in themselves—they were there to process the economic and sociopolitical raw material and to turn out the finished product.[46]

There is more truth and wisdom in this one paragraph than in all of Colletti's strained efforts to excise the dialectic from Marx's reasoning and turn *Capital,* the preeminent model of the method of materialist dialectics, into a learned commentary on alienation and fetishism.

*   *   *

These past and present disputes over the theory of knowledge and the method of *Capital* are not merely a matter of academic interest. They are directly relevant to the solution of pressing social and political problems. The nature of the Soviet Union sixty years after the October revolution is one of the most controversial issues in radical circles today.

According to Moscow's official doctrine, the Soviet Union is socialist from top to bottom and on the way to communism. Peking contends that the Soviet Union is a capitalist, fascist, imperialist state.

Despite their diametrically different conclusions, both of these centers of Stalinist theorizing follow the same logic. They assume that the Soviet Union is a homogeneous whole, possessing an identical content in all respects. This is a formalistic, not a dialectical, method of analyzing its stages of development since 1917.

In reality, the Soviet political structure underwent a deepgoing transformation from the workers' democracy of Lenin's time to the dictatorship of Stalinism. The Soviet Union is an extremely contradictory social formation in which an antisocialist totalitarian political system intermeshes with a postcapitalist nationalized and planned economy. Whereas the ruling bureaucratic caste and its regime are reactionary, the nationalized and planned economy which it mismanages is highly progressive. Although, according to the thought pattern of formalistic thinkers, such a mating of opposites is impossible, this definition corresponds to the real, contradictory state of affairs.

Where does Colletti stand on this crucial question? He does reject the theory that the Soviet Union has restored capitalism. He also considers Trotsky's treatment of the USSR in *The Revolution Betrayed* to be an exemplary model of analysis. But when it comes to drawing a specific conclusion as to the class character of the Soviet state he does not accept Trotsky's dialectical characterization. In an earlier essay, "The Question of Stalin," he did concur with Trotsky that the Soviet Union was a "society of transition" from capitalism to socialism, but he balked at accepting the more concrete materialist definition of a "degenerated workers' state." At the same time, he "cannot propose any more precise definition."[47] This agnostic partisan of Kantian epistemology might find it easier to arrive at an answer if he did not reject the objective reality of contradiction in social structures that accords with the insights of the materialist dialectic.

Colletti sincerely wishes to surmount the stagnation of socialist theory in the West and help resolve the crisis of Marxism. He admits that he cannot yet wholly foresee the outcome of his drastic reconstruction of dialectical materialism. From the orientation of his thinking and the results of his reevaluations to date, the prognosis is none too favorable. He is not following in the footsteps of Marx but departing from his path. In going back to Kant instead of moving forward from Hegel, as Feuerbach, Marx, and Engels did, he is not modernizing and improving Marxism but mutilating its principles and relapsing into outmoded ideas.

That is not all. His retrogression in the philosophical and theoretical spheres has been attended by a political accommodation to reformism. His break from the Stalinist camp has not led forward to revolutionary Marxist positions but backward to Social Democracy.

Colletti has become a supporter of the Italian Socialist Party (PSI), which belongs to the Second International. Nowadays he envisages in Eurocommunism the opportunity for some kind of organic unity between the Socialist and Communist parties, if the CPs move further along in their "affirmation of democracy" and radically revise some essential themes of the doctrines of Marx, Lenin, and Gramsci. This would entail, he argues, opting for the "historical compromise" of CP participation in a coalition government with the Christian Democracy aimed at democratizing rather than combatting the bourgeois state and replacing it with a workers' regime.[48]

*   *   *

The most widely read theorists of Western Marxism deform its principles along two quite different lines. One tendency (the early Georg Lukács, Jean-Paul Sartre, Henri Lefèbvre, the Frankfurt school, et al.) submerges its materialism; the other (Althusser, Colletti, and even Timpanaro) seeks to do away with its dialectical mainspring. Notwithstanding their polemics against one another, both camps strike at dialectical materialism in one or another of its vital parts. The unique philosophical contribution of Marx and Engels was their synthesis of a consistent and comprehensive materialist world view with a theory of universal evolution that was thoroughly dialectical. These two lines of thought had previously been developed separately and were considered incompatible.

To separate one of these components from the other and disparage either is to impair, if not to undo, their achievement.

If Marxism is to retain—and after the debacle of Stalinism, to regain—the scientific rigor of its founders, it must hold fast to both sides of their teachings: the materialist basis and the dialectical mode of thought. These constitute an indissoluble unity, as its most qualified adherents have recognized in the past.

Is Nature Dialectical?

I

Comment on a Debate by George Novack

On December 7, 1961, six thousand young people gathered in a Paris auditorium to listen to a debate on dialectics by four noted French scholars. Such a meeting would be as unlikely in New York as the outdoor recitals poets give before large crowds in Moscow. Different countries, different customs—and different levels of cultural and intellectual development.

The participants in the symposium represented the two most widely discussed philosophies of our time: existentialism and Marxism. Neither trend of thought has the following in the United States that the first has in Western Europe or the second in Communist countries. America's ideological life is provincial and lags far behind the most advanced movements elsewhere.

Jean-Paul Sartre, possibly the most influential living man of letters, and Jean Hyppolite, Sorbonne professor and Hegelian scholar, upheld the existentialist viewpoint. Roger Garaudy of the Political Bureau of the French Communist Party, director of its Center for Marxist Studies and Research, and author of numerous philosophical works, and Jean-Pierre Vigier, one of France's leading theoretical physicists, spoke for Marxism. Their topic was: "Is the dialectic solely a law of history or is it also a law of nature?"

It is possible to hold one of three main positions on this question. The first is that dialectics is sheer metaphysics, a vestige of theology, an aberration of logic, meaningless verbiage which has no reference to reality and is useless for scientific thought in any field. This is the opinion of almost all scholars, scientists, and those trained by them in the universities of the U.S. and England, where empiricism, positivism, and pragmatism hold sway.

Another is that dialectics is valid in certain domains but not in others. Adherents of partial dialectics usually maintain that its laws apply to mental or social processes but not to nature. For them a dialectic of nature belongs to Hegelian idealism, not to a consistent materialism. This position has been put forward by quite a number of Marxists and semi-Marxists. Such is the view taken by the existentialists Sartre and Hyppolite.

The third position is that dialectical materialism deals with the entire universe and its logic holds good for all the constituent sectors of reality which enter into human experience: nature, society, and thought. The laws of dialectics, which have arisen out of the investigation of universal processes of becoming and modes of being, apply to all phenomena. Although each level of being has its own specific laws, these merge with general laws covering all spheres of existence and development, which constitute the content and shape the method of materialist dialectics. This view, held by the creators of scientific socialism and their authentic disciples, was defended in the debate by Garaudy, Vigier, and the chairman, Jean Orcel, professor of mineralogy at the National Museum of Natural History.

An American would consider it strange that the controversy on the question should take place only between two schools of dialecticians, one piecemeal, the other thoroughgoing. Very few people in the United States today are convinced that dialectical logic of any kind is worth serious consideration.

A broad spectrum of attitudes toward Marxism is exhibited in the Soviet Union, the United States, and France. In the U.S., where capitalism reigns supreme, anything associated with socialism and communism is depreciated, if not tabooed. Marxism is regarded as obsolete, its philosophy false.

In the Soviet Union, where the socialist revolution abolished capitalism decades ago, dialectical materialism is the state philosophy. Under Stalin, in fact, it became scholasticized and ossified, as Vigier admits and Hyppolite testifies. The latter tells how during a recent visit the Soviet Academy of Sciences contrived to have him talk to the students about mechanism instead of existentialism, as he wished. However, all the questions after his lecture related to existentialism. "It seems to me that the youth were strongly interested in Sartre's existential philosophy," he dryly observes.

The intellectual and political climate of France stands between those of the major cold war antagonists. There is lively tension and continual intercourse between Marxist and non-Marxist currents of thought, and especially between the politically oriented atheistic existentialists such as Sartre, and various exponents of Marxism. Sartre and C. Wright Mills reflect the ideological differences between their two countries. Mills held a place among radical intellectuals in the English-speaking world like that of Sartre in Europe. Yet in his last work, *The Marxists,* Mills dismissed the laws of dialectics as something "mysterious, which Marx never explains clearly but which his disciples claim to use." Indeed, even this footnote reference was an afterthought added to his original manuscript in deference to friendly critics.

Such a blackout of dialectics would be unthinkable for Sartre. He was educated and lives in an environment where both Hegelian and Marxist philosophies are taken seriously, on a continent where scientific socialism has influenced intellectual and public life for almost a century, and in a country where the Communist Party gets a quarter of the vote and has the allegiance of much of the working class. He has developed his own ideas in contact and contest with Marxism, from the time he propounded the philosophy of existence as its rival to the present stage, when he conceives of existentialism as a subordinate ideology within Marxism which aspires to renovate and enrich it.

Mills took from Marxism only those elements that suited his empirical sociology and New Left orientation. He cut the dialectical heart out of the Marxist method of thought and presented what was left as the whole organism. Sartre has a higher esteem for dialectics. But as we shall see, he too accepts only what can be fitted into his Marxized existentialism.

The transcript of this Paris debate between existentialists and Marxists is worth examining at length because many of the chief objections to materialist dialectics were posed and answered in the light of present-day scientific developments.

Sartre's case against a dialectic of nature is quite different from that of an American pragmatist or positivist. His arguments are distinctively existentialist.

He agrees that history and knowledge are dialectical processes because they are created by humanity and humanity is involved in their development. There is a historical materialism but no dialectical materialism. Dialectics is internal to history. The province of dialectics cannot go beyond human practice. It is illegitimate to extend dialectical laws to nonhistorical, nonhuman phenomena. Sartre presents three main reasons for this restriction:

1. Dialectics deals only with concrete totalities which human beings themselves "totalize" through practice. History and society are such. Nature, on the other hand, does not constitute a single integrated whole. Nature may be infinite, even contain an infinity of infinites. But it consists of fragmented totalities which have no inner unity, no universal and necessary interconnection. The disunity of nature forbids any universal dialectic.

2. The contradictions operating in history cannot be the same as antagonisms in nature. Social contradictions are based upon the reciprocal conditioning and organic interpenetration of their contending sides through human mediation. The opposing forces inside a physical-chemical system are not interactive and interrelated in this way. Brute matter, the "practico-inert," is disjointed, dispersed, resistant to dialectical movement.

3. We can know society and history from the inside, as they really are, because they are the work of humanity, the result of our decision and action. Their dialectical linkages are disclosed through the contradictory interplay of subject and situation. But physical phenomena remain external to us and to other objects. They are opaque to our insight. We cannot penetrate to their real inner nature and grasp their essence.

In sum, nature must be nondialectical because of its disunity, its lack of contradiction, its insurmountable externality and inertia. The only possible dialectical materialism is historical materialism, which views our establishment of relations with the rest of reality from the standpoint of our action upon it.

Orthodox Marxists revert to theology and metaphysics, says Sartre, by extending dialectical laws over nature on purely philosophical or methodological grounds. He does, however, concede that dialectical laws may at some point be found applicable to nature. But only by way of analogy. This presently involves a risky extrapolation, which must await verification through further findings by the natural scientists. And even if they should discover that physical processes resemble the dialectical type and start to use dialectical models in their research, this would provide no insight into the nature of nature, no true knowledge of its essential features.

Thus the existentialist Sartre turns out to be a positivist in his last word on the possible relations of dialectics to the physical world. For him the ideas of this logic can be no more than handy hypotheses in metaphorical dress that may help scientists order and clarify their data but cannot reflect the content of nature.

Sartre is not consistent in his effort to imprison dialectics in the social world and strike it out of prehuman and nonhuman phenomena. His arguments against the dialectics of nature are more fully set forth in his 1960 philosophical work of 755 pages, *Critique of Dialectical Reason*, of which the first part was published here in 1963 under the title *Search for a Method*. There he admits that living matter, at least, may develop dialectically. Sartre writes: "The organism engenders the negative as that which disrupts its unity; disassimilation and excretion are still opaque and biological forms of negation in so far as they are a movement oriented toward rejection." This exception opens a breach in his position. Garaudy correctly observes that once Sartre has recognized that negation and totalization exist in the prehuman state, it will be difficult to stop halfway and keep dialectics confined to biology without extending its jurisdiction to the rest of nature.

In his rejoinder to Sartre, who wishes to see only partial unities or specific totalities in nature, Vigier points out that nature is a whole made up of myriad parts. The reality of the universe we inhabit is both material and dialectical. Its unity is expressed in an infinite series of levels of existence. Each of the specific realms of being which collectively constitute the material universe is finite, partial; it incorporates only a limited aspect of the whole. In itself nature is endless and inexhaustible. It forever generates new properties, modes, and fields of existence. There are no limits to what it has been, to what it now is, to what it may become.

One of the major errors of mechanical and metaphysical thought about nature, Vigier says, is the notion that it is based upon ultimate elements from which everything else issues and with which the rest of reality can be built up. This conception, which goes back to the Greek atomists, has been carried forward by the natural scientists who believed that molecules, atoms, and then "elementary" particles were the basic building blocks of the entire universe.

Actually science has been developing along different lines, both in regard to the universe at large (the macrocosm) and to the subatomic domain (the microcosm). There is no foreseeable end to astronomical phenomena or our discovery of them, as the recently discovered "black holes" indicate. What appears immobile on one level is really in flux at another level. There are in principle no irreducible or immutable elements in nature. This has just been reconfirmed by the acknowledgment that so-called elementary particles can no longer be considered the ultimate objects of microphysics. New microparticles keep turning up which reveal more profound movements and antagonisms.

The history and practice of the sciences demonstrate that various totalities exist in nature as well as in human history. Vigier points out that living organisms are totalities which can be decomposed into finer totalities such as the giant molecules. Farther afield, the earth, the solar system, our galaxy, and all galactic systems taken together can be approached and analyzed as totalities with a disregard for their detailed fluctuations. The distinct totalities which are found all around us in nature are relative, partial, and limited. Yet, far from negating the unity of nature, they constitute and confirm it.

Experiments show that however complicated the biochemistry of life, its processes are fundamentally the same from the algae to the human organism. We ourselves are made of star-stuff. It has been ascertained that the universe has a common chemistry, just as all the diverse forms of life on earth share similar biological laws. The same elements that make up the earth and its inhabitants are present in the most remote stellar regions.

The substantial unity of nature is asserted not only in its structural components, but in its stages and modes of development. Science is rapidly filling in a vast panorama of cosmic advancement. It is uncertain how the observable universe originated, if it did at all. But it has certainly evolved—from the creation of the elements, the constitution of the stellar galaxies, and other celestial phenomena to the birth of our solar system and the formation of the earth's crust and atmosphere. Then it proceeded to the chemical conditions required for the primary reactions leading to the first forms of life, on through the transformations of organic species, up to the advent of humanity. All this has been climaxed by the birth and forward movement of society over the past million-odd years.

This unified process of development is the real basis for the universality of the dialectic, which maintains that everything is linked together and interactive, in continuous motion and change, and that this change is the outcome of the conflicts of opposing forces within nature as well as everything to be found in it.

To assert that everything is in the last analysis connected with everything else does not nullify the relative autonomy of specific formations and singular things. But the separation of one thing from another, its qualitative distinctions from everything else, breaks down at a certain point in time and in space. So long as the opposing forces are in balance the totality appears stable, harmonious, at rest—and is really so. But this is a transient condition. Sooner or later, alterations in the inner relation of forces, and interactions with other processes in the environment, upset the achieved equilibrium, generate instability, and can eventuate in the disruption and destruction of the most hard-and-fast formations. Dialectics is fundamentally the most consistent way of thinking about the universal interconnections of things in the full range of their development.

＊　　　＊　　　＊

In addition to denying the unity of nature, Sartre attempts to erect impassable barriers between different orders of existence by splitting nature from human history. Is this justified by the facts? There was a profound interruption in the continuity of natural evolution, a qualitative jump, when humankind lifted itself above the other primates by means of the labor process. There are basic differences between nature and society; they have different laws of development. But there is no unbridgeable gap between them.

Just as the inorganic gave rise to the organic, that in turn and in time engendered social life, the distinctive field of human action. But all three sectors of reality remain in the closest communion. The chemical elements (nitrogen, carbon, hydrogen, oxygen) which enter into the total metabolism of organisms through food consumption, inhaling, exhaling, internal utilization and breakdown, excretion and elimination, return to the atmosphere, earth, and water for reuse. Our economy as well as our physiology exhibits the unbreakable unity of the diverse levels of being. The farmer furrowing the soil with an animal-drawn plough and seeding it brings together mineral, botanical, zoological, and human forces in the unified process of producing food.

The inanimate, the animate, and the social belong to a single stream of material existence and evolution with endless currents.

Are the oppositions in nature so radically different from contradictions in the life of humanity as Sartre contends? Contradictions on every level of existence have their peculiar characteristics, which must be found out in the course of practical experience and formulated in scientific inquiry. The sociological law that as technology expands, the productive forces of humankind tend to grow beyond and conflict with the relations of production and the property forms in which they have been encased is very different from Isaac Newton's laws of motion.

Does this mean that physical and social processes have no common denominators? Marxism maintains that general laws of being and becoming exist which allow both for the identities and differences, the persistent and the changing, in the real world. They embrace both nature and human life and are capable of expression as laws of logical thought. Included in the inventory of the laws of dialectics are the interpenetration of opposites, the passage of quantity into quality, the negation of the negation, the conflict of form and content, and many others. They are as relevant to nature as to society because they are rooted in the objective world.

Vigier observes that "internal antagonisms (that is to say, the assemblage of forces which necessarily evolve in contrary directions) illustrate the nature of contradiction. . . . The unity of opposites is understood as the unity of elements on one level which engenders the phenomena of a higher level. The transformation of quantity into quality is interpreted as the sudden rupture of equilibrium within a system (for example, the destruction of one of the antagonistic forces), which modifies the equilibrium and gives rise to a qualitatively new phenomenon in the midst of which new contradictions appear."

Vigier cites the advances of modern physics as evidence of the intrinsically contradictory properties of analyzed systems, which contain simplicity and complexity, inertia and violent motion at one and the same time. "The material elements considered inert at one level, for example the macroscopic bodies described by classical physics, are revealed upon analysis to be prodigiously complex and mobile as scientific knowledge progresses. On our scale this table can appear to me inert, but we know it is composed of molecules in extremely complex and violent motion. These molecules themselves can be decomposed into mobile atoms when I push analysis much further. Finally, the atoms themselves split into so-called elementary particles which in their turn disclose equally mobile and complex internal structures."

The motion dealt with in contemporary microphysics is not considered as the simple shift of an inert element from one point to another but rather as a violent oscillating movement which develops at one point to the degree it is destroyed in the immediately preceding position. Each side of this dual process of annihilation and creation reciprocally conditions the other.

The new emerges from the old in nature by way of contradiction, that is to say, by negating the essential properties of the previous form of being and absorbing its reconstituted elements into a higher synthesis. The major leaps from one qualitative state to another take place on the borderlands of evolution where one state of matter passes over into another.

Biochemists are now seeking to ascertain and duplicate the successive steps through which purely chemical reactions produced the first biochemical mechanisms. Although the inorganic is the matrix, the mother of life, life on earth is something radically novel. As a totality it is other and more than a chemical process; it has structures, properties, and powers that go far beyond its predecessor. "It is necessary to seek in the mineral for the origin of the processes and materials of the organic world," says J. D. Bernal, the British physicist, "but life itself represents a capital stage in the evolution of matter: the containment of continual chemical processes in a limited volume."

Formal logic, which is based on abstract, or simple, identity (A equals A), is too one-sided to explain this negation of one state of matter and its transformation into its opposite, in this case the lifeless into the living, because it excludes from its premises real difference and contradiction, which is the extreme development of difference. But the unity of opposites (A equals non-A), which makes contradiction explicit and intelligible, can explain this transition, which actually occurred on earth. The emergence of life from the nonliving in turn substantiates the objective basis in nature of this law of concrete contradiction, a cornerstone of dialectical logic.

According to Sartre, we are barred from knowing the inside of nature because it is not the work of humankind. Are physical-chemical phenomena inaccessible to us because we do not have such direct contact with them as with history? To be sure, remarks Vigier, we have to make and employ experimental devices to delve into the thick of things. But through these instruments we do find out their real properties and inner relations.

How can we be sure that our ideas actually correspond to what nature is "in itself"? This is no new question for philosophy, and Marxism developed a theory of knowledge to answer it. Sartre, like Immanuel Kant, bases his agnosticism upon the supposedly impenetrable character of materiality. Garaudy points out that while relations between the subject and object, the human and nonhuman, may initially be opaque, they can be rendered more and more transparent by practice and theory.

The proof that we know what things really are comes from useful practice. From solar masses to subatomic particles, we handle the materials and direct the operations of nature for our social purposes.

If we project through action an idea or scientific hypothesis about the material world or any portion of it, we receive a response, either negative or affirmative. The idea either fits the situation or it does not. Both responses enable us to deal with, and eventually to understand, the features and functions of nature. They disclose not only the movement but the structure of reality.

A new hypothesis does not simply destroy the old, leading to null results in the history of thought. The superior hypothesis that replaces the cruder and narrower one contains within itself whatever remains valid and valuable in its outworn and discarded predecessor, as an automatic shear retains the cutting edge of chipped stone and Albert Einstein's relativity theory includes and explains what is true and useful in Newtonian physics. Knowledge progresses and accumulates in this dialectical manner. It is thus possible to deepen our understanding and extend our control. Even if we never get to learn everything about nature, the verified knowledge actually gained through endless investigation enables us to probe ever more deeply into its recesses.

The issue in dispute is whether the structure and movement of nature disclosed by science and experiment is such that only a dialectical method of thought renders the phenomena intelligible and manageable. Sartre evades a definite answer to this question by walling up nature in an unbreachable externality with no windows we can look and reach through. He rejects the Marxist conception that human knowledge reflects objective reality.

Garaudy is obliged to clear up two common misunderstandings about this theory which Sartre plays upon. The term "reflection" does not signify that knowledge is a passive phenomenon which merely duplicates the object, like a mirror image, or mechanically reproduces it, like a stamping machine. The process of conception is more complex and active. Arising out of work and everyday practice, stimulated by the predicaments of life, the human mind invents ideas and hypotheses and tries various means of verifying them. Further, knowledge is not simply derived from sensation—which gives immediate contact with the external world—as the original empiricists taught. It is essentially historical, the product of prolonged social practice and intricate modifications of thought in its adjustments to reality, which remain forever incomplete.

This is true of the dialectics of nature as well. It is not imposed a priori or willfully upon nature, as Sartre charges. It represents the verified conclusions, the systematic formulations of practical experience, scientific investigation, and critical thought extending from Heraclitus to Hegel. Like other theoretical acquisitions, it is projected into the future as a guide to further inquiry into concrete reality.

But if Marxism has discarded the passive, oversimplified, and nonevolutionary versions of the thought process held by previous schools of materialism from Epicurus to the eighteenth-century sensationalists, it asserts with them that conceptual reflection does bring out and define the essential qualities and relations of things. Nature is prior to consciousness. There is an internal bond between what exists and what is known—and even how it is known. The order of ideas, as Benedict Spinoza said, does correspond with the order of things.

Hyppolite makes two charges against the Marxist interpretation of dialectics. On the one hand it aims to make nature historical by importing dialectical laws into it, and on the other it tries to "naturize" history by subjecting it to the same laws as the physical world. He wishes to keep history and nature in totally separate compartments.

This is alien to reality. Nature is through and through historical. Vigier emphasizes how, "proceeding from the history of biology and the human sciences, the idea of evolution has step by step invaded the whole of the sciences: after astronomy it is today breaking through into chemistry and physics. . . . This idea of history, of evolution, of analysis in terms of development is for us precisely the profound logical root of the dialectics of nature. It can even be said that in a sense all scientific progress is being achieved along the line of abandoning static descriptions for the sake of dynamic analyses combining the intrinsic properties of the analyzed phenomena. For us, science progresses from Cuvier to Darwin, from the static to the dynamic, from formal logic to dialectical logic."

Nature and society form two parts of a single historical process. But they are basically different, contradictory parts. Other living beings have history made for them; we make our own history.

Animals depend upon the available food and other features of their environment for survival; they cannot alter or discard their specialized organs and ways of life to cope with sudden changes. Entire species can perish when their habitats change too rapidly and radically. Humans, on the other hand, are not subjected to any particular environment or mode of adaptation. We can adjust to new conditions, meet changes, and even institute them by inventing new tools and techniques and producing what we need.

Up to now social development has carried over certain traits of natural development because by and large it has proceeded in an unconscious and uncontrolled manner. The course of society has been determined not by human purposes, but by the unintended results of the operation of the productive forces. But human history has reached the point where it can discard its blind automatism and enter an entirely different type of development. By discovering the laws of social development and collectively acting upon them, we can take control of society and consciously plan its further growth.

*　　　*　　　*

Hyppolite and Sartre accuse Marxism of instituting a new dogmatism by presenting a fixed and finished system of thought about the world. Hyppolite's last words in the debate are: "You risk giving us a sort of dialectics, under the pretext of dialectics of nature, which would be a speculative (i.e., idealistic) thought, in certain respects a theological thought, even though you disclaim such an intention." Sartre contends that Marxist dialectics is a frozen system based upon a limited number of laws, the three mentioned by Engels in *Dialectics of Nature*.

Sartre is right in saying that the laws of logic are not limited. But so does genuine Marxism, even though some doctrinaires of the Stalinist school have sought to limit them. The French philosopher Henri Lefèbvre ridiculed one official of the French Communist Party who smugly declared to him: "The house [of dialectical thought] is finished; there is nothing left to do but put up the tapestries."

"There does not exist a closed, finished, definitive list of dialectical laws," says Garaudy. "The presently known laws constitute a provisional balance sheet of our knowledge. . . . Further social practice and scientific experiment will permit us to enrich and extend them." Although the dialectical laws discovered and formulated to date have a definite content and universal scope, they are neither completed nor unchangeable. The number and the character of the laws of logic have changed over the past 2,500 years. They will continue to be transformed along with the development of nature, society, and knowledge.

Sartre strives to secure an objective basis for dialectics by locating it exclusively within human practice. "If we refuse to see the original dialectical movement in the individual and in his enterprise of producing his life, of objectifying himself, then we shall have to give up dialectic or else make of it the immanent law of History," he writes in *Search for a Method.* This is a very misleading description of dialectical movement even within human history. The dialectical development of society proceeds not from the action and decision of the isolated individual in a concrete situation but from the work of the group, first in the struggle against nature, then in the conflict of classes. Subjective components of the whole—such as individual psychology—which so preoccupy the existentialists, are integral and subordinate elements of this objective historical process and derive their validity and significance from it.

In the reciprocal relationship whereby human practice transforms and masters the environment, nature retains existential priority, however much this offends the subjectivity of the existentialist philosopher.

The origin of human practice itself requires explanation. The distinctive activities that have separated humanity from the animal condition originated with the using and making of tools and weapons to obtain the means of subsistence. But this new kind of activity, which is at the foundation of society, grew out of natural processes that antedate human practice by billions of years.

In the evolutionary scale, animal activity preceded human practice, which was a qualitatively new offshoot of it. When the first fish developed lungs, came to live on dry land, and converted themselves into amphibians, that was a dialectical change in organic nature. Through the natural mechanisms of the evolution of species, the fish, to use Sartre's language, "objectified himself" into something else.

The dialectics of human history grew out of this dialectics of nature. It originated in the conversion of the early primate into the human, the most meaningful of all the contradictory developments of matter. The elevation of humanity above animality was the greatest rupture in the continuity of nature's evolution. The qualitative disjunction between us and other species is so deepgoing that Sartre takes it as the ground for excluding dialectics from nature.

He is here baffled by a genuine contradiction. Human beings are both creatures of nature and a departure from it. When the human is low-rated as nothing but a high-grade animal, different in degree but not in kind from other living beings, the essential and distinctive nature of humanity is obliterated. Human life, which stems from the production of the means of subsistence by tools and weapons, is something radically new compared with the animal foraging for food. The labor process is the beginning of society and provides the platform for the dialectical movement of history. Fundamental changes in the organization of this labor process are the decisive steps in the further advancement of humanity.

But the processes which humanized our primate ancestors were both a prolongation of brute nature and a level above and beyond it. Just as there is both continuity and discontinuity in the transition from ape to human, so there is comparable continuity and discontinuity between the dialectics of nature and that of history. The dialectics of nature has different forms and proceeds according to different laws than the dialectics of social evolution. It is the prehistory of human dialectics, the precondition for it. The one passes over into the other as humanity has created its own characteristics in distinction from the rest of nature.

The evolution of human life through social practice is only the culminating chapter in the evolution of matter. The dialectic of human history, which for Sartre is the be-all and end-all of dialectics, is the latest episode in the universal dialectic.

Sartre's subjectivist and anthropocentric conception of dialectical movement is belied by the latest finding of modern science. Scientists now say that billions of planets are suitable for the creation of life and may very likely be populated by intelligent organisms of some sort. There are a hundred million eligible planets in our galaxy alone! Humanity is only one manifestation of life, inhabiting a small planet of a solar system on the edge of an ordinary galaxy in an explorable universe of billions of galaxies containing other—and in some cases higher—specimens of life.

This remarkable addition to our knowledge does not detract from the value and significance of life on earth for us. After all, the improvement of our own scientific practice and theory has led us to this insight. But it should serve to put our existence into proper cosmic proportion and perspective. Dialectics can no more be restricted to the people on our planet than life and intelligence can be.

The existentialist resents and rejects the rationalism and objectivity of science. It supposedly leads us away from real being, which is to be perpetually sought, though never reached, through the ever-renewed, ever-baffled effort of the individual consciousness to go beyond our human condition. The terrible destiny of the human race is like "the desire of the moth for the star/ the night for the morrow/ the devotion to something afar/ from the sphere of our sorrow."

So the exasperated existentialist Sartre flings as his trump card against the dialectics of nature the current crisis in science. "There has never been, I believe, as grave a crisis as the present one in science," he cries to Vigier. "So when you come to talk to us about your completed, formed, solid science and want to dissolve us in it, you'll understand our reserve."

Vigier calmly replies: "Science progresses by means of crises in the same manner as history; that's what we call progress. Crises are the very foundation of progress." And he concludes: "The very practice of science, its progress, the very manner in which it is today passing from a static to a dynamic analysis of the world, that is precisely what is progressively elaborating the dialectic of nature under our very eyes. . . . The dialectic of nature is very simply the effort of the philosophy of our time . . . of the most encyclopedic philosophy, that is, Marxism to apprehend the world and change it."

This ringing affirmation will appear bizarre to Anglo-American scientists who may respect Vigier for his work as a physicist. They summarily disqualify dialectical logic on the ground that, whatever its philosophical or political interest, it has no value in promoting any endeavor in natural science. If the method is valid, the antidialecticians say, then purposeful application by its proponents should prove capable of producing important new theories and practical results in other fields than the social. Marxists are challenged to cite instances where the dialectical method has actually led to new discoveries and not simply demonstrated after the fact that specific scientific findings conform to the generalizations of dialectical logic.

The most splendid contribution of this kind in recent decades has been Oparin's theories on the origin of life, which are widely accepted and have stimulated fruitful work on the problems of biogenesis and genetics. The Soviet scientist's theory is based on the hypothesis that the random formation and interaction of increasingly complex molecules gave rise to the simplest forms of living matter, which then began to reproduce at the expense of the surrounding organic material.

Oparin consciously employed such principles of materialist dialectics as the transformation of quantity into quality, the interruption of continuity (evolution by leaps), and the conversion of chance fluctuations into regular processes and definite properties of matter, to initiate an effective new line of approach to one of the central problems of science: How did inanimate nature generate life on earth? Such cases would undoubtedly multiply if more practicing scientists were better informed about the Marxist method of thought.

*   *   *

The crisis of method within science is only one aspect of the more general crisis of modern civilization. This has become most excruciating in the deadly consequences of physical science under capitalist auspices. The dialectics of nature exhibited in the fission and fusion of atoms has merged with the dialectics of history in the most monstrous and momentous of all contradictions facing humanity: the threat of self-destruction by nuclear war.

Why have the immense strides in physical knowledge and technology designed to serve humankind become perverted into an intolerable menace to our survival? The H-bomb exemplifies the sociological law that the fast-expanding forces of production have outgrown capitalist relations and are pounding against them for liberation. Used for good or evil, nuclear energy, the greatest source of power at our command, is proving incompatible with private ownership of the economy and capitalist control over the government.

The imperative political conclusion is that the representatives of the money power in the United States must be prevented from pressing the button which can doom us all, as was nearly done in the 1962 missile crisis over Cuba. Capitalism is the last form of socioeconomic organization dominated by laws which operate in an ungovernable way, like laws of nature. The aim of scientific socialism, the task of the proletarian world revolution, is to subdue all the anarchic forces tied up with capitalism which generate insecurity and havoc in our society. The blind drives of class society have pushed humanity to the brink of extinction. Conscious understanding and application of the dialectical laws of evolution—and revolution—can help save us.

Only through public ownership and operation of the economy and democratic direction of state policy can the working people introduce scientific enlightenment into the material foundations of life, overthrow the last entrenchment of automatism in social evolution, and clear the way for the rule of reason in all human affairs.

II

A Comment by Yvonne Groseil

I have just read your article, "Is Nature Dialectical?" in the Summer 1964 issue of the *International Socialist Review*, and I was quite impressed by it.

Although I must plead guilty to a rather superficial knowledge of Marxism, I am very interested in Hegel's work. During my study of Hegel, I have come to the conclusion that the question of the philosophy of nature is a crucial one. In my opinion, Hegel's philosophy falls apart into a dualism of mind and matter instead of being the synthesis he desired just because of the failure of his philosophy of nature.

This failure is not, I submit, a failure of the dialectical method, but the result of the lack of sufficient scientific knowledge at Hegel's time plus Hegel's insistence on bending the inadequate knowledge he did have into his philosophic system. It is the latter fault that makes his philosophy of nature appear downright silly today; but it is only today that we are beginning to attain the scientific knowledge that makes a dialectical view of the facts the only reasonable one.

This part of Hegel's philosophy has been largely neglected, but I consider it vital to a serious consideration of his thought today. Therefore, your article on the dialectics of nature was a very welcome piece of writing to me. On the whole, I agree with your position—the laws of dialectics apply to nature as well as humanity.

The scientific knowledge available now can only be understood thoroughly by the use of dialectics. This appears most obviously in the realm of evolution and biology in general, but the interrelationship of all aspects of our world means that it is applicable to the other sciences as well.

The existentialist position would create a complete alienation between man and the world, and would destroy the objectivity of our knowledge and thus our ability to act. Sartre's position, as described in your article—that humans can never attain to the "reality" of things, that our knowledge and the laws of our (dialectical) logic apply only to humanity and society, etc.— sounds like that of a resuscitated Kant.

It can only lead to a divided world-view, a denial of the possibility of true knowledge and, ultimately, to excesses of subjectivity rather than creative activity. The existentialists may begin their philosophic inquiry from the standpoint of the individual, but that does not mean that they can stop there without losing sight of the essential thing—that we are in and of the world.

The points made by Vigier and Garaudy were, I felt, an excellent rebuttal to Sartre and Hyppolite. There is one point in your article, however, with which I would take some exception. That is when you argue against the antidialecticians by pointing out the advances made in science, especially by Oparin, through the use of dialectical method. Dialectical logic may help the scientist reach some useful hypotheses for later investigation, but this is not the essential point here.

It seems to me that the method or means by which scientific discoveries are made is secondary in this argument. What is really vital is the fact that only a dialectical view of nature can provide an adequate framework in which these new discoveries can be seen in their total relationship. That is, how one gets to the discovery is not so important as the realization that this new "fact" can only be thoroughly explained and related to the rest of our knowledge through a dialectical viewpoint.

There is one other point that seems appropriate to this discussion: I read recently that Roger Garoudy was to write an introduction to a Russian translation of Pierre Teilhard de Chardin's *Phenomenon of Man*. Now Teilhard certainly is not a dialectical materialist in any sense of the word. However, beneath the theological portion of his thought, one finds a view of evolution that is certainly dialectical—in a Hegelian, if not a Marxist, sense. And Teilhard's work seems to have been a little too "materialistic" for the Roman Catholic church.

Teilhard's work in itself deserves study, but simply in connection with the question of the dialectics of nature, it seems to me that it may be a sign that we are approaching a higher synthesis of thought. The static conceptions of "idealism" and "materialism" may give way to a newer, more adequate realization of their interdependence throughout the whole sphere of nature. That can only be achieved if we recognize the objective character of dialectics—that it applies to nature as well as to history. The perpetuation of alienation between "mind" and "matter," humanity and the world, nature and history, can serve no good purpose, but only leads to fragmentation and confusion in philosophy and action.

Dialectics by its nature has to be an "open" system which not only allows for the addition of new knowledge but also admits our freedom and ability to shape history. The recognition of nature as dialectical is the only way to a whole world-view that includes humanity in the world while recognizing our unique position and frees us to control our own future. Your article is an excellent statement of the issues and their importance, and I hope it will precipitate in this country a greater appreciation of the problem and wide discussion of it.

III

George Novack's Response

Here are some comments on the main questions of theoretical interest raised by this friendly comment.

1. Would knowledge of the method of the materialist dialectic, which is based on the most general laws of being and becoming, assist physical scientists in their investigations of nature?

Up to now almost all scientists have carried on their work without conscious understanding of the dialectical laws of universal development, just as most people speak very well without knowing the history or grammar of their language, breathe without awareness of the physiological processes of respiration, and acquire the necessities of life without comprehending the principles of political economy.

Western philosophers and scientists almost unanimously believe that the dialectical view of nature is false, irrelevant, and even positively harmful in the theory and practice of science. This prejudice, rooted in our predominantly empirical and positivist intellectual traditions, has been reinforced by the arbitrary and ignorant interference of the Stalinist bureaucrats with scientific theory, along with their narrowly schematic, distorted, and dogmatic interpretation of Marxist method.

This correspondent has a more favorable attitude toward the dialectical conception of nature. But she suggests that it may be far less important in facilitating progress in physical science than it is for explaining and correlating its discoveries after they have been made.

Such a one-sided emphasis runs the risk of lapsing into the very Kantian dualism which she correctly criticizes in the case of the existentialists. What are here involved are the organic connections between the unity of reality, the sum total of our knowledge, and the scientific inquiry which shuttles from one to the other. If the dialectical method can be useful in clarifying the relationships of the knowledge of nature once it has been acquired, why cannot it be equally valuable in helping scientists to arrive at verified results? After all, the dialectical characteristics which are disclosed in the body of known facts must already have existed and been effective in the objective realities from which they have been derived.

If scientists should approach the problems for which they seek solutions in their particular fields with an informed understanding of the fundamental traits of development formulated in the laws of dialectical logic, why couldn't these serve as a general methodological guide in their concrete inquiries?

In fact, the most creative scientists have assumed the truth of this or that rule of dialectical logic in conducting their work, although they have done so in a piecemeal, haphazard, semiconscious manner. Without referring to past examples, let's take the many non-Marxist scientists around the world who are cooperating with Oparin in studying the specific steps by which the most elementary processes and mechanisms of life have emerged from inanimate matter. Unlike him, they pay no heed to the fact that the transition of the lifeless into the living exemplifies at least two laws of dialectical logic.

One is the unity of opposites, which states that A equals non-A; the other is the transformation of quantity into quality. That is to say, a sufficient aggregate of chemical reactions of a special type gave rise to new properties appropriate to a new and higher state of material existence on this planet, the biochemical level, of which humans are the most complex and advanced embodiment.

Just as Teilhard de Chardin's religious views did not prevent him from participating in the discovery of Peking Man in 1929 and thus adding to our knowledge of human origins, so practicing physicists, chemists, and biologists can and do promote their sciences without any clear notions of the logic underlying their investigations, or even with erroneous ideas of the world. But would not the work of individual scientists benefit—as much as science as a whole—if they could rid their minds of errors and inconsistencies which run counter to a scientific outlook, and thus bring their general ideas about the universe and their logical theory into closer accord with their experimental practice and the requirements of science itself?

That is why Marxists contend that a comprehensive grasp of the logic of dialectical materialism would not only clarify what science has already achieved but enable contemporary scientists to promote and improve their work. Science is still in its infancy and is only now being applied on a grand scale. There are more scientists in the world today than in all previous history. This sudden and sharp jump in the number of scientists and the facilities at their disposal demands a corresponding expansion in their understanding of the logic of evolution, which so far has been best provided by the school of dialectical materialism.

2. The works of Father Teilhard de Chardin can throw light on this matter, although not entirely in the way intended by our correspondent. While Chardin is an inconsistent dialectician, he is not at all a materialist in his philosophy and procedure. One of the world's most eminent biologists, George Gaylord Simpson, who was a friend of Chardin's and has read both his published and unpublished manuscripts, concurs with this judgment in his book *This View of Life*. There, in a chapter entitled "Evolutionary Theology: the New Mysticism," Simpson states that Chardin's ideas are mystical and nonscientific in two major respects. First, he divides all energy into two distinct kinds which cannot be verified: a "tangential" material energy and a "radial" spiritual energy. Second, he advocates orthogenesis as the principal mechanism of evolution. Unlike natural selection, which is based upon random and multidirectional trends of evolution, orthogenesis holds that evolution proceeds in a unidirectional, predetermined, and even purposive manner.

Simpson severely censures Chardin for his spiritualistic "doubletalk," which really has nothing to do with science. He writes that "Teilhard was *primarily* a Christian mystic and only secondarily a scientist."

Roger Garaudy likewise deals with Chardin in his book *Perspectives of Man*. Ironically, this foremost French Communist philosopher is far more conciliatory toward the views of the Jesuit father than is the American biologist Simpson. Garaudy's book undertakes a critical analysis of the main currents of contemporary French thought: existentialism, Catholicism, and Marxism. He claims that all three are engaged in a common effort to grasp "man in his totality," and he seeks to emphasize their "possible convergences." He concludes that radical existentialists, liberal Catholics, and Communists can cooperate "not as adversaries but as explorers in a common venture" which proceeds by different paths toward the same goal.

This theoretical position is the reverse of that taken by Garaudy in the days of Stalin-Zhdanov. It is motivated by the desire for a philosophical rapprochement among these incompatible schools of thought to accompany the CP's quest for a political alliance of all "democratic, progressive, peace-loving" forces as prescribed by the policy of "peaceful coexistence."

Those unorthodox features of Chardin's thought, which scandalize his superiors in the Jesuit order and the church but attract liberal Catholics, lend themselves to this purpose. It is true, as Garaudy points out, that Chardin recognized certain dialectical characteristics in the process of evolution, such as the universal interconnection and reciprocal action of all things, the transformation of quantity into quality in connection with biogenesis (though not in the transition from biological to social life), and the transmutation of matter in an ascending series of higher forms.

But the "finalism" and "vitalism" which permeate his thought—based on the supposition that evolution heads in only one direction, toward greater "centrocomplexity," toward the Omega point where humanity will merge with God—are irreconcilable not only with dialectical materialism but, as Simpson insists, with any acceptable scientific approach to universal evolution.

3. Somewhat in the spirit of Chardin, Yvonne Groseil intimates that "the static conceptions of 'idealism' and 'materialism' may give way to a newer, more adequate realization of their interdependence throughout the whole sphere of nature." A Marxist cannot agree with this for numerous reasons.

First, there is nothing "static" about a consistently dialectical and materialist view of nature, which is based upon the proposition that everything is in flux because of the opposing forces at work within it and in the universe. Materialist dialectics is dynamic, mobile, evolutionary through and through.

Second, the valid and valuable contributions made to the store of human knowledge by the great idealists of the past (like dialectical logic itself) have been—or ought to be—incorporated into the structure of dialectical materialism without surrendering or compromising its fundamental positions: that reality consists of matter in motion, and that social life and intellectuality are the highest manifestations of the development of matter.

Idealism, on the other hand, makes spiritual, supernatural, ideological, or personal forces the essence of reality. Such a fundamentally false philosophy has to be rejected in toto.

Nor can these two opposing conceptions of the world and its evolution be amalgamated into some superior synthesis eclectically combining the "best features of both," as Sartre tries to do with his neo-Marxist existentialism and Father de Chardin in his blend of religious mysticism and evolutionism.

Modern thought and science can be most effectively advanced through a firm repudiation of all religious, mystical, and idealistic notions and the conscious adoption, application, and development of dialectical materialism. Working in equal partnership, Marxist logic and the sciences can enable us to penetrate more surely and deeply into the nature of the world we live in.

*　　　*　　　*

After finishing this reply, I chanced to read "The Emergence of Evolutionary Novelties" by Ernst Mayr, Agassiz Professor of Zoology at Harvard, in *The Evolution of Life*. It deals with the key problem of explaining the origin of entirely new biological phenomena on the basis of random variations.

Mayr points out that "the exact definition of an 'evolutionary novelty' faces the same insuperable difficulty as the definition of the species. As long as we believe in gradual evolution, we must be prepared to encounter mediate evolutionary stages. Equivalent to the cases in which it is impossible to decide whether a population is not yet a species or already a species, will be cases of doubt as to whether a population is already or not yet an evolutionary novelty. The study of this difficult transition from the quantitative to the qualitative is precisely one of the objects of this paper."

Mayr finds that there are three main kinds of evolutionary novelties: cellular biochemical innovations (the uric acid and fat metabolism of the cleidoic egg of the terrestrial vertebrates); new structures (eyes, wings, stings); and new habits or behavior patterns (the shift from water to land or from the earth to air).

The saltationists and mutationists of various schools argued against the natural selectionists that new structures could only have come into existence suddenly and all ready for advantageous use, whereas Charles Darwin held that they would have to be formed by numerous, successive, and slight modifications of preexisting organs. "The problem of the emergence of evolutionary novelties," writes Mayr, "then consists in having to explain how a sufficient number of small gene mutations can be accumulated until the new structure has become sufficiently large to have selective value." He calls this the "threshold problem."

His paper undertakes to demonstrate the ways in which different organisms have actually effected the changeover from one structure to another in the evolutionary process. Mayr's treatment is highly pertinent to our own discussion of logical method in science because it indicates how a biologist concerned with the fundamental problem of evolution has been impelled to invoke the dialectical law of the transformation of quantity into quality in order to explain the generation of novelty in living beings.

Indeed, how would it be possible to comprehend how the mere piling up of quantitative variations could give rise to something decisively different from its antecedents unless this law was operative?

It may be objected that Mayr has not used this law to discover anything new but only to clarify how new biological phenomena come into existence. But, as John Dalton's atomic theory of the chemical elements, Darwin's theory of evolution, and Max Planck's quantum theory testify, the discovery of the general laws at work, the basic features and essential relations in any field of reality, is the highest expression of scientific activity. A correct and comprehensive conception of the production of novelty in organic evolution is more important for the advancement and reinforcement of biological science than the discovery of some new aspect of functional adaptation to a habitat by a particular group of fauna.

Mayr is one of the most eminent of contemporary American biologists. It can be assumed that he is not a Marxist or an adherent of dialectical materialism. He has resorted to one of the major laws of dialectics empirically, without a full awareness of the type of logical thinking he was applying, just as another naturalist of lesser stature might explore a novel type of adaptation of a group of organisms without concerning himself about a general explanation of evolutionary novelty as Mayr had done.

Mayr's acknowledgment of the indispensability of this law of dialectics in solving the problem of the emergence of evolutionary novelties provides involuntary and forceful testimony to its value for the natural scientist.

American Philosophy
and the Labor Movement

"American philosophy and the labor movement . . . How odd to couple these two together!" we can imagine eminent heads in both fields exclaiming. "What can they have in common?"

It must be acknowledged that at present they make an incongruous, even ludicrous, juxtaposition. To most professors, philosophy has no special connection with either politics or the working class. Almost all union leaders believe the labor movement can get along very well without any philosophy. Here as elsewhere, extremes meet. The labor bureaucrats have as little regard for philosophy as the university mandarins have for the labor movement.

Is this estrangement a fixed and permanent feature of American culture? Or is it the product of special, episodic historical conditions? To answer these questions, let us first examine the evolution of the mass labor movement in the United States on its theoretical side, in its two main stages: the Gompers-Green era and the subsequent period of the CIO.

One of the outstanding peculiarities of the American labor movement has been the immense disparity between its strength in industrial action and organization, and its political and theoretical weakness compared with working class movements in other countries.

The American workers possess in full measure all the remarkable qualities which distinguish the American people generally and have been responsible for its colossal achievements. They radiate dynamic energy; they excel in sustained labor and collective organization for the execution of given tasks; they are ingenious, free of routinism, highly cultured in modern technology. They have displayed these capacities not only in working for their bosses but also in the struggles which have created the largest and most powerful trade union structure in the world. These magnificent traits can be counted upon to assert themselves even more forcefully in the decades ahead and will be the source of still greater accomplishments.

At the same time, the development of American labor has suffered from a pronounced unevenness. The growth of its self-awareness as a distinct social force with a world-historical mission has not kept pace with its union organization. Its creativeness in collective thinking has limped far behind its achievements through direct action. Along with its precious positive features our labor movement has inherited the meagerness and immaturity in theoretical matters rooted in the national past.

This defect was crystallized in the craft unionism of the old American Federation of Labor. The original AFL leaders deliberately turned away from any general conceptions of social development and class relations. In his autobiography Samuel Gompers tells how he consciously rejected the Marxism he knew in his younger days, as unsuited to American conditions.

The AFL heads scoffed not only at the ideas of socialism but at any philosophy; such highfalutin matters were no business of organized labor. They lived from hand to mouth, from craft to craft, from contract to contract. The crude tenets of Gompers ("a fair day's pay for a fair day's work"; "reward your friends, punish your enemies") grew out of and corresponded to the primitive organizational setup and class-collaborationist methods of the AFL. When Adolph Strasser, coleader with Gompers of the Cigarmakers, was asked by the Senate Committee on Education and Labor what the ultimate objectives of AFL craft unionism were, he answered: "We have no ultimate ends. We are going on from day to day. We fight only for immediate objects—objects that can be realized in a few years."[1]

Although the AFL leaders themselves felt no need for any theory to explain the role and aims of unionism, certain professors of the John L. Commons school of sociologists, centered at the University of Wisconsin, undertook to fabricate one for them. The Commons conception of U.S. unionism was purely pragmatic in spirit. It fully justified the prevailing practices of the Gompers officialdom, found special virtues in them, and even extended them into the indefinite future. Craft unionism, these scholars declared, was the special form of unionism suited to our distinctive national conditions; industrial unionism was unrealistic, almost un-American. Collective bargaining, craft by craft, would bring about gradual improvement in labor's status and its recognition as an equal of capital.

The narrow outlook of the AFL had much in common with the instrumentalist theories of John Dewey, the highest form of pragmatism. Gompersism and Deweyism were kindred products of the same period in America's social evolution. The principal methods of instrumentalism corresponded on the top level of theory to the everyday practices and outlook of the craft union officials. To be sure, the two sprang from different social strata and did not march closely together. The one stemmed directly from the needs and views of liberal middle class intellectuals; the other came from the habits and interests of the union bureaucracy and the craft aristocracy. Although the former was more volatile and less hidebound than the latter, they converged in the nationally enclosed, opportunist, piecemeal nature of their common ideology.

This kinship has been pointed out by an especially qualified observer, Mark Starr, educational director of the AFL International Ladies Garment Workers Union: "It would, of course, be a mistake to think that there has been a reciprocal interest and a wide conscious study of the philosophy of John Dewey in the ranks of American organized labor, or even in the workers' education section of its activities. However, there is something in common between the economic pragmatism of Samuel Gompers and the philosophic pragmatism of John Dewey. The approach of the American Federation of Labor in working out its theories in the light of daily practice is surely experimentalism. As a matter of fact, just as Dewey has been accused of having no organized body of thought, so the AFL has been accused of emphasizing rule-of-thumb methods to the exclusion of any understanding of ultimate goals."[2]

The two movements were alike not only in their methods of thought but in their underlying aims. Both sought to effect improvements for the lower classes step by step within the settled framework of capitalist institutions. This program of gradual reform necessarily involved accommodation to the political and social bases of capitalism and a deference to its governing bodies.

At critical turning points (wars, sharp clashes between the industrialists and the workers) this attitude of compliance culminated in capitulation to the pressures of the ruling class. Despite recurrent tiffs, grumblings of protest, and threats, both the union leaders and the philosophers, guided by pragmatism, remained loyal oppositionists to the capitalist regime.

The scorn for broad generalizations in historical and social questions was most conspicuous in the Gompers section of the labor movement. But it was an inescapable phenomenon of that entire era. Its prevalence, though in different forms, at the opposite end of the labor movement testified to its deep roots in the objective conditions of American life. Eugene Debs, the revolutionary socialist who was Gompers's lifelong left-wing opponent, exemplified in his own way the low theoretical level characteristic of that time. Debs made his way from trade unionism to socialism under the blows he received through personal participation in the union organizing campaigns and class battles of the 1890s. He learned the real nature of capitalist chicanery and cruelty not so much from books as in the school of hard knocks. In this respect, as in so many others, Debs was genuinely representative of the native laboring masses.

He became a thoroughgoing socialist—and a left-wing one. But, through no fault of his own, he never grew to be a Marxist leader of the highest stature. As a self-educated worker-leader in the provincial America of his day, he could not acquire the theoretical equipment, training, and insight vested in the outstanding figures of the great German and Russian schools of revolutionary socialism who stood at the crossroads of world history in their time. As Debs's best biographer, Ray Ginger, notes: "In his entire life, he never made an important decision on the basis of theoretical study. The facts of his own life kicked him into every step; often he required more than one kick."[3]

This weakness handicapped Debs at many points in his career: in the internal party controversies of the prewar socialist movement, at the time of Wilson's intervention into the First World War, and finally in the developments following the Russian revolution, which required a profound theoretical readjustment in the outlook of all socialists. Debs shared this inadequacy with most of his generation, regardless of their special tendency or affiliation. Similar deficiencies in theory and program were stamped upon the militant ranks of migratory labor and the proletarian fighters of the IWW; they were to prove a decisive factor in the disintegration of this movement after the First World War and the Russian revolution.

Engels, who closely followed the main events in the labor movement here during the last part of the nineteenth century, often emphasized these contradictory aspects of the American character: its strength in practical affairs coupled with its feebleness in theory. "Theoretical ignorance is the attribute of all young peoples," he wrote his friend Friedrich Sorge in the United States, "but so is the speed of development in practice. Just as in England, so all abstractions count for nothing in America until they have been brought forward by factual necessity."[4]

Engels expected that the harsh necessities of the class struggle and the resultant schooling of experience would in time stimulate the American workers' vanguard to gain a clearer, more comprehensive insight into their historical destiny and enable them to overcome their traditional empiricism. Since his death in 1895, our labor movement has taken giant strides forward. But it must be said that for all the advances made in its understanding, these have not kept pace with its organizational gains, and even less with its needs. The union movement is still, in Engels's words, "practically ahead of the whole world and theoretically still in its swaddling clothes."[5]

* * *

The founders of the CIO in the mid-1930s discarded the craft union framework of the AFL—but they did not break with its fundamental ideology. At this great turning point the regenerated ranks of labor needed four major improvements to carry forward their battles for a better life against monopolist rule. These were: an up-to-date union structure in the basic industries; a mass political party to challenge the capitalist two-party system on a national, state, and local level; a program, outlook, and theory on a par with this higher stage in its own development and corresponding to our revolutionary age of transition from one social order to another; and finally, a leadership capable of applying that program in action.

Under CIO auspices American labor succeeded in realizing only the first and most pressing of these objectives. In the 1930s and '40s it built powerful national unions in the key sectors of trustified industry; that has been the imperishable accomplishment of the CIO. But this higher grade of union organization was not extended and fortified by equivalent advances in the political practices, the social views, or the theoretical knowledge of the union leadership.

Even though they captained a far more dynamic and highly developed movement, the general policies and ideological equipment of the top-ranking CIO leaders were little better than those of the old-line AFL bureaucrats. John L. Lewis, the dominant figure in the formative stage of the CIO, carried over into the new movement the basic outlook he had absorbed in the old, so far as his conceptions of its role under capitalism were concerned. To be sure, sensing the stronger position of the organized working class, he demanded a bigger voice for labor within the existing system; this was symbolized by his desire to be nominated as Roosevelt's vice-presidential candidate. But neither Lewis nor his successor, Philip Murray, seriously attempted to pass beyond the two-party setup.

We have pointed out that after organizing basic industry, labor's next urgent task was to cut loose from the capitalist parties and provide an independent medium for the expression of labor politics. Unlike the mine union leaders Lewis and Murray, the auto workers' president, Walter Reuther, who came to head the CIO in the 1950s, was a direct product of the new stage in the labor movement. Originally a socialist, the younger man was familiar with a far wider range of ideas than his predecessors. Yet for all his flexibility he, too, stubbornly resisted being pushed beyond the existing political limits.

Over the years there had been repeated calls from the ranks of the auto workers and the CIO for an independent political policy. Time and again Reuther sidestepped any commitment to a labor party. The debate on this issue held at the thirteenth UAW convention in Cleveland in 1951 affords an excellent insight into the purely pragmatic character of his reasoning.

A minority had submitted a resolution urging the speedy formation of a labor party by the unions in preparation for the national elections in 1952. Reuther resisted this with the following arguments: "We are all opposed to political hacks and we are all opposed to corruption and compromise; but it is not a matter of principle that is being debated here in these two resolutions. The division is not in principle, it is in strategy, in tactics, and that is the keynote to the future development of American political power with respect to the labor movement. I say if you pass the minority resolution you will feel noble, but you will not advance the political struggle to build labor's political power in America. Let us not be generals without an army."[6]

Pragmatism differs from Marxism in its attitude toward principles. Although ordinary pragmatists do not repudiate principles in general, they hold that these must be subordinated to the pursuit of immediate practical aims. Marxism teaches that correct class principles are practically necessary to attain class ends.

Analyzing Reuther's arguments in the light of these contrasting methods, we see that he first of all presents himself as a sturdy fellow who stands firmly upon principle. But then he denies that labor support to the political agencies of the capitalist class is a matter of principle. In reality, opposition to capitalist parties and policies is as vital a principle of working class conduct as opposition to company unions in industry.

The pragmatic Reuther claimed that nothing more was involved than purely practical considerations of strategy and tactics; objective facts, and not noble feelings, must decide the course to take. Although he claimed to be no compromiser or friend of corrupt politicians, his assessment of the prevailing situation compelled him to favor the continuation of the old policy of class collaboration and block the initiation of a labor party.

Thus this opponent of compromise in the abstract turned out to be the proponent of further shameful compromise with Democratic Party politics in the concrete case. While he counterposed his "realism" to the "utopian" labor party advocates, his opportunist maneuver displayed his contempt for principled conduct. Bureaucratic expediency, not working class principle, was his guide.

The irony is that if Reuther had chosen the opposite course at that time, he would have gained more for labor even from the standpoint of practical politics. For the Republican Eisenhower defeated the liberal Democrat Stevenson. Had labor launched its own party in 1951-52, instead of supporting the Democrats and hanging around the anterooms of the capitalist politicians since that time, it would by now be in a stronger position even to make demands upon the older parties. Reuther's opportunistic stand, defended on pragmatic grounds, weakened labor's political position. The trouble with opportunism is that it results in missing so many opportunities.

By 1958 Reuther had become so conservative on this question that when AFL-CIO President George Meany rhetorically threatened the capitalist politicians with secession toward a labor party, Reuther repudiated the idea as un-American. If in 1951 it was merely premature, seven years later the proposal was dogmatically excluded.

*   *   *

The merger of the AFL and CIO in 1955 opened up new possibilities of advancement for labor. So far its leaders have done little to realize them, even in the extension of union organization. They have certainly not raised the level of labor's thought.

Today, insofar as the official labor movement can be said to have any philosophy, it is wholly pragmatic, as it was in both the AFL and CIO phases of its formation. But pragmatism is not a working class philosophy. It is essentially the theory of middle class progressivism, whose basic ideas did not pass beyond the limits of reforming the structure of capitalism. American labor has yet to develop a philosophy of its own; it has borrowed whatever generalizations it needed from the spokesmen for other segments of American society. Or rather, it has neither resisted nor rejected the influences of ideologies which run counter to its fundamental interests and real historical role. How long will American labor continue to operate without a theory of its own or with inadequate ones taken from alien sources? The answer to this question depends on its prospects in the remaining decades of this century.

Seated comfortably in their padded armchairs, the labor executives proceed as though the establishment of industrial unionism was the last major upheaval between the corporations and the workers. Actually, the struggles of the 1930s were the first great step in a process which will have its sequel in a new upsurge of labor radicalism.

The working class is one of the two decisive forces in American society. The unions can maintain their present stability, and their leaders their conservatizing stranglehold, only so long as the capitalist system functions without severe shocks and serious crises. Thus the key to the future of American labor does not lie within itself but rather in the vicissitudes of U.S. capitalism. But

U.S. capitalism is itself subjected to the good or ill fortunes of international capitalism, of which it forms the most important part. So, in order to judge the prospects of the American working class, we must look outside the labor movement and even beyond the United States. We must examine the fundamental trends of world history in our time and the sweeping social changes emerging from them.

The predominant historical movement in the nineteenth century was the building up of capitalist society. Progressivism, Deweyism, Gompersism were manifestations in politics, philosophy, and industry of reactions to this specific stage in the evolution of American and world capitalism. All these were products of the period when American capitalism, emerging from victory after the Civil War, was passing through its democratic, competitive, progressive youth to its reactionary, monopolistic, and imperialistic maturity, while in the world arena capitalism climbed to the peak of its power.

After the First World War and the Russian revolution the further building of capitalism on a global scale was first halted, then reversed. Its structure has been weakened by a series of revolutions which have established postcapitalist regimes from the Elbe River to the Pacific Ocean—and even ninety miles from home, where the first victorious socialist revolution has pierced the Western Hemisphere.

This world anticapitalist revolution is the central tendency of our time. But its first phase has had a contradictory effect upon the position of U.S. capitalism. While the historical system to which it belongs has been falling back on a world scale, U.S. capitalism has been gaining ground.

To be sure, these interlacing processes do not have equal weight. In the long run the advances of the American sector will not compensate for the losses suffered by the capitalist system as a whole. Not only must these in time react upon the United States and drag it down, but the challenge from the Soviet bloc becomes ever greater. Still, among the bourgeois countries, the United States has been the prime beneficiary of the cataclysmic changes that have attended the first period of the transition from capitalism to socialism. It has drawn into itself all the residual vitality of the enfeebled capitalist order and has become preeminent in the imperialist camp. It is this temporarily favorable aspect of the world situation for the American ruling class that has most affected the lives of the American people and been responsible for the inner stability of monopolist rule.

But let us look at the other side of this development. If the United States has been the undisputed victor in the competition among the imperialist nations, it is also a victim of the changed world situation. The totality of capitalist power is contracting, while the strength of the anticapitalist countries and forces is expanding. By having to extend its sphere of influence and military commitments throughout the globe, capitalist America has become inextricably involved in all the convulsions of a chronically sick social system. It has to rush to the rescue of every tottering reactionary relic from Fulgencio Batista to Chiang Kai-shek to Francisco Franco. The Truman Doctrine, the Korean War, the Eisenhower Middle East Doctrine, the Alliance for Progress, are so many milestones along this counterrevolutionary road.

The drive of the U.S. militarists and monopolists for world supremacy, and their ever-deepening involvement in world affairs, has far-reaching implications for the working people. The consequences of the cold war and the threat of hot ones affect all the main aspects of their lives from the tax bite on their weekly paychecks to the degree of their civil liberties. The State Department exerts intense pressure upon the labor leaders to go along with its foreign policies; they eagerly comply and force the ranks to conform. This does not in the least prevent the other arms of the capitalist government from passing and enforcing legislation injuring and endangering the unions (the Taft-Hartley and Kennedy-Landrum-Griffin acts).

This changed situation confronts the labor movement with problems of unprecedented gravity and intricacy. However, its leaders are content to enjoy the ease of the moment without troubling themselves either about the discontents in the ranks or the perils of the future. They remain unaware that any drastic revisions are called for in their outlook or methods. They are as oblivious to dangers ahead as canoers drifting toward rapids hidden around the bend.

The union tycoons pride themselves upon being in step with the times because they hire public relations experts, have chrome-plated offices, and ride in Cadillacs. But their basic ideas about the world, and the place and prospects of labor within it, are as antiquated as the derby hat. Like all pragmatists, they are provincial and short-sighted. They complacently expect that trade union life will remain as it is indefinitely, and whatever changes may be required will be easily handled by their usual methods. On one hand they assume that unionism will continue to roll along the same grooves as in the past. On the other hand they believe that America's future will be shaped along essentially different lines than those revolutionary events which have already upset capitalism in other parts of the world.

It is true that American history has had its peculiarities and will continue to do so. However, these exceptional features have not been great enough in the past to spare the American people from going through two revolutions, one in the eighteenth century and the other in the nineteenth, when capitalism was on the rise in North America. Indeed, these revolutions occurred as they did precisely because of the peculiarities in America's development. So it appears even less likely that the present peculiarities will prevent this nation from being drawn into the revolutionary whirlpool of our age when nuclear energy, rockets, and jet planes have compressed national boundaries and when economics, politics, military strategy, and culture have a global character.

The labor movement needs a far better understanding of its role in American life and world affairs than it has. But it is unlikely to acquire this improved theory until another big shake-up in class relations occurs on the order of the crisis of the 1930s, which brought the CIO into being. When the ranks are again roused into militant action and the fat cats are unseated, labor will begin to cast off its mental sluggishness and absorb new ideas.

The duty of socialists is to foresee this rebirth of mass radicalism and to prepare its advent by developing and disseminating the ideas of Marxism.

Leon Trotsky's Views
on Dialectical Materialism

January 10, 1937—the day after Leon Trotsky and his wife, Natalia Sedova, had landed in Mexico. His party was on the troop-guarded private train sent by the minister of communications to ensure their safe conduct from Tampico to Mexico City. That sunny morning Max Shachtman and I sat with Trotsky in one of the compartments, bringing the exile up to date on what had happened during his enforced voyage from Norway.

Our conversation was animated; there was so much to tell, especially about developments around the Moscow trials. (This was in the interval between the first and second of Stalin's stage-managed judicial frame-ups.) At one point Trotsky asked about the philosopher John Dewey, who had joined the American committee set up to obtain asylum for him and hear his case.

From there our discussion glided into the subject of philosophy, in which, he was informed, I had a special interest. We talked about the best ways of studying dialectical materialism, about Lenin's *Materialism and Empirio-Criticism,* and about the theoretical backwardness of American radicalism. Trotsky brought forward the name of Max Eastman, who in various works had polemicized against dialectics as a worthless idealist hangover from the Hegelian heritage of Marxism.

He became tense, agitated. "Upon going back to the States," he urged, "you comrades must at once take up the struggle against Eastman's distortion and repudiation of dialectical materialism. There is nothing more important than this. Pragmatism, empiricism, is the greatest curse of American thought. You must inoculate younger comrades against its infection."

I was somewhat surprised at the vehemence of his argumentation on this matter at such a moment. As the principal defendant in absentia in the Moscow trials, and because of the dramatic circumstances of his voyage in exile, Trotsky then stood in the center of international attention. He was fighting for his reputation, liberty, and life against the powerful government of Stalin, bent on his defamation and death. After having been imprisoned and gagged for months by the Norwegian authorities, he had been kept incommunicado for weeks aboard their tanker.

Yet on the first day after reunion with his cothinkers, he spent more than an hour explaining how important it was for a Marxist movement to have a correct philosophical method and to defend dialectical materialism against its opponents!

He proved how serious he was about this question three years later by the manner of his intervention in the struggle which convulsed the Socialist Workers Party at the beginning of the Second World War. By this time Shachtman had switched philosophical and political fronts. He was aligned directly with James Burnham and indirectly with Eastman and others against Trotsky, breaking away from the traditional positions of Marxism and the Fourth International on issues extending from the role of philosophy to the class nature of the Soviet Union and its defense against imperialist attack.*

The Burnham-Shachtman opposition sought to separate philosophy from politics in general, and the principled politics of the revolutionary working class movement from Marxist theory in particular. In the spirit of pragmatism, Burnham demanded that the issues in dispute be confined to "concrete questions." "There is no sense *at all*," he declared in "Science and Style," "in which dialectics (even if dialectics were not, as it is, scientifically meaningless) is fundamental in politics, none at all."[1]

In "An Open Letter to Comrade Burnham" Trotsky had pointed out that the experience of the labor movement demonstrated how false and unscientific it was to divorce politics from Marxist sociology and the dialectical method. "You seem to consider apparently that by refusing to discuss dialectic material-

---

*Trotsky's contributions to the theoretical debate are collected in the book *In Defense of Marxism*. Burnham's article "Science and Style" is included as an appendix.

ism and the class nature of the Soviet state and by sticking to 'concrete' questions you are acting the part of a realistic politician. This self-deception is a result of your inadequate acquaintance with the history of the past fifty years of factional struggles in the labor movement. In every principled conflict, without a single exception, the Marxists sought to face the party squarely with the fundamental problems of doctrine and program, considering that only under this condition could the 'concrete' questions find their proper place and proportion."[2]

On the other hand, opportunists and revisionists of every shade avoided discussion of principles and counterposed superficial and misleading episodic appraisals of events to the revolutionary class analysis of the scientific socialists. Trotsky cited examples from the history of the German Social Democracy and from the disputes of the Russian Marxists with the "Economists," the Social Revolutionaries, and the Mensheviks. The Narodnik terrorists, bomb in hand, used to argue: "*Iskra* [Lenin's paper] wants to found a school of dialectic materialism while we want to overthrow Czarist autocracy. . . . It is historical experience," Trotsky observed with characteristic irony, "that the greatest revolution in all history was not led by the party which started out with bombs but by the party which started out with dialectic materialism."[3]

Trotsky attached such great importance to the generalized theory incorporated in Marxist philosophy because of its utility in political practice. "The question of a correct philosophical doctrine, that is, a correct method of thought, is of decisive significance to a revolutionary party just as a good machine shop is of decisive significance to production," he wrote.[4] Many of the now indispensable tools of thought for investigating and analyzing reality were fabricated by the great philosophers before entering into common use. In dialectical materialism, he asserted, Marx and Engels forged the theoretical tools and weapons required by the workers in their struggle to get rid of the old order and build a new one.

*　　　*　　　*

Trotsky never claimed originality for his philosophical views. He was an orthodox Marxist from his conversion to its doctrines in 1898 to his death in 1940. However, he did enrich and extend the teachings of the masters by his far-ranging applications of their method to the complex problems presented by the transition of humanity from capitalism to socialism. His insight and foresight in this field equalled that of any other disciple, Lenin included.

In his four decades of writing he touched upon almost all the principal aspects of materialism, from its insistence upon the primordial reality of nature to its explanation of the supreme products of human thought and artistic imagination. The basis of all life, of all human action and thought, and the object of knowledge, was the being and becoming of the independently existing material world. This universal evolutionary process of material nature was dialectical in character. It proceeded through the conflict of antagonistic forces, which at certain points in the slow accumulation of changes exploded the old formations, bringing about a catastrophic upset, a revolution.

We call our dialectic, materialist, since its roots are neither in heaven nor in the depths of our "free will," but in objective reality, in nature. Consciousness grew out of the unconscious, psychology out of physiology, the organic world out of the inorganic, the solar system out of nebulae. On all the rungs of this ladder of development, the quantitative changes were transformed into qualitative. Our thought, including dialectical thought, is only one of the forms of the expression of changing matter. There is place within this system for neither God, nor Devil, nor immortal soul, nor eternal norms of laws and morals. The dialectic of thinking, having grown out of the dialectic of nature, possesses consequently a thoroughly materialist character.[5]

To clarify the operation of dialectical laws in nature he cited two examples from nineteenth-century science—one from biology, the other from chemistry. "Darwinism, which explained the evolution of species through quantitative transformations passing into qualitative, was the highest triumph of the dialectic in the whole field of organic matter. Another great triumph was the discovery of the table of atomic weights of chemical elements and further the transformation of one element into another."[6]

Materialism provided the only solid theoretical foundation for progress in the sciences, even though many natural scientists might be unaware of this truth or even deny it.

It is the task of science and technology [Trotsky said in a 1926 speech] to make matter subject to man, together with space and time, which are inseparable from matter. True, there are certain idealist books—not of a clerical character, but philosophical ones—wherein you can read that time and space are categories of our minds, that they result from the requirements of our thinking, and that nothing actually corresponds to them in reality. But it is difficult to agree with this view. If any idealist philosopher, instead of arriving in time to catch the nine p.m. train, should turn up two minutes late, he would see the tail of the departing train and would be convinced by his own eyes that time and space are inseparable from material reality. The task is to diminish this space, to overcome it, to economize time, to prolong human life, to register past time, to raise life to a higher level and enrich it. This is the reason for the struggle with space and time, at the basis of which lies the struggle to subject matter to man—matter, which constitutes the foundation not only of everything that really exists, but also of all imagination.

. . . Every science is an accumulation of knowledge, based on experience relating to matter, to its properties; an accumulation of generalized understanding of how to subject this matter to the interests and needs of man.[7]

*   *   *

Trotsky made many such penetrating observations on the materialist approach to the problems of the natural sciences. But his principal contributions to scientific knowledge came from his studies of contemporary society. These were all illuminated and directed by the Marxist method.

Trotsky became engrossed in the problems connected with the materialist conception of history at the early age of eighteen, when he was already involved in the illegal workers' movement of South Russia. From that time on these two sides of his activity—the theoretical investigation of social reality and the practical urge to transform it with the masses along revolutionary lines—went hand in hand.

Trotsky tells in *My Life* how he at first resisted the unified outlook of historical materialism. He adopted in its stead the theory of "the multiplicity of historical factors," which even today is the most widely accepted theory in social science. (Compare the school of Max Weber in Europe or C. Wright Mills in the United States.) His reading of two essays by the Italian Hegelian-Marxist Antonio Labriola convinced him of the correctness of the views of the historical materialists. They conceived of the various aspects of social activity as an integrated whole, historically evolving in accord with the development of the productive forces and interacting with one another in a living process where the material conditions of life were ultimately decisive. The eclectics of the liberal school, on the other hand, split the diverse aspects of social life into many independent factors, endowed these with superhistorical character, and then "superstitiously interpreted their own activity as the result of the interaction of these independent forces."

During his first prison sentence Trotsky wrote a study of Freemasonry, which was later lost, as an exercise in the materialist conception of history. "In the writings of Marx, Engels, Plekhanov and Mehring, I later found confirmation for what in prison seemed to me only a guess needing verification and theoretical justification. I did not absorb historical materialism at once, dogmatically. The dialectic method revealed itself to me for the first time not as abstract definitions but as a living spring which I had found in the historical process as I tried to understand it."[8]

Trotsky employed the newly acquired method to uncover the "living springs" of the class struggle in modern society and, first of all, in tsarist Russia at the turn of the twentieth century, where a revolution was being prepared. The development of his celebrated theory of the permanent revolution was the first result of his researches. This was one of the outstanding triumphs of dialectical analysis applied to the social tendencies and political prospects of prerevolutionary Russia and, in its further elaboration, to the problems confronting backward countries in the imperialist epoch.

Marxists are often accused by their critics of dogmatism, of obsession with abstract schemes of historical development. Some would-be Marxists have been guilty of this fault. Not so Trotsky. He was a consistent practitioner of historical materialism, but within those principled boundaries he was the least formalistic and the most flexible of thinkers.

The materialist dialectic is based upon the existence of conflicting movements, forces, and relations in history, whose contradictions as they develop expose the shortcomings of all fixed formulas. As Trotsky wrote in 1906 in *Results and Prospects,* "Marxism is above all a method of analysis—not analysis of texts, but analysis of social relations."[9]

Trotsky undertook to apply the Marxist method in this materialist manner to the specific conditions of tsarist Russia. He pointed out that the social structure of Russia at the beginning of the twentieth century was a peculiar blend of extremely backward and advanced features. The predominant political and religious backwardness embodied in the Asiatic despotism of the all-powerful monarchy and its servile state church was rooted in the historical and economic backwardness of the country. In Russia there had been no Reformation, no successful bourgeois revolutions, no strong third estate (bourgeoisie) as in Western Europe. The boundless spaces and windswept climate had given rise to nomadic existence and an extensive agriculture, a thin population, a belated and meager feudal development, and an absence of commercial and craft centers. The prevalence of peasant agriculture and home industry self-contained in small villages, of large landed estates, and of administrative-military-consuming cities restricted the domestic market and led to dependence upon foreign capital and culture.

However, with the entry of modern industry, this Asiatic backwardness became complemented and combined with the most up-to-date products of Western European development. Large-scale industry led not only to the fusion of industrial with banking capital and domination of the Russian economy by foreign finance, but ultimately to a proletariat in the major industrial centers, a modern labor movement engaging in political strikes and mass demonstrations, and scientific socialism. These exceptional conditions set the stage for the revolutionary events which were to explode in 1905 and culminate in 1917.

The schematic thinkers among the Russian Social Democrats, who had learned the letter but not the essence of Marx's method and were more or less under bourgeois influence, asserted that Russia would have to follow the trail blazed by Western Europe.

The older capitalist nations had passed from feudalism through a prolonged period of capitalist evolution toward socialism; in politics they had proceeded from rule by the monarchy and landed aristocracy to bourgeois parliamentarism before the workers could bid for supremacy. From this the Mensheviks concluded that the rulership of the bourgeoisie in a democratic republic on a capitalist basis was the logical successor to feudalized absolutism; the workers would have to wait a long while for their turn.

The attempt to impose such a prefabricated sequence upon twentieth-century Russia was arbitrary and false, according to Trotsky. The powerful peculiarities of Russia's past and present made possible, and even inevitable, an unprecedented path of development which opened up immense new prospects for the labor movement. The rottenness of tsarism, the weakness of the bourgeoisie and its institutions, the strategic position of the industrial workers, and the revolutionary potential in the peasantry springing from the unsolved, but urgent, problems of the land question would enable the pending revolution to compress and lead over stages. The workers could place themselves at the head of the insurgent people; they could lead the peasantry in overthrowing the old order and establishing democracy in a higher form under the government of the working class, which would quickly pass over from bourgeois democratic to revolutionary socialist measures. Thus the belated bourgeois democratic revolution would clear the way for and be a direct introduction to the first steps of the socialist revolution.

The political force of the working class could not be viewed in isolation but had to be judged in its relation with all the other factors at work within the country and the world. Although "the productive forces of the United States are ten times as great as those of Russia, nevertheless the political role of the Russian proletariat, its influence on the politics of its own country and the possibility of its influencing the politics of the world in the near future are incomparably greater than in the case of the proletariat of the United States."[10] From all these considerations he drew the conclusion that "the Russian revolution will create conditions in which power can pass into the hands of the workers—and in the event of the victory of the revolution it must do so—*before* the politicians of bourgeois liberalism get the chance to display to the full their talent for governing."[11]

This was the first form of his theory of the permanent revolution. Upon the basis of Russian experience he subsequently extended it to cover the problems and prospects of the revolution in other underdeveloped countries where the workers and peasants must struggle against imperialism and its native agents to extricate themselves from precapitalist barbarism and acquire the benefits of modern economy and culture.

From 1904 to 1917 Trotskyism was identified with the conception that the Russian revolution could end only in the dictatorship of the proletariat, which in its turn must lead to the socialist transformation of society, given the victorious development of the world revolution. This outlook was opposed by the Mensheviks, who could not see beyond the bourgeois democratic republic, and was even unacceptable to the Bolsheviks. However, the young Trotsky was able to see farther than all the others among the

brilliant constellation of Russian Marxists thanks to his preco-
cious mastery of the materialistic and dialectical sides of Marx's
method and his exceptional boldness and keenness of thought.
He was the Columbus of the most extraordinary event in modern
history: the first successful proletarian revolution, in the most
backward country of Europe.

In working out his prognosis of the Russian revolution, Trotsky
utilized the law of uneven and combined development, which he
was later to formulate in general terms. This generalization of the
dialectical intertwining of the backward and advanced features
of the historical process is one of the most valuable instruments
for deciphering the complex relations and contradictory trends of
civilized society.*

*   *   *

The laws of the class struggle constitute the essence of historical materialism applied to civilized society. Liberals and conser-
vatives find this part of scientific socialism impossible to accept;
reformists and Stalinists are unable to carry it through in the
day-by-day struggle against capitalism. The recognition of the
class struggle in its full scope and ultimate consequences was the
very nerve center of Trotsky's thought and action.

The history of the development of human society is the history of the
succession of various systems of economy, each operating in accordance
with its own laws. The transition from one system to another was always
determined by the growth of the productive forces, i.e., of technique and
the organization of labor. Up to a certain point, social changes are
quantitative in character and do not alter the foundations of society, i.e.,
the prevalent forms of property. But a point is reached when the matured
productive forces can no longer contain themselves within the old forms
of property; then follows a radical change in the social order, accompanied by shocks. The primitive commune was either superseded or supplemented by slavery; slavery was succeeded by serfdom with its feudal
superstructure; the commercial development of cities brought Europe in
the sixteenth century to the capitalist order, which thereupon passed
through several stages.[12]

This historical process was propelled forward by the action and

---

*For a full exposition see the chapter entitled "Uneven and Combined
Development in World History" in *Understanding History* by the author.

reaction of one class upon another. The material stake in their struggles was the acquisition and distribution of the surplus product—that portion of the total social product beyond the minimum required for the survival and reproduction of the working force. Possessing and oppressing classes, from the slaveholders to the capitalists, have been distinguished primarily by the different methods of exploitation they have used to extract this surplus from the laboring masses. "The class struggle is nothing else than the struggle for surplus-product. He who owns surplus-product is master of the situation—owns wealth, owns the state, has the key to the church, to the courts, to the sciences and to the arts."[13]

Each society forms an organic whole. The bones of the social organism consist of its productive forces; its muscles are its class (property) relations. The functions and reflexes of all other social organs can be understood only in their connections with the skeletal and muscular systems (the productive forces and property forms) which make up the general structure of the social organism. Since civilized society is split up into classes, the critical point of analysis in scientific sociology has to be

the *class* definition of a given phenomenon, e.g., state, party, philosophic trend, literary school, etc. In most cases, however, the mere class definition is inadequate, for a class consists of different strata, passes through different stages of development, comes under different conditions, is subjected to the influence of other classes. It becomes necessary to bring up these second and third rate factors in order to round out the analysis, and they are taken either partially or completely, depending upon the specific aim. But for a Marxist, analysis is impossible without a class characterization of the phenomenon under consideration.[14]

In order to ascertain the decisive tendencies and the main course of development of any given social formation or nation, the scientific sociologist, according to Trotsky, has to examine its structure and the dynamics of its social forces in their connections with world historical conditions. We must find specific answers to the following questions: What classes are struggling in a country? What are their interrelations? How, and in what direction, are their relations being transformed? What are the objective tasks dictated by historical necessity? On the shoulders of what classes does the solution of these tasks rest? With what methods can they be solved?

During his revolutionary career Trotsky analyzed the situations in many major countries at critical turning points in their evolution, according to this procedure. These included Russia, Germany, France, England, Austria, and Spain in Europe; China and India in Asia; and the United States. The results of his inquiries are contained in a series of works which are models for any aspiring scientific historian or sociologist.

Ever since Marxism stirred up the academicians, much dust has been raised about its conception of the relations between the economic foundations and the rest of the social structure in the process of historical evolution. Trotsky tried not only to clear up the misunderstandings around this question in general, but also to show by example how the material substructure of society, crystallized in the relations of production and its property forms, reacted with other social and cultural phenomena.

"The opinion that economics presumably determines directly and immediately the creativeness of a composer or even the verdict of a judge, represents a hoary caricature of Marxism which the bourgeois professordom of all countries has circulated time out of end to mask their intellectual impotence," he declared.[15] The dialectical approach of Marxism has nothing in common with this crude "economic determinism," so often practiced by the Stalinist school.

The economic foundation of a given society is organically interrelated and continuously interactive with its political-cultural superstructure. But the relations between them can be harmonious or inharmonious, depending upon the given conditions of historical development and the specific combinations of historical factors. In some cases the political regime can be in stark contradiction with its economic basis. Indeed, this is the source of the deepening class antagonisms which generate the need for revolutions. This can hold true not only for capitalist states but for postcapitalist political structures in the period of transition to socialism. In the Soviet Union under Stalin and his heirs, for example, the economic basis of nationalized property and planned production has been increasingly at odds with the autocratic system of bureaucratic rule.

In the long run, economics takes precedence over politics. Political regimes, institutions, parties, and leaders are defined by the roles they play in upholding or changing the existing relations of production. "Although economics determines politics not directly or immediately, but only in the last analysis, *nevertheless economics does determine politics,*" Trotsky affirmed.[16] Capitalist property relations determine the nature of the bourgeois state and the conduct of its representatives; nationalized property determines the nature of the workers' states, however deformed and bureaucratic they may be.

The controversy around "the cult of the individual" provoked by the de-Stalinization campaign in the Soviet bloc has raised again for consideration the question of the role of the individual in history. This much-debated issue has long divided one tendency from another in the social sciences.

Nonmaterialists make one or another of the subjective factors in social life, from ideas to the actions of individuals, paramount in the determination of events. For a historical materialist like Trotsky, the social takes precedence over the individual, the general over the particular, the whole over the part, the material over the intellectual. The individual is important in history. But the extent of his influence depends upon broader historical factors. The strictly personal elements are subordinate to objective historical conditions and the major social forces of which they are a product, a part, and an exemplar.

The Russian Marxists from Plekhanov to Lenin gave considerable attention to this question. In arguing against the Narodnik school of subjective sociology, which in its most extreme expression upheld terrorism as a political means of struggle, the Marxists pointed out that social and political power was not simply an individual attribute; it was at bottom a function of the relations between people and, in the last analysis, between classes. The most prominent personages wield power not solely on their own account, but on behalf of social forces greater than themselves. Even kings, tyrants, dictators represent the material interests of a specific class or combination of classes.

No political institution, for example, fuses the superpersonal forces in history with the personal more than the monarchy. "Monarchy by its very principle is bound up with the personal," wrote Trotsky in *The History of the Russian Revolution.*[17]

Under tsarism the royal family appeared to count as everything, the rest of the nation as nothing. Yet this was only the outward semblance of things.

"The king is king only because the interests and prejudices of millions of people are refracted through his person."[18] The king cannot rule without the tacit consent of nobles, landlords, and other class forces which he serves, or even in the end without the acquiescence of the mass of his subjects. When these refuse any longer to recognize or abide by the royal authority, it is in danger or done for. The first act of the Russian revolution, the overthrow of the monarchy, verified this social basis of personal power.

The Russian revolution, led by the Bolshevik Party of Lenin and Trotsky, abolished both tsarism and capitalism and instituted a workers' and peasants' democracy under the Soviets. This was smashed, and a new despotism came to flourish under Stalin. What was the social basis for Stalin's absolute one-man rule?

Trotsky is often severely condemned for "permitting" Stalin to outwit him in the contest for supremacy after Lenin's death. Critics of this superficial stamp do not understand that the most intelligent individuals with the most correct ideas and strategy are necessarily subordinated to the historical tides of their time and to the prevailing relations of class forces. Power is not a personal possession which can be transported at will like any commodity from one owner to another.

The fundamental factors at work in the world that decide the turn and outcome of great events were then ranged against the cause for which Trotsky fought; they favored and facilitated the advance of Stalin. On the basis of the defeats of the working class in Europe, the isolation of the Soviet Union, and the weariness of the Soviet masses, Stalin was being lifted up and pushed to the fore during the 1920s by the increasingly powerful Soviet bureaucrats and labor aristocrats, backed up and egged on by an acquisitive upper layer of the peasantry. The Left Opposition, headed by Trotsky, which spoke for the revolutionary movement of the world working class and fought for the interests of the Soviet poor, was being pushed aside.

Trotsky explained over and over again that Stalin's triumph and his own defeat did not signify the mere displacement of one individual by another, or even of one faction by another, but the definitive transfer of political power from the socialist working class to the privileged Soviet bureaucracy. He consciously tied his own fate and the fortunes of the Communist Left Opposition to the situation of the world revolution and the Russian working class.

Trotsky had thought profoundly on the dialectical interplay between the individual and the great impersonal driving forces of history. The purely personal characteristics of individuals, he stated, have narrow limits and very quickly merge into the social conditions of their development and collectivity to which they belong. "The 'distinguishing traits' of a person are merely individual scratches made by a higher law of development."[19]

We do not at all pretend to deny the significance of the personal in the mechanics of the historic process, nor the significance in the personal of the accidental. We only demand that a historic personality, with all its peculiarities, should not be taken as a bare list of psychological traits, but as a living reality grown out of definite social conditions and reacting upon them. As a rose does not lose its fragrance because the natural scientist points out upon what ingredients of soil and atmosphere it is nourished, so an exposure of the social roots of a personality does not remove from it either its aroma or its foul smell.[20]

The tsar, as the head of his dynastic caste resting upon the Russian bureaucracy and aristocracy, was a product of its whole historical development and had to share its destiny. The same law held good for his successors at the helm of the Russian state after February 1917. Each of the leading individuals, from Kerensky through Lenin and Trotsky to Stalin, represented and incarnated a different correlation of social forces both national and international, a different degree of determination by the working class, a different stage in the development of the Russian revolution and the state and society which issued from it.

Trotsky was as thoroughgoing a materialist in his psychological observations as in his sociological and political analyses. Stalin as a man, he explained, acquired his definitive historical personality as the chosen leader of the Soviet aristocratic caste. "One can understand the acts of Stalin only by starting from the conditions of existence of the new privileged stratum, greedy for power, greedy for material comforts, apprehensive for its positions, fearing the masses, and mortally hating all opposition," Trotsky told the Dewey Commission in 1937. Stalin's depravity, confirmed two decades afterward by Khrushchev, was not uniquely his own.

The more precipitate the jump from the October overturn—which laid bare all social falsehood—to the present situation, in which a caste of upstarts is forced to cover up its social ulcers, the cruder the Thermidorian lies. It is, consequently, a question not simply of the individual depravity of this or that person, but of the corruption lodged in the position of a whole social group for whom lying has become a vital political necessity. In the struggle for its newly gained positions, this caste has reeducated itself and simultaneously reeducated—or rather, demoralized—its leaders. It raised upon its shoulders the man who best, most resolutely and most ruthlessly expresses its interests. Thus Stalin, who was once a revolutionist, became the leader of the Thermidorian caste.

Conversely, the revolutionary essence of the principles, positions, and social interests that Trotsky consistently embodied and expressed throughout his lifetime made him what he was and placed him where he had to be at each stage. He worked at the side of the Russian working class while it was preparing its first revolutions; he rose to its head in the Soviet of 1905. He remained with its active vanguard during the subsequent reaction. When the revolution surged up to the heights he organized the October insurrection, and then led the Red Army until after the Civil War.

Later, when the workers again became politically passive and prostrate under Stalin's regime, he still stood firmly with them. Throughout this period of reaction he did his utmost to stem the decline of the revolution, rally and educate its forces, and prepare the best conditions for its revival. Trotsky was too much the Marxist to desire or exercise power for any purpose other than to promote socialist aims.

*   *   *

Trotsky's forecast of the Russian revolution was the first triumph of his application of the method of dialectical materialism; his analysis of its degeneration was his final and greatest achievement.

Here Trotsky was confronted with an unprecedented historical phenomenon. To be sure, previous revolutions had mounted to great heights and then receded. But these relapses had taken place within a class society where a new and more progressive—but nevertheless exploiting and oppressing—ruling class had been installed in power. He was familiar with leaderships of other workers' movements which had succumbed to the temptations of privilege and office, abused their authority, become bureaucratized. But these, too, had been beneficiaries and appendages of imperialist capitalism.

The situation in the young Soviet Republic appeared fundamentally different. The workers and peasants, led by the most conscious revolutionary party in history, guided by the scientific doctrines of Marxism, had taken state power and begun to reconstruct society in their own image. For years the leaders and members of the Bolshevik Party had distinguished themselves in battle by their ideas and their program, showing their readiness to sacrifice everything for the cause of socialism.

And yet the viruses of bureaucratism and privilege—"the professional dangers of power," as Christian Rakovsky designated them—had attacked the new rulers of Russia and weakened their resistance to alien class influences. The inroads of infection had been manifest during Lenin's last years, and he had asked Trotsky to join him in combatting their spread.

For someone like Trotsky, who had been so wholly and intimately identified with the revolution and its leadership, it required the utmost objectivity to detach his personal fate from this situation and cope with the problems it presented. He was like a medical scientist who, having detected the presence of a wasting disease in a dear companion, notes its symptoms and makes a diagnosis and prognosis, understanding all the while that the disease may not be arrested and can prove fatal. He followed the unfolding of the bureaucratic reaction step by step, analyzing its causes, pinpointing its results—while prescribing the necessary therapeutic measures to alleviate and cure the disease.

The basic conditions for the growth of bureaucratism, he said, were first of all lodged in the world situation. The failure of the Russian revolution to be matched by the workers in the more advanced industrialized countries of the West, and the temporary stabilization of international capitalism, left the first workers' state in an exposed and weakened position. In the Soviet Union a small working class, exhausted after enormous and sustained exertions, surrounded by a sea of peasantry and poverty, lacking culture, an adequate economic basis, even the elementary necessities of life, had to relinquish the powers and positions it had won to a layer of bureaucratic specialists in administration who wanted rest and the enjoyment of the fruits of the previous revolutionary efforts. The material privileges and narrow political views of this upstart caste came into ever greater conflict with the interests of the masses.

This was the source of the factional conflicts which tore apart the Russian Communist Party and were extended into the Communist International. With the deepening and strengthening of world reaction during the 1930s this process reached its climax in the consolidation of the Stalinist autocracy and the total erasure of Soviet democracy. The ascendancy of Stalinism in the Soviet Union and of fascism in Western Europe were symmetrical historical phenomena. The destruction of bourgeois democracy under the decadence of capitalist imperialism and the destruction of workers' democracy in the Soviet Republic were parallel products of the defeats of the working masses by reaction.

These totalitarian states had, however, completely opposite and historically different economic bases. The fascist dictators Adolf Hitler, Benito Mussolini, and Francisco Franco ruled over states which defended capitalist property relations. Stalin's government, the uncontrolled agent of Soviet bureaucratism, rested upon nationalized property.

Trotsky gave a dialectical, historical, and materialist definition of the Soviet Union. By virtue of its nationalized property, its planned economy, its monopoly of foreign trade, and the socialist consciousness and traditions in the working class, it remained a workers' state. But it was a special type of workers' state in which the political structure contradicted the economic foundations. The policies and activities of Stalinist tyranny not only trampled upon the rights, feelings, and welfare of the masses in whose interests the revolution was made but injured the development of the Soviet economy itself, which required democratic administration by the workers to function most efficiently.

The conflict between Stalin's one-man rule and workers' democracy, between the totalitarian political structure and the economic foundation, was the prime motive force in Soviet society, however much it was repressed and hushed up. The tension between these contending social forces could not endure indefinitely. Either the workers would clean out the bureaucratic usurpers—or the bureaucrats would extrude a wing which would strike at the last remaining achievements of the revolution and clear the way for the return of capitalism from within or from abroad.

Trotsky was no defeatist; he did not declare in advance that the worst would happen. On the contrary, he threw all his forces and resources into the balance to help the favorable outcome prevail. Now, twenty years after his death, his struggle and foresight have been vindicated. While imperialism tore itself to pieces for the second time and was further weakened by the Second World

War, the Soviet state survived, despite all the crimes of Stalinism. After revealing its powers of resistance in the war against Hitlerism, it has displayed amazing capacities for recuperation and swift growth in the postwar years. The socialist revolution itself broke through to new ground, extending into Eastern Europe and Asia and scuttling Stalin's theory of "socialism in one country" as a by-product.

These international and national developments have elevated the Soviet working class to a higher cultural and material level and impelled the most progressive elements in Soviet society to press hard upon the bureaucrats to relax their dictatorship and grant concessions. The drive for de-Stalinization breaks through with such irresistible force that—up to a certain limited point—it has even carried along elements among the bureaucracy. Its momentum testifies to the growing powers and impatience of the socialist elements in Soviet society and confirms Trotsky's analysis of its main motive forces and trends.

Thus far we have seen only the opening events in this new chapter of internal Soviet development, which is heading toward an all-out conflict between the self-appointed successors of Stalin and the resurgent masses. The Soviet workers, intellectuals, and peasants will have to throw off all their overlords and restore democracy on an incomparably higher basis.

The reexamination of values which has been started under the slogan "Return to Lenin" will be supplemented and completed by the slogan "Return to Trotsky." The new leaders of the people in the coming antibureaucratic revolution will reinstate Trotsky's achievements to their proper place and honor him as the initiator, herald, and guide in the fight for socialist freedom and the preservation of the heritage of Marxism and Bolshevism.

*   *   *

Trotsky probed more deeply than any other Marxist thinker into the problems of materialist psychology. In the controversies that counterposed Pavlov's school of conditioned reflexes to the Freudian school of depth analysis he took a third position. While he observed that their respective approaches to the formation of consciousness were different, he did not believe there was an insuperable materialist-idealist conflict between them, as the Stalinists have contended. Both Pavlov and Freud considered that physiology constituted the basis of the higher functions of thought. Trotsky compared Pavlov to a diver who descends to the bottom of the well of the human mind to inspect it from there upwards, while Freud stood above peering through the obscure and troubled waters of the psyche to discern what was at work within its depths.*

The characteristic traits of people are elicited, formed, and perfected by their social environments; even the oddest quirks soon pass over into the behavior and psychology proper to the individual's epoch, group, or class. Certain common characteristics are imposed on people by the mighty forces of historical conditions; similar conditions call forth similar responses and produce similar personality traits. "Similar (of course, far from identical) irritations in similar conditions call out similar reflexes; the more powerful the irritation, the sooner it overcomes personal peculiarities. To a tickle, people react differently, but to a red-hot iron, alike. As a steam-hammer converts a sphere and a cube alike into sheet metal, so under the blow of too great and inexorable events resistances are smashed and the boundaries of 'individuality' lost."[22]

In this way he explained the puzzles of what bourgeois psychologists call "the behavior of crowds," or, more precisely, mass consciousness. Despite all their individual differences and peculiarities, despite their separation in time and place, individuals placed in similar settings and faced with similar problems behave alike.

The so-called faculty psychologists of the nineteenth century split up the human personality and psyche into different factors such as instinct, will, intuition, consciousness, the unconscious, etc., elevating one or another of these elements of human behavior into predominance. Trotsky viewed all these various functions as interpenetrating aspects of a unified physiological-psychological process, materially conditioned and subject to development and change.

Inspiration and intuition are usually regarded as the special

---

*A more complete account of Trotsky's views on this controversy and on other cultural, scientific, artistic, and literary matters is given by Isaac Deutscher in chapter 3 of *The Prophet Unarmed,* entitled "Not By Politics Alone . . .".

province of idealists and mystics. However, Trotsky did not hesitate to come to grips even with these obscure and elusive phases of psychic activity. He noted that the conscious and unconscious coexist in the historical process just as they do within the individuals who compose it. He gave an incomparable definition of their interaction in *My Life*:

Marxism considers itself the conscious expression of the unconscious historical process. But the "unconscious" process, in the historico-philosophical sense of the term—not in the psychological—coincides with its conscious expression only at its highest point, when the masses, by sheer elemental pressure, break through the social routine and give victorious expression to the deepest needs of historical development. And at such moments the highest theoretical consciousness of the epoch merges with the immediate action of those oppressed masses who are farthest away from theory. The creative union of the conscious with the unconscious is what one usually calls "inspiration." Revolution is the inspired frenzy of history.

Every real writer knows creative moments, when something stronger than himself is guiding his hand; every real orator experiences moments when someone stronger than the self of his every-day existence speaks through him. This is "inspiration." It derives from the highest creative effort of all one's forces. The unconscious rises from its deep well and bends the conscious mind to its will, merging it with itself in some greater synthesis.

The utmost spiritual vigor likewise infuses at times all personal activity connected with the movement of the masses. This was true for the leaders in the October days. The hidden strength of the organism, its most deeply rooted instincts, its power of scent inherited from animal forebears—all these rose and broke through the psychic routine to join forces with the higher historico-philosophical abstractions in the service of the revolution. Both these processes, affecting the individual and the mass, were based on the union of the conscious with the unconscious: the union of instinct—the mainspring of the will—with the higher theories of thought.[23]

Trotsky had absorbed the materialist attitude into every fiber of his being; it permeated all his thought and action from his outlook upon human life to his appraisals of the individuals around him. As a consistent materialist he was a proud and avowed atheist. He would not permit himself to be degraded or humanity to be subjugated to any of its own fictitious creations issuing from the barbarous past.

His humanistic profession of faith was frankly stated in the testament he set down a few months before his assassination: "For forty-three years of my conscious life I have remained a revolutionist; for forty-two of them I have fought under the banner of Marxism. . . . I shall die a proletarian revolutionist, a Marxist, a dialectical materialist, and, consequently, an irreconcilable atheist."[24]

He felt no need for the fictitious consolations of personal life after death. Cramped and contaminated though it was by class society, life on earth was enough because of the potential for human enjoyment and fulfillment latent within it. "I can see the bright green strip of grass beneath the wall, and the clear blue sky above the wall, and sunlight everywhere. Life is beautiful. Let the future generations cleanse it of all evil, oppression, and violence and enjoy it to the full." A few days later he added: "Whatever may be the circumstances of my death I shall die with unshaken faith in the communist future. This faith in man and in his future gives me even now such power of resistance as cannot be given by any religion."[25]

Such was the final testimony of the most gifted exponent of the 2,500-year-old materialist philosophy in our time.

NOTES

(In the case of references to works that are listed in the bibliography, the reader is referred to the bibliography for complete publication information.)

My Philosophical Itinerary:
An Autobiographical Foreword

1. Georg Lukács, *The Young Hegel*, p. 97.
2. E. H. Carr, *What Is History?* (New York: Knopf, 1962), p. 165.
3. George Novack, *Origins of Materialism*, pp. 57-58.
4. George Novack, *Pragmatism Versus Marxism*, p. 11.
5. John Lachs, *Marxist Philosophy: A Bibliographical Guide* (Chapel Hill: University of North Carolina Press, 1967), p. 120.

Freedom for Philosophy

1. Cited in Georg Lukács, *The Young Hegel*, p. 261.
2. Barrows Dunham, *Thinkers and Treasurers* (New York: Monthly Review Press, 1955), p. 24.
3. Leszek Kolakowski, "What Is Socialism?" in Edmund O. Stillman, ed., *Bitter Harvest: The Intellectual Revolt Behind the Iron Curtain* (New York: Praeger, 1959), p. 49.
4. Adam Schaff, *Marxism and the Human Individual*, pp. 103-38.
5. Cited in "Dissident Yugoslav Professors Face Renewed Attacks by Regime," *Intercontinental Press*, vol. 12, no. 42 (November 25, 1974), pp. 1574-75.
6. Cited in Dick Fidler, "Yugoslav Professors Reply to Charges," *Intercontinental Press*, vol. 13, no. 6 (February 17, 1975), p. 226.
7. Quoted in *New York Times*, January 10, 1972.
8. Roy and Zhores Medvedev, *A Question of Madness* (New York: Knopf, 1971), p. 209.

9. Leon Trotsky, "Freedom of the Press and the Working Class," in *Writings of Leon Trotsky (1937-38)* (New York: Pathfinder Press, 1970), p. 418.

In Defense of Engels

1. Frederick Engels, *Anti-Dühring: Herr Eugen Dühring's Revolution in Science* (Moscow: Foreign Languages, 1954), p. 14.
2. George Lichtheim, *From Marx to Hegel*, p. 4.
3. Ibid., p. 67.
4. Ibid., pp. 69-70.
5. Georg Lukács, *History and Class Consciousness*, p. xvi.
6. Leszek Kolakowski, *Marxism and Beyond*, p. 78.
7. Alfred Schmidt, *The Concept of Nature in Marx*, p. 193.
8. Alfred Schmidt, *The Concept of Nature in Marx*, p. 193.
9. Cited in ibid., p. 49.
10. Dick Howard and Karl Klare, eds., *The Unknown Dimension*, p. 7.
11. Included in *Understanding History* (New York: Pathfinder Press, 1974).
12. *From Marx to Hegel*, pp. 70-71.
13. Karl Marx, *Capital*, vol. 1 (Harmondsworth: Penguin, 1976), p. 102.
14. Marx and Engels, *Selected Correspondence* (Moscow: Foreign Languages), p. 498, emphasis added.
15. Engels, "Ludwig Feuerbach and the Outcome of Classical German Philosophy" in Marx, *Selected Works*, vol. 1 (New York: International), p. 470.
16. Marx, *Capital*, vol. 1, pp. 423-24.
17. Maurice Merleau-Ponty, *Sense and Non-Sense* (Evanston: Northwestern University Press, 1964), p. 274.
18. Schmidt, *The Concept of Nature in Marx*, p. 195.
19. Loren Graham, *Science and Philosophy in the Soviet Union* (New York: Knopf, 1972), p. 430.
20. Jean-Paul Sartre, *Situations*, vol. 3 (Paris: Gallimard, 1964), p. 213.
21. Leon Trotsky, "Marxism as a Science," in *Writings (1932-33)* (New York: Pathfinder Press, 1972), pp. 200-01.

Georg Lukács as a Marxist Philosopher

1. Georg Lukács, *History and Class Consciousness*, p. xvi.
2. Ibid., p. 222n.
3. Ibid., p. 202.
4. Ibid., p. 229.
5. Ibid., p. xxii.
6. Ibid., p. xxiii.
7. Ibid., p. 132.
8. Ibid., p. 185.
9. Ibid., p. 262, emphasis in original.
10. Ibid., p. 142, emphasis in original.
11. Ibid., p. xxi.

12. Ibid., p. 10.
13. Ibid., p. 27.
14. Ibid., p. 1.
15. Ibid., p. xxvii.
16. Karl Marx, "Theses on Feuerbach," in *Selected Works*, vol. 1 (New York: International), p. 472.
17. Marx, *Economic and Philosophic Manuscripts of 1844* (Moscow: Foreign Languages), p. 111.
18. Leon Trotsky, *Portraits, Political and Personal* (New York: Pathfinder Press, 1977), p. 36.
19. Ibid., p. 40.
20. Trotsky, "On Tolstoy's Death," in *Leon Trotsky on Literature and Art* (New York: Pathfinder Press, 1970), p. 145.

The Jesting Philosopher:
The Case of Leszek Kolakowski

1. Leszek Kolakowski, "What is Socialism?" in Edmund O. Stillman, ed., *Bitter Harvest: The Intellectual Revolt Behind the Iron Curtain* (New York: Praeger, 1959), pp. 48, 49.
2. Leszek Kolakowski, "Intellectuals, Hope and Heresy," an interview in *Encounter*, vol. 37, no. 4, October 1971, p. 48.
3. "A Leszek Kolakowski Reader," *TriQuarterly*, no. 22, fall 1971, p. 5.
4. "What Is Socialism?" in *Bitter Harvest*, p. 48.
5. Leszek Kolakowski, *Marxism and Beyond*, p. 8.
6. Ibid., p. 78.
7. Ibid., p. 77.
8. Ibid., p. 70.
9. Ibid., p. 76.
10. Ibid., p. 87.
11. Ibid., p. 206.
12. Ibid., p. 224.
13. *TriQuarterly*, pp. 112, 115.
14. Ibid., p. 117.
15. *Marxism and Beyond*, p. 82.
16. *TriQuarterly*, p. 177.
17. *Marxism and Beyond*, p. 220.
18. Ibid., p. 227.
19. Leszek Kolakowski, "Intellectuals Against Intellect," in *Daedalus*, vol. 101, no. 3, summer 1972, p. 12.
20. *Encounter*, p. 48.
21. J. T. Baer, "Leszek Kolakowski's Plea for a Non-Mystical World View," *Slavic Review*, vol. 28, no. 3, 1969, p. 476.
22. *TriQuarterly*, p. 36.
23. Ibid., p. 14.
24. Leszek Kolakowski, "The Fate of Marxism in Eastern Europe," in *Slavic Review*, vol. 29, no. 2, June 1970, p. 180.
25. *Encounter*, pp. 44-45.

26. E. P. Thompson, "Open Letter," in *The Socialist Register 1973* (London: Merlin, 1973), pp. 89-90, 93.
27. Isaac Deutscher, "Heretics and Renegades," in *Russia in Transition* (New York: Coward-McCann, 1957), pp. 208-9.
28. Leszek Kolakowski, "On Trotsky and Everything Else," *Partisan Review*, vol. 39, no. 4, fall 1972, p. 595.

Sebastiano Timpanaro's Defense of Materialism

1. Sebastiano Timpanaro, *On Materialism*, p. 230.
2. Ibid., p. 22.
3. Ibid., p. 16.
4. Ibid., p. 34.
5. Ibid., p. 132.
6. Ibid., p. 45.
7. Ibid., p. 169.
8. Ibid., p. 208.
9. Ibid., p. 171.
10. Ibid., p. 193.
11. Ibid., p. 193.
12. Ibid., p. 89.
13. Ibid., p. 132.
14. Ibid., p. 129n.
15. Ibid., p. 113.
16. George Novack, *Humanism and Socialism* (New York: Pathfinder Press, 1973), p. 123.
17. Timpanaro, *On Materialism*, p. 23.
18. Ibid., p. 217.

Back to Kant? The Retreat of Lucio Colletti

1. Lucio Colletti, ed., *Karl Marx: Early Writings* (New York: Vintage, 1975), p. 47.
2. Lucio Colletti, "A Political and Philosophical Interview," *New Left Review*, no. 86, July-August 1974, p. 13.
3. Ibid., pp. 13-14.
4. Ibid., p. 10.
5. Ibid., p. 16.
6. Lucio Colletti, "Marxism and the Dialectic," *New Left Review*, no. 93, September-October 1975, p. 29.
7. "A Political and Philosophical Interview," p. 15.
8. Lucio Colletti, "Rousseau as Critic of 'Civil Society,'" in *From Rousseau to Lenin*, p. 185.
9. Lucio Colletti, "Marxism: Science or Revolution?" in ibid., p. 229, emphasis in original.

10. Lucio Colletti, *Marxism and Hegel,* p. 85.
11. Karl Marx, *Capital,* vol. 1 (Harmondsworth: Penguin, 1976), pp. 102-3.
12. Frederick Engels, *Ludwig Feuerbach and the Outcome of Classical German Philosophy,* in Karl Marx, *Selected Works* (Moscow: Foreign Languages), vol. 1, p. 432.
13. Immanuel Kant, *Critique of Pure Reason* (London: J. M. Dent & Sons, 1934), p. 18, emphasis in original.
14. *Marxism and Hegel,* p. 199.
15. Ibid., p. 213, emphasis in original.
16. "A Political and Philosophical Interview," p. 12.
17. Karl Marx, *Selected Works,* vol. 2, p. 336.
18. Carl J. Friedrich, ed., *The Philosophy of Kant: Immanuel Kant's Moral and Political Writings* (New York: Modern Library, 1949), p. 87.
19. "A Political and Philosophical Interview," p. 10.
20. "Marxism and the Dialectic," p. 6, emphasis in original.
21. *Capital,* vol. 1, p. 198.
22. Frederick Engels, *Dialectics of Nature* (Moscow: Foreign Languages, 1954), p. 65.
23. *Capital,* vol. 1, pp. 99, 102.
24. "Marxism and the Dialectic," p. 9.
25. Ibid., p. 4.
26. Ibid., p. 11.
27. Ibid., p. 18.
28. Ibid., p. 29.
29. Ibid., p. 19, emphasis in original.
30. Karl Marx, *A Contribution to the Critique of Political Economy* (Moscow: Progress, 1970), pp. 20-21.
31. *Capital,* vol. 1, p. 170.
32. Ibid., pp. 165-66.
33. "Marxism and the Dialectic," p. 22.
34. Ibid., p. 20.
35. Ibid., p. 21.
36. See Marx's *Theories of Surplus-Value: Volume IV of Capital* (Moscow: Progress, 1975), Part 3, p. 456.
37. Ibid., p. 276.
38. "Marxism and the Dialectic," pp. 26-27.
39. Ibid., p. 22, emphasis in original.
40. Ibid., p. 29, emphasis in original.
41. Ibid., p. 29.
42. *Capital,* vol. 1, p. 929.
43. Ibid., vol. 1, p. 929.
44. "Marxism and the Dialectic," p. 7.
45. Ibid., p. 29.
46. Isaac Deutscher, "Discovering Das Kapital," in *Marxism in Our Time* (Berkeley: Ramparts Press, 1971), pp. 261-62.
47. "A Political and Philosophical Interview," p. 26.
48. See the joint declaration with the historian Massimo Salvador in the weekly *Espresso,* February 12, 1977, and two statements in *Mondoperaio,*

the monthly magazine of the Italian Socialist Party, January 1977, p. 45, and June 1977, p. 6.

American Philosophy and the Labor Movement

1. Quoted from the *Report of the Senate Committee on Education and Labor*, vol. 1, p. 460, in Philip S. Foner, *The History of the Labor Movement in the United States* (New York: International, 1947), vol. 1, p. 514.
2. Mark Starr, "Organized Labor and the Dewey Philosophy," in Sidney Hook, ed., *John Dewey: Philosopher of Science* (New York: Dial, 1950), p. 185.
3. Ray Ginger, *The Bending Cross* (later published as *Eugene V. Debs: A Biography*) (New Brunswick, N.J.: Rutgers University Press, 1949), p. 19.
4. A slightly different translation appears in "Engels to Sorge," April 29, 1886, in Karl Marx and Frederick Engels, *Letters to Americans* (New York: International, 1953), p. 154.
5. Ibid., p. 248.
6. Taken from the minutes of the UAW 1951 convention.

Leon Trotsky on Dialectical Materialism

1. Leon Trotsky, *In Defense of Marxism,* p. 196.
2. Ibid., pp. 78-79.
3. Ibid., p. 79.
4. Ibid., p. 74.
5. Ibid., p. 51.
6. Ibid., p. 51.
7. Leon Trotsky, "Radio, Science, Technology, and Society," in *Problems of Everyday Life* (New York: Pathfinder Press, 1973), pp. 252-53.
8. Leon Trotsky, *My Life* (New York: Pathfinder Press, 1970 [first published in 1930]), pp. 119, 122.
9. Leon Trotsky, *Permanent Revolution and Results and Prospects* (New York: Merit, 1969 [first published in 1931]), p. 64.
10. Ibid., p. 65.
10. Ibid., p. 65.
11. Ibid., p. 63.
12. Leon Trotsky, *Marxism in Our Time* (New York: Pathfinder Press, 1970 [first published in 1939]), pp. 8-9.
13. Ibid., p. 13.
14. *In Defense of Marxism,* p. 129.
15. Ibid., pp. 118-19.
16. Ibid., p. 119.
17. Leon Trotsky, *The History of the Russian Revolution* (Ann Arbor: University of Michigan Press, 1957 [first published in 1932]), vol. 1, p. 52.
18. Leon Trotsky, "What Is National Socialism?" in *The Struggle*

Against Fascism in Germany (New York: Pathfinder Press, 1971), p. 399.
19. *The History of the Russian Revolution,* vol. 1, p. 52.
20. Ibid., p. 95.
21. Leon Trotsky, *The Case of Leon Trotsky* (New York: Merit, 1968), p. 581.
22. *The History of the Russian Revolution,* vol. 1, p. 93.
23. *My Life,* pp. 334-35.
24. Leon Trotsky, "Testament," in *Trotsky's Diary in Exile—1935* (Cambridge: Harvard University Press, 1958), pp. 165-66.
25. Ibid., p. 167.

Glossary

Absolute Idea—in Hegel's system, the underlying organizing principle of reality. This differs from Plato's "ideas" in that Hegel believed the Absolute Idea to have no existence apart from observable phenomena. Hegel conceived of the working of the Absolute Idea as similar to the innate principle that guides the growth of a seed into a plant. He viewed it as reason inherent in nature and history, guiding their evolution toward self-consciousness. This end product was to result in an identity of subject and object and the end of alienation (*see entry*) and objectification.

abstract labor—under commodity production, human labor embodied in commodities viewed solely from the standpoint of duration in time, i.e., as an interchangeable part of the total labor time available to society.

Adler, Max (1873-1937)—a leading theoretician and philosopher of the Austrian Social Democracy; coeditor with Rudolf Hilferding of *Marx Studien* before 1914.

Adorno, Theodor (1903-1969)—Hegelian-Marxist philosopher and musicologist; staff member of the Frankfurt school from 1938 and its director from 1958 until his death. His best-known book in English is *Negative Dialectics* (1972).

Aleksandrov, Aleksandr Danilo-vich (1912-   )—Soviet mathematician and philosopher, specializing in the mathematics of relativity physics. Aleksandrov is regarded as the founder of the Soviet school of geometry. He was instrumental in the publication of Einstein's collected scientific works in Russian.

alienation—literally, separation from, as in the selling of property or the loss of someone's affection. By extension, the loss of one's creations with a consequent sense of aloneness and powerlessness. This concept is central in twentieth-century existentialism, certain schools of socialist humanism, and various psychological interpretations of Marxism. At the same time, Althusser and the Maoists have tried to extirpate this concept from Marxism, leaving it only in the specific form of the alienation of the product of labor under capitalism. Alienation in the Marxist sense has a double origin, in the powerlessness of human beings to control nature, and, secondly, in class society, in the alienation of labor as well as its product. Marx distinguished here not only the physical appropriation of the products made by the exploited but also the feeling among workers that their laboring activity itself was alien to them and did not satisfy their needs. Additionally there is the sense of separation from humanity as a group, inevitable under class society, and the lack of solidarity with other specific individuals one comes in contact with. Above all, alienation expresses the fact that the objective creations of labor come to dominate their creators so that the market in commodity production stands over them as an alien power.

Althusser, Louis (1918-   )— professor of philosophy at the Ecole normale supérieure in Paris and a member of the French Communist Party since 1948. He rejects both dialectics and humanism, seeking to adapt Marxism to the antievolutionary structuralist school, which examines society primarily on the basis of its existing parts and not as an evolutionary process containing intrinsically contradictory forces. He leans toward Maoism.

Anaxagoras (c. 500-428 B.C.)—Greek materialist philosopher of Clazomenae, later of Athens. He believed natural objects to be composed of minute particles, or "seeds," differentiated by rotary motion initiated by an all-pervading mind. He was charged with blasphemy for his belief that the sun was a fiery stone and the moon was composed of the same materials as the earth. Anaxagoras considered the superiority of humans over animals to rest in the tool-using capacities of the hand.

animism—the belief, common among primitive peoples, that inanimate objects and animals, as well as humans, possess an inner mind or spirit.

anthropocentrism—interpreting nature and the world in terms of human values and experiences.

anthropogenesis—the study of the origin of the human species.

anthropology—that branch of social science concerned with the study of the origin, development, and characteristics of human beings in precivilized societies. In philosophy, an anthropological theory, concerned only with the study of humanity, as distinguished from an ontological theory, which encompasses the nature of being in general, including the inanimate world.

a priorism—deduction from preexisting principles without reference to empirical data for verification. In the case of Kantianism, the assumption that the categories of reason (time, space, number, etc.) are innate and predate all experience.

Aristotelian logic. *See* formal logic.

atomism—the theory that the universe is constructed of invisible, indestructible minute particles. First advanced by the Greek materialist philosophers Leucippus and Democritus (*see entry*) in the fifth century B.C.

Bacon, Francis (1561-1626)—British natural philosopher and statesman. Championed the inductive method of modern science against the a priori, deductive method of medieval scholastics. Bacon was not himself a scientist, and his practical empiricism discounted the value of generalizing theory.

Beauvoir, Simone de (1908-   )— French novelist, essayist, and existentialist philosopher. Her works include *The Second Sex* (1950), *The Mandarins* (1955), and *The Coming of Age* (1970).

becoming—in Hegel's system, the dialectical state transitional between being and nonbeing.

behaviorism—doctrine that psychological science can be reduced to measurable physical behavior of an organism.

Bernstein, Eduard (1850-1932)— leading theoretician of the German Social Democracy and Engels's literary executor. From 1899 he proposed a theory of the gradual transformation of capitalism into socialism and rejected the prospect of socialist revolution as a guide to practical politics.

biologism—belief that social behavior can be explained primarily by biological conditioning and causes.

Bloch, Ernst (1885-   )—a luminary of Marxist culture in Central Europe in the twentieth century, a friend of

Georg Lukács, Bertolt Brecht, Walter Benjamin, and Kurt Weill. After braving persecution by the Nazis, he fell afoul of the East German regime and took refuge in West Germany. His approach to Marxism emphasizes its orientation toward the future and even acquires a somewhat utopian streak in his masterwork, *The Principle of Hope.*

Blokhintsev, Dimitri Ivanovich (1908-   )—Soviet physicist, specialist in quantum mechanics. After 1956, director of the Joint Institute of Nuclear Research at Dubna. He is best known for his theory that the indeterminacy of the position and motion of microparticles—known as the Heisenberg uncertainty principle or relationship—can be modified in the direction of determinate order by the study of the statistical behavior of "ensembles" of particles rather than individual particles.

Bruno, Giordano (1548-1600)— Italian naturalist philosopher and writer. Charged with heresy, Bruno left Italy in 1576 and lived in exile in Paris, London, and Frankfurt. He returned to Venice in 1591, where he was arrested by the Inquisition, imprisoned at Rome for nine years, and then burned. Although something of a mystic, Bruno rejected the Aristotelian cosmology that placed the earth at the center of the universe. He defended and developed the Copernican system (*see entry*), maintaining that the earth was just one of an infinite number of planets circling suns throughout the universe.

Camus, Albert (1913-1960)—French novelist and essayist, generally regarded as an exponent of existentialism although he denied this identification. Born in Algiers, Camus was briefly a member of the French Communist Party in the 1930s. He took part in the underground resistance to the Nazis during World War II. His works developed the idea of the meaninglessness of human existence, tempered by the courageous rebellion of individuals against their circumstances. The best known are the essays *The Myth of Sisyphus* (1942) and *The Rebel* (1951), and the novel *The Stranger* (1942).

categorical imperative—a moral standard that is universally and unconditionally binding.

Chomsky, Noam (1928-   )— American linguist and radical political activist. He developed a system of transformational grammar (*see entry*) in his book *Syntactic Structures* (1957). He is also known for his theory that the underlying logical structure of language stems from biological patterns of perception innate in the brain.

Colletti, Lucio (1924-   )— heterodox Italian Marxist philosopher. He joined the Italian Communist Party in 1950 and was one of its prominent intellectuals until 1964 when he resigned. Influenced as a youth by the Crocean school of historical idealism, he was a disciple of Galvano Della Volpe in the CP. Colletti developed with Della Volpe a positivist strain of Marxism akin to that of Althusser. In 1966-67, he edited the independent Marxist monthly *La Sinistra.* In recent years he has developed important differences with orthodox Marxism, moving in the direction of a return to Kantianism.

concrete labor—under commodity production or capitalism, the human labor embodied in commodities viewed solely from the standpoint of the specific kind of work done (bricklaying, metal working, etc.). As contrasted to abstract labor (*see entry*), concrete labor gives to a commodity its particular utility and hence its use-value, but such labor is not directly comparable with other units of concrete labor.

contradiction—in Hegel's dialectical logic, a state characteristic of all objects and processes in nature, society, and thought, marked by an inner tension between positive and negative poles (unity of opposites) in which, through an accumulation of quantitative changes, the negative pole finally prevails over the positive to establish a new equilibrium (transcendence) in which a new set of contradictions appear. For Hegel, the motor force of such change is the self-expression of reason (Absolute Idea). For Marx, it is the evolution of material forces, and, in civilized societies, the class struggle.

contrariety—as used by Kant and Colletti, clashes between definite existing forces, as distinguished from internal contradiction within a single totality. Synonymous with noncontradictory opposition or "real opposition."

Copernicus, Nicholas (1473-1543)—Polish astronomer and creator of the Copernican system, which constitutes the basis of modern astronomy. Studied in Poland and Italy, settling in Frauenburg, East Prussia, in 1512, where he held clerical office in the local cathedral and practiced medicine. His findings in astronomy were published only on his deathbed, for fear of church reprisals. He postulated that the earth moved around the sun and not the reverse, as had previously been believed. His system still retained the belief that planetary orbits were perfect circles, a serious deficiency that was later rectified by Kepler (*see entry*).

cosmogony—theories on the origin of the universe.

cosmology—the branch of philosophy that seeks to integrate empirical knowledge of nature as a whole with a general theory of the natural order.

critical theory—the name adopted by the Frankfurt school (*see entry*) to describe its distinctive version of Hegelianized Marxism. It stressed the negation through reason and praxis (*see entry*) of existing social reality, dismissing the orthodox Marxist concern with objective conditions as a conservatizing concession to facticity. Although ultimately a rationalistic and subjectivist remodelling of Marxism, the polemics of the "critical theorists" against positivism and against irrationalist creeds

contain many important insights.

Croce, Benedetto (1866-1952)—the most prominent twentieth-century Italian philosopher. An extreme historical relativist and idealist, Croce considered mind to be the only reality and the mental reconstruction of past history to be the highest form of philosophical thought. Croce was much influenced by Hegel and revived interest in Hegel's work, but held that dialectical opposition existed only in counterposed mental propositions, not in empirical fact.

Cuvier, Georges Léopold (1769-1832)—French naturalist, known for his system of zoological classification and contributions to the study of comparative anatomy. He rejected the theory of evolution, explaining the discovery of fossil remains of extinct species by postulating natural catastrophes that had destroyed them outright.

Dalton, John (1766-1844)—English scientist, the first chemist in modern times to revive the atomic theory of the Greek atomists (*see entry*). Based on his study of the behavior of gases, he published the first table of atomic weights in 1805.

Darwin, Charles (1809-1882)—English naturalist, the first to collect and publish substantive documentary evidence for the theory of universal organic evolution. His findings were issued in 1859 in his classic work, *Origin of Species*.

Deborin, Abram Moiseyevich (1881-1964)—leading Soviet philosopher of the 1920s. Briefly a Bolshevik after 1903, Deborin was a Menshevik at the time of the Russian revolution. He joined the CPSU in 1928. He was the leader of the "Deborinist" school of orthodox Marxists in the debate in the 1920s with the mechanists in the USSR. He defended the antireductionist principle that nature, society, and human thought, while all products of matter in motion, each had its own laws. Although supported by the party against the mechanists until 1929, Deborin and his supporters were accused of "idealism" and "Trotskyism" in 1930 and he was forced into obscurity.

deism—a rationalist belief popular in the seventeenth and eighteenth centuries. Stopping short of atheism, the deists rejected organized religion and all supernatural intervention in human affairs. They believed in a god, but held that his actions were limited to the original creation of the natural order.

Della Volpe, Galvano (1895-1968)— Italian philosopher and founder of a positivist interpretation of Marxism. He became interested in Marxism in 1943 and ·joined the Italian Communist Party. Rejected the Hegelian dialectic as inherently idealist and proposed to found a Marxist method on the experimental procedures of Western natural scientists.

de Man, Hendrik (1885-1953)— Belgian Social Democratic theorist and politician. A leader of the right wing of the Belgian Labor Party and minister of finance in the Van Zeeland government (1936-38).

Democritus (c.460-c.370 B.C.)—Greek materialist philosopher. A student of Leucippus of Abdera, he perfected the atomic theory of antiquity. He held that all things are composed of invisible, indestructible atoms, made of matter but of different size and shape. Different aggregations of these atoms produced the impression on the senses of the different objects of perception.

Descartes, René (1596-1650)— founder of the Cartesian philosophical school in France. He held that only mind was knowable, while qualities of matter remained unverifiable. He stressed abstract reason based on the model of mathematical thought.

determinism—the belief that phenomena and events are produced by definite causes. In the philosophical split between determinism and indeterminism, Marxism rejects the view that accident, chance, or free will are domi-

nant, thus belonging firmly to the determinist camp. At the same time, dialectical materialism does not exclude the objective existence of chance, as do some forms of mechanical materialism. Chance and necessity are inseparable and interconvertible features of reality.

Dewey, John (1859-1952)—the most influential twentieth-century American philosopher and educator. Developed the pragmatism of William James and Charles S. Peirce into his own school of "instrumentalism." An Americanized empiricism, Dewey's philosophy was averse to universal generalization and certainty based on causal necessity and lawfulness, and stressed the solution to immediate problems through experiment and practical activity. This mode of piecemeal change is congenial to political liberalism.

diachrony—the analysis of an object through examination of change over time.

dialectical materialism—the philosophical world view of Marx and Engels, encompassing both nature and society. Materialist in that it postulates the existence of nature prior to humanity and views material conditions as the underlying cause and determinant of society and mind; dialectical in that it postulates the study of matter in motion and transformation by way of contradiction from one form or state to another.

dialectics of nature—the position, held by classical Marxism, that evolutionary change through the process of internal contradiction is universal in inanimate and organic nature as well as in society and the human thought process. Hegel also believed in a dialectics of nature, but rooted it in a supposed teleological process in which nature was striving for self-consciousness through higher and higher levels of organization, leading to the realization of the Absolute Idea (*see entry*) in an omniscient and all-powerful subject. Hegelianizers of Marxism retain Hegel's belief that consciousness is required for the existence of contradiction and generally deny that nature apart from human activity is dialectical. Positivistic versions of Marxism reject the dialectics of nature for opposite reasons, maintaining that universal laws of change are incompatible with the findings of the specialized and compartmentalized sciences.

Diderot, Denis (1713-1784)—outstanding French materialist philosopher. A founding editor of the French *Encyclopédie,* Diderot was instrumental in bringing together the writers and philosophers whose work is known as the Enlightenment, which prepared the ideological preconditions of the French revolution. An atheist, Diderot believed that sensation is a property of matter and that mind was a product of complex material evolution.

Dilthey, Wilhelm (1833-1911)—German idealist philosopher, specializing in the history of culture and the effects of psychological factors in history. He assisted in reviving interest in Hegel and Hegel's dialectical logic in Europe.

dualism—the philosophical view that the world is composed of two mutually exclusive types of phenomena, mind and matter, neither of which is the cause or basis of the other.

economic determinism—the belief that economic factors, in particular, immediate economic self-interest, directly decide the conduct of individuals in political life. This view, often falsely attributed to Marxism, is represented among American historians by the school of Charles Beard.

Einstein, Albert (1879-1955)—the most eminent theoretical physicist since Newton. His epoch-making contribution to science was his theory of relativity (*see entry*), which revolutionized the concepts of space and time and laid the basis for modern atomic physics. Born in Germany and raised in Switzerland,

Einstein emigrated to America in 1933 when the Nazis came to power in Germany.

empiricism—the philosophical school founded by John Locke (1632-1704), oscillating between materialism and idealism. It holds that all knowledge originates in experience. Empiricism generally rejects supernatural explanations of phenomena, but its ambiguity as to the determining source of sensations leaves it open to agnosticism.

empiriocriticism—the philosophical school founded by physicist Ernst Mach (1838-1916) that sought to reduce all knowledge to analysis of physical sensations.

Epicurus (341-270 B.C.)—the founder of the epicurean school of Greek materialist philosophy. Epicurus systematized the atomic theories of Leucippus and Democritus (*see entry*), introducing the element of chance into Democritus's overly deterministic system. Epicurus postulated intellectual attainment and human well-being as the principal goals of life, a position later caricatured by his opponents as mere hedonism.

epistemology—the theory of knowledge; in particular, the study of the sources, development, limits, and validity of knowledge.

exchange-value—the common element that permits the exchange, in definite proportions, of commodities that have different physical properties. In Marxist economics, this common, numerically divisible quality of commodities is that they are all products of human labor. The amount of exchange-value possessed by a given commodity is determined by the amount of socially necessary labor-time used in its manufacture, measured as a portion of the total labor-time of society.

existentialism—a humanistic and pessimistic philosophy that holds human existence cannot be understood through either reason or material causation. It conceives of nature and society as dominated by accident and chance and stresses acts of will to recapture human freedom. It has been popularized in the twentieth century by French philosopher Jean-Paul Sartre.

facticity—literally, the state of being a fact, with the connotation of being an unalterable given. As used by Hegelianizers, this term denotes an unwarranted acceptance of existing facts, i.e., of the status quo, and a failure to appreciate the potential for negating the present through revolutionary criticism and praxis.

Feng Yu-lan (1895-   )—China's best-known living philosopher. Feng studied under John Dewey at Columbia University in the 1920s and later taught at various American and Chinese universities. His *History of Chinese Philosophy* (1931) is the most comprehensive account of this subject yet written. Feng remained in China after the revolution of 1949, where in the 1950s his work was published with "self-critical" introductions. A revised edition of his history was suppressed before publication in the Cultural Revolution on the grounds that it reflected the outlook of Liu Shao-ch'i and Teng Hsiao-p'ing. After Mao's death, Feng again came under attack for having agreed to the self-criticisms demanded of him by the Mao faction.

fetishism—attributing to material things human or godlike qualities or powers. In Marx's economic theory, it is the popular tendency under capitalism to believe that value is inherent as a natural quality in things rather than being a reflection of human labor-time and hence of a social relation.

Feuerbach, Ludwig (1804-1872)—German materialist philosopher. Beginning as a Young Hegelian, he discarded Hegel's idealism as well as religion in his 1840 work, *The Essence of Christianity*. Though very influential on the development of the young Marx and Engels, Feuerbach himself developed only a metaphysical, humanistic mate-

rialism, stressing the centrality of humanity in the natural order and proposing literary criticism of religion rather than class struggle.

Fichte, Johann Gottlieb (1762-1814)—German philosopher, founder of "absolute idealism." Intermediary between Kant and Hegel, Fichte sought to overcome Kant's disjunction between theory (noumena) and practice (the realm of phenomena) by postulating human will or ego as the central determinant of reality and viewing history as a struggle of the ego to impose freedom on necessity and morality on nature.

finalism—the belief that events in nature, and particularly natural evolution, are the products of causes that go beyond the apparent physical causes, i.e., the belief that the order of nature is a proof of the guiding hand of God.

Fischer, Ernst (1899-1972)—Austrian Marxist philosopher. After a career as a working class journalist he helped initiate a left-wing opposition within the Social Democratic Party and joined the Communist Party in 1934 when the Viennese workers were crushed in February of that year. A radio commentator in Moscow during World War II, in 1945 he became minister of education in the provisional Austrian government. The most influential of his many literary and theoretical works available in English is *The Necessity of Art* (1959). He broke with the Austrian Communist Party in the late 1960s following the invasion of Czechoslovakia. Subsequently, in his repudiation of Stalinism, he undertook a critical reappraisal of Marxism and Leninism.

Fock, Vladimir Aleksandrovich (1898-   )—Soviet theoretical physicist and philosopher, known for his extensive work in quantum mechanics, electrodynamics, light diffraction, and relativity theory. Although primarily a natural scientist, Fock has written extensively on the philosophic implications of modern physics. From the 1930s he defended the scientific findings of the

Copenhagen school of Niels Bohr, seeking to integrate these with dialectical materialism, despite strong resistance from Communist Party ideologists. He argued that the indeterminate character of subatomic particles was inherent in the physics of the "microlevel," and that it was not a matter of insufficient accuracy of measurement. He held that in quantum physics strict determinism was outmoded, but that dialectical materialism was applicable because the objectivity of atoms remained, as did causality in general.

forces of production—in Marx's economics, the totality of the productive capacity of a given society at a given time. The concept includes not only physical industrial plant and machinery, but also the level of technology and the size and skill of the working population. *See also* means, mode, and relations of production.

formal logic—the first great system of logic, developed by the Greeks and codified by Aristotle. Excluded consideration of indefinite or transitional states or qualitative leaps from one state of being to another. Rests on three basic laws: (1) identity (a thing is always equal to itself, A=A); (2) formal contradiction (things of one type are distinct from those of another type); and (3) the law of the excluded middle (no object may belong to two opposed categories at the same time).

form and content—in dialectical logic, form and content are viewed as an interconnected totality composed of a unity of opposites (*see entry*). Form, or appearance, must ultimately correspond to an object's inner reality or content. The process of change, however, results in a divergence of these two aspects of being which must sooner or later result in a dialectical leap in which the changed content breaks through the old form and establishes a new form corresponding to its altered essence.

Frankfurt school—popular name of the Institute of Social Research, founded in Frankfurt am Main, Germany, in 1923. It developed a Hegelian version of Marxism, stressing dialectics, psychology, and the dehumanizing effects of bourgeois mass culture. Its members rejected the application of dialectics to nature and downgraded the importance of materialism and economic relations in society. It sought to substitute reason and revolutionary will for material interests and the class struggle as motors of social change. Its more prominent members included Max Horkheimer, Theodor Adorno, Herbert Marcuse, and Erich Fromm.

Fromm, Erich (1900-   )—psychoanalyst and author, born in Frankfurt, Germany. Fromm was associated with the Psychoanalytic Institute at Frankfurt (1929-32), where he worked closely with the nearby Institute of Social Research, the Frankfurt school. He joined its staff in emigration in the United States (1934-39). In the 1930s he sought to integrate Marxism with psychoanalysis, producing a number of important essays on mass psychology, character structure, and, in anthropology, in defense of the theory of the matriarchy. In 1939 he broke with the Frankfurt school, developing his own Marxist-tinged theories of society based on the universality of alienation and the quest for redemption through love. Politically, a Social Democrat.

Galileo Galilei (1564-1642)—a great Italian astronomer, mathematician, and physicist. Galileo perfected the modern telescope and with the aid of his instruments discovered the moons of Jupiter, that the Milky Way was composed of individual stars, and that the surface of the moon contained mountains like those of the earth. He was the first to formulate many of the modern laws of motion, holding that celestial mechanics, contrary to the views of Aristotle, operated by the same laws as earthly ones. In 1633 he was tried by the Inquisition in Rome for his heretical defense of the Copernican system, which postulated that the earth revolved around the sun. He was sentenced to house arrest for the remainder of his life.

Garaudy, Roger (1913-   )—in the 1950s and 1960s, the leading ideological spokesman for the French Communist Party. Garaudy was a long-time deputy in the French assembly, elected on the CP ticket; a member of the PCF Politburo from 1961; and director of the party-sponsored Centre d'études et de recherches marxistes. In the 1940s and 1950s he was a rigid Stalinist, but in the 1960s he began to develop differences with the party in the direction of a positivist humanism. He opposed the Soviet invasion of Czechoslovakia in 1968 and was expelled from the party in 1970.

Goethe, Johann Wolfgang von (1749-1832)—German poet, dramatist, and scientist. Noted for his dramatic poem *Faust* and his novel *The Sorrows of Young Werther* which were imperishable contributions to world literature. He was also an accomplished musician, linguist, and naturalist.

Goldmann, Lucien (1913-1970)—one of the leading European praxis philosophers and interpreter of the thought of the young Lukács. Born and educated in Romania, Goldmann headed the Institute of Sociology at the University of Brussels (1946-58) and was director of studies at the Ecole pratique des hautes études in Paris (1958-70). He wrote widely on Marxism and cultural theory, developing a neo-Hegelian Marxism that stressed a humanist evolutionism. He accepted social determinism, but made of this a philosophic category and did not rest it on economic life. He was a champion of the concept of workers'-self-management and held a tragic concept of human existence.

Gramsci, Antonio (1891-1937)—a founder and central leader of Italian Communist Party until his arrest by Mussolini in 1926. Wrote voluminously until his death in prison, developing a subjective Marxism emphasizing the role of praxis (*see entry*), changing of mass consciousness through training of proletarian intellectuals, creation of proletarian culture to contend with bourgeois culture, and organization of workers' committees and councils as a central tactic of class struggle.

Hegel, Georg Wilhelm Friedrich (1770-1831)—the culminating figure of the German idealist school of philosophy that began with Kant. He sought to resolve the traditional philosophical disjunction of mind and matter by postulating a unified, monistic reality in which matter is the "alienated" expression of its own inner organizing force, reason or the Absolute Idea. While reason or mind was predominant in Hegel's system, it viewed reality as undergoing a progressive evolution through the process of dialectical change.

Hegelianizers—within the contemporary Marxist movement, a current that seeks to minimize or discard Marx's materialism and to place human reason and activity at the center of its analysis of society in the manner of the pre-Marxist Young Hegelians. Prominent representatives of this tendency include the young Georg Lukács, Karl Korsch, Max Horkheimer, Theodor Adorno, and Herbert Marcuse.

Heidegger, Martin (1889-1976)—German existentialist philosopher. His ideas were best expounded in *Sein und Zeit (Being and Time,* 1927). A philosopher of irrationalism. Heidegger maintained that the chief impediment to human self-development was reason and science, which led to a view of the world based on subject-object relations. Humans were reduced to the status of entities in the thing-world into which they were thrown (the condition of "thrownness"). This state of unauthentic being could be overcome neither through theory (science) nor social practice, but only by an inward-turning orientation toward one's self, particularly in the contemplation of death. Heidegger was influenced by Kierkegaard and Husserl (*see entries*), and in turn deeply affected the thought of Sartre, Camus, and Marcuse. He was himself a political reactionary, accepting the chair of philosophy at the University of Freiburg in 1928 after his mentor, Edmund Husserl, had been forced to relinquish it by the Nazis. Heidegger supported Hitler, which led to his disgrace at the end of World War II and his retirement in 1951 to a life of rural seclusion.

Heine, Heinrich (1797-1856)— eminent German lyric poet and critic, friend of Marx.

Heraclitus of Ephesus—Greek philosopher of the sixth to fifth century B.C. First to formulate the laws of dialectics, including the idea of the unity of opposites. Described reality as in constant flux and change, though change was regulated by law or *logos*.

Herodotus (484?-425? B.C.)—the founder of modern historiography. His nine volumes were the first attempt to write a comprehensive, secular narrative account of world history.

historical materialism—the application of the dialectical materialist method to the study of the development of society. It holds that ideas and institutions are the product of a definite material and technological base and that the motive force of historical change, in the period following the appearance of governments, is the struggle of contending classes with opposed material interests.

historicity—the general view that societies can be understood only as products of definite laws of historical development and should be studied from the standpoint of process of change over time, leading into the future. (This is contrasted with the view that societies should be seen as fixed structures or organisms in which only the relation of parts to the whole need be considered.) The evolutionary outlook of Marxism places it squarely in the historicist camp.

Hook, Sidney (1902-   )— American pragmatist philosopher; taught at New York University (1927-72) and headed its philosophy department (1948-69). A student of John Dewey at Columbia University in the 1920s, Hook became the foremost of Dewey's disciples. Until 1932-33 he supported the Communist Party and then became a leader of the American Workers Party founded by A. J. Muste. Through his books *Towards the Understanding of Karl Marx* (1932) and *From Hegel to Marx* (1936) Hook became the outstanding American interpreter of Marxism in the 1930s, seeking to blend Marx with Dewey's instrumentalism and the views of the early Lukács. He broke with Marxism at the outset of World War II, becoming a right-wing Social Democrat and an anticommunist publicist.

Horkheimer, Max (1895-1973)— German Hegelian-Marxist philosopher. Born in Stuttgart, Horkheimer received his doctorate from the University of Frankfurt in 1922, participating the next year in the founding of the Institute of Social Research—the Frankfurt school (*see entry*). He became its director in 1930 and was the principal inspirer of its critical theory (*see entry*). He is best known for his books *Eclipse of Reason* (1947) and *Dialectic of the Enlightenment* (with Theodor Adorno, 1947). Horkheimer headed the Frankfurt school in exile in the United States (1934-50), then returned to Germany where it was integrated with the University of Frankfurt. After 1950 Schopenhauer became a more prominent influence in his thought. He concluded that alienation was rooted not in class oppression but in humanity's attempt to dominate nature, which he felt led to the domination of the weak by the strong.

Hume, David (1711-1776)—the culminating figure among the three great founders of British empiricism, after John Locke and George Berkeley. Taking Locke's proposition that all knowledge originates in sense experience, Hume questioned the verifiability of the origins of sensation, becoming the philosopher of extreme skepticism and the inspirer of agnosticism.

Husserl, Edmund (1859-1938)—German philosopher, founder of phenomenology (*see entry*). Trained as a mathematician, Husserl developed his views in several stages. He began with studies of the relations between logic and psychology; proceeded to phenomenology, which he conceived as an intuitive description of the nature of things apprehended, without preconceptions, from their appearances; and concluded after 1907 with an avowed subjective idealism which postulated that objects had no existence outside of consciousness. Husserl profoundly influenced the twentieth-century existentialist movement, primarily through his disciple Martin Heidegger (*see entry*). There have also been attempts to integrate Husserl's phenomenology with Marxism, notably by the writers grouped around the American journal *Telos*. Husserl in 1928 was stripped of his university post in Freiburg because of his Jewish origins. He spent his last years as a pariah in Nazi Germany, although he was not arrested.

Hyppolite, Jean (1907-1968)—French neo-Hegelian philosopher. He was the first to translate Hegel's *Phenomenology of Mind* into French, on the eve of World War II. Hyppolite taught Hegel and Marx at the Sorbonne (1949-54), then was made director of the Ecole normale supérieure (1954-63). His most widely circulated work is his *Studies on Marx and Hegel* (1955). Though sympathetic to Marx, he never considered himself a Marxist. His interpretation of Hegel stressed the anthropological self-creation of humanity through labor; humanism; the necessity for philosophic negation of existing society to bring the future into being; and the impossibility of ever fully overcoming alienation.

idealism—in philosophy, the view that mind, spirit, or God is the dominant feature of reality and that matter is either caused by these spiritual forces or that its nature is inherently unknowable.

identity theory—term denoting the philosophical belief, held by many idealist philosophers, that subject and object either are now or ultimately will become identical. In particular, it refers to Hegel's concept that the separation of subject and object—which separation he identified with both objectification and alienation (*see entries*)—was a temporary stage in the evolution of an infinite subject, the Absolute Idea. The end product of this evolution, for Hegel, was self-knowledge of the infinite subject, leading to an omniscient universal mind. Hegelian distortions of Marxism posit the establishment of communist society as the equivalent of an identity of subject and object. Orthodox Marxism holds that the elimination of class society will remove the roots of alienation, but rejects the notion that human subjectivity can ever be wholly merged with the remaining objective world of nature.

instrumentalism—the variant of pragmatism developed by American educator and philosopher John Dewey (*see entry*). Instrumentalism retained the traditional empiricist opposition to theoretical generalization, to investigation of the whole rather than its parts, and to concern with material causation. It did seek to modernize empiricism by stressing the active and evolutionary elements in cognition, placing practical problem-solving at the heart of its conceptual schema. It remained a semi-materialist anthropology of the reformist-minded U.S. middle class, never acquiring deeper roots in an ontological theory.

irrationalism—those currents in philosophy that deny that science and rational thought can adequately grasp reality and that give priority instead to will, intuition, or accident. It is represented by such figures as Schopenhauer, Nietzsche, Bergson, Heidegger, and the modern existentialists.

Jacobi, Friedrich Heinrich (1743-1819)—German idealist philosopher. Jacobi criticized the rationalism of Spinoza and Kant, objecting particularly to Kant's division of reality into phenomena and noumena. Jacobi, however, proposed to recover an integrated perception of the world by basing all knowledge on intuition and faith.

James, William (1842-1910)—American philosopher and psychologist. James perfected the pragmatic method first projected by Charles Peirce (*see* entry). In applying his psychological insights to philosophy, James sought to recapture a place for free will in face of scientific material determinism—which he generally accepted—by placing human activity at the center of his radical empiricism. James denied that truth or objectivity had any meaning apart from their effectiveness in producing desired results in achieving human goals. Thus James's thought retained the agnostic dualism that characterizes empiricism and positivism, differing from its predecessors primarily in its activist and individualist orientation.

Kant, Immanuel (1724-1804)—the first major figure in the German idealist counterattack on the British empiricist tradition. He sought to rescue universality and reason from the empiricist reaction against scholasticism. Kant granted to the empiricists the unknowability of the origin of sensations, which were the sole source of knowledge of the material world (phenomena), but he maintained that while the "thing-in-itself" was unknowable, morality, faith, and reason were examples of true knowledge in the mental sphere (noumena) where the data of sense impressions were organized and interpreted.

Kedrov, Bonifatiy Mikhailovich (1903-   )—Soviet philosopher of science. Kedrov was removed from his post as editor of *Problems of Philosophy* in 1948 for publishing articles supporting Einstein's views on quantum mechanics. He once again became prominent in Soviet philosophy after Stalin's death and is today a member of the Academy of Sciences and director of its Institute of the History of Science and Technology. He has written widely on the development of the natural sciences, defending Engels and dialectical materialism against Stalinist vulgarization as well as against revision by Western Marxists.

Kepler, Johannes (1571-1630)—German astronomer. Coming midway between Copernicus and Newton, Kepler was one of the major transitional figures in the creation of modern science. Copernicus had challenged the ancient belief that the earth was the immobile center of the universe but he still posited perfectly circular orbits of the planets around the sun as a carryover from Aristotelian cosmology. Kepler was the first to formulate the actual elliptical orbits of planetary bodies.

Kierkegaard, Soren Aabye (1813-1855)—Danish religious existentialist philosopher. Kierkegaard previewed many of the themes of twentieth-century existentialism, although in an explicitly religious context. He stressed that Christianity must be lived and experienced to be "true," rejecting conventional or purely intellectual adherence to faith. He also believed that growing awareness of truth led to personal despair owing to the contrast of the brevity of human life compared to the infinity of God.

Kolakowski, Leszek (1927-   )—dissident Polish Marxist philosopher. Kolakowski joined the Polish Communist Party in 1945 and remained a Stalinist in philosophical questions until the Polish October of 1956, when he went into opposition. In 1968 he left Poland after incessant harassment and has since taught in Western universities in various countries. He has come to reject large parts of the body of Marxist thought, including its materialist basis.

Korsch, Karl (1886-1961)—a founder, with Georg Lukács, of the Hegelian current in twentieth-century Marxism, stressing revolutionary will over objective conditions. A member of the German Communist Party until 1926, he is best known for his book *Marxism and Philosophy* (1923). In exile in the United States after 1936, Korsch renounced Marxism.

Kosík, Karel (1926-   )—Czech Marxist philosopher, notable for his book *Dialectics of the Concrete*, first published in 1963 and issued in an English translation in 1976. As a champion of the humanist, anti-Stalinist trend of thought and a supporter of "socialism with a human face," he has been deprived of his chair in philosophy at Charles University and has suffered persecution by the Husak regime.

Labriola, Antonio (1843-1904)—Italian Marxist philosopher; professor at the University of Rome. He ably disseminated the doctrine of the founders of Marxism through his books *Essays on the Materialist Conception of History* and *Socialism and History*. Labriola polemicized effectively against those in his day who anticipated the Stalinists by seeking to reduce Marxism to simplistic formulas.

law of value—economic law fully expounded by Marx to explain the ratios in which commodities of different types could be exchanged against each other or for a universal equivalent (money). Marx held that the value of a commodity was equivalent to the socially necessary labor-time required for its production or reproduction.

Lefèbvre, Henri (1901-   )—French Marxist philosopher and sociologist. In the 1920s, Lefèbvre's work was influenced by existentialism. In 1929 he joined the French CP, though he main-

tained philosophic differences and later broke with Stalinism. A supporter of the Hegelianizing current in Western Marxism, he rejects the dialectics of nature and "scientific ideology" and stresses human activity and praxis (*see entry*).

Left Hegelians—the radical wing of the Hegelian school in Germany in the 1840s, to which Marx and Engels belonged in their youth. Its most typical representatives were Arnold Ruge, Bruno Bauer, David Strauss, and, before he wrote *The Essence of Christianity*, Ludwig Feuerbach. The strength of the Young Hegelians came from their break with Hegel's belief that the status quo of the Prussian state represented the most progressive achievement to date in the realization of the Absolute Idea. They sought social and political reforms, and their philosophical studies were directed largely toward finding an agency through which such change could be realized. The trenchant criticism of their positions by Marx and Engels in *The German Ideology* (1845) scored their transfiguration of real social and class questions into vague philosophical abstractions and the failure to make any connection between their philosophical criticism of existing society and the social and political practice required to actually change it.

Leopardi, Giacomo (1798-1837)—Italian lyric poet and materialist philosopher. Chronic illness—which led to his early death—drew his attention to humanity's struggle with nature, particularly the prospect of individual mortality. Leopardi developed a philosophy of materialist pessimism centered on humanity's biological frailty.

Lévi-Strauss, Claude (1908-   )—a founder of the structuralist school of anthropology and director of studies at the Ecole pratique des hautes études in Paris. He rejected the historical and evolutionary approach to the study of social development, resting his analysis on the function of existing structures and the role of psychological factors, particularly in the formation of primitive myths.

Lichtheim, George (1912-1973)—German-born Marxist scholar. Lichtheim was close to the left-centrist Socialist Workers Party of Germany in the 1930s, then became an unaffiliated Social Democrat in exile, first in Palestine and then, from the 1940s, in England. In his book *Marxism* (1961) he advanced the thesis that Marxism and liberalism had been twin products of the Enlightenment, both seeking a means to give conscious direction to society. He considered them outmoded by the rise of centralized bureaucratic governments in the twentieth century. An opponent of empiricism, he sought a synthesis of Marxist and Hegelian elements in a new theory on the direction of social evolution. In particular he hoped to find a new agency of social change to replace the industrial proletariat.

Locke, John (1632-1704)—founder of British empiricism. Paralleling the rise of British capitalism, Locke sought to formulate a philosophical defense of bourgeois rights against feudal absolutism and of practical and dynamic activity against the sterile scholasticism of the Middle Ages. He rejected the concept of innate ideas, maintaining that all knowledge was derived from sensation, the raw data of sense experience then being refined and organized by mental reflection. He championed the scientific method and the solution of practical problems, holding that the pursuit of private ends by each individual contributed collectively to the public good.

Lucretius (c 99 B.C.-c 55 B.C.)—Roman materialist philosopher and poet. His great didactic poem, *De rerum natura (On the Nature of Things)*, is the finest exposition of Epicurean atomism in the ancient world and comes close in spirit to modern materialism.

Lukács, Georg (1885-1971)—Hungarian Communist philosopher and cultural critic, best known for his book *History and Class Consciousness* (1923).

Principal inspirer of the Hegelian current in twentieth-century Marxism, stressing revolutionary will over objective conditions. The young Lukács rejected dialectical materialism as a general theory of reality, while in social analysis he placed major emphasis on alienation and cultural phenomena at the expense of productive relations as determinants of social change. He renounced his views in 1933 and grudgingly conformed to Stalinism. In his later years he became a dissident in Stalinist circles in Hungary and returned partially to the orthodox Marxist teachings on dialectical materialism.

Mannheim, Karl (1893-1947)—Austro-Hungarian sociologist and historian. Influenced by Marx, but primarily concerned with the study of the role of social values rather than productive relations in maintaining social cohesion.

Marcuse, Herbert (1898-   )—German Marxist philosopher and long-time staff member of the Frankfurt school (1933-49). His best known works, *Eros and Civilization* (1955) and *One-Dimensional Man* (1964), were written after his break with the Frankfurt school, when he moved to incorporate elements of anarchism and Heideggerian existentialism with his previous views. Though known today as a mentor of the 1960s New Left, Marcuse's works of the 1930s and 1940s hold the most interest. Despite an Hegelianizing bent, books such as his *Reason and Revolution* (1941) are valuable Marxist studies.

Masaryk, Tomas (1850-1937)—Czechoslovak philosopher and politician; first president of Czechoslovakia (1918-35).

materialism—philosophically, the view that all of reality is composed of matter in motion, including mind, which is the product of the physical brain in social life. Materialism rejects all supernatural explanations of phe-

nomena. In contrast to vulgar materialism, Marxism does not reduce phenomena to mechanical motion, but
postulates distinct sets of laws for nature, society, and thought. It holds,
nevertheless, that nature and material
conditions in general have causal priority in explaining the development of
society and thought.

means of production—the tools,
land, buildings, and machinery required
for labor to create the sustenance and
other essential material goods of society.

mechanical materialism—prior to
Marx and Engels, the predominant form
of materialist thought in the bourgeois
era. Its main proponents in modern
times were Hobbes, Spinoza, the
thinkers of the French Enlightenment,
and Feuerbach. Mechanical materialism
defended the proposition that the universe is knowable and lawful. In the
seventeenth and eighteenth centuries, it
modeled its concept of causation on the
laws of mechanics, then the most developed science. Thus mechanical materialism sought to explain all phenomena by
reducing them to the laws of motion of
objects in space and time. Apparent
chance or accident was ascribed to
insufficient data. Dialectical materialism gives place to chance as well as
necessity and allows for qualitative
discontinuity and dialectical leaps as
well as simple straight-line development. Since the development of quantum mechanics and probability theory
modern science has adopted a more
sophisticated concept of determinism
more in accord with the views of dialectical materialism than with the mechanical materialists.

Mehring, Franz (1846-1919)—
German Marxist historian and scholar;
biographer of Karl Marx. One of the
leading theoreticians of the left wing of
the German Social Democracy, siding
with Luxemburg and Liebknecht
against Kautsky and Bernstein in defense of orthodox Marxism. Just before

his death he helped to found the German Communist Party.

meliorism—the belief that the world
tends to become better and better and
that human action can speed this process by gradual means.

Merleau-Ponty, Maurice (1908-
1961)—French existentialist philosopher. Influenced by Husserl's phenomenology (*see entries*), Merleau-Ponty
stressed the primacy of perception as
the means of access to a grasp of reality.
Unlike most phenomenologists, he
granted the prior existence of objective
material reality. This brought him into
sympathy with historical materialism,
but he differed from Marx in giving
much greater weight to mediating factors in the ideological superstructure
that stand between the objective economic base of society and individual
consciousness. This led him in turn to
reject the degree of determinism that
Marxists give to historical evolution,
holding instead that socialism is only
one possible outcome of contemporary
social evolution and that subjective
factors could produce a wide range of
different possible societies in the future.

metaphysics—used in various senses
by different philosophers, usually with
the connotation either of the study of
the general rather than the particular or
of speculation about matters that cannot be verified by experience. Most
commonly used by Marxists to describe
a philosophical system that arbitrarily
divides up reality into a series of externally imposed and unchanging categories.

Milesians—the founders of Greek
philosophy and also of materialism as a
philosophical current. The name is
taken from the city of Miletus in Asia
Minor, where the Ionian school flourished in the sixth and fifth centuries
B.C. Its most prominent representatives
were Thales (*see entry*), Anaximander,
and Anaximenes. The Milesians sought
rational, nonsupernatural explanations
for phenomena, usually in a supposed

primal substance from which the cosmos was derived through natural processes.

Mill, John Stuart (1806-1873)—British philosopher and economist, generally in the empiricist tradition, strongly influenced by the utilitarianism of Jeremy Bentham. His most lasting work is *On Liberty* (1859), a ringing defense of bourgeois democracy and social reform.

Mills, C. Wright (1916-1962)—American sociologist; author of *White Collar* (1951), *The Power Elite* (1956), and *The Sociological Imagination* (1959). Mills was a disciple of Max Weber (*see entry*) who sought to make a radical critique of American society and contemporary sociology in the name of a defense of freedom and reason against the bureaucratic state and the dehumanization of mass culture. Although an admirer of Marx, Lenin, and Trotsky, and a supporter of the Cuban revolution, Mills's sociology differed from Marxism in important respects. He counterposed a theory of multiple, independent sources of social movement in history to the Marxist conception of the primacy of social relations of production and social classes. For the United States, he distinguished a "power elite" composed of independent military, corporate, and government bureaucracies to the Marxist idea of a single capitalist ruling class. Mills's writings have been very influential among theorists of the New Left.

mode of production—the totality of the productive forces and the relations of production among the members of society that form a distinctive socioeconomic pattern at a given point in history. Examples of distinct modes of production include primitive communism, the Asiatic mode of production, pastoralism, slavery, feudalism, capitalism, and socialism.

monism—the philosophical view that the universe is composed of a single basic substance, e.g., for materialists, matter in motion; for consistent idealists, mind, spirit, or God. As contrasted to dualism (*see entry*).

Montaigne, Michel Eyquem, seigneur de (1533-1592)—French essayist, known for his skeptical criticism of received knowledge, which was instrumental in demolishing the smug scholasticism of the Middle Ages.

More, Sir Thomas (1478-1535)—English statesman and author of *Utopia*. A humanist and visionary, More was also a devoted Catholic. This led to a break with his friend King Henry VIII, who had More beheaded for treason when he refused to sanction Henry's rupture from Rome. More was later sainted by the Catholic church.

natural selection—name given by Darwin (*see entry*) to describe the mechanism of organic evolution. Darwin presumed a relative scarcity of food which placed all species in competition. This struggle for existence would be most intense between the most closely related species, as they would share the same environment and feed off the same substances. As statistical aggregates, those populations of individuals best able to adapt to their environment and survive would have the best chance to reproduce. Those species, or individual mutations within a species, less able to adapt and survive would eventually disappear. Mating between survivors would over time produce new traits and whole new species.

Naturphilosophie—a tendency in late eighteenth- and early nineteenth-century German philosophy that emerged as part of the romantic reaction against the Enlightenment. Typified by Goethe and Schelling, the nature philosophers combined genuine study of nature with naive attempts to deduce conclusions based on insufficient evidence. Most frequently, this tendency used analogies from biology to describe all phenomena—growth, decay, the "life force," etc. Anti-Marxists frequently lump Hegelianism and the Marxian dialectics of nature into this category.

negation of the negation—one of the basic laws of dialectics, flowing from the unity and struggle of opposites and the transformation of quantity into quality (*see entries*). Every object or condition is characterized by internal contradiction between a positive and a negative pole—that which exists and that which is coming into being. At the first dialectical leap, or negation, the old framework is broken, the previously subordinate quality or object in the relationship becomes dominant, and a new framework is established with a new set of internal contradictions. In both Hegelian and Marxist dialectics, this rupture is referred to as transcendence, rather than mere empty negation of the previous status quo, because there is an element of continuity and development as well as of destruction. The concept of the negation of the negation traces this element of transcendence over a longer period of time. It is a logical means of conceptualizing evolution over time, on the premise that natural and social processes are sufficiently determinate to show long-term cyclical patterns. Common examples given include the life cycles of living species, where birth represents the breakup of the previous unity of the parent organism for the first negation, with the stage where the progeny reach reproductive age representing the second negation, or the negation of the negation. In social evolution, a common example is the negation of primitive social property by the rise of private property and class society, followed by the eventual emergence of the proletariat, which moves toward the second stage, the negation of private property and the reestablishment of social property on a higher level, for a negation of the negation. From these examples it can be seen that Marx's concept is not purely cyclical but more like a spiral in which the conclusion of the complete process also involves evolution

and progress toward a higher level of organic or organizational complexity, and not mere repetition.

Newton, Isaac (1642-1727)—the dominant thinker in the modern natural sciences before Einstein; professor at Cambridge, England (1669-1701). Newton was the first to formulate the universal laws of gravitation, which explained for the first time the laws governing the motion of falling bodies as well as planetary orbits. Thus Newtonian physics became the basis of all modern astronomy and physics. In addition, he was the inventor of differential and integral calculus and the first to discover that white light is composed of all the colors of the spectrum, a discovery that laid the basis for all technology concerned with radiant energy—from infrared to X-rays. His work was surpassed only in the twentieth century with the formulation of Einstein's theory of relativity and the development of quantum mechanics.

Nietzsche, Friedrich Wilhelm (1844-1900)—German philosopher, best known for his book *Thus Spake Zarathustra*. He developed an antirationalist, atheistic humanism based on an extreme individualism that distrusted all group action. He is best remembered for his concepts of the superman and the will to power. In Nietzsche's writing these were largely meant as a prescription for nonconformist individual fulfillment. His ideas were later adopted in a highly distorted way by the Nazi movement as a rationalization for "Aryan" racism.

noumena—in Kant's philosophical system, the realm of true reality, the "thing-in-itself," which is, except for that portion of it which constitutes the inner moral world of each individual's thought, unknowable. Contrasted to the realm of appearance or phenomena.

object—something that exists independently of mind, as the world of nature, or society in relation to the will of its individual members.

objectification—the process of becoming objective in relation to a subject. While this term can be used to describe the coming into being of anything, it is most often used in Hegel to denote the products of human labor or activity, in which a subjective ability, capacity, or plan is made objective. Marx adopts this term as the heart of his theory of human nature, in which humanity is self-created as a social being (though not as a biological one) through the realization of its inner potential in social labor. Hegelianizing Marxists give two additional meanings to this term that depart from Marx's usage: (1) they place in question the reality or significance of phenomena until they have been "objectified" through human observation and brought into the human world, thus confusing actual creation through labor with mere discovery; and (2) the confusion of objectification with alienation (*see entry*). This second point implies that to be external to humanity is ipso facto to be threatening, an assumption not made by Marx.

objective idealism—one of two fundamental types of idealist thought, exemplified by Hegel. Characterized by the founding of a doctrine of reality on a universal mind or will which exists independently of human beings. As contrasted to subjective idealism (Berkeley, Hume), which takes as the only verifiable reality the individual human mind and is hence skeptical about the existence of all other phenomema.

obscurantism—hostility to the spread of knowledge and enlightenment. Stylistically, writing in such a way as to hide the real meaning, usually through trying to sound learned or mysterious.

Omel'ianovskii, Mikhail Erazmovich (1904-   )—Ukrainian philosopher of science, best known for his work *Philosophic Problems of Quantum Mechanics* (1956). Omel'ianovskii

sought to reconcile the concept of determinism in dialectical materialism with the discoveries of microphysics that it was impossible to simultaneously measure the position and momentum of microparticles. Omel'ianovskii repudiated Stalinist scientists and philosophers who tried to dismiss the problem as due entirely to inadequate measuring instruments. He postulated different sets of causal laws in the micro and macro worlds, granting an inherent uncertainty as to the speed and position of micro particles stemming from their dialectically combining both wavelike and corpuscular features. He held that the requirements of determinism were satisfied by statistical laws and did not require predictability or measurability of individual units.

ontology—the branch of philosophy concerned with the study of real being or existence. The Hegelian current in twentieth-century Marxism generally argues that Marxism should eschew any ontological position, e.g., on the priority of matter and nature over human will and activity, holding that answers to such questions are irrelevant and metaphysical.

Oparin, Aleksandr Ivanovich (1894-   )—Soviet biochemist; graduated from Moscow University in 1917 and subsequently a professor there. Member of the Soviet Academy of Sciences from 1946. Famous for his theories on the origin of life from inorganic matter, first published in 1924 and since very influential throughout the world.

opposites. See *under* unity and struggle of opposites.

orthogenesis—the belief that organic evolution takes place in accord with a predetermined pattern and is not the result of external factors such as natural selection (*see entry*).

Parmenides of Elea—Greek philosopher of the fifth century B.C. On the basis of the law of contradiction of formal logic, Parmenides denied the reality of change, holding that unalterable uniform being was alone real, while becoming and transformation were an illusion.

Pavlov, Ivan Petrovich (1849-1936)—Russian physiologist. Awarded the Nobel prize in 1904 for his experiments in the inducement of conditioned reflexes in animals through repeated external stimuli.

Peirce, Charles Sanders (1849-1914)—American philosopher, logician, and mathematician, inspirer of pragmatism (*see entry*). He worked as a physicist for the Coast Survey for most of his life, lecturing in philosophy only for the years 1879-84. His concept was to base philosophy on the methods of modern science—hence the radical empiricist basis of pragmatism—while deliberately keeping agnostic as to ultimate causes to make possible a reconciliation of science and religion.

phenomena—appearances, observable things and actions. In Kantianism: objects of experience in space and time, as distinguished from things-in-themselves.

phenomenalism—a theory, e.g., of Kant, that limits positive or scientific knowledge to phenomena only.

phenomenology—most broadly, a philosophic method concerned with the description of experience (as in Hegel's *Phenomenology of Mind*). In particular, the philosophic school founded by Edmund Husserl (*see entry*) early in the twentieth century, which was a factor in shaping existentialist thought and was imported into Marxist writing via the Hegelianizing current. Husserl claimed to have discovered a method to supersede both materialism and idealism by rejecting all "presuppositions." He sought to eliminate any theory of knowledge and called for suspending belief about any previously known fact in the study of a particular phenomenon. The internal logic of a phenomenon was to be reconstructed from the appearances of it available to the observer. Thus far

the method appeared to parallel empiricism, but Husserl then posited that the aim of such an investigation was to intuitively grasp the real essence of the phenomena under observation. During the period of study, no consideration was to be given to the reality or nonreality of the object under examination, meaning that dreams, fantasies, and false consciousness were to be examined with seriousness equal to that given to objectively indisputable existences. This approach proved useful in psychology in understanding the logic of aberrant fantasies or in seeing the inner logical connections in irrational social doctrines and movements. It was consciously antimaterialist, however, and in Marxist dress sought to give as much weight to ideological and superstructural factors in social causation as to the material foundations of society and its class structures.

Planck, Max (1858-1947)—German physicist, regarded as the father of quantum theory (*see entry*).

Platonism—after the Greek philosopher Plato (427?-347 B.C.). An idealist view which holds that material phenomena are the reflection of eternally existing nonmaterial forms and qualities (ideas) that predate the material universe and whose combinations make up the perceptions available to the senses.

Plekhanov, George Valentinovich (1856-1918)—the founder of Russian Marxism in 1883. Author of many valuable philosophical works, in particular *The Development of the Monist View of History* and *Fundamental Problems of Marxism*. He remained a central leader of the Russian Social Democracy until 1903, when he sided with the Menshevik faction against Lenin's Bolsheviks. He became a social-patriot in World War I and opposed the Russian October revolution in 1917. Despite this political break, Lenin and Trotsky continued to prize and highly recommend Plekhanov's philosophical writings.

Popper, Karl R. (1902-   )—Anglo-Austrian positivist philosopher. Starting from the standard positivist contention that knowledge must be limited to ascertainable fact and may not include generalized truths or laws, Popper added an intuitive concept of individual genius in the appropriation of knowledge. From this metaphysical and individualist position he polemicized against the notion of the certainty of any piece of knowledge and against all forms of historicism, particularly Marxism, asserting that no lawful development was discernible in history.

positivism—philosophical school founded by Auguste Comte (1798-1857), an offshoot of empiricism, which holds that the only valid knowledge is "positive," i.e., immediately empirically verifiable. Comte envisaged the discovery of laws of social development based on projecting existing trends mechanically into the future. His followers, the neopositivists, reject any general social theories or "value judgments" beyond simple description of actual events and social institutions.

pragmatism—American variant of empiricism, founded by Charles S. Peirce and William James and continued by John Dewey under the name instrumentalism. It stresses the role of thought as a guide to immediate practical individual action and the test of truth by its practical consequences rather than objective realities.

praxis—in general the activity of people in pursuit of their aims. It is popularized by Hegelianizing Marxists to designate social action based on and integrated with theoretical understanding. As they use it, the term implies the ability of revolutionary will to substitute for a lack of propitious objective opportunities.

progressivism—a broadly based middle class reform movement in the United States that arose after the Civil War and reached its height before World War I. Its political leader was Robert M. La Follette, Sr., one-time governor of Wisconsin (1901-6) and later a U.S. senator. Its supporters included literary figures such as Lincoln Steffens and Upton Sinclair. In philosophy, its leading exponent was John Dewey (*see entry*). Its campaigns focused on trust busting, the establishment of a minimum wage, the abolition of child labor, electoral reform, and the institution of social security measures.

quantity and quality—interdependent categories reflecting fundamental features of objective reality. Quality in philosophy is the determinate property of a thing or phenomenon that makes it stable, distinct, and diverse. It is those characteristics of things summed up by the word *quality* that are the province of formal logic (*see entry*). Quantitative definiteness enables things to be divided into homogeneous parts. Materialist dialectics views evolutionary change in nature, society, or human thought, as proceeding through the accumulation of small quantitative changes that, after reaching a specific limit, lead to a qualitative transformation in the essential nature of an object.

quantum theory—the study of the emission and absorption of energy by matter and the motion of material particles. Developed in the first two decades of the twentieth century on the basis of work by Max Planck, Albert Einstein, and Niels Bohr. Physics had previously assumed that energy had no materiality and moved in wavelike formations, while matter was assumed to always occupy a definite spot in space and time. Quantum theory disclosed that subatomic particles emit and absorb energy according to definite laws, but that as a result of these transitions they act sometimes as wavelike bodies and sometimes as particulate bodies, with a degree of inherent indeterminateness as to their speed and position at any given time. This discovery precipitated a major philosophical debate among scientists around the world as to the nature of causation and determinism. Physicist-philosophers such as Werner Heisenberg argued that, since indeterminacy was characteristic of the most elementary building blocks of the material world, all concepts of lawfulness and determinateness were illusory constructions of the human mind. Soviet scientists—after a long initial period under the influence of Stalinist repression, in which they denied outright the validity of the uncertainty principle—began in the 1950s to formulate a new concept of determinism based on the statistical predictability of aggregates of subatomic particles.

Rappoport, Charles (1865-1939?)—Russian revolutionist and publicist. Emigrated to France around the turn of the century and became a leader of the French SP and a founder of the CP. Broke with Marxism at the time of the trial of Bukharin (1938).

rationalism—the reliance upon reason as opposed to sense experience as the source of true knowledge. Classically represented by Spinoza and Leibniz, rationalism polemicized against revelation, mysticism, and irrationalism of all kinds. At the same time, this current is inherently idealist in its deprecation of sense experience. In twentiety-century Marxism, the most openly rationalistic tendency is represented by the Frankfurt school.

real opposition—in Kant and Colletti, a clash of actual forces in life or reality, as contrasted in their view to a dialectical opposition, which they hold to be a mental construct.

reflection, theory of—the basic epistemological assumption of dialectical materialism, that sense perceptions are the doorway to a more or less accurate reflection of the actual material world. The debate over this theory stems mainly from the accusation by the Hegelianizers and neo-Kantians that Engels and Lenin held a passive

"copy theory" of knowledge that failed to take account of Kant's discovery that humans actively assimilate sense data by organizing it into categories of experience. This is an unwarranted distortion of the view of Lenin, who both in his *Materialism and Empirio-Criticism* and in his *Philosophical Notebooks* took account of the active character of interpreting sensory data, rejecting only the notion that Kant's categories were innate or of nonmaterial origin.

reification—attributing materiality to a mental construction; it is a concept closely related to fetishism, which plays a large part in the writings of Lukács. It is most often referred to in discussions of the tendency in thought to reify the capitalist state and its institutions, i.e., to regard them as entities that exist apart from the human beings that administer them.

relations of production—in all human societies, the organized division of labor by which the productive forces are set in motion and human needs satisfied. In class society, this involves different relationships to the means of production for different classes. Such relations in class society are institutionalized and codified in legal property relations. Such an institutionalized structure sooner or later comes in conflict with the expanding forces of production (*see entry*).

relativism—the belief that absolute truth either does not exist or is not at present known, and, in the moral sphere, that no universal and unchanging yardstick exists by which human conduct must be regulated. In its most extreme form, relativism takes the form of subjective idealism, denying the certainty of any knowledge and adopting an indifferent tolerance to all human actions. At the opposite extreme, complete epistemological and moral certitude are to be had only in religion or in the metaphysical systems of the objective idealists. Marxism rests on the assumption of the existence of verifiable truth in epistemology and of objectivity in morality. It retains an important element of relativism in that it recognizes that human knowledge is historically limited and morality is shaped by historical conditions and class divisions.

relativity, theory of—a revolutionary breakthrough in physics developed by Albert Einstein, who published his special theory of relativity in 1905 and his more ambitious general theory in 1916. It superseded Newtonian physics, which had assumed fixed categories such as time, space, mass, energy, etc. Einstein proved that while the universe remained an objective fact with definite laws, time and space were interrelated aspects of the same phenomena. Relative to other objects in the universe moving toward or away from an observer, time can slow down or speed up, and space can literally be shrunk or expanded. Einstein also showed that mass and energy were interconvertible and alternative forms of matter.

Ricardo, David (1772-1823)—British economist. Ricardo, who followed Adam Smith and developed further many of his theories, is regarded with Smith as one of the founders of political economy. Ricardo was the promulgator of the labor theory of value, which appears only in embryo in the works of Adam Smith and which was later perfected by Marx.

Rousseau, Jean-Jacques (1712-1778)—French philosopher and author. Rousseau combined elements of empiricism, rationalism, and romanticism, arguing that society was inherently corrupting and that people should return to a more simple and natural existence. He held that society should be responsible to its members and in *Le Contrat social* (1762) postulated a mythical creation of the state in history through the rational collective decision to form one. Rousseau's criticisms of inequality and his advocacy of representative democracy made him one of the

principal intellectual stimulators of the French and American revolutions.

Royce, Josiah (1855-1916)—American idealist philosopher; taught at Harvard (1882-1916). He held that reality is composed of a living, absolute mind.

Russell, Bertrand (1872-1970)—British philosopher, mathematician, and social reformer; during his long life, a prolific writer on epistemology, metaphysics, logic, mathematics, ethics, and social and political questions. An irreverent iconoclast, he was originally a pacifist who became a crusading antiimperialist in later life. His philosophy was an updated version of empiricism guided by the analytic method. He upheld a view of reality as composed of independent particular facts which were expressible in simple sentences (logical atomism). The work he did on the logical foundations of mathematics with Alfred North Whitehead, *Principia Mathematica* (1910-13), is probably his most enduring achievement. This was the first systematic proof that mathematics is based on the laws of formal logic. It laid the basis for symbolic logic, which, within the limitations of formal logic, permitted the application to language of a rigorous measure of the meaning conveyed by grammar.

saltationism—the belief that biological evolution proceeded by the sudden, direct emergence of one species fullblown from another, as contrasted to the Darwinian theory of the gradual accumulation of quantitative differences through natural selection.

Santayana, George (1863-1952)—Spanish-born American philosopher and man of letters. Santayana sought to fuse elements of materialism and of Platonism (*see entry*) in a romantic synthesis. He granted the material basis of organic life, humanity included, but urged an esthetic transcendence of material existence through the contemplation of distinct qualities of nature which he conceived on the model of Plato's essences or ideas. A professor of philosophy at Harvard (1889-1912), Santayana then returned to Europe where he spent the next forty years in retirement from worldly affairs. He wrote widely in these later years, summing up his thought in the four-volume *Realms of Being* (1927-40).

Sartre, Jean-Paul (1905-   )—the best-known twentieth-century philosopher of nonreligious existentialism. He proposed a doctrine of personal responsibility for human action in a universe without purpose. Sartre originally considered existentialism and Marxism incompatible, but in his *Critique of Dialectical Reason* (1960) sought vainly to reconcile the two world views.

Schaff, Adam (1913-   )—the outstanding contemporary Polish Communist philosopher. He was a member of the Communist Party Central Committee from 1959 to 1968, when he was expelled in the controversy over his book *Marxism and the Human Individual.* He has been chairman of the philosophical committee of the Polish Academy of Sciences and director of the Academy's Institute of Philosophy and Sociology. He has also been editor in chief of the principal Polish philosophical journals. In addition to his post at the University of Warsaw, he is director of the UNESCO-sponsored European Center for the Social Sciences in Vienna. He has recently written on the problem of alienation and on the role of language in human cognition.

Schelling, Friedrich Wilhelm Joseph von (1775-1854)—German idealist philosopher. Schelling's work falls midway in time between Fichte and Hegel. A leader of the romantic movement and a prominent *Naturphilosoph (see entry)*, Schelling viewed the whole of nature as a sort of living organism in the process of growth. He postulated the existence of an "Absolute Ego" that lived in nature in a state of forgetfulness, whose thought process created the phenomenal world and whose gradual awakening was responsible for human history.

Schmidt, Alfred (1931-   )—succeeded Theodor Adorno in 1971 as director of the Institute of Social Research in Frankfurt, West Germany (the Frankfurt school). He is the author of *The Concept of Nature in Marx* (English edition, 1972), in which he denies that laws of nature are dialectical.

Schmidt, Konrad (1863-1932)—German economist and philosopher. As a Social Democrat, Schmidt corresponded with Engels in the latter's last years. He later became a revisionist, adopting neo-Kantian positions.

Schopenhauer, Arthur (1788-1860)—German idealist philosopher, known as the philosopher of pessimism. Schopenhauer accepted Kant's innate categories of logic and fused them into an extreme idealist system in which the highest truth was disembodied "ideas" on the Platonic model *(see entry)*. In a kind of right-wing Hegelianism, he viewed the source of change as an innate "will to life" in all things, but argued that this will in humanity could never be satisfied because human desires are infinite. Schopenhauer proposed an irrationalist quietism, renouncing desire and ego.

scientism—belief that methods of natural sciences are directly applicable to solution of social and philosophical problems.

sensationalism—in epistemology, the doctrine that sensation is the sole source of knowledge. This can lead either to materialism or to subjective idealism depending on what conclusion is then drawn as to the source of sense perceptions.

skepticism—the philosophical tendency that denies the possibility of attaining true knowledge of reality. Considered to have originated in Greece with Pyrrho in the third century B.C. Played a part in the philosophy of Montaigne (1533-1592) in demolishing medieval scholasticism. Most fully developed in modern times by the British empiricist Hume (*see entry*).

Smith, Adam (1723-1790)—Scottish economist who in his 1776 treatise *An Inquiry into the Nature and Causes of the Wealth of Nations* founded the modern science of political economy.

Socrates (469-399 B.C.)—the most famous of all the early Greek philosophers, regarded as the founder of idealism. Socrates sought to turn philosophy from the study of nature to the study of ethics and human conduct, reinterpreting natural events on the model of human activity. He is credited by his disciple Plato with originating the theory of ideal forms as the true essence of all things. A supporter of the Athenian aristocracy, Socrates was put to death by supporters of the democratic camp for his ties to political reaction.

Sophists—originally, wandering scholars in Greece in the fifth century B.C. who charged fees in exchange for lessons. They were critical of many conventional ideas and customs and their arguments and aphorisms exhibited a keen sense of dialectical contradiction. The Sophists acquired their present bad name through their propensity to teach useful political skills such as rhetoric in place of more general truth and their reputed readiness to argue on any side of a question for money.

Spengler, Oswald (1880-1936)—German historian and philosopher, whose outlook is presented at length in *Decline of the West* (1918-22). Spengler's prediction of the imminent decay and fall of Western civilization excited wide interest in the immediate post-World War I period. His philosophical-historical reasoning, however, was based on a crudely cyclical theory of history in which every culture was born, grew old, and died. Each was unique and self-enclosed. This simplistic notion was bolstered by elaborate and far-fetched analogies from many great cultures designed to give the impression that each had followed a precisely similar round of stages in the same span of time.

Spinoza, Benedict (1632-1677)—Outstanding Dutch materialistic and atheistic philosopher. Spinoza denied the existence of God apart from nature and developed a monistic system of thought that explained ideas as a property of nature (matter). Spinoza considered change as mechanical motion and belonged to the rationalist camp in that he believed that true knowledge was derived from reason and not from the senses.

spiritualism—the doctrine that spirit and not matter is the actual substructure of the perceivable universe.

structuralism—view that in social analysis the question of historical evolution is greatly subordinate to examination of existing interrelationship between various institutions and social structures.

structural linguistics—tendency in language analysis founded by Ferdinand de Saussure (1857-1913) that rejected study of evolutionary origins and development of language in favor of examination of different elements within a given linguistic system.

subject—philosophically, that which is capable of conscious thought or action, as contrasted with object (*see entry*).

superstructure—in Marxist social analysis, those sectors of society and social relations ultimately created by the process of direct material production though removed from its immediate sphere. In class society this includes the political state apparatus, social and cultural institutions, schools of thought and ideologies, and other forms of mental and spiritual production. While Marx held that the superstructure was "determined" by the economic base (the level of productive forces, fundamental class relations, etc.), he did not hold that this determination was a direct and mechanical one in which all ideas and political representations could be shown to be an unmediated response to the impact of economic relations.

surplus product—that part of the annual product of a society that is not used for the consumption of the producers or for replacement of the stock of the means of production used in the course of the year. In class society, the social surplus product is appropriated by the property owners of the ruling class.

syncretism—the illegitimate attempt to reconcile conflicting and incompatible beliefs.

synchrony—concern with events at a given time only, ignoring their historical development.

Teilhard de Chardin, Pierre (1881-1955)—French paleontologist and philosopher; ordained as a Jesuit priest in 1911. He took part in the discovery of Peking Man in China (1929). In seeking to reconcile the scientific belief in evolution with church doctrine, he was distrusted by the church because of his evolutionism, but was not accepted as a scientist because of his religious mysticism. His most celebrated work was the posthumously published *The Phenomenon of Man* (1955).

teleology—the belief that nature has an inherent purpose and that natural evolution of social history moves toward a predetermined goal.

Thales (c.636-c.546 B.C.)—the first recorded Western philosopher, founder of materialism and of the Milesian school (*see entry*). He repudiated mythological explanations of natural phenomena and of creation, seeking instead an explanation in some primordial substance. He believed this substance to be water, which through its condensation or rarefaction made up the objects of perception. His innovative method proved to be of extraordinary importance in Western thought even though his answers were naive.

theism—the belief in the existence of God as governor of the universe.

thing-for-us—in Kant's philosophy, the world of appearances, of the superficial knowledge of objects as phenomena. This knowledge might be more or less reliable and of use in achieving desired results through practice, but, for Kant, tells us nothing of the true nature of the "thing-in-itself" (*see entry*).

thing-in-itself—in Kant's philosophy, the true inner nature of objects, the noumenal realm. For Kant, this inner nature is forever unknowable and only phenomenal appearances are available to the mind of the observer.

Thomism—the official philosophy of the Catholic church, formulated by Saint Thomas Aquinas (1225-1274). The greatest of the medieval scholastics, Saint Thomas sought to reconcile faith and reason in a synthesis that would preserve Greek rationalism (Aristotle) in the framework of church doctrine.

Thucydides (c.460-c.400 B.C.)—Greek historian of Athens. Thucydides was, after Herodotus (*see entry*), the most perceptive of the Greek historians of antiquity, famed for his work *The History of the Peloponnesian War*.

Timpanaro, Sebastiano (1923-   )—contemporary Italian Marxist philosopher. Generally an orthodox Marxist and a strong defender of philosophic materialism, although he maintains reservations about the correctness of the dialectical method and its application by Engels in *Dialectics of Nature*.

transcendentalism—American literary and philosophical movement that flourished in New England between the 1830s and the 1860s. Though not a rigorous philosophy, it generally represented an individualistic reaction against the authoritarianism of Calvinist Protestantism. Mystical and romantic in outlook, the transcendentalists stressed self-reliance, individual intuition as the best source of knowledge, and the immanent divinity of humanity and nature. Its best-known exponents were

Ralph Waldo Emerson and Henry David Thoreau.

transformational grammar—a system in linguistics developed by Noam Chomsky (*see entry*) that seeks to extract from surface patterns of speech the underlying logical structures of language, and to generate mathematical rules that can describe transformations of logical "deep structures" into varied surface speech forms.

uneven and combined development—two closely related concepts or laws discerned by Marx and formulated by Trotsky in his theory of permanent revolution. Uneven development concerns the study of the factors producing widely varying rates of social progress in different societies measured by the development of the productive forces, class relations, and social institutions. Combined development refers to social formations that embody interpenetrating institutions or features derived from different stages or levels of historical progression resulting in the creation of a hybrid formation.

unity and struggle of opposites—a concept central to materialist dialectics, which views the internal contradictions of objects as the source of change. All objects, from an atom to a cell to an organism, are composed of a dynamic equilibrium of opposed forces or poles. Over time quantitative changes alter the balance of tension between the opposite poles leading to a qualitative leap in which a new transcendent alignment of forces takes place.

use-value—in a commodity, the specific utility or capacity of the object to satisfy a human need, real or imagined. As distinguished from exchange value (*see entry*).

Vigier, Jean-Pierre (1920-   )—French theoretical physicist; master of research at the National Center for Scientific Research in Paris. A defender of the theory of the dialectics of nature.

vitalism—the belief that life in general and the functioning of living organisms in particular cannot be fully explained by the laws of chemistry and physics but is the result of an inner "life force."

voluntarism—the view that human will can be the dominant factor in social change.

Weber, Max (1864-1920)—German sociologist and economist. Extremely influential in modern sociology, Weber eclectically combined elements from Marxism with various other sources. In contrast to Marx's concept of the centrality of relations of production and class struggle in social development, Weber counterposed a pluralist theory that gave great weight to religious ideology and charismatic leaders as shapers of social development. He developed this approach in his best-known work, *The Protestant Ethic and the Spirit of Capitalism*, where he argued that the material preconditions for the appearance of capitalism had arisen in several disparate societies but it came into being only where the added factor of a congenial religion—Calvinist Protestantism—placed a high value on entrepreneurial activity. His most important contribution to social theory was the stressing of a "social system model," by which a social scientist could, for purposes of analysis, compare the structures of different societies.

Whitehead, Alfred North (1861-1947)—English mathematician and philosopher. He won fame as coauthor with Bertrand Russell (*see entry*) of the *Principia Mathematica* (1910-13), the first rigorous demonstration of the logical basis of mathematics. He developed a metaphysical system which he called the "philosophy of organism"—an anthropological positivism that sought to bridge the materialism-idealism dichotomy by taking as the center of its attention the ongoing process of integrating new experience in human consciousness.

Woltman, Ludwig (1872-1907)— German philosopher and naturalist who wrote on historical materialism and Darwinism from a neo-Kantian viewpoint.

Young Hegelians. *See* Left Hegelians.

A Bibliography in Marxist Philosophy

INTRODUCTORY WORKS

Dewey, John; Novack, George; and Trotsky, Leon. *Their Morals and Ours: Marxist Versus Liberal Views on Morality*. New York: Pathfinder Press, 1969.

Engels, Frederick. *Ludwig Feuerbach and the Outcome of Classical German Philosophy*. New York: International, 1941.

———. *Socialism: Utopian and Scientific*. Various editions—International, Pathfinder.

Mandel, Ernest, and Novack, George. *The Marxist Theory of Alienation*. New York: Pathfinder Press, 1973.

Martel, Harry, and Selsam, Howard, eds. *A Reader in Marxist Philosophy: From the Writings of Marx, Engels, and Lenin*. New York: International, 1963.

Marx, Karl. Preface to *A Contribution to the Critique of Political Economy*. Various editions—Charles H. Kerr, International.

Novack, George. *An Introduction to the Logic of Marxism*. New York: Pathfinder Press, 1969.

Plekhanov, George. "The Materialist Conception of History" and "The Role of the Individual in History," in *Fundamental Problems of Marxism*. New York: International, 1969.

THE ORTHODOX MARXIST TRADITION

Marx and Engels

(Publishing information is generally not provided in this section, since so

327

many different editions have appeared—individually, in anthologies, or in collections such as the *Collected Works* of Marx and Engels.)

Engels, Frederick. *Dialectics of Nature.*

——. *Herr Eugen Dühring's Revolution in Science* (also known as *Anti-Dühring*).

Marx, Karl. *Economic and Philosophic Manuscripts of 1844.*

——. *Grundrisse: Foundations of the Critique of Political Economy.* Harmondsworth: Penguin, 1973.

——. *The Poverty of Philosophy.*

Marx and Engels. *The German Ideology.*

——. *The Holy Family.*

Successors of Marx and Engels

Bukharin, Nikolai. *Historical Materialism: A System of Sociology.* Ann Arbor: University of Michigan Press, 1969.

Kautsky, Karl. *Foundations of Christianity.* New York: Monthly Review Press, 1972.

Labriola, Antonio. *Essays in the Materialist Conception of History.* New York: Monthly Review Press, 1966.

Lenin, Vladimir Ilyich. *Materialism and Empirio-Criticism.* Various editions—Foreign Languages, International.

——. "Philosophical Notebooks," in *Collected Works,* vol. 38. Moscow: Foreign Languages, 1962.

Novack, George. *Empiricism and Its Evolution.* New York: Pathfinder Press, 1971.

——. ed. *Existentialism versus Marxism.* New York: Dell, 1966.

——. *The Origins of Materialism.* New York: Merit, 1965.

——. *Pragmatism versus Marxism.* New York: Pathfinder Press, 1975.

Plekhanov, George. *The Development of the Monist View of History.* New York: International, 1973.

——. *Fundamental Problems of Marxism.* New York: International, 1969.

——. *Materialismus Militans: Reply to Bogdanov.* Moscow: Progress.

——. *Selected Philosophical Works,* vol. 1. Moscow: Progress.

Trotsky, Leon. *In Defense of Marxism.* New York: Pathfinder Press, 1973.

THE PLACE OF HEGEL IN MARXISM

Works by Hegel

Hegel, Georg Wilhelm Friedrich. *Lectures on the Philosophy of History.* New York: Dover, 1956.

———. *Phenomenology of Mind.* New York: Humanities, 1964.

Wallace, William, ed. *The Logic of Hegel.* New York: Oxford University Press, 1975.

Works on Hegel

Lukács, Georg. *The Young Hegel.* Cambridge: MIT Press, 1976.

Mandel, Ernest. *The Formation of the Economic Thought of Karl Marx.* New York: Monthly Review Press, 1971.

Marcuse, Herbert. *Reason and Revolution.* Boston: Beacon Press, 1941.

Mészáros, István. *Marx's Theory of Alienation.* New York: Harper & Row, 1972.

Rosdolsky, Roman. *The Making of Marx's "Capital."* London: Pluto, 1977.

NEO-HEGELIANISM

Initiators of the Subjectivist Revival

Hook, Sidney. *From Hegel to Marx: Studies in the Intellectual Development of Karl Marx.* Ann Arbor: University of Michigan Press, 1962.

———. *Towards the Understanding of Karl Marx.* New York: John Day, 1933.

Howard, Dick, and Klare, Karl, eds. *The Unknown Dimension: European Marxism Since Lenin.* New York: Basic Books, 1972.

Korsch, Karl. *Marxism and Philosophy.* New York: Monthly Review Press, 1970.

———. *Three Essays on Marxism.* New York: Monthly Review Press, 1970.

Lukács, Georg. *History and Class Consciousness: Studies in Marxist Dialectics.* Cambridge: MIT Press, 1971.

———. *Lenin: A Study on the Unity of His Thought.* Cambridge: MIT Press, 1971.

Works on the Frankfurt School

Anderson, Perry. *Considerations on Western Marxism.* London: New Left Books, 1976.

Jay, Martin. *The Dialectical Imagination: A History of the Frankfurt School and the Institute for Social Research, 1923-1950.* Boston: Little, Brown, 1973.

Lichtheim, George. *Collected Essays.* New York: Viking Press, 1973.

————. *From Marx to Hegel.* New York: Seabury Press, 1971.

————. *Marxism: An Historical and Critical Study.* New York: Praeger, 1964.

Works by Members of the Frankfurt School

Adorno, Theodor. *Negative Dialectics.* New York: Seabury Press, 1972.

Habermas, Jürgen. *Knowledge and Human Interests.* Boston: Beacon Press, 1971.

————. *Theory and Practice.* Boston: Beacon Press, 1974.

————. *Toward a Rational Society: Student Protest, Science, and Politics.* Boston: Beacon Press, 1971.

Horkheimer, Max. *Critical Theory.* New York: Seabury Press, 1972.

———— with Theodor Adorno. *Dialectic of Enlightenment.* New York: Seabury Press, 1975.

————. *Eclipse of Reason.* New York: Seabury Press, 1973.

Marcuse, Herbert. *Negations.* Boston: Beacon Press, 1968.

————. *One-Dimensional Man.* Boston: Beacon Press, 1964.

————. *Studies in Critical Philosophy.* Boston: Beacon Press, 1974.

Schmidt, Alfred. *The Concept of Nature in Marx.* London: New Left Books, 1971.

Wellmar, Albrecht. *Critical Theory of Society.* New York: Seabury Press, 1974.

ANTIDIALECTICAL ANTI-HEGELIANISM

Althusser, Louis. *For Marx.* New York: Pantheon Press, 1969.

————. *Lenin and Philosophy, and Other Essays.* London: New Left Books, 1972.

————. *Politics and History: Montesquieu, Rousseau, Hegel, and Marx.* London: New Left Books, 1972.

———— with Etienne Balibar. *Reading Capital.* New York: Pantheon, 1970.

Poulantzas, Nicos. *Political Power and Social Classes.* London: New Left Books, 1975.

TENDENCIES IN EUROPEAN MARXISM

Czechoslovakia

Kosík, Karel. *Dialectics of the Concrete: A Study on Problems of Man and World.* Boston: D. Reidel, 1976.

Svitak, Ivan. *Man and His World: A Marxian View.* New York: Dell, 1970.

Italy

Colletti, Lucio. *From Rousseau to Lenin.* New York: Monthly Review Press, 1972.

———. *Marxism and Hegel.* London: New Left Books, 1973.

Timpanaro, Sebastiano. *On Materialism.* London: New Left Books, 1975.

Poland

Kolakowski, Leszek. *Alienation of Reason: A History of Positivist Thought.* New York: Doubleday, 1968.

———. *Toward a Marxist Humanism: Essays on the Left Today* (published in Britain as *Marxism and Beyond*). New York: Grove Press, 1968.

Schaff, Adam. *Marxism and the Human Individual.* New York: McGraw-Hill, 1970.

———. *A Philosophy of Man.* New York: Monthly Review Press, 1963.

Yugoslavia

Markovic, Mihailo. *From Affluence to Praxis: Philosophy and Social Criticism.* Ann Arbor: University of Michigan Press, 1974.

Stojanoic, Svetoza. *Between Ideals and Reality: A Critique of Marxism and Its Future.* New York: Oxford University Press, 1973.

Index

SOUTH-WESTERN SERIES IN

H R M
HUMAN RESOURCES MANAGEMENT

EMPLOYEE TURNOVER

Peter W. Hom
Department of Management
Arizona State University

Rodger W. Griffeth
Department of Management and
The W.T. Beebe Institute of
Personnel and Employee Relations
Georgia State University

SOUTH-WESTERN College Publishing

An International Thomson Publishing Company

Acquisitions Editor: Randy G. Haubner
Production Editor: Sharon L. Smith
Production House: Fog Press
Cover and Internal Design: Barbara Libby
Marketing Manager: Stephen E. Momper

GJ80AA

Library of Congress Cataloging-in-Publication Date

Hom, Peter W.
    Employee turnover / Peter W. Hom, Rodger W. Griffeth.
        p.   cm. -- (South-Western series in human resources management)
    Includes index.
    ISBN 0-538-80873-X
    1. Labor turnover.   I. Griffeth, Rodger W.   II. Title.
III. Series.
HF5549.5.T8H65 1994   94-33871
658.3'14--dc20   CIP

1 2 3 4 5 6 7 MT 0 9 8 7 6 5 4
Printed in the United States of America

International Thomson Publishing

South-Western College Publishing is an ITP Company. The ITP trademark is used under license.

PREFACE

Katz and Kahn (1968) long observed that the pivotal challenge for organizations was to motivate their members to produce *and* participate. Organizational researchers, who have now adopted this as a guiding principle, have written countless articles on employee performance and turnover, as well as numerous books on their theories about what motivates employees to perform and how to measure their performance. But there are fewer books on organizational participation. Our book seeks to correct this imbalance as we attempt to summarize the immense volume of empirical facts and theories about this significant employee behavior.

Specifically, we update earlier books that dealt with the vast turnover literature (Mobley, 1982; Mowday, Steers, & Porter, 1982; Price, 1977). More than a decade has elapsed since the last book, although surprising new facts and insightful theories on turnover have emerged during this time. This book attempts to review these recent developments and to bring the reader up to the present.

Apart from review, this book is different from others in the field in several respects. First, we provide a meta-analytical review of empirical facts, which is more rigorous than narrative reviews and more comprehensive than earlier meta-analysis (cf. Cotton & Tuttle, 1986). Second, we not only systematically critique various theories but also propose a theoretical integration (Chapter 6), whereas other scholarly books usually emphasize a particular viewpoint. Moreover, this book identifies methods of reducing turnover that are based on empirical research, unlike many popular books whose prescriptions derive from anecdotal evidence or speculations. We also discuss various theories that view turnover as symptomatic of an underlying maladaptation. With the exception of Price and Mueller (1986), books on turnover typically examine *only* turnover and do not consider how it relates to other adaptive responses to work dissatisfaction. Finally, we examine methodological shortcomings of current research and suggest new methods that may overcome those deficiencies. To our knowledge, no existing turnover book evaluates methodologies for investigating turnover.

We are grateful to Jerry Ferris and Ken Rowland, who initiated this project and patiently awaited the arrival of the book. We are also indebted to Tom Lee for his exhaustive review of the preliminary manuscript. The final product benefitted immeasurably from his invaluable suggestions—although we claim all mistakes for ourselves. Luis Gomez-Mejia deserves our eternal gratitude for believing in our book project and reviving it after a false start. We also express our appreciation to Paula Phillips Carson for her diligent efforts on the meta-analysis and to Margaret Harris and Veronica Wan-Huggins for painstakingly double-checking book references. We thank Joyce and Angelo Kinicki for their encouragement and faith in our ability to produce this work. Also without

Jacqui's and Justin's patience and understanding, Dad could not have finished his chapters while entombed in his office. Finally, we credit Chuck Hulin and Bill Mobley for starting us on our decade-long journey on turnover research and to Jim Price for keeping us on this path.

Tempe, Arizona
January 1994

For our biological and intellectual parents:
Nguey Kun Wong and Ting Hom
In Memory of Ann Griffeth
Dean and Vivian Griffeth
Charles Hulin, William Mobley, and James Price

CONTENTS

WHAT IS TURNOVER AND HOW IS IT MEASURED?

WHY THE STUDY OF TURNOVER IS ESSENTIAL

Employee turnover—or voluntary terminations of members from organizations—is a phenomenon of immense interest to employers and organizational scholars alike. Managers have long been interested in turnover because of the personnel costs incurred when employees quit, such as those for recruiting and training new replacements (Cascio 1991). For example, Hom (1992) estimated that turnover cost twenty four mental health agencies more than $3 million in 1991. (Bases for turnover costs are more closely examined in Chapter 2.) Not surprisingly, countless books and articles have appeared over the years to advise employers on how to curb turnover (Bellus 1984; Half 1982; Roseman 1981; Watts and White 1988).

Though pervasive corporate downsizing has dampened recent interest in the subject, turnover among key personnel or groups of strategic employees (Gomez-Mejia and Balkin 1992a) continues to attract the attention of organizations. For instance, the departure of pivotal scientists or engineers from high-tech firms can delay or impede new product development (Turbin and Rossé 1990). Given global competition, the introduction of new products may spell the future of a manufacturing firm. Similarly, 25 percent of all expatriate managers on overseas assignments quit the parent corporation within a year of returning. A multinational company thus loses, not only its $1.2 million investment per offshore assignment, but also invaluable international experience (Gregersen and Black 1992). Though public accounting firms expect most of their staff accountants to leave eventually given only a few can become partners, they are nonetheless distressed about the high attrition rates among third-year senior accountants (Bellus 1984; Hom, Bracker, and Julian 1988). Senior accountants are well-trained veterans who generate $47,000 more in profits than inexperienced accounting graduates do (Sheridan 1992). Thus, even organizations accustomed to (and expecting) excessive quit rates may still worry about the timing: premature turnover may waste their sizeable investment in employee training.

Apart from the departure of special personnel, service organizations—which employ 42 percent of the work force—are becoming concerned about resignations among front-line service personnel (Schlesinger and Heskett 1991). Service firms now recognize that the delivery of services and loyalty of customers may be jeopardized when employees leave(Reichheld 1993). Manpower shortages created by turnover may delay or preclude customer service (Darmon 1990; Machalaba 1993). What is more, inexperienced service providers may be inept or impersonal because they do not know the customers (Darmon 1990). Besides this, the customers, too, may abandon a firm if their attachment had been based on personal ties to former sales personnel (Schlesinger and Heskett 1991).

These trends apart, demographic changes in the work force may rekindle the interest of organizations in the subject of turnover. In particular, the labor shortage that is expected as the population ages and economy revitalizes may prompt companies to worry about keeping their employees. The Bureau of Labor Statistics projects that growth in the work force will slow dramatically from 2 percent a year for the period between 1976 and 1988 to 1.2 percent for the period between 1988 and the year 2000 (Dreyfuss 1990). Certain industries are already facing labor shortages as the economy recovers. Lehman Brothers' chief economist recently warned that the scarcity of long-haul truck drivers represents the "first major, widespread labor shortage since the 1980s" (Machalaba 1993). In the wake of trucking deregulation, many nonunion trucking companies have emerged and expanded demand for truck drivers. Yet the annual turnover of drivers runs to 100 percent or more because of inadequate wages, excessive travel time away from home, and the physical demands of loading and unloading huge amounts of freight. As a result, trucking firms are raising freight rates (so that they can afford higher salaries for the drivers), stopping expansion, or losing long-haul freight to rival railroads. To illustrate, a shortage of drivers during the fall idled 300 trucks belonging to J. B. Hunt Transport Services in Lowell, Arkansas, and reduced its third-quarter revenues by 6 percent.

Organizations may have to compete more aggressively for women and members of racial minorities—the fastest growing segments of the labor market—to fill job vacancies and meet affirmative action goals (Dreyfuss 1990). Yet minorities and women leave corporate America much faster than white males do (Cox and Blake 1991). Despairingly, a visiting professor at Sloan observed that black MBA graduates from Ivy League schools find out, in the workplace, that "they're not where they want to be . . . They're not getting the positions. They're not getting what was promised . . . a chance to really do some cutting-edge work. So there's a lot of disappointment, and a lot of turnover . . . . (Cose 1993, 78–79)." Employers face a daunting challenge in retaining their minority and female employees and may resort to unorthodox methods, such as expanded family benefits and cultural diversity programs, to secure their loyalty (see Chapter 10).

As American firms increasingly hire more foreign nationals abroad, mounting internationalization may reawaken concern about turnover. With competing loyalties to different national cultures, local employees may more readily sever their employment ties to a foreign-based (American) employer. Indeed, the allegiance and retention of local managers of the offshore subsidiaries are essential if U. S. multinational enterprises are to be effective in executing their global business strategies, which demand that the subsidiaries cooperate and that they sacrifice their own goals to achieve the corporation's goals (Palich, Hom, and Griffeth, in press). Moreover, domestic practices that bond American employees to the firm may prove ineffective overseas (Palich, Hom and Griffeth, in press). Despite conventional wisdom about compensation (Gomez-Mejia and Balkin 1992a), Hom, Gomez-Mejia, and Grabke (1993) discovered that various compensation schemes offered by

American owners of manufacturing plants situated along the border between Mexico and the United States failed to curb the 100 percent rates of turnover among Mexican workers.

Notwithstanding waning managerial concern, employee turnover continues to be a lively and enduring subject for academic inquiry, attracting over one thousand studies during this century (Steers and Mowday 1981). Because of its volitional control and ready availability (personnel records), turnover has become a popular criterion to validate (and extend) general theories of motivation, such as expectancy theory (Hom 1980), equity theory (Dittrich and Carrell 1979), and the theory of reasoned action (Hom and Hulin 1981; Prestholdt, Lane, and Mathews 1987). What is more, in theories organizational behavior, turnover is often regarded as one among many outcomes of their motivational processes. For example, these models submit that job characteristics (Griffeth 1985; Hackman and Oldham 1980), organizational demography (Pfeffer 1983; Tsui Egan, and O'Reilly 1992), leader-member exchange (Graen and Ginsburgh 1977), role motivation of managerial effectiveness (Butler, Lardent, and Miner 1983), and person-culture fit (Chatman 1991) may influence employees to leave organizations.

More than this, turnover is a significant motivated behavior in its own right, inspiring theoretical formulations seeking to explain its occurrence. Since March and Simon's (1958) pioneering work, a plethora of complex models have emerged, including Porter and Steers' (1973) met expectation theory, Mobley's (1977) intermediate linkages model, Price and Mueller's (1981) structural theory, Rusbult and Farrell's (1983) investment model, Sheridan's (1985) cusp catastrophe model, and Lee and Mitchell's (1994) unfolding model. In modern times, empirical work on turnover has primarily investigated the validity of these rich conceptualizations about turnover.

Much personnel research has sought to identify predictors that can accurately forecast employment stability (Cascio 1976; Kinicki, Lockwood, Hom, and Griffeth 1990). A large body of applied research has also sought to develop selection procedures that assist companies to reduce turnover. Turnover, in addition to concrete measures of absenteeism and productivity, is one of the few *objective* criteria available to personnel researchers for evaluating the effectiveness of organizational programs and practices. Obviously, turnover rates are the most relevant data for applied research evaluating turnover reduction programs, such as realistic job previews or socialization programs (Kramer 1974; Wanous 1980).

In summary, employee turnover is a critical organizational phenomenon that has evoked considerable managerial and scholarly attention for many decades. Though currently interested in the shrinkage rather than the retention of their work force, organizations are still concerned about turnover among select subpopulations and may devote more attention to the matter in the coming years. Academic interest in turnover continues to flourish, as organizational scholars view turnover as a striking expression of employee malaise or organizational malfunction. The present book more fully describes the theoretical and practical significance of turnover. To quote Porter and Steers (1973), turnover is "a relatively clear-cut act of behavior that has potentially critical consequences for both the person and the organization" (p. 151).

THE PLAN OF THIS BOOK

In the remaining portions of Chapter 1, we define turnover and consider controversies surrounding its measurement. In Chapter 2 we examine the positive and negative consequences of turnover among organizations and individuals. In Chapter 3 we present the results of a comprehensive meta-analysis, summarizing the vast empirical literature on the causes and correlates of turnover. In Chapter 4 we review major theoretical formulations about the cause of turnover, and in Chapter 5 explore new concepts to explain turnover. In Chapter 6 we propose a heuristic model that integrates propositions from prevailing models and empirical findings. In Chapter 7 we discuss research and theory about the relationship of turnover to other employee behaviors. In Chapter 8 we describe methodological problems and advances in empirical investigations of turnover. Chapters 9 and 10 consist of a survey of means to reduce turnover. In Chapter 11 we discuss avenues for future research.

DEFINITION AND MEASUREMENT OF TURNOVER

Following Mobley (1982a), turnover is commonly defined as *voluntary* cessation of membership in an organization by an individual who receives monetary compensation for participating in that organization. This definition emphasizes voluntary behavior because prevailing turnover models primarily seek to explain what *motivates* employees to withdraw from the workplace. Moreover, this conception focuses on *separation* from an organization and *not* on accession, transfer, or other internal movements through an organization. Finally, this notion excludes individuals who work without payment, such as volunteers, students, and members of unions or fraternities who may have quite different reasons for dissolving their affiliation with organizations, though some standard causes of turnover may underlie their departure.

Voluntariness

One of the earliest statements addressing the problem was Price's call (1977) for considering *voluntary* turnover as the appropriate criterion. Until then the conceptualization of the turnover meaning was generally neglected. Taking up Price's call, Mobley, Griffeth, Hand, and Meglino (1979) soon acknowledged criterion definition was troublesome, spawning conflicts within the field about what turnover means. For example, some researchers (for example, Marsh and Mannari 1977) regard pregnancy as a form of voluntary exit; (Mirvis and Lawler 1977; Waters, Roach, and Waters 1976) others exclude pregnant workers. Price (1977) regarded an employee's leaving a job at a spouse's insistence as *involuntary* turnover. Hanisch and Hulin (1990) suggested that early retirement is a form of voluntary quitting.

Apart from inconsistent categorization, the measurement of reasons for leaving is subject to various errors. Most turnover research relies on personnel files to determine the reasons and, thus, whether or not the departure is voluntary (Mobley et al. 1979). Yet such so-called objective records are typically deficient because they fail to capture all the reasons and classify the leavers into a single category—as having left—when various motives may underlie the departure. Organizational records are likely to be biased, although the extent of this bias is unknown. For instance, employers may formally classify a dismissal as a voluntary departure to protect a leaver's reputation (and avoid defamation litigation) or classify a voluntary departure as a layoff to enable a leaver to qualify for unemployment compensation.

Yet former employees' own reports are not necessarily more truthful. Leavers may be reluctant to report negative reasons to avoid endangering their chances of reemployment or employment elsewhere (Price 1977). Employees may, after the fact, develop rationalizations to justify their leaving that do not reflect their original reasons for quitting (Mobley 1982; Mowday, Porter and Steers 1982). Along with such justifications, personally reported reasons are vulnerable to a bias created by social desirability. For example, Mobley, Hand, Baker, and Meglino (1979) found that the Marine Corps was more likely to ascribe recruits' attrition from basic training to their performance deficiencies, such as defective attitudes or laziness. By comparison, departing recruits themselves more often cited homesickness or lack of personal freedom for why they left the Marine Corps. Thus, exiting employees may give more socially desirable, more "volitional" reasons for quitting than do their employers.

To improve the measurement of voluntary turnover, Mobley et al. (1979) suggested using multiple sources to identify the reasons. Because administrative and self-reported reasons for terminations often diverge, uncertainty persists as to which source is valid (Lefkowitz and Katz 1969; Mobley et al. 1979). A wise strategy might be to analyze both criteria seperately for evaluating turnover interventions and the validity of theoretical models (see Mobley et al. 1979). In this way, consistent findings across administrative and self-reported classifications of voluntary turnover would suggest convergent validity for the intervention or model. Along these lines, Price and Mueller (1986) regressed involuntary quits on their turnover model. Their model variables predicted voluntary quits more accurately than they did involuntary quits, a finding that the authors interpreted as supporting their explanatory model of voluntary terminations and, indirectly, validating turnover classifications. Mobley (1982a) recommended follow-up surveys with former employees, especially if they were administered by outside consultants who can guarantee confidentiality (see Mobley et al. 1979; Price and Mueller 1986). Rather than rely on the departing employee's superiors, organizations might entrust personnel specialists (or external consultants) with the responsibility for conducting exit interviews.

In conclusion, turnover researchers and practitioners should, at the very minimum, continue to use *voluntary* turnover when examining causes of motivated behavior. They should also take more precautions to insure that their measures, including more skillful questioning, validly represent voluntary exits. They should attempt to triangulate on the criterion of voluntary turnover using various assessment procedures. Though overlooked, more accurate turnover classifications may well boost the explanatory power of predictor variables as much as the expansion of predictor batteries is expected to. Turnover researchers might tailor models and predictor batteries to correspond to different exit categories. To illustrate, Price and Mueller (1986) removed data on those leavers who quit to follow a relocating spouse before estimating how accurately their model variables, which constitute mainly work-related antecedents, predict voluntary exits. Alternatively, one might include such cases as voluntary quits but expand the prediction equation to capture those environmental influences; one might, for example, ask employees if their spouses plan to relocate or are attending classes—and thus expect to assume a new job elsewhere upon graduation (Price and Mueller 1986).

Recent refinements of the turnover criterion suggest additional considerations for turnover researchers, considerations that are discussed in the following sections.

FUNCTIONAL AND DYSFUNCTIONAL TURNOVER

Several researchers, such as Dalton and Todor (1979), Staw (1980), and Mobley (1982a) discussed potential *positive* organizational consequences of turnover. Departing from conventional beliefs, these writers point out that turnover can prevent stagnation and complacency, facilitate change and innovation, and displace poor performers. Turnover is not inherently negative. Although it creates personnel costs, the "organizational consequences of turnover are dependent on *who* leaves and who stays (Mobley 1982a, p. 42)."

To refine the turnover criterion, Dalton, Todor, and Krackhardt (1982) introduced a taxonomy classifying turnover as either "functional" (poor performers leave or good performers stay) or "dysfunctional" (good performers leave or poor performers stay) (see also Dalton, Krackhardt, and Porter 1981). Figure 1-1 shows this classification scheme. This distinction between functional and dysfunctional turnover assumes that replacements for leavers are at least average performers. The departure of good performers is construed as dysfunctional turnover—representing a loss to the organization—for their replacements are likely to be of lower caliber. The departure of poor performers is viewed as functional turnover—being a beneficial consequence to the organization —because they are apt to be replaced by better performers. Because they benefit firms, superior employees who remain with the organization are classified by this taxonomy with functional turnovers;

Employer's Appraisal of Employee

	Positive	Negative
No initiation of Voluntary Quit	Employee Remains	Employee is Terminated
Initiation of Voluntary Quit	Employee Quits Dysfunctional Turnover	Employee Quits Functional Turnover

Employee's Evaluation of Company

Figure 1-1   Taxonomy of Functional Turnover (Adapted from D. Dalton, W. Todor and D. Krackhardt, "Turnover overstated: The functional taxonomy," Academy of Management Review 7(1982): 118.)

marginal performers who stay (and could be replaced by better performers if they left) with dysfunctional turnovers.

More formally, Hollenbeck and Williams (1986) operationally defined turnover functionality as: $T_{funct} = T_{freq} * Z$. where T_{freq} represents whether or not the employee left the organization (coding stayers +1 and leavers −1) and Z is a standardized performance measure. The product is a continuous variable with positive scores signifying functional turnover, that is, either a high performer stays (positive Z-score * 1 = positive score) or a low performer leaves (negative Z-score * −1 = positive score). Conversely, negative scores indicate dysfunctional turnover; that is, either a high performer leaves (positive Z-score * −1 = negative score) or a low performer stays (negative Z-score * 1 = negative score).

Though an intriguing alternative to traditional turnover indices, the Hollenbeck-Williams index treats a high performing stayer and a poor performing leaver equally. Surely, such individuals face different work conditions and possess dissimilar personal traits. Indeed, the turnover functionality index may be less useful for testing existing turnover models. For example, it is improbable that a high performer who stays and a poor performer who leaves would feel the same job satisfaction and withdrawal cognitions, common precursors of turnover. More plausibly, the stayer would express higher satisfaction and lower withdrawal cognitions than the leaver would, even though the Hollenbeck-Williams index classifies them together. Similarly, this index treats high performing leavers and low performing stayers alike, ignoring crucial experiential and personal differences between these groups.

The turnover functionality index narrowly construes an employee's contribution to the firm, regarding only productivity or performance effectiveness. Yet employees make valuable contributions to organizations in other ways, such as display good citizenship (a desirable trait given the growth of self-managing work teams [Manz and Sims 1989; Organ 1988]), providing creative ideas for new products or labor savings, and mentoring and training new employees. A solution might be to develop different indices of turnover functionality for different contributions. The appraisal literature has long shown, however, that different performance dimensions are distinctive and that employees do some but not all tasks well (Smith 1976). Thus, a productive but unimaginative worker who stays may have a positive turnover functionality index for productivity but a negative turnover functionality index for creativity.

Though inappropriate for testing prevailing theories, a turnover functionality index may measure efficacy of contingent reward systems (Williams and Livingstone 1994). For example, does a merit-pay program effectively reward high performers while penalizing poor performers and, thereby, promote turnover functionality? That is, does the index indicate whether or not a reward system encourages high performers to stay and low performers to leave?

AVOIDABLE AND UNAVOIDABLE TURNOVER

Abelson (1987) further differentiated between organizationally avoidable turnover and organizationally unavoidable turnover. Specifically, he cross-classified leavers according to whether or not they had control over their turnover (a traditional dimension) and whether turnover was avoidable or unavoidable (that is, whether or not the firm had control over turnover). Figure 1-2 shows this taxonomy and various exit reasons illustrating its cross-classifications. For example, organizations cannot control (that is, it is unavoidable) turnover caused by an employee's death—and nor can the employee control it—or by an employee's quitting to trail a relocating spouse, something an employee can control. Testing this classification scheme, Abelson (1987) found little attitudinal differences between the stayers and those whose departure was unavoidable. Nevertheless, both groups differed significantly from those whose departure was avoidable, a group of employees who expressed higher levels of job tension and withdrawal cognitions and lower levels of job satisfaction and commitment to the company .

Turnover researchers are well advised to identify carefully those exits that are avoidable and those that are unavoidable. As Abelson's results (1987) imply, to group both types of leavers together may understate the validity of traditional turnover theories (and the efficacy of managerial interventions to reduce turnover). After all, leavers whose departure is unavoidable resemble stayers more than they resemble the leavers whose departure is avoidable; they do *not* resign because they are unhappy with their jobs. Rather, a superior criterion for testing prevailing turnover models, which generally omit environmental influences, such as family responsibilities (see Price and Mueller 1986), is provided by a definition of turnover that includes only the avoidable departures. Practitioners who fail to subtract instances of unavoidable turnover from turnover statistics may overestimate the severity to equation 1.4. Specifically, R_{pb} from equation 1.4 can be corrected for the dichotomization of a continuous variable using equation 1.1.

To Correct or Not to Correct

Although they are widely prescribed (Hunter and Schmidt 1990a; Kemery, Dunlap, and Griffeth 1988; Steel Shane, and Griffeth 1990), Williams (1990) contends that, for two reasons, corrections of predictor-turnover correlations are unwarranted. First, a dichotomization correction presumes turnover to be simply dichotomized company tenure. Yet turnover represents a different theoretical construct from that of tenure—a distinction implicit in most turnover models that explain *whether* employees quit rather than how long they remain employed. Second, correcting for departures from 50 percent quit base rates may remove nonartifactual variance because study differences in quit rates may reflect valid situational differences, such as varying job markets across settings.

Though Williams's reasoning is persuasive, Steel, Shane, and Griffeth nonetheless argued that turnover researchers may wish to compare turnover base rates across studies as an aid "in estimating the amount of unrestricted criterion variance explainable by model parameters" (1990, p. 185). Bass and Ager (1991) contested Williams's claim that "because differences in turnover can be attributed to meaningful differences in turnover antecedents across studies, there is no defendable theoretical or empirical rational for correcting turnover r_{pb}s for unequal *n*s" (1990, p. 736). Bass and Ager maintained that there are "very compelling reasons to correct turnover r_{pb}s for unequal *n*s (i.e., different turnover base rates)" (1991, p. 596). They declared that the "point-biserial correlation, like any Pearson correlation, is affected by such methodological artifacts as unreliability and restriction of score range, as well as by differences in the marginal distributions of the variables" (ibid.). They further claimed that Williams "confounded nonartifactual differences in conditions across studies with the *effect* of such differences on measurement artifacts" (ibid.). Their rebuttal alleged that Williams erroneously concluded that uneven turnover splits are *purely* authentic (and thus the correction of uneven split r_{pb}s unjustified) just because some situational differences underlie variations in turnover that occurred between studies. Indeed, Williams and Livingstone continued this claim:

> In other words, differences in jobs, organizations, and the economy produce differences in turnover rates and turnover correlations across studies. Because there are real reasons for 1 percent turnover in some jobs and companies, and for 40 percent turnover in others, it does not make sense to correct all correlations to a 50 percent rate of turnover. (1994, p. 10)

All the same, Bass and Ager reasoned that even if the variations in quit rates that do occur between studies arise only from genuine situational differences, the interpretation and comparison of predictor-turnover correlations collected under different conditions remain problematic because the size of the correlations depends partly on base quit rates. Concluding, therefore, that "some sort of correction or standardization is clearly required for comparison purposes" (1991, p. 597), they apply Carroll's correction index (1961):

$$r_{pb} / r_{pbmax}$$

which does not require assumptions of normality of either the predictor or the underlying criterion and enables meaningful comparisons of turnover relationships across settings.

Does one statistically adjust predictor-turnover correlations or not? Although the "methodological artifacts" of turnover dichotomy and skewed turnover distributions are increasingly corrected (Hulin 1991; Jaros, Jermier, Koehler, and Sincich 1993), such corrections—using the Bass-Ager index (1991)—are considered most valuable when one is making cross-study comparisons of predictor-turnover correlations. In other instances, statistical corrections appear less defensible. These corrections presume that turnover is simply dichotomized firm tenure, an implausible assumption (Williams 1990). Indeed, if turnover is merely tenure that is arbitrarily dichotomized, researchers could simply use company tenure as dependent variable—avoiding any loss of statistical power as a result of variable dichotomization—and not worry about correcting their turnover statistics (Price and Mueller 1981). Yet turnover occurrence is likely a different (though related) action—a truly dichotomous theoretical construct—from job longevity and has different root causes (Williams 1990).

As a precaution, turnover researchers might report results with and without such artifactual corrections (Williams and Livingstone, 1994). Alternatively, new methodologies, such as survival analysis, may increasingly be used to analyze turnover data (Morita, Lee, and Mowday 1993). Consequently, this controversy may subside if turnover researchers increasingly relinquish correlational and regresssion analyses, the statistical assumptions or properties of which are threatened by the distributional properties of turnover. In summary, continued thought on the necessity and special conditions for turnover corrections are warranted as is more methodological research, such as Monte Carlo studies.

THE CONSEQUENCES OF TURNOVER

In this chapter, we review the burgeoning conceptual and empirical literature on the consequences of employee turnover (Mobley 1982a; Mowday, Porter, and Steers 1982; Price 1977, 1989; Staw 1980). Pervasive presumptions of the economic costs that turnover engenders for firms—namely, the expenses of recruiting and training replacements—doubtlessly underpin the persistent scholarly inquiry into turnover. In growing numbers, turnover theorists have begun, however, to question this viewpoint (Dalton, Todor, and Krackhardt 1982; Staw 1980). These revisionists contend that the traditional preoccupation with the personnel costs of terminations overstates the adverse effects of turnover and overlooks the positive ramifications for companies and employees alike.

To comprehend the effects, we consider, in this chapter, the various consequences of turnover for companies and individuals who leave them and review the available evidence for those effects. Following Mobley's (1982a) classification scheme, the potential benefits and disadvantages for leavers and employers are summarized in Table 2-1. Whenever possible, we describe how turnover may have curvilinear effects on outcomes or have effects that vary across different conditions (Price 1989; Staw 1980).

NEGATIVE CONSEQUENCES FOR THE ORGANIZATION

This section describes the various adverse repercussions for organizations engendered by employee turnover. To illustrate its financial impact, we report a recent investigation (Hom, 1992) that estimated the personnel expenses incurred by resignations. Besides this, we discuss less familiar economic costs, such as potential productivity losses and impairments to delivery of customer service. In particular, departure of employees—especially experienced or talented ones—may threaten overall firm productivity or client retention. Furthermore, personnel losses may endanger firms' future opportunities in the marketplace or the morale of their remaining work forces.

Economic Costs

Undoubtedly, the financial costs of turnover have attracted the most attention from scholars and practitioners alike (Blakeslee, Suntrup, and Kernaghan 1985; Cascio 1991). Human resource accounting experts define exit expenses as having three main components: costs of separation,

Table 2-1   Consequences of Turnover

	Consequences for Organization	Consequences for Leavers
Negative consequences	Economic costs for separation, replacement, and training Productivity losses Impaired service quality Lost business opportunities Increased administrative burden Demoralization of stayers	Forfeit seniority and fringe benefits Transition stress in new job Relocation costs Teminate personal and family social network Loss of valued community services Disrupt spouse's career
Positive consequences	Displaces poor performers and employees with job burnout Infusion of new knowledge and technology by replacements New business ventures Labor cost savings Enhanced promotional opportunities for stayers Empowerment of stayers	Obtain better job elsewhere Avoid stressful former job Renewed commitment to work Pursue outside endeavors Relocate to a more desirable community Improve spouse's career

(W. Mobley (1982a) *Employee Turnover: Causes, Consequences, and Control,* Reading, MA: Addison-Wesley.)

replacement, and training (Boudreau and Berger 1985; Cascio 1991; Flamholtz 1985). Separation costs are those that quitting produces directly (for example, costs of exit interviews); replacement costs include expenses incurred to replace leavers (such as expenses for advertising job vacancies); training costs consist of the company's expenditures to orient and train replacements and opportunity costs caused by inefficient production.

The various elements comprising each cost category are listed in Figure 2-1. The categories are derived from Hom's study (1992) of the costs of turnover among mental health professionals. This project illustrates specifically how different cost factors are estimated. The basic data were collected from a survey of agency directors who answered a questionnaire about each turnover cost for key clinical positions (reproduced as an appendix on page 315) (see also Cascio 1991; Whiting 1989). Extending previous efforts, Hom's research showed how certain opportunity costs for turnover—namely, the productivity losses long theorized about by human resources accounting scholars—can be estimated (Boudreau and Berger 1985). Leavers may produce fewer goods or services before exiting, and new replacements may perform less efficiently while learning new job skills (Mobley 1982a). Yet turnover costing studies typically omit productivity losses because they are difficult to measure (Cascio 1991). Hom (1992) operationalized these opportunity costs as losses of client revenue. Fewer clients are served while a

Separation Costs

    Exit interviews: Interviewer's and interviewee's time

    Administrative costs: Remove name from records, etc.

    Unused vacation time: Disburse unused vacation time

    Lost client revenues: Service fewer clients during vacancy period

    Overtime pay: Pay employees to assume leaver's work

    Temporary employment: Hire temps to assume leaver's work

    Case consultation: Transfer leaver's clients to others

Replacement costs

    Advertisements: Publicize job vacancies

    Personal recruitment: College recruitment, job fairs, etc.

    Application processing: Process and review applications

    Entrance interviews: Interviewer's time

    Application selection: Interviewer's time

    Miscellaneous costs: Tests, travel, relocation reimbursements, etc.

Training Costs

    Formal orientation: Instructor's and trainee's time

    Formal job training: Instructor's and trainee's time

    Offsite training: Course costs and trainee's time

    On-the-job training: Trainee's time to develop proficiency and informal instruction by superior

    Client revenue loss: Fewer clients serviced by replacements

Figure 2-1   Costs of Turnover Among Mental Health Professionals (P. Hom (1992). *Turnover Costs Among Mental Health Professionals.* Department of Management, Arizona State University. Copyright 1992 Van Nostrand Reinhold. Reprinted by permission.)

position is vacant (because of staff shortages) and new replacements are less productive (because they serve fewer clients as they master their jobs). Thus, the costs of "foregone client revenues" may be more amenable to quantification, especially when service personnel leave (Darmon 1990; Sheridan 1992; Whiting 1989).

Formulas derived from Cascio (1991), for computing separation, replacement, and training costs for a single incidence of turnover in the position Clinician/Counselor II are listed in Figures 2-2 through 2-4. This is a prime position in the mental health field, and incumbents typically maintain caseloads, participate in client staffing, develop treatment plans, maintain client records, and supervise clinical staff. The formulas factored in "fully loaded" compensation—namely, base pay and fringe benefits—and divided each category into its component costs.

For instance, Hom (1992) estimated the costs of orienting and training a replacement by costing out each element:

1.   Formal orientation ([hours to orient new hire × orientation instructor's hourly pay] + [hours to orient new hire × new hire's hourly pay] + costs of training materials)

S1 = Exit Interview Costs = Cost of Interviewer's Time + Cost of Leaver's Time, where interviewer's time cost = interviewer's hourly wage x exit interview time, and leaver's time cost = leaver's hourly wage × exit interview time:
S1 = ($8.73 × 3 hours) + ($12.59 × 3 hours) = $63.96.

S2 = Administrative Costs of Processing Turnover
S2 = $150 for administrative and paperwork costs to remove leaver's name from payroll records, continue group insurance, etc.

S3 = Unused Vacation Time
S3 = Hours of unused vacation x leaver's hourly wage.
S3 = (20 hours x $12.59) = $251.72.

S4 = Lost Revenues due to Vacancy
S4 = Weeks job remains vacant x billable hours per week × hourly rate charged for client services
S4 = (6 weeks x 24 billable hours/week × $66 charge rate) = $9,504.

S5 = Overtime Costs for Extra Help during Job Vacancy
S5 = No. Overtime hours per week × week of vacancy × overtime pay rate × average hourly rate for all employees.
S5 = (0 overtime hours × 6 weeks vacancy) x (0 x $10.85) = $0.00.

S6 = Hiring Temp. Agencies to Serve Clients during Job Vacancy
S6 = Weekly hours of temp. employee × weeks of temp. work × temp. employee's hourly pay.
S6 = (0 × 0 × 0) = $0.00.

S7 = Client Assignment (Transfer Client Records, Case Consultation, Case Learning)
S7 = Clerical costs to transfer client records + (supervisory time for case consultation to staff × supervisor's hourly pay) + (staff time to learn client history × staff hourly pay).
S7 = ($105 clerical cost) + (4 supervisory hours × $15.31) + (4 staff hours × $12.59) = $216.59.

Total separation cost (S1 + S2 + S3 + S4 +S5 + S6 + S7) for Clinician II turnover = $10,186.27.

Figure 2-2 Formulas for Estimating Separation Costs (P. Hom (1992). *Turnover Costs Among Mental Health Professionals.* **Department of Management, Arizona State University. Copyright 1992 Van Nostrand Reinhold. Reprinted by permission.)**

2. Formal training ([hours to train new hire × in-house trainer's hourly pay] + [training hours × new hire's hourly pay])

3. Offsite training ([hours to attend training sessions × new hire's hourly pay] + [tuition charge for training])

4. On-the-job training ([hours to train new hire × supervisor's hourly pay] + [hours to learn agency practices × new hire's hourly pay])

5. Lost revenues during probationary period ([experienced incumbent's billable hours per week – new hire's billable hours per week] × [weeks during probationary period that new hire serves fewer clients × charge rate for client service])

As shown in Figure 2-4, data from a particular agency indicates that the cost of training and orienting a new Clinician II replacement is $14,115.07.

R1 = Advertising Costs to Find Replacements

R1 = $250.

R2 = Job Fairs and College Recruitment

R2 = Hours in the job fairs or college recruitment x agency representative's hourly pay.

R2 = (10 hours × $8.37) = $83.65.

R3 = Processing and Reviewing Job Applications

R3 = (Hours processing resumes × processor's hourly pay) + (hours reviewing resumes × reviewer's hourly pay).

R3 = (6 process hours × $7.38) + (8 review hours × $18.32) = $189.22.

R4 = Inteviewing Applicants

R4 = Number of interviewees × interview time per applicant x first interviewer's hourly pay) + (Number of interviewees × interview time × second interviewer's pay) + (Number of interviewees × interview time × third interviewer's pay), and so on.

R4 = (8 interviewees x 1 hour x $18.12) + (8 interviewees x 1 hour x $13.69) x (8 interviewees x 1 hour x $13.69) + (8 interviewees x 1 hour x $13.69) = $473.47

R5 = Selection of Applicant

R5 = (Hours to select applicants x first selector's hourly pay) + (selection hours x second selector's hourly pay) + (selection hours x third selector's hourly pay).

R5 = (8 hours × $18.12) = $144.96.

R6 = Miscellaneous Replacement Costs

R6 = Employment tests + substance-abuse tests + physical exams + reference checks + fingerprinting costs + credentialing costs + interviewee's travel expenses + relocation expenses + payroll paperwork costs + employment agency fees.

R6 = ($16 reference check + $23 fingerprinting + $125 credentialing + $75 agency fee) = $239.

Total Replacement Cost (R1 + R2 + R3 + R4 +R5 + R6) for Clinician II Turnover = $1,380.30.

Figure 2-3 Formulas for Estimating Replacement Costs (P. Hom (1992). *Turnover Costs Among Mental Health Professionals.* **Department of Management, Arizona State University. Copyright 1992 Van Nostrand Reinhold. Reprinted by permission.)**

The overall turnover cost for this job, the sum of separation, replacement, and training costs, was $25,681.64.

Comparisons between jobs further reveal that turnover costs are not uniform across different occupations (Cascio 1991; Wanous 1980). The different median costs of turnover for various mental health positions is shown in Figure 2-5 (Hom 1992). (For additional comparisons, see Figure 2-6: turnover costs for other occupations derived from other studies [Cascio 1991; Mobley 1982a]). Such occupational variations may reflect disparate recruiting and training costs for jobs varying in labor supply and complexity (Staw 1980). Tight job markets increase selection and recruitment costs, as do less definable criteria for judging candidates for complex occupations, where quick decisions on the applicants may not be possible.

Similarly, job complexity increases training expenses because replacements for complex positions require more time to master their work (Staw 1980). In line with Staw's speculation (1980), dissimilar component

T1 = Formal Orientation

    T1 = (hours to orient new hire × instructor's hourly pay) + (orientation hours × new hire's hourly pay) + (cost of training materials).

    T1 = (2 hours × \$8.73) + (2 hours × \$12.59) + (\$250) = \$292.64.

T2 = Formal Training

    T2 = (hours to train new hire × instructor's hourly pay) + (training hours × new hire's hourly pay).

    T2 = (160 hours × \$18.12) + (160 hours × \$12.59) = \$4,912.87.

T3 = Offsite Training

    T3 = (hours to attend training x new hire's hourly pay) + tuition charge.

    T3 = (8 hours × \$12.59) + (\$200) = \$300.69.

T4 = On-the-Job Training

    T4 = (hours to train new hire x supervisor's hourly pay) + (hours to learn agency practice × new hire's hourly pay).

    Note: T4 = is included only if new hire remains employed throughout probation period.

    T4 = (160 hours × \$18.12) + (160 hours × \$12.59) = \$4,912.87.

T5 = Lost Revenues during Probationary Period

    T5 = (experienced incumbent's billable hours per week – new hire's billable hours per week) × (weeks during probationary period that new hire serves fewer clients × charge rate for client service).

    T5 = (24 billable hours – 10 billable hours) × (4 weeks × \$66 rate) = \$3,696.

Total Orientation and Training Cost (T1 + T2 + T3 + T4 +T5) for Clinician II Turnover = \$14,115.07.

Figure 2-4 Formulas for Estimating Orientation and Training Costs (P. Hom (1992). *Turnover Costs Among Mental Health Professionals.* **Department of Management, Arizona State University. Copyright 1992 Van Nostrand Reinhold. Reprinted by permission.)**

costs for the positions of Clinician II and Psychiatrist, derived from Hom (1992), are shown in Figure 2-7. Training expenses represent the costliest factor when clinicians leave; separation costs the largest expense for psychiatrists.

The full dimensions of turnover costs for organizations are shown in Figure 2-8, which includes data for the overall costs (for all quits from all jobs) for the twenty-three mental health agencies in Hom's study (1992). Indicative of the financial burden was the median agency cost of \$57,902 in 1991. The combined turnover cost for all agencies was \$3,071,484. Hom's estimates were conservative for they excluded costs created by the departures of part-time employees and those providing no direct mental health services, such as janitors and secretaries.

Notwithstanding the costliness of turnover, because of traditional accounting practices, few companies actually track the economics of turnover (Schlesinger and Heskett 1991). Without cost data managers may dismiss (or be unable to justify) interventions, such as improved training or pay, that might reduce exits. They readily attend to program expenses but overlook the costs of job separations that such programs might offset

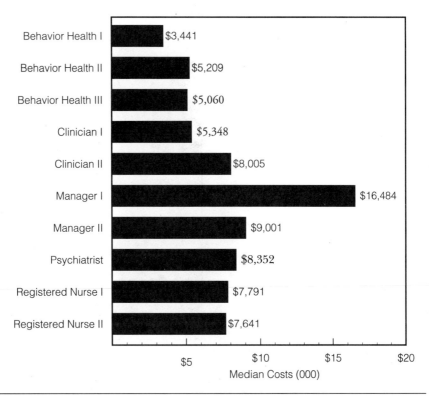

Figure 2-5 Turnover Costs for Mental Health Positions Per One Incidence of Turnover (P. Hom (1992). *Turnover Costs Among Mental Health Professionals.* **Department of Management, Arizona State University.)**

(Reichheld 1993). The perception may, however, be rational when the costs of retaining personnel exceed the savings of preventing turnover (Abelson and Baysinger 1984). That is, "it may be far less expensive to cope with turnover than to prevent it (Dalton and Todor 1979, 200)." All the same, a quantification of termination costs may help firms more precisely balance the costs and benefits of turnover-reduction interventions and therefore wisely decide if they are indeed *cost effective* (Boudreau and Berger 1985). Embodying such foresight, Merck & Company projected that an investment of 50 percent of an employee's salary in measures to lower quits can yield a one-year payback (Schlesinger and Heskett 1991).

Productivity Losses

Other ramifications of turnover that are not beneficial for organizations secured less attention. Some writers on turnover contend that voluntary quits impair organization productivity, which is the ratio of company goods and services to inputs (Price 1977; 1989). Many schools of thought and

Figure 2-6 Turnover Costs in Selected Occupations (Cascio, W. (1991). *Costing human resources: The financial impact of behavior in organizations* **(3rd edition). Boston, MA: Kent Publishing; Hom, P., Bracker, J., & Julian, G. (1988, October). In pursuit of greener pastures.** *New Accountant, 4,* **24–27, 49; Mobley, W. (1982).** *Employee turnover: causes, consequences and control.* **Reading, MA: Addison-Wesley; Wanous, J.P. (1980).** *Organizational entry: Recruitment, selection and socialization of newcomers.* **Reading, MA: Addison-Wesley.)**

indirect evidence (besides cost data [Price 1977]) implicate productivity losses as potential exit outcomes. Specifically, leavers often miss work or are tardy before they depart (Rossé 1988); missing employees obviously produce nothing (Rhodes and Steers 1990). The productivity of leavers may deteriorate before they depart, according to progression-of-withdrawal models (Hulin 1991; Rossé 1988).

New replacements may produce fewer goods or services than the veteran employees who left did (Price 1977), a result that is consistent with positive age and productivity relationships (Waldman and Avolio 1986). In line with this contention, Sheridan (1992) documented that public accounting firms lose $47,000 in profits whenever a new accountant replaces a third-year veteran who leaves. Furthermore, resignations may disrupt other employees'

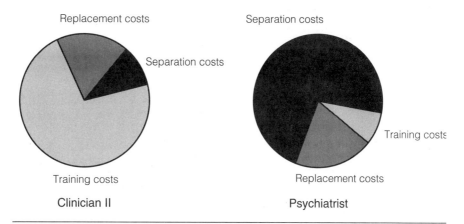

Figure 2-7   Major Constituents of Turnover Costs (P. Hom (1992). *Turnover Costs Among Mental Health Professionals.* **Department of Management, Arizona State University.)**

work if their work depends on the leavers or they must assume the leavers' duties (Mobley 1982a; Schlesinger and Heskett 1991; Staw 1980). Remaining employees must also adjust to the replacements' work style and habits and interrupt work to train them (Louis, Posner, and Powell 1983; Mowday, Porter, and Steers 1982). In summary, turnover may decrease productivity because of the leaver's declining productivity, the inexperience of the replacement, and disruptions of the workflow.

Recently, Ulrich, Halbrook, Meder, Stuchlik, and Thorpe (1991) provided direct evidence that turnover may yield productivity losses. They found that the financially successful Ryder Truck Rental districts had lower termination rates than did the less successful districts. Although it is a noteworthy finding, this preliminary assessment did not statistically control other determinants of performance in firms that might underlie the relationship between performance and quitting.

Functional turnover. Nevertheless, productivity reversals are neither inevitable nor likely consequences of separation. That is, human resource accounting formulas may overstate exit costs because they ignore the identity of the leavers (Dalton, Krackhardt, and Porter 1981). The exit of marginal performers, which may be termed *functional turnover*, benefits employers, who may replace them with superior performers (presuming that productivity gains offset replacement and training expenses [Darmon 1990]). Importantly, several meta-analyses concluded that poor performers are more likely to quit than are good performers, in which case productivity is more likely to improve from turnover (McEvoy and Cascio 1987; Williams and Livingstone, 1994). Thus, as Dalton, Krackhardt, and Porter (1981) documented, gross quit rates are misleading. Their inspection of who left banks revealed that high performers constituted only 58 percent of all quits, a finding that made

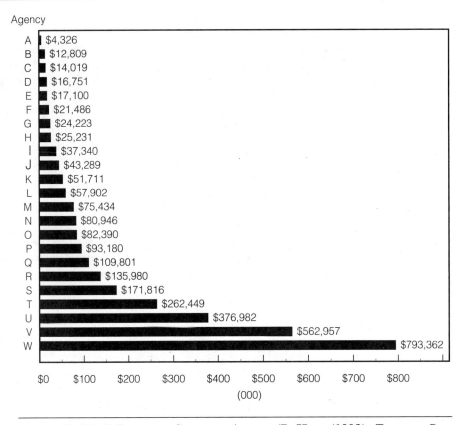

Figure 2-8 Total Turnover Costs per Agency (P. Hom (1992). *Turnover Costs Among Mental Health Professionals.* **Department of Management, Arizona State University.)**

the overall 32 percent quit rate seem less alarming. A computation of *net* performance gains (or losses) that result from hiring replacements who outperform leavers may correct estimates by human resource accounting formulas of the true costs of turnover (Boudreau and Berger 1985).

Moderators. Thus, performance differentials between leavers and replacements may influence whether or not turnover generates economic losses for organizations. Several circumstances may, however, determine the relative effectiveness of these types of employees and thus whether turnover does yield productivity losses. For one, the presence of merit-pay schemes widens the performance differential by distributing fewer incentives to marginal performers who then become dissatisfied and quit (Staw 1980; Williams and Livingstone 1994; Zenger 1992). More valid selection procedures or aggressive recruitment may enhance the quality of new replacements who may outproduce leavers. A shrinking demand for labor may allow companies to hire more qualified replacements for a particular occupation but also may inhibit marginal performers from quitting.

The organizational climate may also influence relationships between performance and quitting. For example, Sheridan (1992) found that ineffective accountants quit more than did effective accountants in public accounting firms that value task achievements. In contrast, varying quit rates between high and low performers were not apparent in firms that endorsed interpersonal relationships, a climate that encouraged both high and low performers to stay on the job longer. By extension, voluntary resignations may thus enhance productivity in firms with task-oriented cultures (assuming that the replacements are better performers) more than they might in firms with interpersonal-relationship cultures.

Staw (1980) proposed that the departures of employees in pivotal rather than peripheral positions interrupt work flows most, given the greater dependency of other employees' work on crucial jobs. Organizations, such as public accounting firms (Sheridan 1992), may anticipate regular exit occurrences and instate contingency plans, using temporary employees or a flexible work force that has been trained in several jobs to offset personnel shortages (Turbin and Rossé 1990).

Impaired Quality of Service

More plausibly, turnover may hinder the delivery of service and retention of customers, additional dimensions of organizational effectiveness (Price 1977; Reichheld 1993). This potential repercussion of turnover increasingly attracts academic and managerial interest as 42 percent of the domestic work force serves food, sells merchandise in retail stores, performs clerical work in service industries, cleans hospitals, schools, and offices, or provides some personal service (Schlesinger and Heskett 1991). Most of all, service occupations accounted for the bulk of the job growth in the 1980s, a trend that will continue until the turn of this century.

Presumably, attrition among service personnel impairs customer service because understaffed offices or stores delay or withhold service (Darmon 1990). Unlike experienced leavers, new employees may also provide less competent or less personalized service because they do not know the clients. Customers may switch firms if their loyalties depend on an affinity with former sales employees (Darmon 1990; Schlesinger and Heskett 1991). Recognizing such loyalty bonds, State Farm recruits new insurance agents who have stable community ties and, thus, long-term relationships with prospective customers, and Olive Garden restaurants hire local managers known and trusted in the community (Reichheld 1993). If satisfied employees make customers feel well treated, disgruntled employees may provide careless service before they leave. (Schneider and Bowen 1992). Turnover also interrupts the transmission of service values and norms, which are essential underpinnings of high quality service, to successive generations of employees (Bowen and Schneider 1988).

Figure 9 summarizes these ramifications, describing how turnover among frontline service workers imperils the quality of service (Schlesinger

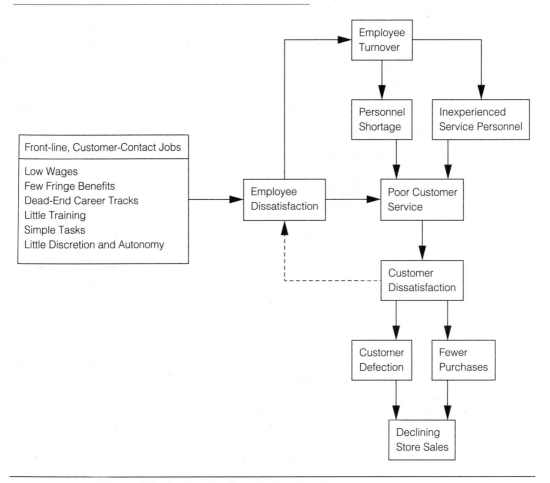

Figure 2-9 Cycle of Failure in Service Company

and Heskett 1991). To begin, most employees in service-sector industries begin working in low-paying and dead-end jobs. Such dissatisfying working conditions breed poor job attitudes and high turnover, eventually jeopardizing customer service. Specifically, uncaring personnel may deliver poor service and turnover also impairs the quality of service because staff shortages delay or withhold service and inexperienced replacements serve clients (Schneider and Bowen 1992). This chain of consequences make the customers dissatisfied (which further compounds the employees' frustration because the customers are complaining) and inclined to make fewer purchases or absent themselves entirely. Through this cycle of failure, dead-end customer-contact jobs eventually diminish sales and company revenues. Reichheld (1993) portrayed a similar scenario relating employee retention to customer retention.

Consistent with this model, Ulrich et al. (1991) documented lower turnover rates in Sears stores delivering good service than in those providing poor service. Similarly, internal research at Automatic Data Processing discerned a strong association between retaining service employees and retaining clients (Shellenbarger 1992). Marriott Corporation projected that a 10 percent in turnover reduction would reduce the incidence of customers' not returning by between 1 percent and 3 percent and raise revenues by between $50 million to $150 million (Schlesinger and Heskett 1991). Despite these promising findings, more research examining the relationship between turnover and quality of service would further validate this portrait of a cycle of service failure triggered by excessive quits.

Professional services. The type of client service, namely, consumer service, as provided by department stores and restaurants, distinguished from professional service, as provided by doctors and lawyers, may influence the degree to which turnover impairs the service. In particular, the departure of deliverers of professional services may most undermine quality of the customers' experience. Because they are less tangible than consumer services, which offer goods, professional services, which are simultaneously produced for and consumed by each consumer, depend more on the presence and actions of the service personnel (Bowen and Schneider 1988).

Several studies have established, consistent with this reasoning, that departures of health or mental health providers diminish the care given to patients (Price 1977). Specifically, Kahne (1968) first suggested that turnover among mental health hospital staff indirectly boosts the incidence of suicides among patients. Although the two were uncorrelated, Kahne nonetheless interpreted the data as hinting that excessive quits overburden hospital staff and distract them from noticing signals of impending suicide. In follow-up research, Coser (1976) found that the departure of a psychiatrist or senior resident—who oversees and trains residents in a mental hospital—preceded every wave of suicide among patients. Presumably, the departure of their superiors impaired the preparation and social support available to psychiatric trainees, and thus their capacity to recognize suicidal clues. Spector and Takada (1991) predicted that the quality of care in eighty nursing homes varied with the turnover among the staff. Their regression disclosed that low turnover among registered nurses enhances the residents' functional skills (their competence in bathing and eating by themselves) more noticeably than other predictors of patient care does.

Murnane, Singer, and Willett (1988, 1989) presented evidence to suggest that attrition among teachers detracts from the students' achievements. The researchers' survival analysis determined that teachers with high aptitude scores left the profession earlier than those with low aptitude scores. The briefer careers of brighter teachers might erode the quality of education as teachers' aptitude scores covary positively with students' achievement scores. Equally alarming, the researchers found that science teachers in particular abandoned education more readily, a tendency that compounds the acute shortage of science teachers and limits the availability of science instruction.

Lost Business Opportunities

Besides affecting the current success of a firm, personnel turnover may hamper the future survival of the organization. Anecdotal evidence abounds about business opportunities lost because key contributors left (Mobley 1982a). For example, the flight of scientists and engineers can delay or prevent the introduction of new products and threaten future profitability in new markets (Gomez-Mejia, Balkin, and Milkovich 1990; Turbin and Rossé 1990). Equally important, expatriates from existing firms may form competing businesses, such as the Silicon Valley firms, Solectron and Lam (Mandel and Farrell 1992).

Increased Administrative Burden

Organizations may expand their administrative staffing to handle the extra recruiting and training created by excessive attrition and research reviews have observed the practice (Price 1977, 1989). Given intense global competition, the effect is especially troublesome because the overhead costs of domestic firms far exceed those of Japanese or German companies (Thurow 1992). No doubt, the current downsizing in corporate America reflects cost-cutting maneuvers to shrink white-collar employment and reduce administrative costs (Henkoff 1990).

Employee Demoralization

Last, turnover may erode the morale and stability of those who remain employed (Mowday, Porter, and Steers 1982). Their morale suffers because they lose friends (O'Reilly, Caldwell, and Barnett 1989; Price, 1977) and may interpret motives for quitting as social criticisms about the job (Mowday, Porter, and Steers 1982). Awareness that a leaver has a better job elsewhere may change employees' perception of jobs. As a result, the stayers may denigrate their present position in the light of superior alternatives (Hulin, Roznoski, and Hachiya 1985) and begin contemplating other employment (Mobley 1982a). In line with these hypothesized effects, research into small groups finds that personnel instability weakens the cohesion of the group (Sundstrom, De Meuse, and Futrell 1990). Turnover studies conclude that work group conflicts and dissatisfaction with coworkers breed dissatisfaction about the job and subsequently, turnover (O'Reilly, Caldwell, and Barnett 1989; Mobley 1982a; Mowday, Porter, and Steers 1982; Pfeffer 1983; Price and Mueller 1981, 1986). Collectively, these findings imply that colleagues' resignations may undermine the employees' social integration and in turn stimulate more turnover (Price 1989). More revealing, Mueller and Price (1989) reported that rising quit rates in hospital units foreshadowed an inability to keep staff, although quit rates did not affect the units' morale or integration.

All the same, the exodus of their colleagues may not invariably demoralize the remaining members of organizations. Krackhardt and Porter (1985) argued that employees may form more positive attitudes toward the job to rationalize their remaining employed while their friends quit. Sustaining this claim, the researchers found that the departure of friends reinforced the stayers' satisfaction and commitment. These provocative findings deserve replication. Krackhardt and Porter sampled adolescents who worked for extra spending money, rather than economic survival, in fast-food restaurants whose turnover ran to 200 percent annually.

Staw (1980) speculated that imputed motives for leaving may dictate whether or not turnover demoralizes stayers. That is, if it is believed that leavers quit for reasons that have nothing to do with the organization (to meet family obligations or relocate to different community), employees may not be induced to rethink their own motives for staying. Besides this, job mobility is a traditional avenue for career advancement in some professions (public accounting [Sheridan 1992, for example]). In such occupations, regular departures may not necessarily undermine the stayers' allegiance to the organization.

POSITIVE CONSEQUENCES FOR THE ORGANIZATION

This section reviews the positive contributions of personnel attrition for organizations, underappreciated effects. Just as it can lower productivity, incur financial costs, and undermine stayers' morale, turnover can have the opposite ramifications under certain circumstances or for certain firms. That is, exits of marginal performers may improve overall firm productivity, while new replacements for leavers can infuse companies with new ideas and technology. Though turnover is obviously costly, personnel shrinkage—especially among administrative staff—can nonetheless reduce overhead costs, a major problem in corporate America. Further, resignations may create more job and empowerment opportunities for employees who remain in firms.

Displacement of Poor Performers

As noted above, several meta-analyses concluded that turnover generally promotes productivity because functional turnover is more common than dysfunctional turnover (that is, the loss of valued personnel) (McEvoy and Cascio 1987; Williams and Livingstone 1994). Besides this, low performers who remain on the payroll because they cannot find other employment may engage in other forms of withdrawal, such as absenteeism and sabotage (Martin and Schermerhorn 1983; Mobley 1982a). Clearly, the absence of such disruptive employees would enhance the organization's effectiveness (Price 1989).

Job burnout. Though turnover of veteran employees may reduce productivity (Price, 1977), job stress or burnout may reverse such productivity losses from turnover. The relationship between job tenure and performance in stressful work (that of traffic controllers), physically demanding work (that of miners and construction workers), technologically changing work (that of electrical engineers), and public service work (that of social workers or nurses) may be modeled by an inverted-U curve (Staw 1980). While lacking experience, new entrants to these stressful occupations are highly motivated or have more current skills, enabling them to outperform seasoned employees. As newcomers accumulate more job seniority, they may also lose their effectiveness; they become sluggish or burn out and their skills atrophy. Resignations by experienced personnel may not invariably yield productivity losses because the conventional J-shaped performance curve—holding that newcomers perform less effectively than veterans do—may not hold in stressful occupations.

Infusion of New Knowledge and Technology

Beyond performance improvements, turnover may benefit firms through the infusion of new knowledge and technology from the newcomers (Price 1977), a contention that reviews of the literature affirm (Mobley 1982a; Mowday, Porter and Steers 1982; Price 1989; Staw 1980). In particular, research on R&D teams indicates that in groups that are excessively long lived or stable, R&D performance decreases (Katz 1980, 1982; Price 1977). Given the importance of external technical knowledge and new ideas, long-lived R&D teams become ineffective because increasingly they rely on customary work patterns and insulate themselves from outside information that might threaten their comfortable, predictable work habits. Derived from Katz's study of fifty R&D teams (1982), 2-10 illustrates this development.

Similarly, exits from top management may lay the groundwork for necessary changes in entrenched but maladaptive company policies (Staw 1980). Finkelstein and Hambrick (1990) found that long-tenured executive teams followed more persistently company strategies that mirrored industry norms, whereas short-tenured teams adopted novel strategies that departed from industry patterns. Such policy changes may occur only if outsiders, rather than insiders, fill vacant executive posts (Staw 1980). The business press has chronicled revolutionary transformations in IBM, Allied-Signal, and other *Fortune* 500 companies wrought by chief executive officers recruited from other firms (Bremner 1991; Stewart 1993).

New Business Ventures

Exiting employees may provide new business to their former employers. For example, staff accountants leaving public accounting often initiate or continue audit work for their former accounting firms with their current business. Similarly, U.S.-trained Chinese returning to Taiwan to develop its high-tech industry often maintained ties to their former companies (Barnathan, Einhorn and Nakarmi 1992).

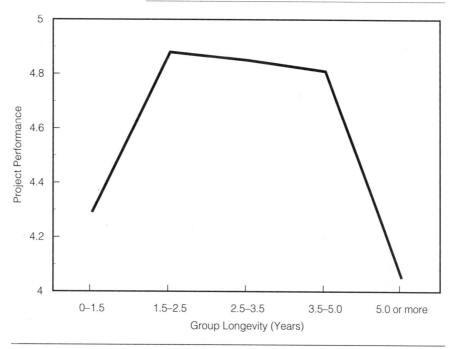

Figure 2-10 **Project Performance of R & D Teams as a Function of Group Longevity (Katz, R. (1982). Effects of Group Longevity on Project Communication and Performance.** *Administrative Science Quarterly, 27,* **81-104.)**

Labor Cost Savings

Voluntary turnover may help corporations control or lower labor costs by reducing the work force as they face stiffer global competition (Balkin 1992; Henkoff 1990; Jacob 1992; Nussbaum 1991). Annual surveys by the American Management Association find that a third of American companies have cut payrolls in the past three years (Henkoff 1990) and that 3.5 million people have lost their jobs since 1987 (Lesly and Light 1992). Voluntary quits represent a less costly way of downsizing than do layoffs, early retirement inducements, or job buy-outs (Balkin 1992; Faltermayer 1992). Though popular, layoffs incur financial charges (for severance pay and outplacement services), demoralize survivors, and damage public relations, (which hurt future recruitment) (Ashford, Lee, and Bobko 1989; Davy, Kinicki, and Scheck 1991; Faltermayer 1992).

Opportunities in Promotion and Empowerment for Stayers

Writers on turnover suggest that there are various advantages for the remaining employees, although the empirical findings are sparse (Price

1977, 1989; Staw 1980). Exits may expand opportunities for promotion among continuing members by opening up the jobs vacated by the leavers and lessening the competition for promotions (Mobley 1982a; Staw 1980). Still, Mueller and Price (1989) did not find turnover rates in hospital units to increase prospects for advancement. In a similar vein, managerial turnover may empower subordinates (Price 1977, 1989). Conceivably, incoming managers feel uncertain about their authority because they are unfamiliar with the position. They may thus initially consult subordinates for background information and advice. Sustaining this view, Price (1977) interpreted several empirical studies as implying that managerial exits and succession decentralize power, while a Phoenix aerospace company recently organized a department of engineers into a self-managing work unit when their manager left, according to the senior author's personal observations. Last, the departure of participants in divisive interpersonal disputes will alleviate tension and conflict among coworkers (Staw 1980).

NEGATIVE CONSEQUENCES FOR THE LEAVER

This section considers the adverse repercussions to employees who quit their jobs. Traditionally, managers and scholars have worried about how turnover harms organizations. Yet attention to negative consequences for leavers may pay dividends for companies. They can forewarn prospective leavers about the full ramifications of their decisions to exit the firm—namely, loss of seniority benefits, transition stress in a new job, relocation costs and family dislocation, and disruption to spouses' careers. Such warnings can help prospective quitters to make wiser decisions about changing jobs as well as deter their exits. Scholarly inquiry into such consequences would refine conceptualizations about turnover, identifying more fully the reasons that inhibit dissatisfied employees from quitting (Mobley, 1977; Rusbult & Farrell, 1983).

Forfeiture of Seniority and Fringe Benefits

Research and anecdotal evidence identify sundry personal disadvantages for leavers, notably the surrender of various rewards of organizational membership (Mobley 1982a; Staw, 1980). Theorists on turnover have long insisted that the expectancy of forfeiting job seniority, unvested pensions, and other fringe benefits deters turnover (Hom and Griffeth 1991; Mobley 1977; Rusbult and Farrell 1983). Quite likely, the loss of health-care benefits would be the most costly to leavers at present. Recent nationwide polls report that between 15 percent and 20 percent of all workers said they or a family member *remained* in a job because of concerns about health benefits (Clements 1993; Lewin 1991). Indeed, a Harvard economist estimates that fear of losing health coverage reduces job mobility by 25 percent (Labor Letter *Wall Street Journal*, November 2, 1993). Explaining what it styled "job-lock," the *New York Times* recounted cases of employees whose cancer or heart disease (or whose dependents' long-term treatment) prevented them from resigning because new insurers would deny them health coverage (Lewin 1991). Another poll determined that the prospect of higher personal expenses for medical coverage at another company does more to discourage employees from quitting than do specific medical conditions (Clements 1993). More convincingly, research by labor economists confirmed that pension and health-care coverage deters job turnover (Ippolito 1991; Mitchell 1983).

Transition Stress in New Employment

Researchers into socialization and turnover further contend that quitters encounter stress during their transition into a new job (Mobley 1982a; Feldman and Brett 1983). Their new employment may disappoint the leavers, failing to confirm their expectations and, therefore, eliciting dissatisfaction and turnover (Wanous 1980; Wanous, Poland, Premack, and Davis 1992). Leavers entering new work roles must repeat basic tasks of socialization, such learning work practices and winning acceptance from new colleagues (Feldman 1975, 1988). Acknowledging this consequence of leaving, Feldman and Brett (1983) documented various strategies for coping with transition stress (such as working longer hours and delegating more responsibilities) used by employees who simply changed jobs within the same company.

Relocation Costs

Leavers may face additional losses if they move to new geographic regions (Mobley 1982a; Mowday, Porter, and Steers 1982; Rusbult and Farrell 1983). Obviously, leavers bear the financial costs of moving, especially if they do not receive full reimbursement from their new employer or if they move to a region where the living costs are higher (Mowday, Porter, and Steers 1982). Apart from moving expenses, relocating leavers may sever their social support networks (Zedeck and Mosier 1990). Various empirical studies implicate this potential exit cost, showing that extensive friendships with coworkers and relatives within a community reinforce the likelihood of remaining in a job (Blegen, Mueller, and Price 1988; Rusbult and Farrell, 1983).

Unfortunately, writers on turnover have neglected to consider the cost of family separation when married leavers relocate but leave their families behind, perhaps because of a spouse's employment or the children's education. The armed services have long known that protracted and repeated family separations caused by military assignments abroad produce not only marital strain but also attrition among soldiers seeking to preserve their marriages (Brown, Carr, and Orthner 1983; Hunter 1983). Researchers on turnover must acknowledge the effects of quitting and relocating on child custody arrangements among divorced leavers. That is, parents who move and do not have custody of their children may find their ties to their children severed; parents who do have custody and relocate may face lawsuits from former spouses trying to preserve visitation rights (Lublin 1992).

Theorists on turnover have also overlooked the ways in which relocation can dissolve the social network of a leaver's family, who must adapt to a new community without support from friends or extended family. Research on expatriate managers attests to such family dislocations in adjusting to new cultural milieus. Indeed, the failure of a family to adapt culturally has prematurely terminated overseas assignments (Dowling and Schuler 1990).

Relocating leavers and their families may lose valued community services, such as those of the family physician and good schools (Abelson and Baysinger 1984; Rusbult and Farrell 1983). Indicative of these costs, Turban, Campion, and Eyring (1992) found that long-term tenure in a *community* discourages people from moving to new jobs elsewhere and Hunter (1983) observed that many navy personnel chose to leave the U.S. Navy because they disliked the frequent moves imposed on their families.

Disruption of Spouses' Careers and Marital Discord

The geographic relocation of leavers who are married to working spouses may disrupt their spouses' careers (Mobley 1982a; Zedeck and Mosier 1990). Attesting to its impact, Turban, Campion, and Eyring (1992) found that more married employees refused offers by employers to relocate than did single employees. Milliken, Dutton, and Beyer (1990) reported that between 25 percent and 30 percent of employees declined promotions that required relocation, mainly to avoid threatening the careers of their spouses. Conversely, members of dual-career couples who resign to follow their relocating spouses may not obtain comparable employment in the new community (Lublin 1993). In particular, trailing husbands adhering to traditional sex roles may feel psychological distress if they cannot find work or become underemployed (Staines, Pottick, and Fudge 1986). Indeed, their wives' employment status would threaten their cherished status as primary breadwinners, and this sex-role reversal would produce marital strain (Lublin 1993; Mirowsky 1987). Nonetheless, this turnover cost may accelerate as men will constitute 25 percent of trailing spouses by the year 2000, according to the Employee Relocation Council, up from 15 percent in 1990 (Lublin 1993).

POSITIVE CONSEQUENCES FOR THE LEAVER

Leavers may reap certain benefits from turnover (Mobley 1982a; Staw 1980). For one, leavers may assume a better position—one that better matches their talents and interests—or escape a stressful job (Mowday, Porter, and Steers 1982). In a national sample of young men, Antel (1991) found that job quitters often obtain higher wages in their new employment, especially if they underwent an intervening period of joblessness. Indeed, a new position may rejuvenate leavers, instilling a greater commitment to work (Mobley 1982a). Moreover, leavers—assuming new (or no) employment that offers a more convenient work schedule—can devote more time to other endeavors, such as family or avocations (Hom and Griffeth 1991; Hulin, Roznowski, and Hachiya 1985). Exit surveys reveal that young female nurses and teachers often resign to bear or raise children (Cavanagh 1989; Murnane, Singer and Willett 1988). A sociological study found that young adults often opt out of full-time employment to attend school (Kandel and Yamaguchi 1987). Relocation may provide leavers and their families with better schools, safer communities, or more attractive climates and recreational opportunities (Cascio 1991; Mowday, Porter, and Steers 1982; Turban, Campion and Eyring 1992).

Leavers, abandoning current positions to trail spouses, who are accepting better career assignments elsewhere, may willingly and gladly assume this sacrifice if they had already fulfilled their career ambitions or if they welcome the opportunity to switch careers—to open a business or return to school perhaps (Lublin 1993). Such "sacrifice" is not uncommon: Exit surveys show that many nurses quit when their spouses relocate (Donovan 1980). Members of dual-career couples may preserve their marriage by quitting firms that request them to transfer. For example, female managers at Mobil Corporation often resigned for fear that their husbands would not go along with the move (Lublin 1993), while military officers often left the armed services to appease spouses who rejected the harsh military life (Hunter 1983).

FUTURE DIRECTIONS FOR RESEARCH

In summary, turnover introduces various contradictory consequences for leavers and employers. Some are advantageous for organizations or individuals, others are not. Such contradictory outcomes make it difficult, however, to forecast the net impact (Staw 1980). Toward this end, we must develop and test more complex conceptualizations of the impact of turnover rather than use simple bivariate associations (see Price 1989). We could then estimate the net effect of turnover on a particular outcome (for example, productivity or satisfaction) by modeling and assessing the opposing intervening processes it stimulates. For example, turnover may increase job satisfaction. When disagreeable colleagues leave and the opportunities for promotion expand, but satisfaction may decrease by prompting employees to question their motivation for staying (ibid.). A structural model test may find, however, that these varied effects cancel one another and that the net effect of turnover on job satisfaction is zero (Podsakoff, Williams, and Todor 1986). Consistent with this approach, Mueller and Price (1989) found that certain consequences of leaving did not materialize once they had statistically controlled other consequences and turnover determinants with multivariate statistical techniques.

Future research might examine turnover effects longitudinally to trace their distribution over time (Price 1989) to reveal that some effects are short term, while others are long term. Beyond this, a particular consequence may manifest *different* effects over time. Thus, some outcomes may appear harmful in the short term but yield long-term benefits. For instance, the departure of top executives from troubled companies may prove temporarily disruptive but pave the way to new strategic initiatives that will revitalize these companies.

Besides longitudinal study, more research on various moderators that shape the effects of turnover will advance the understanding of its consequences, as will examinations of nonlinear effects (ibid.; Staw 1980). Future inquiry must explore the ways in which the effects of turnover change at different levels of analysis (Mueller and Price 1989). For example, turnover among personnel may impair a department's productivity by disrupting production but enhance the corporation's productivity by reducing the work force. Further investigations must differentiate the effects of voluntary and involuntary turnover, which likely diverge. For example, whether quitting demoralizes remaining employees may depend on whether they believed that the leavers departed voluntarily or involuntarily (Staw 1980). More empirical work on the consequences of turnover may also improve managers' projections of the costs and benefits of turnover interventions and alert them to potential side effects (see Staw 1980). To illustrate, some programs may reduce departures but evoke counterproductive effects, such as the retention of marginal employees (Sheridan 1992). Thus, research documenting side effects would help managers make more informed decisions about choosing turnover interventions that yield *net* positive effects for their organizations apart from reducing quits.

CAUSES AND
CORRELATES OF TURNOVER

Many reviews of the antecedents and correlates of turnover have appeared over the years (Brayfield and Crockett, 1955; Hulin, Roznowski, and Hachiya 1985; Mobley 1982a; Mobley, Griffeth, Hand, and Meglino 1979; Muchinsky and Tuttle 1979; Porter and Steers 1973; Price 1977; Steers and Mowday 1981). In this chapter, we update earlier reviews and refine them using meta-analysis, which improves upon traditional or narrative reviews, wherein a reviewer draws conclusions from his or her subjective analysis of empirical findings (Hunter and Schmidt 1990b). For example, a narrative review may conclude that job satisfaction is unrelated to turnover because their correlations often vary widely across different samples. Some studies find positive, others negative, and still others insignificant correlations. These conflicting results may, however, reflect statistical artifacts, such as sampling error and inconsistent instrument reliabilities across studies.

Narrative reviews overlook the small sample sizes of many empirical findings. Yet small samples weaken statistical power, attenuating the statistical significance of variable relationships (Hunter and Schmidt 1990b). Rather than relying on informal inspection, meta-analysis statistically summarizes measures of variable association from different studies. Unlike qualitative reviews, this procedure more precisely estimates the true relationship between two variables (and their generality) by correcting for methodological artifacts. Typically, meta-analysis averages correlations (after weighing them by their sample size) from different studies to correct for sampling error. The mean correlation is then adjusted for random measurement errors and other artifacts (see Hunter and Schmidt 1990b). The result is the correlation coefficient expected in the population. Importantly, this population correlation discloses the magnitude or strength of variable relationships. Narrative reviews generally strive to establish whether or not a relationship exists. Last, meta-analysis estimates the generality of a relationship, determining whether variability in correlations between studies is real or illusory. If it is genuine, other situational or population variables will moderate this relationship. In other words, the association between two variables is not constant but changes across different settings or populations.

Recognizing these advantages, scholars of turnover (including Carsten and Spector 1987; Cotton and Tuttle 1986; Hom, Caranikas-Walker, Prussia, and Griffeth 1992; Mathieu and Zajac 1990; McEvoy and Cascio 1985, 1987; Premack and Wanous 1985; Steel and Griffeth 1989; Steel, Hendrix, and Balogh 1990; Steel and Ovalle 1984; Tett and Meyer 1992; Wanous, et al. 1992; Williams and Livingstone 1994) have increasingly applied meta-analyses to combine research findings. These meta-analyses have, however, investigated a small number of turnover determinants and correlates, such as perceived alternatives (Steel and Griffeth 1989) or organizational commitment (Mathieu and Zajac 1990), rather than summarize a broad array of turnover correlates and causes. Only Cotton and Tuttle (1986) comprehensively reviewed multiple turnover correlates, although they assessed only the *significance* of their relationships to turnover.

In this chapter, we report a comprehensive meta-analysis that covers more turnover predictors and correlates than most meta-analyses. Extending narrative reviews, we estimate the predictive strength of turnover antecedents and determine the generality of correlations between predictors and turnover—that is the existence of moderators that might condition those relationships. We seek to establish a bedrock of empirical facts about turnover, which may refute theoretical propositions or constitute a basis for theoretical interpretation or synthesis.

META-ANALYTICAL PROCEDURE

First, we reviewed the research literature, using computerized sources and a manual search of leading journals in human resource management, industrial/organizational psychology, and organizational behavior, to uncover correlations between turnover and its antecedents (and sample sizes and reliability estimates where available). (If other association indices were reported, we transformed those statistics into correlations using Schwarzer's [1989] meta-analysis program.) We relied on previous turnover meta-analyses and narrative reviews to identify relevant studies. Our review *excluded* studies on aggregate quit rates because our intention was to explain turnover among individuals. Aggregate turnover rates may constitute a different construct and do not directly provide insight into the origins of the decisions that influence turnover among individuals (Mobley et al. 1979). Although aggregate quit rates are computed by combining individual turnover within organizations or departments (Hulin, Roznowski, and Hachiya 1985), the meaning of the turnover construct changes across different levels of aggregation (Rousseau 1985; Terborg and Lee 1984). For example, job vacancy rates correlate differently with aggregate and individual quits (Hulin, Roznowski, and Hachiya 1985; Steel and Griffeth 1989).

Following Hunter, Schmidt, and Jackson's procedure (1982), we corrected correlations and their variances for sampling and measurement errors, the foremost sources of spurious between-study variation (Premack and Hunter 1988). (Regrettably, most studies failed to describe the extent of range restriction in predictor variables.) To correct sampling error, we first averaged correlations between turnover and a given predictor, weighing by sample size. Next, we adjusted this correlation for unreliability by inserting the predictor's reliability coefficient (averaged across different samples) into the classic attenuation correction formula (Hunter and Schmidt 1990b, p. 119). Because of the ongoing controversy surrounding such corrections

(Bass and Ager 1991; Steel, Shane, and Griffeth 1990; Williams 1990), we did not correct turnover for dichotomy or nonoptimal base rate.

Three procedures tested the true generality of each correlation between predictor and quit. These tests estimated nonartifactual variation of this correlation, to detect whether or not (unknown) moderators condition it. One moderator test assessed the degree to which statistical artifacts explain variance in observed correlations (Hunter and Schmidt 1990b). Because our meta-analysis only corrected for sampling error and unreliability, we defined 60 percent (or more) artifactual contribution as signifying *no* moderators (see Hom, Caranikas-Walker, Prussia, and Griffeth 1992; Mathieu and Zajac 1990).

Second, a chi-square test revealed whether between-study variance in observed correlations was solely attributable to sampling error (see Wanous et al. 1992). Third, we computed 95 percent credibility intervals (using variances fully corrected for experimental artifacts) around true population correlations (Whitener 1990). Credibility intervals including zero signal moderators and suggest that correlations can assume signs opposite to that of the population correlation. If these tests collectively reject an invariant relationship, the population estimate constitutes an average of *dissimilar* correlations from distinct subpopulations (Hunter and Schmidt 1990b). To identify these subpopulations, a meta-analytical researcher would pursue additional moderator analyses (see Hom et al. 1992). Such analyses are, however, beyond the scope of this chapter, the primary objective of which is a basic overview of research into turnover.

For the most part, we classified the antecedents of turnover using the taxonomy developed by Mobley et al. (1979). Thus, the chapter is organized into discussion of (1) individual and personal determinants; (2) overall satisfaction; (3) organization and work environment factors; (4) job content factors, and (5) external environment factors. To this taxonomy, we added (6) withdrawal process variables, and (7) other withdrawal behaviors.

In Tables 3-1 through 3-6, we show correlations between antecedents and voluntary quits, reporting the number of samples and overall sample size on which they were based and moderator tests of their between-sample stability. The population correlation (corrected mean *r*) represents the best measure of the relationship between turnover and a determinant because this index was derived from double corrections for measurement and sampling errors. The three moderator tests indicate whether or not this population correlation generalizes across different settings, populations, or circumstances.

On the whole, moderator findings tempered all generalizations, showing that most correlations changed across settings or populations. Specifically, most indices of the contribution of artifactual variance to observed variance fell below the 60 percent threshold value, suggesting that statistical artifacts *did* not entirely account for between-study variation in correlations. Most credibility intervals included zero, and most chi-square tests were significant, indicating that sampling error did not entirely underlie between-study variance. Nevertheless, we proceed with some tentative conclusions about the generality of turnover antecedents and correlates. Given many modest population estimates, we thus suggest possible moderators and potential weaknesses with existing measures or variables. After all, a meta-analysis is only as good as the data available for aggregation.

Demographic and Personal Characteristics

The demographic and personal characteristics of an individual included are cognitive ability, education, training, marital status, kinship responsibility, relatives, children, weighted application blanks (described below), age, sex, and tenure. Most personal attributes modestly predicted resignations, although their predictive strength varied (see Table 3-1).

Contrary to popular stereotypes, women did not quit their jobs more readily than did men; rather, they were more loyal employees ($r = -.07$). Still, kinship responsibility (a complex measure of family obligations based on number of children, their age, and marital status [Blegen, Mueller, and Price

Table 3-1 Individual Demographic and Personal Characteristics

PREDICTOR	k	N	Mean r ($\bar{r}_{obs}$)	Corrected Mean r ($\bar{r}_{cor}$)	Corrected Variance (V_{pop})	Percentage Artifactual Variance	95% Credibility Interval	X^2
Characteristics								
Cognitive ability	2	1,879	−.09	−.09	.0035	30.19	−.19 to .01	6.62*
Education	29	8,915	.07	.07	.0030	52.21	−.04 to .17	55.54*
Training	4	3,394	−.07	−.08	.0074	15.69	−.24 to .09	25.49*
Marital status	23	7,599	.01	.01	.0076	28.48	−.16 to .18	80.76*
Kinship responsibilities	9	5,354	−.10	−.10	.0053	26.90	−.25 to .04	33.46*
Relatives	2	440	.22	.22	.0000	100.00	.22 to .22	1.75
Children	4	727	−.14	−.14	.0000	100.00	−.14 to −.14	.63
Weighted application blanks	6	1,329	.31	.33	.0704	5.84	−.19 to .85	102.73*
Age	29	12,356	−.12	−.12	.0062	26.93	.27 to .03	107.67*
Sex	15	6,748	−.07	−.07	.0134	14.11	−.29 to .16	106.28*
Tenure	36	12,106	−.16	−.17	.0171	16.23	−.39 to .07	221.77*

Note. k = the number of samples; N = the number of employees.
Marital status was coded as Married = low score; Single = high score.
Sex was coded as Male = low score; Female = high score.

Mean r = average correlation across all studies (weighted by their sample size); corrected mean r = average correlation across all studies which has been corrected for measurement errors; corrected variance = variance of corrected correlations across studies; percentage artifactual variance = degree to which statistical artifacts explain variance in observed correlations; 95% credibility interval = interval around the mean corrected correlation which comprises 95 percent of corrected correlations; and X^2 = chi-square test of whether between-study variance in observed correlations is entirely due to sampling error.
*p<.05.

Source. Authors' calculations.

1988]) and number of children improved retention, and the number of relatives in the community accelerated organizational exits. As expected, older employees with long tenure in a company quit less often than younger and short-tenure employees did. This finding possibly reflects a greater long-term job investment by senior personnel (Rusbult and Farrell 1983). The weighted application blank correctly identified mobile personnel. Like an employment test, this procedure scores a job applicant's responses to questions on an application blank based on a scoring key that empirically differentiates between short- and long-term employees (Cascio 1976). (This methodology is described further in Chapter 9.)

Overall Job Satisfaction and Turnover

Consistent with most theoretical perspectives, job dissatisfaction was related ($r = -.19$) to resignations (Mobley 1977; Porter and Steers 1973; Price and Mueller 1986; Steers and Mowday 1981). That is, dissatisfied employees (presumably, reacting to poor working conditions [see Mobley et al. 1979; Price and Mueller 1986]) more readily abandoned their present employment. The relationship between satisfaction and quitting, estimated from seventy-eight studies covering 27,543 employees, is shown in Table 3-2. Surprisingly, this correlation is not substantially different from that determined in two previous meta-analyses (Carsten and Spector 1987; Steel and Ovalle 1984), probably because all these analyses used the same studies.

Our moderator analysis further demonstrated that the correlation between satisfaction and quitting varied across studies. Other meta-analytic research has, however, identified moderators of this relationship by correlating moderator scores with study correlations or comparing correlations from meta-analyses done on subgroups formed by dividing samples according to moderator scores. For instance, Carsten and Spector (1987) and Steel, Hendrix, and Balogh (1990) showed that the association between job satisfaction and turnover is stronger when the time span between administration of the questionnaire and assessment of the turnover is shorter (Mobley et al. 1979). Steel and Ovalle (1984) found a higher agreement between satisfaction and retention for military than for civilian samples, possibly because decisions about reenlistment are more programmed and entail a deeper personal commitment (legal obligation for a lengthy tour of duty) than do civilians' decisions to quit. The correlation is stronger during periods of low unemployment but weaker during periods of joblessness. As Carsten and Spector explained ". . . even though people are not satisfied with their jobs, they will be less likely to quit if there are few (or no) alternatives." (1987, 378). By comparison, Steel and Ovalle (1984) found that between white- and blue-collar occupations distinctions did not moderate the correlations between satisfaction and quitting.

Met expectations—a leading source of job satisfaction according to prevailing thinking (Porter and Steers 1973; Wanous 1980; Wanous et al., 1992)—also predicted turnover ($r = -.13$). Put differently, employees quit

Table 3-2 Job Satisfaction and Organizational and Work Environment Factors

PREDICTOR	k	N	Mean r ($\bar{r}_{obs}$)	Corrected Mean r ($\bar{r}_{cor}$)	Corrected Variance (V_{pop})	Percentage Artifactual Variance	95% Credibility Interval	X^2
Job Satisfaction								
Job satisfaction	78	27,543	−.17	−.19	.0128	19.91	−.37 to .03	391.76*
Met expectations	8	1,435	−.12	−.13	.0086	41.94	−.31 to .05	19.13*
Organization and Work Environment								
Compensation								
Salary	7	3,763	−.06	−.06	.0025	42.59	−.16 to .04	16.44*
Pay satisfaction	16	4,094	−.03	−.04	.0071	41.69	−.20 to .13	38.43*
Distributive justice/ Pay equity	9	4,110	−.07	−.07	.0001	77.22	−.12 to −.02	11.66
Leadership or Supervision								
Participation	5	1,584	−.08	−.08	.0031	53.50	−.19 to .03	9.35
Leader-member exchange	3	161	−.21	−.23	.0167	55.65	−.48 to .03	5.39
Supervisory satisfaction	14	3,002	−.10	−.10	.0018	74.53	−.19 to −.02	18.82
Leader communication	8	5,185	−.11	−.11	.0020	45.71	−.20 to −.03	17.54*
Peer Group Relations								
Cohesion	3	412	−.12	−.14	.0000	100.0	−.14 to −.14	1.90
Integration	4	3,394	−.08	−.10	.0042	29.29	−.22 to .03	13.95*
Coworker satisfaction	11	1,313	−.10	−.10	−.0033	74.19	−.22 to .01	14.84
Role States								
Role clarity	3	391	−.21	−.24	−.0090	100.00	−.21 to −.21	.10
Role overload	3	2,627	.10	.11	.0000	100.00	.11 to .11	.27
Role conflict	2	244	.15	.16	−.0090	100.00	.15 to .15	.90
Company Climate								
Centralization	4	2,506	.08	.09	.0022	46.08	.00 to .18	8.69*
Supportiveness	2	256	.02	.02	.0052	62.47	−.12 to .16	3.20
Promotional Opportunities								
Promotions	24	8,999	−.14	−.15	.024	11.42	−.42 to .15	218.85*
Promotion satisfaction	13	3,276	−.12	−.14	.012	29.25	−.32 to .07	47.87*
Promotional opportunity	8	4,878	−.09	−.10	.007	23.61	−.24 to .06	38.12*
Actual promotions	3	845	−.45	−.45	.034	6.13	−.81 to −.09	48.91*
Actual promotions without outlier	2	657	−.35	−.35	.000	100.00	−.35 to −.35	.15

Note. k = the number of samples; N = the number of employees.

Mean r = average correlation across all studies (weighted by their sample size); corrected mean r = average correlation across all studies which has been corrected for measurement errors; corrected variance = variance of corrected correlations across studies; percentage artifactual variance = degree to which statistical artifacts explain variance in observed correlations; 95% credibility interval = interval around the mean corrected correlation which comprises 95 percent of corrected correlations; and X^2 = chi-square test of whether between-study variance in observed correlations is entirely due to sampling error.

*$p < .05$.

Source. Authors' calculations.

jobs if their work experiences disconfirm the expectations they had about their jobs before taking them up; they remained employed if their experiences confirm their initial expectations. The correlation between met expectation and quitting fell below that between satisfaction and quitting, which suggests that met expectations may affect turnover through job satisfaction (Porter and Steers 1973; Wanous et al. 1992).

Organization and Work Environment

The results calculated from meta-analyses of compensation, leadership and supervision, opportunities for promotion, relations with peer groups, role states, and the climate of the company are also shown in Table 3-2.

Compensation. Although writers on compensation commonly believe that dissatisfaction with salary and pay strongly underlie turnover (Gomez-Meija and Balkin 1992a; Milkovich and Newman 1993), we find very little direct support for this view. The routine omission of other forms of compensation, notably fringe benefits and incentive pay (Heneman 1985), surely understated the effect of compensation. In marked contrast, the popular press and labor economic studies have underscored the ways in which pension and health coverage and profit sharing significantly improve retention rates in the work force (Ippolito 1991; Peel and Wilson 1990). More than this, most turnover scholars have considered pay practices in a single company or occupation. Such limitations possibly underestimated the impact of pay on turnover (Steel and Griffeth 1989).

Distributive justice or inequity. Like dissatisfaction about pay, the perceived fairness of levels of compensation—the justice of the distribution of pay and the equity of rewards—modestly predicted turnover. Here again, the traditional exclusion of fringe benefits and incentive pay doubtlessly underestimated the effects of perceptions of justice on decisions to quit (see Price and Mueller 1981, 1986). Existing studies of turnover neglected to consider the procedural fairness of organizational rules and procedures for allocating rewards (Greenberg 1990). Conceivably, procedures that are perceived as just may do more to encourage employees to stay in their jobs than a just pay distribution does. For instance, Folger and Konovsky (1989) showed that satisfaction with the fairness of a merit-pay distribution did more to promote commitment to the organization than did satisfaction with the amount of the distribution.

Leadership and supervision. The measure styled leader-member exchange predicted turnover more accurately than did measures of participative management, satisfaction with the supervisor, and the leader's communication skills. The latter measures focus on a particular action by a leader or an attitude toward the leader, whereas leader-member exchange is a more general construct summarizing these and other benevolent actions on the part of supervisors. Specifically, leader-member exchange represents the interdependence

between superiors and subordinates and reflects a host of benefits—
including influence on decision making, information, and social support—
given to subordinates who develop high-quality exchanges with their
superiors (Dansereau, Graen, and Haga 1975; Graen and Scandura 1986).

Notwithstanding current findings, future research (and meta-analyses)
may disclose that new forms of participative management may become pivotal deterrents to turnover (Manz and Sims 1989). At present, organizations
are increasingly flattening the management structure and delegating more
authority that was formerly held by supervisors to front-line employees
(Jacob 1992). Modern developments in employee empowerment and self-
management greatly enlarge the workers' sphere of influence beyond that
of conventional participative management, in which workers are given control only over the methods or schedules of their jobs (Hackman and
Oldham 1980).

Peer-group relations. Good peer-group relations, consisting of cohesion among
the work group, integration (the degree to which an individual has close
friends in the organization [Price and Mueller 1981]), and satisfaction with
coworkers decreased turnover. The modest correlations suggest that peer-
group relations are remote causes of turnover and are one source of job satisfaction (ibid. 1986). Nonetheless, in few studies of turnover have the
formation of cohesion in work groups and integration been investigated.
Work in organizational demography, although it has overlooked the underlying mechanisms of value conflicts and miscommunication among heterogeneous members, has demonstrated that heterogeneity within the group
induces decisions to quit (Jackson, Brett, Sessa, Cooper, Julin, and Peyronnin
1991; O'Reilly, Caldwell, and Barnett 1989; Pfeffer 1983). Thus, more inquiry
into the integration of a group's members may identify more potent influences exerted by coworkers on job separations.

Role states. Table 3-2 shows that role clarity (clear perceptions about one's
role in the organization) lowered turnover and that role overload and role
conflict increased it. Even though these results supported theoretical expectations (Katz and Kahn 1978), they are based on only a few studies and so
should be interpreted cautiously. All the same, the size of their modest effect
affirms certain perspectives on commitment and turnover that regard role
states as remote influences that are mediated by cognitions about termi-
nating work and attitudes toward the job (Mathieu and Zajac 1990;
Netemeyer, Johnston, and Burton 1990).

Company climate. Characteristics of an organization only minimally affected
quits, possibly because they are only distal causes (Mobley, Griffeth, Hand,
and Meglino 1979; Price and Mueller 1981, 1986). That is, centralization (or
the degree to which power is concentrated in the higher echelons of management) and supportiveness barely predicted turnover (see Table 3-2).

Though scarcely affecting the departures of individuals, the attributes of a company may still considerably influence aggregate turnover rates (see Alexander 1988; Price 1977; Terborg and Lee 1984). As noted earlier, causal determinants may affect aggregate and individual quits in different ways because the turnover construct may shift in meaning across different levels of aggregation (Price and Mueller 1986; Rousseau 1985).

Given the complexity of organizational climate, our consideration of only two dimensions probably underestimated the impact of climate (see James and James 1989). For instance, Sheridan (1992) considered other attributes of climate and found that new accountants working in firms that valued interpersonal relationships stayed in the jobs there much longer than did those working in firms that emphasized accomplishment of tasks, the median survival time being forty-five months and thirty-one months respectively. Most of all, the *fit* between dimensions of climate and personal values may shape loyalty to a company more than effects of the climate itself. In keeping with this view, Chatman (1991) and O'Reilly, Chatman, and Caldwell (1991) found that new accountants whose personal values matched those of their employers exhibited higher inclinations to stay.

Promotions. The data in Table 3-2 reveal that promotions modestly predicted turnover ($r = -.15$). The inclusion of zero by its credibility interval and the significant chi-square indicate that this relationship varies across different conditions. Perhaps, dissimilar constructs assessed by promotion indices may underpin such between-study variation (Hunter and Schmidt 1990b). That is, current scales might assess different, though related, aspects of job promotions, among them satisfaction with promotion, opportunities for promotion, or actual promotions. As Carson, Carson, Griffeth, and Steel (1993) observed, these operationalizations differ as to whether they measure affect (satisfaction with promotion), beliefs (perceived opportunities for promotion), or behaviors (actual promotion). Moreover, equivalency in measurement cannot be assumed because employees may be dissatisfied with their current rate of promotion but still perceive ample prospects for advancement. Conversely, promoted employees may feel satisfied with their *current rates* of advancement, but expect limited promotional *opportunities* beyond their current position.

Because these operationalizations affect turnover in distinctly different ways, we computed separate meta-analyses for them and present the results in Table 3-2. Here again, satisfaction about promotion and perceived opportunities for promotion modestly predicted turnover. Actual promotions, by contrast, strongly predicted turnover ($r = -.45$). This sizable correlation was derived from three studies; one sample may represent an outlier, its inflated correlation being $-.81$ (Stumpf and Dawley 1981; second sample). After removing this aberrant element, the corrected correlation between actual promotion and turnover shrank from $-.45$ to $-.35$, which still indicates that actual promotions have an appreciable impact on retention.

Table 3-3 Job Content

PREDICTOR	k	N	Mean r ($\bar{r}_{obs}$)	Corrected Mean r ($\bar{r}_{cor}$)	Corrected Variance (V_{pop})	Percentage Artifactual Variance	95% Credibility Interval	X^2
Job Content/Job Characteristics								
Job scope	7	1,604	−.12	−.13	.0261	16.08	−.44 to .19	43.53*
Routinization	6	3,707	.08	.09	.0011	64.69	.03 to −.16	9.35
Work satisfaction	25	7,632	−.16	−.19	.0142	22.50	−.42 to .05	111.13*
Job stress	5	779	.17	.19	.0000	100.00	.19 to .19	1.18
Intrinsic/Internal Motivation	2	1,681	−.12	−.13	.0000	100.00	−13 to −.13	.24
Job involvement	8	2,816	−.13	−.17	.0147	24.04	−.40 to .07	33.27*
Professionalism	4	3,390	−.01	−.02	.0000	100.00	−.02 to −.02	2.77
Managerial motivation	2	753	−.14	−.15	.0001	95.72	−.17 to −.12	2.10

Note. k = the number of samples; N = the number of employees

Mean r = average correlation across all studies (weighted by their sample size); corrected mean r = average correlation across all studies which has been corrected for measurement errors; corrected variance = variance of corrected correlations across studies; percentage artifactual variance = degree to which statistical artifacts explain variance in observed correlations; 95% credibility interval = interval around the mean corrected correlation which comprises 95 percent of corrected correlations; and X^2 = chi-square test of whether between-study variance in observed correlations is entirely due to sampling error.

*p < .05.

Source. Authors' calculations.

Job Content and Intrinsic Motivation

The accuracy of job content and intrinsic motivation as predictors of turnover is shown in Table 3-3.

Job scope. Job scope, the overall complexity and challenge of work duties, sustained job incumbency, although this effect may depend on moderators. A likely moderator is the strength of growth need. Hackman and Oldham (1980) conceptualized that job complexity most enhances satisfaction with work and commitment to the organization in employees who have strong growth needs. Loher, Noe, Moeller, and Fitzgerald's meta-analysis (1985) found that job complexity and job satisfaction correlated .57 for employees with high growth needs but correlated only .32 for those with weak growth needs.

Routinization. Routinization, or the degree to which a job is repetitive (Price and Mueller 1981), has been examined in a few studies. Predictably, employees doing routine work were likely to quit: r = .09.

Work satisfaction. Work satisfaction—reflecting experienced affect to the entire intrinsic attributes of the job—predicted terminations better than did perceptions of specific task attributes. Yet work satisfaction exhibited a weaker relationship to exits ($r = -.19$) than it did in Steel and Ovalle's meta-analysis (1984). Still, the larger number of studies reviewed in this meta-analysis ($k = 25$ compared to $k = 15$) could account for the discrepancy of result. Other moderator tests also suggest variations between studies, which may reflect different unemployment rates across studies and varying time intervals between measurements of satisfaction and turnover across samples (Carsten and Spector 1987; Steel and Ovalle 1984; Steel and Griffeth 1989).

Job stress. Though neglected by researchers, job stress moderately and positively predicts turnover ($r = .19$), a finding that is shown in Table 3-3.

Intrinsic or internal motivation. Theories of job characteristics hold that internal motivation—or self-esteem based on job accomplishments—is derived from doing complex, enriched work (Hackman and Oldham 1980). Because complex jobs bind employees to firms, it is not surprisingly that internal motivation also ($r = -.13$) decreases the incidence of withdrawal from an organization.

Job involvement. Logically, employees who feel involved in their jobs, psychologically identified with their jobs, may feel bound to their jobs (Kanungo 1982). This intuitive hypothesis is supported by data shown in Table 3-3 indicating that involvement with a job ($r = -.17$) moderately predicts a diminishment of turnover.

Professionalism. Many sociologists contend that norms of efficiency and bureaucratic control in the work place clash with professional standards and ethical codes, weakening people's commitment to an organization (Abbott 1988; Kramer 1974; Raelin 1986). Despite those persuasive arguments and observations, our meta-analysis found that professionalism (adherence to professional values and standards) did not affect withdrawal ($r = -.01$). Quite likely, unrepresentative sampling accounts for this null finding, and absence of moderators. All the studies on the relationship between professionalism and turnover were carried out in hospital settings. Because hospitals, especially teaching hospitals affiliated with medical schools, are devoted to patient care, the personnel may face little conflict between their professional standards and practices of the hospitals. In other organizations that value efficiency and bureaucratic control over professional norms, professionalism may influence turnover. The extent to which employers adhere to the professional values and standards of the employees may in part determine whether or not professionalism induces people to seek other jobs.

Managerial motivation. Managerial orientation—or a drive to manage people—slowed the exodus from organizations ($r = -.15$; see Butler, Laurent, and Miner 1983). Notwithstanding the absence of moderators, this

Table 3-4 External Environment Factors

PREDICTOR	k	N	Mean r ($\bar{r}_{obs}$)	Corrected Mean r ($\bar{r}_{cor}$)	Corrected Variance (V_{pop})	Percentage Artifactual Variance	95% Credibility Interval	X^2
Alternative Employment								
Attraction and availability	27	10,447	.10	.11	.0084	28.48	–.07 to .29	96.01*
Comparison of alternatives to present job	7	1,635	.24	.26	.0092	33.44	.08 to .45	21.47*

Note. k = the number of samples; N = the number of employees.

Mean r = average correlation across all studies (weighted by their sample size); corrected mean r = average correlation across all studies which has been corrected for measurement errors; corrected variance = variance of corrected correlations across studies; percentage artifactual variance = degree to which statistical artifacts explain variance in observed correlations; 95% credibility interval = interval around the mean corrected correlation which comprises 95 percent of corrected correlations; and X^2 = chi-square test of whether between-study variance in observed correlations is entirely due to sampling error.

*$p < .05$.

Source. Authors' calculations.

negative correlation may likely vary across occupations. The subjects of all the existing investigations of how managerial orientation deters exits have been military officers. Managerial orientation does persuade people in leadership positions to stay, but the personality trait may not similarly affect those in other jobs.

External Environment

Alternative employment. Organizational scientists and labor economists universally proclaim that employment opportunities stimulate job changes (Forrest, Cummings, and Johnson 1977; Gerhart 1990; Mobley 1977; Mobley et al. 1979; Price and Mueller 1986). Data showing that the perceived attraction and availability of other jobs only modestly encouraged individuals to quit ($r = .11$), a finding that approximates Steel and Griffeth's (1989) estimated .13 correlation, are shown in Table 3-4. This modest effect deviates from the findings of labor economists that there are strong relations between unemployment rates and quit rates (Mobley 1982a; Hulin, Roznowski, and Hachiya 1985) and illustrates the fact that relationships can change across different levels of aggregation (Rousseau 1985).

In a critique, Steel and Griffeth (1989) speculated that several methodological factors may explain why perceived alternatives (PA) modestly impact resignations. For one, most of the studies on PA effects drew samples from one organization, one industry, one region, one occupation, and one time period. Such homogeneous sampling may restrict the variance of the PA measures, attenuating their effects on turnover. By contrast, the studies of labor economists sample broadly across various occupational and geographic lines, contributing variance to aggregate indices of employment opportunity.

Table 3-5 Withdrawal Cognitions

PREDICTOR	k	N	Mean r ($\bar{r}_{obs}$)	Corrected Mean r ($\bar{r}_{cor}$)	Corrected Variance (V_{pop})	Percentage Artifactual Variance	95% Credibility Interval	X^2
Search intentions	24	6,601	.25	.27	.0064	36.00	.12 to .43	66.69*
Quit intentions	70	78,078	.31	.35	.0266	4.81	.03 to .67	2173.10*
Thoughts of quitting	17	5,007	.25	.27	.0203	15.00	−.01 to .55	111.39*
Withdrawal cognitions	4	486	.28	.30	.0022	78.26	.21 to .39	5.12
Probability of finding another alternative	17	5,007	.12	.14	.0026	64.34	.04 to .24	26.42*
Expected utility of alternative	4	2,276	−.01	−.01	.0215	9.51	−.29 to .28	42.08*
Expected utility of present job	4	2,276	.23	.25	.0022	47.03	.16 to .34	8.51*
Expected utility of search	6	1,175	.21	.22	.0072	42.65	.05 to .38	14.19*
Expected utility of quitting	7	1,349	.23	.25	.0000	100.00	.25 to .25	5.62
Organizational commitment	36	13,085	−.17	−.18	.0063	32.22	−.33 to −.03	111.73*

Note. k = the number of samples; N = the number of employees.

Mean r = average correlation across all studies (weighted by their sample size); corrected mean r = average correlation across all studies which has been corrected for measurement errors; corrected variance = variance of corrected correlations across studies; percentage artifactual variance = degree to which statistical artifacts explain variance in observed correlations; 95% credibility interval = interval around the mean corrected correlation which comprises 95 percent of corrected correlations; and X^2 = chi-square test of whether between-study variance in observed correlations is entirely due to sampling error.

*$p < .05$.

Source: Authors' calculations.

In a similar vein, extreme turnover base rates (ordinarily low quit rates) in most studies possibly constrained turnover variance, weakening the relationship between PA and turnover. Although pervading most research, extreme turnover rates may be most problematic in the PA literature where homogeneous occupational sampling *and* low quit base rates restrict the range of both the predictor and the criterion. In such circumstances, the attenuation bias on variable correlations is multiplicative rather than additive. Poor instrumentation may partly underlie the modest correlations between PA and quits (Steel and Griffeth 1989). That is, most investigations used global, one-item PA ratings to assess a complex multifaceted construct (see Mobley et al., 1979). Quite possibly, deficient and unreliable PA scales also underestimate the observed effects of employment alternatives on quits.

Variables of the Withdrawal Process

Withdrawal cognitions. A fundamental tenet of modern thought on turnover is that decisions to withdraw from the work place best portend subsequent withdrawal (Hulin, Roznowski and Hachiya 1985; Mobley et al., 1979; Price and Mueller 1986; Rusbult and Farrell 1983; Steers and Mowday 1981). This

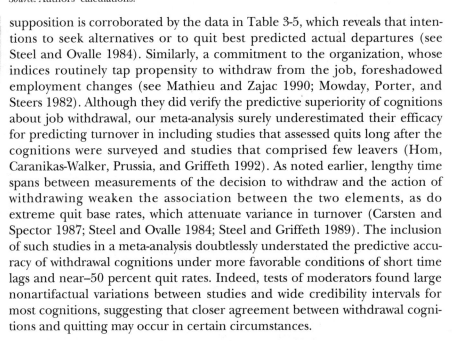

Table 3-6 Other Withdrawal Behaviors

PREDICTOR	k	N	Mean r ($\bar{r}_{obs}$)	Corrected Mean r ($\bar{r}_{cor}$)	Corrected Variance (V_{pop})	Percentage Artifactual Variance	95% Credibility Interval	X^2
Lateness	2	413	.14	.15	.0000	100.00	.15 to .15	.00
Absenteeism	28	4,371	.24	.33	.0079	56.67	.15 to .50	49.41*
Performance	56	15,318	−.16	−.19	.0036	11.87	−.57 to .19	471.97*

Note. k = the number of samples; N = the number of employees.

Mean r = average correlation across all studies (weighted by their sample size); corrected mean r = average correlation across all studies which has been corrected for measurement errors; corrected variance = variance of corrected correlations across studies; percentage artifactual variance = degree to which statistical artifacts explain variance in observed correlations; 95% credibility interval = interval around the mean corrected correlation which comprises 95 percent of corrected correlations; and X^2 = chi-square test of whether between-study variance in observed correlations is entirely due to sampling error.

*$p < .05$.

Source. Authors' calculations.

supposition is corroborated by the data in Table 3-5, which reveals that intentions to seek alternatives or to quit best predicted actual departures (see Steel and Ovalle 1984). Similarly, a commitment to the organization, whose indices routinely tap propensity to withdraw from the job, foreshadowed employment changes (see Mathieu and Zajac 1990; Mowday, Porter, and Steers 1982). Although they did verify the predictive superiority of cognitions about job withdrawal, our meta-analysis surely underestimated their efficacy for predicting turnover in including studies that assessed quits long after the cognitions were surveyed and studies that comprised few leavers (Hom, Caranikas-Walker, Prussia, and Griffeth 1992). As noted earlier, lengthy time spans between measurements of the decision to withdraw and the action of withdrawing weaken the association between the two elements, as do extreme quit base rates, which attenuate variance in turnover (Carsten and Spector 1987; Steel and Ovalle 1984; Steel and Griffeth 1989). The inclusion of such studies in a meta-analysis doubtlessly understated the predictive accuracy of withdrawal cognitions under more favorable conditions of short time lags and near–50 percent quit rates. Indeed, tests of moderators found large nonartifactual variations between studies and wide credibility intervals for most cognitions, suggesting that closer agreement between withdrawal cognitions and quitting may occur in certain circumstances.

Expected utilities of withdrawal acts. Consistent with leading social psychological models (Ajzen 1991; Bagozzi and Warshaw 1990; Fishbein and Ajzen 1975; Triandis 1979), our meta-analysis showed that terminations emerge from conscious calculations of perceived costs and benefits. Rather than quitting impulsively over poor work conditions, many employees formulate decisions to withdraw after considering the possible results. Therefore, they would desert their work place if they believe that job seeking or quitting will be beneficial (if for instance, they could then obtain a better job elsewhere), and if they believe that they can avoid or minimize negative repercussions, such as that of losing a sizable investment in the job.

Other Withdrawal Behaviors

Other forms of withdrawal from the work place—notably, absenteeism ($r = .33$) and lateness ($r = .15$)—that forecast turnover later are shown in Table 3-6. The positive relationship between absence and quitting accords with Mitra, Jenkins, and Gupta's recent meta-analysis (1992). These same researchers found that the duration of a study moderates the correlation between absence and turnover. There is a stronger covariation in short studies that last 12 months or less. They also reported that this relationship is moderated by the type of industry: Stronger associations are to be found in manufacturing settings than in nonmanufacturing settings.

Such positive covariation between milder forms of work avoidance and quitting—the most extreme and irrevocable form of withdrawal—is consistent with a progression-of-withdrawal model (Hulin 1991; Rossé and Miller 1984), that posits dissatisfied employees progressively enacting more extreme manifestations of job withdrawal over time (see Rosse 1988).

We include performance as an act of withdrawal because many theorists submit that passive job behavior reflects dissatisfaction and thus foreshadows quitting (Brayfield and Crockett 1955; Hulin 1991; Mobley 1977; Steers and Mowday 1981; Vroom 1964). Our meta-analysis results reveal a modest negative relationship between job performance and turnover ($r = -.19$), which accords with Williams and Livingstone's recent meta-analysis (1994). This inverse correlation between performance and departure contradicts conventional views that more capable personnel resign—presumably because they have more employment options (see Jackofsky 1984). Nonetheless, tests of moderators suggest that positive correlations between performance and quitting may sometimes emerge (McEvoy and Cascio 1987). Allison (1974) and Schwab (1991) found that productive scholars left research universities more often than less accomplished academicians did.

Rewards that are tied to job effectiveness may moderate relationships between job performance and quitting (Williams and Livingstone 1994). In organizations where rewards were contingent on performance, the better performers (who therefore receive more rewards) would be more satisfied with their jobs and be less likely to quit. Marginal performers in these organizations would receive fewer benefits, become less satisfied with their jobs, and therefore more likely quit. Williams and Livingstone's meta-analysis did, in fact, find that contingent reward systems strengthened negative correlations between performance and turnover.

CONCLUDING REMARKS

These meta-analytical findings carry significant theoretical and practical implications. First, the findings suggest which managerial interventions may be likely to control voluntary quits, a subject addressed in later chapters.

They provide a stronger empirical foundation for prescriptions than do anecdotal evidence or speculation, the prime basis for popular advice. These results also identify robust causal antecedents that any viable model of turnover must incorporate. All the same, we caution that our meta-analyses uncovered limits to our generalizations about the causes of turnover. Many moderator tests indicate that effects of these determinants of turnover, and the direction of those effects, vary across situations and populations. Such persistent evidence of inconsistency suggests that greater theoretical attention might be paid to moderators. All too often, theorists on turnover overstate the generality of their formulations by ignoring boundary conditions. Our meta-analysis also omitted other influential antecedents too rarely examined to be included in a meta-analysis. At the very least, this meta-analysis did call attention to this oversight. Last, even though meta-analysis is, arguably, the most significant methodological breakthrough in the organizational sciences, we must bear in mind the familiar adage, "garbage in, garbage out." After all, it is the quality of empirical studies that determines the validity of conclusions drawn from a meta-analysis.

THEORIES OF
EMPLOYEE TURNOVER

During the past twenty years, turnover researchers have devoted considerable attention to the reasons employees quit jobs. The low turnover predictions by traditional empirical work partly inspired this contemporary theoretical orientation (Locke 1976; Mobley 1977). In this chapter, we review modern conceptual developments, describing and evaluating various theoretical frameworks for understanding turnover. Although turnover has been researched since the turn of the century, March and Simon (1958) pioneered the first formal theory, proposing an *explicit, formal,* and *systematic* conceptual analysis of the withdrawal process.

MARCH AND SIMON: THEORY
OF ORGANIZATIONAL EQUILIBRIUM

In *Organizations,* March and Simon (1958) introduced a general theory of motivation called *organizational equilibrium* (Barnard 1938; Simon 1947), which describes the organization's ability to pay members to motivate them to continue their participation. Each member participates so long as the inducements, such as pay, that are offered match or exceed (measured in terms of the member's values and available alternatives) the member's contributions. Each individual receives a set of inducements from an organization, with each inducement having a separate utility value. In return, the member contributes work, called "contributions," to the organization. Each contribution has its own utility, which is the value of the alternative that an individual forgoes to make the contribution. Both the individual and organization strive for an equilibrium state between inducements and contributions. The ensuing equilibrium assures survival of an organization.

Increases in the balance of inducement utilities over contribution utilities reduce the propensity of the member to leave the organization; decreases in that balance enhance the propensity. The balance between inducements and contributions is a function of two distinct, but interdependent, motivational components: the perceived desirability and the perceived ease of leaving the organization. The root causes of these direct determinants of withdrawal from organizations are portrayed in Figure 4-1.

Perceived Desirability of Movement

The primary influencing factor is the individual's satisfaction with the job. That is, job satisfaction reduces perceived desirability of movement.

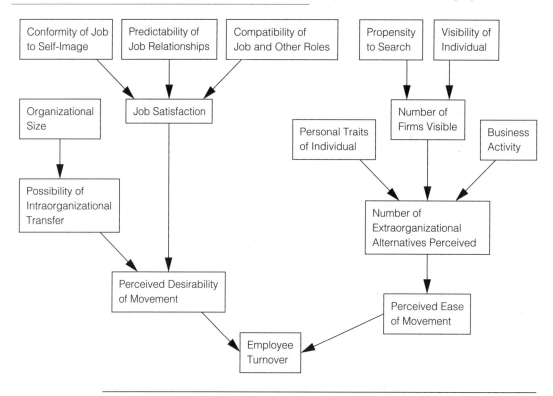

Figure 4-1 March and Simon's Model of Motivation. (Adapted from J. G. March and H. A. Simon, *Organizations.* **New York: Wiley, (1958): 99, 106.)**

March and Simon identified three sources of job satisfaction. First, conformity of job characteristics to self-image enhances job satisfaction: "Dissatisfaction arises from a disparity between reality and the ego-ideal held by the individual. The greater the disparity, the more pronounced the desire to escape from the situation" (1958, p. 94). Relevant dimensions of self-image—namely, self-evaluations of independence, worth, and competencies or interests—are then satisfied (or frustrated) by supervisory practices, wages, participation in job assignments, and educational level. Besides a fit between person and job, predictability in instrumental relationships on the job and compatibility of work requirements with other role requirements promote job satisfaction. Interrole compatibility in turn depends on congruency of work-time patterns with those of other roles and work-group size.

Apart from job satisfaction, organizational size shapes the desirability of moving. The "larger the organization, the greater the perceived possibility or organizational transfer, and therefore, the less the perceived desirability of leaving the organization" (ibid., p. 99). Paradoxically, organizational size may *increase* desirability of movement because organizational and other roles become less compatible in larger firms (creating more dissatisfaction).

Perceived Ease of Movement

Drawing from the well-established tenet that "under nearly all conditions the most accurate single predictor of labor turnover is the state of the economy," March and Simon specified antecedents of perceived ease of movement (ibid., p. 100). They proposed that plentiful extraorganizational alternatives enhance perceived ease of movement. In turn, business activity and personal attributes determine an individual's available extraorganizational alternatives. In particular, young, male, high-status, or short-tenure employees perceive that they have greater ease of movement.

March and Simon further conceptualized that the number of visible firms increases the number of perceived extraorganizational alternatives. In turn, the company's prestige, the size of the organization, the production of a well-known product, the number of high-status occupations and employees, and rapid growth determine the visibility of the firm. In addition, the individual's residence and number of outside organizations to which she belongs increase her personal contacts, which expand the number of visible firms.

Because companies also scan people, an individual's visibility increases the number of visible organizations (who would seek to employ her). Such visibility among individuals may depend on the heterogeneity of personal contacts, high social status, and individual uniqueness. March and Simon posited that the individual's propensity to search them out boosts the number of visible companies. Job satisfaction and habituation in turn shape the propensity to search. "Dissatisfaction makes movement more desirable and also (by stimulating search) makes it appear more feasible" (ibid., p. 105). By contrast, habituation to a particular job, which mounts with age and job tenure, diminishes the propensity to search.

Review

Although few studies *directly* tested March and Simon's model (cf. Mobley 1982a), their conceptualization nonetheless influenced successive generations of theorists. Their seminal work shaped much prevailing contemporary thinking about turnover, including that of Hulin, Roznowski, and Hachiya (1985), Lee and Mitchell (1994), Mobley (1977), and Steers and Mowday (1981). More directly, Jackofsky and her colleagues (1984; Jackofsky and Slocum 1987) incorporated March and Simon's constructs of desirability and ease of movement into a model relating job performance to turnover. This persistent influence over thirty years illustrates the durability of March and Simon's explanatory scheme.

PORTER AND STEERS: MET-EXPECTATION MODEL

Many years elapsed before a new theory emerged. In 1973, Porter and Steers posited that met expectations were the central determinant of decisions about turnover. They argued that, although most employees value pay, promotions, supervisory relations, and peer-group interactions, individuals have distinctive sets of expectations. If an organization fails to meet an individual's set of expectations, dissatisfaction will result, and the probability of withdrawal increase. They view this "as a process of balancing perceived or potential rewards with desired expectations" (1973, p. 171).

More specifically, Porter and Steers suggested that expectations of work rewards are fluid from the beginning of employment to some later period when the individual decides to stay or leave. Two new employees, holding similar job expectations at the outset, may later find their expectations fulfilled in different ways. One employee's expected rewards may be met or exceeded by the job, resulting in satisfaction and participation; the other may discover that the job does not confirm her expectations, inducing dissatisfaction and withdrawal. To summarize, Porter and Steers posited a causal sequence, wherein unmet expectations → job dissatisfaction → turnover.

Review

Porter and Steers's model represents a pivotal theoretical advancement in turnover research. They introduced a parsimonious, integrative construct—namely, met expectations—that summarizes the effects of myriad work-related determinants on turnover (via reward experiences) and acknowledges the existence of personal attributes, which underpin expectation levels. In line with their view, a recent meta-analysis (Wanous, et al., 1992) found that met expectations correlated most closely with job attitudes then with intentions to quit and, last, with turnover. What is more, their model became the dominant explanation for why realistic job previews (RJP) work (Datel and Lifrak 1969; Wanous 1973; Youngberg 1963). RJPs communicate positive and negative features of a job to new employees, and such communication bolsters tenure in the job (Premack and Wanous 1985; Wanous 1992). Supporting the Porter-Steers formulation, various studies have confirmed that RJPs reduce turnover by deflating initial expectations, leading to higher fulfillment of expectations on the job (Premack and Wanous 1985; Hom, Griffeth, Palich, and Bracker 1993).

Some issues continue, however, to elude scholarly scrutiny. One involves the met-expectations concept itself. In its present form, this concept may be too simplistic (Ilgen and Dugoni 1977). According to Festinger (1947), cognitive dissonance occurs when initial expectations are not consistent with later experience. Dissatisfaction results. Dissonance is aroused regardless of whether the disconfirming experience is positive or negative. Dissonance theory predicts dissatisfaction when expectations are unmet or are exceeded and satisfaction when expectations are met. Thus, dissonance theory predicts a quadratic relationship between met expectations and job satisfaction. In contrast, Porter and Steers (1973) hypothesized that most dissatisfaction would arise when expectations are unmet and would decline

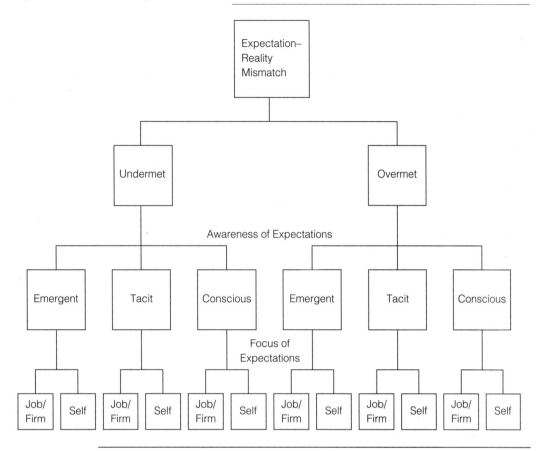

Figure 4-2 Louis' Taxonomy of Unmet Expectations. (M. R. Louis, "Surprise and sense making—what newcomers experience in entering unfamiliar organizational settings," *Administrative Science Quarterly* **25 (1980): 237.)**

(linearly or monotonically) as expectations are met or exceeded. Griffeth (1981) tested these two competing predictions and found stronger support for a curvilinear relationship between dissatisfaction and met expectations.

Louis (1980) further argued that the Porter-Steers notion fails to differentiate between initial expectations that are not fulfilled by the job ("unmet") and those that are surpassed ("overmet"). She reasoned that overmet expectations produce surprise rather than dissatisfaction. She also criticized the Porter-Steers viewpoint as simplistically presuming that all preentry expectations are conscious, clearly defined, and refer to qualities of the job. To overcome the concept's limitations, she introduced a comprehensive taxonomy of different types of unmet expectations based on three dimensions (see Figure 4-2). Besides the direction of the mismatch between expectation and reality, she suggested that expectation has a focus (initial expectations can refer to the self or job) and that there is a level of awareness about expectation (expectations may be conscious or preconscious).

To illustrate awareness in expectation, she discussed possible disconfirmation of unconscious job expectations, such as unexpected features of the job, and quoted a newcomer who said, "I had no idea how important windows were to me until I'd spent a week in a staff room without any" (1980, p. 238). To illustrate expectation focus, Louis mentioned that newcomers may harbor mistaken assumptions about their proficiency ("I'm less competent on this job than I expected to be") or attitudes ("I knew I would put in lots of overtime but I did not expect that sixty-five-hour weeks would be so grueling"). Louis's taxonomy holds great promise for understanding how unmet expectations affect turnover and awaits future validation. Her conceptualization may clarify how RJPs improve job survival because RJPs may also establish entry expectations for the job and the worker, besides promoting met expectations (see Meglino, DeNisi, Youngblood, and Williams 1988).

Though Porter and Steers (1973) acknowledged that unmet expectations do not invariably evoke quits, they did not state why this occurs. Conceivably, some disappointed newcomers do not withdraw because they lack viable alternatives to the present job (Wanous 1973). Thus, Porter and Steers omitted a key moderator of the unmet expectations → turnover pathway: perceived alternatives. Further, they prescribed use of RJPs to deflate newcomers' expectations so that the existing job might more easily fulfill their expectations and improve the chances of their staying on the job. An *increase* in initial job expectations may, however, benefit new entrants to certain occupations. Meglino et al. (1988) showed that an "enhancement" RJP promotes recruits' survival in the Army by reversing overly pessimistic expectations about their ability to complete basic training. Porter and Steers (1973) nevertheless recognized that more theoretical work must examine the psychology of the decisional processes underlying turnover. This call was soon answered by Mobley.

MOBLEY: TURNOVER PROCESS MODEL

In response to Locke's observation (1976) that the relationship between satisfaction and turnover have rarely exceeded .40, Mobley (1977) envisioned a series of intermediate linkages between evaluation of the present job—the result of which is satisfaction or dissatisfaction—and turnover. This decisional sequence is illustrated in Figure 4-3. Job dissatisfaction stimulates thoughts of quitting, which elicit assessments of the utility of seeking other employment (for instance, the chances of finding comparable work) and turnover costs (among them, the loss of unvested pension benefits). If the exit will not be costly, the expectation that it would be beneficial to seek another job will induce intentions of making a search and, thereafter, searching. After finding alternatives, dissatisfied employees will evaluate them and compare them with the present job. When the alternatives are found to be the more attractive, the disparity motivates the employee to quit.

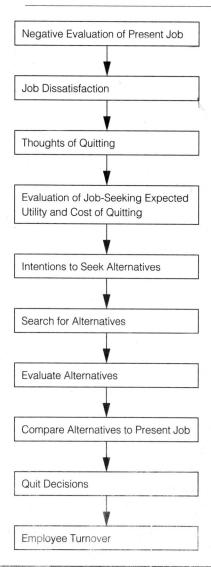

Figure 4-3 Mobley's Intermediate Linkages Model of Turnover. (Adapted from W. H. Mobley, "Intermediate linkages in the relationship between job satisfaction and employee turnover," *Journal of Applied Psychology* **62 (1977): 238. Copyright 1977 by the American Psychological Association. Adapted by permission.)**

Review

In the annals of turnover work, Mobley's theory has most furthered understanding of the withdrawal process and has drawn the most empirical scrutiny. Though March and Simon (1985) provided impetus for modern theory and research, Mobley's 1977 model dominates all work on psychological approaches to turnover. This model stimulated substantial investigations on its validity and inspired subsequent theoretical elaborations or refine-ments. Some theorists (such as Mobley et al. 1979) expanded Mobley's model by introducing more distal determinants of the process from satisfac-tion to quitting. Others have restated or clarified this termination process (Steers and Mowday 1981). Still, other scholars have refined this model by reconfiguring intervening mechanisms that translate dissatisfaction (Hom and Griffeth 1991) yet others regard Mobley's withdrawal sequence as only one of multiple routes to turnover (Lee and Mitchell 1994). If they have not adopted the model in its entirety, other turnover theorists have nonetheless adopted one or more of the theoretical constructs Mobley pioneered—notably, withdrawal intentions (Price and Mueller 1986) and perceived alter-natives (Hulin, Roznowski, and Hachiya 1985; Rusbult and Farrell 1983). In one form or another, Mobley's conceptualization continues to infuse present-day thinking about organizational withdrawal. All told, Mobley's theory is unmatched in its far-reaching and enduring influence.

Early investigations tested an abbreviated version of Mobley's model that Mobley, Horner, and Hollingsworth (1978) had proposed (Coverdale and Terborg 1980; Miller, Katerberg, and Hulin 1979; Mowday, Koberg, and McArthur 1984; Peters, Jackofsky, and Salter 1981; Spencer, Steers, and Mowday 1983). While generally supported (Hom, Caranikis-Walker, Prussia, and Griffeth 1992), tests of the abbreviated 1978 model do not directly sub-stantiate the earlier more elaborate model (Hom, Griffeth, and Sellaro 1984). Though surprisingly scant, the few complete tests of the original 1977 formulation have consistently disputed several model pathways, although upholding most pathways (Griffeth and Hom 1983; Hom, Griffeth and Sellaro 1984; Laker 1991; Lee 1988; Steel, Lounsbury, and Horst 1981). These mixed findings prompted the development of a growing number of alternative structural networks linking Mobley's constructs that secured stronger corroboration than Mobley's original structure (Blau 1993; Hom and Griffeth 1991; Hom, Griffeth, and Sellaro 1984; Hom, Caranikas-Walker, Prussia and Griffeth 1992; Jaros et al. 1993; Sager, Griffeth, and Hom 1992).

HOM AND GRIFFETH: REVISED
INTERMEDIATE-PROCESSES MODEL

Responding to growing challenges to Mobley's structural relations (Hom, Griffeth, and Sellaro 1984; Lee 1988; Steel, Lounsbury, and Horst 1981), Hom, Griffeth, and Sellaro (1984) proposed an alternative network, illustrated in Figure 4-4. They suggested that dissatisfaction evokes thoughts of quitting, which in turn, stimulate decisions to quit and an evaluation of the expected costs and benefits of search and quitting. At this juncture, employees follow one of two paths. Some employees who perceive that alternatives are available undertake a job search. They then compare the alternatives with their present job and, when the alternatives are better, they quit. Other employees, who may expect to find another job easily or who may pursue alternatives

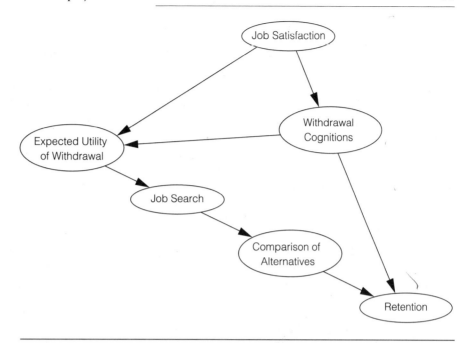

Figure 4-4 Hom and Griffeth's Alternative Linkage Model of Turnover. (P. Hom and R. Griffeth "Structural equations modeling test of a turnover theory," *Journal of Applied Psychology* **76: (1991): 357. Copyright 1991 by the American Psychological Association. Adapted by permission.)**

other than work—simply resign after deciding to quit. The path analytical test by Hom, Griffeth, and Sellaro (1984) supported this causal structure better than Mobley's original model. Nonetheless, several model pathways were empirically derived rather than theorized *a priori* (James, Mulaik, and Brett 1982) and Hom, Griffeth and Sellaro measured employees' generalized impressions of alternative work rather than their perceptions of specific jobs.

Afterward, Hom and Griffeth (1991) attempted to cross-validate the structural alternative proposed by Hom et al. (1984) in two nursing samples, using structural equations modeling (SEM) and more precise measures of specific job offers. In study 1, they investigated the dimensionality of model constructs. Discriminating most constructs, SEM analysis identified, however, a global construct underlying thoughts of quitting, search intentions, and quit decisions. After reconceptualizing withdrawal intentions as different facets of the same construct, Hom and Griffeth supported the structural model shown in Figure 4-4. In study 2, surveying new nurses on three occasions, the researchers tested causal priorities among model variables more rigorously. By and large, this SEM analysis supported the theorized causal directions and demonstrated that some causal effects occur instantaneously and others transpire over time. Moreover, causal effects systematically changed during the assimilation of a newcomer into an organization.

Though their validation is encouraging, Hom and Griffeth's revision of Mobley's withdrawal stages requires further corroboration. Jaros et al. (1993) and Hom, Kinicki, and Domm (1989) similarly verified a global withdrawal cognition, but Sager et al. (1992) upheld a multidimensional conceptualization. The theoretical model merits substantiation in samples of other workers, who may withdraw from organizations for different reasons than nurses do (Hom et al. 1992). More contemporary formulations suggest that Mobley's (and Hom and Griffeth's [1991]) depiction of intervening mechanisms between dissatisfaction and turnover is incomplete. Ironically, Mobley and his colleagues (Mobley et al. 1979; Mobley 1982a) theorized that the attraction of the job—or future improvements in the work role or future attainment of other desirable work roles within the company—may interrupt the translation of dissatisfaction into departure: Dissatisfied employees may decide *not* to leave if they foresee improvements in the job. Similarly, Hulin, Roznowski, and Hackiya (1985) and Steers and Mowday (1981) argued that an alternative reaction to dissatisfaction besides (or before) departure is to improve the workplace—either by eliminating the frustrations of the job or by moving to other positions in the organization. Future investigators might elaborate on the Hom-Griffeth model by introducing other variables that mediate the impact of dissatisfaction on exits.

PRICE: STRUCTURAL MODEL

In a comprehensive review of the literature, the sociologist, James Price, developed a model that integrated past findings about turnover (1977). He theorized that pay, integration, instrumental communication, formal communication, and centralization shape job satisfaction, which influences turnover. Further, opportunity—or the availability of alternative employment—moderates the relationship between satisfaction and turnover. Trial evaluations of this early model subsequently inspired a more comprehensive theory (Bluedorn 1982; Price and Bluedorn 1979; Martin 1979).

Expanding Price's 1977 model, Price and Mueller (1981) proposed that repetitive work reduces satisfaction and that workers who are participating in job-related decisions, receiving work-related information, forming close friendships with others at work, earning good and fair compensation, and enjoying opportunities for promotion are more likely to be satisfied (see Figure 4-5). Job satisfaction, in turn, increases intentions of staying, whereas professionalism, generalized training, and minimal kinship responsibility weaken these intentions. Together, intentions to stay and opportunities for employment elsewhere determine turnover.

Subsequently, Price and Mueller published, in 1986, a revision of their 1981 version. They introduced two antecedents to satisfaction, role overload and family pay, and another determinant of decisions to quit (and, thus, of commitment to the organization), the size of the company and work groups in it. They renamed participation to reflect centralization (the concentration of

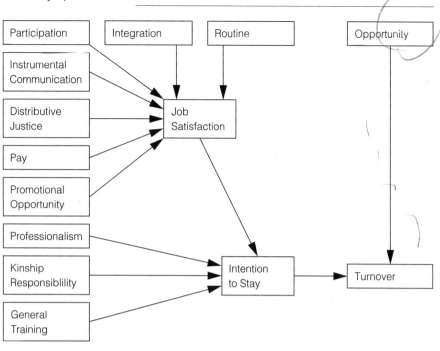

Figure 4-5 Price and Mueller's 1981 Model of Turnover. (Adapted from J. Price and C. Mueller, "A causal model of turnover for nurses," *Academy of Management Journal* 24 (1981): 547.)

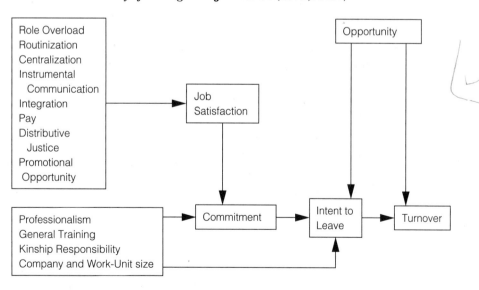

Figure 4-6 Price and Mueller's 1986 Model of Turnover. (Adapted from J. Price and C. Mueller, *Absenteeism and turnover of hospital employees*, Greenwich, Conn.: JAI Press (1986): 10.)

power) and interposed commitment to the organization between job satisfaction and intentions to quit. Their theoretical version is illustrated in Figure 4-6.

Review

Price's theorizing and research represent landmark contributions to research into turnover. Unlike more speculative theorists, he identified in 1977 a comprehensive set of determinants of turnover that was based on a systematic and broad review of the literature of research in labor economics, sociology, and psychology. Thus, his causal determinants are empirically well grounded (based on consistent empirical findings) and include explanatory constructs historically overlooked by organizational researchers. In particular, Price introduced the notions of kinship responsibilities, professionalism, and economic opportunity, which eventually entered the mainstream of modern thought about withdrawal (see Gerhart 1990; Hulin, Roznowski, and Hachiya 1985; Rusbult and Farrell 1983; Steers and Mowday 1981). Moreover, Price and Mueller's empirical investigations of their models (1981, 1986) became hallmarks of methodological rigor. They pioneered causal modeling techniques to assess structural networks, evaluating the nomological validity of a theory as well as its predictive validity, the customary preoccupation. They carefully constructed scales to assess model constructs validly and reliably. For example, they factor analyzed items reflecting the same construct and created reliable factor-based scales of items with high factor loadings (average .75 reliability). Such painstaking validation stands in marked contrast to traditional ad hoc operationalizations and provided psychometrically sound scales for investigations into turnover.

Notwithstanding their rigorous methodology, Price and Mueller found that all the components of the 1981 model together explained only 18 percent of turnover's variance. Importantly, they partially verified theorized causal pathways. Although finding significant estimates for nearly 70 percent of predicted causal effects, their research failed to sustain other expected linkages in the model. Surprisingly, they uncovered significance for 20 percent of the pathways theorized to be absent. To improve predictions about turnover, they recommended that intentions to quit be replaced with commitment to the organization and they reconceptualized the meaning of distributive justice, professionalism, and integration. Even so, the revised (and expanded) 1986 model explained only 13 percent of turnover's variance. Here again, Price and Mueller (1986) partially supported their *a priori* causal structure. They obtained significant estimates for roughly 75 percent of theorized causal pathways, but rejected the remaining pathways. Importantly, approximately 40 percent of supposedly *null* pathways were estimated as statistically significant, which contradicted their theoretical predictions.

In summary, the few research studies of the Price-Mueller models partly affirmed their nomological networks. Besides this, a competitive two-sample test by Griffeth and Hom (1990) found that the Price-Mueller models provide less parsimonious explanations of turnover compared with Hom,

Griffeth, and Sellaro's (1984) variant of Mobley's (1977) model. Still, a joint model synthesizing promising concepts from Mobley's and Price and Mueller's models yielded excellent model fit and parsimony. A promising avenue for future inquiry might be the attempted integration between Price and Mueller's structural formulation and process-oriented models (such as those of Hom and Griffeth [1991], Lee and Mitchell [1994], and Steers and Mowday [1981], that explicate the translation of dissatisfaction into terminations. Future validations of the Price-Mueller theories (or their variants) should be performed on samples of workers other than nurses or hospital personnel, who comprise the validation samples for the original models and may follow a different process of withdrawal than would other members of the work force.

MOBLEY, GRIFFETH, HAND, AND MEGLINO: EXPANDED MODEL

Since proposing the 1977 model, Mobley et al. (1979) reviewed the literature on turnover and organized its causes into a heuristic model reflecting many indirect and direct influences on the phenomenon (see Figure 4-7).

Requisites for Intentions

As in the earlier model, the researchers proposed quit intentions as the immediate precursor to turnover. They further conceived intentions (and turnover) as a function of (1) job satisfaction, (2) expected utility of the present work role, and (3) expected utility of alternative work roles.

Job Satisfaction They defined satisfaction as an affective response resulting from evaluation of the job. Drawing from Locke's theory (1969; 1976), they conceptualized that personal values and job-related perceptions shape job evaluation. Basically, job satisfaction derives from the extent to which an employee's important values are attained in the job (Mobley 1982a). Mobley et al. further theorized that satisfaction is present oriented and generates an approach or avoidance orientation toward the job. However, job dissatisfaction imperfectly foreshadows turnover, which also derives from the employee's expectations of conditions in the organization (Mobley 1982a).

Expected Utility of the Present Role Besides satisfaction, the "expected utility of the present role"—that is, an individual's "expectancies that the job will lead to the attainment of various positively or negatively valued outcomes" and expectancy of retaining the current job—also underpins decisions about turnover (Mobley et al. 1979, p. 518). Thus, an employee may not quit a dissatisfying job if she or he expects the job to lead to future better things, such

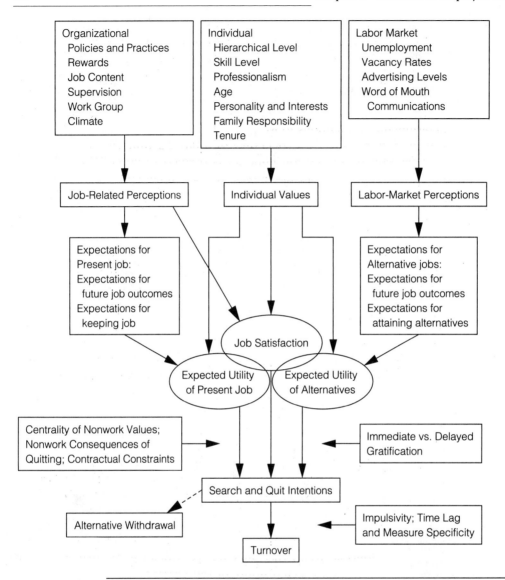

Figure 4-7 Mobley, Griffeth, Hand, and Meglino's Expanded Model of Turnover. (Adapted from W. Mobley, R. Griffeth, H. Hand, and B. Meglino, "A review and conceptual analysis of the employee turnover process," *Psychological Bulletin*, 86 (1979): 517. Copyright 1979 by the American Psychological Association. Adapted by permission.)

as transfer to a better job, promotion, or an improvement in conditions in the organization (Mobley 1982a). The expected utility of the present job thus explains why job satisfaction imperfectly predicts terminations: Optimistic expectations about the job may prevent some dissatisfied employees from leaving; pessimistic expectations about career prospects within the company may induce even satisfied employees to quit.

Expected Utility of Alternative Roles Building on the work of March and Simon (1958), Forrest, Cummings, and Johnson (1977), and Schneider (1976), Mobley et al. posited the expected utility of external alternatives as a third determinant of intentions to withdraw. The expectancy that the alternatives will be better (and the expectancy of attaining those alternatives) also explains why job satisfaction imperfectly predicts turnover. The absence of attractive alternatives may discourage dissatisfied employees from resigning, whereas the availability of desirable employment elsewhere may motivate even satisfied employees to exit (Mobley et al. 1979; Mobley 1982a).

Moderators and Distal Determinants Impulsive quitting, the centrality of non-work values, and a need for immediate gratification moderate the effects of job satisfaction and expected utilities on turnover. Mobley et al. (1979) suggested that employees who cannot secure attractive alternatives may engage in alternative forms of withdrawal, such as absences, accidents, and sabotage. Further, job satisfaction and expected role utilities in turn emanate from various determinants: organizational (for example, policies and practices), occupational (for example, skill level and status), personal (for example, tenure and education), and economic and labor market (for example, unemployment and vacancy rates) factors.

Review

By emphasizing values, expectancies, job-related and external perceptions, and moderators, Mobley et al.'s conceptualization (1979) introduced a welcome multivariate explanation of the turnover process. Unlike Mobley's process-oriented formulation (1977), the later perspective sought to identify a comprehensive set of determinants of turnover and has been hailed by Muchinsky and Morrow as "well developed and highly articulated" (1980, p. 265). Borrowing from expectancy theory, Mobley et al. further popularized notions of the expected utility of the present role and the expected utility of alternatives, which explain why dissatisfied employees do not invariably quit their jobs: the possibility of attractive work roles in the future or the undesirability of external alternatives may discourage dissatisfied employees from severing their employment. Moreover, Mobley et al. emphasized the role of nonwork influences on withdrawal decisions, a concept that now pervades thinking on turnover (see Hom and Griffeth 1991; Hulin, Roznowski, and Hachiya 1985; Steers and Mowday 1981). Notwithstanding these contributions, this comprehensive framework left unspecified the relative impact of the three classes of distal antecedents on job-related perceptions, individual values, and perceptions of the labor market as well as overlooking causal interactions within and between classes of these antecedents.

Two research streams have tested the 1979 theory. Although the tests were not exhaustive, a number of researchers directly investigated portions of the theory: Griffeth and Hom (1988a), Michaels and Spector (1982), Motowidlo and Lawton (1984), and Youngblood, Mobley, and Meglino (1983). Other researchers, among them Arnold and Feldman (1982), and Hom, Griffeth, and Sellaro (1984), borrowed components of the model to validate a different theory. Both approaches affirmed that expected utilities of a work role can improve predictions of turnover decisions and behavior better than measures of job satisfaction can, although the results are neither consistent nor impressive (see Griffeth and Hom [1988a] and Youngblood, Mobley, and Meglino [1983]). Nevertheless, most investigations inadequately operationalized the expected utility of the present work role, emphasizing the present attainment rather than the *future* attainment of role outcomes (Hom, Kinicki, and Domm 1989). In a similar vein, existing studies imprecisely represented the expected utility of alternative jobs, typically measuring the attractiveness of some general alternative rather than considering specific job offers (Griffeth and Hom 1988a). Conceivably, better representations of the original notions of Mobley et al. may enhance the predictive power of the expected utilities of current and other work roles.

Beyond this, many of the model's propositions remain untested. For example, does failure to find attractive alternatives lead to alternative forms of withdrawal as Mobley et al. hypothesized (1979)? Or after failing to find an alternative, do employees reevaluate their present jobs more favorably? No study has attempted to operationalize the model fully. Admittedly, Mobley et al., in providing illustrative components rather than an exhaustive taxonomy, did not specify fully *all* the components of the three sets of distal organizational, individual, and labor-market causes.

MUCHINSKY AND MORROW: MULTIDISCIPLINARY MODEL

Muchinsky and Morrow (1980) conceived economic determinants, such as employment rates and opportunity to obtain work, as immediate precursors of turnover. The rationale for direct employment effects is that most employees will not leave their present job unless alternative opportunities for employment exist. Individual and work-related factors then "flow" through economic opportunity, which acts as a valve to regulate their influence on turnover. That is, when jobs are plentiful, individual and work-related determinants affect turnover more than they do when few jobs exist. As a result, the relationship between job dissatisfaction and quits is stronger for employees that have alternative jobs than for those who do not. Without alternatives, dissatisfied employees are more likely to endure their present situation. Muchinsky and Morrow also acknowledged the likelihood of alternative forms of withdrawal, such as absenteeism or depressed productivity, if employees cannot find more attractive alternatives and argued that individual and work-related factors interact.

Review

Though Muchinsky and Morrow's model (1980) has rarely been tested, Carsten and Spector (1987) examined the thesis that employment moderates relationships between individual and work-related variables. Using meta-analysis, Carsten and Spector considered two correlates of turnover, satisfaction and intentions to quit, during periods of low and high unemployment. Muchinsky and Morrow hypothesized that the relationship would be strong during low unemployment and weak during high unemployment. Generally, the results supported their prediction, although correlations between job satisfaction and turnover ranged from –.18 to –.52, depending upon whether unemployment rates were calculated at state or occupational levels. Relationships between intention and turnover were somewhat lower (–.28 to –.36).

Generalizing from these findings, other scholars substantiated the moderating effects of unemployment on relationships between perceived alternatives and quitting and on structural networks of the causes of turnover (Gerhart 1990; Steel and Griffeth 1989; Hom Caranikis-Walker, Prussia, and Griffeth 1992). These compelling results persuaded organizational psychologists to begin modeling the effects of unemployment rates on turnover among individuals (see Hom Caranikis-Walker, Prussia, and Griffeth 1992; Hulin, Roznowski and Hachiya 1985). Yet theoretical consideration of unemployment rates challenges the prevailing psychological models of turnover, which overlook macro-level determinants (Hom and Hulin 1981; Rousseau 1985).

Conceivably, the unemployment rate affects an individual's turnover because it is a crude proxy for various psychological forces, such as the crystallization of alternatives and the visibility of alternatives (Steel and Griffeth 1989). Additionally, rates of joblessness may indirectly ("spuriously") affect the withdrawal process by impacting the quit base rate (Hom and Hulin 1981). Essentially, high unemployment depresses turnover rates, thereby attenuating relationships between turnover and its antecedents (Steel and Griffeth 1989). Furthermore, high employment may encourage marginal drifters, whose decisions about changing jobs may not be regulated by the same process as those of regular, full-time workers, to join the work force (Hulin, Roznowski, and Hachiya 1985). Once they accumulate sufficient funds, they may simply resign and drop out of the labor market to pursue more "fulfilling" avocations. Therefore, the familiar bases of turnover, which underlie the quit decisions of regular employees, may scarcely determine those of peripheral workers who forsake even satisfying jobs.

Last, scant evidence supports other relationships among the variables, especially interactions, that were depicted in Muchinsky and Morrow's theory (1980). By deemphasizing the process underlying turnover, the Muchinsky and Morrow model represents a content model that catalogues factors of turnover but omitted many essential process determinants, most notably, withdrawal cognitions. Obviously, more research is warranted to validate this model.

FARRELL AND RUSBULT: INVESTMENT MODEL

Farrell and Rusbult (1981) derived a model from social exchange (Homans 1961) and interdependence theories (Thibaut and Kelley 1959; Kelley and Thibaut 1978). From these conceptualizations, they attempted to explain organizational commitment, which is "the binding of the individual to behavioral acts" (Kiesler and Sakumura 1966, p. 349). "Thus, job commitment is related to the probability that an employee will leave his job, and involves feelings of attachment, independent of affect. Job commitment reflects behavioral intention, primarily (but not solely) [the] degree of intention to stay with a job" (Farrell and Rusbult 1981, p. 79).

They proposed various antecedents of commitment, notably, job satisfaction (SAT_x), which they defined as:

$SAT_x = (R_x - C_x) - CL$,
   where R_x is the reward value of an association, defined by
$R_x = E(w_i r_i)$,
   where r_i is the individual's subjective estimate of the reward value of attribute i available from association X and w_i represents its subjective importance, and
$C_x = E(w_j c_j)$,
   where c_j is the magnitude of the subjective costs of association X regarding attribute j and w_j is the importance of the attribute in the association.

CL is the comparison level (Thibaut and Kelley 1959), or internal standard, that the employee has come to expect from associations. That is, "CL is a standard by which the person evaluates the rewards and costs of a given relationship in terms of what he feels he 'deserves'" (Thibaut and Kelley 1959, p. 21). Presumably, job satisfaction arises from a comparison between the CL and the difference between job rewards and costs—called the association outcome value (O_x).

Alternatives, however, undermine commitment. This alternative value (A_y), or the quality of the best available alternative, is defined as:

$A_y = (R_y - C_y) - CL$

   where A_y corresponds to the "Comparison level for alternatives" construct of interdependence theory, which is the standard by which individuals decide whether or not they will remain in an association. That is, A_y is "the lowest level of outcomes a member will accept in the light of available alternative opportunities" (Thibaut and Kelley 1959, p. 21).

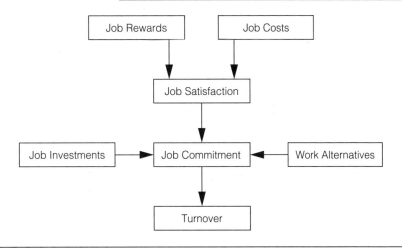

Figure 4-8 Rusbult and Farrell's Investment Model of Turnover. (Adapted from C. Rusbult and D. Farrell, "A longitudinal test of the investment model, *Journal of Applied Psychology* **68 (1983): 429–438.)**

Last, job investments (I_x) reinforce job commitment. These investments comprise resources that are intrinsic to the job, including unvested retirement benefits and nonportable training, and extrinsic resources inextricably tied to the job, such as community services and friends at work, that are relinquished if employees quit their jobs. More formally,

$$I_x = E(w_k i_k),$$

i_k refers to the size of the investment of resource k in relationship X, and w_k refers to the importance of resource k.

To summarize, job commitment (COM_x) is a function of job satisfaction, quality of job alternatives, and size of job investments. In other words, $COM_x = SAT_x + I_x - A_y$. This model is depicted in Figure 4-8.

Review

The investment model is a rich interdisciplinary model predicated on sociological and psychological constructs. Consequently, it is surprising that it has not attracted more research since its inception. In fact, only Farrell and Rusbult have tested the model. In their first study, (Farrell and Rusbult 1981) with a laboratory work simulation and a cross-sectional survey of industrial workers, the major relationships among model variables were sustained. That is, they found that job rewards and costs strongly predicted job satisfaction, that a combination of reward and cost values, the value of alternatives, and investment size strongly predicted job commitment, and that job commitment predicted turnover better than did job satisfaction.

Using a sample of eighty-eight new nurses and accountants, Rusbult and Farrell (1983) next conducted a longitudinal test and found that job satisfaction rose over time as job rewards increased and job cost decreased. Meanwhile, escalating job rewards and investments boosted commitment over time, as did declining costs and quality of alternatives. Importantly, they found that temporal changes in model variables rather than their absolute levels best differentiated between stayers and leavers. For example, job costs and job investments scarcely affected the commitment of newcomers during the initial period of employment. But, as time passed, job costs grew more apparent and investments began accumulating, thereby increasingly shaping the new-comers' commitment. Consequently, temporal *changes* in costs and invest-ments predicted commitment more than did initial job cost and investment values. Most of all, *changes* in job commitment powerfully forecast resignations.

Although their evidence is encouraging, Rusbult and Farrell narrowly construed their commitment construct as primarily withdrawal cognitions. This conceptualization conflicts, however, with more popular, multidimen-sional commitment constructs, which embody, not only withdrawal cogni-tions, but also identification with organizational values and willingness to go beyond formal work-role definitions (Mowday, Porter, and Steers 1982; O'Reilly and Chatman 1986). Whether or not the same model determinants would predict an expanded notion of organizational commitment awaits future research. Rusbult and Farrell's operationalization of job commitment includes both decisions about termination and about search, which other researchers theoretically and empirically distinguish as separate constructs (see Blau 1993; Mobley 1977; Steers and Mowday 1981). The theory oversim-plifies perceived alternatives, considering only the *attractiveness* of other employment opportunities. Yet scholars of turnover envision increasingly more complex, multifaceted conceptualizations of the employment market, taking into account specific job offers (Griffeth and Hom 1988a), the attain-ability of alternatives (Mobley Griffeth, Hand, and Meglino 1979), and the crystallization of alternatives (Steel and Griffeth 1989). Last, one of the main strengths of investment theory—its parsimony—may nonetheless constitute a weakness. In light of more comprehensive formulations (Mobley et al. 1979; Steers and Mowday 1981), the omission from this model of many determi-nants, such as job search and efforts to improve working conditions, weakens its predictive efficacy (see Blau 1993; Hulin Roznowski, and Hachiya 1985).

STEERS AND MOWDAY: MULTI-ROUTE MODEL

Steers and Mowday (1981) advanced another comprehensive turnover model that integrates earlier theories while overcoming their conceptual shortcomings. To clarify its dynamics, they presented this framework in three segments, shown in Figure 4-9.

Origins of Job Expectations and Attitudes

Steers and Mowday theorized that an individual's value system influ-ences his or her expectations about various aspects of a job, such as the

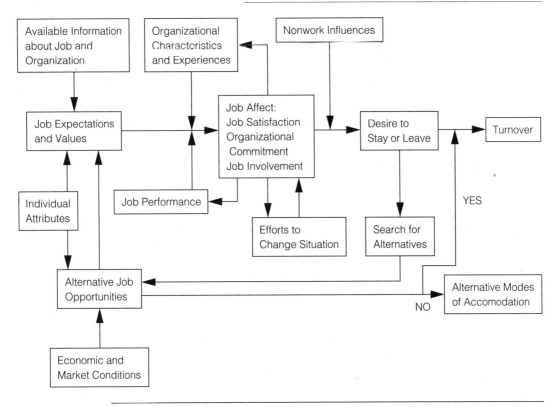

Figure 4-9 Steers and Mowday's Model of Turnover. (R. Steers and R. Mowday, "Employee turnover and post-decision accommodation processes," In L. Cummings and B. Staw (Eds.), *Research in Organizational Behavior,* Greenwich, Conn.: JAI Press; (1981): 242.)

nature of the job and rewards for satisfactory performance. Besides values, personal characteristics—such as age, tenure, and family responsibilities—underpin the expectations of employees by determining "what they expect from a job: what they feel they must have, what they would like to have, and what they can do without" (1981, p. 243). The accuracy of prior information about the job and the company will make the initial expectations more realistic and thereby lower turnover. The alternatives that are available modify expectations about the job because employees who have many attractive options may set higher expectations for their current jobs.

Affective responses to the job. Steers and Mowday conceived affective responses to the job as embodying job satisfaction, organizational commitment, and job involvement. They further hypothesized that job expectations and values would interact with organizational characteristics and experiences, and that job performance would influence affective responses. Extrapolating from met-expectation theory (Porter and Steers 1973), they contended that the more closely preentry expectations align with the work experience, the greater the employee's job satisfaction and propensity to remain in the organization. Job performance also influences affective responses because high performers receive more merit pay (see Lawler 1981) and more job security.

Steers and Mowday further suggested a reciprocal causation between affective responses with job performance and organizational experiences. As previously described, job performance and organizational experiences shape job attitudes, but job attitudes may themselves impact performance and organizational experiences. Moreover, poor attitudes may prompt employees to change the work environment or transfer to other jobs before they decide to leave. If the workplace then becomes more tolerable, attitudes toward their workplace may become positive. A failure to improve the environment would strengthen the employee's resolve to abandon the job, and in the meantime, worsen the attitude toward the job.

How Job Attitudes Affect Intent to Leave

Steers and Mowday further envisioned that job attitudes influence intentions to leave, although outside influences may condition the effect. That is, some employees may tolerate an unpleasant job and remain employed because of circumstances outside the job, such as its instrumentality for future career assignments, or an unwillingness to disrupt a spouse's career or uproot the family from the community.

The Process by Which Intent to Leave Leads to Turnover

The third segment of the framework specifies the ways in which intentions to withdraw induce turnover. Following March and Simon (1958), Steers and Mowday posited that intentions to quit multiplicatively combine with the availability of alternatives. In essence, intentions to quit affect turnover via two causal routes. The formation of a decision to quit may directly trigger the resignation or may indirectly influence turnover by prompting employees to seek alternative jobs. Alternative opportunities partly depend on individual traits, such as age, sex, and occupation, that affect the likelihood of the person's attaining other employment. Failing to find an alternative, a job-seeking employee may revert to other forms of withdrawal, such as absenteeism, sabotage, and alcohol abuse. Dissatisfied individuals, unable to find better alternatives, may accommodate an unpleasant job by rationalizing their reasons for remaining.

Steers and Mowday also noted that employees may be presented with attractive alternatives, which will boost their expectations of their present job. Inflated expectations may, however, translate into frustration (for these expectations are less likely to be realized by the current job), worsening job attitudes and increasing the desire to leave.

Review

The Steers and Mowday model (1981) is a complex representation of the turnover process that pioneered many innovative constructs, including the long-neglected notion that efforts to change the work environment may interrupt the process by which job dissatisfaction develops into departure. Efforts to change the job may also directly affect other determinants of turnover. For instance, Hulin, Roznowski, and Hackiya (1985) implied that efforts to change the job may reduce withdrawal cognitions because dissatisfied employees who manage to improve their working conditions would not quit. Moreover, Steers and Mowday introduced job performance as a determinant of turnover, influencing later writers to give special heed to withdrawal by superior performers whose loss produces sizable costs for the organization (see Jackofsky 1984). Furthermore, their "nonwork influences" construct persuaded other scholars to acknowledge that factors outside organizational boundaries may impel people to quit (see Hom, Kinicki, and Domm 1989). Last, Steers and Mowday rejected Mobley's prevailing view (1977) that dissatisfied employees follow only one course to departure, holding that they actually pursue one of several possible routes. Some dissatisfied employees quit immediately; others undertake the search process described by Mobley (1977). Later portrayals of the translation of dissatisfaction into quitting increasingly included Steers and Mowday's perspective (see Hom and Griffeth 1991; Hom, Griffeth, and Sellaro 1984; Lee and Mitchell 1994; Sager et al. 1992), and in other models, researchers sought to explain why employees simply quit without first seeking alternative jobs (Hulin, Roznowski, and Hachiya 1985).

Though Steers and Mowday's introduction of job performance and nonwork influences extend prior formulations, their conceptualization still demands additional refinement. They proposed that job performance interacts with organizational characteristics and experiences and with job expectations and values but they left unspecified the form of those interactions. Moreover, their definition of nonwork influences is vague, although Lee and Mowday's operationalization (1987) considered perceptions by employees of how various external factors (such as unemployment, personal lifestyle, and time left for the family) influence job affect. This operationalization does not directly reflect attachments to outside pursuits (see Mobley, Griffeth, Hand, and Meglino 1979; Price and Mueller 1981, 1986) or work conflicts with outside interests (Hom and Griffeth 1991; Mobley 1982a); both are more specific and promising constructs of extraneous influences. The determinant, job expectation, originated by Porter and Steers (1973), suffers the same conceptual shortcomings as the original. Indeed, this construct is most relevant to new employees who may respond to unmet expectations by quitting more than veteran employees do (Wanous 1980).

Despite its process orientation, Steers and Mowday's theory imprecisely describes several structural connections among theoretical constructs. In the wake of modern views on varied reactions to dissatisfaction, their formulation explains only incompletely how job affect influences job performance or efforts to change the job, omitting essential behavioral antecedents as perceived consequences to those responses (Rosse and Miller 1984; Withey and Cooper 1989). Nor did Steers and Mowday specify how outside influences moderate the effects of job attitudes on decisions to quit or how performance interacts with attributes of the firm and job expectations to determine job affect (Lee and Mowday 1987). Besides, this model did not identify which particular characteristics of the company and experiences it offers, which attributes of individuals, and which job expectations and values are vital determinants. Are they referring to work values (as defined by Hulin and Blood 1968) or a general structure of values (as conceived by Rokeach 1973)? Steers and Mowday described processes that *mediated* components of their model but, schematically, they represented these processes as *moderators* in their illustration (Figure 4-9).

Several studies (including Arnold and Feldman 1982; Hom, Griffeth, and Sellaro 1984; Hom and Griffeth 1991; and Sager et al 1992) have sustained the prediction by Steers and Mowday that termination cognitions can directly stimulate resignations and predate search decisions. Only Lee and Mowday (1987) fully tested this model, surveying 445 employees of a financial institution. A regression equation comprising information about the job and organization, alternative job opportunities, and personal traits significantly predicted met expectations and job values. However, only available job and firm information explained extra variance in met expectations; alternative job opportunities and personal characteristics did not. Likewise, available information and individual attributes made independent contributions to the prediction of job values; work alternatives did not.

From regression analyses testing the hypothesized multiplicative effect of performance, met expectations, job values, company attributes, and work experiences, the researchers found that the complete model (comprising predictors and interaction terms) significantly predicted each job attitude. Yet these analyses did not estimate additional predictive contributions for the interaction terms, beyond that explained by the main effects (Cohen and Cohen 1983) and did not describe how predictors interacted (though Steers and Mowday never specified their form). Similarly, a full regression equation containing job satisfaction, organizational commitment, job involvement, and nonwork influences—and their interaction terms—significantly predicted decisions to quit. Here again, this analysis did not determine whether interaction terms added any independent predictive variance and did not describe the nature of interactions, although the original theoretical statements are ambiguous in depicting those multiplicative effects. Last, a regression of turnover onto intentions to quit and work alternatives found that only intentions make a significant independent contribution to prediction, and that both predictors accounted for only 5 percent of the variance in turnover.

In summary, the one complete test of the Steers-Mowday model yielded mixed or incomplete support for its validity (Lee and Mowday 1987).

Regression analyses found that each model variable was significantly predicted by its theorized *set* of antecedents. Yet several determinants did not explain independent criterion variance (notably, influences outside work, alternatives, and efforts to change the job). Hypotheses about moderators received incomplete support because the regression analyses did not estimate the special contributions interaction terms made to prediction beyond that predicted by main effects nor described the exact form of their effects. In the examination of the model (James, Mulaik, and Brett 1982), the possibility that causal pathways omitted from this model are truly nonexistent was not tested. Tests of models must validate not only the pathways posited by theorists but also the pathways they specified as absent (see, for example, the "omitted parameters" test of Motowidlo and Lawton [1984]). Intentions to quit and the existence of alternative jobs explained only 5 percent of the turnover variance. Additional research is warranted to validate the Steers-Mowday model. In particular, future replications should refine the operationalizations of nonwork influences, efforts to change the job, and work alternatives because their substantive validity may be better supported by measures that are more psychometrically sound.

SHERIDAN AND ABELSON: CUSP CATASTROPHE MODEL

Deviating from conventional thinking, Sheridan and Abelson (1983) developed a cusp catastrophe model based on two determinants. In their model, organizational commitment and job tension define a two-dimensional control surface, with withdrawal behavior projected as a third, vertical axis (see Figure 4-10). The conceptualization has three characteristics. First, withdrawal behavior is a discontinuous variable with abrupt changes observed between different states of withdrawal. Presumably, employees try to maintain their current employment as long as possible. Once dissatisfaction accumulates (from declining commitment to the company or work stress), the employees abruptly shift states from being determined to stay to being determined to leave. Second, the theory represents a hysteresis zone of behavior as a fold in the behavior surface. Projected as a bifurcation plane on the control surface, this fold reflects the state of transition from retention to termination. Third, divergent behaviors occur on opposite ends of the bifurcation plane. That is, "as an employee approaches the fold region, even small changes in the control variables can result in discontinuous changes from retention to termination" (1983, p. 422). Thus, two employees may have minimally different commitment and stress. Yet if they reside on opposite sides of the bifurcation plane, one may quit, while the other stays. Conversely, two employees expressing quite dissimilar commitment and stress may still exhibit the same withdrawal behavior if they fall on the same side of the bifurcation plane.

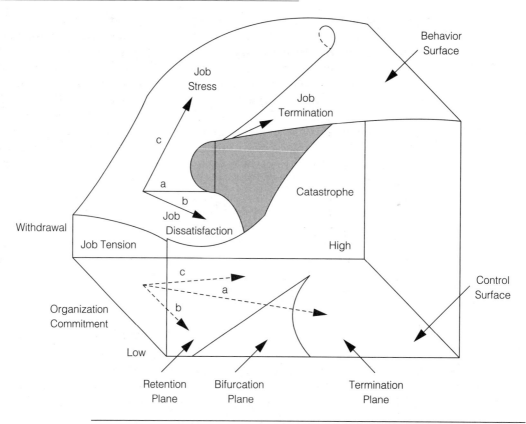

Figure 4-10 Sheridan and Abelson's Cusp Catastrophe Model of Employee Turnover. (J. Sheridan and M. Abelson. "Cusp catastrophe model of employee turnover," *Academy of Management Journal,* **26 (1983): 421.)**

Review

Thus far, two studies have tested the cusp catastrophe model sampling nurses. In the first study, Sheridan and Abelson (1983) assessed job tension and organizational commitment to define the control surface. To test the existence of a bifurcation plane, they compared quit rates on both sides of the bifurcation plane to the total quit rate. The turnover rate in the bifurcation plane was 22 percent (compared to a 17 percent overall quit rate), in the retention plane, 4 percent, and in the termination plane, 41 percent. The total quit rate varied significantly from quit rates in the retention and termination planes, but not the bifurcation plane. Sheridan and Abelson also estimated this model's accuracy in classifying the nurses' employment status in the retention and termination planes. In line with the model, the bifurcation plane accurately differentiated most quitters from stayers in the retention plane, misclassifying merely 4 percent of the quitters as stayers. Still, the bifurcation plane misclassified 59 percent of the stayers as quitters in the termination plane.

Using a panel survey, Sheridan and Abelson further tracked temporal changes in job tension and commitment for stayers and leavers. In general, these tests upheld the cusp catastrophe model, showing that leavers were positioned closer to (or in) the bifurcation plane than were stayers. Over time, the leavers moved into the bifurcation or termination plane, while the stayers barely changed. Regression analyses disclosed that the cusp catastrophe model more correctly classified turnover status (84 percent) than did a linear model (49 percent), although hit rates did not significantly differ. In a study of new nurses (1985), Sheridan replaced commitment to the company with group cohesion as a control surface variable, deeming it a more relevant "attractor" for newcomers than commitment is. From cusp-catastrophe theory, he derived a topological equation describing the cusp-catastrophe surface. This equation predicts withdrawal changes from Time-1 withdrawal actions (declining performance or absenteeism) to Time-2 turnover as a function of the following:

$$B_0 + B_1W_1^3 + B_2W_1^2 + B_3(T \times W_1) + B_4C + B_5T,$$
where W_1 = current Time-1 withdrawal behavior (either poor job performance or absenteeism),
T = job tension, and C = group cohesion.

Using regression analysis, he estimated this equation, running separate analyses for different Time-1 withdrawal acts. The regression equation, including poor performance as the Time-1 withdrawal act, did *not* significantly predict terminations ($R = .129$). However, the equation specifying absenteeism as the Time-1 withdrawal behavior significantly predicted turnover ($R = .207$, $p < .05$). In this equation, the quadratic and cubic components for past absences explained additional turnover variance, suggesting discontinuous transition as withdrawal becomes progressively more extreme. As he did in his 1983 study, Sheridan next examined observations of turnover on the control surface defined by cohesion and job tension. Using cusp-catastrophe criteria, he identified boundaries for retention, termination, and bifurcation regions on the control surface and found that quit rates for these planes were 18 percent, 89 percent, and 33 percent, respectively. Regional location on the control surface accurately forecast turnover status, correctly classifying 86 percent of the participants in the study.

The cusp catastrophe model is a major breakthrough in thinking about turnover. Departing from prevailing linear assumptions, this model depicts quits as a discontinuous function of turnover determinants. As confirmed by two tests, the consideration of nonlinear effects of the antecedents of turnover may enhance predictions of terminations (Sheridan and Abelson 1983; Sheridan 1985). Counteracting modern theoretical developments, this model explains turnover with a parsimonious set of antecedents while retaining predictive power. All too often, in successive generations of theories, explanatory constructs proliferate and how parsimonious a theory accounts for turnover is neglected (Hom and Griffeth 1991). This model considers a broader pattern of withdrawal responses than have previous theories that focus narrowly on turnover. That is, in this theory, resignations are seen as one manifestation of job avoidance and turnover is considered to evolve from less extreme forms, such as absenteeism and poor performance. This model may also explain transitions among the less extreme forms of withdrawal (see Sheridan 1985).

All the same, the cusp catastrophe model merits more empirical and theoretical work. For example, its two determinants (job tension and commitment/cohesion) insufficiently capture the sundry reasons why employees quit, because the vast literature on motives for turnover (Mobley, Griffeth, Hand, and Meglino 1979; Mobley 1982a) has been overlooked. Moreover, Sheridan and Abelson suggested that differences among individuals be taken into account in the model but provided little theoretical guidance. Future tests should include the Time-1 linear term of withdrawal in addition to its quadratic and cubic terms in the *same* regression equation. Though quadratic and cubic terms are posited by cusp-catastrophe theory, true nonlinear effects are revealed after statistically controlling the linear effects (Cohen and Cohen 1983). Indeed, Sheridan's estimated linear interaction models (1985), comprising the Time-1 linear term of withdrawal, job tension, and group cohesion (and their interaction), consistently uncovered linear effects for Time-1 withdrawal behaviors on quits.

This preliminary work possibly overestimated the accuracy of classification in the cusp catastrophe model. The researchers identified the boundaries of the bifurcation plane by inspecting the distribution of observations on turnover in the two-dimensional control space and used the various combinations of threshold scores on the control variables to predict whether or not employees quit. Such *empirical* identification of cutoff scores must be cross-validated on another sample because threshold scores uncovered empirically improve the accuracy of prediction by capitalizing on chance (see Wiggins 1973).

Despite these shortcomings, the cusp catastrophe model is a provocative divergence from traditional linear thinking. More research is needed to test the theory in general and with samples of employees who are not nurses. Though many scholars (Mobley, Griffeth, Hand, and Meglino 1979; Steers and Mowday 1981) have suggested that turnover is a dynamic process, the cusp-catastrophe theory formally models this process and thus becomes a significant theoretical milestone in an understanding of the turnover process.

HULIN, ROZNOWSKI, AND HACHIYA: LABOR-ECONOMIC MODEL

Reviewing empirical tests on job alternatives, Hulin, Roznowski and Hachiya concluded (1985) that perceptual estimates of labor-market prospects have predicted turnover poorly, whereas aggregate labor-market statistics, such as unemployment rates, predicted turnover consistently (and strongly). To account for such discrepant findings, they proposed that work alternatives can directly affect job satisfaction, a reversal of the contention that it is satisfaction that influences alternatives (see Mobley 1977). They also held that job opportunities may directly induce turnover because employees quit when they are sure of an alternative job, not because they surmise from local unemployment data that there is a *probability* of a job. The reconceptualization envisioned a different role in the turnover process for job opportunities (see March and Simon 1958; Mobley 1977). They hypothesized that there were three mechanisms to explain why perceived alternatives minimally affect individual turnover. In the following sections, we review those mechanisms.

Different Economies Produce Different Work Forces

Hulin, Roznowski and Hachiya argued (1985) that economic expansion attracts casual or marginal workers into the labor force. They do not normally work regularly, but prosperous times lure them into full-time employment because the job surplus drives up wages. Nevertheless, marginal employees do not plan to stay employed for very long. After accumulating enough funds, they will quit to pursue more pleasurable or less stressful avocations. Given their weak orientation toward work, these workers are unlikely, when quitting, to engage in the complex cognitive processes theorized by turnover scholars (such as Mobley 1977).

Job Opportunities Directly Influence Job Satisfaction

Drawing from several models (March and Simon 1958; Salancik and Pfeffer 1978; Smith, Kendall, and Hulin 1969; Thibaut and Kelley 1959), the researchers maintained that economic activities, such as employment levels, directly influence job satisfaction. High unemployment in decreasing adaptation and comparison levels for alternatives bolsters job satisfaction. Low unemployment and plentiful alternatives promote dissatisfaction and intentions to quit. More precisely, Hulin, Roznowski and Hachiya conceptualized that foregone alternatives are "opportunity costs" employees incur to maintain membership in their present organization. During good economic times when jobs are abundant, the utilities of foregone alternatives increase, thereby reducing satisfaction with the present job. During economic stagnation, the expected utility of alternatives declines and satisfaction with the present job increases.

Job Opportunities Directly Affect Turnover

Extrapolating from Michaels and Spector's work (1982), Hulin, Roznowski and Hachiya further contended that job opportunities affect turnover directly and not necessarily through intentions to quit. Presumably, most employees do not quit merely on the chance of finding an alternative (that is, because they perceive that alternatives are available) but when they actually secure job offers. Thus, they reasoned, alternative work and dissatisfaction about the job interact in affecting quitting. The more jobs there are available, the more likely it is that dissatisfied employees can find and obtain other jobs and thus can leave their unsatisfactory positions. Job dissatisfaction and job offers must both exist for withdrawal to occur. In passing, the researchers also observed that present-day models of turnover implicitly assume that dissatisfied employees only consider alternative work, failing to recognize that many leavers pursue alternatives other than work, which may also explain why perceptions of alternative work do not readily translate into departures.

Combining these explanations, Hulin, Roznowski and Hachiya designed a model that clarifies the influence of labor-market factors on decisions to quit (see Figure 4-11). Their specification that the availability of alternatives directly influences satisfaction in two ways is consistent with an economic utility theory (for example, March and Simon 1958). Economic conditions affect the value of an employee's contribution of skills, time, and effort to the firm. Low unemployment increases the value of an individual's contributions and the utility of foregone opportunities, making continued membership in a company costly. As a result, job satisfaction declines unless the benefits of membership are equivalently increased. At the same time, the good economic conditions bolster an employee's frame of reference for evaluating the quality of the job. Therefore, the employee devalues the current job and becomes more dissatisfied. Unemployment, by comparison, decreases the utilities of direct and opportunity costs *and* limits the frame of reference for judging the job, thereby boosting job satisfaction.

For many people, dissatisfaction about the job translates directly into decisions to quit. Once dissatisfied, some employees simply form intentions to quit without considering alternatives; others secure alternative offers before quitting. For the latter, the attractiveness of *certain* job offers, rather than the mere probability of a job estimated from local unemployment data, dominates their decision to quit. Still other workers in intolerable jobs may simply decide to quit, assuming that anything would be better than what they are currently doing.

Some dissatisfied employees never make the decision to quit because of various lures or obstacles (perhaps, inertia, low self-esteem, or "golden handcuffs"). Such trapped employees may reduce their dissatisfaction by enacting other withdrawal behaviors, thereby decreasing their job inputs. Given the same level of job outcomes, their satisfaction should grow with declining inputs. Moreover, these withdrawal behaviors may be manifested cyclically, the employees try different responses until they lower their dissatisfaction successfully. Some employees who cope with dissatisfaction by performing other withdrawal acts may be implicitly forming decisions to quit in that their excessive withdrawal behaviors may lead to their dismissal.

Marginal drifters—drawn into regular work by job surpluses—also quit because they are dissatisfied. Yet these individuals would be dissatisfied with any full-time, regular job. They quit, not to take a better job, but because they

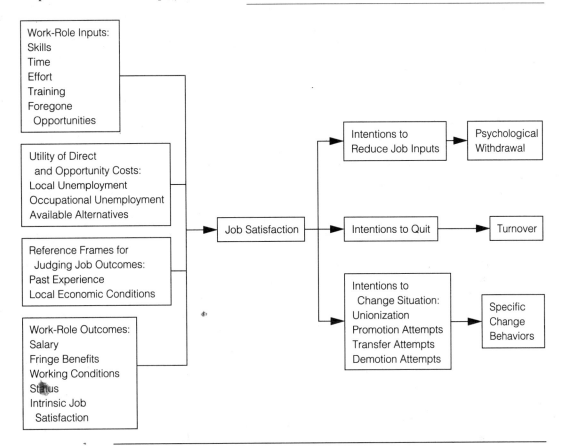

Figure 4-11 Hulin, Roznowski, and Hachiya's Labor-Economic Model of Turnover. (C. Hulin, M. Roznowski, and D. Hachiya, "Alternative opportunities and withdrawal decisions: Empirical and theoretical discrepancies and an integration," *Psychological Bulletin* 97 (1985): 246. Copyright 1977 by the American Psychological Association. Adapted by permission.)

became bored with their present job and assume that any new position will be superior—at least in the short run. Casual workers translate dissatisfaction into decisions to quit because of a general dislike of regular, full-time work.

Review

Hulin, Roznowski and Hachiya (1985), offering a perceptive reexamination of the role of work alternatives in the withdrawal process, resolved a long-standing controversy in the study of turnover. They provided an invaluable taxonomy of the different types of quitters, including marginal drifters and leavers seeking alternatives other than work. These leavers follow a different route to departure from the conventional pathway of job dissatisfaction → job search → quit decisions → quit (Mobley 1977). Their theory explains why job dissatisfaction does not invariably lead to quitting: Employees may respond to dissatisfaction not by quitting but by reducing their job inputs or by changing the current job by way of transfers or unionization. For them, presumably, psychological withdrawal or a change of job would substitute for departure. The formulation reconceptualizes turnover as one among many behavioral reactions to dissatisfaction, thereby going beyond the traditional preoccupation with surface behaviors (Hulin 1991).

Although explaining the different effects of unemployment rates and perceived alternatives on turnover, Hulin and his fellow researchers provided no direct evidence. To date, no research has directly tested the model or its components. Conceivably, notions of adaptation level, comparison level, and the comparison level of alternatives are too generally conceptualized and thus defy ready operationalization. The behavioral responses to dissatisfaction also merit greater clarification for the behaviors that "reduce job inputs" were not specified and other behavioral reactions—namely, alternative acts of withdrawal, such as absences, and other forms of voice (see Farrell 1983)—were omitted. However, Hulin recently (1991) refined his 1985 formulation, expanding and elaborating on behavioral reactions to dissatisfaction to include the following:

> Intentions to increase job outcomes, for example, stealing or moonlighting;
> Intentions to reduce job inputs, for example, long coffee breaks, substance abuse, or gossip;
> Intentions to reduce work-role inclusion, for example, quitting, lateness, absence, or retirement; and
> Intentions to change the work role by, for example, unionizing, transferring, or demotion.

Many scholars, among them Farrell (1983), Rossé and Hulin (1985), Withey and Cooper (1989), are currently developing and validating scales to assess behavioral responses to dissatisfaction. Though not striving for a comprehensive model, Hulin, Roznowski and Hachiya (1985) nonetheless excluded many fundamental explanatory constructs, such as commitment to the organization, outside influences, and job search, that have been affirmed as underpinnings of turnover (Blau 1993; Hom and Griffeth 1991; Lee and Mowday 1987; Price and Mueller 1986).

LEE AND MITCHELL: UNFOLDING MODEL

Lee and Mitchell (1994) generalized Beach's image theory (1991) to further the understanding of termination decisions. Image theory challenges prevailing turnover theories that assume an economic rational basis for decision making (Hulin, Roznowski and Hachiya 1985; Mobley, Griffeth, Hand, and

Meglino: 1979) and presumes that people make decisions by comparing the fit of the options in the decision to various internal images rather than by maximizing the subjective expected utility. Image theory posits that people must filter the constant bombardment of information to select suitable options. This screening is rapid, requires little cognitive effort, and compares the characteristics of options to one of three internal images: value (set of general values and standards that define the self); trajectory (set of goals that energizes and directs individual behavior); or strategic (set of behavioral tactics and strategies for attaining personal goals). This test of compatibility is noncompensatory and requires that the options fit one or more images. If a behavioral option meets the test, the individual compares the alternative to the status quo. Usually, the individual continues with the status quo; sometimes she or he chooses to behave differently. If numerous options survive the screening, a person runs a "profitability" test, choosing the best alternative according to a cost-benefit analysis.

Decision as a Response to Shock

Extending image theory, Lee and Mitchell further proposed (1994) that the entire process of screening and decision making begins with a "shock to the system," a specific event that jars the employee to make deliberate judgments about his or her job and perhaps to consider quitting the job. Lee and Mitchell theorized that the social and cognitive context that surrounds the experienced shock provides a "decision frame"—or frame of reference—with which to interpret the shock along dimensions, such as novelty, favorability, or threat. Then, according to their theory, employees will take one of four ways, "decision paths," to leave their jobs. These different paths to turnover are portrayed in Figure 4-12.

Decision Path 1. In the first path, a shock (diamond *a*) jars an employee to construct a decision frame (box *b*) for interpreting the shock and prompts the employee to search her memory for decisions, rules, or learned responses to similar shocks (box *c*). For example, a shock might be IBM's acquisition of one's smaller company; a rule might be "I will never fit the IBM mold." This probe of memory also brings forth recollections of whether one's previous staying or quitting was appropriate. If the decision frame of the current experience is identical to prior frames and quitting was the appropriate response, then a match (diamond *d*) occurs. Quitting (box *e*) is thus automatically enacted with little mental deliberation ("I have previously quit large corporations"). If a match does not occur, another decision path is initiated. In summary, decision path 1 is basically a script-driven response (involving a match with past decisions) to an experienced shock.

Decision Path 2. In the second decision path, the employee experiencing a system shock (diamond *a*) cannot recall an identical shock that has an appropriate response associated with it or a rule of action (box *c*). Therefore no

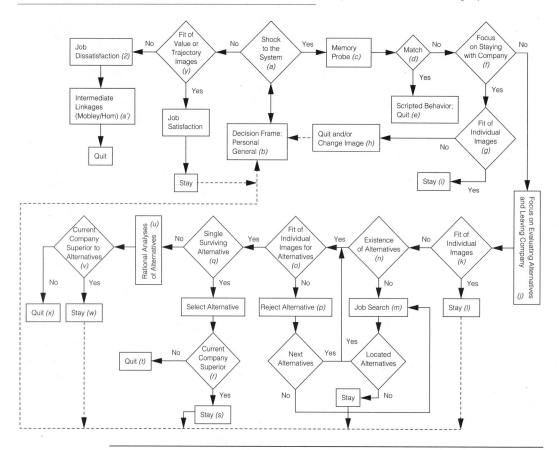

**Figure 4-12 Lee and Mitchell's Unfolding Model of Turnover. (T. Lee, and
T. Mitchell "An alternative approach: The unfolding model of
voluntary employee turnover."** *Academy of Management Review*
19 (1994): 62-63.)

match occurs (diamond *d*). Rather, the employee considers the situation and
frames the shock as a choice, without specific job alternatives in mind, between
staying with or quitting the present firm (diamond *f*). Next, the employee
relies on the value, trajectory, or strategic images to reassess his or her basic
commitment to the company (diamond *g*). If the shock violates these images,
the employee changes the image or leaves (box *h*). If the shock fits, the
employee stays (box *i*). To illustrate, a woman may unexpectedly become pregnant and must decide whether working fits with her images of being a competent mother (value), having a career (trajectory), or continuing in her sales job
(strategy). If the shock violates any image, she will resign her job.

Decision Path 3. Here, a shock (diamond *a*) elicits a memory probe (box *c*) but
a match between the shock currently being experienced and the recall of a
similar shock or an easily accessible rule does not occur (diamond *d*). The

employee frames the shock as a choice between staying with the company or quitting for one or more specific job alternatives (box j). The shock is next judged for image compatibility (diamond k). The employee stays (box l) if the shock fits but considers (diamond n) and seeks alternatives (box m) if it does not. Should the shock violate images, he or she then compares other alternatives to value, trajectory, or strategic images (diamond o) and deletes those failing the compatibility test (box p). If only one alternative fits (diamond q), the employee contrasts this alternative to the benefits of remaining employed (diamond r). The employee stays if the current job provides more benefits (box s) but leaves if the alternative is superior (box t). If numerous alternatives survive the compatibility test, the employee conducts a profitability test, comparing their subjective expected utilities (box u) against that of the present job. If the current job surpasses all alternatives (box v), the employee remains (box w); if an alternative is superior, the employee quits (box x).

Decision Path 4. According to the fourth path, some employees will occasionally reassess their commitment to the company. Their reassessment does not emanate from shock but occurs more routinely or casually. Over time, the employee or company may change and the job no longer fits the employee's value or trajectory images (diamond y). The resulting dissatisfaction (box z) triggers the withdrawal process (box a') described by Mobley (1977) or Hom and Griffeth (1991), wherein employees evaluate their prospects of alternative employment, seek other jobs, compare them to the present job, and form decisions about quitting. This fourth path thus complies with traditional depictions of the translation of dissatisfaction into quitting.

Review

Deviating from the conventional, Lee and Mitchell's theory (1994) contributes many valuable theoretical insights and provides a refreshing new perspective. Their generalization of image theory may depict the procedure of decisions to quit more accurately and comprehensively than does rational expectancy theory, which may more clearly explain only decision path 3, and not all of the decision processes. Lee and Mitchell introduced the notion of scripted (routinized, nonanalytical) turnover behavior, which may underlie impulsive quitting (Mobley 1977) and departures by members of the secondary labor market (Hulin, Roznowski, and Hachiya 1985). Their notion of system shocks—external, unexpected, or random events—accords greater theoretical attention to the origin of the turnover process, an aspect that prevailing formulations neglect (see Baysinger and Mobley 1983). Last, this theory specifies various sequences of withdrawal, broadening the generalizability of the model to more segments of the labor force (Hom and Griffeth 1991; Hulin, Roznowski, and Hachiya 1985).

No empirical research has yet investigated this latest explanation of turnover. The theoretical complexity of their model is daunting, but Lee and Mitchell (1994) have suggested various methodologies, including those of retrospective interviews and protocol analysis, to capture the decision paths. They recommended different statistical procedures to test different processes: survival analysis for decision path 1 and logistic regression for decision paths 1 and 3. We hope that, despite the methodological challenges, such bold theorizing attracts rather than repels further research. Indeed, we expect that the model's creators will begin to evaluate their theory with well-planned and well-executed studies to prevent their novel ideas from withering on the intellectual vine.

NEW EXPLANATORY CONSTRUCTS IN TURNOVER WORK

In this chapter, we review promising theoretical constructs that may advance the understanding of organizational withdrawal. Though not complex models, these constructs may elaborate the meaning of theoretical variables in comprehensive theories, which all too often vaguely specify model constructs. New constructs may supplement conceptual frameworks that, despite their expansive scope, may overlook essential antecedents to turnover. Thus, these constructs are important not only in their own right but also because they may provoke the revision of more complete theoretical formulations of withdrawal.

PERCEIVED ALTERNATIVES TO WORK

Perceived alternatives to work and economic opportunity represent central constructs in leading models of turnover (Farrell and Rusbult 1981; March and Simon 1958; Mobley 1977; Mobley, Griffeth, Hand, and Meglino 1979; Price 1977; Price and Mueller 1981, 1986; Steers and Mowday 1981). Perceived alternatives and economic opportunities constitute different conceptualizations of, at different levels of analysis, the availability of jobs. Economic opportunities refer to an objective condition of the availability of jobs and may affect turnover or moderate its influences. Perceived alternatives represent the employee's perceptions of the labor market. Unfortunately, in organizational research, the effects of perceived alternatives on individual turnover have been found to be weak or nonexistent. This contrast to the findings of the labor economists that unemployment rates have strong effects on quit rates (see Hulin, Roznowski, and Hachiya 1985; Mobley 1982a). We review research on these constructs in the following section.

Griffeth and Hom proposed (1988a) that imprecision, ambiguity, and diversity in operationalizations of perceived alternatives are likely to have resulted in an understatement of its effects on turnover. Different conceptualizations of the construct in various theories partly spawned alternative representations. March and Simon (1958), Price and Mueller (1981; 1986), and Steers and Mowday (1981) considered the number and availability of job opportunities; Farrell and Rusbult (1981) emphasized their quality. Mobley (1977), Mobley, Harner, and Hollingsworth (1978), and Mobley et al., (1979) stressed both the attainability and desirability of alternatives; Billings and Wemmerus (1983) construed perceived alternatives as a personal attribute, hope, arguing that an employee may be optimistic that viable alternatives exist without necessarily knowing the actual number or quality of those alternatives.

Inviting more confusion, empirical operationalizations often misrepresented corresponding conceptual definitions (Griffeth and Hom 1988a). For example, Price and Mueller's concept (1981 1986) embraced both number and availability of alternatives but their measure combined a subjective estimation of job vacancies in the labor market and a personal estimation of chances of finding alternatives (that is, they were measuring hope). Most models imply that specific positions lure employees away from their present job (Hulin et al. 1985), but prevailing measures refer to vague, general impressions of alternatives (see Youngblood, Mobley, and Meglino 1983). Indeed, the typical measurement is determined by simply asking employees to estimate the probability of finding an acceptable alternative (see Mobley, Horner, and Hollingsworth 1978).

Griffeth and Hom (1988a) compared the relative validity of several operationalizations of perceived alternatives within the context of Mobley, Griffeth, Hand, and Meglino's turnover model (1979). They found that no measure of perceived alternatives made a significant independent contribution to the prediction of turnover beyond job satisfaction and expected utility of the present job. Surprisingly, perceptions of specific jobs ("expected utility of alternatives" [ibid.]) predicted intentions to quit less accurately than did more general perceptions of the labor market. Though a pioneering effort, perceived alternatives may have limited influence on decisions to quit in their sample of nurses (who may quit for alternatives apart from work or look for other employment *after* quitting) and deficient representation of alternatives (considering only hospitals within the metropolitan area, thereby excluding jobs outside the city or in different states) likely weakened their measures of perceived alternatives.

Using meta-analysis, Steel and Griffeth (1989) more precisely estimated relationships between perceived alternatives and turnover. Affirming Hulin, Roznowski, and Hachiya's impression (1985), Steel and Griffeth uncovered a modest correlation: r_{mean} = .13. Hulin et al. had suggested several reasons for the minimal impact of perceived alternatives on withdrawal decisions. For one, drifters or casual workers (such as secondary wage earners), who are attracted into full-time employment during economic prosperity (which drives up wages), quit their jobs when they accumulate savings to pursue more enjoyable or less stressful avocations on a full-time basis. These peripheral workers do not quit to take a better, more satisfying job elsewhere; they abhor full-time, regular employment. Similarly, perceptions of the labor market do not underpin the intentions of leavers who are opting out of the work force—permanently or temporarily—to pursue other activities, such as childrearing. Departing from conventional assumptions, Hulin et al. further argued that alternative work may affect quit decisions through job affect. Perceived alternatives scarcely affect turnover because their effects are indirect and depend on transmission by job satisfaction.

Steel and Griffeth further proposed that three methodological problems factors may attenuate relationships between perceived alternatives and turnover. One problem is the predominance of occupationally homogeneous samples in research on turnover, which may restrict variance in perceptions of employment opportunities. Testing this idea, Steel and Griffeth correlated unemployment rates and correlations, derived from various studies, between perceived alternatives and quit rates. They hypothesized an inverse relationship between joblessness and the correlation between alternatives and turnover because as jobs become more plentiful, perceived alternatives should more strongly induce turnover. They were right: Correlations between alternatives and quit rates themselves inversely correlated with national, regional, and industrial unemployment statistics.

Contrary to the hypothesis, the correlations between alternatives and turnover *positively* covaried with occupational unemployment. Suspecting bias, because eight of fourteen occupational studies had sampled nurses, Steel and Griffeth sorted the studies into two subgroups, of nurses and of other workers, and recomputed the statistics. They found that occupational joblessness correlated *negatively* with correlations between alternatives and quit rates for the non-nursing sample ($r = -.76$, $p < .05$), as originally predicted, and positively for the nurses ($r = .83$, $p < .05$). They reasoned that, because the nursing labor market is persistently strong, nurses can readily enter and exit the work force with minimal job search and need for comparison. Because nurses take the job market for granted, perceptions of alternatives do not dominate their decisions to quit (Griffeth and Hom 1988a; Mowday, Koberg and McArthur 1984).

Steel and Griffeth also suggested that turnover base rates may affect the predictive accuracy of perceived alternatives. Testing this moderator, they correlated quit rates across different studies with correlations of perceived alternatives and turnover. The resulting .60 ($p < .01$) correlation indicated that the quit base rate accounted for 36 percent of the variance in this relationship. Thus, a larger variance in turnover (quit rates approaching 50 percent) would boost the estimated effects of perceived alternatives on turnover among other things. What is more, attenuation resulting from extreme base rates is especially acute in the literature on perceived alternatives. Homogenous sampling coupled with low quit rates constrain the variance in the predictor and the criterion. When both variables are restricted, the attenuating effects on relationships among the variables may be multiplicative rather than additive (Alexander, Carson, and Alliger 1987).

Poor instrumentation also possibly weakened the observable influence of perceived alternatives on turnover. Perceived alternatives were typically operationalized by deficient and unreliable measures. Most studies (59 percent) used single-item ratings. Concluding their review, Steel and Griffeth suggested the following avenues for future research on perceived alternatives: (1) sampling a wider range of jobs and occupations, (2) exploring methods to yield more optimal turnover base rates, (3) developing a multivariate conceptualization of alternatives, and (4) improving instrumentation.

Economic Opportunity

Economic opportunity is the objective counterpart to perceived alternatives. Unlike labor-economic studies on this macro construct (Mobley 1982a), relatively few organizational studies examined how economic opportunity affects turnover among individuals. For example, Gerhart (1987) found that regional unemployment rates moderate correlations between satisfaction and turnover. In a meta-analysis, Carsten and Spector (1987) correlated unemployment rates with correlations, derived from various studies, between satisfaction and turnover and also found that economic expansions facilitate the translation of dissatisfaction about the job into departure.

Dreher and Dougherty (1980) found job competition, statistics which they obtained from the United States Department of Labor's *Occupational Outlook Quarterly* (1976), did *not* affect turnover through any interaction with attitudes about the job. Their classification of employment opportunity is noteworthy because the *Occupational Outlook* provides independent evaluations of the supply and demand for most professional and technical jobs. A major drawback is that these projections are made on a national basis (which possibly accounts for the absence of moderators), whereas local or regional job markets may better disclose any moderation of relationships between satisfaction and quitting. Using local unemployment statistics, Youngblood, Baysinger, and Mobley (1985) did find that *both* job satisfaction and joblessness affect turnover and that the relationship between job satisfaction and turnover strengthens during prosperous economic times.

Hom, Caranikis-Walker, Prussia, and Griffeth (1992) used meta-analysis to cumulate studies testing the Mobley, Horner, and Hollingsworth model (1978), depicted in Figure 5-1. They grouped studies by various indices of unemployment to test the way in which unemployment moderates various pathways in the model. Occupational unemployment moderated the pathway between decisions to quit and turnover more than did other joblessness statistics. All forms of unemployment nevertheless conditioned the pathway between satisfaction and withdrawal cognitions (search intentions; quit intentions), although they exerted an opposite moderating impact. That is, depressed occupational labor markets decreased the pathway between satisfaction and thoughts of quitting but heighten the impact of satisfaction on search and quit intentions. In contrast, national and regional unemployment reinforced the pathway between satisfaction and thoughts of quitting while reducing the pathway between satisfaction and decisions to quit. What is more, national unemployment weakened the relationships between probability of alternatives and withdrawal cognitions, whereas occupational joblessness increased them. All forms of unemployment moderated the pathway between search intentions and decisions to quit, though in contrary directions. Expansive occupational markets reinforced this linkage, but prosperous regional and national markets diminished it.

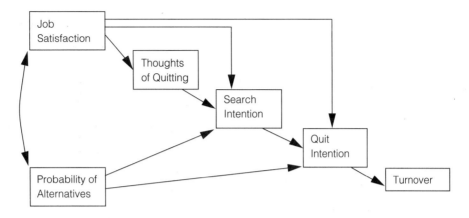

Figure 5-1   Mobley, Horner, and Hollingsworth's Model of Turnover. (W. Mobley, S. Horner, and A. Hollingsworth "An evaluation of precursors of hospital employee turnover," *Journal of Applied Psychology*,, 63 (1978): 410. Copyright 1978 by the American Psychological Association. Adapted by permission.)

Review

Labor economists have long recognized that turnover rates and overall employment conditions strongly relate at the aggregate level (Armknecht and Early 1972; Price 1977; Woodward 1975). These macro-level findings do not, however, help explain the processes underlying the reasons an individual quits, which comprise a different construct from that of organizational or industry turnover rates (Dreher and Dougherty 1980; Rousseau 1985). Recent organizational studies nevertheless suggest that unemployment rates can influence turnover at the individual level by interacting with determinants of turnover, such as job satisfaction, or by directly affecting departures. Hom, Cranikis-Walker, Prussia, and Griffeth (1992) showed that unemployment has more complex effects on the withdrawal process than was previously envisioned (it moderates various steps in the process) and that different forms of unemployment manifest dissimilar effects on withdrawal.

JOB PERFORMANCE

At least four research streams used job performance to clarify the turnover process. In one stream, performance was combined with turnover to define functional or dysfunctional turnover (see Chapter 1).

Performance and Voluntary Quits

At least four research streams used job performance to clarify the turnover process. In one stream, performance was combined with turnover to define functional or dysfunctional turnover (see Chapter 1). In a second, researchers sought to determine if performance and voluntary turnover were reliably related and to identify the sign of this relationship. Early studies characterized this relationship as *negative:* (poor performers quit more often [see, for example, Keller 1984; McEvoy and Cascio 1987; Sheridan and Vredenburgh 1978; Stumpf and Dawley 1981]), or *positive:* (good performers quit more often [see, for example, Allison 1974; Bassett 1967; Blau and Schoenherr 1971; Lazarfeld and Thielens 1958; Pavalko 1970; Pederson 1973]), or even *indeterminate* (see, for example, Mobley 1982a; Price 1977; Bluedorn and Abelson 1981]). Adding to this confusion, some researchers have characterized this relationship as *zero* (Martin, Price, and Mueller 1981). Resolving such conflicting findings, recent meta-analyses (Bycio, Hackett, and Alvares 1990; McEvoy and Cascio 1987; Williams and Livingstone 1994) estimate an *inverse* correlation between performance and turnover, though positive correlations are possible under certain conditions.

Those meta-analyses identified various moderators of the negative correlation between performance and turnover. For one, short time lapses between the measurements of performance and turnover attenuated their association (McEvoy and Cascio 1987). Explaining this moderation, McEvoy and Cascio argued that the relationship appears only after employees decide to leave. After that decision is formed, job performance declines precipitously before the employee quits. McEvoy and Cascio also found that national unemployment rates affect the correlation. Job scarcity increased it so that it became more *negative:* poor performers increasingly leave during poor job markets. Williams and Livingstone (1994) found that contingent pay systems strengthen correlations between performance and quitting, incentive pay accelerating exits by marginal performers.

Performance and Overall Turnover

In a third research stream, Jackofsky's hypothesis (1984), which posits a curvilinear, U-shaped relationship between performance and overall turnover (combining voluntary and involuntary quits) was tested. Extrapolating March and Simon's theory (1958), Jackofsky reasoned that, at low performance levels, involuntary turnover (dismissal) is high. As performance increases to some middle level, both involuntary and voluntary exits decline—presumably because average performers cannot easily find alternatives but neither do they face dismissal. As performance increases beyond the middle range, however, voluntary turnover increases because good performers can change jobs easily.

Testing this curvilinear hypothesis, Jackofsky, Ferris, and Breckenridge (1986) found significant U-shaped curves that accounted for 3 percent and 17.6 percent of the turnover variance among accountants and truck drivers, respectively. This study is noteworthy because the performance of the truckers was measured objectively, by the revenue earned. Later, Mossholder, Bedeian, Norris, Giles, and Feild (1988) replicated those curvilinear relationships in a study of operative electronic employees and textile supervisors. Williams and Livingstone's meta-analysis (1994) summarized the results from eight studies and found that curvilinear relationships between performance and turnover hold reliably.

Interactive Effects of
Performance on Turnover

In a fourth stream, researchers sought to determine if the desirability of job movement (defined as job satisfaction) interacts with performance to affect turnover. Given their greater mobility, effective performers can more easily translate their dissatisfaction with the job into departure than can poor performers. "Thus, the negative relationship between satisfaction and turnover should be stronger for higher, as compared to lower, performers" (Jackofsky 1984, p. 79). Mossholder et al. (1988) tested this prediction with two samples and found that the interaction held for operatives—accounting for 1 percent of the turnover variance—but not for textile supervisors.

Opposing Jackofsky's "perceived alternatives" contention (1984), Lance (1988) advanced a "contingent rewards" rationale (Dreher 1982; Spencer and Steers 1981), theorizing that there is a stronger negative relationship between job satisfaction and turnover for *poor* performers than there is for good performers. Supposedly, most firms retain the good performers by rewarding them more generously than they reward poor performers, which decreases the latters' morale (Zenger 1992). Poor performers are more likely to be "pushed" from the job by dissatisfaction; good performers are readily "pulled" from their present jobs by factors unrelated to their own satisfaction (by, for instance, unsolicited job offers, movement to a higher-level job with another company, or "incidental" job search resulting in an alternative employment opportunity). Using turnover intentions as dependent variable, Lance sustained the "contingent rewards" hypothesis for first-line supervisory and hourly technical groups, but not for other occupational groups.

Review

Job performance exerts complex effects on the turnover process. Nonetheless, the theoretical premise for interactive and curvilinear performance effects is that good performers have more or better alternatives than do poor performers (Jackofsky 1984; Lance 1988). Yet the notion that effective performers have better job opportunities may not always hold. Conceivably, an objective verifiability of job performance would determine whether or not effective performers have more plentiful jobs. Incumbents in many occupations cannot provide any objective documentation of their work achievements to other prospective employers, who must rely on less trustworthy resumes or references to discern an applicant's credentials. University professors can list scholarly publications to document their accomplishments. Schwab found (1991) that accomplished scholars more readily quit for other academic posts than do inept professors. Schwab's finding bears replication for other professionals whose achievements can be authenticated by prospective employers, for example, professional athletes, top executives, scientists and engineers. Future research must assess the greater employability of higher performers directly than rather than infer their marketability from elevated quit rates.

Empirical studies only partially sustained both competing, interactive performance effects. Mossholder et al. (1988) found *some* support for Jackofsky's view (1984) that the negative correlation between satisfaction and quit is higher for effective performers. Lance (1988) found *some* evidence for the "contingent reward" hypothesis, which posits a stronger correlation between satisfaction and quitting for marginal performers. Further scholarly inquiry might explore moderators underlying these discrepant findings. Quite likely, closer examinations of the nature of the reward system (Zenger 1992), type of performance measures, and occupational job markets may uncover promising moderators.

ORGANIZATIONAL COMMITMENT

The popularity of the notion of organizational commitment extends over three decades. Becker (1960) first formally analyzed this construct and proposed the side-bet notion, wherein several conditions under which "side bets" are made by the individual, organization, and culture encourage employees to stay on the job. For example, generalized cultural expectations, impersonal bureaucratic arrangements, individual adjustments to social positions, and face-to-face interactions all involuntarily bind an employee to the company "by default."

In the 1970s, Porter and his colleagues (Porter, Steers, Mowday, and Boulian 1974; Mowday, Porter, and Steers 1982) advanced a new conceptualization, specifying commitment as comprising: (1) a strong belief in and acceptance of the organization's goals and values, (2) a willingness to exert considerable effort on behalf of the organization, and (3) a strong desire to maintain membership in the organization. They developed the Organizational Commitment Questionnaire (OCQ) to assess their concept, and the OCQ eventually became the leading index for testing hypotheses about attachments to companies (see Mathieu and Zajac 1990). Undertaking a longitudinal test, Porter et al. (1974) first demonstrated that commitment more effectively differentiated stayers and leavers than did job satisfaction. Later, Porter, Crampon, and Smith (1976) showed that differences in commitment between stayers and leavers grow as the time lag between turnover and assessments of commitment shrinks.

Subsequently, Steers (1977) proposed and conducted a two-sample test of a model in which organizational commitment mediated three classes of antecedents (personal traits, such as need for achievement and age; job characteristics, such as task identity and feedback; and work experiences, such as group cohesion) and multiple consequences (quit intentions, attendance, turnover, and job performance). Most of the antecedents significantly predicted commitment, but the relationships of commitment to turnover ($r = -.17$, $p \leq .05$) and other outcomes, such as attendance and performance, were low or insignificant. Although partially upheld, Steers's framework (and its later variant [see Figure 5-2]) has activated numerous scholarly explorations of the causes and outcomes of commitment.

In a comprehensive meta-analysis, Mathieu and Zajac (1990) summarized the studies on the antecedents and consequences of commitment, organizing the results according to an expanded framework based on Steers (1977). This framework, including corrected "population" correlations between commitment and its causes or outcomes, is shown in Figure 5-3. Individuals with certain qualities are predisposed to form commitments to a company. Notably, employees who are older ($r = .20$), self-confident ($r = .63$), and work-oriented ($r = .29$) most bond with their firms. Interestingly, the strong self-efficacy influence suggests that employees will make commitments to companies that gratify their needs for growth and achievement.

Employees are also bound to organizations by various dimensions of complexity of job duties, including job scope (overall job complexity, $r = .50$) and challenge ($r = .35$). By comparison, ambiguity ($r = -.22$), conflict ($r = -.27$), and overload ($r = -.21$) in the work role will loosen company affiliations. Leadership, especially leader communication ($r = .45$) and participative management ($r = .39$), and occupational commitment ($r = .44$), job involvement ($r = .44$), and job satisfaction ($r = .53$) reinforce bonds of loyalty. Committed employees quit less often ($r = -.28$) and receive higher performance evaluations ($r = .14$) than do uncommitted employees.

Review

Despite its impressive pattern of relationships, organizational commitment has garnered criticisms on grounds of measurement and conceptualiza-

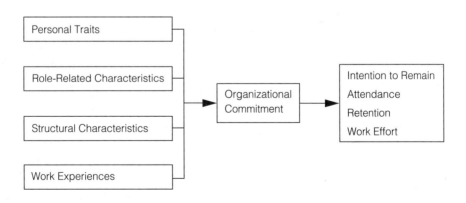

Figure 5-2 Mowday, Porter, and Steers's Model of Organizational Commitment. (Adapted from R. Mowday, L. Porter, and R. Steers, *Employee-Organization Linkages*, New York: Academic Press, (1982): 30.)

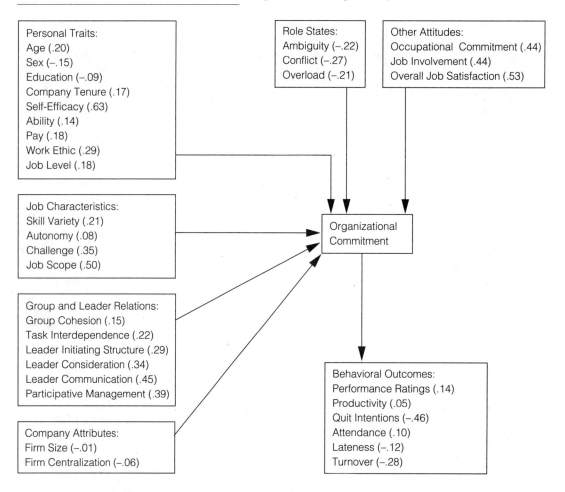

Figure 5-3 Mathieu and Zajac's Meta-analytical Model of Organizational Commitment. (Adapted from J. Mathieu and D. Zajac, "A review and meta-analysis of the antecedents, correlates, and consequences of organizational commitment; *Psychological Bulletin* **108 (1990): 174. Copyright 1990 by the American Psychological Association. Adapted by permission.)**

tion. Though commitment predicts quits better than does job satisfaction, Mobley, Griffeth, Hand, and Meglino (1979) expressed reservations that the inclusion of intentions to quit in the OCQ scale possibly inflated its predictive validity. Hom and his colleagues (Hom and Hulin 1981; Hom, Katerberg, and Hulin 1979) statistically removed an independent measure of intentions to quit from correlations between turnover and attitudes. After those decisions were partialled out, correlations between commitment and quitting did *not* surpass correlations between satisfaction and quitting. Hom and Hulin thus concluded "that the predictive power of OC resides not in its assessing a more relevant employee attitude, but in its assessing intention to withdraw from the organization" (1981, p. 34).

Over the years, other conceptualizations of commitment have surfaced. Reichers (1985) reconceptualized commitment in terms of different constituents, recognizing the influences (values and goals) of multiple reference groups (constituency) and roles in organizations. She posited three definitions: (1) side-bets, or the rewards and costs of membership in an organization, (2) attributions, or the binding of the individual to behavior, and (3) congruence between the goals of the individual and the organization. This concept of "multiple commitments" is a significant theoretical milestone, refining as it does the original global conception of commitment (see Porter et al. 1974) by delineating its multiple facets.

O'Reilly and Chatman (1986) also specified three dimensions of commitment to an organization: (1) compliance (instrumental involvement for extrinsic rewards), (2) identification (involvement based on desire for affiliation), and (3) internalization (involvement predicated on congruence between the values of the individual and the company). They developed an instrument to measure these bases and administered a survey to university personnel. Predictably, factor analysis substantiated three separate factors, and the survey showed that commitment based on internalization or identification increased organizational citizenship and decreased turnover. Compliance, however, weakened decisions to remain with the organization.

Similarly, Allen and Meyer (1993) identified three kinds of commitment: affective, continuance, and normative. Affective attachment corresponds to Porter's conception; continuance refers to the economic, side-bet approach espoused by Becker (1960). Normative commitment, which is defined as moral responsibility to the organization, extends past perspectives. In two studies, Allen and Meyer developed measures of this multidimensional construct and then estimated relationships between these forms and antecedents of commitment. Results differentiated these forms, showing them to be rooted in disparate causes.

In summary, modern theoretical and empirical efforts increasingly suggest that commitment has multiple dimensions. Despite their varying terminology, writers on commitment apparently agree on three dominant dimensions: (1) attitudinal (internalization, identification [O'Reilly and Chatman 1986]; affective [Allen and Meyer 1993]) (2) calculative (compliance [O'Reilly and Chatman 1986]; continuance [Allen and Meyer 1993]); and (3) normative (ibid.). Differentiating attitudinal from calculative commitments, Mathieu and Zajac's meta-analysis (1990) revealed that attitudinal commitment correlated with job satisfaction and quit decisions more than did calculative commitment. Future research should substantiate our crude taxonomy, perhaps by using multitrait-multimethod approaches to establish convergence among different, but parallel constructs. Though increasingly recognizing company commitment, present-day theories of turnover have lagged behind the theoretical development of the concept of commitment (Price and Mueller 1986; Rusbult and Farrell 1983; Sheridan and Abelson 1983; Steers and Mowday 1981). Further refinements of extant turnover models must acknowledge the different forms of commitment and clarify the different ways in which those forms might influence the termination process.

The causal direction of organizational commitment and job satisfaction remains mired in controversy. Early on, Bateman and Strasser's cross-lagged correlation and regression analyses (1984) found that commitment affects satisfaction. Yet two cross-sectional studies using structural equations modeling (SEM) found commitment to be a *consequence* of job satisfaction (Williams and Hazer 1986). Panel research using SEM analysis (Curry, Wakefield, Price, and Mueller 1986; Farkas and Tetrick 1989) found that neither attitude displayed lagged effects on the other attitude. Farkas and Tetrick found synchronous influences between the attitudes but overlooked many causes of both attitudes, testing a misspecified model (Anderson and Williams 1992). Upon reanalysis, new SEM tests rejected even synchronous effects after correlated disturbances were specified to capture omitted causes (ibid.). Mathieu's cross-sectional test (1991) of a nonrecursive model, which included many attitudinal antecedents, uncovered reciprocal causality, albeit one that showed that satisfaction affects commitment more than commitment affects satisfaction. These findings thus tentatively suggest that there is reciprocal *and* synchronous causality between commitment and satisfaction, with satisfaction influencing commitment more than vice versa. This causality accords with the contention held by Price and Mueller (1986) and Rusbult and Farrell (1983) that commitment translates the impact of dissatisfaction into exits.

JOB STRESS AND BURNOUT

Kahn and Quinn (1970) broadly defined job stress as constituting ambiguity in the work role, role conflict, and role overload. Although the contention is intuitively appealing, the few studies available disagree about whether job stress triggers terminations. For example, early research, such as that by Weitz (1956) and Lyons (1971), reported that ambiguity of work role increases turnover. Hamner and Tosi found (1974) that role conflict and ambiguity did not affect turnover. Frese and Okonek found (1984) that job-related stress among shift workers did not boost their departure.

To account for such weak, conflicting findings, organizational researchers deduced that role stress only indirectly induces quits through job dissatisfaction (Gupta and Beehr 1979). Because stress is uncomfortable, employees become dissatisfied and avoid work by tardiness, absenteeism, or quitting. More formally, Bedeian and Armenakis (1981) proposed a causal model describing the effects of role conflict and ambiguity on job tension, job satisfaction, and intentions to quit. This model, which path analyses supported, is shown in Figure 5-4. In another path analytical test, Kemery, Bedeian, Mossholder, and Touliatos (1985) validated this model in three

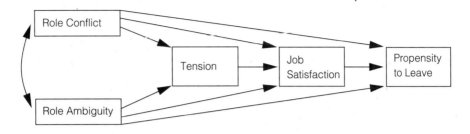

Figure 5-4 Bedeian-Armenakis Model of Role Stress. (Adapted from E. Kemery, A. Bedeian, K. Mossholder, and J. Touliatos, "Outcomes of role stress: A multisample constructive replication," *Academy of Management Journal* **28 (1985): 365.)**

samples of accountants and a hospital sample, finding that most causal pathways were significant across diverse samples.

Netemeyer, Johnston, and Burton (1990), using latent variables SEM methodology, retested the Bedeian-Armenakis model with a salesforce sample. Though validating all indicators, their SEM analysis supported only 50 percent of the causal pathways in the structural model. Specifically, role conflict increased tension and dissatisfaction (though not affecting quit propensity), but role ambiguity did not affect any components of the model. Predictably, tension reduced satisfaction, which in turn, increased propensities to quit. Perhaps occupational differences or SEM controls for measurement errors accounted for the findings by Netemeyer et al., that the model was weaker than Kemery et al. (1985) had found it.

Going beyond conventional research into role stress, Jackson, Schwab, and Schuler (1986) adopted Maslach's model (1982) of job burnout, which embodies emotional exhaustion, depersonalization, and beliefs about lack of personal accomplishment. Their survey revealed that school teachers who remained on the job (or left for other reasons) said that they felt less exhausted than did those leaving for a new teaching job or leaving the teaching profession entirely. Still, depersonalization and feelings of inadequacy did not affect rates of attrition among teachers.

Review

In summary, studies of turnover are preoccupied with role conflict and ambiguity as primary stress-related determinants of withdrawal. Yet other forms of job stress—derived from environmental sources, such as noise, crowding, and threat of criminal assault, and psychological sources, such as time pressure and sexual harassment—might induce people to leave their jobs (see Frese and Okonek 1984). Surely such narrow conceptualizations may explain why mainstream theories on turnover have generally excluded job stress. Quite likely, turnover theorists presume that role strain is no different from job dissatisfaction and that poor work conditions encompass role stress (see Mobley, Griffeth, Hand, and Meglino 1979). Excepting job burnout, factors traditionally associated with role stress thus seem redundant in light of explanatory constructs in models of turnover. Recent theories have introduced new constructs of stress, such as "adaptation" (Hulin 1991), "job tension" (Sheridan and Abelson 1983), and "system shock" (Lee and Mitchell 1994).

Stress researchers universally contend that job stress induces turnover through dissatisfaction. Surprisingly, little research has directly substantiated this assumption. Evaluations of the Bedeian-Armenakis model tested whether job satisfaction mediates the impact of role stress on *intentions* to quit, not on actual turnover. Thus, this critical mediational pathway awaits future corroboration.

Burnout

Though Jackson, Schwab, and Schuler's results (1986) are worthwhile, job burnout seems to be less a cause of turnover than a reaction to more fundamental causes, such as excessive workload and insufficient autonomy on the job. That is, the same factors that induce job burnout may be producing terminations. Reflecting psychological withdrawal from frustrating working conditions, job burnout may simply be an emotional prelude to eventual withdrawal from the job (see Hulin, Roznowski, and Hachiya 1985). Job burnout may accurately foreshadow turnover, but the phenomenon appears to be limited to the care-giving fields (nurses, social workers, and ministers) and is not readily generalizable to other professions.

THE THEORY OF REASONED ACTION

Organizational researchers have extended Fishbein's general attitude-behavior theory (1975) to explain employees' behavior. Drawing from expectancy theory (see Vroom 1964), the "theory of reasoned action" (see Figure 5-5) assumes that people use information rationally to make behavioral decisions. This process of decision making arises from beliefs about behavioral outcomes and social expectations and moves toward behavioral attitudes and social norms, to behavioral intentions, and finally to action (Prestholdt, Lane, and Mathews 1987). Accordingly, the immediate determinant of behavior (*B*) is behavioral intention (*BI*). Intention, in turn, is derived from attitudes toward performing the behavior (*Aact*) and perceptions of social pressure to enact the behavior (*SN*). These relationships are expressed in the following equation:

$B \approx BI = w_1 Aact + w_2 SN,$
> where w_1 and w_2 are relative weights estimated by standardized regression coefficients, signifying causal significance.

The attitudinal and normative components then originate from specific beliefs. Essentially, *Aact* is a function of beliefs about behavioral consequences and evaluation of these consequences. Algebraically, this is expressed:

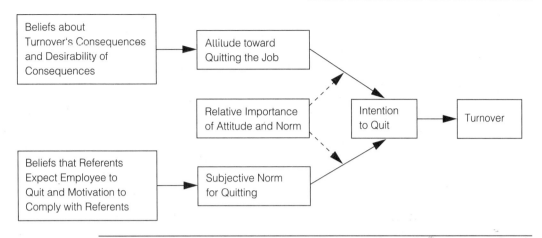

Figure 5-5 Fishbein and Ajzen's Theory of Reasoned Action. (Adapted from M. Fishbein and I. Ajzen, *"Belief, Attitude, Intention and Behavior,"* Reading, Mass: Addison-Wesley, (1975) 334.)

$$Aact = \sum_{i=1}^{n} b_i e_i,$$

where b_i is the expectation that behavioral performance yields outcome i, e_i is the desirability of outcome i, and n is the number of salient outcomes.

Similarly, *SN* depends on beliefs about which referent others want the individual to perform the act and the individual's motivation to comply with the referents. Formally:

$$SN = \sum_{r=1}^{m} NB_r Mc_r,$$

where NB_r is the normative belief that referent r thinks the person should or should not perform the behavior; Mc_r is the motivation to comply with the referent, and m is number of relevant referents.

Four studies have applied Fishbein's theory to turnover. Surveying nursing home employees, Newman (1974) contrasted the predictive utility of an early version of the Fishbein model (1967) to that of job satisfaction. The Fishbein model predicted turnover more accurately than did satisfaction. Hom and his associates (Hom, Katerberg, and Hulin 1979; Hom and Hulin 1981) also compared the relative efficacy of Fishbein's model, organizational commitment, and job satisfaction for predicting reenlistment in the National Guard. The forecast by Fishbein's model (R^2s = .50) was the more accurate.

Prestholdt, Lane, and Mathews (1987) assessed the Fishbein model's effectiveness for predicting turnover among nurses and introduced several modifications. The researchers expanded the model by adding, as another determinant of behavioral intention, the moral obligation to perform the act. Conceivably, feelings of moral obligation in members of an altruistic profession may bolster their decisions to stay. The researchers also assessed the nurses' beliefs about, attitudes toward, and intentions of staying *and* of resigning, computing the scores for differences among the components of the model to predict turnover. They reasoned that decisions to quit implicitly reflect a comparison between the relative attractiveness of staying and leaving (see Hom 1980). Thus, with knowledge of a person's cognitions and affect toward all behavioral options, one would be able to predict the person's behavioral decision more accurately than with knowledge of beliefs and feelings about only one alternative. According to cross-validated hierarchical regression analyses, the Fishbein model (and its refinements) strongly predicted turnover among nurses ($R^2 = .32$).

Review

Overall, the Fishbein model's impressive validity for predicting turnover (R^2s = .50 and .32 for Hom and Hulin [1981] and Prestholdt, Lane, and Mathews [1987], respectively) suggests that, if forecasting turnover were one's goal, Fishbein's model is the model of choice. Besides this, knowledge about employees' beliefs about the consequences of turnover and about which referents urge them to quit can suggest interventions to improve retention (ibid.). If an understanding of the turnover process is one's goal, Fishbein's model has limited value, overlooking, as it does, sources underlying behavioral and normative beliefs. For example, why do resigning nurses believe that by quitting, they will have more time for their family and why are they pressured by their spouses to leave (ibid.)? Are these beliefs rooted in "kinship responsibilities" (Price and Mueller 1986) or "nonwork influences" (Steers and Mowday 1981), both explanatory constructs posited by turnover writers? Such additional explication of the origins of behavioral and normative beliefs (and other determinants of turnover) is the basic objective of most theories of turnover.

Future extensions of the Fishbein model for turnover might consider new theoretical revisions of it. Ajzen (1991) introduced the notion of perceived behavioral control, or beliefs about personal ability to execute the act, to Fishbein's basic theory. Supposedly, beliefs about volitional control over the act reinforce decisions to perform the act through greater perseverance and correct forecasts of behavioral obstacles. Bagozzi and Warshaw (1990) and Triandis (1977) theorized that past actions may directly boost behavioral intentions and occurrences without mediation by mental deliberations of action outcomes or referent demands. These added behavioral precursors may, however, influence certain types of turnover decisions. Perceived behavioral control may best affect decisions about reenlistment, when military organizations can reject soldiers seeking reenlistment because they are incompetent, disabled, or specialized in a military occupation for which demand is declining (see Mobley, Hand, Baker, and Meglino 1979). Similarly, multiple earlier quits may primarily boost terminations by marginal drifters and casual workers (Hulin, Roznowski, and Hachiya 1985).

ATTRIBUTIONS OF PERFORMANCE

According to Weiner's attribution theory (1972, 1979), employees are information processors who seek causal interpretations for their personal achievements. To explain their success or failure, employees invoke the following explanatory factor(s): ability (which is inferred from past successes or failures at similar tasks), task difficulty (which is inferred from the success of others doing the task), luck (which is inferred from a prior pattern of random task outcomes), and effort (which is inferred from task persistence). Weiner classified these attributions along two dimensions: the locus of the causal factor (internal or external to the person) and the stability of the causal factor (a stable or unstable cause). Ability is a stable internal factor, whereas effort is an unstable internal factor; task difficulty is a stable external cause and luck an unstable external cause.

Extending Weiner's theory, Parsons, Herold, and Leatherwood (1985) conceived that demoralizing, perhaps erroneous, personal attributions for job performance by new employees may impel their premature departure. Surveying new female room attendants working for a hotel, Parsons and fellow researchers asked them to think about their performance and identify causal factors responsible for their performance. They found that new employees attributing their performance to luck were more likely to have resigned within six months of starting the job than were those who attributed their performance to ability, effort, or the difficulty of the task. Apparently, when luck is considered to be the explanation of early performance, feelings of achievement are undermined, and insecure newcomers are then motivated to quit prematurely rather than to persist in the job. Positive feedback from the supervisors (based on supervisory reports) increased the newcomers' internal attributions and their tendency to stay. Perhaps employees, receiving performance cues from their supervisors, make causal attributions based on that feedback, and those attributions shape their decisions about quitting.

Review

Parsons, Herold, and Leatherwood's intriguing findings (1985) merit replication and consideration by theorists of turnover. Quite possibly, performance attributions can further account for the causes of turnover in various conceptual schemes. To illustrate, self-explanations of work effectiveness may affect job performance, which, in Steers and Mowday's formulation (1981), is both outcome and cause of job attitudes. That is, dissatisfied employees who habitually attribute their success to hard work or superior ability may be most likely to improve their performance and thus reverse their inferior records and poor attitudes. Dissatisfied employees making such interpretations may also try to change the situation (another response to dissatisfaction) because they feel more optimistic about improving the job given that self-affirming attributions. Yet employees who rely on ability and effort to explain work achievements may hold higher job expectations of the job and feel more dissatisfied (for the job is less likely to meet inflated expectations) (ibid.).

Future work might evaluate attribution-based interventions to stem the early attrition of newcomers (Parsons, Herold, and Leatherwood 1985). Supervisors could encourage trainees to use more performance attributions that are self-enhancing. That is, they might encourage attributions to effort after trainees have turned in a poor performance—by believing, for example, they were insufficiently persistent—and attributions to effort and ability after a good performance (taking more pride in their achievements). By prompting such self-attributions (while discouraging attributions to luck), supervisors might prevent premature resignations among new hires.

CAREER DEVELOPMENT

Krau (1981) conceptualized turnover as a career decision dependent on an employee's career stage. He observed that job changes are commonplace during the exploratory stage of a career and that job stability characterizes the establishment stage. However, a midlife crisis may induce job mobility. If it does not, employees in midcareer enter a maintenance phase, when family responsibilities and life experiences anchor them to the job. Krau further posited that an individual's career type (ascendant or horizontal) and a firm's promotional system (open or inert) shape decisions about quitting. Ascendant individuals (who have a strong orientation toward vocational upward mobility and the qualifications to attain it) would remain in an open system, which provides ample promotions, whereas the horizontally oriented (who lack career ambitions) prefer inert companies, where promotions are rare. Ascendants are, therefore, more likely to quit inert firms; horizontals more readily leave open firms.

To test these hypotheses, Krau first carried out a retrospective study, collecting demographic data on former employees to assess their career stages. This study disclosed that 63 percent of leavers were single and only 15 percent supported several children, indicating that family responsibilities stabilize employment. Workers who had worked in several previous production jobs or acquired more training less readily quit their present job. Most quitters left shortly after entering the firm, and although turnover was higher among younger people, it began to increase again at about age thirty-five.

In a second, longitudinal study, Krau (1981) sampled apprentice lathe operators to examine how career type interacts with promotional system. He first contacted the apprentices after they had completed their schooling and worked for a year. Then he tracked their work history and career development five years later. Apprentices completed a summary measure comprising vocational aptitude (e.g., mechanical reasoning), attitudes toward work and authority figures (using a projective personality test) and vocational interest (measured by reading preferences for book titles), mastery of their vocation (knowledge of lathe technology), initial adaptation (performance during first year on the job), and demographic indices of family ties, by which their career type (ascendant scores) was indexed. Krau then classified these 110 operators as ascendants or horizontals based on their ascendant scores. He regarded promotional systems as open if at least 10 percent of all candidates were promoted to a higher job within a five-year period; otherwise, he deemed the promotional system as inert. Statistical analysis uncovered the predicted interaction between career type and promotional openness on turnover. Expectedly, horizontals were much more likely to quit open systems than inert systems, whereas ascendants were more likely to leave inert systems than open systems.

Review

Krau's career stage is a promising explanatory construct that is inadequately represented by existing formulations of turnover. At best, several theories specify family responsibility and job investments, which may indirectly reflect different career stages (Mobley, Griffeth, Hand, and Meglino 1979; Price and Mueller 1986; Rusbult and Farrell 1983). That is, midlife employees have larger family obligations and more job investments (if they have long tenure in the firm) than do employees in the exploratory stage. Nonetheless, we welcome more direct evidence of the viability of this career construct and its causal impact on turnover. After all, Krau's preliminary study operationalized career stage with demographic proxies and did not demonstrate its predictive validity given retrospective data.

Several frameworks of turnover study have preexisting constructs that made Krau's career type and promotional system redundant. Though Krau's measure comprised an odd concoction of heterogeneous indices, career type seemed akin to promotional aspirations or desires, which several turnover theories already posit. For example, Steers and Mowday (1981) and Mobley, Griffeth, Hand, and Meglino (1979) acknowledged preferences for job outcomes, and by extension, preferences for advancement prospects as attitudinal antecedents. Similarly, Krau's promotional system resembles "promotional opportunities" or "expected utility of the present work role" in prevailing models (Mobley 1982a; Mobley et al. 1979; Price and Mueller 1981; 1986). Nevertheless, we welcome additional validation efforts to refine Krau's index of ascendant career type. Furthermore, future investigations should replicate the predictive validity of this instrument in Western samples. Krau did not differentiate between voluntary and involuntary turnover among his sample of Eastern European workers. He argued that East European managers who refuse to endorse a worker's leaving can make it difficult for him to get another job. Thus, workers often deliberately do a poor job to get managerial approval of their departure. Krau thus assumed that all or most dismissals were "voluntary" quits.

INTEGRATION OF EMPIRICAL FINDINGS AND TURNOVER MODELS

Theoretical models of employee turnover have proliferated since March and Simon's seminal explanation (1958) of organizational participation (Hulin, Roznowski, and Hachiya 1985; Lee and Mitchell 1991, 1994; Mobley 1977; Mobley, Griffeth, Hand, and Meglino 1979; Price and Mueller 1981, 1986; Rusbult and Farrell 1983; Sheridan and Abelson 1983; Steers and Mowday 1981). Rather than introducing another model, our purpose here is to suggest an integrative theoretical framework that builds on contemporary formulations, incorporating constructs and construct linkages that comply with empirical findings. We review, in particular, empirical tests of prevailing theoretical accounts and meta-analyses of turnover correlates. This integrative conceptualization is shown in Figure 6-1, and in the following sections, we discuss the rationale and research for each structural linkage.

JOB ATTITUDES → WITHDRAWAL COGNITIONS

Central to all conceptualizations of turnover, including the present model, is that poor attitudes stimulate the termination process. Traditional thinking (for example, March and Simon 1958; Mobley 1977; Porter and Steers 1973; Price 1977) asserts that job dissatisfaction prompts turnover cognitions, presuming that a dissatisfying work environment motivates the desire to escape (Hulin 1991). Positing that commitment to company values and goals undermines thoughts of withdrawal (Mowday, Porter and Steers 1982), contemporary theorists of turnover (Price and Mueller 1986; Steers and Mowday 1981) have incorporated organizational commitment. Strengthening this expanded set of attitudinal causes, meta-analyses found that both attitudes predict withdrawal cognitions (Hom, Caranikis-Walker, Prussia, and Griffeth 1992; Mathieu and Zajac 1990), while confirmatory factor analyses affirmed their conceptual independence (Brooke, Russell, and Price 1988; Mathieu and Farr 1991). Scholars of commitment agree, contending that commitment predicts quits more accurately than does satisfaction (Porter, Steers, Mowday, and Boulian 1974), because resignation implies a rejection of the company, not necessarily of the job which can be assumed elsewhere (Hom and Hulin 1981). Considering these theoretical rationales and facts, our model includes commitment and satisfaction as affective states initiating withdrawal cognitions.

Contemporary models embrace commitment and satisfaction, but their place in a structural network of withdrawal precursors remains controversial. Early theorists proposed that commitment mediates the influence of satisfaction on terminations (Price and Mueller 1986). Although consistent with cross-sectional recursive models (ibid.; Williams and Hazer 1986), more

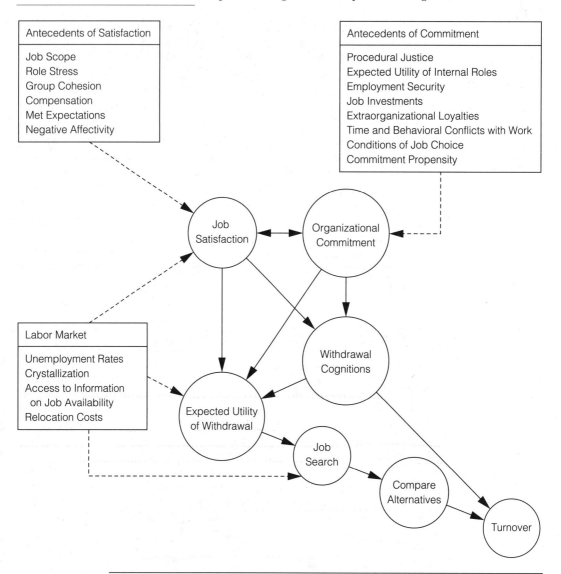

Figure 6-1 Integrative Model of Turnover Determinants

rigorous tests have disputed this preliminary perspective. Most notably, panel research (Farkas and Tetrick 1989) and nonrecursive models (Mathieu 1991) found a reciprocal causality between attitudes and that satisfaction affects commitment more than commitment affects satisfaction (ibid.). Other researchers doubted full mediation through commitment, finding that both attitudes shaped quit decisions independently (Farkas and Tetrick 1989; Vandenberg and Scarpello 1990). On these grounds, our model specifies a reciprocal influence between satisfaction and commitment and their direct effects on withdrawal cognitions (Hom and Griffeth 1991).

WITHDRAWAL COGNITIONS → TURNOVER

Orthodox thinking distinguishes various turnover cognitions, such as thoughts of quitting and search and quit intentions (see Dalessio, Silverman, and Shuck 1986; Hom, Caranikis-Walker, Prussia, and Griffeth 1992). Despite allusions to different acts (quitting and searching), withdrawal cognitions have not been empirically differentiated by recent confirmatory factor analyses (Hom and Griffeth 1991; Hom, Kinicki, and Domm 1989; Jaros et al. 1993). Indeed, several theorists posit a more parsimonious conception, maintaining that molecular withdrawal cognitions represent various facets of a global construct (Miller, Katerberg, and Hulin 1979; Steers and Mowday 1981). Based on these results and reasoning, our conceptual framework offers a general cognition of withdrawal that subsumes specific intentions to withdraw (see James and James 1989).

We agree with Lee and Mitchell (1994), Steers and Mowday (1981), and Hom and Griffeth (1991) that withdrawal cognitions can directly activate turnover. Unlike commonly held viewpoints (those, for example, of Mobley [1977] and Mobley, Griffeth, Hand, and Meglino [1979]), this direct pathway takes into consideration impulsive quitting (Mobley 1977), labor market exits by marginal drifters (Hulin, Roznowski, and Hachiya 1985; Lee and Mitchell 1994), unemployment while searching (Baysinger and Mobley 1983), relocation to distant communities (Hom and Griffeth 1991), and decisions to pursue outside activities (for example, childrearing or childbearing [Hom, Griffeth, and Sellaro 1984; Hom and Griffeth 1991]). Simply stated, this pathway from cognitions of withdrawal to quitting recognizes that many employees depending on various factors including, but not limited to, employment levels in the community, occupational demand, work orientation, and so on, may quit without securing alternative employment.

WITHDRAWAL COGNITIONS → JOB SEARCH

Like Steers and Mowday (1981), we submit in this model that some employees deciding to quit seek other employment before leaving. This route to withdrawal deviates from the conventional tenet that employees develop turnover cognitions after seeking and comparing alternatives (see March and Simon 1958; Mobley 1977; Price and Mueller 1981; Rusbult and Farrell 1983). Indeed, growing empirical evidence refutes this sequence from search to cognitions of withdrawal. For example, Gerhart (1990), Carsten and Spector (1987), and Hom, Caranikis-Walker, Prussia, and Griffeth (1992) found that unemployment rates moderate the impact on turnover of decisions to quit. Yet if employees enter the labor market and form impressions of alternatives before deciding to quit, unemployment rates (a proxy for perceived alternatives) should *not* condition the relationship between the intention to quit and quitting. Rather, observed moderating effects suggest that employees develop intentions to quit before seeking another job. Thus, poor job markets frustrate initial plans to quit work (weakening the relation between intentions of quitting and actually departing), whereas expanding job markets allow premeditated cognitions of withdrawal to be translated into quitting. Moreover, path analytical tests uphold this sequence: withdrawal cognitions → search → quitting (see Griffeth and Hom 1990; Hom, Caranikis-Walker, Prussia, and Griffeth 1992; Hom and Griffeth 1991; Hom, Griffeth, and Sellaro 1984).

EXPECTED UTILITIES OF
WITHDRAWAL → JOB SEARCH

Adopting the rationale of Mobley (1977) and Fishbein and Ajzen (1975), our model posits that prospective quitters evaluate the perceived costs and benefits of quitting and job seeking before pursuing alternatives. Likewise, theories of alternative responses to job dissatisfaction specify that the expected utility (perceived consequences) of those responses dictate their choice (Hulin 1991; Rosse and Miller 1984). Empirical research repeatedly finds that the expected utility of quitting affects terminations (Hom and Hulin 1981; Prestholdt, Lane, and Mathews 1987) and that the expected costs of leaving inhibit a number of exit responses, including job seeking and quitting (Rusbult, Farrell, Rogers, and Mainous 1988; Withey and Cooper 1989).

Straying from popular beliefs of separate expected utilities for job search and quitting (see Hom, Griffeth, and Sellaro 1984; Laker 1991; Lee 1988; Sager, Varadarajan, and Futrell 1988; Steel, Lounsbury, and Horst 1981), we argue that these utilities reflect different aspects of a broader construct of expected utility of withdrawal. Because quit and search decisions are often made simultaneously (Hom and Griffeth 1991), we reason that these expected utilities are inextricably codetermined (see Mobley 1977). This view corresponds with emerging formulations that categorize diverse actions to avoid the job—namely, transfer, job seeking, and turnover—into a general response family, namely exit (see Farrell 1983; Rossé and Hulin 1985; Rusbult et al. 1988; Withey and Cooper 1989). Similarly, Hulin (1991) advocates a general adaptation construct that underlies diverse withdrawal behaviors, including exits. Upholding our global conception, Hom and Griffeth (1991) found in a confirmatory factor analysis that the expected utilities of searching and quitting represented the same latent factor.

Consistent with Mobley (1977) and Steers and Mowday (1981), we propose that positive expected utility of withdrawal stimulates job seeking. After uncovering alternatives, job seekers would then compare them against their present position. Should this comparison favor an alternative, the employee would choose this job and quit. In line with this argument, empirical data substantiated a sequence wherein job search precedes job comparisons (Hom, Griffeth, and Sellaro 1984; Hom and Griffeth 1991; Lee and Mowday 1987; Steel, Lounsbury, and Horst 1981).

OTHER EMPIRICAL SUPPORT
FOR STRUCTURAL NETWORK

Thus far, we discussed empirical support for segments of the proposed nomological network. More direct evidence comes from Hom and Griffeth (1991) and Griffeth and Hom (1992), who completely validated the structural links relating attitudes to quits with structural equation modeling (SEM) procedures. Moreover, meta-analyses of turnover correlates lend greater support to the general causal sequence embedded within our framework: job attitudes lead to withdrawal cognitions, which lead to quitting. Although varying in sample compositions and corrections for statistical artifacts, separate meta-analyses still identically ranked these factors in predictive strength within the same review: Withdrawal cognitions ($r = .30$ [present meta-analysis]; $r = .45$ [Tett and Meyer 1992])—or, more specifically, quit decisions ($r = .35$ [present meta-analysis]; $r = .36$ [Hom, Caranikis-Walker, Prussia, and Griffeth 1992]; $r = .50$ [Steel and Ovalle 1984])—predicted quitting more accurately than did satisfaction ($r = -.19$ [present meta-analysis]; $r = -.18$ [Hom, Caranikis-Walker, Prussia, and Griffeth 1992]; $r = -.28$ [Steel and Ovalle 1984]; $r = -.24$ [Tett and Meyer 1992]) and commitment ($r = -.18$ [present meta-analysis]; $r = -.38$ [Steel and Ovalle 1984]; $r = -.35$ [Tett and Meyer 1992]).

DETERMINANTS OF SATISFACTION

Using a framework established by Mobley, Griffeth, Hand, and Meglino (1979) and Price and Mueller (1981, 1986), we also identify exogenous determinants whose effects on terminations are mediated by job attitudes. Based on theory and research, we classify separate antecedents for job satisfaction and organizational commitment. Given their different foci, we expect specific aspects of the job to shape job satisfaction, whereas organizational characteristics should affect commitment. This taxonomic premise is strengthened by Brooke, Russell, and Price (1988) and Mathieu and Farr (1991) who showed that antecedents correlated differently with commitment and satisfaction. They found that the antecedents correlated with both attitudes, but their analyses did not control interdependency between these attitudes (Mathieu 1991). Given correlated attitudes, a determinant of one attitude may spuriously correlate with the other attitude (Mathieu and Zajac 1990). While we concede the possibility of multiple effects on both attitudes, our taxonomic description of attitudinal causes nevertheless delineates for heuristic purposes the antecedents that most influence a given attitude.

Job Complexity The formulation states that emotional responses to tasks on the job emanate from facets of job complexity. This proposition is derived from theories of task characteristics and holds that core dimensions on the job, such as the identity of the task, its significance, and degree of autonomy, mold job affect by instilling meaning, personal responsibility for outcomes, and knowledge of accomplishments into the work (Hackman and Oldham 1980). Empirical research has established that complexity in a job enhances satisfaction (Fried 1991; Loher et al. 1985) and retention (Griffeth 1985; Katerberg, Hom, and Hulin 1979; McEvoy and Cascio 1985). Still, our proposition, that satisfaction primarily translates the effects of a job's scope into commitment or withdrawal cognitions, remains untested.

Role stress Role stress—namely, ambiguity and conflict in work roles—should diminish job satisfaction. That hypothesis originates from theories of role stress, which submit that ambiguous or conflicting role demands evoke role strain (Kahn, Wolfe, Quinn, Snoek, and Rosenthal 1964; Netemeyer, Johnston, and Burton 1990). Many studies affirmed that role stress fosters dissatisfaction and resignations (Fisher and Gitelson 1983; Jackson and Schuler 1985; Lyons 1971). Affirming satisfaction mediation, recent SEM analyses demonstrated that role stress boosts withdrawal cognitions through job satisfaction (Klenke-Hamel and Mathieu 1990; Netemeyer, Johnston, and Burton 1990).

Group Cohesion Apart from attributes of the work, cohesion among the work group provides job satisfaction, thereby stabilizing employment. Organizational demography theory offers an explanation for our claim (Pfeffer 1983). Demographically dissimilar members of a work group hold different values and outlooks, which lessen mutual attraction and communication within the group. An outcome is weakened cohesion in the group and exacerbated strife, stimulating exits. In line with this supposition, Jackson et al. (1991), McCain, O'Reilly, and Pfeffer (1983), and Tsui, Egan, and O'Reilly (1992) found higher quit rates (or more numerous decisions to quit) in demographically diverse work groups, and O'Reilly, Caldwell, and Barnett (1989) discovered that dissension within heterogeneous groups accelerates the departure of its members. Other research adds credence to our proposition, indicating that satisfaction or integration with coworkers lengthens job retention (Cotton and Tuttle 1986; Price and Mueller 1981, 1986).

Compensation Our theory shares the ubiquitous view that compensation (and compensation satisfaction) builds job longevity through job satisfaction (Hulin, Roznowski, and Hachiya 1985; Price and Mueller 1981 1986). Borrowing from social-exchange and equity models, many authors on turnover insist that inadequate financial reward for employees' contributions to the firm engenders feelings of inequity that, in turn, induce the employees to leave (Hulin, Roznowski, and Hachiya 1985; Rusbult and Farrell 1983). Management and labor-economic studies support this contention, finding that low pay or dissatisfaction about pay create job dissatisfaction (Ironson, Smith, Brannick, Gibson, and Paul 1989; Lawler 1971,

1981) and turnover (Blakemore, Low, and Ormiston 1987; Cotton and Tuttle 1986; Mobley 1982a; Wilson and Peel 1991). Motowidlo (1983) and Price and Mueller (1981, 1986) have directly validated our mediational sequence: pay → satisfaction → quitting.

Leader-Member Exchange We further contend that poor leader-member exchange (LMX) may instigate dissatisfaction, and hence, turnover (Graen and Scandura 1986). According to Graen and his associates (Dansereau, Graen, and Haga 1975; Graen and Scandura 1986), superiors develop more effective working relationships (trust, for example) with select subordinates (high LMX). Leaders exchange various incentives, such as latitude on the job and influence on decision making, beyond the formal employment contract with these select employees. In return, high-LMX subordinates reciprocate with higher contributions toward the functioning of the unit. This mutual interpersonal exchange fosters, in turn, the subordinates' morale and loyalty. Empirical data (Ferris 1985; Graen and Ginsburgh 1977; Graen, Liden, and Hoel 1982; Graen, Novak, and Sommerkamp 1982) have borne out the validity of this notion. Empirical findings on the satisfaction mediation of LMX effects are equivocal and scant. Ferris (1985) and Graen, Liden, and Hoel (1982) found that partialling out overall job satisfaction did not negate correlations between LMX and turnover, which suggests that satisfaction does *not* fully mediate LMX's influence. Yet Williams and Hazer (1986) upheld a causal network wherein leader consideration (an aspect of LMX) bolsters satisfaction and thus decisions to stay.

Met Expectations We agree with Porter and Steers' theory (1973) of met expectations, which declares that new employees become dissatisfied (and hence withdraw) if the job refutes their initial expectations. Supporting this view, Wanous et al. (1992) found by meta-analysis, that met expectations do strengthen satisfaction and retention, but affect the former more. Recent SEM tests more directly verified that job affect translates the effects of met expectation into exits (Bacharach and Bamberger 1992; Farkas and Tetrick 1989; Hom et al. 1993).

Negative Affectivity Negative affectivity—a personality predisposition reflecting the chronic tendency to evaluate oneself, others, and situations (such as, work settings) unfavorably—may shape feelings toward the job (Staw, Bell, and Clausen 1986). Although empirical work confirmed that negative affectivity arouses dissatisfaction (Staw, Bell, and Clausen 1986) and decisions to quit (George 1989), Judge discovered (1993) that this personality syndrome conditions the way in which dissatisfaction develops into exits. Dissatisfaction more readily evoked resignations among *positively* affective employees than among negatively affective ones. Happy employees are, presumably, more likely quit a bad job—which provides a sharp contrast with other, pleasant aspects of their lives; unhappy employees do not view a bad job as anything unusual. Given their inclination toward disparaging their jobs, we would expect negatively affective employees to feel job dissatisfaction more readily, but positively affective employees to abandon poor jobs more promptly.

DETERMINANTS OF COMMITMENT

Procedural Justice Our conceptualization further states that procedural justice—that is, fair procedures for allocating rewards in the organization—should underpin commitment to a company and thereby bolster participation in the organization (Folger and Greenberg 1985; Folger and Konovsky 1989). This hypothesis is based on Folger and Konovsky's rationale (1989) that procedural equity instills confidence in the employees that their employers will distribute rewards fairly in the long run. Lacking faith in the reward system, employees would not commit themselves to the firm and so discontinue their careers there. Supporting this perspective, Folger and Konovksy (1989) documented that an equitable distribution of pay raises strengthens bonds of loyalty between employees and company. Relatedly, Miceli, Jung, Near, and Greenberger (1991), using SEM analysis, validated a causal pathway in which fairness in the pay system improves satisfaction, which, in turn, reduces intentions to quit.

Expected Utility of Internal Roles. Prospects for attaining desirable work roles inside a company may engender commitment to the firm and stability (Mobley 1982a). The expectation of assuming a desirable position inside the firm—the "expected utility of internal roles," such as promotion—may explain, as Mobley and his associates (1982a; Mobley et al. 1979) postulated, why some dissatisfied employees do not quit. Similarly, Hulin, Roznowski, and Hachiya (1985) suggested that "efforts to change the work situation"—through transfers, promotions, or demotions—represent alternative ways to leave an unpleasant job, a formulation that thus implies that successful changes of job within the organization reduce termination decisions (Jackofsky and Peters 1983b).

Various streams of research corroborate commitment-binding effects of attractive roles within the firm. Several empirical studies reveal that lack of promotion underlies decisions to quit (Cotton and Tuttle 1986) and weakens company commitment (Mathieu and Zajac 1990). Although specifying other mediators as well, recent SEM tests also support a basic pathway from promotions to commitment to turnover (Griffeth and Hom 1990; Price and Mueller 1986). Hom, Kinicki, and Domm's (1989) confirmatory factor analysis did not, however, distinguish between the expected utility of other internal roles and job satisfaction. Considering its prominence in modern thought (see, for example, Hulin 1991; Mobley, Griffeth, Hand, and Meglino 1979), the construct of the expected utility of internal roles nonetheless warrants additional research on its explanatory power.

Employment Security Employment security may be a primary base for commitment. We build this contention on Ashford, Lee, and Bobko's (1989) reasoning that employees who perceive their companies as unreliable in carrying out personnel obligations would lose trust in and commitment to companies. Subscribing to this view, Kerr and Slocum (1987) described an employee's commitment to the firm as an exchange for the firm's long-term commitment to the individual: job security. Observers of Japanese firms widely claim that the venerated loyalty and productivity of Japanese workers stem from the promise of lifetime employment in corporations (Lincoln 1989; Lincoln and Kalleberg 1985; Marsh and Mannari 1977). Ashford, Lee, and Bobko (1989) discovered that employees who fear layoffs felt less committed to the employer and planned to quit, and Davy, Kinicki, and Scheck (1991) documented that feelings of insecurity about the job weakened commitment and decisions to stay among survivors of corporate layoffs.

Job Investments Our framework also recognizes job investments, such as nontransferable pension benefits, job-specific training, and seniority perks, as an essential basis for organizational commitment and retention. Theorists on turnover suggest that turnover may be deterred by the fear of losing one's job investments (Mobley 1977; Rusbult and Farrell 1983), and that such fears are the basis for the well-supported association between job tenure and turnover (Cotton and Tuttle 1986; Mobley 1982a). Researchers on commitment similarly conceive of compliance or calculative commitment as identification based on extrinsic inducements (Mathieu and Zajac 1990; Meyer, Allen, and Gellatly 1990; Meyer, Paunonen, Gellatly, Goffin, and Jackson 1989; O'Reilly and Chatman 1986), an association originating from Becker's side-bet notion (1960). In this form of commitment, employees become bound to a firm because they have a personal investment in it and fear losing those investments (Mathieu and Zajac 1990). Supporting this investment factor, turnover studies found that the perceived costs of quitting reduced the number of resignations (Hom, Griffeth and Sellaro 1984; Lee 1988; Rusbult and Farrell 1983; Steel. Lounsbury, and Horst 1981), and Mathieu and Zajac's meta-analysis (1990) found calculative commitment to be inversely associated with withdrawal intentions and actions.

Extraorganizational Loyalties Outside loyalties represent another antecedent of commitment. Theorists of turnover contend that competing commitments, such as professionalism and family responsibilities, jeopardize loyalty to the company (Mobley 1982a; Mobley, Griffeth, Hand, and Meglino 1979; Price and Mueller 1981 1986; Steers and Mowday 1981). Indeed, psychological attachment to outside pursuits represents a fundamental idea behind several conceptions of influences other than work (Lee and Mowday 1987; Price and Mueller 1981, 1986). In a similar vein, scholars on professionalism have long maintained that the loyalty of professionals to their occupation can interfere with loyalties to the company because of conflicting values and norms (Dean, Ferris and Konstans 1988; Raelin 1986; Von Glinow 1988). To illustrate,

Kramer (1974) observed that nursing school graduates are often disheartened when a hospitals' norms of efficiency and bureaucratic control interfere with their ability to serve patients according to professionally prescribed standards.

Still, empirical findings failed to provide evidence for the presumed detrimental effects of competing attachments outside work on job incumbency (Blegen, Mueller, and Price 1988; Lee and Mowday 1987; Price and Mueller 1981, 1986). Contrary to sociological observations, empirical investigations regularly find that professional and organizational commitments do not necessarily clash and that professionalism is inversely related to turnover (Aranya, Pollock, and Amernic 1981; Curry, Wakefield et al. 1985; Ferris and Aranya 1983; Mathieu and Zajac 1990; Price and Mueller 1981; Morrow and Wirth 1989).

Similarly, common demographic proxies of family responsibility, such as marital status and family size, have not shown clear-cut effects on turnover (Mobley 1982a; Mobley, Griffeth, Hand, and Meglino 1979; Morita, Lee, and Mowday 1993; Muchinsky and Tuttle 1979; Porter and Steers 1973). Rather, these demographic effects may vary with gender and family composition. For example, family size and marital status may influence women to quit their jobs, because they traditionally carry the primary family obligations, but inhibit turnover among men, who are traditionally the primary family breadwinners (see Mobley 1982a; Porter and Steers 1973). In a similar fashion, family composition displayed inconsistent effects. Quite likely, conflicting definitions of family size may underlie their variable effects. The size of the *nuclear* family (especially, the number and presence of young children) accelerates turnover among women, whereas the size of the *extended* family (comprising relatives) in the community prolongs company tenure for both sexes (Blegen, Mueller, and Price 1988; Donovan 1980; Gerson 1985; Huey and Hartley 1988; Price and Mueller 1981). In summary, simple demographic indexes often misrepresent family responsibility. Their extensive usage suggests an oversimplification of their meaning because marital status and family size may historically symbolize family obligations for women (a symbol that is, however, changing as more women go out to work), but not for men.

To establish the effects of family obligations more firmly, future research must develop more direct measures of them or develop more valid demographic indices showing how they reflect family burdens (see Blegen, Mueller, and Price 1988). For example, Kossek (1990) recommends measuring the configuration of children's ages rather than merely counting the number of children (infants require a different level of care from toddlers, who are different from school-age children, and so on) and the configuration of employment in the household rather than marital status (single parents have greater family responsibilities than do parents in traditional nuclear families).

Time and Behavior Conflicts Based on our limited review, we contend that studies of turnover overlook interrole conflict—the interference from work with commitments outside the organization (Hom and Griffeth 1991; Mobley 1982a; Ralston and Flanagan 1985). Conflict between the job and nonjob domains may arise from conflicts of time or demands for incompatible behavior (O'Driscoll, Ilgen and Hildreth 1992; Zedeck and Mosier 1990). Thus, competing loyalties will speed turnover (and, perhaps, departure from the work force) only if work schedules interfere with participation in outside activities (Gerson 1985; Hom and Griffeth 1991) or if behaviors at work conflict with values outside the organization. These two sources of job conflicts parallel the traditional dimensions of role stress: role overload (insufficient time to do the job) and conflict between the person and the role (a perceived incongruency between role requirements and personal values) (Miles 1976). Although still scarce, there is mounting evidence to show that conflict between the job and endeavors outside the organization (including those generated by professional standards; Aranya and Ferris 1983 promote withdrawal cognitions and weaken commitment to the organization (Bacharach and Bamberger 1992; Hom, Kinicki, and Domm 1989). More revealing, a recent path analytical test confirmed that when time spent working is excessive to the point that the job interferes with other activities, commitment is thereby diminished (O'Driscoll, Ilgen, and Hildreth 1992).

Contradictory findings about the effects of attachments outside the organization on withdrawal may be explained by the existence of interrole conflicts. That is, employees dedicated to other endeavors, such as childrearing, leisure, or community service, are motivated to quit only if their present work hours are excessive or inconvenient enough to hamper or preclude their involvement in those undertakings (Mobley 1982a). Similarly, professionals committed to their occupation will more readily change jobs if they cannot apply professional standards in their current job duties (see Hom, Griffeth, Palich, and Bracker 1993; Huey and Hartley 1988). All told, neglected time-based or behavioral conflicts may moderate the effects of extraorganizational interests on turnover. To comprehend extraorganizational influences thoroughly , future investigations should consider, not only conflicts between work and family, but also other pursuits, such as leisure and involvement in community activities (O'Driscoll, Ilgan, and Hildreth 1992; Hom, Kinicki, and Domm 1989).

Initial Job Choices We further submit that circumstances surrounding the initial decision to join an organization underpin commitment to that organization. Theorists on commitment argue that forces binding newly hired employees to their initial decisions to join a company later induce company loyalty by way of a retrospective rationality (Mowday, Porter, and Steers 1982; Salancik 1977). Previous studies have established that newcomers making irrevocable, free, and public choices about a job become psychologically attached to their firms (Kline and Peters 1990; Lee, Ashford, Walsh, and Mowday 1992; Meyer, Bobcel, and Allen 1991; O'Reilly and Caldwell 1981).

Propensity to Commitment Following Mowday, Porter, and Steers (1982), we include the predisposition of individuals to form organizational commitment. Several studies on socialization disclosed that some personal characteristics predispose new employees to develop company attachments. Most persuasively, Lee et al. (1992) recently assessed the propensity for commitment of new recruits to a military academy, measuring their desire for a military career, familiarity with the military, confidence of success at the academy, preentry expectations, and job-choice influences. A composite of these personal traits and other factors predicted the cadets' initial and subsequent commitment to the military academy.

LABOR AND MARKET DETERMINANTS

Last, we observe that job-market determinants—encompassing various factors as suggested by different theorists—exert multiple, complex effects on the termination process (Hom, Caranikis-Walker, Prussia, and Griffeth 1992; Steel and Griffeth 1989). Like Hulin, Roznowski, and Hachiya (1985), we posit labor-market influences on job satisfaction, asserting that attractive perceived alternatives lower the valuation of the present job (the "greener grass" syndrome; see Schneider 1976). We adopt Mobley's reasoning (1977) that unemployment rates, especially rates in the community or in a specific occupation (Hulin, Roznowski, and Hachiya 1985), diminish the expected utility of job seeking. Job-market factors (notably, relocation costs) enter into the mental calculations of the costs and benefits of quitting (Hom and Griffeth 1991; Steel and Griffeth 1989) as do job investments via commitment. Besides this, labor-market antecedents may shape the course of the job search (Hom, Caranikis-Walker, Prussia, and Griffeth 1992; Mobley, Griffeth, Hand, and Meglino 1979; Steers and Mowday 1981). Limited information about available positions or low vacancy rates may undermine search for a job, preventing job seekers from finding suitable alternative employment.

Unfortunately, research studies find that current measures of perceived alternatives poorly or inconsistently predict turnover or moderate quit determinants (Hom, Caranikis-Walker, Prussia, and Griffeth 1992; Hulin, Roznowski, and Hachiya 1985; Steel and Griffeth 1989). Explaining disappointing findings, Griffeth and Hom (1988a) and Steel and Griffeth (1989) maintained that common scales inadequately represent the complex, multifaceted employment market. By comparison, objective indices of joblessness have moderated the impact of attitudes and quit decisions and directly affected quits (Carsten and Spector 1987; Gerhart 1990; Hom, Caranikis-Walker, Prussia, and Griffeth 1992). We still recommend the development of measures to assess varied perceptions of the labor market directly, instead of relying on indirect proxies based on unemployment rates, to verify theoretical propositions about work alternatives (Steel and Griffeth 1989).

Although rooted in existing research and theory, our modest efforts at theoretical integration await further rigorous validation. Our formulation overlooked many explanatory constructs, among them job performance (Steers and Mowday 1981) and attempts to change the work role or switch to other internal roles (Hulin, Roznowski, and Hachiya 1985) and intervening processes, such as comparison of alternatives based on compatibility of images (Lee and Mitchell 1994) and the discontinuous progression of job withdrawal (Sheridan and Abelson 1983). Thus, we invite others to refine and elaborate our conceptual framework. Perhaps a theory initiates its prime legacy rather than its ultimate validity.

<table>
<tr><td>CHAPTER

7</td><td><h1>TURNOVER AND
OTHER BEHAVIORS;
TURNOVER AND
MALADAPTATION</h1></td></tr>
</table>

In various lines of academic inquiry, researchers have examined the question of whether quitting employees behave differently from those who stay. Hulin (1991) has considered whether terminations relate to other forms of disengagement from the job. The research presumes that dissatisfied employees engage in "short-term" quits, such as absences, before leaving, or if they cannot quit, temporarily escape from aversive work conditions through absence or lateness. Other investigators, prompted by concern over whether or not effective performers resign more often than poor performers do, explored relationships between voluntary turnover and job performance (McEvoy and Cascio 1987). Recently, more complex behavioral models have emerged in which turnover is conceptualized as one of many responses to dissatisfaction or maladaptation (Hulin 1991; Hulin, Roznowski, and Hachiya 1985; Rossé and Miller 1984; Rusbult et al. 1988). Alienated employees may reduce their contributions to the job or modify work conditions before or instead of leaving. In this chapter, we review research and theory on how turnover relates to other behaviors in the work place.

RESPONSE FAMILY OF WITHDRAWAL BEHAVIORS

Turnover is commonly viewed as belonging to a family of withdrawal behaviors that physically distance employees from unpleasant work settings. Serving a common psychological function, withdrawal actions reduce the time spent in an aversive environment and thus reduce job dissatisfaction. Different models, however, conceive of different patterns of association between termination and other acts of withdrawal (Hulin 1991; Rossé and Miller 1984). Five models of the structural relationships among withdrawal behaviors have been conceptualized.

An "independent-form" model posits that withdrawal actions are unrelated to one another because their antecedents and consequences differ (Hulin 1991; Porter and Steers 1973; Rossé and Miller 1984). Explaining their independence, Mobley (1982a) speculated that absence and turnover may not ordinarily correlate positively when, (1) one behavior arises from positive attraction rather than avoidance, (2) absence serves nonjob demands, (3) one act is constrained, (4) either occurs impulsively, (5) the job allows discretionary time away from work, (6) unused sick pay can be reimbursed when the employee leaves, or (7) absence is a safety value that reduces the chances of quitting.

A "spillover" model asserts a positive covariation among withdrawal acts because aversive jobs elicit a generic avoidance tendency that expresses itself in manifold ways (Hulin 1991). That is, enacting one withdrawal act increases the likelihood of other withdrawal acts. Two models specify negative response covariations (ibid.; Rossé and Miller 1984). The "alternative-forms" version submits that withdrawal behaviors are substitutable and that environmental constraints on one behavior evoke less constrained behaviors. For example, dissatisfied employees who cannot resign because the job market is depressed may miss work more often. The "compensatory" model presumes that all withdrawal responses provide a relief valve for escaping noxious circumstances at work. If one response relieves dissatisfaction, then that response will compensate for other responses, making them unnecessary (Hulin 1991). A "progression-of-withdrawal" model posits a hierarchical response sequence ranging from minor, such as tardiness, to extreme work avoidance, that is, departure. Over time, very dissatisfied employees manifest increasingly more extreme withdrawal with frequent absences and tardiness before leaving.

Limitations of Empirical Evidence

Validating a family of withdrawal responses requires evidence of their communality and mutual dependency on job dissatisfaction (revealing a shared psychological function); verifying their structural interconnections demands complex statistical tests of behavioral patterns (Hulin 1991; Rossé and Hulin 1985). Unfortunately, empirical tests are limited and plagued by methodological weaknesses (Hulin 1991). With few exceptions (Clegg 1983; Rossé 1988), research studies primarily examined quits and absenteeism, neglecting other expressions of work avoidance (Hulin 1991). The distributional properties of withdrawal acts often jeopardize the validity of statistical conclusions. Many commonly studied withdrawal behaviors occur rarely, the mean 4.7 percent absenteeism rate among American workers being a case in point (Rhodes and Steers 1990). Infrequent acts produce highly skewed and noncontinuous frequency distributions, which attenuate Pearson product-moment correlations (Bass and Ager 1991; Harrison and Hulin 1989; Hunter and Schmidt 1990a). What is more, responses whose frequency distributions are skewed in opposite directions further deflate correlations between them. In the same manner, abnormal response distributions can bias estimates of regression parameters (Harrison and Hulin 1989; Hulin 1991).

In a provocative simulation, Hulin (1991) showed how discrete, non-normal behavioral distributions undermine the corroboration of a withdrawal response family. He initially specified that continuous, normally distributed action tendencies underlie absenteeism, tardiness, and turnover and have sizable (.4 to .6) factor loadings on a latent withdrawal construct. From each normal response distribution, he derived a frequency distribution for its observed behavioral manifestation. In essence, he divided the continuum of each response propensity, using various threshold values, to produce the skewed frequency distributions typical of withdrawal acts. Then, he correlated these observed responses and found trivial correlations (.04 to .08) between them. His demonstration also uncovered weak correlations between satisfaction and withdrawal, even though he specified satisfaction to reflect the same withdrawal construct. Hulin concluded that "empirical correlations among this sample of infrequent withdrawal behaviors with badly skewed distributions provide little information about the underlying relations" (1991, p. 474).

To overcome such distributional problems, scholars routinely aggregate data on absences or lateness over arbitrary time periods. Unfortunately, the aggregation of data over long periods of time may weaken the relevance of withdrawal determinants (Harrison and Hulin 1989). Though useful for predicting absenteeism the next day or a week later, job satisfaction on a given day may be unable to forecast absence a month later or an aggregated month's worth of absences. Misclassifications of the voluntariness of withdrawal acts may underestimate covariation between responses for these acts supposedly voluntarily taken to relieve dissatisfaction (Hulin 1991).

Withdrawal Responses

Given these caveats, existing research does yield tentative conclusions about a taxonomic family of withdrawal actions (ibid.; Rossé and Miller 1984). Inspections of the relations between satisfaction and withdrawal indicate whether responses reflect the same functional meaning of work avoidance (Rossé and Miller 1984). Sustaining this interpretation, several meta-analyses clearly established that job satisfaction (especially overall and work-content satisfaction) moderately correlates with quits (Carsten and Specter 1987; Hom et al. 1992; Steel and Ovalle 1984; Tett and Meyer 1992). Other meta-analyses found weaker but still inverse correlations between satisfaction and frequent absence (Hackett 1989; Hackett and Guion 1985; Scott and Taylor 1985). To illustrate, Hackett's comprehensive review estimated that work and overall satisfaction correlated –.21 and –.15, respectively with absences. In narrative reviews, negative but weak associations between lateness and satisfaction were addressed (Hulin 1991; Rossé and Miller 1984). Such associations are less consistent, but also less studied (Adler and Golan 1981; Clegg 1983; Rossé and Hulin 1985).

Correlations among avoidance reactions further uphold a shared behavioral family. In empirical studies, positive, modest correlations between absence and turnover and between absence and lateness are typically reported (Lyons 1972; Rossé and Hulin 1985; Rossé and Miller 1984). More revealing, Mitra, Jenkins, and Gupta's meta-analysis (1992) established a .33 correlation between absences and terminations based on 5,316 employees from thirty-three samples. Although sparse, examinations of relations between lateness and turnover provisionally suggest weak positive correlations (Rossé and Hulin 1985; Rossé and Miller 1984). Collectively, these findings suggest that tardiness, absences, and turnover are manifestations of a general latent withdrawal trait (Hulin 1991).

Structural Models

Notwithstanding their limitations, observed covariations between withdrawal responses may provide tentative evidence about the relative validity of the five structural models. The preponderance of positive response correlations disputes the independent-forms and alternative-forms models (ibid.). These findings, however, do not necessarily uphold the spillover model, which oversimplifies job withdrawal by overlooking labor-market determinants. For example, the spillover model implausibly implies that dissatisfied people, who cannot leave because the job market is depressed, would repress other avoidance actions. More likely, disgruntled employees will express withdrawal in other ways if they cannot resign (ibid.), although Markham and McKee (1991) found that absenteeism fell during rising unemployment.

Though disputing other models, first-order cross-sectional correlations between responses inadequately test compensatory and progression-of-withdrawal models. Partial correlations, holding job satisfaction constant, would correctly test the compensatory model (Hulin 1991). Positive first-order correlations also do not differentiate withdrawal progression from the spillover phenomenon (ibid.). Apart from ambiguity, traditional cross-sectional correlations mask the way in which withdrawal responses become progressively extreme over time (Rossé 1988). Indeed, zero or negative correlations are consistent with the progression of withdrawal if they are computed from behavioral data aggregated over short intervals (ibid.). For example, employees cannot simultaneously arrive at work late, miss a day's work, and quit all in a single day.

To test withdrawal progression more rigorously, Rossé examined relationships between absenteeism, tardiness, and turnover on a weekly basis rather than between their aggregated forms. He collected weekly response data on sixty-three hospital employees for seven weeks and computed the conditional probability of a subsequent response, given the antecedent response. The existence of progressive avoidance is illustrated in Figure 7-1: Employees have a higher conditional probability (.34) of being absent if they had been late even once during the previous two weeks, the absence base rate being .14. Employees who missed work twice in one week are more likely to have resigned two weeks later, a finding that is shown in Figure 7-2. Indeed, 40 percent of those absent twice in one week quit within two weeks. Likewise, employees who were late twice or more in a, week were also more likely to have quit two weeks later. In summary, Rossé's provocative findings lend impressive support to the progression-of-withdrawal model.

Research Evaluation

While encouraging, the empirical evidence reviewed above only partially affirmed a withdrawal response family. Yet scholars of turnover have long envisioned other withdrawal actions besides absence, lateness, and turnover (Farrell 1983; Hulin 1991; Mobley 1982a). Rossé and his col-

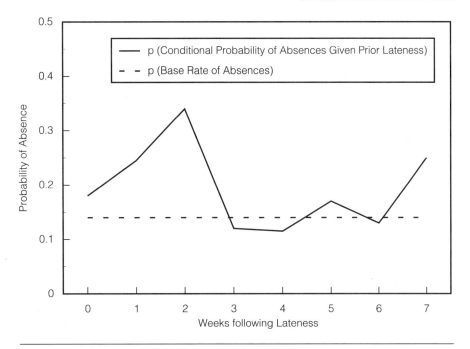

Figure 7-1 The Conditional Probability of Absence Following a Single Episode of Lateness. (J. Rosse, Relations among lateness, absence, and turnover: Is there a progression of withdrawal. *Human Relations,* **41 (1988): 523.)**

leagues (Rossé & Hulin 1985; Rossé and Miller 1984) suggested lengthy work breaks, leaving work early, or psychological withdrawal (drug taking, daydreaming); Hanisch and Hulin (1990) in light of the legal abolition of mandatory retirement, advanced voluntary retirement as a candidate for this behavioral family. More research on other withdrawal behaviors is warranted if we are to specify completely the domain of the behavioral withdrawal construct.

Although current evidence upholds the progression-of-withdrawal model more than it does competing structural models, this model and the alternatives merit more rigorous investigation. To handle their unusual distributional properties, survival analysis should be extended to analyze dynamic relationships among withdrawal acts (Fichman 1988; Harrison and Hulin 1989). Survival analysis may find that survival functions on company tenure may decline more precipitously over time for the frequently absent employees than for rarely absent employees (see Morita, Lee, and Mowday, 1993). Though the subject is controversial (Bass and Ager 1991; Williams 1990), Hulin (1991) and Hunter and Schmidt (1990a) have suggested that correlations involving turnover and other dichotomous acts might be corrected for extreme base rates and dichotomy to improve their strength. Assessments, made by the

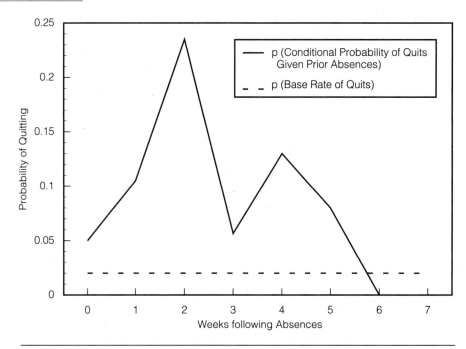

Figure 7-2 The Conditional Probability of Turnover Following Multiple Absences. (J. Rosse, Relations among lateness, absence, and turnover: Is there a progression of withdrawal. *Human Relations*, 41 (1988): 523.)

employees themselves, of their withdrawal actions (to *supplement* personnel records) may improve accuracy in classifying the voluntariness of actions and reasons for their occurrence (see Rossé and Hulin 1985). Structural models may hold up better when involuntary responses from statistical analyses are discarded as the models presume that all acts of avoidance are voluntary.

TURNOVER AND PERFORMANCE EFFECTIVENESS

Many researchers into turnover have explored the relationship between turnover and job performance (McEvoy and Cascio 1987). Their interest arises from growing doubts that turnover is necessarily a disadvantage. Organizational scientists realize that whether or not turnover impairs company performance depends on who quits (Boudreau and Berger 1985). The exodus of effective performers would be harmful. But when marginal or poor employees leave voluntarily, the firms benefit if they can find more productive replacements fairly easily and inexpensively (Hollenbeck and Williams 1988; Mobley 1982a). Beyond this practical concern, modern theories of turnover have incorporated job performance as an additional determinant to improve explanatory power (Jackofsky 1984; Steers and Mowday 1981).

The association between performance and turnover has drawn much academic inquiry. Summarizing this growing literature, three meta-analyses concluded that job performance and voluntary turnover correlate negatively, albeit modestly (Bycio, Hackett, and Alvares 1990; McEvoy and Cascio 1987; Williams and Livingstone, 1994). The most comprehensive meta-analysis, cumulating data from 15,138 employees from fifty-five samples, estimated that work effectiveness correlated –.16 with voluntary exits (Williams and Livingstone, 1994). *Marginal* performers voluntarily quit more often than do high performers. Not surprisingly, job performance correlates strongly with involuntary quits (Bycio, Hackett, and Alvares 1990; McEvoy and Cascio 1987). To illustrate, Bycio and fellow researchers, studying ten firms employing a total of 2,744 employees, reported a –.52 correlation between involuntary terminations and performance. Correlations between voluntary departures and performance were generally negative, but the meta-analyses further revealed that positive correlations are possible: Superior performers more readily quit under some circumstances (Bycio, Hackett, and Alvares 1990; Williams and Livingstone, 1994).

Beyond empirical demonstrations, theorists tried to explain the psychological mechanisms responsible for associations between performance and exit. Jackofsky (1984) proposed the most elaborate account, depicted in Figure 7-3. Drawing from March and Simon (1958), she reasoned that job performance affects turnover (via quit decisions) through desirability and perceived ease of movement. The availability of rewards that depend on performance determines how job performance translates into the desire to change jobs. Incentive systems distribute more rewards to superior performers, making them more satisfied and less anxious to leave. Merit-pay schemes drive out marginal performers, who receive fewer incentives and feel more dissatisfied about their rewards. Effective performers feel short-changed when their rewards are not commensurate with their relatively large contributions to the job. Noncontingent reward systems definitely make them think about changing jobs.

Its impact on desires to move does depend on available incentive pay, but performance invariably bolsters ease of movement according to Jackofsky (1984). Owing to personal achievements (and greater skills and ability), effective workers can find alternative employment more easily than their ineffective counterparts can. Jackofsky also theorized that effectiveness in work decreases involuntary separations. Most likely, poor performance eventually leads to dismissals or layoffs. Indeed, marginal performers may decide to "voluntarily" resign rather than face such sanctions.

Jackofsky's model has prompted several investigations. Most scholarly inquiries tried to verify her prediction that the relationship between performance and overall turnover (including voluntary *and* involuntary exits) is curvilinear: poor and good performers quit more frequently than average performers do. Supposedly, ineffective performers are more likely to be fired or to expect to be dismissed, and effective performers find it easier to leave because job opportunities are plentiful for them. Moderate performers are

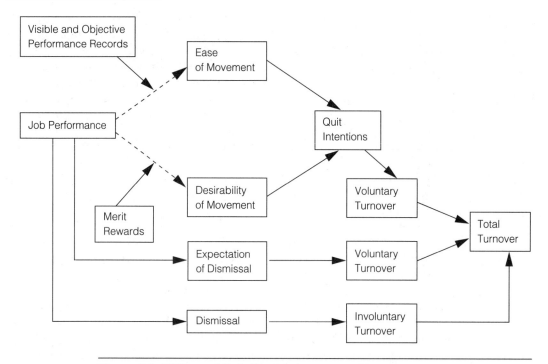

Figure 7-3 Effect of Job Performance on Turnover. (E. F. Jackofsky. Turnover and job performance: An integrated process model. *Academy of Management Review,* **9 (1984): 78.)**

the least likely to leave because they do not face imminent dismissal nor do they have a plethora of job options. In an early test, Jackofsky, Ferris, and Breckenridge (1986) confirmed this U-shaped relationship between performance and quitting for accountants and truck drivers.

Summarizing eight tests, Williams and Livingstone's meta-analysis (1994) more firmly established this curvilinearity between performance and voluntary quits and that reward systems that are dependent on performance reinforce the relationship between performance and turnover, another of Jackofsky's principles. The corrected correlation between voluntary exits and performance was −.27 when contingent rewards exist, but only −.18 when they do not. Poor performers are most likely to resign voluntarily when firms reward accomplishments. But then they also resign more frequently than superior performers do, even without performance incentives. Jackofsky and Slocum (1987) found that good performers felt more job satisfaction and were more optimistic about job opportunities.

Recently, Schwab (1991) challenged the generality of Jackofsky's view that productive employees enjoy more job mobility than unproductive employees do. In line with Dreher's (1982) observations, he reasoned that successful incumbents in most occupations cannot objectively document their performance to inform other prospective employers of their accomplishments. Generally speaking, effective performers are *not* more mobile, which explains the relative scarcity of positive correlations between performance and turnover (Bycio, Hackett, and Alvares 1990; Williams and Livingstone, 1994). Nonetheless, career achievements in some professions are public or objective, facilitating job mobility for high performers. Testing this idea, Schwab (1991) examined turnover among university professors whose publications may be measured objectively and are externally visible to prospective employers—other research institutions. He found that departures among tenured faculty (who usually leave voluntarily) correlate positively (.30) with the scholars' external reputation, as indexed by the frequency with which their publications are cited by other scholars. (This latest finding is incorporated in our depiction of Jackofsky's model.)

Research Evaluation

Although studies upheld the hypothesized U-shaped relationship between performance and turnover, further research on Jackofsky's theory should directly assess its posited mechanisms for translating the effects of job performance into turnover. Despite the theoretical significance, few studies have directly evaluated the possibility that desirability and ease of movement truly mediate between performance and voluntary exits. Such model tests assume greater urgency in the wake of Schwab's contention (1991) that ease of movement is not typically higher for effective performers (excepting university professors). Beyond model tests, additional research assessing job performance with objective measures would more definitively establish the relationship between performance and quitting. Unfortunately, most studies used supervisors' ratings (Bycio, Hackett, and Alvares 1990; Williams and Livingstone, 1994), which are subject to well-known biases (Bernardin and Beatty 1984). It may be that other mechanisms account for the covariance between job performance and turnover. For example, supervisor's affinity for a subordinate may spuriously underlie their relations (Tsui and Barry 1986): Supervisors may judge the performance of subordinates they dislike more harshly and may withhold rewards from them, prompting the subordinates to quit "voluntarily." Alternatively, relationships between performance and quitting may be illusory because negative affectivity increases quitting while contributing to poor performance evaluations. That is, negatively affective employees are more dissatisfied and thus more resign readily (George 1989, 1990). Yet they also express their dissatisfaction more visibly and thereby earn low ratings from their supervisors for poor job attitudes (Smither, Collins, and Buda 1989).

Reward systems merit more scholarly attention, given Williams and Livingstone's finding (1994) that incentive pay conditions the relationship between performance and quitting. Future research must determine if reward satisfaction and perceived distributive equity are truly behind the observed moderation by merit-pay schemes (ibid.). Along these lines, future replications should consider other features of merit-pay schemes and how they might moderate relationships between performance and quitting. For instance, Zenger (1992) discovered that some companies apply contracts that most reward outstanding performers, which induce *moderate* and poor performers to leave. Consideration of different distribution formulas in incentive programs may extend Jackofsky's (1984) formulation (see Gomez-Mejia and Balkin 1992a; Milkovich and Newman 1993). Replications of Schwab's (1991) unusual discovery of positive correlations between performance and quitting with data taken from other professions that objectively track success (scientists and engineers, top executives, professional athletes), are warranted. Such verifications would further uphold Jackofsky's (1984) claim that high performers enjoy greater ease of movement.

TURNOVER AS ONE RESPONSE TO DISSATISFACTION

An emerging school of thought regards turnover as simply one among many alternative responses to dissatisfaction and maintains that prevailing theories of turnover are considering surface variables instead of the behavioral patterns that represent broader theoretical constructs (Hulin 1991; Rusbult et al. 1988; Rossé and Hulin 1985). Rossé and Hulin argued that "surface behaviors should be judged on their scientific merit as an indicator of an underlying construct rather than whether they are costly, attention-getting, or popular research topics" (1985, p. 325). Such narrow perspectives also have practical drawbacks. For instance, in clinical psychology, it is held, treatments for mental-health problems that address symptoms, instead of the underlying causes, may evoke substitute symptoms. Likewise, absent knowledge about how turnover relates to other reactions to dissatisfaction, managerial interventions that reduce only resignations, such as overusing "golden handcuffs," may unwittingly trigger other dysfunctional responses (Rusbult et al. 1988). In line with this possibility, Meyer et al (1989) found that employees bound to companies by extrinsic inducements performed their jobs less satisfactorily than did those who express less calculative commitment. To overcome these shortcomings, two new theoretical approaches have emerged that conceive turnover as one of many actions that relieve dissatisfaction. Unlike simpler models of structural relations among acts of withdrawal, these integrative formulations posit a complex interdependency among broad *families* of reactions to dissatisfaction.

Exit-Voice-Loyalty-Neglect (EVLN) Model

Taking a preliminary step toward this expanded conception, Farrell (1983) developed a taxonomy of behavioral responses to dissatisfaction that includes quitting. Drawing from Hirshman (1970), he posited an exit-voice-loyalty-neglect (EVLN) model, in which he identified four classes of reaction to dissatisfaction:

Exit: Quitting a job, transferring, and seeking different jobs

Voice: Actively improving work conditions through discussions with supervisors, solving problems, and seeking help from outside agencies

Loyalty: Passively but optimistically waiting for conditions to improve, such as giving public and private support to the company, waiting for change, or practicing good citizenship

Neglect: Passively allowing conditions to deteriorate through reduced effort, chronic absenteeism, personal business on company time, or increased error rates

To validate these behavioral constructs, Farrell wrote twelve descriptions of behavior that exemplify each response type and recruited management scholars to sort these descriptions, written on separate cards, into separate categories. By and large, expert judges sorted similar responses into the same clusters. To identify the cognitive structures behind these response clusters, Farrell then had one hundred eighty-five employees compare the similarity of EVLN acts in a multidimensional scaling (MDS) task. This MDS uncovered four behavioral clusters and suggested two dimensions—passive and active and destructive and constructive—differentiating those clusters. A simplified typology of the MDS findings is shown in Figure 7-4, although MDS results actually assigned acts of loyalty to the passive/destructive quadrant.

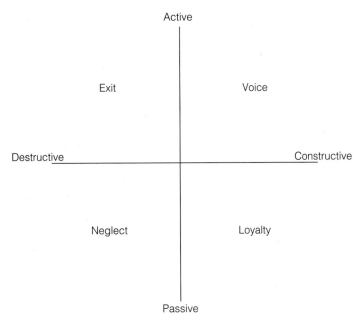

Figure 7-4   Typology of responses to Dissatisfaction. (D. Farrell, "Exit, voice, loyalty and neglect as responses to job dissatisfaction: A multidimensional scaling study." *Academy of Management Journal,* **26 (1983): 603.)**

Thus, voice responses are active and constructive, exit behaviors are active and destructive, loyalty is passive and constructive, and neglect is passive and destructive.

In a follow-up study, Rusbult et al. (1988) extended the Rusbult-Farrell turnover model (1983) to explain EVLN choice. They proposed that dissatisfaction promotes destructive responses (exit and neglect), and satisfaction elicits constructive responses (voice and loyalty). Presumably, satisfied employees are motivated to upgrade their working conditions or be optimistic about future job improvements. Rusbult et al. further reasoned that employees heavily invested in their jobs (those with firm-specific training and unvested pensions) behave constructively: They can lose many benefits if they quit or are dismissed (because they are showing neglect). Those lacking job investments can easily afford to enact exit or neglect responses. Job opportunities increase exit or voice reactions. Having alternatives empowers employees to do something ("shape up or ship out"), freeing them from relying on their current position for employment. Without alternatives, employees can only wait passively for work conditions to improve (loyalty) or allow conditions to decline (neglect).

Rusbult et al. carried out laboratory simulations and a survey of union members to test these propositions. They found that the hypothesis holds: Job satisfaction enhances constructive responses but inhibits destructive activities. Predictably, job investments elicited constructive and suppressed destructive actions, whereas employment prospects increased exit and voice. However, job availability did not diminish neglect, contesting a popular view that neglect substitutes for exit during periods of high unemployment (Rossé and Miller 1984). Investment size most fostered voice given high job satisfaction. Quite likely, voice is a difficult, costly act performed only by heavily invested employees who are sufficiently motivated to improve their jobs.

In a panel study, Farrell, Rusbult, Lin, and Bernthall (1990) then more rigorously tested the causal assumptions behind this EVLN model. They surveyed union locals on two occasions (assessing how often EVLN responses are made and their determinants) and used cross-lagged panel correlations to infer causal direction. Their comparisons of cross-lagged correlations upheld the following hypothesized causality: Satisfaction decreases exit; investments promote loyalty; and job availability increases exit and voice. Even so, most statistical comparisons found either no lagged causal impact or even reverse causality—satisfaction reducing voice and job opportunities increasing loyalty.

Extending Rusbult et al.'s model (1988), Withey and Cooper (1989) introduced additional antecedents of EVLN choice (see Figure 7-5). They conceptualized that employees choose a particular response to dissatisfaction after considering this action's costs, its efficacy for restoring satisfaction, and the attractiveness of the setting in which the action occurs. Basically, the perceived costliness of an act inhibits its occurrence in favor of less costly acts; its perceived efficacy for restoring satisfaction bolsters its selection. Thus, dissatisfied employees optimistic about improving work conditions prefer voice or loyalty; pessimistic people are more likely to leave or to allow circumstances to deteriorate (neglect). Employees who are committed to the company, finding the workplace attractive, prefer to improve their working conditions through voice or loyalty rather than abandon the company or let it decline.

Withey and Cooper further theorized that employment opportunities shape EVLN choice indirectly via three immediate response antecedents. That is, job availability enhances exit and neglect by reducing their costliness (people with options do not fear losing their jobs) and job attraction (employees devalue their jobs in light of other alternatives). In turn, declining job attraction decreases voice and loyalty: Uncommitted employees do not strive to improve their working conditions. Withey and Cooper also envisioned a potential countervailing effect, wherein work alternatives *increase* voice. Conceivably, employees who can easily find employment elsewhere feel empowered and therefore less fearful of retaliation from the employer for attempting change.

Testing their model, Withey and Cooper surveyed a large college alumni population and employees of an accounting firm on two separate occasions. They adopted Farrell's scales (1983) to assess EVLN acts and operationalized most response determinants, although only exit (that is, sunk costs and job investments) and voice costs. The alumni survey findings, depicting the correlations between Time-1 antecedents and Time-2 EVLN behaviors, and the multiple correlations yielded by all Time-1 predictors, are shown in Table 7-1. Upholding the Withey-Cooper model, dissatisfied employees enacted more responses of exit and neglect than responses of voice. Predictably, the perceived costliness of exit and voice lowered their occurrence, boosting the less costly loyalty and neglect.

Employees confident about the possibility of job improvements (that is, response efficacy) preferred voice rather than exit or neglect. Committed

Table 7-1   Correlations between Model Components and ELVN. (M. J. Withey and W. H. Cooper, "Predicting exit, voice, and loyalty, and neglect," *Administrative Science Quarterly*, 34 (1989): 530.)

| | Time-2 EVLN Responses | | | |
Time-1 Model Predictors	Exit	Voice	Loyalty	Neglect
Exit; sunk costs	−0.21*	0.05	0.08*	0.07
Exit; investments	−0.14*	0.10	−0.14*	−0.13*
Voice costs	0.29*	−0.19*	0.27*	0.18*
Job satisfaction	−0.51*	0.20*	−0.29*	−0.35*
Optimism about change	−0.37*	0.24*	−0.25*	−0.21*
Company commitment	−0.48*	0.20*	−0.23*	−0.19*
Job alternatives	0.25*	−0.07	0.01	0.12*
Adjusted multiple R^2	0.26	0.05	0.13	0.12

*$p < .05$.

employees attracted to their setting also opted for voice over exit or neglect. People with job opportunities were more likely to desert their jobs or let their jobs deteriorate; they did not, however, try to change their work conditions. Confounding model predictions, job satisfaction, optimism about improvements, and commitment *decreased* loyalty. The survey of accountants mostly replicated the findings among the alumni, albeit reporting fewer significant findings as the sample was smaller.

For additional insight, Withey and Cooper classified employees into "exiters," "neglecters," "voicers," or "loyalists," based on which EVLN response they predominantly chose. Then, they compared how those groups scored on the causal antecedents of EVLN choice. The score profiles for the four kinds of people are shown in Figure 7-6. Exiters encountered the lowest sunk costs; neglecters reported the fewest job investments. Not surprisingly, voicers did not consider voice responses as costly options and they experienced the highest job satisfaction, whereas exiters and loyalists expressed the lowest morale. Voicers expected future improvements in work conditions; exiters and loyalists felt more pessimism about change. Exiters were the least committed to their companies and believed that positions elsewhere were more attractive than their present job; voicers had the least inflated perceptions of alternative employment.

Though these findings were encouraging, other results suggest some theoretical revision of the Withey-Cooper formulation. For one, the model explained merely 5 percent of the voice variance, quite possibly omitting crucial influences on voice, such as sponsorship, interpersonal barriers, and the inertia of coworkers. Employees may feel reluctant to voice complaints unless they have a sponsor to protect them from potential retaliation (Withey and Cooper 1989). Employees may not voice complaints at all unless they believe that supervisors will listen (interpersonal barriers do not obstruct voice). Individuals may engage in costly voice actions if they feel personally responsible for solving work problems, an obligation that arises when other colleagues ignore it (the inertia of coworkers.)

Empirical tests further disputed Withey and Cooper's predictions about the reasons employees adopt loyalty responses. Indeed, the pattern of

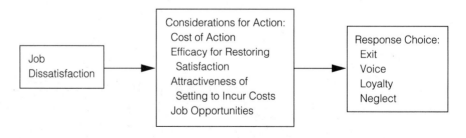

Figure 7-5 Model of Choice of EVLN Response. (M. J. Withey and W. H. Cooper, "Predicting exit, voice, loyalty, and neglect," *Administrative Science Quarterly,* **34 (1989): 522–525.)**

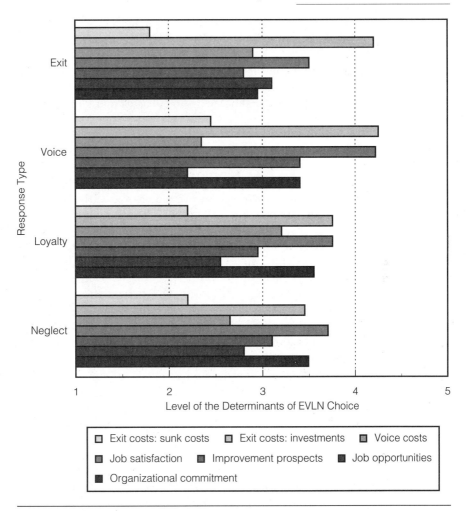

Figure 7-6 Profile of EVLN Response Types. (M. J. Withey and W. H. Cooper, "Predicting exit, voice, loyalty, and neglect," *Administrative Science Quarterly,* **34 (1989): 531. Copyright 1989 by administrative Science Quarterly. Adapted by permission.)**

correlations between antecedents and loyalty resembled that for correlations between antecedents and neglect (see Table 7-1), and the antecedent-score profiles of loyalists and neglectors closely corresponded (see Figure 7-6). These findings contradict the conventional portrait of loyalists as people who quietly support the company through hard times (Farrell 1983; Hirshman 1970). Interpreting these results, Withey and Cooper pointed out that the traditional depiction of loyalty actually embodys conflicting qualities: quiet passivity and active support for the firm. On the former measure, loyalty is indistinguishable from neglect, being a mild variant of it. Yet the latter measure—proactive loyalty—is unlike voice in that it maintains the status quo, whereas voice seeks to change or overthrow existing conditions. These data likening loyalists to neglectors may imply that Farrell's loyalty scale (1983) is deficient as it omits active forms of loyalty, such as working hard to get the job done or doing things beyond the call of duty. In summary, loyalty may best be construed as a form of *proactive* action (akin to organizational citizenship) and measurement of this reconceptualization may improve the capacity of Withey-Cooper's theoretical framework to account for loyalty.

Employee Adaptation Models

Taking a different approach, Rossé and his colleagues (Rossé and Hulin 1985; Rossé and Miller 1984) viewed job withdrawal as a more general process of adaptation to work. They defined work-role adaptation as the process by which relative dissatisfaction is reduced through behavioral or cognitive mechanisms. According to their conceptualization (shown in Figure 7-7), stimulus events precipitate an evaluation of the job. The resulting evaluation may bring about *relative* dissatisfaction when one learns that the current state of affairs is deficient and can be improved. A dissatisfied employee then considers various remedial strategies: work avoidance, which includes behavioral withdrawal (putting physical distance between oneself and the work setting), psychological withdrawal (reducing work awareness through daydreaming, diversions, or substance abuse), and retaliation against the firm, or attempts to change the current situation. The unhappy employee chooses an adaptive behavior to end the source of relative dissatisfaction or to alter this source constructively.

Rossé and his colleagues conceived four determinants of adaptive responses. (1) Past reinforcement history guides response selection. People who previously performed certain responses learn about their relative utility and later choose those responses having maximum utility. (2) Individuals may observe role models and emulate actions that successfully resolved past dissatisfaction. (3) Social norms prohibiting or proscribing certain actions in a given context may dictate adaptive choices. (4) Perceived constraints on behaviors (both personal and environmental barriers) influence adaptive responses. Simply put, employees do not choose to do things they cannot do.

If the initial response fails, a dissatisfied employee repeats this adaptive cycle, selecting another (or the same) adaptive response. An adaptive behavior may, however, trigger a "deviation-amplifying" cycle. For example, a disgruntled employee may miss work periodically and face penalties imposed by his or her employer. Enraged, the disciplined employee may perform more extreme adaptive behaviors, invoking even stronger sanctions. This cycle of infraction and sanction continues until it is broken when the employee leaves. Repeated adaptive attempts may fail to restore satisfaction and thus produce job stress—feelings of hopelessness about one's inability to adapt to unsatisfactory conditions. Expanding this adaptation

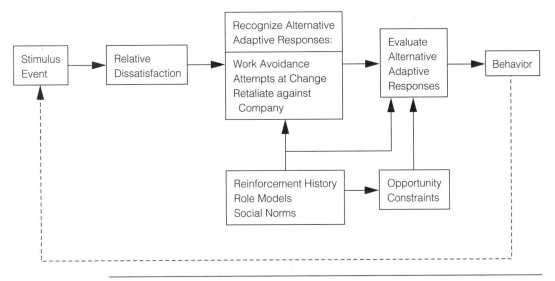

Figure 7-7 Model of Employee Adaptation. (J. Rosse and H. Miller Relationship between absenteeism and other employee behaviors. In P. Goodman, R. Atkin, and Associates (Eds.), *Absenteeism* **(p. 208). San Francisco: Jossey–Bass.)**

model, Hulin (1991) introduced attempts to increase job outcomes (stealing or moonlighting) and psychological job withdrawal (long coffee breaks or substance abuse) as means to relieve dissatisfaction.

Rossé and Hulin (1985) first investigated this adaptation theory using a longitudinal design. Assessing job affect and adaptive responses, they interviewed new hospital employees on several occasions during their first six months of work and solicited biweekly supervisory reports about withdrawal behaviors. As predicted, job attitudes inversely correlated with withdrawal acts and a complex, self-reported measure of avoidance and retaliation responses. Refuting theoretical expectations, it was found that job affect *increased* self-reported attempts at change. Dissatisfied employees who performed few adaptive behaviors suffered severe symptoms of mental and physical ill health.

Research Evaluation

These explanatory accounts of varied manifestations of dissatisfaction broaden our thinking about turnover, positing as they do quitting as symptomatic of dissatisfaction that finds expression whenever other routes to restore satisfaction are blocked. While encouraging, empirical support for adaptation and EVLN models still lags. In particular, future researchers must clarify the meaning of these behavioral taxonomies to resolve conflicting conceptualizations of response families. To illustrate, EVLN theorists overlook psychological avoidance, aggression toward employers, and attempts to increase job outcomes; adaptation theorists (Hulin 1991; Rossé and Hulin

1985) omit loyalty as a possible adaptive response. Compounding this confusion, different theoretical schools define similar response clusters differently. For example, EVLN taxonomies classify turnover and absences into different families (exit and neglect, respectively); adaptation taxonomies categorize both acts together under "behavioral job withdrawal." EVLN theorists conceive job transfer as an exit response; adaptation theorists regard this act as an "attempt to change the work role" rather than as a form of behavioral withdrawal. Instead of intuition, stronger theoretical justifications for classifying responses are clearly merited. That is, we will benefit from more explicit criteria that differentiates between behavioral families.

Besides resolving such conceptual ambiguities, we need more development and validation of measures of response families. As a start, future investigations might refine the most popular measure, Farrell's scales (1983). Farrell's measures were derived from a sound theoretical basis and have shown promising construct validity (see also Withey and Cooper 1989). In view of the potential redundancy between passive loyalty and neglect (ibid.), we might revise Farrell's operationalization of loyalty to emphasize *proactive* company support. Existing validated measures of organizational citizenship may better approximate this conception of loyalty (Organ 1990). We might also expand Farrell's scales to accommodate other adaptive reactions, such as the aggression and psychological withdrawal conceived of by adaptation theorists (Hulin 1991).

Additional validations of self-reported measures of adaptive responses with external criteria (such as performance ratings, personnel records, and productivity); Withey and Cooper (1989) would dispel criticism that common method bias underpins corroboration of the models (Rusbult et al. 1988). We must establish whether EVLN or adaptation models can actually predict overt behaviors rather than self-reported acts. Only Rossé and Hulin (1985) showed that their adaptation formulation predicts objective records of tardiness, absences, and turnover. Yet objective behavioral assessments are essential: Survey respondents may readily deny neglectful or withdrawal behaviors because of concerns about the way they are presenting themselves or fears of incrimination (Hessing, Elffers, and Weigel 1988). Given the likely falsification of self-reported "misdeeds," EVLN or adaptation models may not be able to forecast overt adaptive responses (Hom, Sutton, and Tehrani 1992).

Longitudinal examinations must also substantiate causal assumptions behind these theories. Unlike existing panel work, future panel research must apply more powerful SEM analyses (see Williams and Podsakoff 1989) and collect response data during more propitious time intervals (Hom and Griffeth 1991). It is quite likely that deficient panel analyses and inopportune measurement intervals may underlie the equivocal support for causal effects provided by EVLN determinants (see Farrell et al. 1990). We recommend longitudinal research on the causal interaction among adaptive responses (Withey and Cooper 1989). EVLN and adaptation models imply that dissatisfied employees substitute alternative behaviors if their initial response fails to resolve their dissatisfaction (Rossé and Hulin 1985; Withey and Cooper 1989)—an untested implication.

Maladaptation

Conceptual developments in modern social psychological explanations of relationships between attitude and behavior may enrich theories about how employees cope with maladaptation to work. Most notably, theories of reasoned action deserve special consideration (Ajzen 1991; Bagozzi and Warshaw 1990; Fishbein and Ajzen 1975; Koslowsky, Kluger, and Yinon 1988; Triandis 1979). These models propose that the expected utility of the act (including the perceived benefits and costs of the act *and* a valuation of those consequences), social pressures to enact the behavior (and motivation to

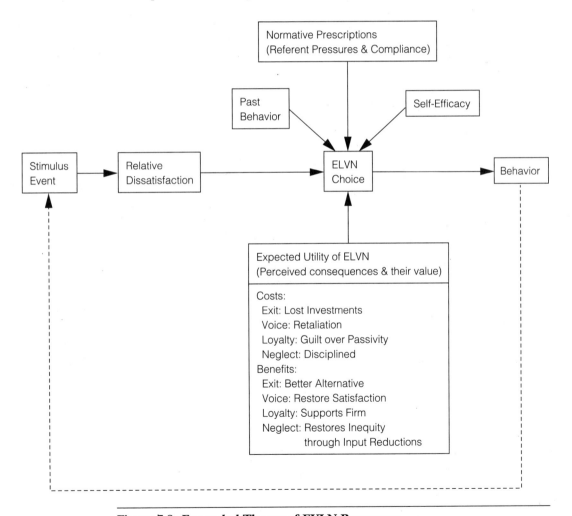

Figure 7-8 Expanded Theory of EVLN Responses.

comply with these demands), perceived ability to perform the act (belief in self-efficacy), and previous behavioral occurrences ("habit" [Bagozzi and Warshaw 1990; Triandis 1979] or behavioral investments [Koslowsky, Kluger, and Yinon 1988]) dictate behavioral choice. These models (Ajzen 1991; Sheppard, Hartwick, and Warshaw 1988; Triandis 1979; Zalesny 1985) have successfully predicted diverse human activities including exit—that is, turnover (Hom and Hulin 1981; Prestholdt, Lane, and Mathews 1987)—and loyalty—that is, organizational citizenship (Becker, Randall, and Riegel 1992).

We thus adapt a contemporary theory, illustrated in Figure 7-8, of reasoned action to explain EVLN responses and elaborate on EVLN and adaptation models. (Note that this model begins with EVLN responses as a preliminary, but not exhaustive, behavioral taxonomy.) Although commonly applied to explain specific behaviors, the theory of reasoned action can be generalized to predict general categories of behavior (Ajzen and Fishbein 1980). Indeed, this perspective may explicate EVLN response selections better than current viewpoints do by specifying more proximal and complete behavioral determinants. This theoretical view accounts for Rusbult et al.'s finding (1988) that dissatisfaction promotes destructive responses, the presumption being that the expected utility of those acts underlies the effects. Disgruntled employees take actions of neglect or exit because they perceive that such acts harm their employer *and* that they (the employees) value that damage (the actions have a positive utility). Similarly, the theory of reasoned action can explain why job investments deter acts of exit and neglect (ibid.). Supposedly, job incumbents who are heavily invested in the job do not behave destructively because they fear forfeiting their job investments; for them, destructive acts have a negative utility. The expected utility of exit and voice and self-efficacy of voice—constructs from the theory of reasoned action—may account for Rusbult et al.'s finding (1988) that job opportunities reinforce exit and voice. Employees who have alternatives face fewer costs in leaving (for them, there is less threat of unemployment) or of voice (and less fear of dismissal) (Withey and Cooper 1989), while the availability of work elsewhere empowers them (increasing their self-efficacy) to voice complaints.

Moreover, the theory of reasoned action elaborates Withey and Cooper's constructs. Like Withey and Cooper's framework, this model specifies perceived action costs but also considers the valuation of those costs, which vary among employees. This formulation may explain Withey and Cooper's contention that an individual's expectations that colleagues will not do anything can impel that individual into action. Essentially, inertia among coworkers represents a referent pressure prescribing *neglect* responses. Yet an employee may *not* comply with such implicit social demands because the passivity of coworkers about deteriorating conditions subjects her and others to continued suffering. Assuming personal responsibility, this person thus undertakes voice responses to correct circumstances. The theory of reasoned action regards "efficacy of response for restoring satisfaction" as a primary *voice* consequence. Unlike Withey and Cooper's view, our conception of expected utility embraces other positive consequences of the voice response (and their relative desirability) besides "efficacy for restoring satisfaction." For example, this model conceives sponsors as another beneficial voice outcome: protection from reprisals for voicing complaints. Furthermore, our theory construes interpersonal barriers to voice as merely *one* of many constraints reducing the perceived self-efficacy of voice (i.e., lowering one's perceived ability to perform the act).

This model further conceptualizes job availability and organizational commitment as distal rather than proximal EVLN antecedents (ibid.). Expected utility and normative prescriptions explain why committed employees respond constructively to dissatisfaction. They choose voice or loyalty because they believe that such actions benefit their company. They value that outcome and more readily comply with managerial expectations for constructive acts. The expected utility of destructive acts underlies the reason that ample work opportunities promote destructiveness: The availability of other jobs reduces the costliness of exit and neglect, making those responses more probable.

Our formulation considers previous behavioral occurrences as a EVLN determinant (Fredricks and Dossett 1983; Koslowsky, Kluger, and Yinon 1988; Triandis 1979). Employees may perform some EVLN responses habitually, without conscious deliberation about behavioral contingencies or social expectations. Instead of rational decision making, individuals, being script driven may automatically select behaviors that match previous successful responses (Lee and Mitchell 1994). In line with this conjecture, Withey and Cooper (1989) reported high temporal stability for EVLN acts; a response made previously is likely to be repeated. Following Bagozzi and Warshaw's reasoning (1990), we also contend that previous EVLN responses boost future EVLN responses whenever intentions are unclear, behavioral expected utility and social norms are changing, or expected utility incompletely reflects self-generated inferences from past responses.

Our extension of the theory of reasoned action resembles adaptation models (Hulin 1991; Rossé and Hulin 1985; Rossé and Miller 1984). Thus, normative prescriptions represent role models and social norms in adaptation models and past behavior corresponds to reinforcement history. The self-efficacy construct parallels opportunity constraints in adaptation models. Adaptation theorists also acknowledge the notion of behavioral expected utility as a major antecedent of response choice (Hulin 1991; Rossé and Miller 1984).

Though similar, the theory of reasoned action provides more precise conceptual and operational definitions for theoretical variables than do existing adaptation models. For example, this model specifies perceived behavioral prescriptions of individual referents; adaptation theories do not describe how to operationalize social norms and role models, corresponding social determinants (Rossé and Miller 1984). Over the years, empirical tests of the theory of reasoned action have also developed and refined measurement operations for components of the model (Ajzen and Fishbein 1980). Given its conceptual clarity and its refined measurement operations, this model is potentially more testable. Admittedly, operationalizing the theory of reasoned action for general classes of behavior is more cumbersome than testing its predictions of specific behavior (ibid.). For example, an ideal but impractical assessment of response utility would operationalize the utilities of all behaviors in a response family rather than a generic (potentially vague) utility for the whole family. Ajzen and Fishbein (1975) suggest procedures for inductively identifying salient behavioral consequences and referent others.

Although promising, the theory of reasoned action doubtlessly overemphasizes rational decision making (Lee and Mitchell 1994). Dissatisfied employees may not always choose adaptive behaviors after careful, mental deliberation about their costs and benefits. In contrast with this economic view of decision making, Lee and Mitchell (ibid.) described the less rational and more automatic processes by which employees decide how to behave. Drawing from image theory, they argued that people often choose behaviors after evaluating the compatibility of such action with personal values and goals ("images"). Such assessments of compatibility occur quickly and involve simply determining violations of fit (with the images) by behavioral options. Lee and Mitchell further reasoned that nonanalytical judgments are more routine than are elaborate, conscious calculations of behavioral outcomes and prescriptions and may typify certain individuals. Several behavioral options that survive the screening for image fit may, however, later be subject to a more rational cost-benefit analysis before a behavioral choice is made. The introduction of alternative decision-making strategies portrayed by image theory would further extend our preliminary theoretical framework for EVLN choice.

METHODOLOGICAL PROBLEMS IN TURNOVER RESEARCH

In this chapter, we review the limitations of prevailing research methodologies for studying turnover. Specifically, we describe deficiencies in current procedures for validating measures of causes of turnover, validating theories of structural relations among antecedents of turnover, and verifying causal priorities and causal lag times among determinants of turnover. Later, we suggest alternative methods to offset these shortcomings that might provide greater insight into the phenomenon called turnover.

MEASUREMENT PROBLEMS

Although new explanatory constructs are proliferating, research into turnover have universally neglected to evaluate whether measures truly represent those turnover antecedents. With rare exceptions (for job satisfaction [Kinicki, Carson, and Schriesheim 1990] and organizational commitment [Mowday, Porter, and Steers 1982]), operationalizations of most determinants of turnover have largely escaped construct validation. Researchers often used ad hoc scales with unknown validity or indirectly represented constructs with standard scales (Griffeth and Hom 1988a). Such arbitrary measurements doubtlessly reflected the omission of measurement operations or vague conceptual definitions in the theories (Bagozzi and Phillips 1982). Questionable assessment procedures may underlie the mounting evidence disputing the substantive validity (Schwab 1980) of many models of turnover (Griffeth and Hom 1990; Hom, Griffeth, and Sellaro 1984; Lee 1988; Lee and Mowday 1987; Price and Mueller 1981, 1986). In the following section, we review existing approaches for construct validation and their weaknesses.

Scale Unidimensionality

All too often turnover researchers simply assume, rather than test, that a scale's items are unidimensional (Marsh and Hocevar 1988). That a scale's items measure the same construct is the "most critical and basic assumption of measurement theory" (Hattie 1985, p. 49). Indeed, unidimensionality of scale is a prerequisite for construct validity (Gerbing and Anderson 1988). Items on a scale must estimate the same concept before its conceptual meaning can be ascertained (Hattie 1985).

Exploratory factor analysis (EFA) and estimates of reliability have primarily evaluated the unidimensionality of the scale. To illustrate, Price and Mueller (1981, 1986) used EFA to show that a set of items purportedly measuring the same thing loaded on a common dimension. After deleting poor loading items, they estimated internal consistency reliabilities for the remaining items. Though commonplace, these approaches test scale unidimensionality poorly for they neglect the "external consistency" criterion (Gerbing and Anderson 1988). This criterion requires that measures of the same construct have parallel patterns of correlations with measures of *other* constructs. That is, indicants of other factors help determine the unidimensionality of items defining a given scale.

Thus, EFA and reliability estimates omit tests of external consistency because they overlook relations between a given item set and other item sets. Even when used to analyze multi-item sets, EFA still violates the notion of unidimensionality by estimating items' loadings on multiple dimensions, not one dimension. Furthermore, reliability estimates *assume*, but do not assess, unidimensionality.

Beyond those limitations, EFA typically unearths fewer factors than exist in data (Hunter and Gerbing 1982). Underfactoring poses a serious problem for models of the turnover process that specify closely coupled, correlated causes (Mobley 1977). As a result, EFA would collapse highly correlated but distinctive causes into one factor. Further, EFA offers no "residual" factor for bad items (Hunter and Gerbing 1982). Because every item must sizably load on some factor, EFA assigns bad items to some factors. In short, EFA inadequately validates scales, although it aids in the construction of scales (Gerbing and Anderson 1988).

Convergent and Discriminant Validity

Moreover, scholars of turnover have neglected to verify the convergent and discriminant validity of measures of turnover causes. Here again, this oversight frustrates the confirmation of a theory. For example, examinations of the same model may produce conflicting interrelationships between constructs because they operationalize model concepts differently (see Dalessio, Silverman, and Schuck 1986; Griffeth and Hom 1988a; Steel and Griffeth 1989). That is, alternative translations of the same constructs may lack convergent validity and reflect different concepts. Likewise, measures lacking discriminant validity may undermine support for the theory. Essentially, indices of purportedly dissimilar constructs may actually reflect the same construct and display similar patterns of correlations with other variables, refuting theoretical expectations of different relationships for those indices (see Baysinger and Mobley 1983).

Besides oversight, the few available tests of convergent and discriminant validity have been inadequate. To illustrate, some researchers interpreted high correlations among similar indicators as showing convergent validity (Hom, Griffeth, and Sellaro 1984), while taking modest correlations among dissimilar indicators as signs of discriminant validity (Price and Mueller 1981, 1986). Such informal inspections are not only imprecise but also misleading. According to Campbell and Fiske (1959), the proper diagnosis of discriminant validity requires the comparison of heterotrait correlations with convergent validities. This comparison may find that *modest* heterotrait correlations exceed convergent validities, implying that there is no discriminant validity. (Bollen and Lennox [1991] showed that even this test can mislead because correlations between indicants of different factors may surpass correlations between indicants of the same factor when the factors correlate highly and factor loadings are uneven.) Such informal tests overlook shared method bias (Williams, Cote, and Buckley 1989). Common or correlated assessment methods inflate correlations among common-construct indicants, overstating convergent validity. Conversely, method bias understates discriminant validity by inflating heterotrait correlations.

Construct Differentiation and Dimensionality

In the wake of the growing complexity and scope of theories of turnover, construct validation is increasingly necessary in order to substantiate independent concepts (see Mobley, Griffeth, Hand, and Meglino 1979; Price and Mueller 1981, 1986; Steers and Mowday 1981). Theorists on turnover often introduced explanatory constructs without justifying their independent existence (Schwab 1980). Multiplying constructs invite confusion rather than understanding if the new constructs overlap or duplicate (using different construct names) existing ones (Hom, Kinicki, and Domm 1989). Indeed, fundamental model support requires the empirical differentiation of a model's theoretical terms (Bacharach 1989; Bagozzi and Phillips 1982). Demonstrations that model variables are redundant can promote theoretical parsimony and counterbalance modern trends for ever-expansive conceptualizations (Hom and Griffeth 1991).

Apart from concept differentiation, examinations of theory have overlooked the development of higher-order integrative concepts (ibid.; James and James 1989). The formulation and validation of general concepts that summarize lower-order (even distinctive) concepts would advance parsimonious thinking on turnover (Stein, Newcomb, and Bentler 1988; James and James 1989). Such higher-order concepts may more readily than lower-order concepts disclose substantive validity (Friedman and Harvey 1986; Hunter and Gerbing 1982). Compared with construct variance, scale-specific variance often dominates measures of lower-order concepts, obscuring linkages between constructs (Rossé and Hulin 1985).

Similarly, substantiation for complex, abstract constructs in many formulations of turnover is amiss (Hom, Kinicki, and Domm 1989). Although they serve as valuable organizing frameworks (Osigweh 1989), some molar concepts resemble collections of diverse concepts rather than being unitary concepts (Brooke 1986) or unifying concepts underlying distinctive, related subdimensions (James and James 1989). Echoing Goodman, Ravlin, and Schminke (1987), many models of turnover that identify general classes of causes are "heuristic". For example, prevailing conceptualization of perceptions of the labor market are oversimplified and overly abstract (Steel and

Griffeth 1989). Impressions held by employees comprise varied beliefs, such as the crystallization of alternatives, information about the availability of jobs, and ease of movement, components that may be sufficiently distinctive to warrant being treated as separate constructs (Hom, Kinicki, and Domm 1989; Morrow 1983).

Besides obscuring meaning, broad categories consisting of heterogeneous components may confound estimates of substantive validity because they have different nomological networks (Hunter, Gerbing, and Boster 1982). Indeed, Marsh, Barnes, and Hocevar (1985) contend that construct validation of a concept's dimensionality must precede valid research on its linkages with other constructs. Construct validation is urgently needed to address the question of whether concepts of turnover causes are differentiable or redundant and ascertain their level of abstraction—whether they are general concepts or distinctive subcomponents. Such refinement of concepts is a precondition for correctly embedding them within a nomological network (Schwab 1980).

Measurement Bias

With rare exceptions (Graen and Ginsburgh 1977; Laker 1974), turnover researchers routinely employ one method—namely, survey methodology—to operationalize causal constructs. This dependency on a single-method threatens construct and substantive validity. Shared biases in assessments undermine the determinations of convergent and discriminant validity. In the same manner, common bias in method distorts substantive validity by inflating the estimated structural relations among constructs (Bagozzi, Yi, and Phillips 1991). Some researchers cope with this error by including several scale formats in a survey instrument. Even so, reactivity and response biases still pervade these formats (Webb, Campbell, Schwartz, Sechrest, and Grove 1981).

Furthermore, survey (or other verbal self-report) methodology may produce self-generated validity (Feldman and Lynch 1988). Merely interrogating respondents about workplace attitudes, beliefs, or intentions may create cognitions. These artificially induced cognitions may in turn imply answers to later questions about the job. In this way, self-report procedures create relations that might not otherwise exist in the absence of obtrusive measurement. Even if such cognitions already reside in memory, questions early in the survey may boost their accessibility and overstate their effects on answers to later questions (Srull and Wyer 1979). In short, survey assessments may spuriously produce or inflate relations among the antecedents of turnover, overestimating the validity of models of turnover.

CONFIRMATORY FACTOR ANALYSIS

In this section, we describe more rigorous construct validation procedures. We recommend a special application of structural equation modeling

(SEM)—known as confirmatory factor analysis (CFA) (Long 1983)—that offers particular advantages for construct validation. In testing a hypothesized factor structure, CFA better substantiates scale unidimensionality and convergent and discriminant validity (Anderson and Gerbing 1988). CFA can assess concept redundancy and validate higher-order constructs (Stein, Newcomb, and Bentler 1988). With multiple operational procedures, CFA can also assess the extent to which bias in the method affects the indicators and can control the effects of bias on estimates of causal interrelations in turnover models (Glick, Jenkins, and Gupta 1986; Schmitt and Stults 1986).

A Priori Measurement Model

Unlike EFA, CFA requires a theoretically prescribed factor structure—that is, an explicit measurement model. For this method, CFA users must specify in advance the number of factors, whether or not the factors are correlated, and pattern of indicator loadings on factors. For an *a priori* measurement model, CFA users must designate which parameters are fixed (set, for example, at zero) and which are freed for estimation. Generally speaking, free parameters are factor loadings—estimating how well indicants measure certain factors—and factor correlations. Fixed parameters include factor loadings that are set to 0 for indicators that supposedly do *not* reflect certain factors and 1.0 factor loadings for reference indicators, whose factor loadings are fixed to 1.0 to set a scale for each factor (Hayduk 1987). CFA then estimates the free parameters and the fit of this measurement model to the data.

In Figure 8-1, we depict a hypothetical measurement model for two antecedents of turnover: organizational commitment and job satisfaction. Suppose two indicators assess each construct. For example, attitudinal and behavioral indices might assess commitment (see O'Reilly and Chatman 1986); affective and cognitive indices measure satisfaction (Fishbein and Ajzen 1975). In Figure 8-1, factors are depicted by circles and indicators by boxes. Curved arrows indicate correlations between factors, and straight arrows represent the factors' effects on indicators (factor loadings). Short, unlabeled arrows without source variables signify the indicators' measurement-specific factors *and* random measurement errors.

This measurement model posits that attitudinal and behavioral indicators load (λ) only on the commitment construct, whereas affect and cognitive indicators measure the satisfaction construct. In contrast to EFA, this model proposes that commitment indicators have zero loadings on satisfaction and that satisfaction indicators have zero loadings on commitment. (The absence of arrows linking indicators to factors represents zero factor loadings.) Depending on one's theory about oblique or orthogonal factors, this model submits either correlated or uncorrelated factors (ϕ). Using one of several procedures for estimation (e.g. maximum likelihood), CFA then estimates theorized factor loadings, factor intercorrelations, and measurement error variances. Given the restricted parameters, CFA estimates the free

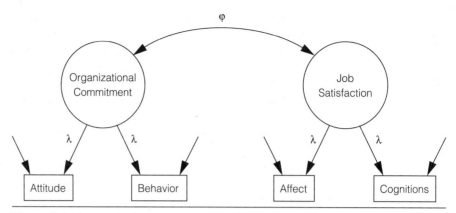

Figure 8-1 An a priori Measurement Model for CFA Evaluation

(and constrained) parameters so that they maximally reproduce observed covariances among indicators (Anderson and Gerbing 1988).

Three kinds of indices assess model fit: omnibus fit indices, individual parameter estimates, and nested model comparisons.

Omnibus Fit Indices The most popular overall fit index is a chi-square test, which statistically compares the covariance matrix implied by the measurement model with the observed covariance matrix. (Although SEM procedures assume input covariances, SEM users routinely analyze correlations, which can distort SEM results [Cudeck 1989].) A nonsignificant chi-square indicates that the measurement model accurately reproduces covariances, whereas a significant chi-square signals significant departures between covariances implied by the model and those observed. Unfortunately, large samples and/or departures from normality may inflate the chi-square, rejecting an otherwise acceptable model (Joreskog and Sorbom 1989). Indeed, because models only approximate reality, all models are a priori false and, with sufficiently large samples, will be rejected (Marsh 1989).

Because of the chi-square's limitations, alternative fit indices have emerged. In particular, many CFA users have interpreted the normed fit index (NFI [Bentler and Bonett 1980]). We compute the NFI by subtracting the model's chi-square from the chi-square of a null model—that posits mutually uncorrelated variables and no factors—and then dividing by the null model's chi-square. The NFI compares the measurement model to a null model, which provides the worst fit with the data and yields the largest chi-square (James, Mulaik, and Brett 1982). The NFI thus compares the lack of fit (that is, the chi-square) of the measurement model with that of the worst-fitting null model. The NFI approaches unity when a plausible measurement model greatly reduces the lack of fit relative to the maximal lack of fit possible—that of the null model. NFIs exceeding .90 signal a good fit (Bentler and Bonett 1980).

Nonetheless, small sample sizes depress the mean of the sampling distribution of the NFI (and other normed indices that are bound between 0 and 1), although sample size does not enter into its calculation (Bollen 1989, 1990b). By comparison, sample size influences the calculated values of nonnormed fit indices—which may exceed 1—but barely affects their sampling-distribution means (Bollen 1990b). Because their weaknesses are different, Bollen prescribed both normed and nonnormed indices to compensate for their different sample-size biases. For example, Mathieu (1991) and Hom, Caranikis-Walker, Prussia, and Griffeth (1992) interpreted the NFI (a normed index) along with a nonnormed "incremental fit index" (IFI [Bollen 1989]). The IFI is a variant of the NFI but its denominator subtracts the measurement model's degrees of freedom from the chi-square of the null model. This index offsets the NFI's small-sample bias to approximate better the asymptotic NFI value (Marsh, Balla, and McDonald 1988; Mulaik, James, Van Alstine, Bennett, Lind, and Stillwell 1989).

Bentler (1990) introduced the comparative fit index (CFI), which estimates a population parameter unlike other descriptive statistics of fit. His simulation study found that the CFI more accurately estimates true model fit than do other indices of fit, especially in small samples. Indeed, the CFI shows less sampling variability than do the NFI or IFI. Unlike the IFI, the CFI also never exceeds 1 and avoids the NFI's small-sample underestimation of model fit. Despite varying formulas, these three indices of fit are nevertheless asymptotically equivalent (ibid.).

Parameter Estimates Individual estimates of model parameters complement overall indices of fit (James, Mulaik, and Brett 1982), which only test the validity of fixed parameters, such as factor loadings that are set to zero. Significant (sizable) factor loadings support the factor model and convergent validity, affirming that the indicators mirror the underlying constructs (Anderson and Gerbing 1988; Bollen 1989). Bagozzi and Yi (1990) further recommended an examination of the possibility that parameter estimates might be illogical or fall outside conventional acceptability. Such "improper" estimates (such as standardized factor loadings > 1.0) may emanate from misspecified models. Inspections of estimated factor correlations may further test the measurement model. Low correlations indicate discriminable factors; excessively high correlations suggest redundant factors. To test discriminant validity precisely, CFA users can compute a confidence interval around the correlation between two factors; the inclusion of unity denotes equivalent factors (ibid.).

Nested Model Comparisons Nested model comparisons can evaluate a measurement model, verifying the necessity of a parameter set. For this test, we specify one or more restricted versions of the basic measurement model by fixing (or constraining) some parameters to certain values, such as zero. These restricted versions are termed "nested" models because they are derived from the original model. Then we statistically compare each nested model with the original model by subtracting their chi-squares, the difference also being a chi-square (James, Mulaik, and Brett 1982). The difference between the degrees of freedom in the models is the degree of freedom for this "difference chi-square." A significant difference chi-square rejects the more restrictive model and its extra parameter restrictions, a finding that validates the parameters fixed in the nested model but freed in the original model. A nonsignificant chi-square upholds (or fails to reject) the restrictive model, which is favored over the original model due to parsimony. In this event, parameters fixed in the nested model but freed in the original model are superfluous. Moreover, NFI or CFI difference between models indicates practical differences in fit (Glick, Jenkins, and Gupta 1986; Hom and Griffeth 1991; Widaman 1985) and may resist sample-size bias more than the difference chi-square would (Marsh 1989).

Estimation procedures Most CFA users assess a measurement model with maximum likelihood estimation. Given parameter restrictions, this procedure seeks maximum likelihood estimates of free parameters that minimize discrepancies between observed and model-implied covariances (Hayduk 1987). Yet this method assumes a multivariate normal distribution of observed variables. Maximum likelihood parameters are robust against departures from multinormality (Anderson and Gerbing 1988; Huba and Harlow 1987). Non-normal data do, however, bias—albeit a conservative bias—parameter standard errors and overall chi-square test.

New estimation procedures have emerged, relaxing the multinormality assumption. One promising alternative is elliptical estimation, which requires zero skewness but not normal-variable kurtosis (Bentler 1985; Bollen 1989). Variables can have platykurtic or leptokurtic distributions, although their kurtosis must be equal. The least restrictive procedure is the distribution-free method, which is asymptotically insensitive to variable distribution. In other words, variables can have any distributional form. All the same, these new methods demand much larger sample sizes than does maximum likelihood estimation, limiting their use (Anderson and Gerbing 1988; Bollen 1989).

Convergent and Discriminant Validity

As stated above, CFA assessment of an *a priori* measurement model can test convergent and discriminant validity (Anderson and Gerbing 1988). Significant factor loadings reveal convergent validity for indicators. Confidence intervals around factor correlations excluding 1.0 suggest discriminant validity. Beyond this, nested model comparisons can augment evidence for discriminant validity (ibid.). To illustrate this approach with our running example, we would specify perfect correlation between the two factors in Figure 8-1 ($\phi = 1.0$) to generate a nested (one-factor) measurement model. Then, we compute differences in fit statistics between the original two-factor and one-factor models. Meaningful differences between models in fit reject the constraint of perfect factor correlation and disclose discriminably different factors, whereas minimal model differences support this parameter restriction and oppose discriminant validity. To test models with three or more factors, Anderson and Gerbing (ibid.) recommended testing the discriminant validity between each pair of factors rather than simultaneously testing all the factors.

Concept Differentiation and Redundancy

Nested model comparisons can similarly verify theoretical independence or redundancy among model concepts. For example, Hom and Griffeth (1991) used CFA to test the conceptual distinctions between thoughts of quitting, search decisions, and intentions to quit. They compared nested models, which equated pairs of withdrawal cognitions, with a baseline model positing all three cognitions. Equating these concepts did not materially degrade fit relative to this baseline model. That is, nested model comparisons countered these popular theoretical distinctions (Mobley 1977; Mobley, Griffeth, Hand, and Meglino 1979), prescribing a global withdrawal cognition instead. CFA tests of concept differentiation thus advance theoretical parsimony by identifying redundant concepts. That said, CFA comparisons of alternative measurement models may advance our thinking about turnover just as competitive theory testing does (Hom and Griffeth 1991; Hom and Hulin 1981).

Scale Unidimensionality

CFA tests scale unidimensionality more rigorously than does EFA or reliability estimation (Gerbing and Anderson 1988). CFA explicitly determines whether all scale items represent the same factor, whereas EFA estimates item loadings on all factors. To illustrate, suppose our measurement model of the item structure specifies that each scale comprises two items, as depicted in Figure 8-2. For CFA this model further theorizes that the items reflect only their factor (scale) and have zero loadings on other "irrelevant" scales. CFA would thus test those prespecified factor loadings. Significant (strong) factor loadings would support item assessment of factors; good indices of fit would uphold the validity of *a priori* null factor loadings—that items do not reflect extraneous factors. More than this, CFA of multifactor models can verify the external consistency standard for scale unidimensionality. According to Gerbing and Anderson (1988), overall statistics of fit indicate whether items from the same scale have a parallel pattern of correlations with items from other scales.

Noninterval scales   It is quite likely that the dichotomous, or categorical, nature of most item measures violates the statistical assumptions of CFA. Prevailing SEM estimation procedures assume interval-level scales, but most scales for psychological measurement lack this property of measurement (Ghiselli, Campbell, and Zedeck 1980). Fortunately, Muthen's LISCOMP (1987) and Joreskog and Sorbom's LISREL 7 (1989) can handle categorical data or mixtures of categorical and continuous variables. The procedure pre-

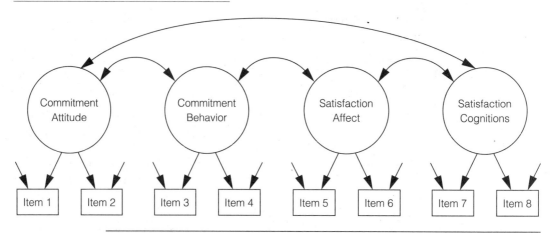

Figure 8-2 Measurement Model of Scale Items

sumes that normally distributed latent variables underlie observed categorical variables and analyzes polychoric correlations (between categorical variables) and polyserial correlations (relating categorical and continuous variables) (Bollen 1989; Schoenberg 1989). This categorical procedure requires larger samples than does maximum likelihood (Joreskog and Sorbom 1989).

Bollen (1989) summarized the simulation research on the effects of treating ordinal indicators as though they were continuous variables. First, excessive kurtosis or skewness of indicators adversely affects the chi-square and z tests of the statistical significance of maximum likelihood estimators. Second, kurtosis and skewness of ordinal variables rather than the number of their categories most bias the chi-square test. Third, fewer numbers of categories of ordinal indicators attenuate standardized coefficient estimates. All told, item indicators having few categories and/or exhibiting severe skewness and kurtosis may most bias CFA tests of scale unidimensionality.

Multitrait-Multimethod Analysis

As stated earlier, common or correlated assessment methods overestimate convergent validity but underestimate discriminant validity (Kenny and Kashy 1992). Different operationalizations of each construct that do not share the same methodological weakness can offset method bias. Given dissimilar measurements of multiple constructs, we can derive a multitrait-multimethod (MTMM) matrix comprising correlations among different assessment methods. This matrix reveals the extent of convergent validity—different measures of the same construct converge—and discriminant validity—different measures of dissimilar constructs diverge. Over the years, many procedures have evolved to analyze MTMM correlations (Kinicki, Bannister, Hom, and DeNisi 1985; Schmitt and Stults 1986).

Presently, CFA has become the method of choice for analyzing MTMM data (Bagozzi, Yi and Phillips 1991; Kenny and Kashy 1992; Schmitt and

Stults 1986). Apart from assessing convergent and discriminant validity, CFA can evaluate the effects of bias in method and control method effects on estimates of validity. For MTMM analysis, we specify a measurement model, shown in Figure 8-3, positing latent factors for different assessment procedures and traits (e.g. commitment and satisfaction) (known as the complete model [Kenny and Kashy 1992] or Model 3C [Widaman 1985]). Each indicator loads on a particular trait factor *and* a method factor. Although allowing method factors to correlate, this model mandates zero correlations between trait and method factors to avoid identification problems (Kenny and Kashy 1992; Widaman 1985). CFA evaluation of this model then estimates convergent and discriminant validity and method bias. Specifically, factor loadings measure the extent to which indicators reflect the trait (validity) and method (systematic error) factors. Here again, significant (large) trait loadings indicate convergent validity; low trait correlations (that differ significantly from 1.0) signal discriminant validity (Bagozzi, Yi and Phillips 1991). A measure's loading on a method factor reveals its susceptibility to method bias (Bagozzi and Yi 1990).

Given a plausible MTMM model, we can compare nested models to test convergent and discriminant validity further. Following Widaman (1985), we assess convergent validity by comparing Model 3C (the complete model) against a nested model positing method and no trait factors. (This Methods-Only Model is shown in Figure 8-4.) Dissimilar fit between this model and

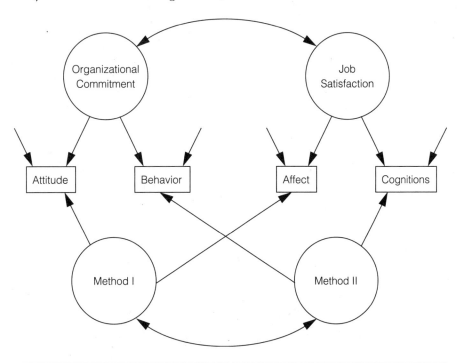

Figure 8-3 Measurement Model with Trait and Method Factors

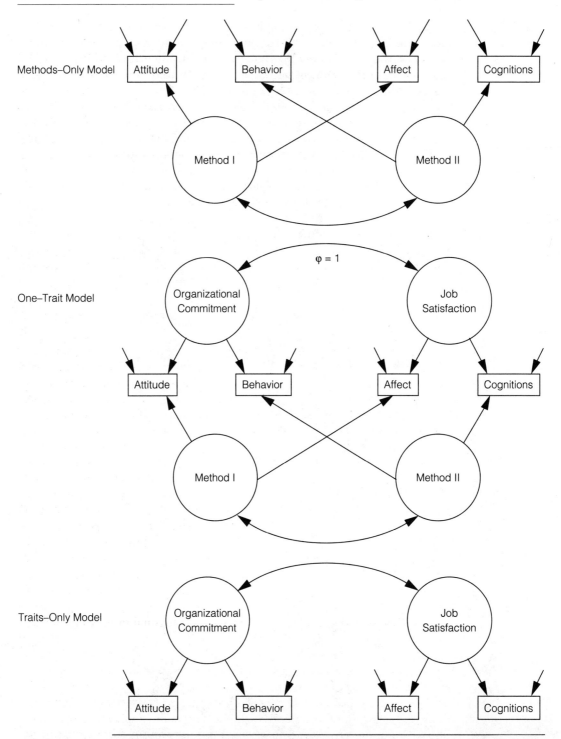

Figure 8-4 Nested Models for Testing Convergent and Discriminant Validity

Model 3C indicates that trait factors (i.e., job attitudes) are essential for model fit; no difference in fit suggests that they are dispensable (Bagozzi, Yi and Phillips 1991). Testing discriminant validity, we next compare Model 3C against a model specifying perfectly correlated traits (the One-Trait Model, see Figure 8-4). Different model fits indicate discriminably different traits, whereas similar fits suggest redundant traits (Bagozzi and Yi 1990). Last, we compare Model 3C against a model (the Traits-Only model; see Figure 8-4) postulating no method factors. A poorly fitting Traits-Only Model reveals significant method covariance among measures, whereas no fit decrement discloses little method bias (ibid.).

Other MTMM Models   Despite its advantages, the complete trait-method model often yields improper solutions (negative variances or correlations exceeding 1.0) or fails to converge (Kenny and Kashy 1992). To overcome these limitations, CFA researchers advanced various MTMM models. Kenny and Kashy (ibid.) compared various MTMM models and concluded that Marsh's (1989) "correlated uniqueness" model best surmounts problems of estimation. This model, shown in Figure 8-5, proposes estimating only trait factors and no method factors. To represent systematic error, this model correlates the disturbance (or unique factor) of each measure with disturbances of other measures using the same method. Covariation between unique factors thus assesses method effects, sizable covariances signifying large method bias. In the illustration, correlated disturbances are depicted as curved lines between sourceless arrows. Reanalyzing MTMM data, Kenney and Kashy showed that this model yielded fewer estimation difficulties and more reasonable parameter estimates than did the standard Model 3C.

Moreover, Model 3C confounds random measurement error with unique true-score variance specific to a measure, such as item wording (Bagozzi, Yi and Phillips 1991). Reviewing alternative corrections for this weakness, Bagozzi and fellow researchers (ibid.) concluded that Kumar and Dillon's (1990) First-Order, Multiple-Informant, Multiple-Item (FOMIMI) Model best disentangles random error from unique test variance. Like Model 3C, the FOMIMI Model specifies trait and method factors and posits further measure-specific factors to isolate specific test variance from random measurement error. As illustrated in Figure 8-5, this model posits that each measure consists of trait, method, test-specific, and random-error components (the last are not shown). Specific factors are not related by curved arrows because theoretically, the factors are orthogonal to one another and to trait and method factors. This illustration specifies that two distinct methods, survey and interview, assess organizational commitment, focusing on different expressions (attitude, behavior, or intention) of commitment. For example, an interviewer might ask employees how they feel about the firm (affect), how often they perform tasks that go beyond their job descriptions (behavior), and whether they intend to remain employed there (intention). Common survey and interview questions about company attitudes may reflect the same measure-specific factor (Specific Factor 1). Yet the

Correlated Uniqueness Model

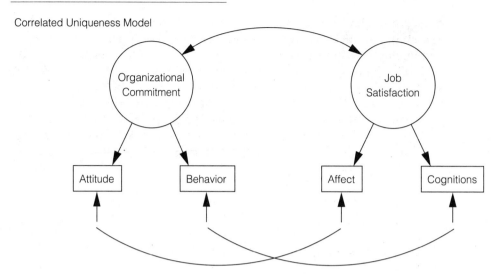

First–Order, Multiple–Informant, Multiple–Item Model

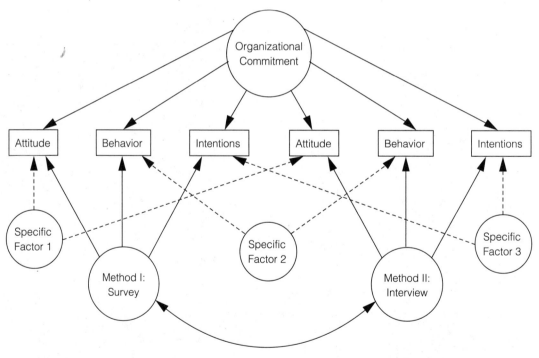

Figure 8-5 Alternative Multitrait-Multimethod Models

FOMIMI model demands three times as many measures as Model 3C does, requiring at least three items for each combination of trait and method to achieve identification.

Model 3C presumes that variation in measures is a linear combination of traits, methods, and error (Bagozzi and Yi 1990). In some circumstances, method factors may *multiplicatively* interact with trait factors. For example, high relationships between traits may boost method effects. Presuming only additive effects for traits and methods, the traditional MTMM model may yield poor fit and biased estimates if methods do interact with traits. To permit interactions between trait and method, Bagozzi and Yi (ibid.; Bagozzi, Yi and Phillips 1991) proposed the Direct Product Model. Bagozzi and Yi (1990, 1991) describe how to analyze this model. Analyzing many MTMM matrices, they showed that the Direct Product Model fit data better than Model 3C does when nonadditive effects are present. They recommended first determining whether method effects are additive or multiplicative before assessing construct validity.

Higher-Order CFA

Earlier we argued that the development of general concepts to subsume lower-order concepts may advance theory parsimony and more readily reveal substantive validity (Hunter and Gerbing 1982; James and James 1989). Higher-order CFA can establish their viability. For example, a global attitude that may account for job satisfaction and commitment (see Steers and Mowday 1981) is shown in Figure 8-6. This Second-Order Model proposes that a general factor "causes" lower-order factors (i.e., commitment and satisfaction), which in turn affect indicators. (This model is formally a structural model, which is more fully described below.) Depicted as dependent variables, lower-order factors also have disturbance terms (shown as sourceless arrows) that embody causal influences other than the general attitude. (For identification, a factor loading for each lower-order concept and the higher-order factor variance must be fixed at 1.0 [Bollen, 1989].)

Higher-order CFA would estimate the general factor's causal effects, indicator loadings, and overall model fit. Besides, we can contrast this model to a nested model, also shown in Figure 8-6, positing only correlated first-order factors (First-Order Model) (James and James 1989). Thus, the more parsimonious Second-Order Model becomes plausible if it closely matches the fit of the First-Order Model (Marsh and Hocevar 1985). In this event, lower-order factors are hierarchically arranged and reflect different facets of a higher-order factor. If the higher-order factor in the (well-fitting) Second-Order Model also sizably impacts the lower-order factors, a simpler unidimensional representation becomes plausible, wherein a general factor so dominates first-order factors as to erase their distinctiveness. This form of the Second-Order Model thus implies that the first-order factors are equivalent and equally reflect the general construct.

Concept Dimensionality   Conversely, higher-order CFA may validate existing abstract concepts of turnover causes, testing various measurement structures of concept dimensionality. Marsh and Hocevar (ibid.) identified three leading structures for comparison: unidimensional structure, multidimensional conception with hierarchically arranged, distinctive components, and multidimensional structure with independent subdimensions. To illustrate this application, a Second-Order model depicting Mobley's (1977) global conception of withdrawal expected utility, underlying expected utilities of quitting and job-seeking, is shown in Figure 8-7. Testing his notion, Hom, Kinicki, and Domm (1989) surveyed employees to measure their attitude toward those acts of withdrawal and the perceived consequences of the acts (see Ajzen and Fishbein 1980). Using CFA, they then compared Mobley's implicit Second-Order Model with a less restricted measurement model having two first-order (correlated) expected-utility factors. The Second-Order Model fit data worse than did the First-Order Model, thereby rejecting Mobley's abstract conception. These findings suggested that this global construct might be decomposed into two separate (albeit correlated) lower-order concepts (Hunter, Gerbing, and Boster 1982).

CAUSAL ANALYSIS

Apart from breadth and scope, modern theories of turnover formulate elaborate networks of structural associations among concepts (Price and Mueller 1981, 1986; Steers and Mowday 1981). Notwithstanding their complexity, prevailing models must undergo more theoretical refinement before they can be subject to proper confirmatory testing. Essentially, most theories of turnover fall short on one or more of the conditions that James, Mulaik, and Brett (1982) outlined for confirmatory analysis:

1. Formal statement of theory as a structural model
2. Theoretical rationale for causal hypotheses
3. Specification of causal order
4. Specification of causal direction
5. Self-contained functional equations
6. Specification of boundaries
7. Stability of structural model

For example, Mobley, Griffeth, Hand, and Meglino (1979) and Hulin, Roznowski, and Hachiya (1985) specified causal order and directionality for sets of theoretical variables rather than for each variable. Still, they overlooked the way in which each component in an antecedent set impacts the components of a consequent set. By contrast, Price and Mueller (1981, 1986) more fully described causality, but left unspecified the way in which organizational conditions translate into job dissatisfaction, or how dissatisfaction translates into withdrawal decisions. Though confirmatory analysis does not require assessment (and representation) of micromediational mechanisms,

Second–Order Factor Model

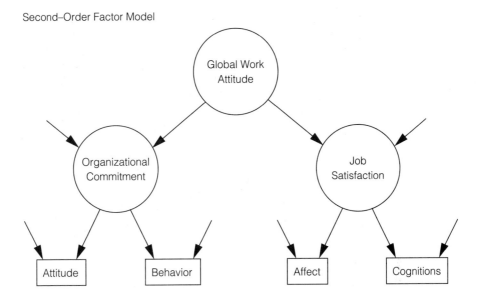

First–Order Factor Model

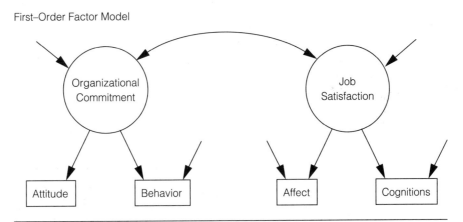

Figure 8-6 Measurement Models for Testing Viability of Higher-Order Factor

such specifications nonetheless furnish a theoretical rationale for causal connections (James, Mulaik, and Brett 1982).

Most theorists of turnover assume, but do not justify, self-containment. Confirmatory analysis requires a self-contained theory that specifies all the relevant causes of each endogenous variable (ibid.). A relevant cause is an influence of an endogenous variable that covaries with its other influences. Omission of relevant causes can, however, bias estimates of the impact of measured causes (ibid.). Most theorists implicitly consider their models to generalize over time (stationarity) and across occupations and organizations

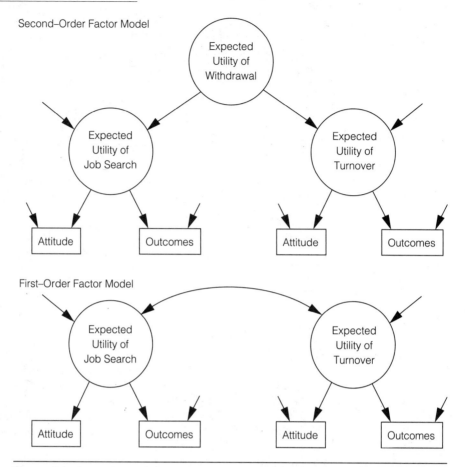

Figure 8-7   Measurement Models for Testing Concept Dimensionality

(limitless boundary conditions), assumptions that are increasingly being challenged (Cotton and Tuttle 1986; Hom and Griffeth 1991; Hom, Caranikis-Walker, Prussia, and Griffeth 1992). In summary, the seven conditions delineated by James, Mulaik, and Brett (1982) are essential for the proper confirmatory validation of turnover theories. Nevertheless, empirical testing of turnover models has proceeded despite paltry evidence or rationale for those preconditions.

In addition, examinations of theory have often applied inappropriate or inefficient statistical approaches (James, Mulaik, and Brett 1982). In particular, exploratory path analysis has often been used to evaluate models, each turnover determinant being regressed onto *all* the preceding antecedents (Hom, Griffeth, and Sellaro 1984; Mobley, Horner, and Hollingsworth 1978; Price and Mueller 1981; Lee 1988). This application of path analysis does not, however, represent confirmatory analysis, which prescribes the testing of theoretically dictated pathways, not every possible one (James, Mulaik, and Brett 1982). Apart from such misuse, researchers generally neglect to validate pathways that are omitted by their formulations ("the omitted parameters test," ibid.). Most theories, especially parsimonious ones, imply the *absence* of causal connections, in addition to specifying connections. Yet the validity of so-called null pathways usually goes untested. Ordinary path analysis does not control random measurement error, which biases estimates of parameters. Measurement error can attenuate or inflate causal parameters, make estimates of zero parameters nonzero, or yield estimates with the wrong sign (Williams and Hazer 1986).

Single-sample model tests typically lack sufficient statistical power (Hunter and Schmidt 1990b). It is quite likely that weak statistical power undermines tests of structural networks in turnover theories. Because well-articulated causal networks imply highly correlated causes (hence, multicollinearity), large samples are necessary to insure stable parameter estimates (Hom, Caranikis-Walker, Prussia, and Griffeth 1992). Along these lines, small-sample tests may generate inconsistent parameter estimates, suggesting uneven model support across studies (see Dalessio, Silverman, and Shuck 1986). Yet fluctuating parameters may reflect error in the sampling rather than inconstancy in the model (Hunter and Schmidt 1990b).

Structural Equation Modeling

Structural equation modeling (SEM) can overcome several of the aforementioned shortcomings of traditional model testing. SEM analysis requires an explicit declaration of the theory as a structural model and the justification of its causal hypotheses. Unlike path analysis, SEM can more accurately estimate the causal effects among constructs in turnover models by controlling random and systematic measurement errors (Bagozzi 1980; Dwyer 1983; Glick, Jenkins, and Gupta 1985). A two-stage SEM application that initially tests and refines the measurement model before evaluating the structural model can produce better support for the theory (Anderson and Gerbing 1988): The prior validation of indicants may enhance substantive validity (Schwab 1980). SEM can analyze panel data more powerfully to verify the causal assumptions of turnover models (Anderson and Williams 1992; Williams and Podsakoff 1989) and can assess more precisely the boundary conditions (Palich, Hom, and Griffeth, in press) and the stability of the model over time (Hom and Griffeth 1991).

To control measurement error, SEM users must assess each construct with multiple indicators and then estimate a measurement model (relating indicators to constructs) that disattenuates structural relationships from random errors (Dwyer 1983). (An alternative method is to test a path model with one indicator per construct [the "manifest variables" model] using SEM to set measurement parameters based on reliabilities [see Williams and Hazer 1986].) SEM analysis then simultaneously estimates both measurement and structural models, which together constitute the Latent Variables (LV) Structural Model. An LV turnover model, in which latent variables (factors) are depicted with circles and manifest variables (indicators) with boxes, is shown in Figure 8-8. Straight arrows from circles to boxes represent indicator loadings on latent variables; straight arrows among circles represent causal effects among latent variables. Curved arrows portray correlations among exogenous causes and short arrows without source variables and pointing toward boxes signify measurement errors. Arrows impinging on circles signify disturbances—other omitted causes of endogenous variables. Like the CFA measurement model, the measurement submodel prescribes a certain pattern of factor loadings (λ) between indicators and latent factors. (To define its metric, each factor must have one factor loading fixed at 1.0 [Hayduk 1987].) The structural submodel of the LV Model depicts theorized structural relations (ßs: causal effects) among factors. The structural submodel essentially embodies the substantive theory.

Using one of several estimation methods (e.g., maximum likelihood), SEM simultaneously derives estimates for the measurement and causal parameters that maximally recompute observed covariances. Here again, we interpret omnibus fit indices and parameter estimates to judge model fit. Acceptable fit statistics support the overall LV Model. Significant (sizable) factor loadings uphold the measurement submodel; significant causal parameters (carrying the correct signs) uphold the structural submodel. Nested model comparisons further test the turnover theory (Anderson and Gerbing 1988). James, Mulaik, and Brett (1982) prescribed the following sequence (shown in Figure 8-9) of nested models: Measurement Model; LV Structural Model; and a Structural Null Model. The LV Structural Model is actually nested within the Measurement Model, specifying certain but not all, relationships among factors according to the substantive theory. First we validate the Measurement Model. Anderson and Gerbing (1988) suggested testing various measurement models to find the best-fitting one. Though exploratory, separate estimation, and possibly respecification, of the measurement model before assessing the structural model may reduce "interpretational confounding."

Finding a tenable measurement model, we compare that model to the LV Structural Model. Minimal differences between the models indicate that the more restricted, causal structure accurately (and more parsimoniously) explains covariances among latent factors. Given a well-fitting LV Structural Model, we then contrast it with Structural Null Model that is nested within the LV Structural Model, with all causal parameters set to zero. This comparison measures the variance explained by the set of causal parameters. A large disparity between models would require the rejection of the Structural Null Model and prescribes the structural parameters as essential for model fit.

Williams and Hazer (1986) further proposed testing less restrictive versions of the LV Structural Model. Testing omitted parameters, these versions introduce superfluous causal pathways not posited in the turnover theory (James, Mulaik, and Brett 1982). In our example, an alternative structural model might prescribe that satisfaction and extra work conflict directly affect withdrawal cognitions. SEM assessment of this model that reveals these extra

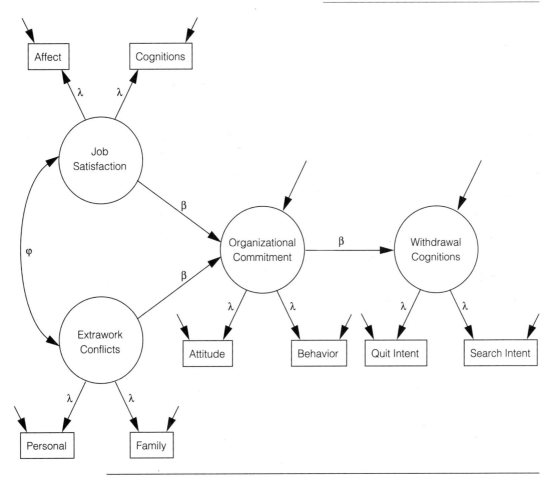

Figure 8-8 Latent Variables Structural Model

pathways to be nonsignificant then further corroborates the original structural model, which supposes no direct effects for satisfaction and conflict on withdrawal cognitions.

Competitive Testing   Most examinations of theory try to validate a single turnover model. The examined model may plausibly fit data, but untested alternatives may provide even closer fits (Hom, Caranikis-Walker, Prussia, and Griffeth 1992; Mobley and Meglino 1979). Thus, a comparison of alternative formulations would more conclusively establish the relative validity of models (Platt 1964). Given the burgeoning numbers of turnover models, competitive testing is becoming imperative so that less valid models might be discarded in favor of more valid ones.

SEM can facilitate competitive theory testing in two ways. First, SEM supplies more diagnostic indices of model fit. The few comparative examinations of turnover models that have been made have focused exclusively on

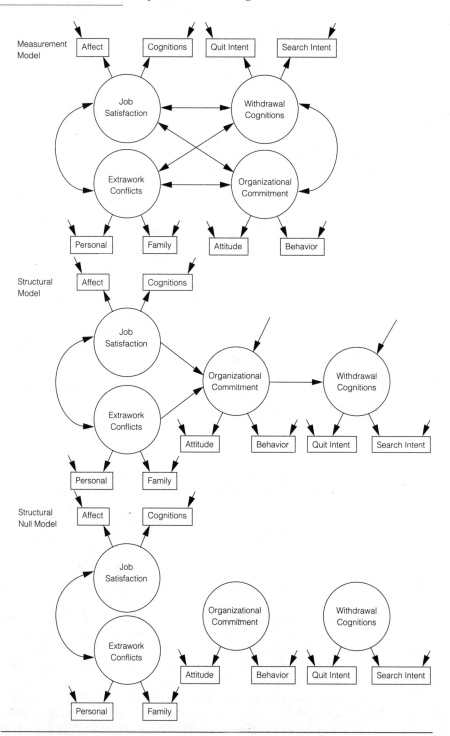

Figure 8-9 Nested Model Sequence

predictive validity (Hom and Hulin 1981), neglecting substantive or nomological validity (Griffeth and Hom 1990). SEM analysis can assess the relative nomological validity across models, using parameter estimates and omnibus fit indices (James, Mulaik, and Brett 1982). Second, SEM can statistically compare competing models that are nested within one another (Netemeyer, Johnson, and Burton 1990; Williams and Hazer 1986).

To illustrate this SEM application, we report a study (Griffeth and Hom 1990) comparing two leading turnover models: a variant of Mobley's 1977 model produced by Hom, Griffeth, and Sellaro (1984), and Price and Mueller's models (1981, 1986). In spite of the extensive research on which they are based, these models have not been directly compared in one study. The comparison constituted a relatively fair competitive test (Cooper and Richardson 1986). Given the development and refinement of model measures over a long period, both models can be operationalized with considerable, if not equal, fidelity and care (Hom, Caranikis-Walker, Prussia, and Griffeth 1992; Dalessio, Silverman, and Schuck 1986; Mobley, Horner, and Hollingsworth 1978; Price and Mueller 1981, 1986). The Price-Mueller and Hom, Griffeth, and Sellaro models are shown in Figures 8-10 and 8-11, respectively. Griffeth and Hom (1990) found similar predictive validities for both models but higher nomological validity for Hom, Griffeth, and Sellaro's theory. Because these models emphasize different withdrawal stages, Griffeth and Hom then designed an integrated model, shown in Figure 8-12, combining promising constructs from both models (ibid). SEM tests upheld the predictive and nomological validity of this synthesis. Although it is not an inevitable outcome, competitive testing can generate an unifying framework integrating several theories.

Along similar lines, SEM competitive testing can compare concepts from different theories to identify potential construct redundancy (Griffeth and Hom 1988a). Such examinations may reverse the growing confusion when different theorists name similar concepts differently (see Baysinger and Mobley 1983). Using SEM, Cabrera, Castaneda, Nora, and Hengstler (1992) tested the equivalence between concepts from two theories of student attrition from college. Both models, proposing that student feelings of belongingness to the college reinforce student retention, defined and measured the concept differently: one as institutional commitment, the other as institutional fit. To measure components of these models, Cabrera and his colleagues administered a survey to 466 entering college freshmen and accessed personnel files to learn about their grade point averages and their continued enrollment a year later. Analyzing these data, the researchers set up several nested measurement models to test the convergence of concepts from different theories of college attrition. Taking a concept from each model, the initial model posited two correlated factors (institutional commitment and institutional fit) and their respective measures as indicants of those factors. This model was then compared with an orthogonal two-construct model (positing uncorrelated factors) and a one-construct model (positing perfect correlation). SEM tests rejected the orthogonal factor

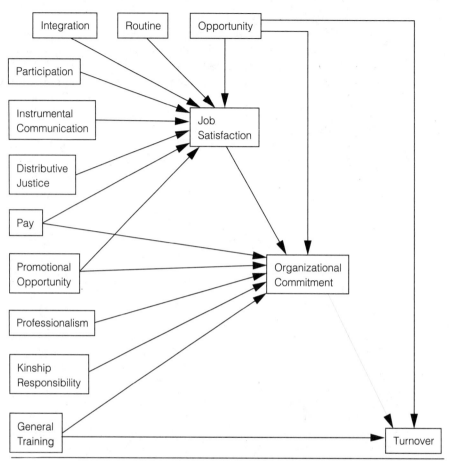

Figure 8-10 Revised Price-Mueller 1981 Model of Turnover. (J. Price and C. Mueller, "A causal model of turnover for nurses." *Academy of Management Journal,* **24 (1981): 547.)**

model but sustained the initial and one-construct models. Because the latter two models fit data equally well, these results imply that institutional commitment and fit were equivalent concepts. SEM can detect equivalence in constructs from different models that may be defining and operationalizing those constructs differently. An SEM approach may develop an integrative framework in which models may be combined (ibid.), thereby eliminating superfluous models and concepts in order to generate more parsimonious explanations.

Method Bias   If constructs are represented by various different assessment procedures, SEM can control for method bias in estimating structural parameters (Glick, Jenkins, and Gupta 1986). For example, we might test the MTMM model in Figure 8-3 but specify the causal effects among the traits, such as commitment affecting satisfaction. SEM could estimate the structural

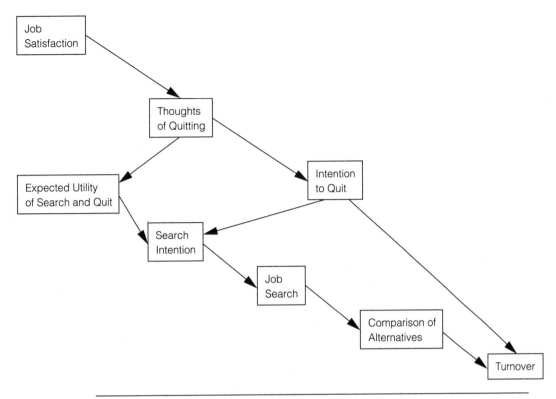

Figure 8-11 Hom, Griffeth, and Sellaro's Model of Turnover. (P. W. Hom, R. W. Griffeth, C. L. Sellaro, "The Validity of Mobley's model of employee turnover." *Organizational Behavior and Human Performance,* **34 (1984): 166.)**

parameters, adjusting for the biasing effects of systematic and random measurement errors.

Categorical Variables   Many authors have condemned the use of an ordinary least-squares regression to predict a binary dependent variable such as turnover (Harrison and Hulin 1989; Huselid and Day 1991) because it produces severe statistical problems. First, predicted turnover values may fall outside 0–1 boundaries, generating meaningless results. Second, heteroscedastic and nonnormal errors derived from the analysis of a dichotomous dependent variable may well invalidate coefficient *t* tests. Third, estimates of the marginal effects of an independent variable may be biased because they depend on the mean value of the dependent variable. Illustrating this pitfall, Huselid and Day (1991) showed dramatically divergent conclusions yielded by a least-squares regression and a more correct logistic regression.

The same objections extend to SEM tests of turnover models because SEM procedures assume continuous interval-scaled variables (Jaros et al.

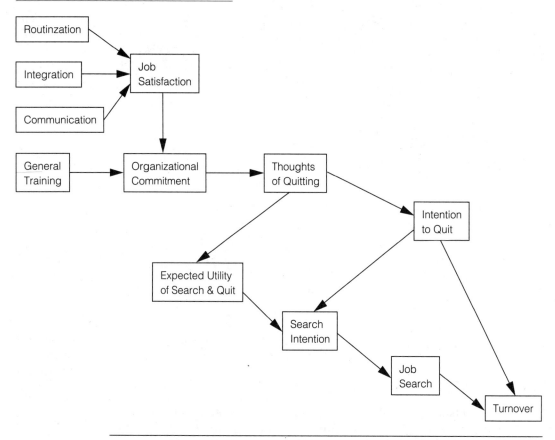

Figure 8-12 Integrated Model of Turnover. (R. W. Griffeth, and P. W. Hom (1990, August). Competitive examination of two turnover theories: A two-sample test. Paper presented at the annual convention of the Academy of Management, San Francisco, CA: 21.)

1993). To offset this limitation, Muthen (1987, LISCOMP) and Joreskog and Sorbom (1989, LISREL 7) developed new estimation procedures that handle categorical (binary, ordinal) variables and analyze polyserial and polychoric correlations derived from observed categorical data. For example, Hollis and Muthen (1987) compared LISCOMP and LISREL maximum likelihood estimates for clearly categorical data and found that LISCOMP produced more efficient (and less biased) estimates of parameters and a more valid model chi-square test and standard errors.

To show its relevance for turnover, we estimated a simple model, on a large sample of four hundred retail store employees, comparing LISREL 7's categorical-data option with its maximum likelihood method (which presumes interval scales). The model proposes that job satisfaction impacts withdrawal cognitions, which in turn affects quits. Moreover, satisfaction directly influences turnover. The model is illustrated in Figure 8-13, in which the categorical parameter estimates are noted; the maximum likelihood parameters having been included in parentheses. Factor loadings were consistent across both estimation procedures. The structural parameters, especially those for the direct effects of antecedents on turnover, diverged. The categorical method estimated larger parameters and superior fit statistics:

categorical $x^2(33) = 91.68$ ($p < .05$) and Goodness-of-Fit = .991

compared with

maximum likelihood $x^2(33) = 209.39$ ($p < .05$) and Goodness-of-Fit = .904.

In conclusion, new categorical SEM procedures may reveal a higher substantive validity for turnover theories because they relax unrealistic interval-scaling requirements (see Jaros et al. 1993). Still, these methods demand larger samples, limiting their usage (Joreskog and Sorbom 1989). Our illustration disclosed that maximum likelihood estimates of structural relations among turnover causes and the measurement structure closely matched categorical estimates, although they underestimated the linkages between antecedents and quit. Generalizing from this simple demonstration, we may say that the maximum likelihood procedure most attenuates the direct causal effects from the antecedents to turnover. It may, however, produce reasonably correct estimates of structural relations among determinants, the substance of most turnover formulations, as well as factor loadings. All the same, some authors contend that turnover is truly a categorical variable, disputing LISCOMP and LISREL 7 corrections that presume turnover to be a continuous variable formed by dichotomizing company tenure (Williams 1990).

Cautionary Remarks   With the growing popularity, SEM tests of turnover models risk becoming abused. Unidentified models and unmeasured variables are most likely to plague current SEM analyses. For one, SEM applications usually do not verify model identification to establish that model parameters can be uniquely estimated given the information available in the covariance matrix (Bollen 1989). Without such preliminary scrutiny, SEM assessments of under identified models may yield misleading parameter estimates. Thus, SEM users should establish model identification before evaluating turnover models (ibid.). Moreover, SEM investigations of withdrawal models routinely neglect (or incompletely state) the theoretical rationale for the self-containment of functional equations. As James, Mulaik, and Brett (1982) warned, the omission of relevant causes biases estimates of causal effects among measured determinants. To satisfy this condition, prevailing frameworks may well demand additional theoretical refinement and extension. It is more than likely that current theories do not specify *all* the relevant causes of each and every endogenous variable in their conceptualizations.

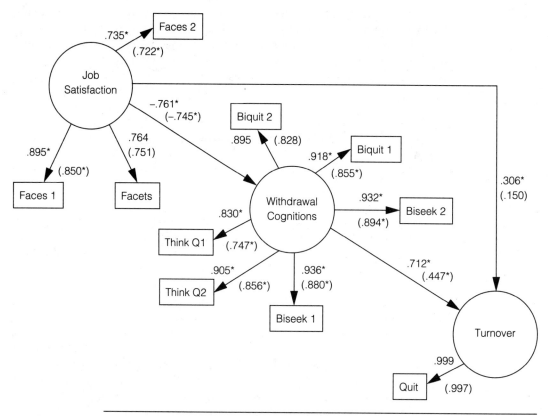

Figure 8-13 Lisrel Analysis of Categorical Variables

PANEL ANALYSES

Causal priorities in turnover models are rarely validated. Given pervasive cross-sectional surveys, turnover researchers assume that causal order and direction hold while they are testing their models (Mobley 1982a). While unable to rival true experimentation for causal inference, panel designs—repeated administrations of a survey—can estimate causal effects more accurately than can ubiquitous cross-sectional designs (Aronson, Ellsworth, Carlsmith, and Gonzales 1990; Dwyer 1983). Cross-sectional assessments substitute observed *intraindividual* changes for observed *interindividual* differences (Dwyer 1983). Several longitudinal studies have documented the bias in this substitution (Bateman and Strasser 1983, 1984; Curry, Wakefield, Price, and Mueller 1986; Farkas and Tetrick 1989). Even so, panel research remains underused.

Uncertainty over the timing of surveys and the appropriate statistical analyses partly explain why panel data are rarely collected. Turnover theories universally neglect causal lag times (Sheridan and Abelson 1983), providing no guidelines on time intervals between survey waves to capture lag times.

Considerable controversy has raged over proper panel analyses. Traditionally, in panel research, correlations between variables assessed at different times have been compared. Yet differing variable stabilities and variances can bias such cross-lagged panel correlations (Rogosa 1980). More recent tests have applied cross-lagged regression (Bateman and Strasser 1983, 1984) or path analysis (Curry et al. 1986; Farkas and Tetrick 1990) to evaluate lagged causal impact of Time-1 variables on Time-2 variables. Though superior to cross-lagged correlations, these procedures do not control autocorrelated measurement errors, emanating from repeated model assessments, which can distort causal estimates (Anderson and Williams 1992; Dwyer 1983).

Structural Equation Modeling for Panel Data

Williams and Podsakoff (1989) proposed Latent Variables (LV) SEM as a more powerful procedure for analyzing longitudinal data and for empirically specifying temporal parameters in turnover formulations. We next describe this promising approach.

Causal Order and Direction   Suppose we seek evidence about causal priority between two latent constructs: job satisfaction and organizational commitment. We would undertake a panel survey and measure these constructs, using multiple indices, on two occasions. Then, we develop a baseline LV Structural Model, such as that shown in Figure 8-14. Unlike a cross-sectional model, this panel model can control autocorrelated measurement errors—a bias introduced by repeating measures (Bentler 1987; Hom and Griffeth 1991)—by estimating correlations between errors across occasions (portrayed by arrows connecting two boxes). This model also specifies the time-lagged effect of each variable onto itself, the source of its temporal stability. For instance, Time-1 satisfaction is depicted as impacting Time-2 satisfaction. The specification of the effect of Time-1 satisfaction on Time-2 commitment and of the impact of Time-1 commitment on Time-2 satisfaction in this model estimates lagged causal effects.

Other nested models, which are shown in Figure 8-15 without measurement submodels, verify causal order and direction. The first model (reciprocal causation) posits a lagged reciprocal causation between attitudes and is the baseline model against which others are compared. Assuming that the baseline model fits the data, we compare it to the satisfaction causation model, specifying only a lagged satisfaction effect. If this model matches the baseline model's fit and its causal parameter is significant, satisfaction "causes" commitment. If the commitment causation model approximates the baseline model's fit better than does the satisfaction causation model and yields a significant commitment lagged influence, commitment "affects" satisfaction. Reciprocal causation is, however, indicated by the superior fit in the baseline model relative to the other models and significant estimates for its two lagged causal parameters. All causal lagged effects are refuted if the baseline model badly fits data and it estimates no significant causal influences.

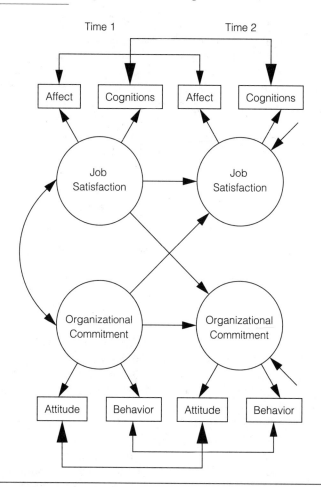

Figure 8-14 Panel Model Showing the Causality Latent Variables

Dwyer (1983) demonstrated, however, that alternative, spurious models may underlie significant cross-lagged causal influences. Two such models, which may simulate lagged effects between satisfaction and commitment, are shown in Figure 8-16. Model I is a synchronous, common-factor model, in which a common factor underlies all attitudinal measures. Model II is an unmeasured variables model, wherein X and Y are unmeasured variables related to all Time-1 variables. The latter model specifies that X exerts lagged effects on Time-2 satisfaction indices and Y has lagged effects on Time-2 commitment proxies, generating specious effects between attitudes. Besides testing substantive theory, Dwyer (ibid.) recommended that spurious models be assessed and refuted to validate more rigorously lagged causation.

Along similar lines, longitudinal models of causation between employee attitudes are generally misspecified because they often exclude many causes, including common antecedents of attitudes (Anderson and

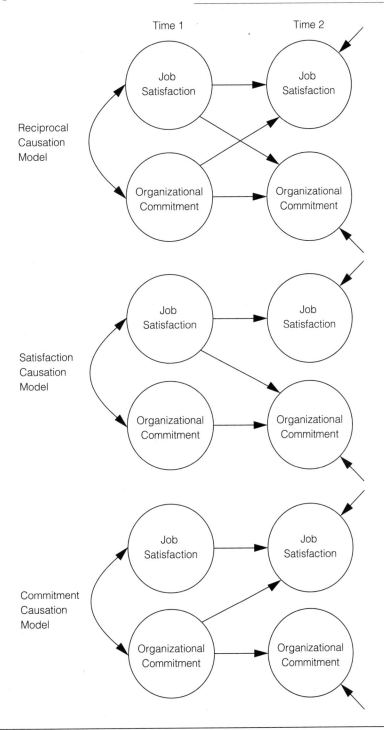

Figure 8-15 Causality Compared in Nested Models

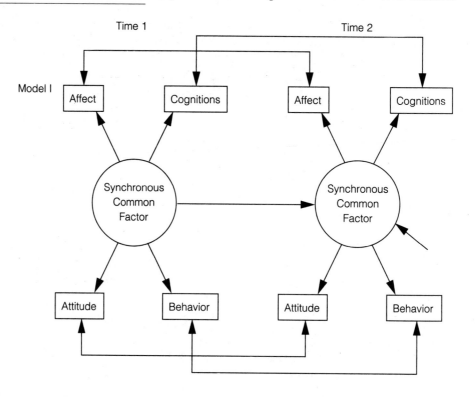

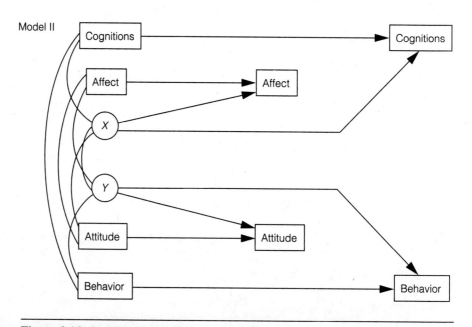

Figure 8-16 Spurious Models

Williams 1992). If stable, these unmeasured causes can induce correlations between disturbances across time periods and thus distort estimated lagged causal effects. Anderson and Williams (ibid.) compared two panel models of reciprocal effects between satisfaction and commitment, one with and one without correlated disturbances. The model specifying no correlated disturbances—an invalid assumption given the exclusion of many attitudinal causes—estimated lagged causal effects; the (correct) model, which did have correlated disturbances (to represent omitted causes), revealed few lagged effects. Consequently, Anderson and Williams recommended that SEM users estimate between-time (and within-time) correlations among disturbances if their panel models exclude relevant (and stable) causes. By taking into account disturbance correlations, SEM tests of even misspecified models that omit relevant causes would more accurately assess lagged causal influences.

Notwithstanding its rigor, SEM panel analysis necessitates certain tradeoffs. To control and estimate autocorrelated errors (and random errors), we require several indicators per concept to secure identification. On top of this, we must measure *all* the relevant causes of each endogenous variable to avoid the problem of unmeasured variables (James, Mulaik, and Brett 1982). Yet the addition of multiple indicators may compound panel attrition because the survey is so long (Dillman 1978; Kessler and Greenberg 1981). As a compromise, we might limit the length of the survey to indicants of a few model constructs and initially test causality among those few constructs rather than evaluate an entire structural network (Farkas and Tetrick 1989). Conceivably, an SEM test of the panel model might reduce bias caused by unmeasured variables by estimating correlated disturbances (Anderson and Williams 1992).

Causal Lag   Because temporal parameters are missing from turnover models (Miller, Katerberg, and Hulin 1979), SEM analysis might empirically specify causal lags (Kessler and Greenberg 1981; Morita, Lee, and Mowday 1989). Sims and Szilagyi (1979) pioneered an empirical method to estimate causal lag times. They reviewed cross-lagged correlations based on varying measurement lags from multiple studies. They pinpointed the causal lag as that measurement lag yielding the largest cross-lagged correlation difference.

Refining this approach, Williams and Podsakoff (1989) applied SEM analysis to estimate causal lag times from several waves of observations taken at equal time intervals. A three-wave LV panel model specifying causal influence from satisfaction to commitment is shown in Figure 8-17. Like a two-wave model, this model specifies covariances between measurement errors and autoregressive effects between adjacent time periods. Assuming that satisfaction causes commitment (and not the reverse), this model estimates brief (first-order effects between adjacent periods, such as: Time-1 satisfaction affects Time-2 commitment) and extended (second-order effect from Time-1 variable to Time-3 variable, such as: Time-1 satisfaction affects Time-3 commitment) lagged effects for satisfaction.

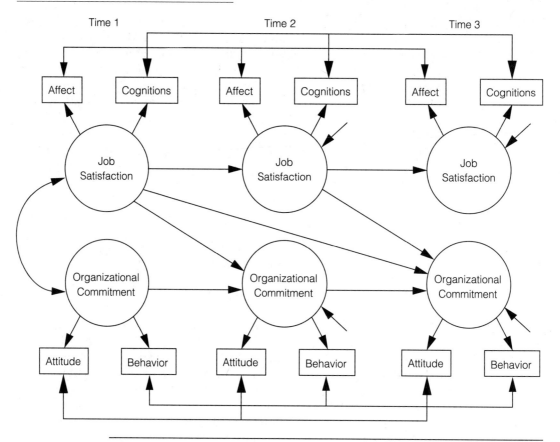

Figure 8-17 LV Panel Model Showing Causal Lag Time

This panel model serves as the baseline model for comparisons with the nested models shown in Figure 8-18 without the measurement submodel. Assuming the baseline model (Model I) fits data, we test a nested model (Model II) specifying only first-order lagged effects. If this model explains data as closely as Model I does and estimates significant lagged estimates, the causal interval falls between adjacent observation periods (that is, first-order). Conversely, the causal lag spans the first and third observation times if Model III (positing only a second-order lagged impact) matches Model I's fit and yields a significant lagged effect. Poor fitting Models II and III and all significant lagged parameters in a well-fitting Model I suggest a distributed lagged effect. That is, the influence of satisfaction on commitment is distributed over a period of time rather than occurring at one time (Kessler and Greenberg 1981). Last, if Model I estimates no significant causal parameters, lagged effects are nonexistent.

This empirical approach is not without its limitations. We can rely on background knowledge and intuition, but the specification of survey timing is still somewhat arbitrary. If measurement lags are too long, we might miss

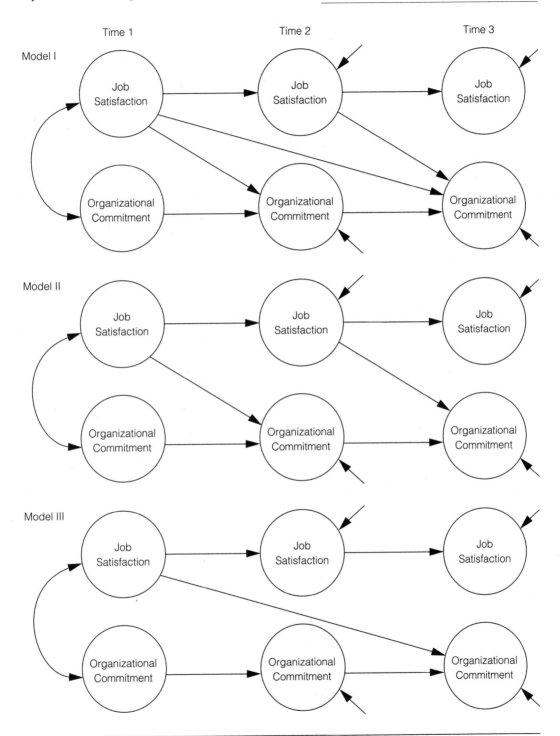

Figure 8-18 Comparisons with Nested Models to Identify Causal Lags

the causal duration (Curry et al. 1986; Farkas and Tetrick 1989) and falsely conclude that there is no lagged causation (Anderson and Williams 1992). As a possible remedy, we might measure theoretical constructs more often—over more closely spaced intervals of time (see Rossé 1988). Although difficult, finer panel measurement may more precisely pinpoint the actual causal lag time or trace the shape of distributed causal effects.

SEM Tests of Boundary Conditions

Most theorists on turnover neglect boundary conditions for models, implicitly assuming model universality. Growing evidence of correlations between predictors and turnover (Cotton and Tuttle 1986) and structural relations in models (Dalessio, Silverman, and Shuck 1986; Hom, Caranikis-Walker, Prussia, and Griffeth 1992) diverging across occupational lines contravenes this assumption. On rare occasions, researchers have evaluated model generality by estimating a model separately in subpopulations and comparing causal relationships (Dalessio, Silverman, and Shuck 1986; Peters, Jackofsky, and Salter 1981). Several methodological weaknesses plague this approach. Multiple comparisons may not be independent and inflate Type-I error rates (Palich, Hom and Griffeth in press). Unequal scale validity or reliability across subgroups may exaggerate variations in structural networks between groups (see Hunter and Schmidt 1990b; Schaubroeck and Green 1989).

SEM analysis can more efficiently and validly compare model parameters between subpopulations (Bollen 1989). Controlling Type-I error, SEM can compare entire sets of structural parameters across subgroups by comparisons of nested models (James, Mulaik, and Brett 1982). This procedure can correct for varying qualities of instrumentation across subpopulations (Bollen 1989). To illustrate, we relate an example from Palich, Hom and Griffeth (in press), who tested the generality of a measurement model across different cultures before comparing the structural model. That is, they used LISREL 6's multisample option to investigate a series of nested comparison models, that successively constrain measurement parameters to be equal between cultural subgroups (Bollen 1989; Podsakoff, Williams, and Todor 1986). These comparison models used for testing the stability of a measurement model for organizational commitment and its antecedent between subpopulations varying on the Power Distance Index (PDI, Hofstede 1980) are shown in Figure 8-19. (Power distance is a cultural dimension that describes the extent to which members of a given culture accept unequal distribution of institutional and organizational power. Thus, the United States has a low PDI score but Japan has a high PDI score.) In Comparison Model I, factor loadings (indices of validity) and measurement error variances (inversely related to reliabilities) differ between high- and low-PDI subsamples. Palich, Hom and Griffeth found that this model explained data and produced all significant factor loadings. They next evaluated Comparison Model II, in which factor loadings are equated across cultural subgroups. Model II reproduced data as well as Model I did, implying that factor loadings across PDI subgroups are

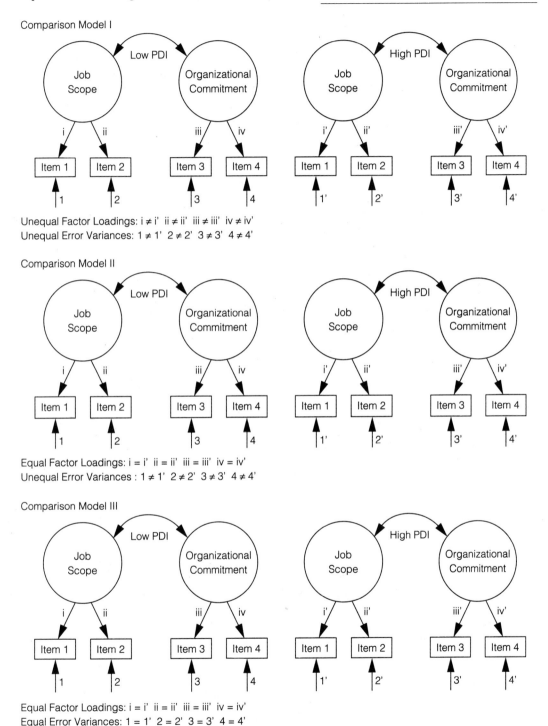

Figure 8-19 Nested Model Sequence to Test Moderation of Measurement Model.

constant and that the meaning of the scale is culturally invariant. Comparison Model III, in which equal factor loadings and measurement error variances across cultural subgroups are specified, approximated Model II's fit, signaling culturally consistent reliabilities. If scale attributes had changed across cultures, subsequent SEM tests of the structural model could adjust for psychometric variation by letting measurement parameters vary between cultures.

Palich, Hom and Griffeth (ibid.) then evaluated the cross-cultural generality of the structural model. They hypothesized that PDI moderates the effects of job scope and participation on organizational commitment, but not the impact of role clarity and extrinsic inducements. Testing these hypotheses, they specified another set of comparison models, shown in Figure 8-20 without measurement submodels. They first tested Comparison Model A, which permits all structural parameters to vary across PDI subgroups. Because of its good fit, they next compared Comparison Model A with Comparison Model B, in which some causal parameters are equal across PDI subgroups whereas others vary. Comparison Model B constrained *culturally independent* parameters (*c*: role clarity; *d*: extrinsic rewards) so that they were equal across cultural subgroups but allowed culturally moderated parameters (*a*: job scope; *b*: participation) to diverge. Model B fit the data as accurately as Model A did, sustaining the implicit hypothesis that PDI does *not* affect parameters (*c* and *d*) constrained in Model B. Last, they contrasted Model B with Model C, in which *all* causal parameters are equated across PDI subgroups. This comparison tested hypotheses of cultural moderators, prescribing that PDI moderates parameters (*a* and *b*) fixed in Model C but freed in Model B. Because Models B and C equally explained data, the power-distance dimension did *not* moderate the causal determinants of organizational commitment. In sum, this approach illustrates a powerful means for testing the generality of turnover models.

META-ANALYTICAL TEST

By joining meta-analysis to SEM analysis, we derive a more powerful methodology for testing theories of turnover (Hom, Caranikis-Walker, Prussia, and Griffeth 1992; Premack and Hunter 1988). Meta-analysis greatly multiplies the statistical power for tests of models through the accumulation of correlations from many studies. This procedure, for example, produces a more stable estimate of variable relationship by averaging correlations taken from several samples, after weighing the correlations by sample size (Hunter and Schmidt 1990b). Besides correcting sampling error, meta-analysis provides additional corrections for statistical artifacts, such as unreliability and range restriction. These refinements bolster the magnitude of correlation indices that are attenuated by random errors of measurement and restricted score variance. Consequently, such data aggregation and statistical corrections yield more valid measures of "true" correlations between variables.

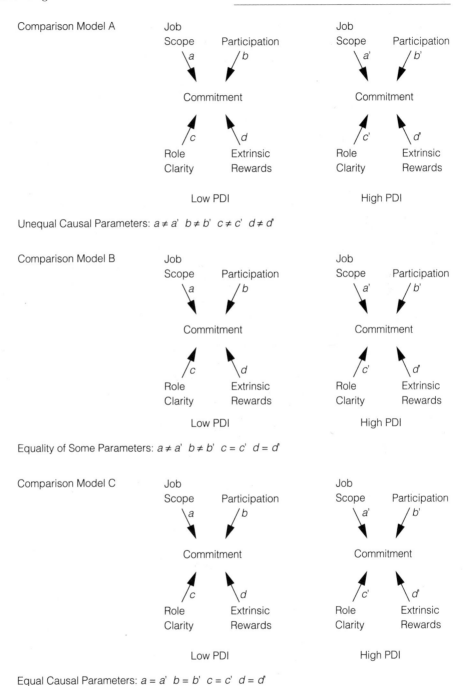

Figure 8-20 Nested Model Sequence to Test Moderation of Structural Model.

Afterward, SEM can analyze correlations that are purified of methodological artifacts and may uncover higher model validity (see Hom, Caranikis-Walker, Prussia, and Griffeth 1992; Premack and Hunter 1988).

Meta-analytical example

To demonstrate this joint methodology, we describe Hom, Caranikis-Walker, Prussia, and Griffeth's investigation (1992) of Mobley, Horner, and Hollingsworth's 1978 model (see Figure 8-21). Previous investigations disputed the causal network and generalizability of this model. Dalessio, Silverman, and Shuck (1986) reanalyzed data from five samples and counted how often the model's parameters were significant and had correct signs in five regression tests. They found conflicting support for the model's pathways. Three of five tests, for instance, showed that satisfaction impacts quit decisions. (Figure 8-21 reports the number of times each causal parameter was upheld by Dalessio, Silverman, and Shuck's five regression tests in parentheses.) Parameter estimates, too, fluctuated widely across regression tests. For example, they reported that the estimated effects of quit intentions on turnover ranged from .18 to .61. Though intuitively appealing, Dalessio et al.'s method of counting significant results generated misleading conclusions: Causal parameters may appear significant in large-sample tests but not in small-sample tests. Given modest sample sizes (and modest statistical power), most tests may fail to detect significance even for a valid parameter (Hunter and Schmidt 1990b).

Instead of this counting method, Hom, Caranikis-Walker, Prussia, and Griffeth (1992) applied meta-analysis to cumulate studies before model estimation, taking into account the uneven sample sizes across the studies

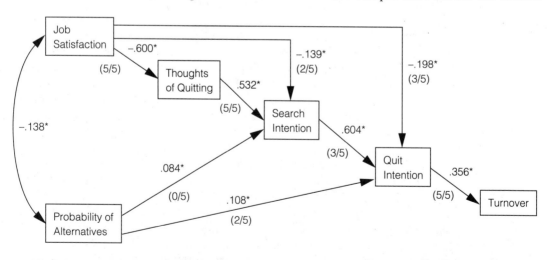

Figure 8-21 Meta-analysis of Mobley, Horner, and Hollingsworth's Model of Turnover (1978)

(Premack and Hunter 1988). Correcting for sampling and measurement errors, they aggregated correlations from seventeen samples ($N = 5,013$) testing Mobley, Horner, and Hollingsworth's (1978) model with Hunter and Schmidt's procedures (1990b; Hunter, Schmidt, and Jackson 1982). They then evaluated a model based on corrected correlations. As a result, they uncovered acceptable statistics of fit (NFI = .916; CFI = .916) and found that all parameter estimates were statistically significant and carried theoretically correct signs (shown in Figure 8-21). These findings are impressive because no other research study (Dalessio, Silverman, and Shuck 1986; Hom, Griffeth, and Sellaro 1984; Lee 1988; Steel, Lounsbury, and Horst 1981), including Mobley, Horner, and Hollingsworth's original test (1978) has ever verified each and every model pathway.

Meta-analysis may also refine examinations of model generality by controlling differential statistical artifacts across subpopulations (Hunter and Schmidt 1990b). That is, meta-analysis can adjust correlations from different samples for different reliabilities of scale and restriction of range before testing to ascertain whether a turnover model generalizes across subgroups (Hom, Caranikis-Walker, Prussia, and Griffeth 1992). In this way, variability in statistical artifacts between groups does not overstate inconstancy of the model. After correcting correlations within each subpopulation, SEM can more precisely evaluate the invariance of the model's parameters across subpopulations (ibid.).

Limitations

Though powerful, a meta-analytical SEM test requires ample findings from multiple studies to minimize second-order sampling error (Hunter and Schmidt 1990b). Yet complete tests of conceptualizations—that assess all the components of a model—about withdrawal remain rare. Nonetheless, empirical data on formulations made by Price and Mueller (1981, 1986), Mobley (1977), and Farrell and Rusbult (1981) are growing. These models may eventually prove amenable to meta-analytical SEM testing. Alternatively, meta-analysis might aggregate correlations between model variables from studies that do not directly test that model (Premack and Hunter 1988). This practice yields correlations derived from incomplete data, a violation of the presumption held by current SEM statistical theories that data are complete (Bentler and Chou 1987). To date, the repercussions of analyzing incomplete-data correlation matrices are unknown.

More importantly, SEM procedures assume covariance matrices, but meta-analysis typically, and perhaps unavoidably, cumulates correlations. But correlations as SEM input may generate the wrong omnibus test statistics or standard errors (except those for scale-invariant models) (Cudeck 1989). All the same, Hom, Caranikis-Walker, Prussia, and Griffeth (1992) found that least squares parameter estimates (which do not require input covariances) virtually matched maximum likelihood SEM estimates. Thus, input correlations may not necessarily distort tests of models. To cross-check SEM results, turnover researchers might thus apply least squares regressions to analyze meta-analytical correlations (Premack and Hunter 1988). Though not yet widespread, newer SEM techniques can correctly analyze correlation matrices (Cudeck 1989).

PREDICTION OF TIMING OF TURNOVER

The prevailing cross-sectional methodology—surveys of employees on one occasion to forecast who quits after some elapsed time—has increasingly drawn criticism (Morita, Lee, and Mowday 1989, 1993; Peters and Sheridan 1988; Singer and Willett 1991). Typically, the dates for beginning and ending a cross-sectional study are arbitrary. Yet the particular calendar period chosen can dramatically alter a study's findings on correlations between predictors and quitting (Murnane, Singer, and Willett 1988). Short measurement periods weaken correlations because fewer employees leave in any one brief period, and the smaller numbers of quitters shrink variance in turnover. By contrast, more employees will be quitting over a longer time, the higher numbers bolstering the correlations—if there has been no erosion of predictive power over that time (Harrison and Hulin 1989). Thus, the predictive efficacy of determinants of turnover may hinge more on arbitrarily chosen measurement intervals than on their true predictive validity. Carsten and Spector (1987) estimated an $-.51$ correlation between the time period of data collection and relationships between satisfaction and turnover; job satisfaction best predicts quits when the time span is short.

This cross-sectional approach also distorts results by arbitrarily dictating which participant in a study is a stayer and which a leaver (Murnane, Singer, and Willett 1988; Peters and Sheridan 1988). Stayers are merely those employees who happened not to have quit by the time the study ended; leavers are those who left during the study period. If, a study had terminated earlier, some leavers—who had not by that time quit—would have been classified as stayers; a study ending later would result in some stayers having become leavers. Such shifting employment status (and hence, changing base rate and variance in criterion) spuriously alters the estimated predictive power of turnover causes (Morita, Lee, and Mowday 1993, Peters and Sheridan 1988).

Most of all, this cross-sectional methodology neglects the timing of resignations (Morita, Lee, and Mowday 1989), treating an employee who quits after ten years of tenure on the same level as one who quits after a few days (Murnane, Singer, and Willett 1988). It is quite likely that this methodological tradition inhibited the consideration of dynamic relationships in prevailing theories and overlooked the temporal dimension of withdrawal (Mobley 1982; Morita, Lee and Mowday 1993; Sheridan and Abelson 1983). Current theories strive to explain whether turnover occurs (Williams 1990), not when turnover occurs, with the result (Singer and Willett 1991) that the 100 percent job turnover rates found among certain workers, such as certified public accountants (Peters and Sheridan 1988) and registered nurses

(Huey and Hartley 1988), are given short shrift. For such jobs, predictions of *when* employees will quit rather than *if* they will quit would be more useful to organizations (Murnane, Singer, and Willett 1989).

To offset such methodological inadequacies, several scholars introduced "survival analysis" to examine turnover timing (Morita, Lee, and Mowday 1989, 1993; Murnane, Singer, and Willett 1989; Peters and Sheridan 1988; Sheridan 1992). This technique comprises a family of actuarial methods used in the biomedical life sciences to track the life expectancies of patients with life-threatening diseases. By treating employment duration as analogous to a lifetime, survival analysis can trace retention rates during employment, estimate quit rates at various stages of tenure, and identify peak termination periods (Singer and Willett 1991).

The following passage describes a nonparametric survival analysis based on life-table analysis (Peters and Sheridan 1988). For this analysis, we chose a particular calendar date and sampled all the new hires from that time until the study ended, recording their company tenure. Stayers—those continuously employed throughout the study period—yield "censored" observations because they will leave (if at all) *after* the measurement window is closed (Singer and Willett 1991). For them, retention time is the length of their employment until the study's end. Involuntary quits are likewise "censored" when one is studying voluntary quits because how long the subjects would have remained voluntarily had they not been fired is unknown (Morita, Lee and Mowday 1993). In survival analysis, unlike in traditional procedures, data from involuntary quitters is used partially rather than being discarded (Sheridan 1992): the data are included in the tenure intervals that they completed (their retention time is at least their dismissal date) but are discarded from tenure periods they missed.

The procedure next divides the duration of the study into time (tenure) intervals, such as weeks or months, and estimates the following probability statistics for each interval.

1. The total number of employees exposed to "termination risk" during each tenure interval i (r_i):
   r_i = Total number of employees – one-half of employees whose data entering tenure interval are censored at this interval

2. The probability that employees quit in tenure interval i (q_i):
   q_i = (Number of terminations [t_i] occurring in tenure interval i) ÷ (Number of employees exposed to termination risk in that interval)

3. The probability that employees remain employed ("survive") during tenure interval i (p_i):
   $p_i = 1 - q_i$

4. The cumulative survival rate (S_i) = the probability of staying to the end of tenure interval i:
   $S_i = p_1 \times p_2 \times p_3 \times p_4 \dots \times p_i$

5. The hazard rate (λ) = the probability of quitting (per unit of time) during tenure interval i:

λ_i = (Probability of quitting [per time unit] in tenure interval i) ÷ (Probability of staying to the midpoint of tenure interval i)

= $(2 \times q_i) / h_i \times (1 + p_i)$, where h_i = length of tenure interval in time units.

The hazard rate is thus a conditional probability that employees will quit during a given time interval among those who stayed employed up to that time (that is, members of the "risk" set) (Singer and Willett 1991).

Importantly, survival analysis provides informative graphs. A graph of the cumulative probability of staying (i.e., that is, of the survival function) over time shows the proportion of new hires remaining after reaching a particular tenure. This graph also identifies retention half-life, or the tenure period at which 50 percent of employees stay (ibid.). In Figure 8-22, the retention experiences of one hundred fifty-eight new nurses in Cleveland (cf. Hom et al., 1993), of whom 84 percent remained after the first year, are shown. More revealing, a graph of the hazard rate shows how propensities to quit change each week and pinpoints when quitting most occurs (ibid.). That the nurses' quit rates peak during the fourteenth and fifty-second weeks of their employment is shown in Figure 8-23. These peaks coincide with the three-month probationary period and the annual appraisal review, which may encourage poor performers to leave (Morita, Lee, and Mowday 1993).

Survival analysis can estimate the temporal effects of a turnover cause on survival and hazard profiles (see Murnane, Singer, and Willett 1989). We can compare different subgroups that have different values for a prospective determinant and ascertain if their survival (or hazard) profiles differ. If they do, this subgrouping variable is a "predictor" of the survival profile. To illustrate, the survival rates of two cohorts of new staff accountants—one of which received a realistic job preview (RJP) when they began work, the other of which (the control group) did not (Hom et al. 1993)—are shown in Figure 8-24. A nonparametric chi-square test found that the tenure of the two groups differed significantly (Lee and Desu 1972): Survival analysis disclosed that RJPs prolonged employment, a disclosure complementing traditional evidence showing that RJPs reduce turnover rates (Premack and Wanous 1985).

Graphic comparison between subgroups that have different predictor values may disclose that a predictor's relationship to quits changes over time (Singer and Willett 1991). We might, for example, investigate the predictive efficacy of college internship among new accounting graduates. We would form two subgroups—one of accountants who had had internships, another of accountants without the experience—and contrast their survival rates. A graph of the data derived from Hom et al.'s work (1993) is shown in Figure 8-25. We see that the survival curves of the groups overlapped until the third month, after which survival rates for those without internships declined. The

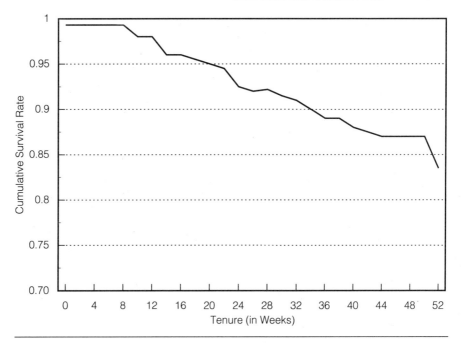

Figure 8-22 Job Tenure Survival Rates for Nurses.

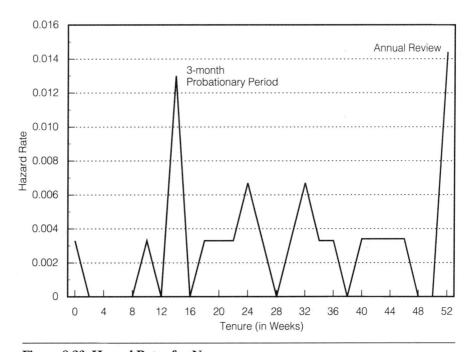

Figure 8-23 Hazard Rates for Nurses.

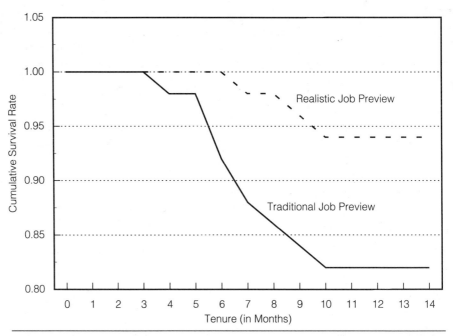

Figure 8-24 Survival Rates for New Staff Accountants as Functions of RJPs and Job Tenure.

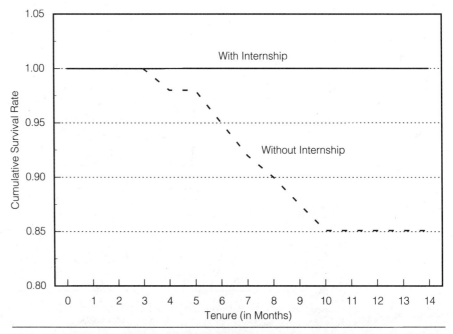

Figure 8-25 Survival Rates for New Staff Accountants as Functions of Prior Internships and Job Tenure.

survival distributions differed significantly. A traditional static correlation between internship and turnover during the first year overlooks the fluctuating predictive validity of internships, whose impact became evident after the third month of tenure. Survival analysis reveals dynamic changes in predictive strength more efficiently than does the correlation of predictor scores with quits at varying tenure periods (see Porter, Steers, Mowday and Boulian 1974).

Proportional Hazard Model

While informative, profile comparisons are ill-suited for estimating the temporal effects of continuous predictors and of several predictors simultaneously (Singer and Willett 1991). Statistical models, known as proportional hazard models can better model the relationship between a predictor, such as RJP status, and the whole hazard profile (which is more informative than the survival function that confounds incidence with duration) (Morita, Lee, and Mowday 1993; Singer and Willett 1991). Consider Figure 8-26, in which it is shown that the RJP predictor (assigning control subjects zeros and RJP subjects ones) roughly displaces two hazard profiles vertically relative to each other (using data from Hom et al.'s [1993] study). This profile elevation indicates that the RJP variable affects quit rates; that is, the hazard profile for control subjects who did not get RJPs (RJP score = 0) consistently exceeds the hazard profile for RJP recipients (RJP score = 1). The higher the displacement, the stronger a predictor's (RJP) impact. To represent algebraically the dependence of profile elevation on a predictor, a proportional hazard model uses regression-like formulas, such as:

$$\log h(t) = \beta_0 t + \beta_1 (RJP),$$

where $h(t)$ is the entire population hazard profile. (Hazard models analyze logarithmic transformation of the hazard because probability scores assume only nonnegative values [Singer and Willett 1991].) This equation resembles a regression equation except that the dependent variable is an entire hazard function (Morita, Lee and Mowday 1993; Singer and Willett 1991). $\beta_0 t$ is the baseline log-hazard profile and represents the value of the dependent variable (entire hazard function) when the predictor score is zero. That is, $\beta_0 t$ describes the temporal pattern of quits among control subjects. β_1 measures vertical displacement of the hazard profile due to the RJP predictor.

Essentially, the proportional hazard model assumes that a predictor shifts the hazard profile up (RJP = 0) or down (RJP = 1) depending on predictor scores and that each subject's hazard function is some constant multiple (proportional constant) of the baseline hazard function (Morita, Lee and Mowday 1993). This statistical model can be used to examine multiple predictors of varying measurement properties (continuous as well as categorical scales), estimating each predictor's unique effect while statistically

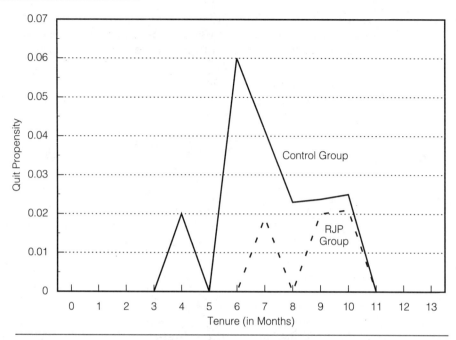

Figure 8-26 Hazard Profiles of RJP and Control Accountants: Quit Propensities at Various Stages of Tenure.

controlling other predictors (ibid.). Hazard models can also be used to examine predictors whose values change over time and also forecast quit rates on a given date (Darden, Hampton, and Boatwright 1987).

Predictors' estimated ßs are interpreted as regression weights (Singer and Willett 1991). Each ß represents the difference in elevation of the log-hazard profile for a one-unit difference in the predictor; large ßs indicate strong predictors that produce larger profile displacements. Alternatively, the hazard equation can be transformed back into a more familiar probability metric by antilogging:

$$h(t) = e^{\beta_0 t} \times e^{\beta_1 RJP},$$

where the hazard function, $h(t)$, is $e^{\beta_0 t}$ for the control group (whose RJP score = 0) and $e^{\beta_0 t} \times e^{\beta_1}$ for the RJP group (RJP score = 1). Thus, the RJP hazard profile is the control profile multiplied by e^{β_1}. Basically, the exponential value of the predictor coefficient is a multiplier of the baseline hazard function, with positive signs indicating increased hazards and negative signs indicating decreased hazards (Kandel and Yamaguchi 1987; Morita, Lee, and Mowday 1993; Singer and Willett 1991). If hypothetically, ß = –.50, then $e^{-.50}$ = .61. Thus, RJP subjects have .61 times the risk (of quitting) than do control subjects. (Alternatively, the hazard function for the control group is the baseline function multiplied by e^0 or 1.) Stated differently, the realistic job preview reduces the likelihood of quitting by a factor of .61. We can also interpret a predictor's significance with the following formula for percentage change in hazard rates for unit change in a given predictor:

$$\%h(t) = 100 \times (e^\beta - 1).$$

In our running example, the RJP (a unit change in the predictor) decreases the termination hazard by 39 percent (Allison 1984). One can test the overall model with a global chi-square test (that all predictor coefficients are zero) and test the significance of individual coefficients (Morita, Lee, and Mowday 1993).

Although promising, proportional hazard models assume that all log-hazard profiles for different predictor values have the same shape and are mutually parallel (Singer and Willett 1991). Nonetheless, Singer and Willett found plentiful examples of violations of this assumption. Thus, they recommended that investigators always test this assumption by subdividing samples by predictor values and comparing hazard profiles, or else, they might estimate predictor X time interactions in hazard models. Because proportional hazard models however assume that predictor effects are constant over time (hence, parallel hazard profiles), this assumption can be tested by estimating predictor X time interaction terms for these models. Fully parameterized hazard models however do not assume constant hazards. These models however are less accessible and require fitting a functional form for the hazard function (see O'Reilly, Caldwell, and Barnett 1989).

In conclusion, survival analysis offers a powerful technique for disclosing the temporal dimension of the withdrawal process. This method is superior to cross-sectional methodology at uncovering dynamic relations between turnover and its antecedents. For example, Morita, Lee, and Mowday (1989) demonstrated that overall quit rates for two subgroups differing on a predictor variable can be identical even though their quit rates vary at different times. Traditional analytical procedures may mask the impact of a causal antecedent on termination rates at varying tenure stages. Moreover, the inclusion of a dichotomous dependent variable (turnover) into regression analyses violates the statistical assumptions of continuous dependent variable and normally distributed errors, thereby producing biased estimates (Huselid and Day 1991). Morita, Lee and Mowday (1993) demonstrated how such violations render invalid conclusions by regression analysis compared with survival analysis. Survival analysis also treats missing or censored data more efficiently (Morita, Lee and Mowday 1989).

Despite these advantages, current applications of survival analysis in turnover remain limited in scope (Darden, Hamplin, and Boatwright 1987; Kandel and Yamaguchi 1987; Murnane, Singer, and Willett 1989; O'Reilly, Caldwell, and Barnett 1989; Sheridan 1992). To date, these studies have investigated the effects of a few predictors on survival rates, failing to test complete turnover models. Yet survival analytical tests of turnover formulations may extend their capacity to explain not only if, but also when, turnover occurs. Quite likely, many explanatory constructs in prevailing models, such as organizational commitment can forecast exit times as well as exit occurrences (Morita, Lee, and Mowday 1989; 1993). This methodology, given its ability to handle multiple quit incidences, promotes the development of theories of intrafirm mobility (see Fichman 1988; Harrison and Hulin 1989; Murnane, Singer, and Willett 1988). By examining an individual's pattern of quitting, we might develop dispositional explanations for unstable work histories (see Kandel and Yamaguchi 1987). The approach may identify valid predictors of employment duration to help firms select more stable employees, especially in settings characterized by excessive turnover, such as public accounting (Sheridan 1992) or *maquiladora* factories (Hom, Gomez-Mejia, and Grabke 1993).

ROBUST METHODS OF
CONTROLLING TURNOVER

Prescriptions for reducing employee turnover abound (Bellus 1984; Gardner 1986; Half 1982; Moore and Simendinger 1989; Roseman 1981; Watts and White 1988). However popular, such advice often rests on dubious or nonexistent empirical underpinnings. All too often, practical remedies are derived from case studies or anecdotal evidence. Rigorous research on practical interventions—especially those using quasi-experimental or experimental designs—is remarkably scarce (McEvoy and Cascio 1985). In the following chapter, we review "robust" interventions for curtailing exits supported by quasi-experimental or experimental research. Supplementing this discussion, we consider interventions that influence reliable precursors of turnover (namely, job satisfaction and withdrawal cognitions) even if experimental studies did not assess their impact on quits. In the next chapter, we consider interventions suggested by the wider body of organizational research on predictors of turnover. While not necessarily testing interventions, nonexperimental studies still suggest practical remedies (termed "promising" methods of turnover reduction).

REALISTIC JOB PREVIEWS

Existing academic inquiry has primarily evaluated realistic job previews (RJPs) for reducing turnover (Rynes 1990; Wanous and Collela 1989). Presumably, extensive and realistic communications about a new job to prospective or new employees during recruitment or orientation may improve their tenure (Wanous 1980). Sample statements from RJP booklets for nursing and accountancy taken from Hom et al. (1993) are reproduced in Figure 9-1. Unlike traditional job portrayals, RJPs show both the positive and negative features of the new job.

By now, extensive research has corroborated the efficacy of RJPs for reducing early attrition in many occupations (McEvoy and Cascio 1985; Premack and Wanous 1985; Reilly, Brown, Blood, and Malatesta 1981; Wanous and Collela 1989; Wanous 1992). Even so, the impact is modest: $r = .12$ between RJP and retention (Wanous and Collela 1989). Moreover, the effectiveness of RJPs varies with job survival rates, being most effective under poor conditions for survival (Premack and Wanous 1985). Despite these promising findings, the underlying reasons for the success of RJPs and their optimal design remain lively topics of debate. In the following section, we review these persistent controversies.

Nursing

The provision of nursing care is a constant challenge in this teaching hospital with its variety of patients and its introduction of new medical procedures, technology, drugs, and equipment. In addition, nurses can make many autonomous and independent decisions regarding patient care and are part of an interdisciplinary team where everyone's input (from aides to nursing directors) is considered. Since nurses apply a large variety of skills within a given day and care for patients having varied and unusual problems, there are numerous opportunities to learn much here and to use the skills and knowledge acquired in nursing school.

Most nurses love their work here, but feel that there is too much of it—sometimes feeling overwhelmed by responsibilities. Nursing can be hard, physically and mentally demanding work, with nurses often performing the work of others to ensure that patients do not suffer. Thus, some nurses find it difficult to "shrug off" a stressful day and worry after work about things they were unable to do during work hours. Further, nurses receive little feedback about their job performance or little praise for good work from supervisors: However, informal performance feedback often comes from the nurse's peers and patients, and the nurse values their feedback most.

Accountancy

Students may anticipate having to work long hours and to carry heavy workloads, but they still will have difficulty adjusting. "Knowing it is one thing, living through it is another."

Often lost in the details of the audit, new staff often do not see the big picture or fully understand the audit's objectives.

Even though they were good students in college, new staff may be inefficient or technically incompetent at work.

New staff are rarely their own boss, in charge of a job from beginning to end.

Firms doubt whether first-year staff can creatively suggest more efficient or correct ways to audit an area for last year's workpapers.

Public accounting work is highly diverse since clients are so different. This diversity can be both frustrating and challenging.

New staff often do "grunt work" (xeroxing, carrying audit bags, being gofers).

Firms often set time budgets too low for jobs. Unforeseen circumstances or client differences frequently prevent staff from doing the job within budgeted time.

Staff work is stressful since there are always pressures to meet job deadlines and to finish jobs within time budgets.

Multiple reviews of workpapers usually catch staff errors but also expose staff to criticism from multiple reviewers.

Clients' employees may feel the auditor is "out to get them." They feel their job is threatened if the auditor detects errors in the accounting system.

Clients may procrastinate in supplying the needed information. This can ruin the auditor's time budget (makes the auditor look bad) and waste the auditor's own time (spends unproductive time waiting).

Generally speaking, partners do not take new staff under their wings.

Figure 9-1 Sample Statements from Realistic Job Previews. (P. Hom, R. Griffeth, L. Palich, and J. Bracker (1993). "Realistic job previews: Two-occupation test of mediating processes." College of Business, Arizona State University, Tempe, Arizona.)

Theoretical Explanations

Met Expectations   The prevailing explanation for the efficacy of RJPs is derived from the theory of met expectations (Porter and Steers 1973). Presumably, new employees hold naive and inflated expectations about their new jobs (Wanous 1980) and later are shocked to learn that their new work roles do not conform to their initial expectations (Dean, Ferris, and Konstans 1988). Unmet expectations, in turn, induce dissatisfaction and resignations (Premack and Wanous 1987). RJPs can forestall the reality shock by forewarning newcomers about the unpleasant realities of the work. With initial expectations deflated, the job can more easily meet newcomers' expectations, and disillusionment and organizational withdrawal be prevented.

Supporting this process, a meta-analysis by Premack and Wanous (1985) revealed that RJPs deflate initial expectations, and a meta-analysis by Wanous et al. (1992) affirmed that met expectations (whether manipulated or measured) enhance satisfaction and job survival. Notwithstanding such impressive evidence, empirical support primarily comes from testing the impact of RJPs on initial expectations (Hom et al. 1993; Rynes 1990). Existing research may overstate the validity of this mediating process because preemployment and met expectations represent different constructs (Louis 1980). The few studies of met expectations report an inconsistent impact by RJPs on the construct (Colarelli 1984; Horner, Mobley, and Meglino 1979; Ilgen and Dugoni 1977; Reilly et al. 1981).

Commitment to Choice of Organization   According to another theory, RJPs strengthen job incumbency by reinforcing commitment to the original choice of the organization (Ilgen and Seely 1974; Meglino et al. 1988). New employees who are fully informed while choosing the job feel that they have more freedom in making their choices (Meglino and DeNisi 1988; Wanous, 1977, 1980) and thus they feel more personally responsible and committed to the decision (O'Reilly and Caldwell 1981; Salancik 1977). Job candidates who accept the job despite warnings in RJPs about its drawbacks feel more bound to their choice, if only to ameliorate dissonance (Ilgen and Seely 1974): Employees who did receive RJPs feel cognitive dissonance about their initial decision when, later, they confront disagreeable work conditions. To resolve that dissonance, they rationalize their decision by overemphasizing the positive qualities of the job they have chosen, while deemphasizing its negative qualities (Vroom and Deci 1971).

That RJPs develop commitment is shown in the meta-analysis by Premack and Wanous (1985). Here again, the studies reviewed primarily measured organizational commitment rather than commitment to the original job decision (Dean and Wanous 1984; Horner, Mobley, and Meglino 1979; Meglino et al. 1988; Reilly et al. 1981). Though related, these forms of attachment constitute psychological bonds to different acts that have dissimilar origins (Kline and Peters 1991; Mowday, Porter, and Steers 1982; O'Reilly and Caldwell 1981; Wanous 1992). Only Colarelli (1984) operationalized commitment to job choice—and found no stronger commitment among RJP recipients.

Self-Selection   RJPs may improve the fit between person and job through applicant self-selection (Vandenberg and Scarpello 1990; Rynes 1990; Wanous 1980). According to this rationale, RJPs describe the rewards available in a job, thus allowing prospective employees to make better decisions about whether or not the job satisfies their personal needs. If this theory holds, those newcomers who received RJPs will fit the job better than will naive newcomers. If the rewards of the job do satisfy their preferences, they will develop higher levels of job satisfaction and loyalty (Locke 1976). Candidates who lack realistic information make unwise choices and take jobs for which they are less well suited.

The meta-analysis by Premack and Wanous (1985) disclosed that applicants given previews are more likely to refuse job offers. Job refusal rates indirectly test the hypothesis of self-selection, which implies that samples of candidates who received RJPs are made up of different kinds of people from samples of control candidates who did not (Zaharia and Baumeister 1981). The former should experience a higher congruency between their personal needs and the organizational climate than the latter, but will not necessarily turn down job offers (Wanous 1973). Varying rates of job refusal may mirror a different process, by which it is the RJPs that drive away qualified candidates but leave the less employable (and hence, more loyal) to take the job (Rynes 1990). Only Wanous (1973) has assessed job preferences, and found *no* dissimilar preferences between RJP and control subjects.

Value Orientation   RJPs might modify desires for job outcomes if newcomers are uncertain about what constitutes a "good return" on an outcome from a job (Ilgen and Dugoni 1977). RJPs may intensify the newcomers' desires for what is available but dampen desires for what is absent (Meglino et al. 1988)—the latter devaluation occurring to avoid disappointment (Horner, Mobley, and Meglino 1979; Meglino and DeNisi 1987). RJPs may, as a result, narrow the gap between the experienced and the desired levels of job outcomes, boosting satisfaction (Locke 1976). Though scarce, some studies showed that RJPs can shape preferences for rewards (Horner, Mobley, and Meglino 1979; Miceli 1985).

Perceived Employer Concern and Honesty   RJPs may also promote beliefs that the employer is trustworthy and concerned about the newcomer's welfare, which would make the job more attractive (Dugoni and Ilgen 1981). This perception of benevolence may also foster feelings of obligations to reciprocate with continued affiliation (Meglino et al. 1988; Meglino, DeNisi, Ravlin, Tomes, and Lee 1990). Past research (Dean and Wanous 1984; Dugoni and Ilgen 1981; Horner, Mobley, and Meglino 1979; Premack and Wanous 1985) disputed this mechanism, but recent studies relate that RJPs do foster perceptions that the company is candid and supportive (Meglino et al. 1988;

Suszko and Breaugh 1986) and enhance impressions of representatives of the firm (Colarelli 1984; Ilgen and Dugoni 1977).

Coping Efficacy   RJPs may help newcomers cope with their new work roles because warnings of potential stress will allay disquiet (Ilgen and Dugoni 1977; Wanous and Collela 1989) and permits rehearsals of methods for handling it (Breaugh 1983). A meta-analysis (Premack and Wanous 1985) estimated, however, that RJPs only negligibly bolster coping effectiveness, although four studies accounted for the estimate. Since that review, Suszko and Breaugh (1986) found that recipients of RJPs managed stress better and felt less distress than did nonrecipients, and Meglino et al. (1988, 1990) discerned that RJP recipients worried more about stressful events.

In conclusion, empirical support for mediating processes is indirect, equivocal, or meager. Most researchers examined initial rather than met expectations; the few assessments of the latter construct did not reveal any consistent effects of RJPs. Likewise, studies have largely measured commitment to the company rather than commitment to the job decision; the sole inquiry on the latter did not discern that RJP recipients were any more committed (Colarelli 1984). Tests of self-selection primarily considered job acceptance rates rather than the psychological match between individual needs and an organization's climate (Premack and Wanous 1985). Only two tests corroborated the effect of value orientation, and the few tests of coping efficacy yielded conflicting results, the later tests being more supportive than were the early ones. Past research has rejected the notion that RJPs augment perceptions that the employer is honest and concerned, but current work finds that RJPs can enhance such perceptions of the firm or its representatives.

Past analysis has been inadequate in showing that mediators intervene between RJPs and withdrawal. With few exceptions (Dilla 1987; Dugoni and Ilgen 1981), researchers have assessed the impact of RJPs on mediators and turnover. Yet documentation for complete mediation of the type $X \rightarrow M \rightarrow Y$ requires that *four* conditions hold: (1) that $X \rightarrow Y$ is significant; (2) that $X \rightarrow M$ is significant; (3) that $M \rightarrow Y$ is significant; and (4) that X has no direct effect on Y when M is held constant (Baron and Kenny 1986; James and Brett 1984). Unfortunately, traditional approaches have tested the first two conditions but overlooked the third and fourth. Current statistical procedures have failed to capture some of the more elaborate mediation processes that have long been posited, among them the notion that RJP mediators influence quits through satisfaction and withdrawal cognitions (see Horner, Mobley, and Meglino 1979; Wanous 1980).

Test of a Comprehensive Model of Mediation

To overcome these methodological shortcomings, Hom et al. (1993) revisited the five principal reasons for how RJPs given after an employee is hired will strengthen job incumbency—namely, met expectations, commitment to the choice of job, value orientation, perceptions of the company's concern, and coping efficacy (Horner, Mobley, and Meglino 1979; Ilgen and Dugoni 1977; Ilgen and Seely 1974; Meglino and DeNisi 1987; Meglino et al. [1988, 1990] further subdivided these processes). Posthire previews, by experimentally controlling self-selection and postdecisional dissonance reduction, may better clarify how these mediators operate (Horner, Mobley, and Meglino 1979). Hom and colleagues extended structural equations modeling (SEM) to validate a theoretical framework encompassing all mediating processes (see Figure 9-2). Although emerging over a decade ago (ibid.; Wanous 1980), comprehensive formulations about preview mediation have escaped confirmatory assessment. Their conceptualization further elucidated RJP translation by interposing job satisfaction and withdrawal cognitions between RJP mediators and exits. This extended mediation reflected the view of many that RJP mediators activate a withdrawal sequence culminating in job separations (Horner, Mobley, and Meglino 1979; Vandenberg and Scarpello 1990; Wanous 1980, 1992). The model further proposed a causal flow: satisfaction → termination cognitions → quits (Hom, Caranikis-Walker, Prussia, and Griffeth 1992; Hom and Griffeth 1991; Price and Mueller 1986; Williams and Hazer 1986).

After showing that RJPs impact quits (condition one), Hom et al. (1993) tested conditions two, three, and four by evaluating their model with SEM analysis. Confirmatory methodology assessed the mediators' pathways to the RJP treatment and termination process, fulfilling conditions two and three (Fiske, Kenny, and Taylor 1982). To meet condition four, they introduced direct linkages between RJP and withdrawal to this mediation model to verify the hypothesized *absence* of any direct effects of RJPs (Bollen 1989). Their SEM application also addressed the question of whether or not RJP mediators indirectly affect quits by way of satisfaction and turnover cognitions (Baron and Kenny 1986). Sustaining the hypotheses about mediating processes, Hom et al. validated this structural model with a sample of registered nurses. Another sample of accountants (possibly because of delayed surveys, which overshot the occurrence of mediating processes) did not provide supporting evidence.

Practical Design and Implementation

Unlike mediational tests, research on the design and implementation of RJPs is sparse. Understanding may improve the execution of RJPs (Rynes 1990), but attention to practical issues may yield more immediate payoffs. In the following section, we review other conditions that influence the effectiveness of RJPs.

RJP Timing   Job candidates can receive RJPs while they are being recruited—before they decide whether or not to accept the job—or during orientation—after they have chosen the job (Wanous and Collela 1989). Presumably, job previews are most effective in reducing turnover when they are delivered *before* the choice is made (Breaugh 1983), when there is still time for self-selection and postdecisional dissonance to operate (Ilgen and Seely 1974; Wanous

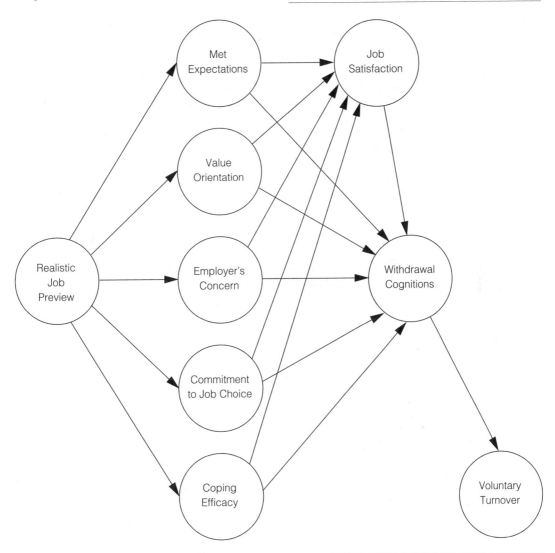

Figure 9-2 Theory of Processes Mediating the Influence of Posthire Realistic Job Previews on Turnover. (P. Hom, R. Griffeth, L. Palich, and J. Bracker (1993), "Realistic job previews: Two-occupaton Test of mediating precesses." College of Business, Arizona State University, Tempe, Arizona: 40.)

and Collela 1989). That is, job applicants can only select themselves out of a job or feel dissonance about their decision to take the job if they receive RJPs before they make the choice. Even so, many studies find that posthire RJPs can reduce quits (Dugoni and Ilgen 1981; Hom et al. 1993; Horner, Mobley, and Meglino 1979; Meglino et al. 1988). In no study has the timing of RJPs been directly compared, and the question merits further investigation.

Communication Modes   RJPs have been presented in various modes of communication, including booklets, audiovisual media, work samples, and interviews (Wanous and Collela 1989). The booklet, being easily developed and convenient to administrate, is by far the most popular medium. These practical advantages notwithstanding, Premack and Wanous (1985) found that booklet RJPs decreased exits as effectively as did audiovisual RJPs, which also improved job performance.

In a rare test, Colarelli (1984) compared two modes of delivering realistic previews, booklet and presentations by employees contending that the latter are more effective. Face-to-face interactions make the applicants pay attention and improves their comprehension. Employees, in addressing each applicant's particular concerns, communicate more relevant information. Employees are also more candid than booklets, from which facts that the company does not want to acknowledge formally may be omitted, and are more credible sources because they occupy positions sought by applicants. Predictably, Colarelli found that RJPs given by employers reduced resignations among new bank tellers (3-month quit rate: 14.6 percent) more than did booklet previews (44.9 percent quit rate).

Developmental Procedures   The present-day construction of RJPs (especially as booklets) increasingly follows content validation methods to insure that they accurately and completely reflect the job content. For example, the development of a booklet requires a survey of many current employees and their superiors, who will independently verify the accuracy of statements about the job that were drawn from preliminary interviews (Dean and Wanous 1984; Reilly, Tenopyr and Sperling 1979). Majority opinion (a 70 percent consensus) determines which statements are included in the booklet. This painstaking development process may benefit from additional refinement from further research comparing various ways of compiling RJPs (see the development procedures for behaviorally anchored rating scales [Bernardin, LaShells, Smith, and Alvares 1976]). Developmental procedures for other RJP media remain unexamined and warrant future evaluation.

RJP Content   Uncertainty over which dimension of job content—specificity, favorability, occupational focus, or subjective reality—should be emphasized in RJPs persists. Addressing one dimension, Dean and Wanous (1984) compared a RJP booklet containing specific information about bank tellers with a more general RJP booklet. Surprisingly, the specific RJP did *not* reduce turnover any more than the generic preview did. Comparing another dimension, Meglino et al. (1988) exposed army trainees to one of three audiovisual RJPs differing in favorability. One of these audiovisual RJPs, like most, embodied a "reduction" preview, primarily portraying problems in the workplace. Another was an "enhancement" preview, emphasizing the positive attributes of the job. The third was a comprehensive RJP combining the other two.

The combined RJP lowered attrition the most among military trainees. The enhancement RJP reduced exits more than the reduction RJP did, leading one to speculate that enhancement RJPs may help new entrants in demanding jobs (such as military training) by modifying their overly pessimistic expectations (Wanous and Collela 1989). Surprisingly, among recipients of the reduction RJP, retention was poorer than it was in a control group. Conceivably, this RJP exacerbated already negative expectations about basic training, arousing fears and inducing early departures (Meglino et al. 1988). Still, the reduction preview did improve the retention of recruits who were *committed* to the army.

Considering another dimension of content, Hom et al. (1993) designed a preview about an occupation rather than a specific job in a particular company. They initially interviewed supervisors and accountants from several public accounting firms about accounting work and compiled their statements into a survey. Then they surveyed accountants in other firms, who confirmed the veracity of each statement. Comprising statements that 70 percent (or more) of the survey participants deemed valid, the RJP booklet thus described standard features of the accounting *profession* across twenty-seven firms. A later field experiment established that this occupational preview reduced voluntary exits among new accountants.

Most RJPs describe objective work conditions and employees' impressions, but subjective impressions of reality in the workplace may benefit newcomers most (Wanous 1989). Socialization studies show that new recruits are usually more ignorant of the intrinsic job content (for example, boring tasks and rare performance feedback) than of extrinsic work features (such as pay rates) (Wanous 1980). Thus, RJPs about how employees *feel* about the intrinsic qualities of work activities would most inform newcomers because these attributes are less visible and more abstract (ibid.)

Moderators of RJP Efficacy

Early reports about the uneven effectiveness of RJPs stimulated conceptualizations of situational and personal moderators of their impact. In particular, RJPs may work best if newcomers are naive about the job and can freely choose to select themselves out of jobs they have previewed—that is, if they have other options (Breaugh 1983). Yet traditional RJPs primarily portray "simplistic and highly visible" service jobs, suggesting that many samples of RJP recipients already have relatively accurate expectations (Wanous and Collela 1989). Such visibility might explain why some tests report that RJPs fail for some jobs, such as those of bank tellers (Reilly et al., 1981). High unemployment may prevent the recipients of RJPs from declining job offers even when they discern a misfit between their needs and the organizational climate. Weak job markets may shortcircuit the self-selection process and thus undermine the effectiveness of RJPs (Wanous 1973).

Job Complexity   Theorists have long maintained that RJPs most assist new entrants to complex roles (McEvoy and Cascio 1985; Reilly et al. 1981). They presume that complex jobs comprise more varied, enriched tasks than do simple jobs. Because intrinsic work content is inherently abstract (Wanous 1980), the nature of complex work is thus less visible to outsiders (Wanous and Collela 1989) So realistic portrayals of complex work would prove more informative and reduce turnover better than previews of simple work do. McEvoy and Cascio (1985) and Reilly et al. (1981) found RJPs did benefit employees in complex work roles most, but Premack and Wanous (1985) did not.

Notwithstanding such conflicting evidence, Hom et al. (1993) argued that the predominance of simple jobs in past studies of RJPs understated moderating effects, restricting variance in job complexity (Rynes 1990; Wanous and Colella 1989): Range restriction attenuates not only predictor strength but also moderator effects (Hunter and Schmidt 1990b). In prior meta-analytical comparisons of the effects of RJPs across jobs of varying complexity, the jobs were categorized subjectively (McEvoy and Cascio 1985; Premack and Wanous 1985; Reilly et al. 1981). Without precise definitions of job complexity, such arbitrary classifications conceivably underlaid contradictory findings about the usefulness of RJPs for complex work (Wood, Mento, and Locke 1987).

Going beyond traditional hourly jobs (Rynes 1990), Hom et al. (1993) developed RJPs for accountants and registered nurses (RNs), whose occupations are more complex than those formerly examined and which may more readily disclose the superiority of RJPs for complex jobs. These professional RJPs reduced voluntary turnover among nurses—8.5 percent of whom quit as compared with 17.1 percent of a control group (χ^2 [1, $N = 158$] $= 2.62$, $p < .10$)—and certified public accountants (CPAs)—5 percent of whom quit as compared with 17 percent of a control group ($\chi^2[1, N = 109] = 4.03$, $p \leq .05$). Just the same, the mean effect size for professional previews ($r = .154$) did not significantly differ from previous estimates (.087, McEvoy and Cascio 1985; .06, Premack and Wanous 1985). Hom et al. assigned professional jobs and those from earlier RJP studies into groups of complex and simple jobs using *Dictionary of Occupational Titles* ratings (Avolio and Waldman 1990; Schaubroeck and Ganster 1993). Despite the objective job classification, the new meta-analysis did not generate larger correlations between RJPs and retention for complex jobs.

Organizational Commitment   Organizational commitment may, according to Meglino and DeNisi (1987), moderate the efficacy of RJPs. They theorized that RJPs immediately deflate attraction to the new job and motivate early withdrawal. During early employment, employees who received RJPs must somehow be bound to a job whose allure the RJP has tarnished. Only then can they later experience the ameliorating processes set in motion by the RJPs (met expectations, coping ability, and so on) and thus survive longer than employees who were not given RJPs. Meglino and DeNisi (ibid.) conceived of several factors that bind new hires during early employment: high unemployment rates, attractive jobs, and contractual obligations.

Empirical work found mixed support for the moderation of RJP success by commitment, which bonds newcomers during initial employment. Meglino et al. found that RJPs bolstered retention more for committed army recruits than for the uncommitted recruits (1988), and no difference among committed and uncommitted correction officers (1990). Hom et al. (1993) found that RJPs lowered quits more for committed than uncommitted CPAs but benefitted uncommitted RNs more than the committed. To explain such discrepancies, Hom et al. (ibid.) proposed that the relevant moderator is *occupational* rather than organizational commitment. Studies of CPAs and military recruits that report beneficial effects for committed newcomers were measuring occupational attachment; studies, in which the moderating effects of commitment were not disclosed, had been measuring organizational commitment among RNs and correction officers.

JOB ENRICHMENT

Job enrichment is another promising intervention for reducing turnover (McEvoy and Cascio 1985). According to prevailing models of task design, employees find work motivating and attractive to the extent that they learn (by knowing the results) that they themselves (being personally responsible) performed well on a job they care about (felt as meaningful) (Hackman and Oldham 1976, 1980). These "critical psychological states" derive from certain characteristics of a job: variety of skill (using various skills and talents); task identity (doing a whole and identifiable piece of work); task significance (doing work that substantially affects the work or lives of others); autonomy (freedom to schedule work and work procedures); and job feedback (obtaining direct and clear information about performance) (Hackman and Oldham 1980).

Several research streams indicate that job enrichment can curb turnover. Correlational studies find that employees holding complex jobs are less likely to quit (Katerberg, Hom, and Hulin 1979; Price and Mueller 1981, 1986). McEvoy and Cascio's meta-analysis (1985) revealed that field experiments enriching jobs reduced turnover more effectively than did RJPs. That is, the effect of job enrichment ($r = .17$) exceeded the effect of RJPs ($r = .09$). Even so, the former estimate was based on only five studies, and only two of them randomly assigned participants to treatments (one experiment found no impact on turnover [Locke, Sirota and Wolfson 1976]). Nonetheless, Griffeth (1985) did randomly assign part-time university desk receptionists to enriched or unenriched work conditions. Following Hackman and Oldham's implementing principles (1980), he enriched the job—upgrading skill variety, task significance, and job feedback—and found that enriched work indeed reduces turnover.

WORKSPACE CHARACTERISTICS

Oldham and his colleagues (1988; Oldham and Fried 1987; Oldham, Kulik, and Stepina 1991; Oldham and Rotchford 1983) theorized that physical characteristics of the work environment shape attitudes to work and withdrawal behavior. Drawing from overstimulation theory, Oldham reasoned that certain features in a workplace excessively stimulate employees, producing a psychological state of stimulus overload that evokes dissatisfaction and work avoidance. Social density, the total number of people in a work area, overly stimulates employees, who feel overcrowded and engage in more interpersonal conflicts (Oldham and Fried 1987). Dim lighting and drab wall colors increase perceptions of spatial restriction, inducing overstimulation (ibid.). Office enclosures, walls or partitions surrounding a work area, limit unwanted or unexpected intrusions and insure privacy. Distance from colleagues in the work place reduces perceptions of crowding and distractions.

Besides affecting morale, attributes of the workspace shape perceptions about the job (Oldham and Rotchford 1983). For example, employees working in open offices that have few interior walls or partitions may feel less autonomous because unwanted intrusions interfere with their freedom to work. They may also feel less task identity because they notice the work of others and the continuous work flow in the office. If they view the product of the entire office as the whole unit of work, they may see their own contribution as only a small piece of this product. Open offices also affect perception of the significance of the task. By observing how their work affects others, employees in open offices may regard their own jobs as more or less significant, depending on its actual effects. Oldham's model of workplace overstimulation is summarized in Figure 9-3.

Testing this theory, Oldham and his colleagues (Oldham and Fried 1987; Oldham and Rotchford 1983) demonstrated that attributes of the workspace explained 31 percent of the variance among clerical workers' work satisfaction. The combined effects of dark rooms, few enclosures, close work areas, and overcrowded offices most elicited dissatisfaction. Oldham and Rotchford (1983) showed that characteristics of the task at hand partly mediated the effect of unpleasant workspaces. Offices with few interior boundaries reduced task significance, autonomy, and task identity, and darkness lowered autonomy. Open offices enhanced task significance. Oldham and Fried (1987) found that the main and interactive effects of the attributes of an office explained 24 percent of turnover variance, with multiple conditions of overstimulation increasing turnover most.

Using a quasi-experiment, Oldham (1988) further examined the effects on insurance claims adjusters of changes in the layout of three open-plan offices lacking interior walls or partitions. Two of the offices were changed from the open-plan design, one to a partitioned design, the other to a low-density open-plan design. The third office remained unchanged. Adjusters moving to the new office configurations that reduced overstimulation reported improvements in privacy, task communication, and crowding. Employees moving to the low-density open office felt more work satisfaction than did those who moved to the partitioned office or those who did not move.

Stimulus-screening skills and job complexity moderate reactions to distractions in the workplace (Oldham, Kulik, and Stepina 1991). *Screeners* are

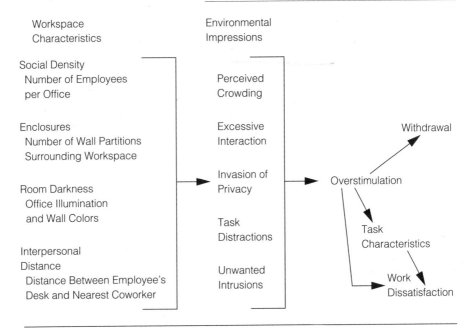

Figure 9-3   Theory of Workspace Overstimulation. (G. R. Oldham, and N. L. Rotchford, "Relationships between office characteristics and employee reactions: A study of the physical environment" *Administrative Science Quarterly,* **28 (1983): 542–547.)**

more adept than *nonscreeners* are at filtering out extraneous intrusions and thus feel less perturbed when working in dense, crowded offices without interior walls. Employees doing simple jobs may be more disturbed by unshielded environments than are those with complex jobs because the work is not psychologically absorbing. Oldham, Kulik, and Stepina (1991) found that government employees with poor screening skills or doing simple tasks were less happy if their offices were crowded, had few enclosures, or had not much space separating them from their fellow workers.

Given these encouraging findings, workplace protections against stimulus overload may enhance retention. Future inquiry must substantiate this possibility directly. To date, most research studies have considered attitudinal responses to invasive office settings (Oldham 1988) or predictions of turnover from attributes of workspaces (Oldham and Fried 1987). Field experiments (or quasi-experiments) must directly verify that improvements restricting unwanted or unexpected intrusion in offices do truly diminish turnover.

SOCIALIZATION PRACTICES

Turnover is primarily concentrated among new employees (Mobley 1982a; Murnane, Singer, and Willett 1988; Wanous 1980) whose morale and

commitment fall precipitously during early tenure (Hom and Griffeth 1991; Wanous 1980). Excessive premature quits implicate inadequate or incomplete organizational socialization as a fundamental cause (Feldman 1988; Fisher 1986). In the following section, we review socialization programs that might facilitate the difficult, stressful adaptation to new work roles. According to many socialization scholars, newcomers must define the work role, win collegial acceptance, resolve conflicting demands, and develop proficiency in the job to become established (ibid.). Attesting to the benefits of assistance in socialization, Corning Glass Works found that an improved orientation program saved over $250,000 per year in turnover costs among new professionals (Turbin and Rossé 1990).

Socialization Programs

Though theories about organizational socialization abound, descriptions about successful practices are scarce. To close this knowledge gap, Louis, Posner, and Powell (1983) surveyed new business graduates, who reported on the availability and helpfulness (using a five-point scale) of various socialization practices and their own attitudes to work. The results of the survey are shown in Figure 9-4: Peers, supervisors, and senior coworkers offered newcomers the most assistance. Surprisingly, business graduates regarded formal programs, such as on-site orientation and offsite residential training, as less helpful and despite popular writings, mentors or sponsors were neither available nor helpful to new graduates (see Kantor 1977).

Correlations indicating which socialization practices promoted job satisfaction and tenure intentions are shown in Figure 9-5. Although not widely endorsed by graduates, favorable offsite residential training and business trips most improved morale and intentions of staying. Louis, Posner, and Powell's findings (1983) are intriguing but warrant experimental or quasi-experimental replications to validate whether these socialization practices truly aid retention.

Reality Shock Programs

Using quasi-experimental designs, several studies evaluated special orientation programs to help nursing graduates adjust to hospital life. Kramer and Schmalenberg's "bicultural training" (1977) is the most acclaimed program, serving as model for others. Once a week during the first six weeks of employment, nursing graduates attend ninety-minute "rap sessions," at which they share problems and ways to cope with them (and develop a "same boat consciousness," Van Maanen and Schein 1979, p. 233). During the fourth week, new nurses read Kramer and Schmalenberg's workbook descriptions of common forms of reality shock, such as infrequent feedback and feelings of incompetence. Between four and five months after entry, the nurses also attend conflict-resolution workshops—first separately and later with their

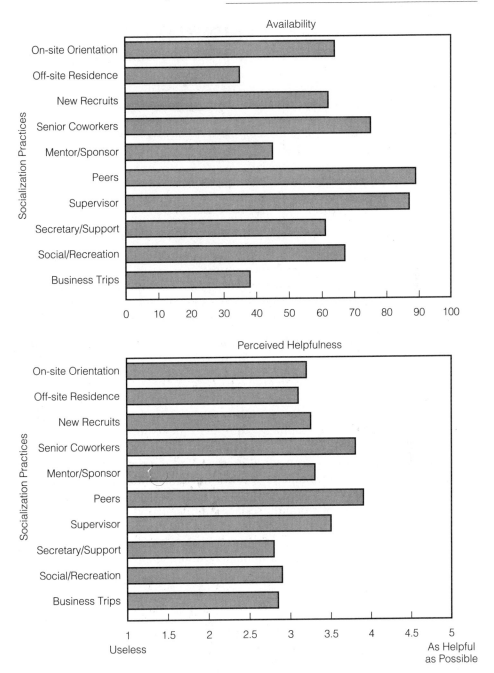

Figure 9-4 **Availability and Helpfulness of Socialization Practices. (M. R. Louis, B. Z. Posner, and G. N. Powell, "The availability and helpfulness of socialization practices."** *Personal Psychology,* **36 (1983): 861.)**

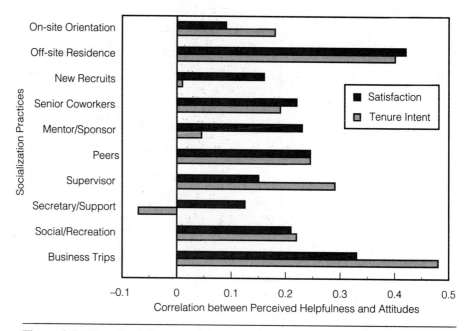

Figure 9-5 How Socialization Practices Affect Job Satisfaction and Tenure Intentions. (M. R. Louis, B. Z. Posner, and G. N. Powell, "The availability and helpfulness of socialization practices." *Personal Psychology,* **36 (1983): 863.)**

head nurses—at which they role play ways to deal with routine conflicts, a common developmental hurdle for newcomers (Feldman 1976, 1988).

Kramer (1977) first evaluated bicultural training by recruiting 260 new RNs from eight medical centers. Half these RNs received bicultural training, while others received a traditional orientation. After a year, 90.2 percent of the biculturally trained nurses remained employed, whereas 60.2 percent of the control-group nurses had quit. Similarly, Holloran, Mishkin, and Hanson (1980) found that only 3 percent of the nurses who completed the bicultural training resigned; the quit rate before the program began had been 42 percent. Many hospital orientations now include "reality shock" components (lectures, rap sessions) and instruction in clinical skills (addressing graduates' insecurities about their professional competence [Borovies and Newman 1981]). Reviewing these programs, Weiss (1984) concluded that comprehensive orientations reduced turnover: Seven percent of the trained nurses (compared with 31 percent of the nurses hired without this training) quit.

Coping Skills

Socialization theorists describe assimilation as a stressful time for newcomers (Feldman and Brett 1983) who may find their personal resources taxed or exceeded and their mental well-being endangered (Lazarus and Folkman 1984). Feldman and Brett (1983) documented the fact that new

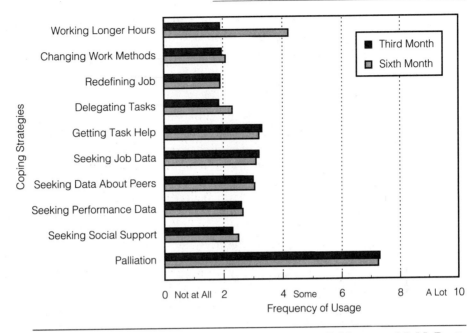

Figure 9-6   Coping Strategies of New Hires. (D. C. Feldman and J. M. Brett, "Coping with new jobs: A comparative study of new hires and job changers," *Academy of Management,* **26 (1983): 268.)**

hires often practice many coping strategies during the early months of employment, such as soliciting help from others and palliation (reducing anxiety through chemical substances) (see Figure 9-6).

Self-management training may assist newcomers to develop mechanisms for coping with transition stress and improve their job survival (Manz 1991; Manz and Sims 1980; Manz and Sims 1989). This training is based on social learning theory, which submits that perceived self-efficacy and outcome expectancies underlie motivation (Frayne and Latham 1987). Self-efficacy is the personal belief that one can successfully execute the behavior and it influences behavioral choice and effort. But people must also expect rewarding consequences from performing the act—that expectancies for the outcomes will be more positive rather than negative. Otherwise, they have little incentive to execute the behavior.

Designed to surmount problem behaviors, self-management training instructs individuals in various cognitive and behavioral strategies designed to change their beliefs about self-efficacy and their expectancies for the outcomes of those behaviors. Individuals may follow a strategy of self-observation to collect systematic data about the problem behavior. Such data provide feedback for later self-reinforcement and may pinpoint underlying behavioral causes. People can set specific goals (including intermediate behavioral goals) to overcome behavioral problems and thus enhance their self-efficacy. With cueing strategies, they can develop self-efficacy by limiting their exposure to environmental cues that encourage the maladaptive behaviors, while increasing their exposure to cues that evoke the desired actions. People can gain more behavioral control through rehearsal, systematically practicing a competing, more desirable act. Individuals can also improve outcome expectancies by identifying and administering reinforcers for behavioral improvements (Manz 1991b). Many clinical interventions involving self-management practices have helped individuals cope with weight loss and smoking (Frayne and Latham 1987).

Adapting self-management to the workplace, Frayne and Latham (ibid.; Latham and Frayne 1989) trained twenty unionized state-government employees to reduce absenteeism. The trainees received eight weekly, one-hour, group sessions at which they learned to set proximal and distal goals for attendance, write a behavioral contract with themselves for dispensing self-chosen reinforcers and punishers, monitor their own attendance behavior, administer incentives, and brainstorm about potential interference with adherence to this training and find solutions for the problem. Trainees attended work more regularly than did an untrained control group over a twelve-week period after training and maintained their superior attendance record nine months later (ibid.).

Extending self-management theory and training, Manz and Neck (Manz 1992; Manz and Neck 1991; Neck and Manz 1992) developed a "thought self-leadership" (TSL) program to foster constructive thinking patterns (Judge and Locke 1993). They reasoned that maladaptive behaviors are rooted in distorted and unrealistic beliefs that undermine self-efficacy and outcome expectancies (Burns 1980). To modify dysfunctional thinking, Manz and Neck (1991) proposed that employees facing stressful events first observe and record their existing beliefs, self-verbalizations, and mental imagery patterns. For example, a new employee may feel anxious about an upcoming presentation to higher management. She may feel that this presentation will be poorly received by the audience (belief), may tell herself that she cannot speak effectively (self-talk), or may imagine hostile reactions from the audience (mental imagery).

The TSL program next prescribes that employees analyze the functionality and constructiveness of those beliefs, self-talk, or imagery. Employees would challenge the validity of their distorted beliefs by identifying the form of dysfunctional thinking that they mirror. Various dysfunctional beliefs chronicled by Burns (1980) are shown in Figure 9-7. Continuing with our example, the employee's belief that the audience would dislike her presentation may represent "jumping to conclusions." By identifying a belief's dysfunctional form, employees can develop more functional, constructive thinking patterns to replace the dysfunctional thought. That is, using various techniques, they might generate plausible counterarguments to refute an irrational belief (see Burns 1980, 1988). For example, the anxious speaker might convince herself that her fears are groundless because she has delivered well-received presentations in the past. Last, the TSL program requires continued monitoring over time of one's thinking pattern.

All or Nothing Thinking
    Viewing things as black or white
Over-generalization
    Specific failure is seen as endless pattern of defeat
Mental Filter
    Excessive dwelling on single negative detail
Disqualifying Positives
    Discount positive aspects in an event
Jumping to Conclusions
    Drawing negative conclusions without concrete evidence
Magnifying and Minimizing
    Exaggerate importance of negatives but minimize positives
Emotional Reasoning
    Interpret reality through negative emotions
Should Statements
    Use "should" and "must" to motivate
Labeling and Mislabeling
    Describing oneself or others with negative labels
Personalization
    Blaming oneself for negative event even though not primarily responsible

Figure 9-7 Forms of Dysfunctional Thinking. (D. Burns, *Feeling good: The new mood therapy*, NY: William Morrow and Company, Inc. (1980): 42–43.)

Recently, Neck (1992) evaluated TSL training in a field experiment. He recruited forty-eight employees of an airline operating under bankruptcy regulations, randomly assigning twenty-four to training and twenty-four to a control group. During a six-week period, the trainees were enrolled in two-hour sessions in which he instructed them on self-talk, mental imagery, managing beliefs and assumptions, thought patterns, and preventing relapse. Afterwards, the trainees expressed more positive moods and higher job satisfaction than the control group did and maintained higher affective states a month after training. Though Neck found no evidence that training affected turnover, no research participant had left during the study. Given the ongoing recession, employees probably felt pessimistic about finding other employment in a bleak job market in the airline industry—a pessimism surely compounded by their firm's bankruptcy.

Although unproven for socialization problems, self-management training (including TSL) may well help newcomers adapt to the new job. This application might first identify the socialization tasks that are customarily difficult and stressful for newcomers to a given job. For example, Kramer and Schmalenberg (1977) identified common frustrations for new nurses, such as dealing with older coworkers and having insufficient time for quality patient care. A self-management program would help newcomers develop behavioral strategies to cope with those situations, including

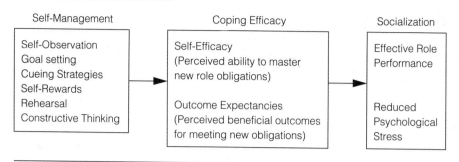

Figure 9-8 Coping with Newcomer Stress.

changing the work environment (Feldman and Brett 1983). What is more, a TSL component would reduce newcomers' stress by helping them challenge their illogical interpretations (often the result of exaggerated feelings of inadequacy or pessimism) of socialization difficulties (Burns 1980; Lazarus and Folkman 1984). Parsons, Herold, and Leatherwood (1985) found that new employees attributing their performance to luck (possibly an irrational belief) were more likely to resign than were those explaining their performance in terms of ability. Judge and Locke (1993) found that habitually dysfunctional thinkers felt more job dissatisfaction, avoided work more frequently, and spent more time thinking about quitting. A prospective self-management program to help new employees deal with transition stress and improve their job survival is shown in Figure 9-8. The determination of whether self-management (and TSL) can reduce turnover, especially among newcomers, awaits future scholarly inquiry.

LEADER-MEMBER EXCHANGE

Graen and his associates developed a theory about leadership that emphasizes a superior's role in the assimilation and retention of newcomers (Dansereau, Graen, and Haga 1975; Graen and Scandura 1989⁶). During the socialization period, superiors initiate special working relationships—or high "leader-member exchanges" (LMX)—with some new subordinates and offer them inducements, such as job latitude, decision-making influence, information, and support, that go beyond the formal employment contract. In return, high-LMX subordinates express higher commitment and assume more unit responsibilities. With other, low-LMX subordinates, superiors rely on formal authority rather than social exchange to elicit role compliance.

According to socialization theories, high-LMX exchanges may facilitate a newcomer's adaptation (Feldman 1988; Fisher 1986). Superiors communicate more often with high-LMX newcomers, which improves role definition—a vital developmental stage (Dansereau, Graen, and Haga 1975).

Moreover, high-LMX newcomers negotiate their work roles with superiors and thus obtain tasks that they value and can do, thereby becoming initiated into the task, another developmental milestone (Feldman 1988). Superiors also express more social support for high-LMX newcomers, alleviating transition stress. With the enhanced socialization, research finds higher job satisfaction and retention among high-LMX than among low-LMX subordinates (Dansereau, Graen, and Haga 1975; Ferris 1985; Graen and Ginsburgh 1977; Graen, Liden, and Hoel 1982).

Drawing from LMX research, Graen, Novak, and Sommerkamp (1982) designed a leadership program that, in six two-hour sessions, trains managers to form high-quality social exchanges with subordinates. Using lecture and role playing, this program instructs superiors about the LMX model, active listening skills, techniques for exchanging mutual expectations and resources, and developing and practicing one-on-one sessions. Then managers meet with each subordinate and they follow a prepared script to communicate their concerns and expectations about each other's job and their working relationship.

An initial field experiment found that LMX training increases productivity over a twelve-week period and improves the subordinate's job satisfaction and perceived job complexity (Graen, Novak, and Sommerkamp 1982). Following this test, Scandura and Graen (1984) showed that the training can reverse initially poor dyadic exchanges between superiors and low-LMX members and ultimately boost the subordinates' morale and productivity. Graen, Scandura, and Graen (1986) found that subordinates having strong growth needs most welcomed LMX training for their leaders who engaged in more collaboration and developed interdependent working relationships with them, enriching their work. Subordinates with high growth needs who were working for LMX-trained superiors outproduced subordinates with low growth needs by 55 percent.

In conclusion, LMX training holds great promise for sustaining job tenure. Although there are no experiments showing that LMX training reduces exits, field experiments affirm that this training promotes the quality of work life for subordinates—an essential basis for loyalty to the firm (McEvoy and Cascio 1985)—and correlational studies verify that subordinates engaging in high-quality dyadic exchanges with leaders are less likely to leave.

EMPLOYEE SELECTION

Biographical Predictors

To insure a more stable, satisfied work force (Kinicki, Lockwood, Hom, and Griffeth 1990), employers typically screen out job applicants when they evince job instability—popularly known as the "hobo syndrome" (Hulin 1991; Ghiselli 1974)—or the likelihood that they will not find satisfaction on the job (Judge 1992). To date, the weighted application blank (WAB) has yielded the most accurate predictions of turnover (Cascio 1976; Cotton and

Tuttle 1986; Schmitt, Gooding, Noe, and Kirsch 1984). WABs are application forms converted into tests. For this conversion, we first examine current and former employees' past answers to items on an application blank completed during their hiring. We seek items that elicited different responses from long- and short-term employees (Gatewood and Field 1987). After identifying the discriminating items, we derive a key that assigns different scores to the two groups' dissimilar answers. Summing scores on these particular items generates a test score indicating propensity for turnover. After the WAB is developed, candidates fill it out and those whose computed WAB scores suggest job instability would be screened out.

Fearing charges of discrimination, few companies actually use WABs, despite their predictive validity (Gatewood and Fields 1987). Inquiries about some demographic traits violate state fair-employment statutes, and screening based on certain background attributes (such as residence) may disproportionately reject minority or female applicants (ibid.). Besides, the apparent irrelevance of certain questions and potential invasion of privacy may prompt discrimination lawsuits (Breaugh and Dossett 1989). Companies may face impaired public relations and sizable litigation costs to defend so-called unfair questions. In spite of evidence that the questions are related to the job, some federal courts have even overturned WABs because firms failed to defend WABs as the best selection device by proving that alternative selection methods with less adverse impact do *not* exist (Arvey and Faley 1988; Breaugh and Dossett 1989).

To expand the use of WABs, Breaugh and Dossett (1989) advanced a more rational basis for choosing biographical data. Traditional empirical approaches provide little understanding about the reasons that biodata items predict turnover and they require large samples from which scoring keys may be developed. Breaugh and Dossett recommended that WABs include only biodata items that are verifiable (to encourage honesty among applicants) *and* that are known, according to accepted psychological theories, to underlie turnover. The selection of such items would improve the face validity of WABs, making them less objectionable to applicants.

Following these criteria, Breaugh and Dossett designed a WAB to predict turnover among bank tellers. They chose tenure on the previous job as a predictor, a choice that accords with the maxim: "Past behavior is the best predictor of future behavior." They also selected employee referrals (a recruitment source) and relevance of prior work experience to index the realism of expectations, an underpinning—according to met-expectation theory (Wanous 1980)—of job survival. Last, they added educational attainment, presuming that educated applicants are more likely to quit because they have better job opportunities elsewhere (Cotton and Tuttle 1986). Altogether these biodata items moderately predicted turnover ($R = .44$). The Breaugh-Dossett method represents a practical (because it avoids the large-sample requirements of empirical scoring keys) and defensible (because it uses theory-based item selection) way to design WABs and may overcome resistance from employers.

Personality Predictors

In contrast to the efficacy of WABs, traditional research reports disappointing predictive validity for personality measures and interest inventories (Griffeth and Hom 1988b; Mobley 1982a; Mowday, Porter, and Stone 1978; Muchinsky and Tuttle 1979; Porter and Steers 1973). Generally speaking, early studies showed that personality tests provided modest or insignificant predictions of turnover. For example, Griffeth and Hom (1988b) calculated that the widely fluctuating correlations reported in published reports averaged *merely* .18. Such ubiquitous findings thus motivated Muchinsky and Tuttle to conclude that personality has a "very marginal impact on turnover (1979,p. 48)."

In the wake of modern personality research, pessimistic conclusions about personality predictions of quits are nevertheless premature. For one, conventional narrative reviews underestimated predictive validity (and overestimated inconsistency in predictors) because they did not take into account statistical artifacts, such as unreliability, range restriction, and sampling error (Hunter and Schmidt, 1990b). Recent meta-analyses conclude that personality tests do reliably predict turnover (Barrick and Mount 1991; Schmidt et al. 1984). Schmidt and his colleagues estimated (1984) a sample-weighted mean validity coefficient of .121 between personality tests and job retention. This validity (corrected only for sampling error) does not exceed Griffeth and Hom's (1988a) .18 estimate, but early reviewers misinterpreted the utility of so-called modest predictive validities (Premack and Wanous 1985). After all, a predictor's true usefulness depends, not only on its predictive validity, but also on selection ratio (proportion of applicants hired to those applying) and base rate (proportion of employees who quit) (Arvey and Faley 1988). To illustrate, Premack and Wanous (1985) showed that an .12 correlation between RJP and job survival (which scarcely differs from existing personality validities) translates into a 6 percent improvement in job survival due to RJPs if the job survival rate is 80 percent (a high base rate), and an impressive twenty-four percent gain for a 20 percent survival rate (a low base rate).

Early critics condemned personality inventories as susceptible to falsification by job applicants, who present themselves in a favorable light to obtain employment (Bernardin 1987). Contemporary investigations dispute this claim, documenting that job applicants do not usually distort descriptions of themselves any more than incumbents do (Hough, Eaton, Dunnette, Kamp, and McCloy 1990). Tett, Jackson, and Rothstein's meta-analysis (1991) concluded that personality scales do *not* predict recruits' performance less validly than that of current employees, contradicting accepted wisdom that recruits tend to falsify self-descriptions to obtain employment and thus undermine the validity of personality scales. Hough et al. (1990) found that a measure of social desirability (or the deliberate self-inflation of personal qualities) barely moderated the predictive validity of personality inventories. That is, the criterion-related validity of personality scales was only slightly lower for employees given to inflated self-descriptions than for employees who accurately describe themselves.

In traditional work, personality measures were often adopted arbitrarily without much thought being given to their theoretical correspondence to turnover or job behaviors (Tett, Jackson, and Rothstein 1991; Weiss and Adler 1984). Yet Tett, Jackson, and Rothstein's meta-analysis (1991) revealed much stronger predictive validities (.294) when personality scales were chosen for their clear conceptual linkages to performance criteria than when empirically chosen without any rationale for their performance linkages (.121). Trait measures selected on the basis of job analysis that identified a job's personality requirements produced a mean predictive validity of .375. Barrick and Mount's meta-analysis (1991) reported higher validity coefficients when personality tests matched occupational requirements. For instance, extraversion positively related to sales effectiveness but negatively to professional performance (where work is often done alone).

In traditional reviews, predictive validities were collapsed across different personality dimensions, the possibility that some dimensions predict turnover more accurately than do others being overlooked. Present-day meta-analyses estimating predictive validities for the "Big Five" personality dimensions—an emerging taxonomy for classifying personality traits—disclose different validities (Barrick and Mount 1991; Tett, Jackson, and Rothstein 1991). Barrick and Mount (1991) discovered that conscientiousness (for which the average correlation was .12, after correcting for sampling error, range restriction, and measurement error), agreeableness (corrected correlation = .09), and openness to experience (corrected correlation = −.11) best predicted job retention across various occupations. Extraversion (correlation = −.03) and emotional stability (correlation = .02) barely predicted tenure.

Affective Disposition Contemporary dispositional research also suggests that personality traits might influence job stability. In particular, a growing body of research has implicated "negative affectivity" (NA) (Staw, Bell, and Clausen 1986) as a dispositional source of job satisfaction. A person with a NA personality evaluates oneself, others, and situations unfavorably, and thus experiences negative emotional states (Brief, Burke, George, Robinson, and Webster 1988; George 1990). Prone to cynicism, NA individuals process work cues negatively and thus feel more job dissatisfaction (Staw, Bell, and Clausen 1986). In a striking study, Staw and colleagues showed that NA measures taken during adolescence reliably forecast job attitudes in adulthood—predicting satisfaction as long as fifty years later: The adolescents who had viewed life negatively eventually judged their adult work unfavorably. Other research extended these findings, showing that the NA trait encourages absenteeism and intentions to quit, while discouraging prosocial actions (George 1989, 1990).

Nevertheless, Judge (1992, 1993) identified many conceptual and methodological pitfalls in studies on dispositional sources of job satisfaction.

Specifically, popular NA measures confuse affect intensity and affect frequency and presume a false dichotomy between negative and positive affectivity. Most of all, NA research mainly demonstrates how subjective well-being rather than affective traits shapes morale (Judge and Locke 1993). Dispositional studies do not distinguish between a general disposition to be satisfied (affective disposition) and how happy an individual currently is with his or her life (affective state) (Judge, 1992; Judge and Hulin 1993).

Judge (1993) proposed an alternative index of affective disposition adapted from Weitz (1952). Weitz's "gripe index" assesses satisfaction with forty-four items common in everyday life, such as the way people drive and the income tax. This index may measure the dispositional trait of affective orientation better than do existing NA indices, which reflect experienced affect. After adapting Weitz's scale (deleting confounded and irrelevant items and modernizing the wording), Judge (1992, 1993; Judge and Locke 1993) showed that this measure discriminably differed from subjective measures of well-being (which included negative and positive affectivity scales). Importantly, Judge and Locke (ibid.) found that this dispositional index influenced job satisfaction and work avoidance indirectly through subjective well-being.

Recently, Judge (1993) demonstrated that the Weitz scale moderates the translation of job dissatisfaction into exits. Extending Weitz's reasoning (1952), Judge argued that employees positively disposed toward life are more likely to quit a dissatisfying job than are the negatively predisposed employees. Relative to other things in their lives, happy individuals feel more dissatisfied with a bad job than do unhappy individuals, for whom job dissatisfaction is no more meaningful or exceptional than other dissatisfying events in their lives. Judge found higher correlations between job satisfaction and voluntary quits for medical clinic personnel with positive orientations than for the negatively disposed employees.

Person-Environment Fit   The research stream on the fit between person and environment also suggests that personality can forecast quits (Chatman 1991). Following interactional psychology (Schneider 1985), O'Reilly, Chatman, and Caldwell (1991) reasoned that shared and deeply held values of the members of an organization embody the organizational culture and that an employee's adherence to those cultural values fosters his or her commitment to the company (O'Reilly and Chatman 1986). To assess the fit between a person and a company, O'Reilly, Chatman, and Caldwell (1991) introduced the Organizational Culture Profile (OCP). The OCP compares people and organizations according to values (enduring preferences for a specific mode of conduct or end-state of existence [Rokeach 1973]) that are relevant and commensurate descriptors of both individuals and companies.

The OCP identifies value profiles for the individual and the firm and uses a template-matching procedure to assess the similarity of their profiles

(Caldwell and O'Reilly 1990; O'Reilly, Chatman, and Caldwell 1991). To generate a personal profile, an employee is asked to use a Q-sort procedure to classify fifty-four value statements (drawn from extensive writings about corporate culture) into nine categories, ranging from the most to the least descriptive of her *ideal* company, and to allocate a specified number of statements into each category. Specifically, a respondent sorts fewer items into the extreme categories and more items in the middle categories, following this distribution for items: 2-4-6-9-12-9-6-4-2. For a profile of the firm, senior managers sort value statements according to which they describe the firm following the same distribution pattern. The correlation between individual and firm profiles then yields a person-company fit score. An idiographic approach, the OCP is a methodological breakthrough over customary personality tests because it assesses the relative salience and configuration of variables (values) *within* entities (persons or firms) rather than the relative standing of entities across variables (Caldwell and O'Reilly 1990). O'Reilly, Chatman, and Caldwell (1991) and Chatman (1991) further validated the OCP, showing that person-culture fit among new accountants predicted job attitudes and retention, albeit the latter modestly ($r = .16$).

Operationalizing person-job fit differently, Bernardin (1987) designed a forced-choice personality inventory to screen out job applicants ill-suited for work as customer service representatives. A forced-choice inventory controls falsification by having respondents choose a descriptor from a pair of descriptors matched on social desirability—only one of which is a valid choice. Bernardin interviewed employees and superiors to identify discomforting work events and wrote statements about those events. He also generated statements about discomforting situations that were irrelevant to the job and had judges rate the discomfort levels of both the relevant and irrelevant statements. The final inventory comprised pairs of relevant and irrelevant statements matched for discomfort levels. Respondents would choose statements depicting events most distressing them. For example, a job applicant would circle two of the following situations that would most discomfort her (a valid item is indicated with a v):

1. You must be indoors on a sunny day (v)
2. You are stood up for an appointment
3. You hear your neighbors argue (v)
4. You are the only employee to forget to get the boss a birthday card.

Using a concurrent validation design, employees completed the personality inventory. It transpired that those selecting many valid discomforting descriptions resigned more often ($r = .31$). In essence, this personality scale identifies people who would fit the job poorly because they would be disturbed by stressful events that are part of the job and would more readily withdraw from the occupation.

Personality Testing and Retention

Modern research has established that personality scales, given methodological and theoretical advancements, can predict terminations. Barrick and Mount (1991) validated conscientiousness, openness to experience, and agreeableness as robust predictors. Yet employers may best increase the predictive validity of personality tests by identifying the personality requirements of a given job by analyzing the job and then choosing (or developing) valid measures of *relevant* personality constructs (Tett, Jackson, and Rothstein 1991). Employers might safeguard themselves against applicants who distort their self-descriptions by including social desirability scales, even though current research refutes the persistent myth that the falsification of personality scales is pervasive or that it automatically threatens predictive validity (Hough et al., 1990). Such scales may identify dishonest job candidates (motivating a closer scrutiny of other hiring criteria) and may statistically adjust personality scores for intentional falsifications (Bannister, Kinicki, DeNisi, and Hom 1987). Employers might develop forced-choice personality inventories to control for social desirability bias (Bernardin 1987). That said, we urge future research that uses predictive validation designs to substantiate directly these guidelines for identifying valid personality predictors of turnover.

Rather than selection, employers might use measures of affective traits (or states) to assign negatively oriented newcomers to work groups that have positive affective tones (that is, shared norms of positive affectivity) to curb their morose affect (George 1990). Mood elevation may in turn reduce work avoidance. OCP company profiles may serve as realistic organizational previews for prospective employees, enabling them to better self-select themselves for preferred organizational cultures (Sheridan 1992).

Measures of dispositional affect might identify those employees who would most benefit from morale-lifting interventions, although recent work finds that affective dispositions do not constrain the impact of job enrichment (Arvey, Bouchard, Segal, and Abraham 1989; Judge 1992). Beneficial treatments may do most to raise the morale of positively affective employees who currently dislike their jobs and to retain them because it is they who are prone to abandon dissatisfying work (Judge 1992, 1993). Judge and Locke (1993) recommended training employees to overcome dysfunctional thinking about their jobs and lives in general in order to increase their subjective well-being and job satisfaction (ultimately reducing job avoidance [Judge 1992]). Despite the claims of many dispositional researchers (Arvey et al. 1989; Staw, Bell, and Clausen 1986), affective states and dispositions are not immutable, as Neck (1992) impressively demonstrated.

In summary, there are various "robust" methods for controlling turnover:

Realistic job previews
Job enrichment
Protection of the workspace against overstimulation
Reality-shock orientation
Self-management coping strategies
Leader-member exchange training
Biographical prdictors
Personality selection and placement

More experimental tests of these methods are nonetheless warranted because only RJPs have been extensively tested using field experiments that randomly assign employees to different treatment conditions and monitor their impact on job tenure.

PROMISING METHODS
OF TURNOVER REDUCTION

In this chapter, we review some promising methods that might curb unwanted turnover. The empirical underpinnings for these interventions, unlike those described in Chapter 9, are more limited. Rather than experimental or quasi-experimental research, the efficacy of these approaches for reducing turnover is primarily corroborated by cross-sectional correlational studies, opinion surveys, or informal observations. The wealth of such supportive but weak evidence is impressive and suggests that these methods may be useful.

COMPENSATION PRACTICES

Employers universally regard low or uncompetitive wages as a leading cause of turnover. To illustrate, partners in public accounting firms recounted in a statewide survey that dissatisfaction about pay is one of the principal reasons that their staff quits (Hom, Bracker, and Julian 1988). Indeed, the widespread presumption that pay induces loyalty to a firm underlies the customary salary surveys, which insure that current wages are competitive (Milkovich and Newman 1993). Sharing this view, employees often mention pay as being central to their quit decisions. Many exit surveys find that former employees often blame their resignations on poor salaries or fringe benefits (Donovan 1980; Huey and Hartley 1988; Sigardson 1982).

Notwithstanding such testimonials, scholars of turnover have, for several reasons, generally ignored compensation or downplayed its impact. For one, most turnover scholars received their professional training in sociology or psychology (rather than in economics or business) so their turnover models largely reflect prevailing motivational theories that view pay as being immaterial to the work force (see Mobley 1977). Prevailing motivational models emphasize intrinsic motivation, such as self-actualization, while holding that lower-order physiological and security needs are less salient in our prosperous modern society (Brief and Aldag 1989). Research has reinforced the neglect of pay, generally finding weak correlations between pay and resignations by individuals (Mobley 1982a).

New research has challenged the conventional presumptions about the unimportance of pay. Brief and Aldag (1989) reviewed studies showing that pay can satisfy higher-order needs, such as achievement needs, a contradiction of the myth that pay meets only lower-order needs. In the wake of the past recession and with relentless global competition, compensation has become increasingly valued by Americans as their standard of living steadily declines (O'Reilly 1992; Smith 1992). Previous findings that people rank pay lower than they rank other attributes of a job understate extrinsic motivation, reflecting an artifact of social desirability (Lawler 1971). Policy-capturing studies—that lessen respondent tendency to present a favorable impression to investigators as one not driven by greed—reveal stronger pay preferences (Brief and Aldag 1989). Research on satisfaction with life and subjective well-being denotes income as a prime basis for happiness (Aldag and Brief 1989; Diener 1984; Judge 1992). Though not primarily underpinning happiness, work nonetheless renders economic benefits that enable people to enjoy more valued pursuits outside work, such as family activities and hobbies.

Methodological artifacts may have underestimated correlations between pay (and pay satisfaction) and individual quits (Moble, Griffeth, Hand, and Meglino 1979; Mobley 1982a; Motowidlo 1984; Weiner 1980). Turnover research generally examines one job or organization, restricting pay variance and hence correlations between pay and quitting (Steel and Griffeth 1989). Labor-economic studies on nationwide samples drawn from diverse firms and communities reveal that pay has bigger effects (Blakemore, Low, and Ormiston 1987; Shaw 1987). The routine measurement of base salary (Price and Mueller 1981, 1986) overlooks fringe benefits and incentive pay, rising expenditures in pay packages and growing concerns to employees (Fernandez 1986; Lewin 1991; Milkovich and Newman 1993). Turnover research often sampled secondary wage-earners and young employees who have fewer financial needs (Donovan 1980; Hom, Kinicki, and Domm 1989). It is the family breadwinners and midcareer adults—those bearing sizable financial obligations—who may most value pay and readily quit over poor incomes (Brief and Aldag 1989).

Model of Pay Effects on Turnover

We propose a model, illustrated in Figure 10-1, summarizing prior conceptualizations (Heneman 1985; Lawler 1981; Miceli and Lane 1991). This framework explicates the ways in which pay (and pay practices) can affect turnover and suggests ways to promote retention. This model differentiates between attitudes toward variable and base pay and specifies common antecedents, although their effects on those attitudes are likely to vary (Heneman, Greenberger, and Strasser 1988; Miceli and Lane 1991; Scarpello, Huber, and Vandenberg 1988). For example, job responsibilities may influence expectations about salary, whereas effectiveness in performing those duties may affect expectations about pay increases (Milkovich and Newman 1993). (Like Miceli and Lane [1991], we posit another model for the effects of fringe benefits.) Satisfaction about pay should be derived from perceived fairness in pay practices (procedural justice) and pay amounts (distributive justice) (Folger and Greenberg 1985; Greenberg and McCarty 1990).

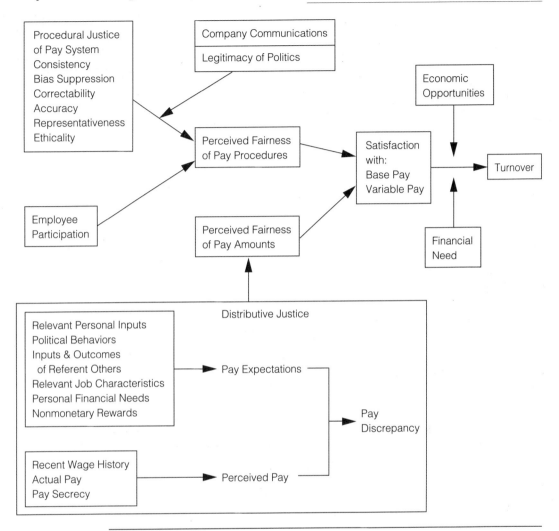

Figure 10-1 Effects of Pay on Turnover

We theorize that discrepancy between expected (base or variable) pay and the amount received determines the perception of distributive justice (Lawler 1971, 1981) because pay equity occurs when one gets what one deserves (Berkowitz, Fraser, Treasure, and Cochran 1987). In line with Miceli, Jung, Near, and Greenberger (1991), this model contends that over-payment evokes satisfaction, not guilt (Miceli and Lane 1991). Pay expectations depend, in turn, on personal job inputs (such as job performance) and the job characteristics (such as working conditions) that employees deem *relevant* contributions to the firm. Heneman, Greenberger, and Strasser (1988) and Miceli et al. (1991) found that the belief that pay is based on personal accomplishments enhances pay satisfaction and fairness. Organizations may base pay on different criteria (or weight them differently [Greenberg and McCarty 1990]) from those that are important to employees, thereby confounding the employees' pay expectations.

This model recognizes political behaviors as potential pay bases, conforming to Gould and Penley's (1984) research showing that salaries increased most for managers who openly agreed with their superiors' opinions or who flattered them. Employees' own comparisons of the contributions of and inducements offered to others shape pay expectations (Heneman 1985; Lawler 1971; Miceli and Lane 1991). Countless studies revealed that the belief that others doing similar work (in or outside the firm) earn higher pay is demoralizing, as are perceptions that friends and relatives are getting higher wages (Miceli et al. 1991; Miceli and Lane 1991; Scholl, Cooper, and McKenna 1987; Sweeney, McFarlin, and Interrieden 1990).

This framework also suggests that expectations about pay stem from financial needs (such as family size and mortgage), which economic misery (inflation, for instance) exacerbates (Miceli and Lane 1991; Scholl, Cooper, and McKenna 1987). Three national surveys disclosed, after controlling pay, greater pay dissatisfaction when earnings do not meet current expenses (Sweeney, McFarlin, and Lane 1990). Men adhering to the traditional role of the breadwinning sex may feel more financial need (and expect higher pay) if their wives work or earn higher wages than they do themselves (Mirowsky 1987; Staines, Pottick, and Fudge 1986). Nonmonetary rewards (status symbols) may partially substitute for compensation and thus lower pay expectations (Lawler 1971). An opinion survey found that intrinsic rewards promote satisfaction about pay (Berkowitz et al. 1987), and a laboratory experiment showed that high-status job titles may compensate for extra job duties—in lieu of more pay—and thereby insure feelings of equity (Greenberg and Ornstein 1983).

This model further identifies sources of perceived earnings, pinpointing real wages as a prime cause (Lawler 1971; Miceli and Lane 1991). Actual base pay dictates the meaningfulness of a pay hike (Lawler 1981). Prior wage history—especially in recent jobs—also modifies perceived pay amounts because previous salaries set a frame of reference for judging the value of current wages (Hulin 1991; Smith, Kendall, and Hulin 1969). Two national surveys showed that higher past income made current pay seem small in comparison (Sweeney, McFarlin, and Lane 1990). (Earlier salaries may also inflate expected pay because formerly well-paid people become accustomed to costly lifestyles or internalize inflated views of their self-worth [Lawler 1971; Miceli and Lane 1991]).

Secrecy about pay policies may color pay perceptions (Lawler 1971), though this influence hinges on whether employees over or underestimate others' pay. Underestimating others' earnings raises one's own perceived pay (and pay satisfaction); overestimating lowers one's perceived pay (Miceli and Lane 1991). Economic troubles, such as spiraling inflation, shrink pay perceptions by eroding the employee's purchasing power (Heneman 1990).

Table 10-1 Procedural Rules of Justice for Compensation

Rules of Justice	Setting Base Pay	Pay Increases
Consistency Allocation procedures are consistent across persons and/or time	Apply same job evaluation to all jobs	Apply same performance standards to all subordinates
Bias-Suppression Minimize personal self-interest in allocation procedure	Safeguards against depressed evaluation of jobs dominated by women	Performance ratings are free from personal prejudice
Accuracy Base allocation on accurate information	Base job evaluation on accurate up-to-date job descriptions	Document performance ratings with behavioral examples
Correctability Opportunities to modify or reverse allocation decisions	Employee opportunity for job audits if jobs are placed in wrong pay grades	Employee opportunity to disagree with performance rating
Representativeness Allocation process represents concerns of all recipients	Job evaluation committee includes representatives from all functional areas	Multiple-rater appraisal comprises ratings from knowledgeable raters
Ethicality Allocations do not violate prevailing moral standards	Company complies with stated objective of equitable pay differentials	Maintain confidentiality of individual employees' performance ratings

Beyond distributive-justice bases, our conceptualization specifies that the rules of procedural justice underpin perceptions of fairness in pay practices (Folger and Greenberg 1985; Miceli and Lane 1991). Drawing from Leventhal (1980), those rules are defined in Table 10-1 and their applicability for setting base pay and pay raises illustrated. Folger and Konovsky (1989) found that fair appraisal procedures—among them, feedback and planning—improve satisfaction about pay raises, as did the perceived fairness of the raise. Miceli et al. (1991) found that federal managers regard their merit-pay plan as fair if their superiors follow formal performance-appraisal standards.

Employee participation in pay design also fosters perceptions of procedural fairness (Miceli and Lane 1991), an observation that is consistent with a "fair process effect," wherein people feel committed to outcomes they chose (Greenberg and McCarty 1990). Laboratory experiments affirm this phenomenon, showing that subjects view reward outcomes—even bad outcomes—as more fair and satisfying whenever they believe that they have a say in allocation decisions (even though their influence is, experimentally, held immaterial) (Folger and Greenberg 1985). Field studies reveal that, when workers participate in pay designs, pay satisfaction is increased, and when subordinates are given the opportunity to share their opinions about performance during appraisal interviews, their satisfaction with merit-pay decisions is enhanced (Folger and Konovsky 1989; Jenkins and Lawler 1981).

The present perspective further posits communications about pay practices and the legitimacy of politicking as moderating procedural justice. Without widespread communication, even fair practices cannot induce impressions of fairness (Miceli and Lane 1991), an observation that is borne out by studies from which it was found that open policies elicit satisfaction about pay (Greenberg and McCarty 1990; Miceli and Lane 1991). Explanations (or excuses) about wage setting may soften employees' hostility toward unpopular pay decisions (Greenberg and McCarty 1990). Besides this, personal values about the legitimacy of politics may decide whether or not violations of just allocation rules are offensive (Miceli and Lane 1991). If politics dominate pay decisions, employees morally opposed to political bases may regard procedural infractions (uneven standards, rating biases) as unfair.

Alternative economic opportunities and financial needs may moderate the effects pay attitudes have on turnover. Employees dissatisfied with their earnings quit more readily if they can obtain better pay elsewhere (Motowidlo 1983) or if they have urgent financial obligations (Brief and Aldag, 1989). Lawler (1971) argued that dissatisfaction about pay most induces quits if pay is personally important. Using this framework, we describe, in the following section, methods for improving attitudes toward pay (and ultimately, retention) and how they work.

Pay Structures

Traditional Pay Structures   Our model suggests that pay structures affect turnover through base-pay satisfaction (Milkovich and Newman 1993). Companies usually set the base pay for jobs through job evaluation and salary surveys (Henderson 1989; Milkovich and Newman 1993). An internal compensation committee or a consulting firm designing and applying a job evaluation plan may differ from employees in rating and weighting compensable factors (pay bases). Nurses have long complained that prevailing job evaluation plans, such as the Hay Plan, undervalue nursing work because they neglect responsibility for human life (Comp Worth Study: "Nurses really underpaid", 1984). Given discrepant pay bases, job evaluation procedures might place a lower value on jobs than would the incumbents and set base salaries that fall below the incumbents' pay expectations. Pay dissatisfaction thus results because the pay is not commensurate with employee perceptions of the requirements and demands of the job.

Pay structure may induce exits if pay differentials between pay grades do not correspond to the incumbents' views of the relative grade differences in job worth (Miceli and Lane 1991). As Scholl, Cooper, and McKenna (1987) found, employees' comparisons with inputs and outcomes of others shape their pay satisfaction. Incumbents doing more demanding work may feel underpaid if their pay is not *sufficiently* higher than that of those holding simpler jobs. Despite a similar (or lesser) internal job worth, pay for male-dominated jobs is often more than for female-dominated jobs, thereby inducing women's advocacy for comparable worth (Milkovich and Newman 1993). Similarly, labor shortages for some jobs may drive up hiring rates for new hires faster than the pay increases for seasoned employees in higher pay grades, compressing pay differentials (ibid.). To illustrate, Gomez-Mejia and Balkin (1987) found that senior business faculty became dissatisfied with their pay when incoming new Ph.D.s earned similar salaries because of a faculty shortage. Turbin and Rosse (1990) attributed the exodus of young engineers in high-technology firms (who lose a third of their recent graduates) to pay compression created by higher wages offered to new hires.

Common salary-survey practices may also disconfirm pay expectations. Often, organizations survey other companies competing in their product, service, or labor market (Belcher, Ferris, and O'Neill 1985; Milkovich and Newman 1993). This sampling design may omit firms considered by employees as pay referents and thus produce market wages that fall below employees' estimates. Employees may not use surveyed (benchmark) jobs for their external pay comparisons. For example, Sweeney, McFarlin, and Lane (1990) found that employees compare their incomes to those earned by incumbents in *different* jobs. Given discrepant market estimates, wage surveys may set wages that violate the employees' pay expectations. Customary means to develop pay structures may not yield entirely fair wages, thwarting employees' pay expectations and weakening loyalty to the company.

Fair Pay Structures   Traditional compensation management seeks distributive justice, though not necessarily meeting this goal. Present-day compensation theorists increasingly prescribe various ways to enhance procedural fairness (Milkovich and Newman 1993). Employees might write or update their job descriptions, which are then signed off by their superiors, as input for job evaluations (Gomez-Mejia, Page, and Tornow 1982). Employee representatives might serve on compensation committees to develop job evaluation plans and rate positions (ibid.; Milkovich and Newman 1993). Companies might solicit the input of employees on which firms to include in wage surveys (Milkovich and Newman 1993). Firms may grant employees the opportunity to appeal or review the job classifications (ibid.) Extensive communications to demystify compensation practices would enhance beliefs in their fairness (Greenberg and McCarty 1990).

Skill-Based Pay   New approaches for wage setting, known as skill-based or knowledge-based pay plans, may improve procedural and distributive justice (Lawler 1990; Ledford 1991). Unlike traditional job-based plans, these alternative pay structures base pay on what employees know rather than what they do (Milkovich and Newman 1993). These programs distribute pay for *depth* of knowledge in one professional or technical job (Northern Telecom [Leblanc 1991]) or for *breadth* of knowledge of several production jobs, cor-

Table 10-2 Job Based and Knowledge-Based Pay.
(G. Milkovich and J. Newman. *Compensation* (3rd. Edition).
Homewood, IL: Irwin: p. 86.)

	Job-Based Pay	**Knowledge-Based Pay**
Pay Structure	Higher pay for jobs having more demands and responsibilities	Higher pay for jobs requiring higher or different skills
Salary Progression	Job promotion	Skill acquisition
Valuation Procedure	Job evaluation	Skill certification
Benefits	Pay based on value of work done	Flexibility in scheduling reduced work force
Disadvantages	Inflexibility, Bureaucracy	Training costs, Topping out on pay

responding to different stages in a continuous-process technology (General Mills [Ledford and Bergel 1991]) or manufacturing assembly (Honeywell [Ledford, Tyler, and Dixey 1991]). In Table 10-2, a comparison between knowledge-based and traditional job-based pay is shown.

Preliminary studies (Lawler 1990; Ledford 1991; Milkovich and Newman 1993) suggest higher distributive justice in knowledge-based pay plans because employees earn bigger paychecks (A more flexible, leaner work force also permits higher earnings per employee.) These programs accelerate salary growth because employees can progress as fast as they can master new skills or receive additional training. Traditional plans usually reserve major pay hikes for promotions, which hinge on available job openings over which the employees lack control. Skill-based pay also enhances perception of procedural fairness because salary increases follow clear and possibly, more acceptable criteria: the acquisition of skills as judged by supervisors, colleagues, or special committees (Ledford 1991). Job-based pay assigns salaries on criteria (compensation factors) and evaluations (judgments by anonymous compensation committees) that are usually obscure to employees (Miceli and Lane 1991). Skill-based pay plans provide significant training resources to employees and require experienced members to train others (Lawler 1990; Ledford, Tyler, and Dixey 1991). The intrinsic rewards derived from peer training and job rotation may further promote pay satisfaction (Berkowitz et al. 1987). Some plans pay production workers to learn administrative tasks, thus providing opportunities for autonomy and self-management (Lawler 1990). Many skill-based plans pay competitive market wages and may offer merit pay (Ledford 1990).

Skill-based pay may also directly increase the loyalty of the work force. By broadening their skills, workers can transfer to other jobs in which there is more work rather than face layoffs, during business downturns (Milkovich and Newman 1993). Such greater job security reinforces inclinations to stay (Davy, Kinicki, and Scheck 1991). Multiskilled employees may stay in the jobs they have because they cannot find comparable pay in other firms that offer separate, and lower, wages for distinct jobs (Lawler 1990). Though sparse, empirical studies do suggest that pay-for-knowledge systems can enhance morale and retention. Ledford and Bergel (1991) found more satisfaction with pay and pay administration in the General Mills plan, and Leblanc (1991) reported that the Northern Telecom plan halved voluntary turnover. A study of twenty skill-based plans found higher levels of commitment and satisfaction among workers (Milkovich and Newman 1993).

Variable Pay

Variable pay—tying financial rewards to performance of the job or of the firm—can potentially reduce quit by effective performers (Dalton, Todor, and Krackhardt 1982; Lawler 1990; Mobley 1982a). Research studies establish that contingency pay schemes bolster functional quits, motivating marginal performers to quit more readily (Bishop 1990; Williams and Livingstone 1994; Zenger 1992). Other research finds that group incentives, delivering higher pay to most employees, can reduce overall quit rates (Blakemore, Low, and Ormiston 1987; Wilson and Peel 1991).

Nonetheless, merit-pay programs—the most common form of allocating variable pay—often do not increase productivity, and hence, may not deter dysfunctional quits (Gomez-Mejia and Balkin 1992a; Lawler 1990; Meyer 1991; Schwab 1991). Heneman's review (1990) of twenty-two field studies found that merit-pay programs produce few or inconsistent gains in performance. The chief reason behind their general ineffectiveness is a reliance on performance judgments, which are often biased or defective (DeVries, Morrison, Shullman, and Gerlach 1981; Lawler 1990). As a result, employees do not hold "line of sight" beliefs that effort translates into monetary rewards (Lawler 1981). Without such perceptions, merit-pay programs cannot lower dysfunctional turnover because effective performers do not expect financial rewards for their superior accomplishments and thus quit (Lawler 1971). Illustrating this weakness, the Wyatt Company found, in a broad survey, that only 27 percent of the work force felt rewarded for doing a better job (Bleakley 1993).

Drawing from research on employees' reactions to appraisal practices, we review in the next section some ways to improve merit-pay programs (Bernardin and Beatty 1984; Murphy and Cleveland 1991). Through more valid and credible appraisals, their improvement would increase procedural and distributive justice, enhancing the retention of superior performers.

Appraisal Reviews Early survey research found higher satisfaction among employees who express their own views and discuss plans for performance improvements during appraisal sessions (Dipboye and Pontbriand 1981; Landy, Barnes, and Murphy 1978). A more recent survey on procedural fairness reports that employees' ability to challenge ratings, employees' input

Performance Measurement
   Consistent performance standards
   Relevant performance dimensions
   Behavioral performance dimensions
   Subordinates' views solicited
   Frequent supervisory observations
   Supervisory knowledge of job requirements
   Performance obstacles accounted for

Performance Feedback
   Frequent feedback
   Specific feedback for behavioral change
   Rationale for performance rating

Performance Planning
   Specific and clear goals set
   Plans for performance improvements discussed
   Difficulties about job duties resolved
   Periodic review of goal progress

Recourse
   Expressions about performance rating permitted
   Opportunity to appeal performance rating provided

Figure 10-2 Credible and Fair Appraisal Interview Practices

before the final ratings are determined, superiors' familiarity with employees' work, and the consistent application of standards underpin employees' impressions of fair appraisals (Greenberg 1986). Folger and Konovsky (1989) found that perceived feedback, planning, observation, and recourse during appraisal sessions increased satisfaction with pay raises and commitment to the company.

Experimental studies on performance appraisal corroborated these survey findings. Ivancevich (1982; Ivancevich and Smith 1981) showed that managerial training in goal setting and feedback delivery enhanced the reactions of subordinates, including their perceptions of the fairness of the appraisal. He also found (1980) that engineers evaluated by a behaviorally anchored rating system—with more relevant performance standards—had better perceptions of the appraisal's fairness than had those evaluated by a trait-based rating system. These credible and fair appraisal interview practices are summarized in Figure 10-2.

Variable Pay Allocation   Heneman (1990) summarized reward distribution practices that promote line-of-sight views. Predictably, contingent-pay schemes that objectively tie pay to performance foster those beliefs. Meaningful pay increases for high performance and sufficient variability of pay hikes also reinforce line-of-sight perceptions. Yet many merit-pay schemes customarily restrict raises to between three and five performance categories and cluster 80 percent of the yearly salary increases to within 2 percent of the mean increase (Zenger 1992). In addition, merit guide charts usually tie pay hikes to performance ratings *and* salary position in the pay grade (Lawler 1990; Milkovich and Newman 1993). Controlling expenses, such salary guidelines restrict pay raises for those earning high salaries, undermining their motivation (Heneman 1990). Some firms avoid demotivation by granting one-time merit bonuses to employees whose salaries are near the top of their pay range.

Moreover, merit bonuses reinforce the perceived instrumentality of performance for pay more than do merit raises, which are permanently folded into base salaries (Lawler 1990). Instead of becoming annuities, one-time bonuses must be earned again by meritorious performance every year (Heneman 1990). The lump-sum distribution of a merit raise is more likely to sustain belief in instrumentality of performance for incentives than is burying the raise across several pay checks in the coming year (ibid.; Lawler 1981). Merit-pay programs must also pay competitive salaries to sustain line-of-sight perceptions (Heneman 1990).

Aside from the issue of procedural justice, fair and valid performance appraisals bolster pay-for-performance perceptions (ibid.; Lawler 1990). Written performance standards, the adherence to performance standards, and reliable measures of performance boost line-of-sight cognitions (Heneman 1990). Open pay policies may develop perceptions of performance instrumentality by communicating the criteria for merit pay (Lawler 1981). Such policies may, however, inhibit superiors from granting varying raises to avoid challenges to their decisions on the matter (ibid.; Zenger 1992). Perhaps, communications about the range and size of merit awards and the decision-making procedure instead of public identification of the award recipients may maintain line-of-sight perceptions without incurring the costs of pay justifications (Lawler 1981). If such features were built into merit-pay programs, they might encourage functional quits while discouraging dysfunctional quits.

Key Contributors   High-technology and military organizations pioneered special financial incentives to retain personnel (Cascio 1990). The armed services offer reenlistment bonuses and use enlistment bonuses and educational benefits to lure new recruits (Hand, Griffeth, and Mobley 1978; Lakhani 1988; Gilroy, Phillips, and Blair 1990). High-tech firms award various incentives to technical employees ("key contributors"), whose special skills or proprietary knowledge contribute to the firm's performance (Cascio 1990; Gomez-Mejia, Balkin, and Milkovich 1990). Many high-tech firms give large cash awards for outstanding scientific achievements. To cultivate a sense of ownership, small private firms grant stocks to their technical professionals; public corporations award unit performance shares or phantom stocks (Cascio 1990). Scientists and engineers may receive special budgets for equipment purchases or conference travel. Some high-tech firms fund their key contributors' new ventures (Barnatham, Einhorn, and Nakarmi 1992; Gomez-Mejia, Balkin, and Milkovich 1990). Such intrapreneurship satisfies their intellectual and entrepreneurial pursuits while discouraging their exits.

Group Incentive Plans   Increasingly, incentive pay is based on company performance (Gomez-Mejia and Balkin, 1992a; Milkovich and Newman 1993), a bonus being based on controllable costs or, units of output (efficiency plans), or the firm's profitability (profit-sharing plans) (Lawler 1990). Many reviews attest to the productivity gains resulting from group incentive plans, though methodological problems temper this conclusion (Blinder 1989; Bullock and Lawler 1984; Cascio 1990; Lawler 1990; Welbourne and Gomez-Mejia 1988; White 1979). Using a large sample and statistical controls, Gerhart and Milkovich (1990) nevertheless confirmed that firms offering long-term incentives to managers realized higher returns on investments.

Group incentive schemes may also improve retention by increasing pay satisfaction. In particular, efficiency-based plans most promote perceptions of the procedural fairness of pay through their emphasis on the employees' involvement (Irrgang 1972; Lawler 1990; Lincoln 1951; White 1979). The Scanlon plan uses a screening committee, comprising labor and top management, to review workers' suggestions for plantwide efficiency improvements and to administer the bonus plan (Frost 1978; Lesieur 1958). Group incentive plans may also heighten perceptions of distributive justice if they deliver sizable bonuses, as the Lincoln Electric Company does (Balwin 1982). Supporting our reasoning, Wilson and Peel (1991) found that profit sharing in British firms reduced overall voluntary quits.

Group incentive plans may reduce turnover by providing greater job security (Gomez-Mejia and Balkin 1992a; Irrgang 1972). By reducing fixed labor costs (base salary and indirect benefit costs), organizations, rather than lay off personnel, can withhold incentive pay during economic recessions (Lawler 1990). Higher job security, in turn, improves loyalty to the company (Davy, Kinicki, and Scheck 1991; Greenhalgh and Rosenblatt 1984). A Rutgers study concluded that companies whose profit sharing consisted of cash payouts had one-third fewer layoffs during economic downturns than did competitors in the same industry (Cascio 1990).

Stock Ownership   Stock ownership—through stock grants, such as employee stock-ownership plans [ESOPs], or stock purchase plans—may foster company loyalty by several mechanisms (Klein 1987). ESOP shares (which vest over time) and stock options (or restricted stock) possibly prolong job tenure because employees must remain employed for a certain time to receive their fully vested ESOP shares or to exercise the options (ibid.; Lawler 1990). Stock ownership may reduce unfriendly takeovers by outsiders, because employees can vote on who runs the firm, and so prevent the downsizing or dismantling that often follows takeovers (Faltermayer 1992). Heightened job security then builds loyalty to the firm (Davy, Kinicki, and Scheck 1991). The receipt of stock options granted for performance may discourage superior performers from leaving, although stock prices depend more on vagaries of the financial market than on the performance of individuals (Lawler 1990). Klein (1987) found that employees who were receiving large ESOP contributions felt more committed to their firms, and Wilson and Peel (1991) showed that firms that offered stock ownership to their employees endured fewer quits.

Research Needs   Though current research affirms that merit-pay schemes reduce dysfunctional quits, the identification of which features help to bond superior performers to organizations awaits further inquiry (Williams and Livingstone 1994; Zenger 1992). In particular, we suggest more research into whether pay practices promoting line-of-sight beliefs also reduce dysfunctional quits. Essentially, do effective merit pay programs that motivate and reward superior performers also sustain their attachment to the job? Further inquiry must also consider the relative efficacy of various pay-for-performance prescriptions for reducing dysfunctional quits. Some prescriptions, such as an open pay policy and differential merit pay, may work at cross-purposes. Similarly, we welcome more direct research to assess the impact of group incentive plans on turnover and verify the routes (procedural justice, for instance) through which they decrease turnover. Beyond testimonials, the efficacy of incentives for key contributors and stock ownership for retention merits more scholarly attention. Except for military studies, anecdotal evidence primarily suggests that special incentives can retain technical personnel in high-tech firms (Cascio 1990; Turbin and Rosse 1990). More organizational-level research on the effects of pay on quit rates (see Gomez-Mejia 1992; Hom 1992) would provide the most relevant data for wholesale interventions by the firm (Hom, Gomez-Mejia, and Grabke 1993).

Fringe Benefits

Employers expend considerable funds—38 percent of payroll costs in 1990—to provide fringe benefits to improve morale, attraction, and retention in the work force (Milkovich and Newman 1993). With few exceptions (Hulin, Roznowski, and Hachiya 1985), turnover researchers overlooked the role of fringe benefits in retaining employees. Although Milkovich and Newman concluded that "there is at best only anecdotal evidence that employee benefits are cost justified" (1993, p. 409), prevalent reports by journalists and opinion polls forcefully show that benefits do sustain loyalty to a firm. According to the popular press, fears that pensions will be reduced discourage early retirement (Cahan 1986; Stricharchuk 1987) and the feared loss of health benefits restrains employees from quitting (Clements 1993; Lewis 1991). Many opinion polls and surveys chronicle the widespread premium the American populace places on fringe benefits, especially for health coverage (Clements 1993; Dwyer and Garland 1991).

Theoretical Framework   In this section, we describe a model derived from Miceli and Lane's framework (1991) to explain the origins of satisfaction

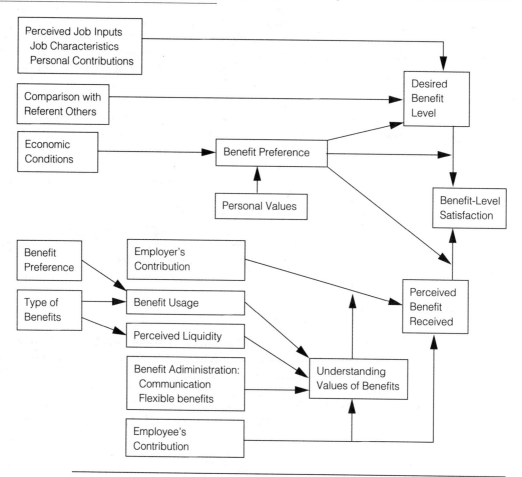

Figure 10-3 (M. Miceli and M. C. Lane. "Antecedents of pay satisfaction: A review and extension." In G. Ferris and K. Rowland (Eds.), *Research in Personnel and Human Resources Management,* (1991) Vol. 9.)

about benefits and how benefits can sustain loyalty (see Figure 10-3). Following Lawler (1971), in this model, we contend that discrepancy between desired and perceived benefit levels underpins satisfaction about benefits. In turn, preferences for benefits moderate this impact; desired but unmet benefit levels create despair only if employees value that benefit (Locke 1976). We further posit various determinants of desired benefit levels, among them perceived job inputs, such as personal contributions and doing disagreeable or difficult jobs. For example, many firms tie the levels of some benefits—typically, pensions and vacation time—to length of employment (Milkovich and Newman 1993). Employees may compare their benefits to those of others and expect similar levels (Miceli and Lane 1991). Desired benefit levels also derive from benefit preferences, which in turn are shaped by economic circumstances and personal traits (ibid.). Unemployment may raise the demand for more unemployment insurance; married employees, unlike single employees, may want more health coverage for their dependents.

The formulation likewise specifies various causes of perceived amount of benefit received, positing that the firm's contribution represents the key antecedent. Dreher, Ash, and Bretz (1988) found that benefit coverage modestly increased benefit satisfaction, and an understanding of the benefits strengthened this effect. This model also submits that employees who understand the benefit scheme are more likely to recognize (if not better appreciate) contributions from the employer. The workers' own contributions to the benefit lower the perceived benefit levels (Miceli and Lane 1991; Milkovich and Newman 1993, Dreher, Ash, and Bretz 1988). All the same, employees who contribute to the costs of the benefit may understand it better and appreciate the company's contribution (Wilson, Northcraft, and Neale 1985).

Certain administrative practices may improve understanding of the benefits (Miceli and Lane 1991). Effective communication programs, such as small group meetings and personalized benefit statements will clarify their values and expand awareness of the firm's contribution (Milkovich and Newman 1993). Indeed, communication about benefits is essential in promoting satisfaction about them because most employees are ignorant about or underestimate their benefits (Wilson, Northcraft, and Neale 1985). Flexible benefit plans—providing the employee with a choice of benefits—may enhance knowledge about them and increase the level of desired benefits (Miceli and Lane 1991). Barber, Dunham, and Formisano (1992) found that the introduction of a cafeteria benefit plan raised satisfaction with and understanding of the benefits.

The frequency with which benefits are used (due to personal preference) should enhance awareness of the value of the benefits. Understanding of benefits depends on the type because some benefits are used more often or are more "liquid" than others (Miceli and Lane 1991). Frequently used benefits, such as parking, are more appreciated than the ones used less, such as life insurance, as illustrated in the sick-leave abuser's confession that "it is not a benefit if I don't use it" (ibid., p. 296). Liquid benefits, such as vacation days, are more easily translated into a cash value than are others; such translation makes their value more readily understood than that of nonliquid benefits.

Reducing Turnover   The model suggests that benefit coverage can inhibit employees from leaving (Barber, Dunham, and Formisano 1992; Ippolito 1991; Williams and Dreher 1992). Dreher, Ash, and Bretz (1988) found that broad coverage elevates satisfaction about benefits, which according to Hulin, Roznowski, and Hachiya (1985) may enhance job stability. Williams and Dreher (1992) showed that banks that provide more generous fringe benefits attract more job applicants. More directly, labor economists find that pension coverage and accumulation deter quits (Ippolito 1991; Mitchell 1983).

The tying of benefit levels, such as pension and vacation time, to tenure on the job may dissuade employees from leaving (Milkovich and Newman 1993). While acknowledging that premature quits (before full vesting) incur loss of pensions, scholars of turnover (and employees) may not realize that exits even after full vesting can impose sizable losses in pensions, which grow with tenure (Ippolito 1991). Common defined-benefits plans distribute smaller pensions to vested employees who quit before retirement age because pension formulas peg benefits to the level of their most recent wages—which freezes at the exit date and loses its purchasing power over time—and years of service (benefits are reduced as service declines) (Milkovich and Newman 1993). Amazingly, job-hoppers who fully vest in several pension plans earn less in pension benefits than do employees spending their entire career in one firm (ibid.). Documenting such potential costs, Ippolito (1991) calculated pension capital losses for 6,416 employees in 109 pension plans and found that if the pension subject to forfeiture is sizable, tenure will be prolonged. His finding may underlie one of the most durable facts about turnover: Quits decline with increasing seniority in a firm (Mobley 1982a).

This framework further suggests that some fringe benefits may promote satisfaction and retention more than others (Miceli and Lane 1991). Opinion polls identify health coverage as the most prized benefit (Clements 1993), but the preferences of employees for this and other benefits will surely vary with personal values (risk aversion, leisure demands), family responsibilities, and age (Miceli and Lane 1991; Milkovich and Newman 1993). Williams and Dreher (1992) found that banks providing more paid time off more readily filled vacant teller positions because this mostly female work force valued time off to meet their parental duties. To provide valued benefits, firms must identify the employees' preferences, perhaps by using surveys for diagnosis (Barber, Dunham, and Formisano 1992; Milkovich and Newman 1993).

According to our thinking, benefit coverage, however generous, fosters satisfaction and retention only if employees understand and appreciate their benefits (Dreher, Ash, and Bretz 1988; Miceli and Lane 1991). As noted above, most employees do not know or they underestimate their fringe benefits (Wilson, Northcraft, and Neale 1985), and such ignorance or misunderstanding can offset the benefit coverage (Dreher, Ash, and Bretz 1988). Effective communication programs—notably, small group meetings and personalized benefit statements—can foster satisfaction about benefits by informing employees of those that are available and the costs to the firm to procure the benefits (Barber, Dunham, and Formisano 1992; Miceli and Lane 1991; Wilson, Northcraft, and Neale 1985).

This model also suggests that employers must limit benefit expenses imposed on employees, who increasingly share the cost of coverage (Dreher,

Ash, and Bretz 1988; Milkovich and Newman 1993). Dreher, Ash, and Bretz (1988) showed that costs paid by employees, such as high premiums and deductibles, diminish satisfaction with the benefit. Conversely, contributions from workers would expand their understanding of the benefits and improve benefit coverage (Wilson, Northcraft, and Neale 1985). Flexible benefit plans may improve knowledge about benefits and the attainment of desired benefits (Barber, Dunham, and Formisano 1992; Miceli and Lane 1991). Williams and Dreher (1992) found that flexible benefits reduced the length of time in which bank-teller positions were vacant, implying that flexible benefits can keep tellers on the job.

In summary, future research must validate the practical implications of this benefit-satisfaction model for curbing turnover. The state of knowledge about the effects of benefits would expand with more investigations into how specific attributes of benefit packages (rather than simple global satisfaction [Heneman 1985]) affect the decisions of individuals to quit. We require more organizational-level studies describing how benefit packages affect quit rates (Dreher, Ash, and Bretz 1988; Hom 1992). Researchers might survey compensation directors (Gomez-Mejia 1992) or access data about firms gathered by compensation consulting firms (Gerhart and Milkovich 1990) which may provide more complete and accurate descriptions about benefit packages than those obtained from individual employees.

Compensation Strategies

The emerging discipline of compensation strategy may suggest new avenues by which compensation can reduce organizational quit rates (Gomez-Mejia and Balkin 1992a; Milkovich and Newman 1993). This perspective defines compensation strategy as the "deliberate utilization of the pay system as an essential integrating mechanism through which the efforts of various subunits and individuals are directed toward the achievement of an organization's strategic objectives" (Gomez-Mejia and Balkin 1992a, p. 35). This conceptualization presumes that the effective implementation of corporate strategy depends on the *appropriate* pay strategy, implying that no single pay strategy is best for all organizations.

For a preliminary test, Hom (1992) investigated the way in which pay strategy affects quit rates. The directors of mental health agencies completed a survey assessing, not only compensation levels, but also decisions and practices about pay—including administrative procedures and criteria for pay increases—that support business strategy (see Gomez-Mejia and Balkin 1992a). Then, Hom correlated the survey responses with overall quit rates among the agencies. The pay strategies that promoted retention of the work force are shown in Table 10-3. Surprisingly, an emphasis on performance incentives rather than on base pay or fringe benefits lowered turnover rates. Pay and benefits that were generous compared with prevailing rates decreased exit rates. Compensation procedures that provide employees with

**Table 10-3 Compensation Practices and Turnover Rates Among
Mental Health Agencies. (P. W. Hom (1992).
Turnover costs among mental health professionals.
College of Business, Arizona State University, Tempe, Ariz.: 102.)**

Compensation Practices	Definition of Compensation Practices	Correlation with Turnover Rates
Pay Mix	Relative emphasis on pay and benefits in total pay package	−.40
Pay Incentives	Emphasis on incentives in employees' earnings	−.60
Risk-Sharing	Employees' earnings vary with success of the organization	−.35
Internal Pay Equity	Pay system emphasizes internal pay equity	−.08
Pay Secrecy	Pay policies and practices are not openly disclosed	.14
Performance-Based Rewards	Job performance rather than job seniority is rewarded	−.33
Pay Centralization	Compensation system is centralized	−.21
Executive Perks	Availability of "perks" (special rewards) to a few employees—i.e., top managers	−.20
Market Competitiveness	Pay and benefits exceed those offered by other employers	−.24
Participative Design	Employees have a say in pay policies	−.29
Job-Based Pay	Pay rates reflect job duties and responsibilities rather than job incumbent's ability or skills	−.25
Long-Term Orientation	Pay system rewards employees for long-term accomplishments	.09
Frequency of Reward	Pay system offers frequent incentives or bonuses	.10
Intrinsic Rewards	Company emphasizes intrinsic rewards, e.g., job enrichment	.16
Bureaucratic Pay Policies	Compensation structure is regimented, with carefully defined procedures	−.18

a voice in pay policies and wages that are based on the responsibilities of the job lessened turnover rates, as did centralized pay policies and the availability of executive perks. Compensation strategy research represents a new paradigm for studying the effects of pay on the overall termination rates of companies and identifying attributes of a pay system, besides the amount of compensation, that reduce quits. Future research should replicate Hom's (1992) exploration with other industries because effective pay strategies that reinforce loyalty are likely to vary across different industries and with different corporate strategies.

DEMOGRAPHIC DIVERSITY

Diversity in race, gender, ethnicity, and nationality increasingly characterizes the modern American work force (Cox 1991). This demographic and cultural heterogeneity will accelerate as women and nonwhite men will constitute 85 percent of the net addition to the labor force between now and the year 2000 (Cox, Lobel, and McLeod 1991; "Pay Equity Makes Good" 1990). Given such demographic trends and a shrinking labor supply, employers will face stiff competition to attract and retain women and members of minorities ("One Company's Approach" 1991; Fisher 1992; "Promoting Women to Upper" 1990). Despite the changing composition of labor, turnover researchers have rarely examined quits among minorities and women or the reason for their quitting (Nkomo 1992). Myriad case studies and journalistic accounts report elevated levels of turnover among minorities and women (Gleckman, Smart, Dwyer, Segal, and Weber 1991; Schwartz 1989). National statistics indicate that Afro-Americans quit 40 percent more frequently than whites do and statistics gathered by Corning Glass and Monsanto show that female professionals leave at twice the rate shown by men (Cox and Blake 1991; Fisher 1992). According to exit surveys of minority and female leavers (James 1988; Schwartz 1989), that exodus may arise from discrimination—real or imagined.

Although the issue is beyond the scope of this book, the well-known racial and gender disparities in pay and rates of promotion do not automatically signal discrimination (Becker 1991; Milkovich and Newman 1993). For one, other factors, such as differences in industry or human capital ("Black College Graduates" 1991; Lobel and St. Clair 1992; Milkovich and Newman 1993), may account for women and minorities earning lower wages or occupying fewer managerial and professional jobs (Morrison and Von Glinow 1990). Even after controlling extraneous factors, statistical findings of unequal outcomes still do not clearly implicate discrimination (Gerhart and Rynes 1991; "Pay Equity Makes Good" 1990; Morrison and Von Glinow 1990). Quite often, aggregate economic statistics poorly proxy or omit nondiscriminatory causes, only partly adjusting those confounds (Brimelow and Spencer 1993; Milkovich and Newman 1993).

Though no longer a matter of dispute, the *extent* of discrimination continues to spur debate (Gerhart and Milkovich 1989). Some pay studies conclude that sexism minimally explains pay gaps, such as young, college-educated women earning 10 percent less pay than their male counterparts (Koretz 1990); others incriminate gender bias as a chief cause, underlying between one-half and one-quarter of pay disparities for women and nonwhites ("Pay Equity Makes Good" 1990). In a rigorous test, after holding constant human capital attributes, family power (the percentage of the family income earned), willingness to relocate, and industry, Stroh, Brett, and Reilly (1992) recently estimated that sex explained a 2 percent unique variance in salary growth among managers in twenty *Fortune*-500 firms. Female managers following the male model of career advancement (college graduation, stable work patterns, employment in higher-paying industries, job relocation, providing the main financial support for the family) still lagged behind male managers in salary. Perhaps the safest conclusion that can be deduced from existing data is that gender and racial gaps reflect both discriminatory and nondiscriminatory causes. With this caveat, we next discuss factors stimulating turnover among minorities and women, recognizing that perceptions of discrimination—whether rooted in reality or not— govern termination decisions. Those potential sources of discrimination are summarized in Figure 10-4.

Supervisor's Bias   The business press pinpoints poor or indifferent treatment from supervisors as prompting minorities and women to quit. Minority leavers describe their supervision as arbitrary and unfair (Gleckman et al. 1991), and 81 percent of surveyed CEOs of *Fortune* 1000 firms believed that stereotyping blocked career advancement for women ("Upward Mobility for Women" 1991). More revealing, organizational studies uncovered evidence that supervisors generally deflate the performance evaluations of minorities and women (Sackett, DuBois, and Noe 1991) and that managers underestimate the accomplishments of their black subordinates, although they favored women over men (Tsui and O'Reilly 1989).

Heilman's "lack of fit" model (1983) parsimoniously explains bias among supervisors. A perceived lack of fit between the requirements of powerful, high-status, high-income jobs and the personal attributes of minorities and women underlies their exclusion from such positions and their deficient performance appraisals (see Figure 10-5). Superiors consider that minorities and women have traits that are stereotypical of their groups and that deviate from the perceived requirements of professional or managerial jobs. Asians or women may be overlooked for management because they are seen as representatives of self-effacing or docile groups that cannot meet the responsibilities of leadership (Mandel and Farrell 1992; Watanabe 1973). A Taiwanese engineer who left Silicon Valley to open up a company overseas recounted how, "No matter how hard I worked, I always remained a technical contributor" (Barnathan, Einhorn, and Nakarmi 1992). Indeed, the token representation of minorities or women in managerial ranks exacerbates the lack-of-fit stereotyping (Kantor 1977; Stockdale 1993). Dominants, that is, white males, more readily attribute stereotyped group attributes to token representatives because there are so few of them—too few to provide enough examples to contradict generalizations. Documenting the effects of tokenism, Sackett, DuBois, and Noe (1991) found that women in work groups in which less than 20 percent of the members are female receive inferior performance appraisals.

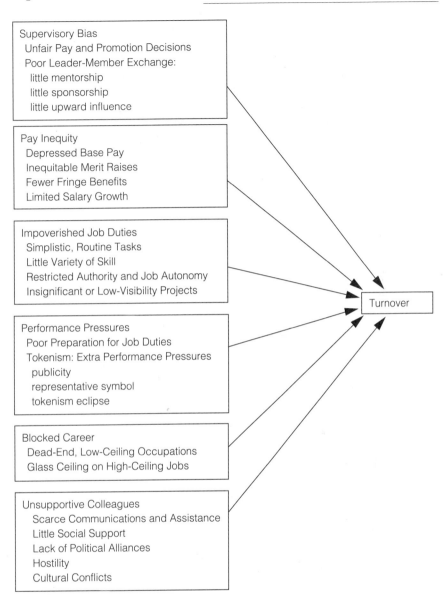

Figure 10-4   Potential Causes of Turnover among Minorities and Women.

Superiors may attribute effective performance by managerial or professional women or minorities to luck rather than ability because their success violates preexisting expectations (Heilman 1983). Superiors may act (or not act) toward minorities or women in ways that undermine their performance, thereby realizing the initial expectations of lack of fit (a self-fulfilling prophecy). They may meet infrequently with those subordinates and inade-

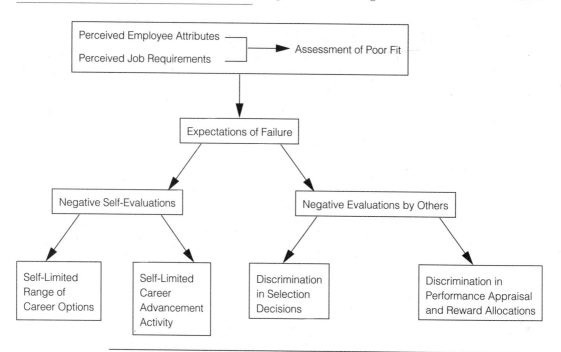

Figure 10-5 Heilman's Lack of Fit Model. (M. E. Heilman, "Sex bias in work settings: The Lack of Fit model," *Research in Organizational Behavior,* **5 (1983): 281.)**

quately communicate the role expectations that would direct their subordinates toward meeting the work goals (Tsui and O'Reilly 1989). Minorities and women may internalize beliefs about their incompetence in nontraditional jobs, thereby suppressing their aspirations for such jobs or doing them less well (Heilman, Rivero, and Brett 1991; Parsons, Herold, and Leatherwood 1985).

Beyond imagined incompetence, minorities and women may not fit managerial occupations because they are not considered trustworthy. According to Kantor (1977), the fundamental problem of managing uncertainty in complex organizations has historically resulted in "homosexual reproduction" in managerial promotions. Because evaluative criteria for managers are indefinite, executives often base their decisions about promotions on trustworthiness and loyalty. White male executives thus select other white men who can be trusted to assume discretionary, responsible positions and share similar attitudes and values (Tsui and O'Reilly 1989). Indeed, the director of executive education at MIT exclaimed, "In tough times, top management prefers to entrust the risks that accompany decision making at the highest levels to a known quantity—meaning someone like themselves. A man" (Fisher 1992).

Heilman (1983) reviewed many studies showing that presumptions that women were not fit for male, sex-typed occupations impaired their employment conditions. Lobel and St. Clair (1992) found that family-oriented women (mostly managers) with preschool children received *higher* merit increases than did family-oriented men with preschoolers, but that career-oriented women with preschoolers received *lower* merit increases than did career-oriented men with preschoolers. Ironically, conformity to traditional gender-role stereotypes (being a family-oriented mom) may offset adverse treatment toward women entering male-dominated careers.

Minorities and women may develop poor leader-member exchanges with their superiors, thereby imperiling their progress. More than 70 percent of *Fortune*-1000 top executives have had mentors (Graen and Scandura 1986; Kantor 1977; Thomas 1993). Yet minorities and women have fewer or less positive mentorships because white male executives prefer to mentor subordinates with whom they can identify (Kantor 1977; Morrison and Von Glinow 1990; Thomas 1993; Tsui and O'Reilly 1989). A third of the CEOs questioned in a recent poll taken by *Fortune* magazine believed that lack of informal advice and sponsors stymie women's careers (Fisher 1992). Given inferior leader-member exchanges, female and minority managers lack influence with their superiors, so their capacity for managing their own subordinates is hampered (Kantor 1977). Besides this, minority and female managers may lack sponsors among top management who could defend them at contested meetings and offer career-enhancing job opportunities (ibid.). These "godfathers" or "rabbis" can also help junior managers bypass the organizational hierarchy—by, for instance, providing inside information—and empower them through "reflected power" (ibid.).

Depressed Earnings   Low or inequitable pay may also escalate quits among women and people of color (Gleckman et al. 1991). Typically, they earn less because they mostly work in low-paying secondary (hourly) jobs (Bovee 1991; Hom 1979; Kantor 1977; Morrison and Van Glinow 1990; Gleckman et al. 1991). Despite their growing admission to management and male-dominated professions, women and minorities still earn less and express more dissatisfaction about their pay ("Black College Graduates" 1991; Morrison and Von Glinow 1990). Morrison and Von Glinow (ibid.) reported that female vice presidents earn 42 percent less than their male peers, and Gerhart and Rynes (1991) found that female MBA graduates who negotiated salary offers attain lower payoffs than did male graduates. Stroh, Brett, and Reilly (1992) impressively demonstrated that female managers earn less than male managers do despite their similar education, family power, industry, employment patterns, and willingness to relocate.

Career Blocks   Limited or blocked promotions underlie turnover, and especially for minority and female departures. Women and minorities primarily hold secondary, hourly jobs, from which advancements are limited or scarce (Cox 1991; Hom 1979; Kantor 1977). Even those assuming professional or managerial jobs progress more slowly than white men do, and the promotions are eventually halted by a "glass ceiling" (Fisher 1992; Morrison and

Von Glinow 1990). No doubt, the limited advancement of women trapped in white-collar "ghettos" (Konrad 1990; Morrison and Von Glinow 1990; Gleckman et al. 1991) and Asians in technical professions (Duleep and Sanders 1992; Mandel and Farrell 1992) reflects occupancy in short-ladder occupations. Cose (1993) termed the predominance of black executives in departments of community relations and public affairs as "pigeon-holing."

Regardless of the reasons that careers stall, a myriad statistics attest to blocked promotions for people of color and women. For instance, women occupy merely 1.7 percent of corporate officerships in the companies comprising the *Fortune* 500 (Morrison and Van Glinow 1990). The Pacific Studies Center concluded that, despite Asians' large presence in Silicon Valley firms, they accounted for less than 10 percent of the management ranks (Mandel and Farrell 1992). More revealing, an inquiry made by the Department of Labor in 1991 uncovered much lower glass ceilings than formerly thought that were restricting women from entering mid- and upper-level management (Garland 1991). Exit surveys of minority and female professionals and managers disclose that blocked careers are a prime reason for escaping corporate life (Cox and Blake 1991; James 1988; Mandel and Farrell, 1992). One-third of 100 leading corporate women profiled in a survey by *Business Week* in 1976 had left corporate America ten years later (Morrison and Von Glinow 1990).

Limited career mobility for minorities and women may also prompt involuntary quits because limited advancement breeds a cycle of disadvantage, reconfirming the belief that they are only competent to work in dead-end jobs. Kantor (1977) observed that women placed on dead-end tracks develop less commitment to the company, downplay their career aspirations, withdraw from extra responsibilities at work, and doubt their competence. As a result, they become undesirable candidates for promotion. If the alienation becomes acute, they are eventually dismissed.

Work Activities   Minorities and women often occupy less intrinsically satisfying jobs, which weaken their loyalty to the organization (Mathieu and Zajac 1990). Many hold hourly jobs, exposing them to routine work in which they have little discretion (Hom 1979; Morrison and Von Glinow 1990). Even female and minority professionals and managers take on less enriched, less challenging work (Cose 1993; Kantor 1977; Morrison and Von Glinow 1990). Nonwhite or female managers may have less authority and autonomy because they lack informal "empowering" alliances with mentors and peers (Cleveland and Kerst 1993; Kantor 1977). Doubting the competence of minorities and women in nontraditional roles (Heilman, Rivero, and Brett 1991), superiors may also give them fewer challenging assignments that solve urgent problems in the organization (Kantor 1977; "Upward Mobility for Women" 1991). Several studies recount how women enjoy fewer developmental assignments involving start-ups, troubleshooting, or international experiences (Morrison and Von Glinow 1990; "OFCCP Glass Ceiling Initiative" 1991). Depriving nonwhites and women of such opportunities makes them less visible to top management and less prepared for executive posts (Garland 1991).

Acceptance by Coworkers   Harassment by white or male coworkers may induce minorities and women to resign. The business press reports widespread antagonism or indifference from white male colleagues (James 1991; Morrison and Von Glinow 1990, who are motivated by prejudice (Heilman 1983; Jones 1972; Stockdale 1993) and dissimilar cultural values (Cox, Lobel, and McLeod 1991; O'Reilly, Caldwell, and Barnett 1989; Tsui and O'Reilly 1989). Angered over pay inequity and the implied rejection by his white colleagues, a black attorney in a law firm declared that he would "go to [his] own people for acceptance" (Cose 1993). Well-publicized affirmative-action programs may arouse a backlash from white men who resent incoming people of color or women, viewing them as unqualified or as jeopardizing their own jobs (Brimelow and Spencer 1993; Cox 1991; Gates 1993; Gleckman et al. 1991; Solomon 1991).

Whatever its origin, rejection from Anglo males impedes the careers of women and minorities, driving them out of the company. Peers facilitate not only the socialization of newcomers but also their effectiveness at work (Cleveland and Kerst 1993; Feldman 1988). Coworkers provide vital information about the job including career advice (Lobel 1993; Luthans, Rosenkrantz, and Hennessey 1985). Professionals and managers require the cooperation of their peers on joint projects and acquire needed power through informal alliances and coalitions with peers (Cleveland and Kerst 1993; Kantor 1977). Superiors often solicit input from coworkers, including reports about collegiality (a critical basis for managerial promotions), for performance evaluations (Cleveland and Kerst 1993; Kantor 1977). Not surprisingly, women queried in a survey by Honeywell cite personal relationships as essential for upward mobility (Konrad 1990).

Performance Pressures   The extra pressures to perform that are imposed on women and nonwhites in nontraditional careers may prompt them to leave the company. They may have been promoted into managerial jobs, for which they lack sufficient experience or training, because the firm is being pressured to achieve affirmative-action goals (Brimelow and Spencer 1993; Gates 1993). Tokens in traditional white male occupations may feel that they must excel (Kantor 1977; Thomas 1993). Basically, tokenism itself induces special performance pressures because of publicity, representative symbolism (being viewed as a symbol of a race or gender category rather than as an individual), and tokenism eclipse (the token's extraneous attributes blotting out the token's achievements) (Kantor 1977). Token minorities or women are highly visible due to their race or gender uniqueness (Morrison and Van Glinow 1990). In the limelight, they face more pressures to conform and to avoid mistakes, which will be glaringly obvious (Kantor 1977). Such conformity may trigger an identity crisis; a black vice president who, because he rarely spoke out against racism (to avoid being typecast as a troublemaker and to further his career), expressed guilt about not "being black" (Cose 1993).

Tokenism enhances the perception—when there are only a few minorities or women in a firm—of their being representative of a category.

Regarded more as symbols than as individuals, tokens strive to be exemplary models to prove that their group can succeed in jobs from which they have been historically excluded. Failure may risks prospects of other representatives of the category. A token's secondary characteristics may obscure his or her accomplishments as an individual. Made distinctive by gender or race, tokens must overachieve to make their performance more noticeable than their auxiliary traits are. Cose (ibid.) writes about an Afro-American woman, a Harvard-educated lawyer, who carries a Bally bag when visiting exclusive shops to assure clerks that she is fit to shop there.

Nonwhite and female newcomers may feel the need to overachieve to avoid being stigmatized by aggressive (and well-publicized) affirmative-action programs (Heilman, Block, and Lucas 1992; Morrison and Von Glinow 1990; Solomon 1991). Minorities or women who have been preferentially selected may feel less competent and devalue their accomplishments more than do those chosen on merit (Heilman, Rivero, and Brett 1991). As a black journalist put it, "Your achievement is defined by your color and its limitation. And even if in reality you've met your fullest potential, there's an aggravating, lingering doubt . . . because you're never sure" (Cose 1993, p. 58). Therefore, member of racial minorities and women must excel to reverse the beliefs of others and themselves that they were unqualified for admission to formerly exclusive jobs (Gleckman et al. 1991).

Sexual Harassment   Sexual harassment is a form of sex discrimination that motivates many women to quit (Gutek and Koss 1993; "How Employees Perceive Sexual Harassment" 1992). Summarizing polls and surveys in the past decade, Fitzgerald and Shullman (1993) estimated that one of every two women has been sexually harassed at some time during her working life. Similarly, in a telephone survey using random-digit dialing of a national sample of working women, it was disclosed that 18 percent have encountered sexual harassment (Gutek and Koss 1993). A poll taken by UCLA in 1992 of women executives (vice presidents and higher) at fifteen hundred major corporations revealed that 59 percent had been sexually harassed at work and that 5 percent of them coped with harassment by leaving (Swingle 1993). According to many broad surveys, 10 percent of harassed women have left employment (Guteck and Koss 1993). A government study projected that the sexual harassment of federal employees cost, over a two-year period, $200 million because of the cost to replace leavers, higher medical-insurance claims and sick leave benefits, and productivity losses (Fitzgerald and Shullman 1993).

Increasingly, firms implement various strategies to deal with sexual harassment and many organizations have enacted policies prohibiting it (Fitzgerald and Shullman 1993; Gutek and Koss 1993). More effective than written policies are personal statements from executives, like that of the CEO of a midwestern utility who circulated a brochure and letter to all seven thousand employees publicizing his "zero tolerance for sexual harassment" (Segal 1992). Employees often complain that management "doesn't walk what it talks" (Pryor, Lavite, and Stoller 1993). Another popular remedy has been sensitivity training for men, the chief culprits of sexual harassment (Cleveland and Kerst 1933), who may mistake friendliness in a woman for sexual overtures and who tend to condone or tolerate sexual harassment (Deutschman 1991; Stockdale 1993). At a minimum, organizations should monitor sexual harassment using psychometrically sound instruments, such as Fitzgerald and Shullman's Sexual Experience Questionnaire (1993) that measures various forms of harassment.

Organizations might screen out job candidates—especially those seeking managerial posts—who might sexually harass others. For this selection, employers might consider Pryor, Lavite, and Stoller's scale, Likelihood to Sexually Harass (LHS) (1993), which has men imagine themselves in ten situations where they control rewards for attractive women and project their likelihood of using rewards to exploit the women sexually. Survey research finds that high-LHS men hold adversarial sexual beliefs and express stronger intentions of rape. Laboratory experiments reveal that high-LHS men (acting as trainers) sexually touched a female trainee more frequently than did low-LHS men after they had earlier witnessed an authority figure sexually harassing the trainee (ibid.).

Employers might structurally change the workplace by improving the balance of females to males in work groups, especially in male sex-typed occupations. Research established that sexual harassment increases with a token female presence in work groups and female incumbency in nontraditional jobs (Deutschman 1991; Fitzgerald and Shullman 1993; Lach and Gwartney-Gibbs 1993). The promotion of more women into management may lessen sexual harassment because, ironically, women working for male superiors face more sexual harassment from their coworkers (Fitzgerald and Shullman 1993). Grievance procedure for filing harassment claims—and safeguards against retaliation—may curb turnover (Gutek and Koss 1993). Anecdotal and survey data reveal that slow-responding complaint systems in which there is no guarantee of confidentiality or protection from reprisal disillusion victims, motivating their departure (Deutschman 1991; Gutek and Koss 1993; "How Employees Perceive Sexual Harassment" 1992; Lach and Gwartney-Gibbs, 1993). A Boston law firm has an ombudsperson counsel victims privately; a Minnesota utility company lets victims file complaints with their superiors, the human resource department, or a panel of peers (Segal 1992); DuPont has a confidential twenty-four hour hotline offering advice on personal safety and sexual harassment (Deutschman 1991).

As firms rush to restrain sexual harassment, certain sociodemographic trends outside the workplace may frustrate these efforts (Lobel 1993). Rising female representation in organizations increases contact between men and women, engendering more nonharassing *and* harassing sexual behavior. The AIDS panic may encourage people to date coworkers, and the escalating divorce rate may encourage the development of more intimate relationships at work to replace dissolving affective relationships at home. According to a recent Gallup poll and not surprisingly, 57 percent of employed Americans view workplace dating as acceptable (ibid.). To deter sexual harassment without interfering with office romances, employers might introduce policies restricting certain forms of sexual behaviors rather than trying to eradicate sexuality from the workplace (ibid.; Segal 1992). In particular, they might prohibit superiors from dating subordinates (which arouses the most collegial resentment and legal suits) and have in place policies embodying definitions by women of unsuitable forms of sexuality in the workplace. A "reasonable woman" standard that sets company norms may best combat sexual harassment because it is women—more readily than men—who interpret certain acts as sexual harassment (Segal 1992; Stockdale 1993).

In the wake of the confirmation hearings for Clarence Thomas and the Navy's Tailhook scandal, many companies have hurriedly initiated training to combat sexual harassment. Yet a recent review of the sexual harassment literature concluded that "virtually no attempt has been made to evaluate the outcomes of sexual harassment training interventions" (Fitzgerald and Shullman 1993, p. 16). Echoing this complaint, we further recommend evaluations of sexual harassment programs for reducing turnover among women and men.

White Male Flight   Paradoxically, the entry of minorities and women into the workplace may induce exits among white men by dissolving group cohesion—because there are more conflicts and miscommunications with different peoples—threatening their self-identity (Tsui, Egan, O'Reilly 1992). Self-categorization theory implies that people often base their identify on social categories, such as gender and race (ibid.), preferring homogeneous groups of others who are similar because these groups contain the "self" (Nkomo 1992). They view out-group members as being different from and less attractive than their in-group. Because social identity is derived from membership in homogeneous groups, the members will maintain their standing and protect the group from undesirable outsiders. The changing demographic composition of the referent group—the White Male Club—undermines the group as a basis for social identify and self-esteem. Some white men may thus ask themselves, "Do I belong here?," and decide to resign.

Upholding this theory, Tsui Egan, and O'Reilly (1992) found that growing female representation in 151 work units diminished the men's commitment to the organization and their inclination to stay. Increasing minority concentration in the units intensified white flight. These provocative findings question the conventional assumption behind the cultural diversity movement that heterogeneity inevitably enhances harmony between races and between the sexes. In fact, it is neglected facilitating conditions, such as superordinate goals, that best surmount tension between heterogeneous members of a group.

Imagined or actual reverse discrimination may motivate white men to desert companies that are aggressively promoting affirmative action. Many white men feel that affirmative-action programs have become a means to discriminate against them rather than a way to eradicate racial and sexual discrimination (Gates 1993). One white male in ten expressed, in a poll taken in 1984, the belief that quotas had cost them promotions (Brimelow and

Spencer 1993). Similarly, a national poll taken by *Newsweek* magazine revealed that 48 percent of white men believe that "white males should fight against affirmative-action programs"; only 36 percent rejected this opinion (Cose 1993). Such sentiments are, no doubt, fueled by employers who notify white male applicants that they were denied employment so that the company might meet affirmative-action goals (ibid.; Solomon 1991). Though face-saving, this rationale surely infuriates the excluded white males, who feel that they unfairly lost jobs or promotions to unqualified minorities or women. Perceived or real reverse discrimination may thus dissolve the commitment of white men to organizations.

Immigration and Foreign Ownership   Rising immigration—new immigrants generated 39 percent of the total population growth between 1980 and 1990—threatens native-born Americans (Mandel and Farrell 1992). Quite likely, the growing presence of immigrants in the domestic workplace may breed higher turnover among immigrants and Americans alike. Increasing cultural heterogeneity in work groups may produce more interpersonal conflicts and quits (O'Reilly, Caldwell, and Barnett 1989; Tsui and O'Reilly 1989). Many immigrant scientists and engineers have abandoned Silicon Valley firms to set up their own businesses because they faced impediments to their careers (Mandel and Farrell 1993). Paradoxically, immigrants may encounter more hostility from minorities than from Anglo-Americans as immigrants and minorities often compete in the same labor markets. For example, a Harris poll relates that 73 percent of blacks believe that business would rather hire immigrants than black Americans (Mandel and Farrell 1992).

Conversely, Americans increasingly work for foreign-owned companies that, owing to cultural prejudice, may discriminate against them (Palich, Hom, and Griffeth in press; Payson and Rosen 1991). The Japanese Labor Ministry estimated that 57 percent of 331 Japanese firms operating in America face discrimination lawsuits (Payson and Rosen 1991). For $2.7 million, Sumitomo Corp. settled a suit brought by female secretaries charging denial of promotions and pay raises in favor of male Japanese coworkers. A federal court ruled that Quasar discriminated against Americans by reserving certain managerial posts for Japanese nationals (ibid.) Honda of America resolved a $6 million case over allegations that its hiring requirement—that workers live within thirty miles of its plant (even *before* applying for a job)—adversely impacted the employment of minorities (ibid.).

Cultural Diversity Management

Responding to changing demographics in the work force, many large corporations have sought to improve their management of cultural diversity, Cox (1991) developed a taxonomy of cultural diversity management and catalogued practices that advance the goals of cultural diversity. Cox's typology of diversity management techniques and the objectives they serve are summarized in Figure 10-6. He proposed pluralism as a primary corporate objective:

Goals	Implementation Procedures
I. Pluralism Aid minority culture Influence on company norms and values	A. Managing/valuing diversity training B. New member orientation C. Language training D. Diversity on key committees E. Advisory groups to top management F. Diversity in mission statements
II. Structural Integration Representation at all job levels and functions	A. Educational programs B. Affirmative action C. Targeted career development D. Managerial appraisals and rewards for diversity goals E. Flexible work schedules
III. Integration into Informal Networks Remove barriers to entry and participation	A. Mentoring programs B. Sponsored social events
IV. Cultural Tolerance Reduce prejudice	A. Equal-opportunity seminars B. Focus groups C. Bias-reduction training D. Internal research on status of minorities and women
V. Intergroup Cooperation Reduce conflict among demographically different Reduce white-male backlash	A. Education for white males about inferior status and progress of minorities and women B. Conflict-management training

Figure 10-6 Managing Cultural Diversity. (T. Cox, "The Multicultural Organization," *Academy of Management Executive,* **5 (2) (1991): 41.)**

the valuing of cultural differences to the extent of permitting minority culture to shape company culture. Attesting to the significance of this goal, a black woman leaving corporate America believed that there her race was seen not as an asset but as something she had to overcome (Cose 1993). To further pluralism, Cox recommended specific training, such as managing and valuing training in cultural diversity (communications about the cultural norms of different groups), the orientation of new members (help for minority and female workers to adjust to their new jobs), and language training (for instance, English instruction for immigrants). Beyond training, Cox argued that support from top management is essential in fostering pluralism. Toward this end, he prescribed that minorities and women be represented on key committees, the inclusion of goals for diversity in mission statements, and the establishment of advisory groups—comprising minorities and women—for senior management to provide advice on improving diversity in the work force. (Avon's Multicultural Participation Council or U.S. West's Pluralism Council are examples.)

Cox (1991) also suggested structural integration—the broad representation of minorities and women at all organizational levels and functions—as another goal of diversity. This suggestion accords with perspectives on power conflicts, which contend that the abolition of the racial division of labor in firms will attack the basic source of discrimination: the desire of management to weaken the workers' collective strength and to preserve its domination (Nkomo 1992). Affirmative action for top-level jobs ("Moving Past Affirmative" 1990), educational efforts to develop the skills of minorities, special career-development programs (McDonald's "Black Career Development Program"), inclusion of diversity management in managerial appraisals and rewards, and introduction of flexible work arrangements and schedules (to reduce the conflicts between work and family that burden women) can further structural integration. Xerox is striving for a 35 percent female representation in 300 top executive jobs in one division by 1995 and holds managers accountable for that goal ("Moving Past Affirmative" 1990). Baxter International and Monsanto tie managers' raises to affirmative-action goals (Fisher 1992; Konrad 1990).

Besides this, cultural-diversity programs might promote integration in informal networks (Cox 1991). Mentoring programs, company-sponsored social events, and support groups (associations sharing information and social support) for minorities can further the involvement of minorities in networks. Security Pacific's "Black Officers Support System" recruits and retains blacks (Morrison and Von Glinow 1990); Honeywell and Pacific Bell team promising women and minorities with experienced executives who coach them on career strategies and corporate politics (Fisher 1992; Konrad 1990). Sustaining the validity of such prescriptions, surveys describe effective diversity programs as embodying networking, mentorships, and the requirement that management be accountable for achieving results in diversity ("Managing Diversity: Success" 1991).

Effective diversity management must also combat prejudice. Seminars on equal opportunity, focus groups (small groups confronting attitudes and feelings about differences within the group, such as Digital's "Valuing Differences" groups ["Moving Past Affirmative" 1990]), bias-reduction training (attacking prejudice), and company reports on the progress of the careers of minority and female employees may lessen bigotry in the work force. Some companies have instituted a tracking system for minority and female managers to insure that they acquire enough developmental experience to move up the corporate ladder ("One Company's Approach" 1991; "OFCCP's Glass Ceiling" 1991). A task force organized by Equitable Financial ("Women's Business Resource Group") addresses women's problems identified by its surveys. Finally, effective diversity management should minimize conflict within groups (Solomon 1991). In particular, communiques describing the special difficulties of minorities and women at work or combating misperceptions of their reputed incompetence may temper white male

Policy	Maximum Score
Flexible Schedule	105
Family Leave	40
Financial Assistance	80
Corporate Giving and Community Service	60
Dependent-Care Services	155
Management Change	90
Work-Family Stress Management	80
Total Possible Score	610

Figure 10-7 Index of Corporate Family-Friendliness. (A. Bernstein, J. Weber, and L. Driscoll. "Corporate America is still no place for kids," *Business Week*, Reprinted from page 236 of November 25, 1991 issue of Business Week by special permission, copyright © 1991 by McGraw-Hill, In.c.

backlash, and conflict-resolution training may help supervisors to manage conflicts among different ethnic groups. Cox (1991) proposed a family of promising techniques for promoting cultural diversity that may help minorities and women stay on the job. Given the growing significance of cultural diversity, further research must validate those methods (Morrison and Von Glinow, 1990) for supportive evidence comes mostly from testimonials ("Managing Diversity: Success" 1991; "One Company's Approach" 1991).

MANAGING INTERROLE CONFLICT

The massive entry of women into the work force further compels organizations to accommodate conflicts between work and family (Galen 1993). Mothers of preschool-aged children are the fastest growing segment of the labor force (Milliken, Dutton, and Beyer 1990). On top of these developments, representatives of single-parent and dual-income families in the workplace now outnumber representatives of traditional nuclear households (Bernstein, Weber, and Driscoll 1991; Farrell 1992; Galen 1993; Zedeck and Mosier 1990). Twenty-five percent, double that in 1980, of the working-age population now cares for aging relatives (O'Reilly 1992; Shellenbarger 1992). These demographic trends portend increasing conflicts between and work and family for employees, and especially for women who traditionally bear domestic obligations (Kossek 1990; Ralston and Flanagan 1985; Zedeck and Mosier, 1990). The Department of Labor found that, of all women opting out of work in 1986, 33 percent did so to devote more time to the family; of all men who did so, 1 percent cited that reason (Mattis 1990). Likewise, a survey by Yankelovich Clancy Shulman disclosed that nearly 33 percent of working mothers want to quit to become full-time homemakers (Spiers 1992).

Such escalating interrole conflict may be likely to translate into higher quits, especially among women (O'Driscoll, Ilgen, and Hildreth 1992; Galen 1993; Hom, Kinicki, and Domm 1989; Kossek 1990). Long-term career studies find that many teachers and nurses leave their professions to satisfy domestic duties (Donovan 1980; Murnane, Singer, and Willett 1989). A survey by a public utility found that many working women contemplate quitting to rear children (Kossek 1990). Addressing this cause of turnover, firms have introduced various interventions to help employees balance the responsibilities of career and family (Bernstein, Weber, and Driscoll 1991; Galen 1993; Schwartz 1992). The National Council of Jewish Women found, in a nationwide study of twenty-six hundred pregnant women, that women working in firms that accommodated pregnancy prolonged their employment by one and a half months. An inquiry by the U.S. Census Bureau showed that 71 percent of women who received maternity benefits, but only 43 percent of those without benefits, returned to work within six months of childbirth (Trenk 1990). In the following section, we discuss promising approaches catalogued by Zedeck and Mosier (1990): maternity and parental leave; child- and dependent-care services; alternative work schedules; and telecommuting. The Families and Work Institute used these strategies to devise an overall company index, shown in Figure 10-7, of family-friendliness (Bernstein, Weber, and Driscoll 1991).

Family Leave

Exit interviews and surveys find that may women forsake the workplace—temporarily or permanently—to bear or raise children (Gerson 1985; Huey and Hartley 1980). Maternity or parental leave would doubtlessly reduce exits (Cook 1989; Johnson 1990). In particular, the 1993 Family and Medical Leave Act may sustain loyalty by guaranteeing women *and* men twelve weeks of unpaid leave for childbirth or family sickness. This bill ensures that the same or a similar job is available upon return and that health-insurance coverage continues during the leave. Though they ease conflicts between work and family, these federal provisions are still limited. The law excludes firms employing fewer than fifty workers, and unlike many European laws, does not mandate *paid* leave. Some firms offer more generous benefits than the law requires, especially informally (Bernstein 1991b). Forty percent of working women have partial or full *paid* maternity leave, which they largely receive as a disability or sickness benefit. New parents at AT&T can receive up to a year's unpaid leave (Galen 1993; Zedeck and Mosier 1990).

Notwithstanding their promise (Nobile 1990), there is little corroboration that family leave policies truly reduce exits, a prime motive for their adoption (Bernstein, Weber, and Driscoll 1991; Galen 1993). Because other family-responsive measures were implemented simultaneously, the studies mentioned above merely suggest that accommodation for pregnancy lowers quits (Trenk 1990). Aetna Life & Casualty introduced family leave because 23 percent of the women returning to work after childbirth left later (ibid.)

This leave—allowing new mothers up to six months off without pay—and accommodation for part-time work halved turnover. Similarly, the availability of extended parental leave possibly explained why 90 percent of new mothers returned to AT&T within six months of delivery (Galen 1993).

Child & Dependent Care Services

Increasingly, business provides daycare services, usually in the form information and referral programs or flexible spending accounts (Goff, Mount, and Jamison 1990; O'Reilly 1992; Zedeck and Mosier 1990). Most employees with children prefer on- or near-site childcare, which is also the costliest daycare service (Kossek 1990; Zedeck and Mosier 1990, Yalow 1990). Even though Goff, Mount, and Jamison (1990) found that on-site child-care did not decrease conflicts between work and family, the Campbell Soup Company claimed that on-site child-care at its headquarters lowered quits (Yalow 1990). More convincingly, Milkovich and Gomez (1976) showed that mothers who enrolled their children in company-sponsored daycare quit less often than did mothers who did not. Youngblood and Chambers-Cook (1984) discerned that the availability of daycare decreased employees' intentions to withdraw.

Alternative Work Schedules

Alternative work schedules may help employees balance home and work duties. Experimental tests find that flexitime does not impact quits (Dalton and Mesch 1990; Ralston and Flanagan 1985). Compressed work schedules—longer hours but for fewer days—may build company loyalty by giving the employees more days to handle other duties (Pierce and Dunham 1992). Compressed work weeks—with recuperative days off—can compensate for the disruptive effects—psychological and for the family—of shift rotation, a leading cause of turnover (Choi, Jameson, Brekke, Podratz, and Mundahl 1986; Newby 1980; Zedeck, Jackson, and Summers 1983). Pierce and Dunham (1992) showed that police officers on shorter work weeks experienced higher morale and greater ability to handle outside demands.

Case studies and other empirical work indicate that part-time work and job-sharing—two employees share a full-time position—can reduce resignations (Galen 1993; Shellenbarger 1992; Zedeck and Mosier 1990). Hospitals have long experimented with part-time and temporary work to retain nurses and lure inactive nurses back into nursing (Bogdanich 1991; Huey and Hartley 1988; Laird 1983; Newby 1980; Wandelt, Pierce, and Widdowson 1981). Many mothers in other occupations credit part-time schedules and job-sharing for their return to work (Johnson 1990; Mattis 1990). In a national survey taken in 1990, 39 percent of women endorsed part-time work for women with children (Bernstein 1991a). In professional firms, woman lawyers and certified public accountants can, increasingly, work part-time and benefit from extended paths to partnership (Ehrlich 1989), although such "mommy tracks" may derail their careers (Schwartz 1989). Sixty-eight percent of the employers surveyed by Catalyst believed that part-time work and job-sharing improve the retention of women employees. NationsBank Corp offers valued employees job-sharing to retain them (Shellenbarger 1992).

Telecommuting

Telecommuting—working at home and electronically transferring the results to the office—helps working parents because they are more available during the day and do not have to commute (Zedeck and Mosier 1990). In an early study, interviews with female office employees disclosed that telecommuting allowed them to care for children and strengthened their commitment to the organization (Olson and Primps 1984). Yet they earned lower pay and fewer benefits and faced *more* conflict over the simultaneous demands of work and family. Male professionals reported less work stress (for interruptions were fewer and office politics less demanding), and commuting stress, while enjoying more leisure opportunities—weekday recreation avoids weekend crowds.

Many businesses are experimenting with family-assistance programs to help employees balance their personal lives with their work. Evaluations of these efforts have primarily examined the overall impact of a host of family-responsive measures. Seventy-one percent of Johnson & Johnson employees using flexitime and family leave stated that these programs were "very important" in their decisions to stay; Continental Corporation's family-friendly programs, including job-sharing and telecommuting, halved its voluntary exit rates (Galen 1993). A Duke Power customer-service center reduced turnover after introducing a child-care center and compressed work weeks and eliminating shift rotations; its annual quit rate was 12 percent compared with typical quit rates of 40 percent in telephone-call centers nationwide (ibid.).

Despite these impressive statistics, more rigorous experimental (or quasi-experimental) tests of how effectively family-responsive measures deter resignations are sparse. To date, validation rests mainly on testimonials of successful examples (which may not be representative cases) (Goff, Mount, and Jamison 1990; Kossek and Grace 1990). The few empirical evaluations that do exist are plagued by various methodological shortcomings. lacking control groups and statistical controls for extraneous confounds (Miller 1984). Companies usually instate several family benefits simultaneously, making it difficult to isolate the efficacy of a particular intervention (see Trenk 1990). In the light of rising demands in the work force for family benefits, more scholarly inquiry is urgently warranted to determine which approaches promote job tenure (Kossek and Grace 1990).

FUTURE DIRECTIONS
IN TURNOVER RESEARCH

In this last chapter, we suggest an agenda for future research on employee turnover. What topics merit further attention from organizational scholars? Having reviewed the field, we would venture that the following topics are worthy of attention: the development and testing of theories; methods of reducing turnover; models of the consequences of turnover; and research on alternative responses to dissatisfaction.

Our review of current research on predictors of and theories about turnover suggests that there is more room for theoretical advancement. In particular, a theoretical synthesis of the varied existing formulations might develop more comprehensive formulations and shrink the plethora of alternative conceptualizations. For example, future research might build on Griffeth and Hom's integration (1990) of Mobley's and Price and Mueller's models (1977 and 1986, respectively) or the current model inductively derived from our meta-analysis of turnover predictors. Similarly, Lee and Mitchell (1994) construed Mobley's withdrawal process (1977) as representing one of four different decision paths by which employees relinquish their jobs.

Although theoretical parsimony is desirable, we must also consider new explanatory constructs or processes overlooked by prevailing thinking about withdrawal. In particular, the way in which prospective leavers form impressions of the labor market is critically important for the development of theory given the centrality of this construct in modern conceptualizations (Steel and Griffeth 1989). Steel and Griffeth (1989), took a preliminary step in this direction by identifying various elements that are possibly underlying impressions of alternative jobs and Lee and Mitchell (1994) pioneered the notion of the "shock to the system" as a means by which the labor market can affect withdrawal. Turnover models must elaborate the search and evaluation of work alternatives. To date, representation of this process is oversimplified (Hom and Griffeth 1991) or underrepresented (Price and Mueller 1986). Lee and Mitchell (1994) recently proposed that employees perform tests of compatibility and profitability to compare alternatives. The determination that such judgmental processes posited in image theory truly underlie termination decisions awaits further scholarly inquiry. The growing research on job-search and job-choice processes may enrich formulations of turnover, although most of this work has described the ways in which new entrants to the work force seek work rather than the ways in which people already in the labor force switch jobs (Schwab, Rynes, and Aldag 1987).

Writers on turnover increasingly acknowledge the essentiality of commitments outside the workplace but fail to specify precisely how they influence the withdrawal process (Hom, Caranikis-Walker, Prussia, and Griffeth 1992; Hulin, Roznowski, and Hachiya 1985; Mobley, Griffeth, Hand, and Meglino

1979; Price and Mueller 1986; Steers and Mowday 1981). Do employees who are resigning to meet external commitments undergo a different process of withdrawal from those who are seeking alternative work? Unlike job-seeking leavers, they may likely *not* proactively seek outside pursuits (as they would other jobs) nor directly compare them (on commensurate dimensions) with their current employment. Even so, sociological descriptions of women's decisions to abandon employment disclose that they do compare the relative costs and benefits of continued participation in the work force and the income foregone to raise or bear children (Gerson 1985). Do leavers seeking different outside pursuits undertake different termination processes? Do, for instance, quitters returning to college withdraw from the workplace in a different way from those who quit to bear children? Taking a novel approach, Lee and Mitchell's unfolding theory (1994) suggests that nonwork factors affect resignations through shocks and checks for image violations.

Adaptation models may refine prevailing turnover models, explaining why dissatisfaction does not automatically engender resignation. Conventional thinking holds that only failure to find other employment interrupts the translation from dissatisfaction to exit (see Mobley 1977). Yet this presumption of a passive (escape) response to deteriorating work conditions overlooks proactive attempts to change work conditions or affective states (Hulin, Roznowski, and Hachiya 1985). Researchers must consider how other adaptive responses to dissatisfaction (voice, loyalty, neglect, and other exit acts, such as absenteeism) can also abort the termination process. For example, do voice responses increase the "expected utility of internal roles" (that is, improve future work conditions), thereby reducing withdrawal cognitions and quitting (Hom, Kinicki, and Domm 1989)? Alternatively, do dissatisfied employees who "neglect" their job duties (decrease their job inputs) relieve dissatisfaction (ending the withdrawal process [Hulin 1991]) or do performance declines represent the first step toward eventual withdrawal from the job (McEvoy and Cascio 1987)? Adaptation theories may reformulate existing turnover models, specifying why some dissatisfied employees quit immediately, while others perform other adaptive responses before leaving.

Turnover models must further clarify the *process* by which distal causal determinants shape attitudes toward a job. Two schools of theory development dominate present-day perspectives on turnover. One school emphasizes the process by which causes affect exits (Lee and Mitchell 1994; Mobley 1977; Rusbult and Farrell 1983); the other strives to specify exhaustively the content of turnover determinants (Mobley, Griffeth, Hand, and Meglino 1979; Price and Mueller 1981, 1986; Steers and Mowday 1981). Future theory-building efforts must merge both approaches to enrich our understanding of turnover. Griffeth and Hom (1990) combined Mobley's process model (1977) with Price and Mueller's content model (1986). Though encouraging, this integrated model still did not explain the *process(es)* by which immediate determinants of job satisfaction and organizational commitment influence those attitudes. Do poor wages diminish job satisfaction because of a discrepancy in the perceived and desired levels of rewards or because of inequity between job inputs and reward outcomes? This question deserves further atention and it is possible that sociopsychological writings on attitude formation would have some bearing on it. Comprehensive accounts of the mechanisms through which distal antecedents translate into job attitudes may implicate several processes, such as equity comparisons and unmet expectations, and better clarify how individual differences affect the withdrawal process (see Griffeth and Hom 1988b; Mobley 1977; Steers and Mowday 1981).

THEORY TESTING

Our review of extant tests of turnover theories suggests the usefulness of more panel investigations (applying structural equations modeling [SEM] techniques) to validate their causal assumptions and to trace causal lag times of the determinants. Future work should use survival analysis to test theoretical models, which thus far have simply estimated the predictive efficacy of an arbitrary set of predictors of turnover (see Morita, Lee, and Mowday 1993). We might extend their ability to predict not only the occurrence of turnover, but also its timing. Additionally, SEM tests that compare and contrast the differences and similarities of turnover models can further their theoretical integration (Cabrera, Nora, and Casteneda 1993).

We recommend more causal modeling extensions of traditional meta-analyses to validate turnover models (Hom, Caranikis-Walker, Prussia, and Griffeth 1992). Procedures that combine the strengths of meta-analysis and SEM techniques may bolster methodological rigor in testing complete models (ibid.) SEM meta-analytical tests can evaluate models that, in most studies, have been only partially assessed or have *never* been directly tested (see Premack and Hunter 1988). This new methodological strategy does, however, create other methodological problems, among them, the potential distortion of SEM results that stem from the analysis of correlations (rather than covariances) derived from incomplete data. We welcome more methodological research on ways to correct biases in SEM estimates that are based on such common meta-analytical data.

Although mundane, more construct validation would advance understanding of the turnover process as well as improve the validation of turnover formulations. As discussed earlier, construct validation would decide whether determinants of turnover are truly distinctive or are redundant constructs. Such investigations may also reveal that apparently dissimilar explanatory constructs reflect a common higher-order construct, thereby yielding more parsimonious theoretical constructs (James and James 1989). Further efforts at construct validation should operationalize model variables with maximally heterogeneous methods to verify convergent validity. In the wake of Feldman and Lynch's methodological critique (1988), scholars of turnover must vigorously undertake safeguards against shared-method bias in tests of construct and substantive validity.

Future research should investigate the generality of withdrawal theories. Most theorists of turnover presume that their models hold universally, overlooking the possibility that formulations may falter in some subpopulations or settings (see Lee and Mitchell 1994; Palich, Hom, and Griffeth in press). Given the growing diversity of the domestic work force, the generality of models across different genders and ethnic minorities (including new immigrants) will doubtlessly become a pivotal concern in turnover research. To be sure, theorists of turnover should explicitly acknowledge discrimination (including sexual harassment) in the workplace as a prospective source of resignations by women and minorities. Future work must then determine if discrimination only affects the withdrawal process by inducing job dissatisfaction. If it does, process models of turnover may generalize for women and racial minorities; if it does not, the dominant conceptualizations may require more substantive revision (Hom, Caranikis-Walker, Prussia, and Griffeth 1992).

American firms are internationalizing and employing more local nationals abroad (Palich, Hom, and Griffeth in press). To illustrate, American-owned assembly plants, *maquiladoras*, along the U.S.-Mexican border employ roughly half a million Mexicans (Hom, Gomez-Mejia, and Grabke 1993). This global development raises skepticism about the cross-cultural stability of domestic models of turnover and domestic methods to control turnover (Palich, Hom, and Griffeth in press). A recent examination of incentives in the *maquiladoras* contradicted conventional assumptions about material inducements for workforce loyalty, finding that only a few incentives effectively diminished rates of quitting among Mexican workers, which routinely exceed 100 percent annually (Hom, Gomez-Mejia, and Grabke 1993). Foreign owners are increasingly hiring Americans and still expect to be able to apply home-country practices to induce corporate fidelity. Our turnover models may misportray the process of withdrawal from foreign employers who may be culturally distant from their American work force. In particular, Japanese "welfare corporatism" has evoked much controversy about the capacity of Japanese factory owners to build company commitment among American workers (Lincoln 1989). Turnover scholars should find out whether their formulations generalize to offshore settings and to employment within foreign-owned corporations.

Global competition has accelerated the employment of part-time and contingent employees as companies strive to control labor costs and downsize their work force. Temporary work has accounted for 28 percent of the growth of new jobs in the U.S. economy during the 1993 recovery ("Joyless Recovery" 1993). In growing numbers, writers on turnover suspect that current formulations of turnover misrepresent organizational withdrawal among marginal drifters and workers in secondary labor markets (see Hulin, Roznowski, and Hachiya 1985; Lee and Mitchell 1994). We must attempt to validate or extend our conceptions to include this rising segment of the working population. Admittedly, turnover researchers must initially show that the attrition of peripheral workers is costly to firms. The burgeoning temporary-help industry may welcome scholarly explorations into why "temps." quit work and how to retain them.

Turnover researchers must design more comprehensive models of turnover rates at the organization level (see Terborg and Lee 1984). Existing research on turnover among individuals or between industries may not generalize to the firm level, where many managerial decisions about wholesale interventions to lower quits are made (Hom, Gomez-Mejia, and Grabke 1993). The derivation of companywide prescriptions from prevailing psychological or labor-economic evidence may risk the ecological fallacy (Rousseau 1985). Work on quits by individuals may suggest prospective sources of variations in rates of turnover across companies (see Terborg and Lee 1984), but organizational theories may identify more crucial determinants of companywide quit rates (Price 1977). Once developed, organizational-level models may fill a void in our knowledge about organizational-level turnover and suggest more effective means to combat elevated organizational rates of turnover.

TURNOVER REDUCTION METHODS

In our review of the means of managing turnover, we concluded that nonexperimental or anecdotal data primarily upheld their validity. Future inquiry should apply quasi-experimental and experimental evaluations to determine more rigorously whether promising interventions can promote job survival. Rather than more tests on realistic job previews and job enrichment, we prescribe more investigations on alternative methods of turnover reduction that may better retain employees. In particular, we recommend more evaluation research on workspace protections against overstimulation, socialization practices, and leader-member exchanges.

Beyond this, future tests might redress the traditional overemphasis on intrinsic approaches for curbing exits (Brief and Aldag 1989). More studies on the efficacy of pecuniary inducements would be useful. In particular, the new discipline of compensation strategy suggests various economic interventions (apart from pay raises) for boosting retention rates in a firm (see Hom 1992). To deploy pay strategies effectively, turnover scholars must identify those that are compatible with the company's strategy (Gomez-Mejia and Balkin 1992a; Milkovich and Newman 1993). Gomez-Mejia and Balkin (1992a) demonstrated that business strategy determines the pay strategies that promote organizational effectiveness. By implication, an ideal pay strategy that deters turnover for all organizations may not exist. Consequently, turnover researchers must discover which compensation strategies "fit" which type of organizations (and which business strategy) to maximize the retention of the work force. Here again, the development of theories of organizational-level quit rates might identify appropriate pay strategies.

We further prescribe the consideration of financial incentives that retain highly skilled and very proficient employees—key-contributor awards and variable-pay schemes, respectively. In the wake of corporate downsizing and depressed job markets, managerial and academic interest in how to reduce overall quit rates has sharply eroded. Interest may shift to the problem of preventing the resignations of valuable employees. Turnover researchers must investigate pay incentives that reinforce the company loyalty of desired personnel, while encouraging the flight of undesired personnel (Williams and Livingstone 1994).

Turnover scholars must begin to consider specific methods for decreasing attrition among women and racial minorities, whose quit rates greatly surpass that of white men (Cose 1993). In particular, more turnover work should be done to evaluate which of the plethora of cultural-diversity programs truly bind women and minorities to firms and to pinpoint the psychological mechanisms for their efficacy. Such evaluations should also consider whether diversity programs inadvertently induce white male flight or whether they sustain company loyalty among *all* members of the work force (Tsui, Egan, and O'Reilly 1992). Turnover research should investigate the process by which the sexual harassment of men as well as of women encourages terminations and the forms of prohibitions against sexual harassment that best enhance job incumbency. As family benefits pervade the workplace, tests of their ability to build company commitment become ever more important.

As attested to by traditional work on weighted application blanks, it is quite likely that more selection research would maximize payoffs for turnover management (Muchinsky and Tuttle 1979). Turnover researchers have neglected this methodology because of its reputed dustbowl empiricism and the potentially adverse impact on the employment of women and minorities. Yet biographical predictors can be chosen according to theoretical considerations (following speculations about the types of people who are happy in a given job) and discriminatory items discarded (Breaugh and Dossett 1989; Gatewood and Feild 1987). Biodata methodology using broad autobiographic measures of an applicant's background may further enhance predictions of turnover. Although less verifiable and more subjective than weighted application blanks are, biodata questions (such as self-reported satisfaction with previous jobs) may better detect the elusive "hobo syndrome" or negative affectivity (Hulin 1991; Judge 1992). The predictive accuracy of biodata questions may vary different jobs (see Gatewood and Feild 1987). Survival analysis may disclose whether biographical predictors can forecast turnover timing and multiple turnover episodes (Morita, Lee, and Mowday 1993; Singer and Willett 1991).

We must also reconsider the possibility that current retention-building practices are no longer effective in the wake of widespread corporate restructuring (shrinking promotional opportunities) and downsizing (reducing job insecurity). Japanese scholars have long observed that Japanese firms earn the commitment of workers in exchange for guarantees of permanent employment (Lincoln 1989; Lincoln and Kalleberg 1985) When such fundamental underpinnings of organizational loyalty are steadily eroding, can existing enticements still retain employees or must we revise our commitment-boosting practices (offer, for instance, more monetary inducements in lieu of stable employment), or devise new approaches? The emergence of self-managing work teams may develop into a new means of binding employees to companies (Manz and Sims 1993). These work teams promise more social rewards, job enlargement, and empowerment for team members, possibly replacing the status and perks of declining opportunities for managerial advancement (Hom and Miller 1992).

MODELING TURNOVER CONSEQUENCES

Our review further recommends more scholarly exploration into the consequences of turnover for individuals and organizations. Beyond the simple effects, more elaborate conceptualizations that take into account all the possible ramifications of turnover may more precisely project its net impact. Such modeling efforts may identify countervailing trends that are activated by turnover and work at cross-purposes to it, possibly cancelling out any impact. Longitudinal research is warranted to track the consequences of turnover over time; short-term effects may differ from long-term effects. The exodus of top executives from a corporation may prove temporarily disruptive but eventually insure the long-term survival of the firm as incoming executives revitalize a declining business with new strategies. More research on identifying the moderators of the consequences of turnover is merited.

ALTERNATIVE RESPONSES TO DISSATISFACTION

Adaptation theories about how different response families relieve dissatisfaction constitute probably the most promising theoretical developments in turnover thinking. Disputing traditional perspectives of withdrawal as a surface phenomenon, this school of thought contends that turnover is symptomatic of maladaptation (Hulin 1991). This rethinking promises several benefits. First, in conceiving quits as one form of withdrawal and withdrawal as one of several response families that lessen disaffection among employees, we might derive more parsimonious but far-reaching formulations. Unlike prevailing accounts of turnover, these alternative viewpoints strive to explain a wider array of reactions to dissatisfaction. Second, these reconceptualizations yield practical insights, suggesting that other adaptive actions (including short-term withdrawal and worsening performance) may provide early signals of impending job exits.

These theoretical views suggest that interventions that combat turnover may breed unfavorable side effects. For example, employees who are "handcuffed" to their jobs (because they receive generous compensation benefits) may express their dissatisfaction in frequent absenteeism or poorer performance. Attesting to such unintended consequences, Meyer, et al. (1989) found that employees whose organizational commitment was derived from extrinsic bases performed their jobs less effectively than did employees who were emotionally attached to their company. Theories of work adaptation argue that successful managerial interventions target the underlying alienation instead of its behavioral symptoms. Construct validation of a taxonomy of response families must proceed before additional research on adaptation models is undertaken. Perhaps, this avenue of research can follow previous work validating a withdrawal-response family. Future validations must show that actions belonging to the same family covary *and* that all families represent ways to relieve dissatisfaction—that is, they share this psychological function (Hulin 1991).

Turnover is a fertile field for continued academic inquiry. Despite the voluminous literature on the subject, much scholarly explorations remain to further our understanding of this pivotal organizational behavior.

REFERENCES

Abbott, A. D. 1988. *The System of Professions.* Chicago, Il.: University of Chicago Press.

Abelson, M. A. 1987. Examination of avoidable and unavoidable turnover. *Journal of Applied Psychology,* 72:382–86.

Abelson, M. A., and B. D. Baysinger. 1984. Optimal and dysfunctional turnover: Toward an organizational level model. *Academy of Management Review,* 9:331–41.

Adler, S., and J. Golan. 1981. Lateness as a withdrawal behavior. *Journal of Applied Psychology,* 66 (5):544–54.

Ajzen, I. 1991. The theory of planned behavior. *Organizational Behavior and Human Decision Processes,* 50:179–211.

Ajzen, I., and M. Fishbein. 1975. A Bayesian analysis of attribution processes. *Psychological Bulletin,* 82 (2):261–77.

———— 1980. *Understanding Attitudes and Predicting Social Behavior.* Englewood Cliffs, N.J.: Prentice-Hall.

Alexander, J. A. 1988. The effects of patient care unit organization on nursing turnover. *Health Care Management Review,* 13:61–72.

Alexander, R. A., K. P. Carson, and G. M. Alliger. 1987. Correcting doubly truncated correlations: An improved approximation for correcting the bivariate normal correlation when truncation has occurred on both variables. *Educational and Psychological Measurement,* 47:309–15.

Allen, N., and J. P. Meyer. 1993. Organizational commitment: Evidence of career stage effects? *Journal of Business Research,* 26 (1):49–61.

Allison, P. D. 1974. *Inter-Organizational Mobility of Academic Scientists.* Paper presented at annual meeting of the American Sociological Association, Montreal, Canada.

———— 1984. *Event History Analysis: Regression for Longitudinal Event Data.* Beverly Hills, Calif.: Sage.

Anderson, J. C., and D. W. Gerbing. 1988. Structural equation modeling in practice: A review and recommended two-step approach. *Psychological Bulletin,* 103 (3):411–23.

Anderson, S. E., and L. J. Williams. 1992. Assumptions about unmeasured variables with studies of reciprocal relationships: The case of employee attitudes. *Journal of Applied Psychology,* 77 (5):638–50.

Aranya, N., and K. R. Ferris. 1983. Organizational-professional conflict among U. S. and Israeli professional accountants. *Journal of Social Psychology*, 119 (2):153–61.

Aranya, N., J. Pollock, and J. Amernic. 1981. An examination of professional commitment in public accounting. *Accounting, Organizations and Society*, 6:271–80.

Armknecht, P. A., and J. F. Early. 1972. Quits in manufacturing: A study of their causes. *Monthly Labor Review*, 95 (11):31–37.

Arnold, H. J., and D. C. Feldman. 1982. A multivariate analysis of the determinants of job turnover. *Journal of Applied Psychology*, 67:350–60.

Aronson, E., P. C. Ellsworth, J. M. Carlsmith, and M. H. Gonzales. 1990. *Methods of Research in Social Psychology*. New York: McGraw–Hill.

Arvey, R. D., T. J. Bouchard, N. L. Segal, and L. M. Abraham. 1989. Job satisfaction: Environmental and genetic components. *Journal of Applied Psychology*, 74:187–92.

Arvey, R. D., and R. H. Faley. 1988. *Fairness in Selecting Employees*. Reading, Mass.: Addison-Wesley.

Ashford, S. J., C. Lee, and P. Bobko. 1989. Contention, causes, and consequences of job insecurity: A theory–based measure and substantive test. *Academy of Management Journal*, 32:803–29.

Avolio, B. J., and D. A. Waldman. 1990. An examination of age and cognitive test performance across job complexity and occupational types. *Journal of Applied Psychology*, 75 (1):43–50.

Bacharach, S. B. 1989. Organizational theories: Some criteria for evaluation. *Academy of Management Review*, 14 (4):496–515.

Bacharach, S., and P. Bamberger. 1992. Causal models of role stressor antecedents and consequences: The importance of occupational differences. *Journal of Vocational Behavior*, 41:13–34.

Bagozzi, R. P., and L. W. Phillips. 1982. Representing and testing organizational theories: A holistic construal. *Administrative Science Quarterly*, 27 (3):459–89.

Bagozzi, R. P., and P. R. Warshaw. 1990. Trying to consume. *Journal of Consumer Research*, 17:127–140.

Bagozzi, R. P., and Y. Yi. 1989. The degree of intention formation as a moderator of the attitude-behavior relationship. *Social Psychology Quarterly*, 52 (4):266–79.

———— 1990. Assessing method variance in multitrait-multimethod matrices: The case of self-reported affect and perceptions at work. *Journal of Applied Psychology*, 75 (5):547–60.

Bagozzi, R. P., and Y. Yi. 1991. Multitrait-multimethod matrices in consumer research. *Journal of Consumer Research*, 17:426–39.

Bagozzi, R. P., Y. Yi, and, L. W. Phillips. 1991. Assessing construct validity in organizational research. *Administrative Science Quarterly*, 36 (3):421–58.

Balkin, D. B. 1992. Managing employee separations with the reward system. *The Executive*, 6:64–71.

Balwin, W. 1982. This is the answer. *Forbes* (5 July): p. 51.

Bannister, B., A. Kinicki, A. DeNisi, and P. Hom. 1987. A new method for the statistical control of rating error in performance ratings. *Educational and Psychological Measurement*, 47:583–96.

Barber, A. E., R. B. Dunham, and, R. A. Formisano. 1992. The impact of flexible benefits on employee satisfaction: A field study. *Personnel Psychology*, 45:55–75.

Barnard, C. I. 1938. *The Functions of the Executive*. Cambridge, Mass.: Harvard University Press.

Barnathan, J., B. Einhorn, and L. Nakarmi. 1992. Bringing it all back home. *Business Week* (7 December): p. 133.

Baron, R. M., and D. A. Kenny. 1986. The moderator-mediator variable distinction in social psychological research: Conceptual, strategic, and statistical considerations. *Journal of Personality and Social Psychology*, 51:1173–82.

Barrick, M. R., and M. K. Mount. 1991. The big five personality dimensions and job performance: A meta-analysis. *Personnel Psychology*, 44:1–26.

Bass, A. B., and J. Ager. 1991. Correcting point–biserial turnover correlations for comparative analysis. *Journal of Applied Psychology*, 76:595–98.

Bassett, G. A. 1967. *A Study of Factors Associated with Turnover of Exempt Personnel*. Crotonville, N.Y.: General Electric.

Bateman, T. S., and S. Strasser. 1983. A cross-lagged regression test of the relationships between job tension and employee satisfaction. *Journal of Applied Psychology*, 68 (3):439–45.

———— 1984. A longitudinal analysis of the antecedents of organizational commitment. *Academy of Management Journal*, 27 (1):95–112.

Baysinger, B., and W. Mobley. 1983. Employee turnover: Individual and organizational analysis. In *Research in Personnel and Human Resources Management*, ed. K. Rowland and G. Ferris. Vol. 1:269–319. Greenwich, Conn.: JAI Press.

Beach, L. R. 1990. *Image theory: Decision Making in Personal and Organizational Contexts.* Chichester, England: Wiley.

Becker, G. S. 1991. Working women's staunchest allies: Supply and demand. *Business Week* (2 December): p. 18.

Becker, H. S. 1960. Notes on the concept of commitment. *American Journal of Sociology,* 66:32–42.

Becker, T. E., D. M. Randall, and C. D. Riegel. 1992. A competitive evaluation of the multidimensional view of commitment and the theory of planned behavior. Unpublished manuscript. Department of Management and Systems, College of Business and Economics, Washington State University.

Bedeian, A. G., and A. A. Armenakis. 1981. A path-analytic study of the consequences of role conflict and ambiguity. *Academy of Management Journal,* 24 (2):417–24.

Belcher, D. W., N. B. Ferris, and J. O'Neill. 1985. How wage surveys are being used. *Compensation and Benefits Review,* (September–October):34–51.

Bellus, D. 1984. Turnover prevention: Third–year staff accountants. *Journal of Accountancy,* 158:118–22.

Bentler, P. M. 1990. Comparative fit indexes in structural models. *Psychological Bulletin,* 107 (2):238–46.

Bentler, P. M., and D. G. Bonnett. 1980. Significance tests and goodness of fit in the analysis of covariance structures. *Psychological Bulletin,* 88 (3):588–606.

Bentler, P. M., and C. Chou. 1987. Practical issues in structural modeling. *Sociological Methods and Research,* 16:78–117.

Berkowitz, L., C. Fraser, F. P. Treasure, and S. Cochran. 1987. Pay, equity, job gratifications, and comparisons in pay satisfaction. *Journal of Applied Psychology,* 72 (4):544–51.

Bernardin, H. J. 1987. Development and validation of a forced choice scale to measure job-related discomfort among customer service representatives. *Academy of Management Journal,* 30:162–73.

Bernardin, H. J., and R. W. Beatty. 1984. *Performance Appraisal: Assessing Human Behavior at Work.* Boston: Kent.

Bernardin, H. J., M. B. LaShells, P. C. Smith, and K. M. Alvares. 1976. Behavioral expectation scales: Effects of developmental procedures and formats. *Journal of Applied Psychology,* 61 (1):75–79.

Bernstein, A. 1991a. Do more babies mean fewer working women? *Business Week* (5 August):49–50.

———— 1991b. Family leave may not be that big a hardship for business. *Business Week* (3 June):28.

Bernstein, A., J. Weber, and L. Driscoll. 1991. *Business Week* (25 November):234–37.

Billings, R., and V. Wemmerus. 1983. The role of alternatives in process models of employee withdrawal. *Proceedings of the 26th Annual Conference of the Midwest Academy of Management*:18–29.

Bishop, J. H. 1990. Job performance, turnover, and wage growth. *Journal of Labor Economics,* 8:363–86.

Black college graduates in today's labor market. 1991. *Fair Employment Practices* (18 February): p. 15.

Blakemore, A., S. Low, and M. Ormiston. 1987. Employment bonuses and labor turnover. *Journal of Labor Economics,* 5:124–35.

Blakeslee, G. S., E. L. Suntrup, and J. A. Kernaghan. 1985. How much is turnover costing you? *Personnel Journal* (November):98–103.

Blau, G. 1993. Further exploring the relationship between job search and voluntary individual turnover. *Personnel Psychology,* 46:313–30.

Blau, P. M., and R. Schoenherr. 1971. *The Structure of Organizations.* New York: Basic Books.

Bleakley, F. R. 1993,. Many companies try management fads, only to see them flop. *Wall Street Journal* (6 July):1.

Blegen, M. A., C. W. Mueller, and J. L. Price. 1988. Measurement of kinship responsibility for organizational research. *Journal of Applied Psychology,* 73:402–409.

Blinder, A. S. 1989. Want to boost productivity? Try giving workers a say. *Business Week* (17 April):10.

Bluedorn, A. C. 1982. A unified model of turnover from organizations. *Human Relations,* 35:135–53.

Bluedorn, A. and M. Abelson. 1981. Employee performance and withdrawal from work. Unpublished manuscript. College of Business Administration, Pennsylvania State University.

Bogdanich, W. 1991. Danger in white: The shadowy world of 'temp' nurses. *Wall Street Journal* (1 November):B1.

Bollen, K. A. 1989. *Structural Equations with Latent Variables.* New York: Wiley.

———— 1990a. A comment on model evaluation and modification. *Multivariate Behavioral Research,* 25:181–85.

———— 1990b. Overall fit in covariance structure models: Two types of sample size effects. *Psychological Bulletin,* 107:256–59.

Bollen, K., and R. Lennox. 1991. Conventional wisdom on measurement: A structural equation perspective. *Psychological Bulletin,* 110 (2):305–14.

Borovies, D. L., and N. A. Newman. 1981. Graduate nurse transition program. *American Journal of Nursing* (October):1832–35.

Boudreau, J. W., and C. J. Berger. 1985. Decision-theoretical utility analysis applied to employee separations and acquisitions. *Journal of Applied Psychology,* 70 (3):581–612.

Bovee, T. 1991. Black, white pay unequal, study says. *Arizona Republic* (20 September): p. C1.

Bowen, D. E., and B. Schneider. 1988. Services marketing and management: Implications for organizational behavior. In *Research in Organizational Behavior,* ed. B. Staw and L. Cummings, 10:43–80. Greenwich, Conn.: JAI Press.

Brayfield, A. H., and W. H. Crockett. 1955. Employee attitudes and employee performance. *Psychological Bulletin,* 52:396–424.

Breaugh, J. A. 1983. Realistic job previews: A critical appraisal and future research directions. *Academy of Management Review,* 8 (4):612–19.

Breaugh, J. A., and D. L. Dossett. 1989. Rethinking the use of personal history information: The value of theory–based biodata for predicting turnover. *Journal of Business and Psychology,* 3:371–85.

Bremner, B. 1991. Tough times, tough bosses. *Business Week* (25 November):174–79.

Brief, A. P., and Aldag, R. J. 1989. The economic functions of work. In *Research in Personnel and Human Resources Management,* ed. G. Ferris and K. Rowland, 7:1–24. Greenwich, Conn.: JAI Press.

Brief, A. P., M. J. Burke, J. M. George, B. S. Robinson, and J. Webster. 1988. Should negative affectivity remain an unmeasured variable in the study of job stress? *Journal of Applied Psychology*, 73:193–98.

Brimelow, P., and L. Spencer. 1993. When quotas replace merit, everybody suffers. *Forbes* (15 February):80–102.

Brooke, P., D. W. Russell, and J. L. Price. 1988. Discriminant validation of measures of job satisfaction, job involvement, and organizational commitment. *Journal of Applied Psychology*, 73:139–45.

Brown, R. J., R. Carr, and D. K. Orthner. 1983. Family life patterns in the air force. In *Changing U.S. Military Manpower Realities*, ed. F. Margiotta, J. Brown, and M. Collins:207–20. Boulder, Colorado: Westview Press.

Bullock, R. J., and E. E. Lawler. 1984. Gainsharing: A few questions, and fewer answers. *Human Resource Management*, 23:23–40.

Burns, D. 1980. *Feeling good: The new mood therapy*. New York: William Morrow and Company.

———— 1988. *The feeling good workbook*. New York: New American Library.

Burns, T. J. 1988. Learning what workers think. *Nation's Business* (August):33.

Butler, R. P., C. L. Lardent, and J. B. Miner. 1983. A motivational basis for turnover in military officer education and training. *Journal of Applied Psychology*, 68:496–506.

Bycio, P., R. D. Hackett, and K. M. Alvares. 1990. Job performance and turnover: A review and meta-analysis. *Applied Psychology, An International Review*, 39 (1):47–76.

Cabrera, A. F., M. B. Castaneda, A. Nora, and D. Hengstler. 1992. The convergence between two theories of college persistence. *Journal of Higher Education*, 63:143–65.

Cabrera, A. F., A. Nora, and M. B. Castaneda. 1993. College persistence: Structural equations modeling test of an integrated model of student retention. *Journal of Higher Education*, 64:123–40.

Cahan, V. 1986. The shrinking nest egg: Retirement may never be the same. *Business Week*. (8 December):114–16.

Caldwell, D. F., and C. A. O'Reilly. 1990. Measuring person–job fit with a profile–comparison process. *Journal of Applied Psychology*, 75:648–57.

Campbell, D. T., and D. W. Fiske. 1959. Convergent and discriminant validity by the multitrait-multimethod matrix. *Psychological Bulletin*, 56:81–105.

Carroll, J. B. 1961. The nature of the data, or how to choose a correlation coefficient. *Psychometrika*, 26:347–72.

Carson, P. P., K. D. Carson, R. W. Griffeth, and R. P. Steel. 1993. Promotion and employee turnover: Critique, meta-analysis, and implications. *Journal of Business and Psychology*, 8:245–256.

Carsten, J. M., and P. E. Spector. 1987. Unemployment, job satisfaction, and employee turnover: A meta-analytic test of the Muchinsky model. *Journal of Applied Psychology*, 72:374–81.

Cascio, W. F. 1976. Turnover, biographical data, and fair employment practice. *Journal of Applied Psychology*, 61:576–80.

———— 1990. Strategic human resource management in high technology industry. In *Organizational Issues in High Technology Management*, ed. L. Gomez-Mejia and M. Lawless. Greenwich, Conn.: JAI Press.

———— 1991. *Costing Human Resources: The Financial Impact of Behavior in Organizations*. 3rd. ed. Boston, Mass.: Kent.

Cavanagh, S. J. 1989. Nursing turnover: Literature review and methodological critique. *Journal of Advanced Nursing*, 14:587–96.

Chatman, J. A. 1991. Matching people and organizations: Selection and socialization in public accounting firms. *Administrative Science Quarterly*, 36:459–84.

Choi, T., H. Jameson, M. L. Brekke, R. O. Podratz, and H. Mundahl. 1986. Effects on nurse retention: An experiment with scheduling. *Medical Care*, 24:1029–43.

Clegg, C. W. 1983. Psychology of employee lateness, absence, and turnover: A methodological critique and an empirical study. *Journal of Applied Psychology*, 68:88–101.

Clements, M. 1993. Fear of losing aid chains some to jobs. *USA Today* (1 March):B1–B2.

Cleveland, J. N., and M. E. Kerst. 1993. Sexual harassment and perceptions of power: An under-articulated relationship. *Journal of Vocational Behavior*, 42:49–67.

Cohen, J., and P. Cohen. 1983. *Applied Multiple Regression/Correlation Analysis for Behavioral Sciences*, 2d ed. Hillsdale, N.J.: Erlbaum.

Colarelli, S. M. 1984. Methods of communication and mediating processes in realistic job previews. *Journal of Applied Psychology*, 69:633–42.

Comp worth study: "Nurses really underpaid." 1984. *American Journal of Nursing* (February): p. 256.

Cook, A. H. 1989. Public policies to help dual–earner families meet the demands of the work world. *Industrial and Labor Relations Review,* 42:201–15.

Cooper, W. H., and A. J. Richardson. 1986. Unfair comparisons. *Journal of Applied Psychology,* 71 (2):179–84.

Cose, E. 1993. *The Rage of a Privileged Class.* New York: HarperCollins.

Coser, R. L. 1976. Suicide and the relational system: A case study in a mental hospital. *Journal of Health and Social Behavior,* 17:318–27.

Cotton, J. L., and J. M. Tuttle. 1986. Employee turnover: A meta-analysis and review with implications for research. *Academy of Management Review,* 11:55–70.

Coverdale, S., and J. Terborg. 1980. A re-examination of the Mobley, Horner, and Hollingsworth model of turnover: A useful replication. Paper presented at the annual meeting of the Academy of Management, Detroit, Mich.

Cox, T. H. 1991. The multicultural organization. *Academy of Management Executive,* 5:34–47.

Cox, T. H., and S. Blake. 1991. Managing cultural diversity: Implications for organizational competitiveness. *Academy of Management Executive,* 5:45–56.

Cox, T. H., S. A. Lobel, and P. L. McLeod. 1991. Effects of ethnic group cultural differences on cooperative and competitive behavior on a group task. *Academy of Management Journal,* 34 (4):827–847.

Cudeck, R. 1989. Analysis of correlation matrices using covariance structure models. *Psychological Bulletin,* 105 (2):317–27.

Curry, J. P., D. S. Wakefield, J. L. Price, C. W. Mueller. 1986. On the causal ordering of job satisfaction and organizational commitment. *Academy of Management Journal,* 29:847–58.

Curry, J. P., D. S. Wakefield, J. L. Price, C. W. Mueller, and J. C. McCloskey. 1985. Determinants of turnover among nursing department employees. *Research in Nursing and Health,* 8:397–411.

Dalessio, A., W. H. Silverman, and J. R. Schuck. 1986. Paths to turnover: A re–analysis and review of existing data on the Mobley, Horner, and Hollingsworth turnover model. *Human Relations,* 39:245–63.

Dalton, D. R., D. M. Krackhardt, and L. W. Porter. 1981. Functional turnover: An empirical assessment. *Journal of Applied Psychology,* 66:716–21.

Dalton, D. R., and D. J. Mesch. 1990. The impact of flexible scheduling on employee attendance and turnover. *Administrative Science Quarterly,* 35:370–87.

Dalton, D. R., and W. D. Todor. 1979. Turnover turned over: An expanded and positive perspective. *Academy of Management Review,* 4:225–35.

Dalton, D. R., W. D. Todor, and D. M. Krackhardt. 1982. Turnover overstated: A functional taxonomy. *Academy of Management Review,* 7:117–23.

Dansereau, F., G. Graen, and W. J. Haga. 1975. A vertical dyad linkage approach to leadership within formal organizations. *Organizational Behavior and Human Performance,* 13:46–78.

Dansereau, F., Jr., J. Cashman, and G. Graen. 1974. Expectancy as a moderator of the relationship between job attitudes and turnover. *Journal of Applied Psychology,* 59:228–29.

Darden, W. R., R. D. Hampton, and E. W. Boatwright. 1987. Investigating retail employee turnover: An application of survival analysis. *Journal of Retailing,* 63:69–88.

Darmon, R. Y. 1990. Identifying sources of turnover costs: A segmental approach. *Journal of Marketing,* 54:46–56.

Datel, W. E., and S. T. Lifrak. 1969. Expectations, affect change, and military performance in the army recruit. *Psychological Reports,* 24:855.

Davy, J. A., A. J. Kinicki, and C. L. Scheck. 1991. Developing and testing a model of survivor responses to layoffs. *Journal of Vocational Behavior,* 38:302–17.

Dean, R. A., and J. P. Wanous. 1984. Effects of realistic job previews on hiring bank tellers. *Journal of Applied Psychology,* 69:61–68.

Dean, R. A., K. R. Ferris, and C. Konstans. 1988. Occupational reality shock and organizational commitment: Evidence from the accounting profession. *Accounting, Organizations and Society,* 13:235–50.

Deutschman, A. 1991. Dealing with sexual harassment. *Fortune,* (4 November):145.

DeVries, D. L., A. M. Morrison, S. L. Shullman, and M. L. Gerlach. 1981. *Performance Appraisal on the Line.* New York: John Wiley.

Diener, E. 1984. Subjective well-being. *Psychological Bulletin,* 95 (3):542–75.

Dilla, B. L. 1987. Descriptive information in a realistic job preview. *Journal of Vocational Behavior,* 30 (1):33–48.

Dillman, D. A. 1978. *Mail and Telephone Surveys: The Total Design Method.* New York: Wiley.

Dipboye, R. L., and R. de Pontbriand. 1981. Correlates of employee reactions to performance appraisals and appraisal systems. *Journal of Applied Psychology,* 66:248–51.

Dittrich, J. E., and M. R. Carrell. 1979. Organizational equity perceptions, employee job satisfaction, and departmental absence and turnover rates. *Organizational Behavior and Human Performance,* 24:29–40.

Donovan, L. 1980. What nurses want. *RN* 43:22–30.

Dowling, P. J., and R. S. Schuler. 1990. *International Dimensions of Human Resource Management.* Boston, Mass.: PWS–Kent.

Dreher, G. F. 1982. The role of performance in the turnover process. *Academy of Management Journal,* 25:137–47.

Dreher, G. F., R. A. Ash, and R. D. Bretz. 1988. Benefit coverage and employee cost: Critical factors in explaining compensation satisfaction. *Personnel Psychology,* 41:237–54.

Dreher, G. F., and T. W. Dougherty. 1980. Turnover and competition for expected job openings: An exploratory analysis. *Academy of Management Journal,* 23:766–72.

Dreyfuss, J. 1990. Get ready for the new work force. *Fortune* (23 April):165.

Dugoni, B. L., and D. R. Ilgen. 1981. Realistic job previews and the adjustment of new employees. *Academy of Management Journal,* 24:579–91.

Duleep, H.O., and S. Sanders. 1992. Discrimination at the top: American-born Asian and white men. *Industrial Relations,* 31:416–32.

Dwyer, J. H. 1983. *Statistical Models for the Social and Behavioral Sciences.* New York: Oxford University Press.

Ehrlich, E. 1989. The mommy track. *Business Week* (20 March): 126.

Faltermeyer, E. 1992. Is this layoff necessary? *Fortune* (June):71.

Farkas, A. J., and Tetrick, L. E. 1989. A three–wave longitudinal analysis of the causal ordering of satisfaction and commitment on turnover decisions. *Journal of Applied Psychology,* 74:855–868.

Farrell, C. 1992. Where have all the families gone? *Business Week* (29 June): 90–91.

Farrell, D. 1983. Exit, voice, loyalty, and neglect as responses to job dissatisfaction: A multidimensional scaling study. *Academy of Management Journal,* 26:596–607.

Farrell, D., and C. E. Rusbult. 1981. Exchange variables as predictors of job satisfaction, job commitment, and turnover: The impact of rewards, costs, alternatives, and investments. *Organizational Behavior and Human Performance,* 28:78–95.

Farrell, D., C. E. Rusbult, Y. H. Lin, and P. Bernthall. 1990. Impact of job satisfaction, investment size, and quality of alternatives on exit, voice, loyalty, and neglect responses to job dissatisfaction: A cross-lagged panel study. *Proceedings of the Academy of Management* (August):211–15.

Feldman, D. C. 1976. A contingency theory of socialization. *Administrative Science Quarterly,* 21:433–52.

———— 1988. *Managing Careers in Organizations.* Glenview, Ill.: Scott, Foresman.

Feldman, D. C., and J. M. Brett. 1983. Coping with new jobs: A comparative study of new hires and job changers. *Academy of Management Journal,* 26:258–72.

Feldman, J. 1975. Considerations in the use of causal-correlational technique in applied psychology. *Journal of Applied Psychology,* 60 (6):663–70.

———— 1981. Beyond attribution theory: Cognitive processes in performance appraisal. *Journal of Applied Psychology,* 66 (2):127–48.

Feldman, J. M., and J. G. Lynch. 1988. Self-generated validity and other effects of measurement on belief, attitude, intention, and behavior. *Journal of Applied Psychology,* 73 (3):421–35.

Fernandez, J. P. 1986. *Child Care and Corporate Productivity.* Lexington, Mass.: Lexington Books.

Ferris, G. R. 1985. Role of leadership in the employee withdrawal process: A constructive replication. *Journal of Applied Psychology,* 70 (4):777–81.

Ferris, K. R., and N. Aranya. 1983. A comparison of two organizational commitment scales. *Personnel Psychology,* 36 (1):87–98.

Festinger, L. 1957. *A Theory of Cognitive Dissonance.* Evanston, Ill.: Row, Peterson.

Fichman, M. 1988. Motivational consequences of absence and attendance: Proportional hazard estimation of a dynamic motivation model. *Journal of Applied Psychology,* 73 (1):119–34.

Finkelstein, S., and D. C. Hambrick. 1990. Top–management–team tenure and organizational outcomes: The moderating role of managerial discretion. *Administrative Science Quarterly*, 35:484–503.

Fishbein, M. 1967. Attitude and the prediction of behavior. In *Readings in Attitude Theory and Measurement*, ed. M. Fishbein: 477–92. New York: Wiley.

Fishbein, M., and I. Ajzen. 1975. *Belief, Attitude, Intention and Behavior: An Introduction to Theory and Research.* Reading, Mass.: Addison–Wesley.

Fisher, A. B. 1992. When will women get to the top? *Fortune* (21 September):44.

Fisher, C. D. 1986. Organizational socialization: An integrative review. In *Research in Personnel and Human Resources Management*, ed. K. Rowland and G. Ferris, 4: 101–46. Greenwich, Conn.: JAI Press.

Fisher, C. D., and R. Gitelson. 1983. A meta-analysis of the correlates of role conflict and ambiguity. *Journal of Applied Psychology*, 68:320–33.

Fiske, S. T., D. A. Kenny, and S. E. Taylor. 1982. Structural models for the mediation of salience effects on attribution. *Journal of Experimental Social Psychology*, 18 (2):105–27.

Fitzgerald, L. F., and S. L. Shullman. 1993. Sexual harassment: A research analysis and agenda for the 1990s. *Journal of Vocational Behavior*, 42:5–27.

Flamholtz, E. 1985. *Human Resource Accounting.* San Francisco. Jossey–Bass.

Folger, R., and J. Greenberg. 1985. Procedural justice: An interpretive analysis of personnel systems. In *Research in Personnel and Human Resources Management*, eds. K. Rowland and G. Ferris, 3:141–83. Greenwich, Conn.: JAI Press.

Folger, R., and M. A. Konovsky. 1989. Effects of procedural and distributive justice on reactions to pay-raise decisions. *Academy of Management Journal*, 32:115–30.

Forrest, C. R., L. L. Cummings, and A. C. Johnson. 1977. Organizational participation: A critique and model. *Academy of Management Review*, 2:586–601.

Frayne, C. A., and G. P. Latham. 1987. Application of social learning theory to employee self-management of attendance. *Journal of Applied Psychology*, 72 (3):387–92.

Fredericks, A. J., and D. L. Dossett. 1983. Attitude-behavior relations: A comparison of the Fishbein-Ajzen and the Bentler-Speckart models. *Journal of Personality and Social Psychology*, 45 (3):501–12.

Frese, M., and K. Okonek. 1984. Reasons to leave shiftwork and psychological and psychosomatic complaints of former shiftworkers. *Journal of Applied Psychology,* 69 (3):509–14.

Fried, Y. 1991. Meta-analytic comparison of the Job Diagnostic Survey and Job Characteristics Inventory as correlates of work satisfaction and performance. *Journal of Applied Psychology,* 76 (5):690–97.

Friedman, L., and R. J. Harvey. 1986. Factors of union commitment: The case for a lower dimensionality. *Journal of Applied Psychology,* 71 (3):371–76.

Frost, C. F. 1978. The Scanlon plan: Anyone for free enterprise? *MSU Business Topics* (Winter):25–33.

Galen, M. 1993. Work and family. *BusinessWeek* (28 June):80.

Gardner, J. E. 1986. *Stabilizing the workforce: A complete guide to controlling turnover.* Westport, Conn.: Quorum.

Garland, S. B. 1991. Throwing stones at the "glass ceiling." *Business Week* (19 August): p. 29.

Gates, D. 1993. White male paranoia. *Newsweek* (29 March): 48.

Gatewood, R. D., and H. S. Feild. 1987. *Human Resource Selection.* Hinsdale, Ill.: The Dryden Press.

George, J. M. 1989. Mood and absence. *Journal of Applied Psychology,* 74:317–24.

——— 1990. Personality, affect, and behavior in groups. *Journal of Applied Psychology,* 75:107–16.

Gerbing, D. W., and J. C. Anderson. 1988. An updated paradigm for scale development incorporating unidimensionality and its assessment. *Journal of Marketing Research,* 24:186–92.

Gerhart, B. 1987. How important are dispositional factors as determinants of job satisfaction? Implications for job design and other personnel programs. *Journal of Applied Psychology,* 72 (3):366–73.

——— 1990. Voluntary turnover and alternative job opportunities. *Journal of Applied Psychology,* 75:467–76.

Gerhart, B., and G. T. Milkovich. 1990. Organizational differences in managerial compensation and financial performance. *Academy of Management Journal,* 33:663–91.

Gerhart, B., and S. Rynes. 1991. Determinants and consequences of salary negotiations by male and female MBA graduates. *Journal of Applied Psychology*, 76 (2):256–62.

Gerson, K. 1985. *Hard Choices*. Berkeley, Calif.: University of California Press.

Ghiselli, E. E. 1963. Moderating effects and differential reliability and validity. *Journal of Applied Psychology*, 47:81–86.

——— 1974. Some perspectives for industrial psychology. *American Psychologist*, 80:80–87.

Ghiselli, E. E., J. P. Campbell, and S. Zedeck. 1981. *Measurement Theory for the Behavioral Sciences*. San Francisco: W. H. Freeman.

Gleckman, H., T. Smart, P. Dwyer, T. Segal, and J. Weber. 1991. Race in the workplace. *Business Week* (8 July): p. 50.

Glick, W. H., G. D. Jenkins, and N. Gupta. 1986. Method versus substance: How strong are underlying relationships between job characteristics and attitudinal outcomes? *Academy of Management Journal*, 29:441–64.

Goff, S. J., M. K. Mount, and R. L. Jamison. 1990. Employer supported child care, work/family conflict, and absenteeism: A field study. *Personnel Psychology*, 43:793–809.

Gomez-Mejia, L. R. 1992. Structure and process of diversification, compensation strategy, and firm performance. *Strategic Management Journal*, 13:381–97.

Gomez–Mejia, L. R., and D. B. Balkin. 1987. The causes and consequences of pay compression in business schools. *Compensation and Benefits Review*, 19(5): 43–55.

——— 1992a. *Compensation, Organizational Strategy, and Firm Performance*. Cincinnati: South-Western.

——— 1992b. Determinants of faculty pay: an agency theory perspective. *Academy of Management Journal*, 35:921–55.

Gomez–Mejia, L. R., D. B. Balkin, and G. T. Milkovich. 1990. Rethinking your rewards for technical employees. *Organizational Dynamics*, 18:62–75.

Gomez–Mejia, L. R., R. C. Page, and W. Tornow. 1982. A comparison of the practical utility of traditional, statistical, and hybrid job evaluation approaches. *Academy of Management Journal*, 25:790–809.

Goodman, P. S., E. Ravlin, and M. Schminke. 1987. Understanding groups in organizations. In *Research in Organizational Behavior*, ed. L. Cummings and B. Staw, 9:121–73. Greenwich, Conn.: JAI Press.

Gould, S., and L. E. Penley. 1984. Career strategies and salary progression: A study of their relationships in a municipal bureaucracy. *Organizational Behavior and Human Performance,* 34 (2):244–65.

Graen, G. B., and S. Ginsburgh. 1977. Job resignation as a function of role orientation and leader acceptance: A longitudinal investigation of organizational assimilation. *Organizational Behavior and Human Performance,* 19:1–17.

Graen, G. B., R. Liden, and W. Hoel. 1982. Role of leadership in the employee withdrawal process. *Journal of Applied Psychology,* 67:868–72.

Graen, G. B., M. A. Novak, and P. Sommerkamp. 1982. The effects of leader-member exchange and job design on productivity and satisfaction: Testing a dual attachment model. *Organizational Behavior and Human Performance,* 30 (1):109–31.

Graen, G. B., and T. A. Scandura. 1986. A theory of dyadic career reality. In *Research in Personnel and Human Resources Management,* ed. K. Rowland and G. Ferris, 4:147–181. Greenwich, Conn.: JAI Press.

Graen, G. B., T. A. Scandura, and M. R. Graen. 1986. A field experimental test of the moderating effects of growth need strength on productivity. *Journal of Applied Psychology,* 71:484–91.

Greenberg, J. 1986. Determinants of perceived fairness of performance evaluations. *Journal of Applied Psychology,* 71:340–42.

———— 1990. Employee theft as a reaction to underpayment inequity: The hidden cost of pay cuts. *Journal of Applied Psychology,* 75 (5):561–68.

Greenberg, J., and C. L. McCarty. 1990. Comparable worth: A matter of justice. In *Research in Personnel and Human Resources Management,* ed. G. R. Ferris and K. Rowland, 8:265–301. Greenwich, Conn.: JAI Press.

Greenberg, J., and S. Ornstein. 1983. High status job title compensation for underpayment: A test of equity theory. *Journal of Applied Psychology,* 68 (2):285–97.

Greenhalgh, L., and Z. Rosenblatt. 1984. Job insecurity: Toward conceptual clarity. *Academy of Management Review,* 9:438–48.

Gregersen, H. B., and J. S. Black. 1992. Antecedents to commitment to a parent company and a foreign operation. *Academy of Management Journal,* 35:65–90.

Griffeth, R. W. 1981. *An Information Processing Model of Employee Turnover Behavior.* Unpublished doctoral diss. University of South Carolina, Columbia.

———— 1985. Moderation of the effects of job enrichment by participation: A longitudinal field experiment. *Organizational Behavior and Human Decision Processes,* 35:73–93.

Griffeth, R. W., and P. W. Hom. 1988a. A comparison of different conceptualizations of perceived alternatives in turnover research. *Journal of Organizational Behavior,* 9:103–11.

———— 1988b. Locus of control and delay of gratification as moderators of employee turnover. *Journal of Applied Social Psychology,* 18:1318–33.

———— 1990. Competitive examination of two turnover theories: A two–sample test. Paper presented at the annual convention of the Academy of Management, San Francisco, Calif. (August).

———— 1992. Predictive and nomological validity of two turnover theories: A two-sample competitive examination. Department of Management, Georgia State University, Atlanta, Georgia.

Griffin, R. W. 1987. Toward an integrated theory of task design. In *Research in Organizational Behavior,* ed. L. L. Cummings and B. M. Staw, 9:79–120. Greenwich, Conn.: JAI Press.

Guion, R. M. 1965. *Personnel Testing.* New York: McGraw-Hill.

Gupta, N., and T. A. Beehr. 1979. Job stress and employee behaviors. *Organizational Behavior and Human Performance,* 23 (3):373–87.

Gutek, B. A., and M. P. Koss. 1993. Changed women and changed organizations: Consequences of and coping with sexual harassment. *Journal of Vocational Behavior,* 42:28–48.

Hackett, R. D. 1989. Work attitudes and employee absenteeism: A synthesis of the literature. *Journal of Occupational Psychology,* 62 (3):235–48.

Hackett, R. D., and R. M. Guion. 1985. A reevaluation of the absenteeism-job satisfaction relationship. *Organizational Behavior and Human Decision Processes,* 35 (3):340–81.

Hackman, J. R., and G. R. Oldham. 1976. Motivation through the design of work: Test of a theory. *Organizational Behavior and Human Performance,* 16 (2):250–9.

———— 1980. *Work Redesign.* Reading, Mass.: Addison–Wesley.

Half, R. 1982. Keeping the best—employee retention in public accounting. *The CPA Journal,* 52:34–38.

Hamner, W. C., and H. L. Tosi. 1974. Relationship of role conflict and role ambiguity to job involvement measures. *Journal of Applied Psychology*, 59 (4):497–99.

Hand, H. H., R. W. Griffeth, and W. H. Mobley. 1978. Military enlistment, reenlistment, and withdrawal research: A critical review of the literature. *Journal Supplemental Abstract Series Catalog of Selected Documents in Psychology*, 8:74–75.

Hanisch, K. A., and C. L. Hulin. 1990. Job attitudes and organizational withdrawal: An examination of retirement and other voluntary withdrawal behaviors. *Journal of Vocational Behavior*, 37 (1):60–78.

Harrison, D. A., and C. L. Hulin. 1989. Investigations of absenteeism: Using event history models to study the absence-taking process. *Journal of Applied Psychology*, 74 (2):300–16.

Hattie, J. A. 1985. Methodology review: Assessing unidimensionality of tests and items. *Applied Psychological Measurement*, 9 (2):139–64.

Hayduk, L. 1987. *Structural Equation Modeling with LISREL*. Baltimore, Md.: Johns Hopkins Press.

Heilman, M. E. 1983. Sex bias in work settings: The lack of fit model. In *Research in Organizational Behavior*, ed. L. Cummings and B. Staw, 5:269–98. Greenwich, Conn.: JAI Press.

Heilman, M. E., C. J. Block, and J. A. Lucas. 1992. Presumed incompetent? Stigmatization and affirmative action efforts. *Journal of Applied Psychology*, 77 (4):536–44.

Heilman, M. E., J. C. Rivero, and J. F. Brett. 1991. Skirting the competence issue: Effects of sex-based preferential selection on task choices of women and men. *Journal of Applied Psychology*, 76:99–105.

Henderson, R. 1989. *Compensation Management*. Englewood Cliffs, N.J.: Prentice–Hall.

Heneman, H. G. 1985. Pay satisfaction. In *Research in Personnel and Human Resources Management*, ed. K. M. Rowland and G. R. Ferris, 3:115–40. Greenwich, Conn.: JAI Press.

Heneman, R. L. 1990. Merit pay research. In *Research in Personnel and Human Resources Management*, ed. G. R. Ferris and K. Rowland, 8:203–63. Greenwich, Conn.: JAI Press.

Heneman, R. L., D. B. Greenberger, and S. Strasser. 1988. The relationship between pay-for-performance perceptions and pay satisfaction. *Personnel Psychology*, 41 (4):745–59.

Henkoff, R. 1990. Cost cutting: How to do it right. *Fortune* (April):40.

Hessing, D. J., H. Elffers, and R. H. Weigel. 1988. Exploring the limits of self-reports and reasoned action: An investigation of the psychology of tax evasion behavior. *Journal of Personality and Social Psychology,* 54 (3):405–13.

Hirschman, A. O. 1970. *Exit, Voice, and Loyalty: Responses to Decline in Firms, Organizations, and States.* Cambridge, Mass.: Harvard University Press.

Hofstede, G. 1980. Motivation, leadership and organizations. *Organizational Dynamics,* 9:42–63.

Hollenbeck, J. R., and C. R. Williams. 1986. Turnover functionality versus turnover frequency: A note on work attitudes and organizational effectiveness. *Journal of Applied Psychology,* 71:606–11.

Hollis, M., and B. O. Muthen. 1987. *Structural covariance models with categorical data: An illustration involving the measurement of political attitudes and belief systems.* Paper presented at annual meeting of the American Political Science Association, Chicago, Ill.

Holloran, S. D., B. H. Mishkin, and B. L. Hanson. 1980. Bicultural training for new graduates. *Journal of Nursing Administration,* 10:17–24.

Hom, P. W. 1979. Effects of job peripherality and personal characteristics on the job satisfaction of part-time workers. *Academy of Management Journal,* 22:551–65.

——— 1980. Expectancy predictions of reenlistment in the National Guard. *Journal of Vocational Behavior,* 16:235–48.

——— 1992. Turnover costs among mental health professionals. College of Business, Arizona State University, Tempe, Ariz.

Hom, P. W., J. S. Bracker, and G. Julian. 1988. In pursuit of greener pastures. *New Accountant* (October)4:24.

Hom, P. W., F. Caranikas–Walker, G. E. Prussia, and R. W. Griffeth. 1992. A meta-analytical structural equations analysis of a model of employee turnover. *Journal of Applied Psychology,* 77:890–909.

Hom, P. W., L. Gomez-Mejia, and A. Grabke. 1993. Do certain maquiladora compensation practices reduce turnover among production workers? Paper read at the 7th National Symposium on Hispanic Business and the Economy, Mexico City.

Hom, P. W., and R. Griffeth. 1991. Structural equations modeling test of a turnover theory: Cross–sectional and longitudinal analyses. *Journal of Applied Psychology,* 76:350–66.

Hom, P. W., R. W. Griffeth, and P. P. Carson (in press). Turnover of Personnel. In *Handbook of Public Personnel Administration and Labor Relations,* ed. J. Rabin, T. Vocino, W. B. Hildreth, and G. Miller. New York: Marcel Dekker.

Hom, P. W., R. W. Griffeth, L. E. Palich, and J. S. Bracker. 1993. Realistic job previews: Two-occupation test of mediating processes. College of Business, Arizona State University, Tempe, Ariz.

Hom, P. W., R. W. Griffeth, and C. L. Sellaro. 1984. The validity of Mobley's 1977 model of employee turnover. *Organizational Behavior and Human Performance,* 34:141–74.

Hom, P. W., and C. L. Hulin. 1981. A competitive test of the prediction of reenlistment by several models. *Journal of Applied Psychology,* 66 (1):23–39.

Hom, P. W., R. Katerberg, Jr., and C. L. Hulin. 1979. Comparative examination of three approaches to the prediction of turnover. *Journal of Applied Psychology,* 64:280–90.

Hom, P. W., A. Kinicki, and D. Domm. 1989. Confirmatory validation of a theory of employee turnover. In *Proceedings of the 49th Annual Conference of the Academy of Management,* ed. F. Hoy, 219–23. Ada, Ohio: Academy of Management.

Hom, P. W., and J. S. Miller. 1992. Determinants of product commitment in concurrent engineering teams. In *Integrated Design,* ed. J. Ettlie, G. Boer, P. Hom, and J. Miller, Report No. DDM–907043. Washington, D. C.: National Science Foundation.

Hom, P. W., C. Sutton, and M. Tehrani. 1992. Toward an understanding of lenient peer appraisals: A comparative examination of theories of rater motivation. Department of Management, Arizona State University, Tempe, Ariz.

Homans, G. C. 1961. *Social Behavior: Its Elementary Forms.* New York: Harcourt, Brace and World.

Horner, S. O., W. H. Mobley, and B. M. Meglino. 1979. An experimental evaluation of the effects of a realistic job preview on Marine recruit affect, intentions, and behavior (Technical Report 9). Columbia, S.C.: Center for Management and Organizational Research, University of South Carolina.

Hough, L. M., N. K. Eaton, M. D. Dunnette, J. D. Kamp, and R. A. McCloy. 1990. Criterion-related validities of personality constructs and the effect of response distortion on those validities. *Journal of Applied Psychology*, 75:581–95.

How employees perceive sexual harassment. 1992. *Harvard Business Review* (March-April): p. 23.

Huba, G. J., and L. L. Harlow. 1987. Robust structural equation models: Implications for developmental psychology. *Child Development*, 58 (1):147–66.

Huey, F. L., and S. Hartley. 1988. What keeps nurses in nursing. *American Journal of Nursing*, 88:181–88.

Hulin, C. L. 1991. Adaptation, persistence, and commitment in organizations. In *Handbook of Industrial and Organizational Psychology*, ed. M. D. Dunnette and L. M. Hough, 2d ed. Vol. 2. Palo Alto, Calif.: Consulting Psychologists Press.

Hulin, C. L., and M. R. Blood. 1968. Job enlargement, individual differences, and worker responses. *Psychological Bulletin*, 69:41–55.

Hulin, C. L., M. Roznowski, and D. Hachiya. 1985. Alternative opportunities and withdrawal decisions: Empirical and theoretical discrepancies and an integration. *Psychological Bulletin*, 97:233–50.

Hunter, E. J. 1983. Family power: An issue in military manpower management. In *Changing U.S. Military Manpower Realities*, ed. F. Margiotta J. Brown, and M. Collins, 195–206. Boulder, Colorado: Westview Press.

Hunter, J. E., and D. W. Gerbing. 1982. Unidimensional measurement, second order factor analysis, and causal models. In *Research in Organizational Behavior*, ed. B. Staw and L. L. Cummings. 4:267–320. Greenwich, Conn.: JAI Press.

Hunter, J. E., D. W. Gerbing, and F. J. Boster. 1982. Machiavellian beliefs and personality: Construct validity of the Machiavellianism dimension. *Journal of Personality and Social Psychology*, 43 (6):1293–1305.

Hunter, J. E., and F. L. Schmidt. 1990a. Dichotomization of continuous variables: The implications for meta-analysis. *Journal of Applied Psychology*, 75 (3):334–49.

——— 1990b. *Methods of Meta-analysis*. Newbury Park, Calif.: Sage Publications.

Hunter, J. E., F. L. Schmidt, and G. B. Jackson. 1982. *Meta-analysis: Cumulating Research Findings Across Studies*. Beverly Hills, Calif.: Sage Publications.

Huselid, M. A., and N. E. Day. 1991. Organizational commitment, job involvement, and turnover: A substantive and methodological analysis. *Journal of Applied Psychology,* 76:380–91.

Ilgen, D. R., and B. L. Dugoni. 1977. Initial orientation to the organization. Paper presented at the annual meeting of the Academy of Management, Kissimmee, Fla. (August).

Ilgen, D. R., and W. Seely. 1974. Realistic expectations as an aid in reducing voluntary resignations. *Journal of Applied Psychology,* 59:452–55.

Ippolito, R. A. 1991. Encouraging long-term tenure: Wage tilt or pension? *Industrial and Labor Relations Review,* 44:520–35.

Ironson, G. H., P. C. Smith, M. T. Brannick, W. M. Gibson, and K. B. Paul. 1989. Construction of a job in general scale: A comparison of global, composite, and specific measures. *Journal of Applied Psychology,* 74:193–200.

Irrgang, W. 1972. The Lincoln Incentive Management Program. Lincoln Lecture Series, College of Business, Arizona State University, Tempe, Ariz.

Ivancevich, J. M. 1980. A longitudinal study of behavioral expectation scales: Attitudes and performance. *Journal of Applied Psychology,* 65:139–46.

———— 1982. Subordinates' reactions to performance appraisal interviews: A test of feedback and goal-setting techniques. *Journal of Applied Psychology,* 67:581–87.

———— J. M., and S. V. Smith. 1981. Goal setting interview skills training: Simulated and on-the-job analyses. *Journal of Applied Psychology,* 66 (6):697–705.

Jackofsky, E. F. 1984. Turnover and job performance: An integrated process model. *Academy of Management Review,* 9:74–83.

Jackofsky, E. F., K. R. Ferris, and B. G. Breckenridge. 1986. Evidence for a curvilinear relationship between job performance and turnover. *Journal of Management,* 12 (1):105–11.

Jackofsky, E. F., and L. H. Peters. 1983a. The hypothesized effects of ability in the turnover process. *Academy of Management Review,* 8:46–49.

———— 1983b. Job turnover versus company turnover: Reassessment of the March and Simon participation hypothesis. *Journal of Applied Psychology,* 68:490–95.

Jackofsky, E. F., and J. W. Slocum. 1987. A causal analysis of the impact of job performance on the voluntary turnover process. *Journal of Occupational Behavior* 8 (3):263–70.

Jackson, S. E., J. F. Brett, V. I. Sessa, D. M. Cooper, J. A. Julin, and K. Peyronnin. 1991. Some differences make a difference: Individual dissimilarity and group heterogeneity as correlates of recruitment, promotions, and turnover. *Journal of Applied Psychology,* 76:675–89.

Jackson, S. E., and R. Schuler. 1985. A meta-analysis and conceptual critique of research on role ambiguity and role conflict in work settings. *Organizational Behavior and Human Decision Processes,* 36:16–78.

Jackson, S. E., R. L. Schwab, and R. S. Schuler. 1986. Toward an understanding of the burnout phenomenon. *Journal of Applied Psychology,* 71:630–40.

Jacob, R. 1992. The search for the organization of tomorrow. *Fortune* (May):92.

James, F. E. 1988. More blacks quitting white-run firms. *Wall Street Journal* (7 June):B1.

James, L. A., and L. R. James. 1989. Integrating work environment perceptions: Explorations into the measurement of meaning. *Journal of Applied Psychology,* 74:739–51.

James, L. R., S. A. Mulaik, and J. M. Brett. 1982. *Causal Analysis: Assumptions, Models, and Data.* Beverly Hills, Calif.: Sage Publications.

Jaros, S. J., J. M. Jermier, J. W. Koehler, and T. Sincich. 1993. Effects of continuance, affective, and moral commitment on the withdrawal process: An evaluation of eight structural models. *Academy of Management Journal,* 36:951–95.

Jenkins, G. D., and E. E. Lawler. 1981. Impact of employee participation on pay plan development. *Organizational Behavior and Human Performance,* 28 (1):111–28.

Johnson, A. A. 1990. Parental leave—is it the business of business? *Human Resource Planning,* 13:119–31.

Jones, J. M. 1972. *Prejudice and Racism.* Reading, Mass.: Addison-Wesley.

Joreskog, K. G., and D. Sorbom. 1989. *LISREL 7.* Chicago, Ill.: SPSS.

"Joyless recovery": Well-paying, full-time jobs still scarce. 1993. *The Arizona Republic* (5 September): A4.

Judge, T. A. 1992. The dispositional perspective in human resources research. In *Research in Personnel and Human Resources Management,* ed. G. R. Ferris and K. M. Rowland, 10:31–72. Greenwich, Conn.: JAI Press.

———— 1993. Does affective disposition moderate the relationship between job satisfaction and voluntary turnover? *Journal of Applied Psychology,* 78:395–401.

Judge, T. A., and C. L. Hulin. 1993. Job satisfaction as a reflection of disposition: A multiple source causal analysis. *Organizational Behavior and Human Decision Processes,* 56:388–421.

Judge, T. A., and E. A. Locke. 1993. Effect of dysfunctional thought processes on subjective well-being and job satisfaction. *Journal of Applied Psychology,* 78:475–90.

Kahn, R. L., and R. P. Quinn. 1970. Role stress: A framework for analysis. In *Mental Health and Work Organizations,* ed. A. McLean. Chicago: Rand McNally.

Kahn, R. L., D. N. Wolfe, R. P. Quinn, J. D. Snoek, and D. A. Rosenthal. 1964. *Organizational Stress: Studies in Role Conflict and Ambiguity.* New York: John Wiley.

Kahne, M. J. 1968. Suicides in mental hospitals: A study of the effects of personnel and patient turnover. *Journal of Health and Social Behavior,* 9:255–66.

Kandel, D. B., and K. Yamaguchi. 1987. Job mobility and drug use: An event history analysis. *American Journal of Sociology,* 92 (4):836–78.

Kantor, R. M. 1977. *Men and Women of the Corporation.* New York: Basic Books.

Kanungo, R. N. 1982. Measurement of job and work involvement. *Journal of Applied Psychology,* 67:341–49.

Katerberg, R., P. W. Hom, and C. L. Hulin. 1979. Effects of job complexity on the reactions of part-time workers. *Organizational Behavior and Human Performance,* 24:317–32.

Katz, D., and R. L. Kahn. 1978. *The Social Psychology of Organizations,* 2d ed. New York: John Wiley.

Katz, R. 1980. Time and work: Toward an integrative perspective. In *Research in Organizational Behavior,* ed. B. Staw and L. L. Cummings, 2:81–127. Greenwich, Conn.: JAI Press.

———— 1982. The effects of group longevity on project communication and performance. *Administrative Science Quarterly,* 27:81–104.

Keller, R. T. 1984. The role of performance and absenteeism in the prediction of turnover. *Academy of Management Journal,* 27:176–83.

Kelley, H. H., and J. W. Thibaut. 1978. *Interpersonal relations: A theory of interdependence.* New York: Wiley.

Kemery, E. R., A. G. Bedeian, K. W. Mossholder, and J. Touliatos. 1985. Outcomes of role stress: A multisample constructive replication. *Academy of Management Journal,* 28 (2):363–75.

Kemery, E. R., W. P. Dunlap, and R. W. Griffeth. 1988. Correction for range restrictions in point-biserial correlations. *Journal of Applied Psychology,* 73:688–91.

Kenny, D. A., and D. A. Kashy. 1992. Analysis of the multitrait-multimethod matrix by confirmatory factor analysis. *Psychological Bulletin,* 112 (1):165–72.

Kerr, J., and J. W. Slocum. 1987. Managing corporate culture through reward systems. *Academy of Management Executive,* 1:99–108.

Kessler, R. C., and D. F. Greenberg. 1981. *Linear Panel Analysis: Models of Quantitative Change.* San Diego, Calif.: Academic Press.

Kiesler, C. A., and J. Sakumara. 1966. A test of a model for commitment. *Journal of Personality and Social Psychology,* 3:349–53.

Kinicki, A., K. Carson, and C. Schriesheim. 1990. *Psychometric properties of the job descriptive index.* Unpublished manuscript, Department of Management, Arizona State University, Tempe.

Kinicki, A. J., B. D. Bannister, P. W. Hom, and A. S. DeNisi. 1985. Behaviorally anchored rating scales vs. summated rating scales: Psychometric properties and susceptibility to rating bias. *Educational and Psychological Measurement,* 45 (3):535–49.

Kinicki, A. J., C. A. Lockwood, P. W. Hom, and R. W. Griffeth. 1990. Interviewer predictions of applicant qualifications and interviewer validity: Aggregate and individual analyses. *Journal of Applied Psychology,* 75:477–86.

Klein, K. J. 1987. Employee stock ownership and employee attitudes: A test of three models. *Journal of Applied Psychology,* 72:319–32.

Klenke-Hamal, K. E., and J. E. Mathieu. 1990. Role strains, tension, and job satisfaction influences on employees' propensity to leave: A multi-sample replication and extension. *Human Relations,* 43:791–808.

Kline, C. J., and L. H. Peters. 1991. Behavioral commitment and tenure of new employees: A replication and extension. *Academy of Management Journal,* 34 (1):194–204.

Konrad, W. 1990. Welcome to the woman-friendly company where talent is valued and rewarded. *Business Week* (6 August):48.

Koretz, G. 1990. Women still earn less, but they've come a long way. *Business Week* (24 December):14.

Koslowsky, M., A. N. Kluger, and Y. Yinon. 1988. Predicting behavior: Combining intention with investment. *Journal of Applied Psychology,* 73 (1):102–106.

Kossek, E. E. 1990. Diversity in child-care assistance needs: Employee problems, preferences, and work–related outcomes. *Personnel Psychology*, 43:769–91.

Kossek, E. E., and P. Grace. 1990. Taking a strategic view of employee child-care assistance: A cost–benefit model. *Human Resource Planning*, 13:189–202.

Krackhardt, D., and L. W. Porter. 1985. When friends leave: A structural analysis of the relationship between turnover and stayers' attitudes. *Administrative Science Quarterly*, 30:242–61.

Kramer, M. 1974. *Reality Shock: Why Nurses Leave Nursing.* St. Louis, Mo.: Mosley.

———— 1977. Reality shock can be handled on the job. *RN*, 63:11.

Kramer, M., and C. Schmalenberg. 1977. *Paths to Biculturalism.* Wakefield, Mass.: Contemporary Publishing.

Krau, E. 1981. Turnover analysis and prediction from a career development point of view. *Personnel Psychology*, 34:771–90.

Kumar, A., and W. R. Dillon. 1990. On the use of confirmatory measurement models in the analysis of multiple-informant reports. *Journal of Marketing Research*, 27 (1):102–11.

Labor letter. 1993. *Wall Street Journal.* (2 November): 1.

Lach, D. H., and P. A. Gwartney-Gibbs. 1993. Sociological perspectives on sexual harassment and workplace dispute resolution. *Journal of Vocational Behavior*, 42:102–15.

Laird, D. D. 1983. Supplemental nursing agencies—a tool for combatting the nursing shortage. *Health Care Management Review*, 8:61–67.

Laker, D. R. 1974. *The influence that perceptions of alternative employment, past search activities and feedback from the job search have upon the turnover decision process.* Ph.D. diss., University of Illinois., Champaign, IL.

———— 1991. Job search, perceptions of alternative employment and the turnover decision. *Journal of Applied Business Research*, 7:6–16.

Lakhani, H. 1988. The effect of pay and retention bonuses on quit rates in the U. S. Army. *Industrial and Labor Relations Review*, 41:430–38.

Lance, C. E. 1988. Job performance as a moderator of the satisfaction-turnover intention relation: An empirical contrast of two perspectives. *Journal of Organizational Behavior*, 9 (3):271–80.

Landy, F. J., J. Barnes, and K. Murphy. 1978. Correlates of perceived fairness and accuracy of performance appraisals. *Journal of Applied Psychology*, 63:751–54.

Latham, G. P., and C. A. Frayne. 1989. Self-management training for increasing job attendance: A follow-up and a replication. *Journal of Applied Psychology*, 74 (3):411–16.

Lawler, E. E. 1971. *Pay and Organizational Effectiveness: A Psychological View*. New York: McGraw–Hill.

———— 1981. *Pay and Organizational Development*. Reading, Mass.: Addison–Wesley.

———— 1990. *Strategic Pay*. San Francisco: Jossey–Bass.

Lazarsfeld, P. F., and W. Thielens. 1958. *The Academic Mind: Social Scientists in a Time of Crisis*. Glencoe, Ill: The Free Press.

Lazarus, R. S., and S. Folkman. 1984. *Stress, Appraisal, and Coping*. New York: Springer.

Leblanc, P. V. 1991. Skill–based pay case number 2: Northern Telecom. *Compensation and Benefits Review*, 23:39–56.

Ledford, G. E. 1991. Three case studies on skill–based pay: An overview. *Compensation and Benefits Review*, 23:11–23.

Ledford, G. E., and G. Bergel. 1991. Skill–based pay case number 1: General Mills. *Compensation and Benefits Review*, 23:24–38.

Ledford, G. E., W. R. Tyler, and W. B. Dixey. 1991. Skill–based pay case number 3: Honeywell ammunition assembly plant. *Compensation and Benefits Review*, 23:57–77.

Lee, E. T., and M. M. Desu. 1972. A computer program for comparing K samples with right censored data. *Computer Programs in Biomedicine*, 2:315–21.

Lee, T. W. 1988. How job satisfaction leads to employee turnover. *Journal of Business and Psychology*, 2:263–71.

Lee, T. W., S. J. Ashford, J. P. Walsh, and R. T. Mowday. 1992. Commitment propensity, organizational commitment, and voluntary turnover: A longitudinal study of organizational entry processes. *Journal of Management*, 10:15–32.

Lee, T. W., and T. R. Mitchell. 1994. An alternative approach: The unfolding model of voluntary employee turnover. *Academy of Management Review*, 19:51–89.

Lee, T. W., and R. T. Mowday. 1987. Voluntarily leaving an organization: An empirical investigation of Steers and Mowday's model of turnover. *Academy of Management Journal,* 30:721–43.

Lefkowitz, J., and M. L. Katz. 1969. Validity of exit interviews. *Personnel Psychology,* 22:445–55.

Lesieur, F. G. 1958. *The Scanlon Plan: A Frontier in Labor-Management Cooperation.* Cambridge, Mass.: MIT Press.

Lesly, E., and L. Light. 1992. When layoffs alone don't turn the tide. *Business Week* (7 December):100–101.

Leventhal, G. S. 1980. What should be done with equity theory? In *Social Exchange,* ed. K. Gergen, M. S. Greenberg, and R. H. Willis. New York: Plenum Press.

Lewin, T. 1991. High medical costs hurt growing numbers in U.S. *The New York Times* (28 April):1.

Lincoln, J. F. 1951. *Incentive Management.* Cleveland, Ohio: Lincoln Electric Company.

Lincoln, J. R. 1989. Employee work attitudes and management practices in the U.S., and Japan: Evidence from a large corporation survey. *California Management Review* 31:89–106.

Lincoln, J. R., and A. L. Kalleberg. 1985. Work organization and workplace commitment: A study of plants and employees in the U. S. and Japan. *American Sociological Review,* 50:738–60.

Lobel, S. A. 1993. Sexuality at work: Where do we go from here? *Journal of Vocational Behavior,* 42:136–52.

Lobel, S. A., and L. St. Clair. 1992. Effects of family responsibilities, gender, and career identity salience in performance outcomes. *Academy of Management Journal,* 35:1057–69.

Locke, E. A. 1969. What is job satisfaction? *Organizational Behavior and Human Performance,* 3:309–36.

———— 1976. The nature and causes of job satisfaction. In *Handbook of Industrial and Organizational Psychology,* ed. M. D. Dunnette: 1297–1350. Chicago: Rand McNally.

Locke, E. A., D. Sirota, and A. D. Wolfson. 1976. An experimental case study of the successes and failures of job enrichment in a government agency. *Journal of Applied Psychology,* 61 (6):701–11.

Loher, B. T., R. A. Noe, N. L. Moeller, and M. P. Fitzgerald. 1985. A meta-analysis of the relation of job characteristics to job satisfaction. *Journal of Applied Psychology,* 70:280–89.

Long, J. S. 1983. *Confirmatory Factor Analysis.* Beverly Hills, Calif.: Sage Publications.

Louis, M. R. 1980. Surprise and sense making—what newcomers experience in entering unfamiliar organizational settings. *Administrative Science Quarterly,* 25:226–51.

Louis, M. R., B. Z. Posner, and G. N. Powell. 1983. The availability and helpfulness of socialization practices. *Personnel Psychology,* 36:857–66.

Lublin, J. S. 1992. After couples divorce, long-distance moves are often wrenching. *Wall Street Journal* (20 November):1.

——— 1993. As more men become "trailing spouses," firms help them cope. *Wall Street Journal* (13 April):1.

Luthans, F., S. A. Rosenkrantz, and H. W. Hennessey. 1985. What do successful managers really do? An observation study of managerial activities. *Journal of Applied Behavioral Science,* 21 (3):255–70.

Lyons, T. F. 1971. Role clarity, need for clarity, satisfaction, tension, and withdrawal. *Organizational Behavior and Human Performance,* 6:99–110.

——— 1972. Turnover and absenteeism: A review of relationships and shared correlates. *Personnel Psychology,* 25:271–81.

McCain, B. E., C. O'Reilly, and J. Pfeffer. 1983. The effects of departmental demography on turnover: The case of a university. *Academy of Management Journal,* 26:626–41.

McEvoy, G. M., and W. F. Cascio. 1985. Strategies for reducing employee turnover: A meta-analysis. *Journal of Applied Psychology,* 70:342–53.

——— 1987. Do good or poor performers leave? A meta-analysis of the relationship between performance and turnover. *Academy of Management Journal,* 30:744–62.

Machalaba, D. 1993. Trucking firms find it is a struggle to hire and retain drivers. *Wall Street Journal* (28 December):1.

Managing diversity: Successes and failures. 1991. *Fair Employment Practices* (5 August): p. 90.

Mandel, M. J., and C. Farrell. 1992. The immigrants. *BusinessWeek* (13 July):114.

Manz, C. C. 1991a, September. Developing self-leaders through superleadership. *Supervisory Management,* 36:3.

—— 1991b, November. Helping yourself and others to master self-leadership. *Supervisory Management* 36:8–9.

—— 1992. Self-leading work teams: Moving beyond self-management myths. *Human Relations,* 45 (11):1119–40.

Manz, C. C., and C. P. Neck. 1991. Inner leadership: Creating productive thought patterns. *Academy of Management Executive,* 5:87–95.

Manz, C. C., and H. P. Sims. 1980. Self-management as a substitute for leadership—a social learning theory perspective. *Academy of Management Review,* 5:361–67.

—— 1989. *Super Leadership.* New York: Prentice Hall Press.

—— 1993. *Business without Bosses.* New York: John Wiley.

March, J. G., and H. A. Simon. 1958. *Organizations.* New York: John Wiley.

Markham, S. E., and G. H. McKee. 1991. Declining organizational size and increasing unemployment rates: Predicting employee absenteeism from within—and between—plant perspectives. *Academy of Management Journal,* 34:952–65.

Marsh, H. W. 1989. Confirmatory factor analyses of multitrait-multimethod data: Many problems and a few solutions. *Applied Psychological Measurement,* 4:335–61.

Marsh, H. W., J. R. Balla, and R. P. McDonald. 1988. Goodness-of-fit indexes in confirmatory factor analysis: The effect of sample size. *Psychological Bulletin,* 103 (3):391–410.

Marsh, H. W., J. Barnes, and D. Hocevar. 1985. Self-other agreement on multidimensional self-concept ratings: Factor analysis and multitrait-multimethod analysis. *Journal of Personality and Social Psychology,* 49 (5):1360–77.

Marsh, H. W., and D. Hocevar. 1985. Application of confirmatory factor analysis to the study of self-concept: First- and higher-order factor models and their invariance across groups. *Psychological Bulletin,* 97 (3):562–82.

—— 1988. A new, more powerful approach to multitrait-multimethod analyses: Application of second-order confirmatory factor analysis. *Journal of Applied Psychology,* 73 (1):107–17.

Marsh, R. M., and H. Mannari. 1977. Organizational commitment and turnover: A prediction study. *Administrative Science Quarterly,* 22:57–75.

Martin, T. N., J. L. Price, and C. W. Mueller. 1981. Job performance and turnover. *Journal of Applied Psychology,* 66:116-19.

Martin, T. N., and J. R. Schermerhorn. 1983. Work and nonwork influences on health: A research agenda using inability to leave as a critical variable. *Academy of Management Review*, 8 (4):650–59.

Martin, T. N., Jr. 1979. A contextual model of employee turnover intentions. *Academy of Management Journal*, 22:313–24.

Maslach, C. 1982. *Burnout: The Cost of Caring*. Englewood Cliffs, N.J.: Prentice-Hall.

Mathieu, J. E. 1991. A cross–level nonrecursive model of the antecedents of organizational commitment and satisfaction. *Journal of Applied Psychology*, 76:607–18.

Mathieu, J. E., and J. L. Farr. 1991. Further evidence for the discriminant validity of measures of organizational commitment, job involvement, and job satisfaction. *Journal of Applied Psychology*, 76:127–33.

Mathieu, J. E., and D. Zajac. 1990. A review and meta-analysis of the antecedents, correlates, and consequences of organizational commitment. *Psychological Bulletin*, 108:171–94.

Mattis, M. C. 1990. New forms of flexible work arrangements for managers and professionals: Myths and realities. *Human Resource Planning*, 13:133–46.

Meglino, B. M., and A. S. DeNisi. 1987. Realistic job previews: Some thoughts on their more effective use in managing the flow of human resources. *Human Resource Planning*, 10:157–67.

Meglino, B. M., A. S. DeNisi, E. C. Ravlin, W. E. Tomes, and J. Lee. 1990, August. The effects of realistic job preview and prior job experience on the retention of correctional officers. Paper presented at annual convention of the Academy of Management, San Francisco, Calif.

Meglino, B. M., A. S. DeNisi, S. A. Youngblood, and K. J. Williams. 1988. Effects of realistic job previews: A comparison using an enhancement and a reduction preview. *Journal of Applied Psychology*, 73:259–66.

Meyer, H. H. 1991. A solution to the performance appraisal feedback enigma. *Academy of Management Executive*, 5:68–76.

Meyer, J. P., N. J. Allen, and I. R. Gellatly. 1990. Affective and continuance commitment to the organization: Evaluation of measures and analysis of concurrent and time–lagged relations. *Journal of Applied Psychology*, 75:710–20.

Meyer, J. P., S. V. Paunonen, I. R. Gellatly, R. D. Goffin, and D. N. Jackson. 1989. Organizational commitment and job performance: It's the nature of commitment that counts. *Journal of Applied Psychology*, 74:152–56.

Miceli, M. P. 1985. The effects of realistic job previews on newcomer behavior: A laboratory study. *Journal of Vocational Behavior,* 26 (3):277–89.

Miceli, M. P., I. Jung, J. P. Near, and D. B. Greenberger. 1991. Predictors and outcomes of reactions to pay–for–performance plans. *Journal of Applied Psychology,* 76:508–21.

Miceli, M., and M. C. Lane. 1991. Antecedents of pay satisfaction: A review and extension. In *Research in Personnel and Human Resources Management,* ed. G. R. Ferris and K. M. Rowland, 9:235–309. Greenwich, Conn.: JAI Press.

Michaels, C. E., and P. E. Spector. 1982. Causes of employee turnover: A test of the Mobley, Griffeth, Hand, and Meglino model. *Journal of Applied Psychology,* 67:53–59.

Miles, R. H. 1976. Role requirements as sources of organizational stress. *Journal of Applied Psychology,* 61:172–79.

Milkovich, G. T., and L. Gomez. 1976. Day care and selected employee work behavior. *Academy of Management Journal,* 19:111–15.

Milkovich, G., and J. Newman. 1990. *Compensation* (Third Edition). Homewood, Ill.: Irwin.

Milkovich, G. T., and J. M. Newman. 1993. *Compensation* (Fourth Edition). Homewood, Ill: BPI/Irwin.

Miller, H. E., R. Katerberg, and C. L. Hulin. 1979. Evaluation of the Mobley, Horner, and Hollingsworth model of employee turnover. *Journal of Applied Psychology,* 64:509–17.

Miller, T. I. 1984. The effects of employer–sponsored child care on employee absenteeism, turnover, productivity, recruitment or job satisfaction: What is claimed and what is known. *Personnel Psychology.* 37:277–89.

Milliken, F., J. E. Dutton, and J. M. Beyer. 1990. Understanding organizational adaptation to change: The case of work–family issues. *Human Resource Planning,* 13:91–107.

Mirowsky, J. 1987. The psycho-economics of feeling underpaid: Distributive justice and the earnings of husbands and wives. *American Journal of Sociology,* 92 (6):1404–34.

Mirvis, P. H., and E. E. Lawler. 1977. Measuring the financial impact of employee attitudes. *Journal of Applied Psychology,* 62 (1):1–8.

Mitchell, O. S. 1983. Fringe benefits and the cost of changing jobs. *Industrial and Labor Relations Review,* 37:70–78.

Mitra, A., G. D. Jenkins, and N. Gupta. 1992. A meta-analytic review of the relationship between absence and turnover. *Journal of Applied Psychology*, 77:879–89.

Mobley, W. H. 1977. Intermediate linkages in the relationship between job satisfaction and employee turnover. *Journal of Applied Psychology*, 62:237–40.

———— 1982a. *Employee Turnover: Causes, Consequences, and Control.* Reading, Mass.: Addison–Wesley.

———— 1982b. Some unanswered questions in turnover and withdrawal research. *Academy of Management Review*, 7:111–16.

Mobley, W. H., R. W. Griffeth, H. H. Hand, and B. M. Meglino. 1979. Review and conceptual analysis of the employee turnover process. *Psychological Bulletin*, 86:493–522.

Mobley, W. H., H. H. Hand, R. L. Baker, and B. M. Meglino. 1979. Conceptual and empirical analysis of military recruit training attrition. *Journal of Applied Psychology*, 64:10–18.

Mobley, W. H., S. O. Horner, and A. T. Hollingsworth. 1978. An evaluation of precursors of hospital employee turnover. *Journal of Applied Psychology*, 63:408–14.

Mobley, W., and B. Meglino. 1979, August. *Toward further understanding of the employee turnover process.* Paper presented at the 39th annual meeting of the Academy of Management, Atlanta, Ga.

Moore, T. F., and E. A. Simendinger. 1989. *Managing the Nursing Shortage.* Rockville, Md.: Aspen Publishers.

Morita, J. G., T. W. Lee, and R. T. Mowday. 1989. Introducing survival analysis to organizational researchers: A selected application to turnover research. *Journal of Applied Psychology*, 74:280–92.

———— 1993. The regression-analog to survival analysis: A selected application to turnover research. *Academy of Management Journal*, 36:1430–64.

Morrison, A. M., and M. A. Von Glinow. 1990. Women and minorities in management. *American Psychologist*, 45 (2):200–208.

Morrow, P. C., and R. E. Wirth. 1989. Work commitment among salaried professionals. *Journal of Vocational Behavior*, 34:40–56.

Mossholder, K.W., A. G. Bedeian, D. R. Norris, W. F. Giles, and H. S. Feild. 1988. Job performance and turnover decisions: Two field studies. *Journal of Management*, 14 (3):403–14.

Motowidlo, S. J. 1983. Predicting sales turnover from pay satisfaction and expectation. *Journal of Applied Psychology,* 68:484–89.

———— 1984. Does job satisfaction lead to consideration and personal sensitivity? *Academy of Management Journal,* 27 (4):910–15.

Motowidlo, S. J., and G. W. Lawton. 1984. Affective and cognitive factors in soldiers' reenlistment decisions. *Journal of Applied Psychology,* 69:157–66.

Moving past affirmative action to managing diversity. 1990. *Fair Employment Practices* (17 September): 109.

Mowday, R. T., C. S. Koberg, and A. W. McArthur. 1984. The psychology of the withdrawal process: A cross–validation test of Mobley's intermediate linkages model of turnover in two samples. *Academy of Management Journal,* 27:79–94.

Mowday, R. T., L. W. Porter, and R. M. Steers. 1982. *Employee-Organization Linkages.* New York: Academic Press.

Mowday, R. T., L. W. Porter, and E. F. Stone. 1978. Employee characteristics as predictors of turnover among female clerical employees in two organizations. *Journal of Vocational Behavior,* 12:321–32.

Mowday, R. T., and D. G. Spencer. 1981. The influence of task and personality characteristics on employee turnover and absenteeism incidents. *Academy of Management Journal,* 24:634–42.

Muchinsky, P. M., and P. C. Morrow. 1980. A multidisciplinary model of voluntary employee turnover. *Journal of Vocational Behavior,* 17 (3):263–90.

Muchinsky, P. M., and M. L. Tuttle. 1979. Employee turnover: An empirical and methodological assessment. *Journal of Vocational Behavior,* 14:43–77.

Mueller, C. W., and J. L. Price. 1989. Some consequences of turnover: A work unit analysis. *Human Relations,* 42:389–402.

Mulaik, S. A., L. R. James, J. Van Alstine, N. Bennett, S. Lind, and C. D. Stillwell. 1989. Evaluation of goodness-of-fit indices for structural equation models. *Psychological Bulletin,* 105 (3):430–45.

Murnane, R. J., J. D. Singer, and J. B. Willet. 1988. The career paths of teachers. *Educational Researcher,* 17, 22–30.

———— 1989. The influences of salaries and "opportunity costs" on teachers' career choices: Evidence from North Carolina. *Harvard Educational Review,* 59:325–46.

Murphy, K. R., and J. N. Cleveland. 1991. *Performance Appraisal.* Needham Heights, Mass.: Allyn and Bacon.

Muthen, B. O. 1987. *Liscomp.* Mooresville, IN: Scientific Software.

Neck, C. P. 1992. *Thought self-leadership: The impact of mental strategies training on employee cognitions, behaviors, and emotions.* Ph.D. diss., Arizona State University, Tempe, Ariz.

Neck, C. P., and C. C. Manz. 1992. Thought self-leadership: The influence of self-talk and mental imagery on performance. *Journal of Organizational Behavior,* 13:681–99.

Netemeyer, R. G., M. W. Johnston, and S. Burton. 1990. An analysis of role conflict and role ambiguity in a structural equations framework. *Journal of Applied Psychology,* 75:148–57.

Newby, J. M. 1980. Study supports hiring more part–time RNs. *Hospitals* (1 September):71–73.

Newman, J. E. 1974. Predicting absenteeism and turnover: A field comparison of Fishbein's model and traditional job attitude measures. *Journal of Applied Psychology,* 59:610–15.

Nkomo, S. M. 1992. The emperor has no clothes: Rewriting "Race in Organizations." *Academy of Management Review,* 17 (3):487–513.

Nussbaum, B. 1991. I'm worried about my job! *Business Week* (7 October):94.

O'Driscoll, M. P., D. R. Ilgen, and K. Hildreth. 1992. Time devoted to job and off–job activities, interrole conflict, and affective experiences. *Journal of Applied Psychology,* 77:272–79.

OFCCP's glass ceiling initiative. 1991. *Fair Employment Practices* (2 September): p. 102.

Oldham, G. R. 1988. Effects of changes in workspace partitions and spatial density on employee reactions: A quasi-experiment. *Journal of Applied Psychology,* 73:253–58.

Oldham, G. R., and Y. Fried. 1987. Employee reactions to workspace characteristics. *Journal of Applied Psychology,* 72:75–80.

Oldham, G. R., C. T. Kulik, and L. P. Stepina. 1991. Physical environments and employee reactions: Effects of stimulus-screening skills and job complexity. *Academy of Management Journal,* 34 (4):929–38.

Oldham, G. R., and N. L. Rotchford. 1983. Relationships between office characteristics and employee reactions: A study of the physical environment. *Administrative Science Quarterly*, 28:542–56.

Olson, M. H., and S. B. Primps. 1984. Working at home with computers: Work and nonwork issues. *Journal of Social Issues*, 40:97–112.

One company's approach to valuing workforce diversity. 1991. *Fair Employment Practices* (25 April): 48.

O'Reilly, B. 1992. How to take care of aging parents. *Fortune* (18 May):108–112.

——— 1992. The job drought. *Fortune* (24 August):62.

O'Reilly, C. A., and D. F. Caldwell. 1981. The commitment and job tenure of new employees: Some evidence of postdecisional justification. *Administrative Science Quarterly*, 26 (4):597–616.

O'Reilly, C. A., D. F. Caldwell, and W. P. Barnett. 1989. Work group demography, social integration, and turnover. *Administrative Science Quarterly*, 34:21–37.

O'Reilly, C. A., and J. Chatman. 1986. Organizational commitment and psychological attachment: The effects of compliance, identification, and internalization. *Journal of Applied Psychology*, 71:492–99.

O'Reilly, C. A., J. Chatman, and D. F. Caldwell. 1991. People and organizational culture: A profile comparison approach to assessing person–organization fit. *Academy of Management Journal*, 34:487–516.

O'Reilly, J. P., K. A. Tokuno, and A. T. Ebata. 1986. Cultural differences between Americans of Japanese and European ancestry in parental valuing of social competence. *Journal of Comparative Family Studies*, 17 (1):87–97.

Organ, D. W. 1988. A restatement of the satisfaction-performance hypothesis. *Journal of Management*, 14 (4):547–57.

——— 1990. The motivational basis of organizational citizenship behavior. In *Research in Organizational Behavior*, ed. B. Staw and L. L. Cummings, 12:43–72. Greenwich, Conn.: JAI Press.

Osigweh, C. A. 1989. Concept fallibility in organizational science. *Academy of Management Review*, 14 (4):579–94.

Palich, L. E., Hom, P. W., and Griffeth, R. W. (in press). Managing the international context: Testing the cultural universality of an organizational commitment model. *Journal of Management*.

Parsons, C. K., D. M. Herold, and M. L. Leatherwood. 1985. Turnover during initial employment: A longitudinal study of the role of causal attributions. *Journal of Applied Psychology,* 70:337–41.

Pavalko, R. M. 1970. Recruitment to teaching: Patterns of selection and retention. *Sociology of Education,* 43:340–53.

Pay equity makes good business sense. 1990. *Fair Employment Practices* (3 September): 103.

Payson, M. F., and P. B. Rosen. 1991. Playing by fair rules. *HR Magazine,* 36:42–43.

Pederson, D. G. 1973. Approximate method of sampling on multinomial population. *Population Biometrics,* 29:814–21.

Peel, M. J., and N. Wilson. 1990. Labor absenteeism: The impact of profit sharing, voice and participation. *International Journal of Manpower,* 11:17–24.

Peters, C. C., and W. R. Van Voorhis. 1940. *Statistical Procedures and Their Mathematical Bases.* New York: McGraw-Hill.

Peters, L. H., E. F. Jackofsky, and J. R. Salter. 1981. Predicting turnover—a comparison of part-time and full-time employees. *Journal of Occupational Behavior,* 2:89–98.

Peters, L. H., and J. E. Sheridan. 1988. Turnover research methodology: A critique of traditional designs and a suggested survival model alternative. In *Research in Personnel and Human Resource Management,* ed. K. M. Rowland and G. R. Ferris, 6:231–62. Greenwich, Conn.: JAI Press.

Pfeffer, J. 1983. Organizational demography. In *Research in Organizational Behavior,* ed. L. L. Cummings and B. M. Staw, 5:299–357. Greenwich, Conn.: JAI Press.

Pierce, J. L., and R. B. Dunham. 1992. The 12–hour work day: A forty eight-hour, eight-day week. *Academy of Management Journal,* 35:1086–98.

Platt, J. R. 1964. Strong inference. *Science,* 146:347–53.

Podsakoff, P. M., L. J. Williams, and W. D. Todor. 1986. Effects of organizational formalization on alienation among professionals and nonprofessionals. *Academy of Management Journal,* 29 (4):820–31.

Porter, L. W., W. J. Crampon, and F. J. Smith. 1976. Organizational commitment and managerial turnover: A longitudinal study. *Organizational Behavior and Human Performance,* 15:87–98.

Porter, L. W., and R. M. Steers. 1973. Organizational, work, and personal factors in employee turnover and absenteeism. *Psychological Bulletin,* 80:151–76.

Porter, L. W., R. M. Steers, R. T. Mowday, and P. V. Boulian. 1974. Organizational commitment, job satisfaction, and turnover among psychiatric technicians. *Journal of Applied Psychology,* 59:603–609.

Premack, S. L., and J. E. Hunter. 1988. Individual unionization decisions. *Psychological Bulletin,* 103:223–34.

Premack, S. L., and J. P. Wanous, 1985. A meta-analysis of realistic job preview experiments. *Journal of Applied Psychology* 70:706–19.

Premack, S., and J. Wanous. 1987, August. *Evaluating the Met Expectations Hypothesis.* Paper presented at the national meeting of the Academy of Management, New Orleans, La.

Prestholdt, P. H., I. M. Lane, and R. C. Mathews. 1987. Nurse turnover as reasoned action: Development of a process model. *Journal of Applied Psychology,* 72:221–27.

Price, J. L. 1977. *The Study of Turnover.* Ames, Iowa: Iowa State University Press.

——— 1989. The impact of turnover on the organization. *Work and Occupations,* 16:461–73.

Price, J. L., and A. C. Bluedorn. 1979. Test of a causal model of turnover from organizations. In *The International Yearbook of Organizational Studies,* ed. D. Dunkerley and G. Salaman. London and Boston: Routledge and Kegan Paul.

Price, J. L., and C. W. Mueller. 1981. A causal model of turnover for nurses. *Academy of Management Journal,* 24:543–65.

——— 1986. *Absenteeism and Turnover of Hospital Employees.* Greenwich, Conn.: JAI Press.

Promoting women to upper management. 1990. *Fair Employment Practices* (19 July): p. 86.

Pryor, J. B., C. M. LaVite, and L. M. Stoller. 1993. A social psychological analysis of sexual harassment: The person/situation interaction. *Journal of Vocational Behavior,* 42:68–83.

Raelin, J. A. 1986. *The Clash of Cultures.* Boston, Mass.: Harvard Business School Press.

Ralston, D. A., and M. F. Flanagan. 1985. The effect of flexitime on absenteeism and turnover for male and female employees. *Journal of Vocational Behavior,* 26:206–17.

Reichers, A. E. 1985. A review and reconceptualization of organizational commitment. *Academy of Management Review,* 10:465–76.

Reichheld, F. F. 1993. Loyalty-based management. *Harvard Business Review,* 71:64–73.

Reilly, R. R., B. Brown, M. R. Blood, and C. Z. Malatesta. 1981. The effects of realistic previews: A study and discussion of the literature. *Personnel Psychology,* 34:823–34.

Reilly, R. R., M. L. Tenopyr, and S. M. Sperling. 1979. Effects of job previews on job acceptance and survival of telephone operator candidates. *Journal of Applied Psychology,* 64 (2):218–20.

Rhodes, S. R., and R. M. Steers. 1990. *Managing Employee Absenteeism.* Reading, Mass.: Addison–Wesley.

Rogosa, D. 1980. A critique of cross-lagged correlation. *Psychological Bulletin,* 88 (2):245–58.

Rokeach, M. 1973. *The Nature of Human Values.* New York: Free Press.

Roseman, E. 1981. *Managing Employee Turnover.* New York: AMACOM.

Rossé, J. G. 1988. Relations among lateness, absence, and turnover: Is there a progression of withdrawal? *Human Relations,* 41:517–31.

Rossé, J. G., and C. L. Hulin. 1985. Adaptation to work: An analysis of employee health, withdrawal, and change. *Organizational Behavior and Human Decision Processes,* 36 (3):324–47.

Rossé, J. G., and H. E. Miller. 1984. Relationship between absenteeism and other employee behaviors. In *Absenteeism: New Approaches to Understanding, Measuring, and Managing Employee Absence,* ed. P. S. Goodman and R. S. Atkin. San Francisco: Jossey–Bass.

Rousseau, D. 1985. Issues of level in organizational research: Multi–level and cross–level perspectives. In *Research in Organizational Behavior,* ed. L. L. Cummings and B. M. Staw, 7:1–37. Greenwich, Conn.: JAI Press.

Rusbult, C. E., and D. Farrell. 1983. A longitudinal test of the investment model: The impact on job satisfaction, job commitment, and turnover of variations in rewards, costs, alternatives, and investments. *Journal of Applied Psychology,* 68:429–38.

Rusbult, C. E., D. Farrell, G. Rogers, and A. G. Mainous. 1988. Impact of exchange variables on exit, voice, loyalty, and neglect: An integrative model of responses to declining job satisfaction. *Academy of Management Journal,* 31:599–627.

Rynes, S. L. 1990. Recruitment, job choice, and post-hire consequences: A call for new research directions. In *Handbook of Industrial and Organizational Psychology,* ed. M. D. Dunnette and L. Hough, 2d ed.: 399–444. Palo Alto, Calif.: Consulting Psychologists Press.

Sackett, P. R., C. L. DuBois, and A. W. Noe. 1991. Tokenism in performance evaluation: The effects of work group representation on male-female and white-black differences in performance ratings. *Journal of Applied Psychology*, 76 (2):263–67.

Sager, J., R. W. Griffeth, and P. W. Hom. 1992. A structural model assessing the validity of turnover cognitions. Department of Marketing, University of North Texas, Denton, Texas.

Sager, J., P. Varadarajan, and C. Futrell. 1988. Understanding salesperson turnover: A partial evaluation of Mobley's turnover process model. *Journal of Personal Selling and Sales Management,* 8:20–35.

Salancik, G. R. 1977. Commitment and the control of organizational behavior and belief. In *New Directions in Organizational Behavior,* ed. B. Staw and G. Salanick, 1–54. Chicago, Ill: St. Clair Press.

Salancik, G. R., and J. Pfeffer. 1977. An examination of need-satisfaction models of job attitudes. *Administrative Science Quarterly,* 22 (3):427–56.

Scandura, T. A., and G. B. Graen. 1984. Moderating effects of initial leader–member exchange status on the effects of a leadership intervention. *Journal of Applied Psychology,* 69:428–36.

Scarpello, V., V. Huber, and R. J. Vandenberg. 1988. Compensation satisfaction: Its measurement and dimensionality. *Journal of Applied Psychology,* 73 (2):163–71.

Schaubroeck, J., and D. C. Ganster. 1993. Chronic demands and responsivity to challenge. *Journal of Applied Psychology,* 78:73–85.

Schaubroeck, J., and S. G. Green. 1989. Confirmatory factor analytic procedures for assessing change during organizational entry. *Journal of Applied Psychology,* 74 (6):892–900.

Schlesinger, L. A., and J. L. Heskett. 1991. The service-driven service company. *Harvard Business Review,* (September–October) 69:71–81.

Schmitt, N., R. Z. Gooding, R. D. Noe, and M. Kirsch. 1984. Meta-analyses of validity studies published between 1964 and 1982 and the investigation of study characteristics. *Personnel Psychology,* 37:407–22.

Schmitt, N., and D. M. Stults. 1986. Methodology review: Analysis of multitrait-multimethod matrices. *Applied Psychological Measurement,* 10 (1):1–22.

Schneider, B. 1985. Organizational behavior. *Annual Review of Psychology,* 36:573–611.

—— 1987. The people make the place. *Personnel Psychology,* 40:437–53.

Schneider, B., and D. E. Bowen. 1985. Employee and customer perceptions of service in banks: Replication and extension. *Journal of Applied Psychology,* 70:423–33.

——— 1992. Personnel/human resources management in the service sector. In *Research in Personnel and Human Resources Management,* ed. G. Ferris and K. Rowland, 10:1–30. Greenwich, Conn.: JAI Press.

Schneider, J. 1976. The "greener grass" phenomenon: Differential effects of a work context alternative on organizational participation and withdrawal intentions. *Organizational Behavior and Human Performance,* 16:308–33.

Schoenberg, R. 1989. Covariance structure models. *Annual Review of Sociology,* 15:425–40.

Scholl, R. W., E. A. Cooper, and J. F. McKenna. 1987. Referent selection in determining equity perceptions: Differential effects on behavioral and attitudinal outcomes. *Personnel Psychology,* 40 (1):113–24.

Schwab, D. P. 1980. Construct validity in organizational behavior. In *Research in Organizational Behavior,* ed. B. Staw and L. Cummings, 2:3–43. Greenwich, Conn.: JAI Press.

——— 1991. Contextual variables in employee performance–turnover relationships. *Academy of Management Journal,* 34:966–75.

Schwab, D. P., S. L. Rynes, and R. J. Aldag. 1987. Theories and research on job search and choice. In *Research in Personnel and Human Resources Management,* ed. K. M. Rowland and G. R. Ferris, 5:129–66. Greenwich, Conn.: JAI Press.

Schwartz, F. N. 1989. Management women and the new facts of life. *Harvard Business Review* (January–February):65–76.

Schwartz, R. H. 1992. Is Holland's theory worthy of so much attention, or should vocational psychology move on? *Journal of Vocational Behavior,* 40 (2):79–187.

Schwarzer, R. 1989. *Meta.* Durham, N.C.: National Collegiate Software.

Scott, K. D., and G. S. Taylor. 1985. An examination of conflicting findings on the relationship between job satisfaction and absenteeism: A meta-analysis. *Academy of Management Journal,* 28 (3):599–612.

Segal, U. A. 1992. Values, personality and career choice. *Journal of Applied Social Sciences,* 16 (2):143–59.

Shaw, K. 1987. The quit propensity of married men. *Journal of Labor Economics,* 5:533–60.

Shellenbarger, S. 1992. Managers navigate uncharted waters trying to resolve work–family conflicts. *Wall Street Journal* (7 December):B1

Sheppard, B. H., J. Hartwick, and P. R. Warshaw. 1988. The theory of reasoned action: A meta-analysis of past research with recommendations for modifications and future research. *Journal of Consumer Research,* 15 (3):325–43.

Sheridan, J. E. 1985. A catastrophe model of employee withdrawal leading to low job performance, high absenteeism, and job turnover during the first year of employment. *Academy of Management Journal,* 28:88–109.

———— 1992. Organizational culture and employee retention. *Academy of Management Journal,* 35:1036–56.

Sheridan, J. E., and M. A. Abelson. 1983. Cusp catastrophe model of employee turnover. *Academy of Management Journal,* 26:418–36.

Sheridan, J. E., and D. J. Vredenburgh. 1978. Usefulness of leadership behavior and social power variables in predicting job tension, performance, and turnover of nursing employees. *Journal of Applied Psychology,* 63:89–95.

Sigardson, K. M. 1982. Why nurses leave nursing: A survey of former nurses. *Nursing Administration Quarterly,* 7 (Fall):20–24.

Simon, H.A. 1947. *Administrative Behavior.* New York: Free Press.

Sims, H. P., and A. D. Szilagyi. 1979. Time lags in leader reward research. *Journal of Applied Psychology,* 64 (1):71–76.

Singer, J. D., and J. B. Willett. 1991. Modeling the days of our lives: Using survival analysis when designing and analyzing longitudinal studies of duration and the timing of events. *Psychological Bulletin,* 110 (2) 268–90.

Smith, L. 1992. Are you better off? *Fortune* (24 February):38–42, 46, 48.

Smith, P. C. 1976. Behaviors, results, and organizational effectiveness: The problem of criteria. In *Handbook of Industrial and Organizational Psychology,* ed. M. D. Dunnette. Chicago: Rand McNally.

Smith, P. C., L. M. Kendall, and C. L. Hulin. 1969. *The Measurement of Satisfaction in Work and Retirement.* Chicago: Rand McNally.

Smither, J. W., H. Collins, and R. Buda. 1989. When ratee satisfaction influences performance evaluations: A case of illusory correlation. *Journal of Applied Psychology,* 74 (4):599–605.

Solomon, C. M. 1991. Are white males being left out? *Personnel Journal* (September):88.

Spector, W. D., and H. A. Takada. 1991. Characteristics of nursing homes that affect resident outcomes. *Journal of Aging and Health,* 3:427–54.

Spencer, D. G., and R. M. Steers. 1981. Performance as a moderator of the job satisfaction–turnover relationship. *Journal of Applied Psychology,* 66:511–14.

Spencer, D. G., R. M. Steers, and R. T. Mowday. 1983. An empirical test of the inclusion of job search linkages into Mobley's model of the turnover decision process. *Journal of Occupational Psychology,* 56 (2):137–44.

Spiers, J. 1992. The baby boom is for real. *Fortune* (10 February):101.

Srull, T. K., and R. S. Wyer. 1979. The role of category accessibility in the interpretation of information about persons: Some determinants and implications. *Journal of Personality and Social Psychology,* 37 (10):1660–72.

Staines, G. L., K. J. Pottick, and D. A. Fudge. 1986. Wives' employment and husbands' attitudes toward work and life. *Journal of Applied Psychology,* 71 (1):118–28.

Staw, B. M. 1980. The consequences of turnover. *Journal of Occupational Behavior,* 1:253–73.

Staw, B. M., N. Bell, and J. A. Clausen. 1986. The dispositional approach to job attitudes: A lifetime longitudinal test. *Administrative Science Quarterly,* 31:56–77.

Steel, R. P., and R. W. Griffeth. 1989. The elusive relationship between perceived employment opportunity and turnover behavior: A methodological or conceptual artifact? *Journal of Applied Psychology,* 74:846–54.

Steel, R. P., W. H. Hendrix, and S. P. Balogh. 1990. Confounding effects of the turnover base rate on relations between time lag and turnover study outcomes: An extension of meta-analysis findings and conclusions. *Journal of Organizational Behavior,* 11:237–42.

Steel, R. P., and N. K. Ovalle II. 1984. A review and meta-analysis of research on the relationship between behavioral intentions and employee turnover. *Journal of Applied Psychology,* 69:673–86.

Steel, R. P., G. S. Shane, and R. W. Griffeth. 1990. Correcting turnover statistics for comparative analysis. *Academy of Management Journal,* 33:179–87.

Steel, R., J. Lounsbury, and W. Horst. 1981. A test of the internal and external validity of Mobley's model of employee turnover. *Proceedings of the 24th Annual Conference of the Midwest Academy of Management,* ed. T. Martin and R. Osborn, College of Business Administration, Southern Illinois University, Carbondale, Ill.

Steers, R. M. 1977. Antecedents and outcomes of organizational commitment. *Administrative Science Quarterly,* 22 (1):46–56.

Steers, R. M., and R. T. Mowday. 1981. Employee turnover and postdecision accommodation processes. In *Research in Organizational Behavior,* ed. L. Cummings and B. Staw, 3:235–81. Greenwich, Conn.: JAI Press.

Stein, J. A., M. D. Newcomb, and P. M. Bentler. 1988. Structure of drug use behaviors and consequences among young adults: Multitrait-multimethod assessment of frequency, quantity, work site and problem substance use. *Journal of Applied Psychology,* 73 (4):595–605.

Stewart, T. A.. 1993. The king is dead. *Fortune* (11 January): 34.

Stockdale, M. S. 1993. The role of sexual misperceptions of women's friendliness in an emerging theory of sexual harassment. *Journal of Vocational Behavior,* 42:84–101.

Stricharchuk, G. 1987. Retirement prospects grow bleaker for many as job scene changes. *Wall Street Journal* (26 August):1

Stroh, L. K., J. M. Brett, and A. H. Reilly. 1992. All the right stuff: A comparison of female and male managers' career progression. *Journal of Applied Psychology,* 77 (3):251–60.

Stumpf, S. A., and P. K. Dawley. 1981. Predicting voluntary and involuntary turnover using absenteeism and performance indices. *Academy of Management Journal,* 24:148–63.

Sundstrom, E., K. P. DeMeuse, and D. Futrell. 1990. Work teams: Applications and effectiveness. *American Psychologist,* 45 (2):120–33.

Suszko, M., and J. A. Breaugh. 1986. The effects of RJPs on applicant self-selection and employee turnover, satisfaction, and coping ability. *Journal of Management,* 12:513–23.

Sweeney, P. D., D. B. McFarlin, and E. J. Inderrieden. 1990. Using relative deprivation theory to explain satisfaction with income and pay level: A multistudy examination. *Academy of Management Journal,* 33 (2):423–36.

Swingle, C. 1993. Sexism still an obstacle. *USA Today* (30 June):1.

Terborg, J. R., and T. W. Lee. 1984. A predictive study of organizational turnover rates. *Academy of Management Journal,* 27:793–810.

Tett, R. P., D. N. Jackson, and M. Rothstein. 1991. Personality measures as predictors of job performance: A meta-analytic review. *Personnel Psychology,* 44:703–42.

Tett, R. P., and J. P. Meyer. 1992. *Job satisfaction, organizational commitment, turnover intention, and turnover: Path analyses based on meta-analytic findings.* Department of Psychology, University of Western Ontario, London, Ontario, Canada.

Thibaut, J. W., and H. H. Kelly. 1959. *The Social Psychology of Groups.* New York: Wiley.

Thomas, D. A. 1993. Racial dynamics in cross-race developmental relationships. *Administrative Science Quarterly,* 38:169–94.

Thorndike, R. L. 1949. *Personnel Selection.* New York: Wiley.

Thorndike, R. M. 1978. *Correlational procedures for research.* New York: Gardner Press.

Thurow, L. C. 1992. *Head to head: Coming economic battles.* New York: Warner Books, Inc.

Title VII's overseas reach; upward mobility for women. 1991. *Fair Employment Practices* (16 September): 105.

Trenk, B. S. 1990. Future moms, serious workers. *Management Review* (September):33–37.

Triandis, H. C. 1977. *Interpersonal behavior.* Monterey, Calif.: Brooks/Cole.

———— 1979. Values, attitudes, and interpersonal behavior. In *Nebraska Symposium on Motivation,* ed. H. E. Howe, Jr., 159–259. Lincoln, Nebr.: University of Nebraska Press.

Tsui, A. S., and B. Barry. 1986. Interpersonal affect and rating errors. *Academy of Management Journal,* 29:586–99.

Tsui, A. S., and C. A. O'Reilly. 1989. Beyond simple demographic effects: The importance of relational demography in superior-subordinate dyads. *Academy of Management Journal,* 32 (2):402–23.

Tsui, A. S., T. D. Egan, and C. A. O'Reilly. 1992. Being different: Relational demography and organizational attachment. *Administrative Science Quarterly,* 37:549–79.

Turban, D. B., J. E. Campion, and A. R. Eyring. 1992. Factors relating to relocation decisions of research and development employees. *Journal of Vocational Behavior,* 41:183–99.

Turbin, M. S., and J. G. Rossé. 1990. Staffing issues in the high technology industry. In *Organizational Issues in High Technology Management,* ed. L. Gomez-Mejia and M. Lawless, 227–41. Greenwich, Conn.: JAI Press.

U.S. Department of Labor. 1976. *Occupational Outlook Quarterly*, 20:2–28.

Ulrich, D., R. Halbrook, D. Meder, M. Stuchlik, and S. Thorpe. 1991. Employee and customer attachment: Synergies for competitive advantage. *Human Resource Planning*, 14:89–103.

Van Maanen, J., and E. H. Schein. 1979. Toward a theory of organizational socialization. In *Research in Organizational Behavior*, ed. B. Staw, 1:209–64. Greenwich, Conn.: JAI Press.

Vandenberg, R. J., and V. Scarpello. 1990. The matching model: An examination of the processes underlying realistic job previews. *Journal of Applied Psychology*, 75:60–67.

Von Glinow, M. A. 1988. *The New Professionals*. Cambridge, Mass.: Ballinger.

Vroom, V. H. 1964. *Work and Motivation*. New York: Wiley.

Vroom, V. H., and E. L. Deci. 1971. The stability of post-decisional dissonance: A follow-up study of the job attitudes of business school graduates. *Organizational Behavior and Human Performance*, 6:36–49.

Waldman, D. A., and B. J. Avolio. 1986. A meta-analysis of age differences in job performance. *Journal of Applied Psychology*, 71:33–38.

Wandelt, M. A., P. M. Pierce, and R. R. Widdowson. 1981. Why nurses leave nursing and what can be done about it. *American Journal of Nursing*, (January) 81:72–77.

Wanous, J. P. 1973. Effects of realistic job preview on job acceptance, job attitudes, and job survival. *Journal of Applied Psychology*, 58:327–32.

——— 1977. Organizational entry: Newcomers moving from outside to inside. *Psychological Bulletin*, 84 (4):601–18.

——— 1980. *Organizational Entry: Recruitment, Selection and Socialization of Newcomers*. Reading, Mass.: Addison–Wesley.

——— 1989. Installing a realistic job preview: Ten tough choices. *Personnel Psychology*, 42:117–34.

——— 1992. *Organizational Entry*, 2d ed. New York: Addison-Wesley.

Wanous, J. P., and A. Colella. 1989. Organizational entry research: Current status and future directions. In *Research in Personnel and Human Resources Management*, ed. G. Ferris and K. Rowland, 59–120. Greenwich, Conn.: JAI Press.

Wanous, J. P., T. D. Poland, S. L. Premack, and K. S. Davis. 1992. The effects of met expectations on newcomer attitudes and behaviors: A review and meta-analysis. *Journal of Applied Psychology*, 77:288–97.

Watanabe, C. 1973. Self-expression and the Asian-American experience. *Personnel and Guidance Journal*, 51:390–96.

Waters, L. K., D. Roach, and C. W. Waters. 1976. Estimates of future tenure, satisfaction, and biographical variables as predictors of termination. *Personnel Psychology*, 29 (1):57–60.

Watts, L. R., and E. C. White. 1988. Assessing employee turnover. *Personnel Administrator*, 33:80–85.

Webb, E. T., D. T. Campbell, R. D. Schwartz, L. Sechrest, and J. B. Grove. 1981. *Nonreactive Measures in the Social Sciences*. Boston, Mass.: Houghton Mifflin Company.

Weiner, B. 1972. *Theories of Motivation: From Mechanism to Cognition*. Chicago: Rand McNally.

———— 1979. A theory of motivation for some classroom experiences. *Journal of Educational Psychology*, 71:3–25.

Weiner, N. 1980. Determinants and behavioral consequences of pay satisfaction: A comparison of two models. *Personnel Psychology*, 33:741–57.

Weiss, H. M., and S. Adler. 1984. Personality and organizational behavior. In *Research in Organizational Behavior*, ed. B. M. Staw and L. L. Cummings, 6:1–50. Greenwich, Conn.: JAI Press.

Weiss, S. J. 1984. The effect of transition modules on new graduate adaptation. *Research in Nursing and Health*, 7:51–59.

Weitz, J. 1952. A neglected concept in the study of job satisfaction. *Personnel Psychology*, 5:201–205.

———— 1956. Job expectancy and survival. *Journal of Applied Psychology*, 40:245–47.

Welbourne, T. M., and L. R. Gomez–Mejia. 1988. Gainsharing revisited. *Compensation and Benefits Review*, 20:19–28.

Wells, D. L., and P. M. Muchinsky. 1985. Performance antecedents of voluntary and involuntary managerial turnover. *Journal of Applied Psychology*, 70:329–36.

White, J. K. 1979. The Scanlon plan: Causes and correlates of success. *Academy of Management Journal*, 22:292–312.

Whitener, E. M. 1990. Confusion of confidence intervals and credibility intervals in meta-analysis. *Journal of Applied Psychology,* 75:315–21.

Whiting, L. 1989. Turnover costs: A case example. Ohio Department of Mental Health, Columbus, Ohio.

Widaman, K. P. 1985. Hierarchically nested covariance structure models for multitrait-multimethod data. *Applied Psychological Measurement,* 9 (1):1–26.

Williams, C. R. 1990. Deciding when, how, and if to correct turnover correlations. *Journal of Applied Psychology,* 75:732–37.

Williams, C. R., and L. P. Livingstone. 1994. Another look at the relationship between performance and voluntary turnover. *Academy of Management Journal,* 37:269–98.

Williams, L. J., J. A. Cote, and M. R. Buckley. 1989. Lack of method variance in self-reported affect and perceptions at work: Reality or artifact? *Journal of Applied Psychology,* 74 (3):462–68.

Williams, L. J., and J. T. Hazer. 1986. Antecedents and consequences of satisfaction and commitment in turnover models: A reanalysis using latent variable structural equation methods. *Journal of Applied Psychology,* 71:219–31.

Williams, L. J., and P. M. Podsakoff. 1989. Longitudinal field methods for studying reciprocal relationships in organizational behavior research: Toward improved causal analysis. In *Research in Organizational Behavior,* ed. L. Cummings and B. Staw, 11:247–92. Greenwich, Conn.: JAI Press.

Williams, M. L., and G. F. Dreher. 1992. Compensation system attributes and applicant pool characteristics. *Academy of Management Journal,* 35:571–95.

Wilson, M., G. B. Northcraft, and M. A. Neale. 1985. The perceived value of fringe benefits. *Personnel Psychology,* 38:309–20.

Wilson, N., and M. J. Peel. 1991. The impact on absenteeism and quits of profit–sharing and other forms of employee participation. *Industrial and Labor Relations Review,* 44:454–68.

Withey, M. J., and W. H. Cooper. 1989. Predicting exit, voice, loyalty, and neglect. *Administrative Science Quarterly,* 34:521–39.

Wood, R. E., A. J. Mento, and E. A. Locke. 1987. Task complexity as a moderator of goal effects: A meta-analysis. *Journal of Applied Psychology,* 72 (3):416–25.

Woodward, H. M. 1975. Criterion-referenced testing and the measurement of language growth. *Volta Review,* 77 (4):229–40.

Yalow, E. 1990. Corporate child care helps recruit and retain workers. *Personnel Journal* (June):48–55.

Youngberg, C. F. 1963. *An experimental study of job satisfaction and turnover in relation to job expectations and self-expectations.* Ph.D. diss., New York University, N.Y.

Youngblood, S. A., and K. Chambers–Cook. 1984. Child care assistance can improve employee attitudes and behavior. *Personnel Administrator,* 29:45.

Youngblood, S. A., W. H. Mobley, and B. M. Meglino. 1983. A longitudinal analysis of the turnover process. *Journal of Applied Psychology,* 68:507–16.

Youngblood, S., B. Baysinger, and W. Mobley. 1985, August. *The role of unemployment and job satisfaction on turnover: A Longitudinal Study.* Paper presented at the national meeting of the Academy of Management, San Diego, Calif.

Zaharia, E. S., and A. A. Baumeister. 1981. Job preview effects during the critical initial employment period. *Journal of Applied Psychology,* 66 (1):19–22.

Zalesny, M. D. 1985. Comparison of economic and noneconomic factors in predicting faculty vote preference in a union representation election. *Journal of Applied Psychology,* 70 (2):243–56.

Zedeck, S., S. E. Jackson, and E. Summers. 1983. Shift work schedules and their relationship to health, adaptation, satisfaction, and turnover intention. *Academy of Management Journal,* 26:297–310.

Zedeck, S., and K. L. Mosier. 1990. Work in the family and employing organization. *American Psychologist,* 45:240–51.

Zenger, T. R. 1992. Why do employers only reward extreme performance? Examining the relationships among performance, pay, and turnover. *Administrative Science Quarterly,* 37:198–219.

TURNOVER COST OF
A CLINICAL POSITION

1. Job title: _____

   Circle the job title below that most closely matches the job title in your agency.

01. Behavioral Health Worker I	08. Psychologist
02. Behavioral Health Worker II	09. Staff Psychiatrist
03. Behavioral Health Worker III	10. LPN
04. Clinician/Counselor I	11. RN I
05. Clinician/Counselor II	12. RN III
06. Program Coordinator/Manager I	13. Occupational/Recreational/
07. Program Coordinator/Manager II	Speech Therapist

2. What is the entry-level annual salary for this job? $ _____

3. What is the average annual salary for this job? $ _____

4. What percentage of salary does fringe benefits represent?   _____%

5. How many employees with this job title were employed in your agency on Jan. 1, 1991?   _____

   Number of Women with this job title   _____
   Number of Blacks with this job title   _____
   Number of Hispanics with this job title   _____
   Number of American Indians with this job title   _____
   Number of Asians with this job title   _____

6. How many employees with this job title were employed in your agency on Dec. 31, 1991?   _____

   Number of Women with this job title   _____
   Number of Blacks with this job title   _____
   Number of Hispanics with this job title   _____
   Number of American Indians with this job title   _____
   Number of Asians with this job title   _____

7. How many employees with this job title voluntarily
   quit during 1991? _____

   Of these, how many leavers were satisfactory
   (or better) performers? _____

   What was the average annual salary of these leavers? $ _____

8. How many employees with this job title were
   dismissed or laid off during 1991? _____

9. How many employees were hired for this job in 1991?   _____

10. What was the average (hiring) salary of new
    replacements for this position in 1991? $ _____

I.   SEPARATION COSTS

1. If you conduct exit interviews with departing
   employees, what is the average length of time for
   an interview?   _____ hours

2. What is the typical annual salary of the person
   (e.g., personnel, agency manager) conducting the
   exit interview? $ _____

3. Approximately, how much are administrative and
   paperwork costs of processing one individual
   turnover (e.g., continued group insurance,
   removing quitter's name from personnel records)? $ _____

4. Maintaining Client Services During Position Vacancy

   a.   Temporary Agencies

        If your agency contracts for services to fill vacant
        positions with this job title, how many hours per
        week, on average, do you use temporary
        employees to fill a full-time vacancy?   _____ hours

        Typically, for how many weeks do you employ
        a temp?   _____ weeks

        What is the typical hourly wage of a temporary
        employee in this position? $ _____

b.   Assignment of Clients to Other Employees

If currently employed mental health professionals assume some or all clients of the leaver, what are costs of case consultation and transfer?

What is the typical clerical cost to transfer client records (of a leaver) to other mental health professionals? $ _____

What is the typical annual salary of the supervisor providing case consultation to other employees? $ _____

On average, how many total hours does this supervisor spend on case consultation for other employees?   _____hours

c.   Overtime Pay for Heavier Client Load

Does your agency pay overtime for this position?   Yes   No

If yes, how many total overtime hours per week are typically paid to other employees to assume the leaver's duties and clients?   _____hours

What is this position's overtime pay rate:

(Circle your answer)   Straight Time
                                                 Time-and-a-half
                                                 Double-time
                                                 Other _____

5.   Lost Patient Revenues during Position Vacancy

Does your agency experience any lost client revenues during the time period when this particular job is vacant due to turnover? For example, do clients of a leaver stop using agency services or does your agency turn away clients due to vacancy? For us to estimate this lost client revenue, please provide the following estimates:

a.   On average, how many weeks does this position remain vacant before a replacement is hired to fill the vacancy?   _____weeks

b.   In this particular job, how many work hours are billable hours per week?   _____hours

c. What is typical unit rate for client service by
   incumbents in this job? $ _____ rate

6. Disbursement of Unused Vacation Time:

   a. If employees accrue unused vacation time, can
      they redeem those hours for cash upon
      termination?   Yes   No

   b. If yes, how many hours of vacation time,
      on average, do departing employees generally
      accrue?   _____hours

II. REPLACEMENT COSTS

1. Seeking Replacements from Advertising

   What are the cost of advertising to fill *one* vacancy
   for this job? (newspaper and journal ads, writing ad,
   updating job descriptions) $ _____

2. Seeking Replacements from Job Fairs or College Placements

   Does your agency send representatives to job fairs
   or colleges to recruit applicants for this job title?   Yes   No

   a. If yes, what is the representative's annual salary? $ _____

   b. On average, how many hours are spent recruiting
      through job fairs or colleges to fill a vacancy in
      this job?   _____hours

3. Processing and Reviewing Applications

   What are the clerical and personnel costs of processing resumes and applications for
   this job (e.g., communications with applicants, writing acknowledgments, filling out
   affirmative action reports)?

   a. Typical annual salary of the processor: $ _____

   b. Average time to process resumes for this job
      vacancy: _____hours

What are labor costs of an agency manager who reviews resumes/applications for jobs with this job title?

a. Typical annual salary of reviewer for this job: $ _____

b. Average time to review resumes for one job
    vacancy: _____hours

4. Interviewing Applicants

What are the labor costs of interviewing applicants? Please describe below interview time and interviewers' wages.

a. On average, how many applicants are interviewed
    to fill one vacancy on this job
    (number of interviewed applicants per vacancy)?   _____

b. What is the typical annual salary of managers
    interviewing applicants for this job? $ _____

c. On average, how many hours does a manager
    spend to interview one applicant for this job?   _____hours

d. What are annual salaries of other interviewers and their average interview time with
    one job applicant?

    Second interviewer   Annual pay _____   Interview hours _____
    Third interviewer   Annual pay _____   Interview hours _____
    Fourth interviewer   Annual pay _____   Interview hours _____

5. Selecting Applicants

What are the labor costs of final selection of candidates to fill one vacant position with this job title?

a. What is the typical salary of the selector? $ _____

b. On average, how much time does he or she
    spend choosing an applicant for this job?   _____hours

c. If others are involved in selection, what are their annual salaries and the average
    time they spend to choose a new hire?

    Second selector   Annual pay _____   Selection hours _____
    Third selector   Annual pay _____   Selection hours _____

6. Miscellaneous Hiring Costs

Please estimate any miscellaneous hiring costs (including out-of-pocket expenses and administrative costs) to hire one new employee for this job:

Employment tests	$ _____
Substance-abuse testing	$ _____
Physical exams	$ _____
Reference-checking	$ _____
Fingerprinting	$ _____
Credentialing costs	$ _____
Travel expenses for interviewees	$ _____
Employment agency fees	$ _____
Paperwork to get staff on payroll	$ _____
Relocation expenses for new hire	$ _____
Other costs: _____	$ _____
Other costs: _____	$ _____

III.   ORIENTATION AND TRAINING COSTS

1. Formal Orientation

What are labor costs to orient a new employee in this particular job?

a. What is the annual salary of the person
    conducting orientation? $ _____

b. On average, how many total hours are spent to
    orient a new employee?   _____ hours

c. Please estimate the dollar costs of booklets,
    manuals, reports, etc. for orienting and training a
    new employee: $ _____

2. Formal Job Training

What are the average costs of providing in-house and offsite formal training to a new employee in this job?

a. What is the annual salary of the in-house trainer? $ _____

b. On average, how many total hours does this trainer
    spend to train a new employee?   _____ hours

c.   How much money does your agency spend to
     provide offsite training for a new employee
     in this job? $ _____

d.   If a new employee attends offsite training during
     work hours, how many work hours are spent in
     training?   _____ hours

3.   Familiarizing New Employees

     How costly is it for a new employee to become familiar with agency practices?

     a.   On average, how many total hours are required
          for a new employee to learn the agency's internal
          system and external environment to do the job
          properly?   _____ hours

     b.   How many weeks does this learning period
          typically last?   _____ weeks

     c.   In 1991, how many new hires for this job
          remained employed in your agency beyond this
          learning period (number of new hires who
          remained employed)?   _____

     d.   On average, how many total hours does a
          manager (or senior employee) spend to
          familiarize a new employee with agency
          policies and practices, and patients (e.g., case
          consultation)? $ _____

4.   Lost Patient Revenues during New Staff Orientation and Familiarization

     Does your agency experience any client revenue loss during this orientation and familiar-
     ization period? That is, do new employees see fewer clients or charge fewer billable hours
     during this time? For us to calculate these costs, please provide the following estimates:

     a.   Does a new employee serve fewer clients (compared
          with experienced incumbents) during this
          familiarization period?   Yes   No

     b.   If yes, how many weeks does a new employee serve
          fewer clients during this period?   _____ weeks

     c.   During this familiarization time, how many hours
          in an average week are billable hours for a new
          employee?   _____ hours

AUTHOR INDEX

SUBJECT INDEX